# Canadian Retailing

# CANADIAN RETAILING

**J. Barry Mason**

**Morris L. Mayer**

**Hazel F. Ezell**

**Michel Laroche**
*Concordia University*

**Gordon H. G. McDougall**
*Wilfrid Laurier University*

**IRWIN**

Burr Ridge, Illinois
Boston, Massachusetts
Sydney, Australia

Front cover: © Peter Christopher/Masterfile
Back cover: © Lloyd Sutton/Masterfile
© Richard D. Irwin, Inc., 1990 and 1993

Senior sponsoring editor:  Roderick T. Banister
Product manager:  Murray D. Moman
Project editor:  Jess Ann Ramirez
Production manager:  Ann Cassady
Designer:  Mercedes Santos
Art coordinator:  Heather Burbridge
Compositor:  The Clarinda Co.
Typeface:  10/12 Times Roman
Printer:  R.R. Donnelley & Sons Company

ISBN 0-256-12358-6

Library of Congress Catalog Number: 92-74989

*Printed in the United States of America*
3  4  5  6  7  8  9  0  DOC  0  9  8  7  6  5  4

This book is
dedicated to Anne
Laroche and Betty,
Michael, and Sandy
McDougall

Since the first edition of *Canadian Retailing* was published, the world of Canadian retailing has experienced many traumatic events, from the recession in the early 1990s to the combined effects of cross-border shopping, the Canada–U.S. Free Trade Agreement (FTA), and the federal Goods and Services Tax (GST). These factors, in turn, have forced inefficient retailers out of business, and prompted many others to rethink their basic strategic approach, including a better focus on good customer service. Retailers who followed this road did well, even during the recession.

The second part of this decade will bring more challenges, particularly for the astute entrepreneur who understands retailing in the Canadian environment within a more globalized economy. What kinds of new retailing concepts will be introduced, particularly to lower distribution costs? How far will the concept of controlled environment be extended, and will the future bring more megamalls like the West Edmonton Mall or the Mall of America? How far will the information society go, what new technologies will be introduced, and how will this affect the management of retail institutions, or create new ones? Will cross-border shopping continue as strongly as before, or will it fade away? How will consumer environmental concerns affect retailing in Canada?

Answers to these and other questions will determine which retailing institutions will survive in a highly competitive and globalized economy. This text emphasizes a managerial, practical approach to retailing, focusing directly on the strategic issues faced by the owner, the manager, or the employee of a retail institution for the rest of the 1990s and beyond. It assumes no prior knowledge of retailing, and it covers the conceptual and analytical foundations necessary to understand all aspects of retail management in the current Canadian environment. This is done from a practical point of view, in simple straightforward language, and with many real-life examples.

Each chapter starts with a Retailing Capsule that sets the stage for the material in the chapter. Throughout the chapter, numerous examples and Retail Highlights reflecting recent events have been added to provide an in-depth look at important issues and applications. Each chapter ends with detailed chapter highlights, a list of key terms, eight discussion questions, three application exercises, and suggested cases. The complete package is intended to maximize learning while doing. Enhanced pedagogical features have been added to improve student access to important details: page references for end-of-chapter key terms and suggested cases, an end-of-text glossary, as well as new figures, tables, and exhibits.

The book follows a logical sequence toward strategy development for the retail firm.

In Part I, *The World of Canadian Retailing,* five chapters provide a broad perspective on the institutions, economy, and markets in the Canadian environment. Chapter 1 introduces the student to retailing in Canada—its history, role, and evolution. Chapter 2 provides an overview of trends, social dimensions, and prospects that affect retailing, including the emerging services retailing. Chapter 3 covers the critical environmental factors affecting retail strategy development (legal, economic, demographic, competitive, and technological). Understanding the retail customer is critical to the success of the retail strategy, including individual factors (Chapter 4) and social influences (Chapter 5).

In Part II, *Developing the Retail Strategy,* the conceptual, financial, and organizational aspects of the retail strategy are logically developed. Chapter 6 deals with the development of strategic planning, as a method of defining the objectives of the firm and deciding how to compete. To compete successfully, retailers need to understand how to finance and organize a business (Chapter 7). Franchising as a means of owning and operating a retail firm is examined in detail (Chapter 8). Chapter 9 discusses the critical issues in the recruitment, selection, training, and motivation of retail employees. Knowledge of markets is essential to strategy development, and the retail research methods used to obtain this knowledge are covered in Chapter 10.

In Part III, *Designing the Retailing Mix,* the various decisions on the key variables of the retailing mix are discussed. The key issues in retail location decisions are covered in Chapter 11. Store design, layout, and merchandise presentation decisions are covered in Chapter 12. Merchandise and expense planning decisions are the subject of Chapter 13. Buying, handling, and inventory management decisions are explained in Chapter 14. Determining retail prices is the topic of Chapter 15. In order to successfully promote their products or services, retailers need to help their employees develop the keys to successful selling (Chapter 16); design effective programmes in retail advertising, sales promotion, and publicity (Chapter 17); and instill in their employees a customer-focused culture (Chapter 18).

In Part IV, *Evaluating the Retail Strategy,* the tools used to determine how well the retail strategy is doing are explained. Internal evaluation is critical to the retail manager, including the elements involved in developing control systems (Chapter 19), and evaluation of performance through an accounting system (Chapter 20).

Following Chapter 20, an appendix on careers in retailing is provided to help students make informed decisions about the many facets of working in retailing.

Another strong feature of the text is the set of cases and exercises. These are among the best case materials available in Canada, and they cover all aspects of the text. The cases are keyed to each chapter, and some cases can be used to cover several topics. Some cases were contributed by Canadian academics, and many others by the authors of the text. The mix of cases provides instructors with some that are very comprehensive and others that are of more restricted scope; the remainder can be used to focus on very specific issues. Thus, a wide range of teaching material is provided to maximize learning.

Available for the instructor is an Instructor's Manual including detailed course outlines, suggested answers to discussion questions, answers to cases, solutions to chapter problems, and transparency masters. New to this edition are a testbank of approximately 1,600 true/false and multiple choice questions and the computerized version of the testbank, CompuTest 3. CompuTest 3 is available on both 3½-inch and 5¼-inch diskettes. CompuTest 3 enables the instructor to create up to 99 versions of the same test, and add or edit questions.

In the preparation of this edition, many people have provided encouragement, suggestions, and material, and we are most grateful for their assistance. Professor Lanita S. Carter, Memorial University of Newfoundland, Professor Margaret A. Sutcliffe, Ryerson Polytechnical Institute, and Ms. Glenna Urbshadt, British Columbia Institute of Technology, reviewed the first edition of *Canadian Retailing*. Development of the second edition owes much to the thoughtful and thorough reviews of Mr. Aldo Cimpello, Algonquin College; Mr. Drew Evans, Red River Community College; Mr. Rob Jakes, SIAST; Ms. Pat Kolodjieski, Mohawk College; and Ms. Jessie Pendygrasse, Capilano College. Many thanks also to Professor Chung K. Kim, Concordia University, for useful feedback, and to all the case contributors who provided material for the book.

The production of this manuscript involved other individuals to whom we are most grateful. Many thanks to Elsie Grogan and Lori Kapshey, who proved once again to be cheerful, professional individuals who met both reasonable and other deadlines. We would like to acknowledge the excellent editing provided by Rosalyn Sheff. As well, the financial support of Irwin is very gratefully acknowledged.

Finally, we hope this revised edition of *Canadian Retailing* will provide you with a useful and rewarding learning experience for many years to come.

**Michel Laroche**
**Gordon H. G. McDougall**

# CONTENTS

**PART IV**

**EVALUATING THE RETAIL STRATEGY**

## 19   Evaluation and Control of Merchandise and Expense Planning   517

## 20   Performance Evaluation   531

## Appendix   Careers in Retailing   554

## Cases   565

# I THE WORLD OF CANADIAN RETAILING

The five chapters in Part I provide a broad perspective of the types of retailers, the economy, and the markets in the Canadian environment. Chapter 1 introduces the student to retailing in Canada and its history, role, and evolution. Chapter 2 provides an overview of trends, social dimensions, and prospects that affect retailing, including the emerging services retailing. Chapter 3 covers the critical environmental factors (legal, economic, social, and technological) affecting retail strategy development. Understanding the retail customer is critical to the success of the retail strategy, including individual factors (Chapter 4) and social influences (Chapter 5).

# 1   INTRODUCTION TO CANADIAN RETAILING

## Chapter Objectives

After reading this chapter, you should be able to:

1 Relate retailing to the marketing discipline.
2 Explain and describe the descriptive classifications of retail structure.
3 Explain and describe the strategic classifications of retail structure.
4 Review the explanations of retail structural change.

**Retailing Capsule**

In the recession of the early 1990s, thousands of Canadian retailers went bankrupt. From small independents to large, well-known chains like Town & Country, Maher, Elks, Bargain Harold's, and A&A, these retailers were unable

*BiWay adds stores targeted at the price segment of the retail market.*

SOURCE: Courtesy BiWay.

To set the stage, we offer the following overview of retailing in Canada:

- Retailing employs more Canadians than any other industry. Over 1.6 million people, or approximately 13 percent of Canada's work force, work in retailing.
- Total retail sales in Canada are over $230 billion annually; on average, each Canadian spends over $8,600 on retail goods and services in stores from Prince George (population 70,000 and annual retail sales of over $620 million) to Sydney (population 120,000 and annual retail sales of over $780 million).
- Over 100,000 stores dot the Canadian landscape. While independent retailers account for the majority of total retail sales (because of their sheer numbers), much of the buying power is in the hands of a few large chains that are well known to most Canadians (Table 1–1).

*Retailing Capsule continued*

to compete in the hostile economic climate brought on by the recession, rising consumer taxes, the GST, restrictions on Sunday shopping, and cross-border shopping. For thousands of other retailers, survival was the name of the game as they fought for their share of fewer consumer dollars.

Yet, amidst this retail wreckage, some retailers grew and prospered. While many Canadian clothing retailers went bankrupt or lost money, Reitmans (a 600-store women's clothing chain) increased revenues with a strategy that offered reasonable prices and average styles to a target market of "Honest, Hard-Working People Looking for Good Value." BiWay, a discount chain in the Dylex group, added stores to capture a greater share of the price segment of the market. BiWay's president, reflecting on the troubled times, said, "The ultimate survivors and winners are those who offer real value, recognize the needs of the consumer, and respond quickly."

Whether times are good or bad, a group of retailers led by McDonald's continually outperforms its competitors. McDonald's continues to outpace its rivals in the highly competitive fast-food business with strategies and tactics that include adding new outlets, locating in unique, nontraditional sites (e.g., hospitals, train stations, and the SkyDome), and adding new product lines like salads and pizza. While other competitors occasionally flounder, McDonald's monitors the environment for opportunities that lead to sales of over $1 billion each year.

Sources: John Heinzl, "Retail Industry Still on Rocks," *Globe and Mail,* March 10, 1992, pp. B1, B10; Mathew Ingram, "Reitmans: A Retailer ahead of the Pack," *Financial Times,* January 20, 1992, pp. 1, 4; and Barrie McKenna, "Rag Trade Facing Disaster," *Globe and Mail,* May 12, 1992, p. B6.

- Canadians spend over 50 percent of their retail dollars in shopping centres. From the West Edmonton Mall with over 600 stores and a vast amusement complex to the 28-store Millbrook Mall in Corner Brook, the more than 1,200 shopping centres are the shopping destinations for the majority of Canadians.
- Canadians respond to new retailing concepts. When Price Club (the no-frills giant warehouse outlet) entered the Canadian market, it generated over $1 billion in sales in its first full year of operations.
- Canadian retailers face many challenges and opportunities, including cross-border shopping, new forms of competition, and shifting demographics (Retail Highlight 1–1).

Retailing in Canada is a competitive, dynamic business. As the above examples show, retailers must continually adjust to an environment where consumers, segments, and competitors are constantly changing. Success in retailing is not easy, but it's always exciting.

**TABLE 1-1   Major Canadian Retail Chains**

| | Revenue (000) | Comments |
|---|---|---|
| **Department Stores** | | |
| Hudson's Bay Company | $5,000,000 | Comprises three chains, The Bay (89 stores), Zellers (272 stores), and Fields (124 stores). Employs over 60,000 people. |
| Sears Canada | 4,100,000 | Has 106 retail stores and 1,595 catalog units across Canada. Employs approximately 48,000 people. |
| Woolworth | 2,100,000 | U.S.-owned chain operates Woolco and Woolworth stores in Canada. |
| Kmart Canada | 1,200,000 | U.S.-owned 123-store chain is currently spending $200 million to reposition its stores in Canada. |
| Eaton's | N/A | Probably Canada's best-known department store chain, a private company. |
| Woodward's | 600,000 | Dominant in western Canada, this 100-year-old chain of 26 stores is facing an uncertain future. |
| **Clothing Stores** | | |
| Dylex | 1,800,000 | Operates 16 chains, including Fairweather, Suzy Shier, Harry Rosen, Tip Top, Steel, BiWay, Club Monaco, and Thrifty's. Has over 1,300 stores. |
| Reitmans | 300,000 | Its two major chains are Reitmans (384 stores) and Smart Set (201 stores). |
| Mark's Work Wearhouse | 240,000 | Calgary-based chain of over 140 corporate and franchise stores. |
| Château Stores | 150,000 | Operates 155 stores across Canada. |
| Dalmys | 138,000 | Operates three major chains across Canada: Dalmys (108 stores), Astels (71 stores), and Cactus (19 stores). |
| **Specialty Stores** | | |
| Canadian Tire | 3,000,000 | A Canadian landmark with over 400 stores. |
| Shoppers Drug Mart | 3,000,000 | Part of the Imasco Group, includes over 670 franchise Shoppers Drug Mart and Pharmaprix stores. |
| Kinney Canada | 620,000 | The leading footwear chain in Canada. |
| Henry Birks | 390,000 | The leading jewellery chain in Canada. |
| Leon's Furniture | 260,000 | Operates 27 company-owned and 21 franchise stores. |

SOURCE: *Report on Business Magazine,* July 1992 and various annual reports 1991, 1992.

**Retailing** consists of all activities involved in the sale of goods and services to the ultimate consumer. A retail sale occurs whenever an individual purchases groceries at a supermarket, a compact disc at Sam the Record Man, a coffee at Tim Horton Donuts, a haircut at Magicuts, or a membership at a fitness centre. Not all retail sales are made in stores. Some are made by door-to-door salespeople employed by firms such as Avon, by mail-order firms such as Eddie Bauer, by telemarketers such as the Canadian Home Shopping Network, by the use of automatic vending machines, or by farmers selling produce at the roadside.

**Marketing** is the process by which individuals and groups obtain what they need and want through creating and exchanging products and value with others. Retailing is the final part of that process, satisfying individual and organizational objectives through exchanges.

# The Retailing Challenges for the 1990s

- *Economic environment*. The recession of the early 1990s reduced the profitability of most retailers. The challenge is to manage a retail business in a slow-growth environment where consumers have become more value conscious.

- *Demographic environment*. The Canadian population is aging, nontraditional household groups are emerging, and ethnic markets are increasing. The challenge is to respond to the diverse needs of these new market segments.

- *Competitive environment*. New forms of competition, including cross-border shopping, foreign retailers, entering the Canadian market, and off-price retailers, are changing the competitive landscape. The challenge is to identify the competition and revise retail strategy to reflect this new retailing era.

- *Customer satisfaction*. Many consumers have expressed dissatisfaction with the merchandise, value, and service offered by retailers. The challenge is to address these consumer concerns by focusing on customer satisfaction through the merchandise mix and services offered, including retail staff training.

- *Store location*. Shopping centres have lost their glamour for a number of Canadians. The challenge is to rejuvenate these centres by rethinking the store mix, store cluster, and physical design.

- *Positioning*. A number of Canadian retailers do not create a clear image in the consumer's mind. The challenge is to design and implement a positioning strategy that presents the consumer with a complete picture of what the retailer offers.

**Structure** is the arrangement of parts, elements, or constituents considered as a whole rather than a single part. Thus, the retailing structure comprises all the outlets (organizations, establishments) through which goods or services move to the retail customer. The structure is complex and can be classified in various ways to help understand its components.

Retailing is thus a part of marketing from a process point of view and is a complex structure from an institutional perspective. Finally, retailing is primarily carried out by organizations that link manufacturers to consumers in the distribution channel. **Channels of distribution** are systems through which products or services are marketed. Figure 1-1 presents a diagram of the place of retailing in the classic marketing channels of distribution.

## Alternative Ways to Classify the Retail Structure

The complexity and dynamics of retailing can best be understood by analyzing its structure. Analyzing retail structure and understanding competition are critical to developing and implementing retail strategies. By analyzing the structure, better ways of serving consumer needs through new types of retailing organizations may be revealed. These new approaches can serve as a competitive advantage that may be difficult for competitors to copy in the short run.

*Hermès enters the Canadian market with a strong image.*

SOURCE: Courtesy Hermès.

   The retailing structure can be classified in various ways, and for two broad purposes—for describing and understanding and for strategy assistance.

**FIGURE 1–1**

*Typical channel structures*

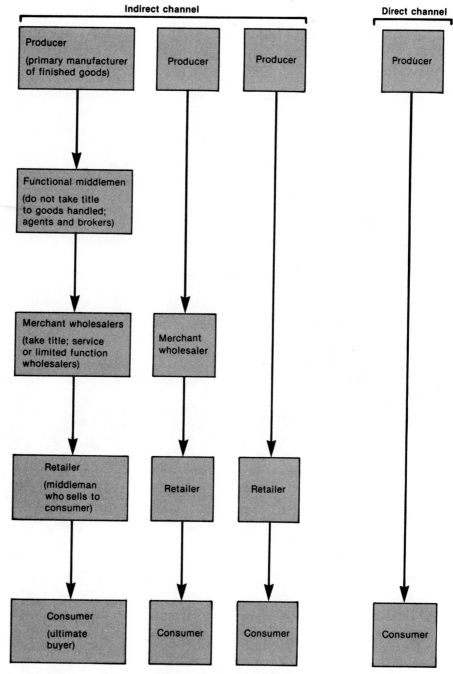

Indirect channel --Involves the use of intermediaries between producer and consumer.
Direct channel --Allows the movement of goods or services directly from producer to consumer.

*Descriptive
Classifications*

The five main descriptive ways of classifying retail structures are (1) type of owner-ship, (2) variety and assortment, (3) kind of business, (4) location, and (5) nonstore retailing.

### Type of Ownership

The most common classification is based on ownership, and the two major types are independent and chain. The *independent,* with a single store, constitutes around 58 percent of total retail sales.[1] Single-unit organizations tend to be small businesses operated by family members.

The small, independent store can compete with chains because (1) the store's cost of doing business is usually low due to low rents, location in a lower-traffic neighbourhood or rural area, and ownership by the proprietor; (2) the store is often located closer to customers than are larger chain stores; (3) a personal relationship between customers and the manager is more likely to occur, allowing the smaller store to develop a unique personality, and (4) the manager can be very flexible in meeting the needs of customers. Still, the failure rate among small, independent retail stores remains high. Such failures can be attributed to inexperience, incompetence, or other management shortcomings.

*Most stores in Canada are independents.*

SOURCE: Photo by James Hertel.

A **chain** is a retail organization consisting of two or more centrally owned units that handle similar lines of merchandise. In food retailing and the general merchandising field, chain stores control a substantial proportion of the market. The six largest department store chains—The Bay, Sears Canada, Woolworth, Kmart, Woodward's, and Eaton's—have total sales exceeding $15 billion annually.[2] Three of these chains—The Bay, Eaton's, and Woodward's—have operated in Canada for close to 100 years or more and have historical importance (Retail Highlight 1–2). The large supermarket chains, including Safeway, Loblaws, Provigo,

# Canadian Department Stores: The Originals

Two of Canada's department store chains, The Bay and Eaton's, have considerable importance from an historical perspective. The Hudson's Bay Company is Canada's oldest enterprise. The original charter, granting it trading rights in Hudson's Bay, was given on May 2, 1670. During its first century, the company established forts on the bay and traded with the Indians. The merger of the company with a rival trading firm in 1821 led to the Hudson's Bay Company. The company played an important role in Canada's development from its early inception to today. It is now a conglomerate with sales exceeding $5 billion annually.

Timothy Eaton, generally acknowledged as the "father of the department store" in Canada, opened his first store in 1860 in St. Mary's, Ontario. Nine years later, he opened a store on Yonge Street in Toronto, and in early 1870, he added a slogan to his handbills and advertisements that was to revolutionize Canadian retailing:

"Goods Satisfactory or Money Refunded." By 1929, three chains, one being Eaton's, accounted for 80 percent of all department store sales. Today, Eaton's is one of the largest department store chains in Canada, with over 100 retail outlets and sales exceeding $2 billion each year.

Another early Canadian retailer, Charles Woodward, began the Woodward's department store chain by opening his first store in Vancouver in 1892. He was the originator of the one-price sale days, beginning with the 25-Cent Day in 1910. The idea—of offering a wide range of items for one price—proved to be very successful and was imitated by retailers throughout North America. Woodward's continued this tradition, and $1.49 Days were popular with customers in western Canada for many years after the Second World War. In recent years, Woodward's has suffered losses, and the future of this 100-year-old chain is uncertain.

Source: *Hudson's Bay Company,* Annual Report, 1991; William Stephenson, *The Store That Timothy Built* (Toronto: McClelland and Steward, 1969); *Department Stores in Canada: 1923–1976* (Ottawa: Statistics Canada, 1979); Douglas E. Harker, *The Woodwards* (Toronto: Mitchell Press, 1976); and Bob Mackin, Jr., "Western Canada's Department Store Spans a Century," *Marketing,* June 15, 1992, p. 22.

Atlantic & Pacific, Sobeys, and the Oshawa Group, have achieved dominance in food retailing through vertical integration and buying power.

A number of specialty retail chains have become major forces in Canadian retailing—Dylex, Grafton Group, Reitmans, and Dalmys in the clothing field, Beaver Lumber in the home improvement area, and Canadian Tire in the automotive and hardware business. The size of these chains provides them with many opportunities, including buying power, advertising economies, and in-store specialists. Overall, these chains can use their size to create efficiencies in distribution, management, and purchasing. At times, these chains may be bureaucratic and lack the flexibility to meet the needs of local markets.

Retail stores can be owned by manufacturers, such as Bata Shoes, owned by governments, such as provincial-owned liquor stores, or consumer-owned. **Consumer cooperatives** are retail stores owned by consumers and operated by a hired manager. Co-ops have prospered in some rural areas of Canada where the benefits of group buying are more important than in larger communities. However, some co-ops have been successful in larger communities, such as Co-op Atlantic, with its reduced prices to members and its slogan "It Pays to Belong."[3]

### Variety and Assortment

**Variety** is the number of lines of merchandise carried—hence, the term *variety store*. **Assortment** is the choice offered within a line. *Variety* can be thought of as the width or breadth of a store's merchandise selection, and *assortment* can be thought of as the depth of a store's selection, including sizes, colours, and types of material. Figure 1–2 illustrates the concept of width and depth for sports shoes

**FIGURE 1–2**

*Types and brands of sports shoes offered*

| Types of Sports Shoes | Specialty Store | Eaton's | Zellers |
|---|---|---|---|
| Running | Reebok<br>Nike<br>Brooks<br>Adidas<br>Asics<br>Saucony<br>New Balance<br>Avia<br>(47 items) | Reebok<br>Nike<br>Brooks<br><br><br><br><br><br>(18 items) | Nike<br>Brooks<br>Venture<br><br><br><br><br><br>(22 items) |
| Basketball | Nike<br>Reebok<br>Adidas<br>Converse<br>Asics<br>(26 items) | Nike<br>Reebok<br><br><br><br>(4 items) | Nike<br>Adidas<br>Converse<br>Venture<br><br>(19 items) |
| Cross-training | Nike<br>Reebok<br>Avia<br>(30 items) | Nike<br>Reebok<br><br>(12 items) | Nike<br>Venture<br><br>(14 items) |
| Tennis | Adidas<br>Nike<br>Reebok<br>(14 items) | | |
| Volleyball | Asics<br>Kangaroo<br>(3 items) | | |
| Soccer | Reebok<br>Nike<br>Mitre<br>Adidas<br>(32 items) | | |
| Golf | Nike<br>Reebok<br>(4 items) | | |

*A specialty store carries a deep range of jogging shoes.*

SOURCE: Photo by James Hertel.

carried in a specialty store, a department store (Eaton's), and a discount department store (Zellers).

In this example, the number of items reflects the models offered by each manufacturer. The specialty store carries more types of shoes (width) and more depth (brands and items) within each type than either Eaton's or Zellers. The width of Eaton's and Zellers sports shoe lines are the same, but Zellers offers more depth, including a store brand (Venture). The specialty store, with its wide and deep line, provides a wider choice, which is appealing to customers, but it requires more inventory. The strategy is to attract more customers and hopefully generate more sales because of the variety and assortment.

### Kind of Business

Outlets may also be classified by kind of business or merchandise group. Such a classification is helpful to management in analyzing retail sales by merchandise groups such as drugstores, shoe stores, men's clothing stores, women's clothing stores, and the like.

### Location

An analysis by location is helpful in establishing long-term trends in regional levels of retail sales. The three major types of locations are the central business district, shopping centres, and stand-alone locations. As mentioned earlier, shopping centres account for over 50 percent of all retail sales in Canada, but many retailers do very well by locating in the downtown area or a stand-alone location. The characteristics of these locations and trends within these locations are discussed in Chapter 11. Trading area, another concept dealing with locations, is also discussed in Chapter 11.

### Nonstore Retailing

The four major types of **nonstore retailing,** or direct retailing, are (1) mail order, (2) telephone shopping, (3) door to door (direct selling), and (4) vending machines.

*Mail Order.*    Historically, mail-order retailing thrived in rural areas where consumers had few shopping alternatives. Today, mail-order operations also serve the specialty needs of urban areas. Sears Canada, the industry leader, sends out 10 different catalog editions to 3.5 million homes and generates between 30 and 40 percent of its total sales through catalog sales. In addition to its massive 800-page Sears Catalog, Sears also mails out smaller catalogs such as its tool catalog to consumers who show interest in that product category.[4] Other Canadian retailers, notably Canadian Tire, Mark's Work Wearhouse, and Consumers Distributing, use catalogs as part of their retail mix, although the customer visits the store to purchase items shown in the catalog.

Catalog retailing has become very popular in the United States, and some well-known retailers such as Lands' End and L. L. Bean are now targeting Canadian consumers. These direct-mail retailers appeal to convenience-oriented Canadian consumers who are looking for products not available in Canada. About 60 percent of Canadians make at least one catalog or mail-order purchase each year.[5]

*Telephone Shopping.*    Telephone shopping has increased in popularity. General merchandise enterprises such as Sears maintain catalog desks at their local retail outlets. In addition, Canadians who have access to cable television can purchase merchandise by phone when viewing the Canadian Home Shopping Network. In 1991, it had sales of $67 million and, for the first time in its five-year history, made a profit of $3 million.

The future of telephone shopping may be in a form developed by Bell Canada. This direct-marketing tool brings all the goods of a shopping mall into a customer's home (see Retail Highlight 1–3).

*Door to Door.*    The variations of the house-to-house canvassing (such as Avon) include party-plan selling (such as Tupperware and Mary Kay) and home calls made after advance prospecting over the telephone. The direct-selling industry is in transition because of changing environmental conditions. Some direct sellers, including marketers of children's products, are experiencing growth because

**Retail Highlight 1–3**

# Electronic Home Shopping: The Future of Retailing?

In 1990, Bell Canada launched Alex (named after Alexander Graham Bell), a direct marketing tool that brings all the goods and services of a shopping mall into a customer's home.

Consumers dial a telephone number on a rented terminal, or a modem-equipped personal computer, to connect with Bell's interactive videotex network, enabling them to order from home shopping catalogs and connect with information databases on a 24-hour, seven-days-a-week basis. Alex lists more than 400 on-line databases, and consumers can make a reservation from an auto-rental agency, check weather forecasts, perform routine bank transactions, locate winning lottery numbers, scan stock markets, or reach out and touch someone on a video chat line.

The terminal rents for $7.95 a month, on top of which a user's fee is added. Total average cost is estimated to be $25 a month.

As in a shopping mall, "tenants" will rent space (a minimum 10 screens will cost $15,300 annually), while Bell Canada as "mall operator" will manage the merchandiser's customer service, order processing, and catalog design and maintenance. All goods purchased are paid electronically by credit card, and next-day delivery is guaranteed.

To date, about 31,000 Canadians have subscribed to the service, but only about 10 percent actually use the system. While some experts feel that Alex represents the future of retailing, others feel that the system will not catch on with many consumers.

Source: Colin Languedoc, "Jury Is Still Out on the Prospects for Bell's Alex," *Globe and Mail,* September 10, 1991, pp. C1, C7.

working mothers find it convenient to shop at home.[6] However, other direct sellers have declining sales because of the large number of women who have entered the work force. Direct sellers are investigating new ways of reaching consumers, including telemarketing, catalogs, and staging parties in offices and factories.

*Vending Machines.*    Sales by vending machines total more than $440 million for products ranging from coffee to sandwiches. Vending machines are typically located in factories, offices, hospitals, and colleges. The primary appeal of vending machines is convenience for the customer in terms of location and time—vending machines are open 24 hours a day.

*Strategic Classifications*

The following strategic classifications help explain retailing and also assist retailers in achieving differential advantages in the market. The classifications include strategic dimensions that may provide helpful ideas for achieving a competitive advantage.

## The Margin-Turnover Classification

The margin-turnover framework for retail structure may be applied to all types of outlets. The framework is useful in strategy formulation rather than in data reporting and analysis.

**Margin** is defined as the difference between the cost and the selling price, or as the percentage markup at which the inventory in a store is sold, and **turnover** is the number of times the average inventory is sold, usually expressed in annual terms.

Figure 1–3 diagrams four quadrants, defined by margin and turnover, into which any retail outlet can be placed. Typically, the low-margin, high-turnover retailer focuses on price, offers few services, and carries a large variety of merchandise. Two of the leading Canadian retailers, Zellers and Sears, have adopted this strategy. The high-margin, high-turnover retailer focuses on convenience by having numerous locations and extensive open hours, charges prices

**FIGURE 1–3**

*The margin–turnover classification*

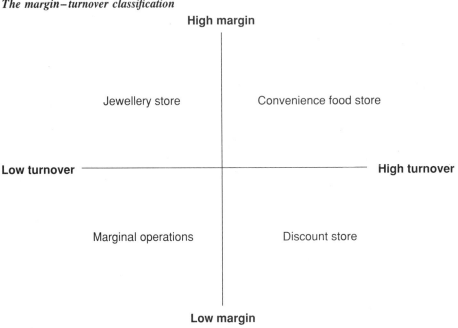

| Strategic dimensions | Low margin– High turnover | High margin– Low turnover | High margin– High turnover |
|---|---|---|---|
| Merchandise | Presold or self-sold | Sold in store | Presold or self-sold |
| Services | Few | Many | Many |
| Locations | Stand-alone | Cluster | Numerous |
| Organization | Simple | Complex | Simple |
| Variety | Large | Small | Large |
| Assortment | Small | Large | Small |
| Prices | Very competitive | Less competitive | Less competitive |
| Promotion | Price focus | Merchandise focus | Minimal |

above the market, and provides a large variety of merchandise, considering the store size. Mac's Milk, 7-Eleven, and a host of convenience stores pursue this strategy. The high-margin, low-turnover store focuses on service, charges prices above the market, and offers a limited variety of merchandise, often on an exclusive basis. Birks, a Canadian retail institution, typifies this category. The low-margin, low-turnover retailer has a poor strategy that requires adjustment to regain profitability.

### Retail Price and Service Strategy Classification

A second classification utilizes two major value dimensions—price and service. In Figure 1–4, Quadrants 1 and 4 are not viable in the long run and are, in fact, traps. Quadrants 2 and 3 are promising strategic options.

In Quadrant 1, even though customers would be pleased with high service and low prices, the strategy would be unwise for the retail firm because it is unlikely to generate sufficient profits. Customers would not be interested in Quadrant 4's poor value of low service at high prices. Retailers must monitor this strategy carefully as they reduce service in an attempt to be more price competitive. A popular strategy recently has been that illustrated by Quadrant 3 and represented by such firms as Price Club and Costco. Zellers and Kmart also fit into that quadrant.

Quadrant 2, high price and high service, illustrates the business practices of firms such as Birks and Liptons, and Lands' End in catalog retailing.

**FIGURE 1–4**

*The retail price service strategy classification*

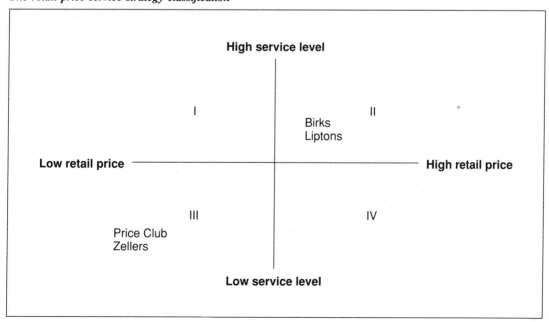

## Retail Structural Change

Figure 1–5 illustrates selected changes in the retail institutional structure that have occurred during the past 100 years. The **life cycle** describes the stages a retail institution goes through, from its beginning to its decline and possible disappearance from the retailing scene. In general, the life cycle has four stages: (1) introduction, where the new form begins (e.g., the West Edmonton Mall, which combined retail and amusement concepts in 1979); (2) growth, where new competitors enter the market (e.g., the current situation with wholesale clubs); (3) maturity, where intense competition is often the major characteristic (e.g., electronic superstores, with their advertising and price wars); and (4) decline, where the store type slowly fades from the landscape (e.g., variety stores). In Figure 1–5, we indicate the period of fastest growth for each type of institution, the stage in the life cycle of

**FIGURE 1–5**

*Selected changes in retail institutional structure*

| Institutional Type | Period of Fastest Growth | Period from Inception to Maturity (years) | Stage of Life Cycle | Examples of Explanatory Hypotheses* | Representative Firms† |
|---|---|---|---|---|---|
| General store | 1800–40 | 100 | Declining/obsolete | Ra | A local institution |
| Single-line store | 1820–40 | 100 | Mature | Ab | Sam the Record Man |
| Department store | 1860–1940 | 80 | Mature | Dp | Eaton's |
| Variety store | 1870–1930 | 50 | Declining/obsolete | Ab | Kreske |
| Mail-order house | 1951–50 | 50 | Mature | Ab | Gifts Unlimited |
| Corporate chain | 1920–30 | 50 | Mature | Ab | The Bay |
| Discount store | 1955–75 | 20 | Mature | Ab, Dp | Kmart |
| Conventional supermarket | 1935–65 | 35 | Mature/declining | Dp | Loblaws |
| Shopping centre | 1950–65 | 40 | Mature | Ab | Oakridge |
| Co-operative | 1930–50 | 40 | Mature | Ab | Home Hardware |
| Gasoline station | 1965–75 | 45 | Mature | Dp | Esso |
| Convenience store | 1960–75 | 20 | Mature | Ra | Mac's Milk |
| Fast-food outlet | 1965–80 | 15 | Mature | Dp | McDonald's |
| Home improvement centre | 1975–85 | 15 | Late growth | Ra | Beaver Lumber |
| Super specialist | 1975–85 | 10 | Growth | Ra | One Stop Battery |
| Warehouse retailing | 1970–80 | 10 | Maturity | Wr | Leon's |
| Regional shopping mall (megamall) | 1979–90 | ? | Late growth | Ab | West Edmonton Mall |
| Computer store | 1980–87 | 7 | Mature | Ra | Computerland |
| Electronics superstore | 1982–88 | 6 | Mature | Ra | Futureshop |
| Off-price retailer/ factory outlet | 1980– | ? | Growth | Dp | Apparel Clearance Centre |
| Hypermarche | 1986– | ? | Late growth | Ra | Real Canadian Superstore |
| Electronic home shopping | 1987– | ? | Introduction | Ab | Canadian Home Shopping Network |
| Wholesale club | 1990– | ? | Introduction/Growth | Wr | Price Club |

*Ra = Retail accordion; Ab = Adaptive behaviour; Dp = Dialectic process; Wr = Wheel of retailing.

†These firms are representative of institutional types and are not necessarily in the stage of life cycle specified for the institutional group as a whole.

each store type, our own explanation for the development of each type, and an example of each. The table provides a framework for the discussion that follows.

No single theory can explain the evolution of all types of retail outlets. At best, the existing theories discussed are descriptive and perhaps somewhat explanatory. Certainly, they are not predictive of institutional change.

# Theories of Retail Institutional Change

## *The Wheel of Retailing*

The **wheel of retailing** hypothesis is the best-known explanation for changes in the structure (Figure 1–6). This theory states that new types of retailers enter a market as low-margin, low-priced, low-status merchants. Gradually, they add to their

FIGURE 1–6

*The wheel of retailing*

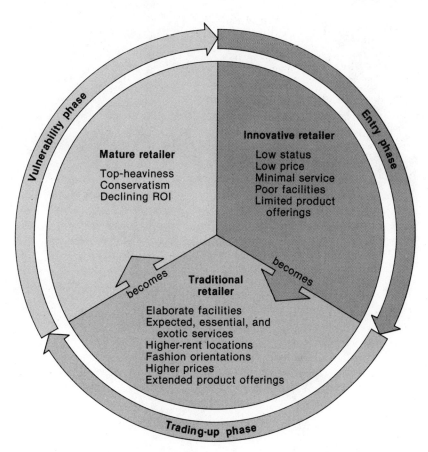

SOURCE: Dale Lewison and Wayne Delozier, *Retailing* (Columbus, Ohio: Charles E. Merrill, 1982), p. 37.

operating costs by providing new services and improving their facilities in the trading-up phase. Over time, they become high-cost merchants and are vulnerable to new types of competition that enter the marketplace as low-cost, no-frills competitors. Recently, the warehouse club has entered the low-priced, low-status area. Both Costco and Price Club have proven to be formidable competitors in Canada, resulting in a strong reaction from many existing competitors, including Canadian Tire and Loblaws.

This theory has been criticized because not all institutions begin as low-margin outlets with few services.[7] Department stores did not follow this model, but other types of institutions have.

*Price Club, a U.S. warehouse club, entered the Canadian market with a low-price, no-frills strategy.*

SOURCE: Courtesy Price Club.

## The Retail Accordion

An alternative explanation for change is the concept of the **retail accordion** (Figure 1–7). Proponents of the theory argue that changes in the merchandising mix, not prices and margins, are a better explanation for changes in retail institutional structure than the wheel of retailing. The accordion theory is based on the premise that retail institutions evolve over time, from broad-based outlets with wide assortments to outlets offering specialized, narrow lines. Over time, the outlets again begin to offer a wide assortment, thus establishing a general-specific-general pattern. This evolution suggests the term *accordion,* which reflects a contraction and expansion of merchandise lines.

For example, modern retailing in Canada began with the general store; a one-stop outlet with wide assortments of merchandise. Then came the urbanized department stores, more specialized than the general store. As urbanization continued, **single-line** and **specialty** stores (e.g., bookstores and drugstores) emerged. More recently, the single-line and specialty stores added complementary lines. For example, grocery stores over time added faster-moving merchandise to the traditional lines. Some stores added small appliances, convenience-food items, and paper products. Many supermarkets now offer nonfood items such as drugs and cosmetics, and discount stores offer a variety of soft goods.

## Further Theories

Two further theories have been proposed to explain changes in retailing. One theory, the **dialectic process,** is based on the adage, "If you can't beat them, join them."[8] As a new store—for example, the discount store—gains share at the expense of existing stores—for example, department stores—a new form emerges that is a blend of both stores—for example, discount department stores such as Kmart and Zellers. The second theory, the **adaptive behaviour** explanation, suggests that the retailing institutions that can most effectively adapt to economic, competitive, social, technological, and legal environmental changes are the ones most likely to survive.[9] The variety store is often cited as an institution that failed to adapt to the changing environment and is seldom seen today. On the other hand, video stores grew rapidly with the advent of videocassette recorders.[10]

**FIGURE 1–7**

*The retail accordion*

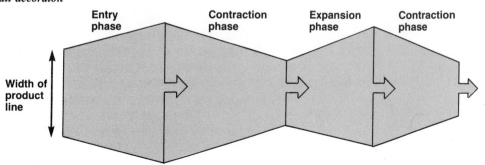

# Chapter Highlights

- Marketing is the process by which individuals and groups obtain what they need and want through creating and exchanging products and value with others. Retailing is the final part of the process, satisfying individual and organizational objectives through exchanges.

- The dynamics of retailing can best be understood by analyzing its structure, which also helps illustrate the strategies by which retailers compete in the marketplace.

- Descriptive classifications of retailing structure include ownership, variety and assortment, kind of business, location, and nonstore retailing.

- Strategic classifications include margin-turnover and price and service.

- The retail structure is dynamic. Retail types appear to follow a pattern of evolution, but no single theory explains the evolution of all types of retail outlets. The existing theories are, at best, descriptive and perhaps somewhat explanatory.

- The wheel of retailing theory is based on the premise that retailers evolve through three phases: entry, trading-up, and vulnerability. A second explanation for change is the retail accordion, where retail institutions evolve from broad-based outlets with wide assortment patterns to specialized narrow lines and then return to the wide-assortment pattern.

- Two further theories are the dialectic process ("If you can't beat them, join them") and the adaptive behaviour explanation (those that most effectively adapt to the changing environment will survive).

# Key Terms

Adaptive behaviour    21
Assortment    12
Chain    10
Channels of distribution    7
Consumer cooperative    11
Dialectic process    21
Life cycle    18
Margin    16
Marketing    6

Nonstore retailing    14
Retail accordion    21
Retailing    6
Single-line store    21
Specialty store    21
Structure (retail institutional)    7
Turnover    16
Variety    12
Wheel of retailing    19

# Discussion Questions

1. Explain the following concepts: retailing, marketing, retail structure, and channels of distribution.

2. Why is it important to classify the retail institutional structure?

3. Discuss the margin-turnover classification model (Figure 1–3). Give an example of a retail outlet that may exist in each of the four quadrants of the margin-turnover model.

4. What are the differences in the operating characteristics of a low-margin, high-turnover retail firm and a high-margin, low-turnover firm?

5. Describe the classification of retail stores based on ownership of the establishment.

6. What are some bases for the classification of retail outlets other than margin-turnover and ownership of the establishment?

7. How might the owner of an existing store benefit from a study of retail structure in a given market area?

8. What three environments are emerging as retail challenges for the 1990s?

## Application Exercises

1. Select a full city block or a shopping centre in your city. Classify each store according to its margin-turnover classification scheme.

2. Place five different stores in your community in each quadrant of the margin-turnover figure (Figure 1–3). Explain the reasons for their placement.

3. Using the classification schemes in the text, choose the major stores in the retail structure in your community and make a complete classification chart of the structure. Then draw some strategic conclusions.

## Suggested Cases

1. Videofile    565
2. Retailing Newswatch    569

## Endnotes

1. *Retail Chain Stores* (Ottawa: Statistics Canada, Catalog 63-210), annual, 1991.
2. *The Financial Post 500* (Toronto: Maclean Hunter, Summer 1992).
3. Sandra Porteous, "Three-Sided Grocery War Rages in Moncton," *Marketing,* October 15, 1990, p. 28.
4. Susan Thorne, "Retailers Cash In with Catalogues," *Globe and Mail,* October 22, 1991, p. B4.
5. Jennifer Pepall, "Selling by the Book," *Profit,* December 1990, pp. 40–41.
6. Ellen Roseman, "Burp That Tupperware, Pamper That Skin: Home Shopping Is Back," *Globe and Mail,* December 23, 1988, p. B4.
7. Rom J. Markin and Clovin P. Duncan, "The Transformation of Retailing Institutions: Beyond the Wheel of Retailing and Life Cycle Theories," *Journal of Macromarketing,* Spring 1981, pp. 58–66; Stephen Brown, "The Wheel of Retailing,"

*International Journal of Retailing* 3, no. 1 (1988), pp. 16–37; and Stephen Brown, "Variations on a Marketing Enigma: The Wheel of Retailing Theory," *Journal of Marketing Management* 7 (1991), pp. 131–55.
8. Thomas J. Maronick and Bruce J. Walker, "The Dialectic Evolution of Retailing," *Proceedings: Southern Marketing Association* (Atlanta: Georgia State University, 1975), pp. 147–51.
9. A. C. R. Dressmann, "Patterns of Evolution in Retailing," *Journal of Retailing* 44 (Spring 1968), pp. 64–81.
10. For more information on the evolution of retail institutions, see Adam Finn and John Rigby, "West Edmonton Mall: Consumer Combined-Purpose Trips and the Birth of the Mega-Multi-Mall," *Canadian Journal of Administrative Sciences,* June 1992, pp. 134–145.

# 2 CONTEMPORARY ISSUES AND TRENDS IN CANADIAN RETAILING

## Chapter Objectives

After reading this chapter, you should be able to:

1 Understand the broad changes affecting Canadian retailers, including the globalization of markets.

2 Understand the meaning of the shift from a merchandising to a marketing orientation in strategy development.

3 Describe key merchandising trends.

4 Discuss the changes occurring in the external environments that can affect retail strategy.

5 Describe emerging retailing strategies in response to changes in the external environments.

6 Discuss the rapid growth of services retailing.

7 Describe the key issues in the consumerism movement and management responses to consumer dissatisfaction.

***

**Retailing Capsule**

Retailers must constantly monitor and be able to respond to changes in the Canadian environment. It is important to spot important trends early on and develop sound strategies. One such recent (but fluctuating) trend centres around public concerns about the ecology. Some examples and responses follow:

- The Body Shop, a Canadian retailer of skin and hair products, was one of the first Canadian retailers to use biodegradable plastic bags. These bags are made of a combination of starch and polymers that, when buried, break down completely in two to three years, compared to 100 years for regular plastic bags. This is in keeping with the firm's traditional concern for environmental issues. The firm uses only recycled paper, sells only biodegradable products, and develops synthetic alternatives to cosmetic ingredients from animals. Also, under study is a biodegradable plastic bottle.

*The Body Shop offers products for the environmentally concerned consumer.*

SOURCE: Photo by Sandy McDougall.

*Continued on next page.*

*Retailing Capsule continued*

- Under pressure from environmental groups, and with public opinion polls showing that the environment was the number one concern of Canadian consumers, food retailers are beginning to introduce products that are "friendly" to the environment **(green marketing).** In January 1989, the Loblaws chain introduced a line of products with the label "Green Environmental Friendly." Under the slogan "Something Can Be Done," and under its President's Choice label, Loblaws has over 100 environmental- and body-friendly products. Four weeks after the launch, 84 percent of Canadians were aware of the Green line, and 27 percent had purchased at least one Green product. The first year, Loblaws sold $60 million worth of Green products; it sold $80 million the second year (although this was $40 million below forecast).

- In 1988, the federal Minister of the Environment introduced a new seal of approval (called **EcoLogo**[M]) programme for products that do not damage the environment, as shown in the advertisement reproduced in Figure 2–1. Each dove represents a sector of society: consumer, industry, and government. The doves intertwine, symbolizing that these sectors must work together to improve the quality of Canada's environment.

  The objectives of that programme are:

1. To raise the environmental consciousness of Canadian consumers.
2. To empower the consumer to pull industry toward the production of products and processes that are environmentally sound in their use and disposal.
3. To identify products and packaging through a universal logo to appear on Canadian consumer products.
4. To encourage environmental safeguards at the manufacturing and packaging levels.

In the first two years of operation, only 26 products were approved and allowed to use the EcoLogo. However, public awareness of the EcoLogo is generally low, and the advertising campaign illustrated in Figure 2–1 is an attempt to raise it.

Sources: "Body Shop Makes Mother Nature Glad," *Marketing,* January 18, 1988, p. 7; see also Philip DeMont, "And This Is Our Biodegradable, Solar-Cell, CFC-Free Model," *Financial Times of Canada,* April 24, 1989, p. 5; Craig McInnes, " 'Green' Products May Offer More for Conscience than Environment," *Globe and Mail,* June 5, 1989, p. A13; Gordon H. G. McDougall, "The Green Movement in Canada: Implications for Marketing Strategy," *Journal of International Consumer Marketing* 5, no. 3 (1992); and Bettylynn W. Stoops, *Environmentally Friendly Products Program: Conceptual Framework* (Ottawa: Environment Canada, 1988), p. 2.

**FIGURE 2–1**

*Advertisement showing the design selected for the environmental choice programme (ECP) logo and explaining the programme*

# Trends in Canadian Retailing

Retailing is an exciting, dynamic part of the business world. Retailing strategies probably change more quickly than any other component of the business structure. The reason is that retailing is closer to the consumer than any other part of the corporate world.[1] As a consequence, retailing strategies are constantly changing in response to shifts in the external environment and as new forms of competition such as biodegradable bags and Green or environmentally friendly products are developed to meet consumer needs.

In this chapter, we introduce you to the trends that are likely to affect retail strategies and employment opportunities in the 1990s.

### *Environments Are Changing at a Fast Pace*

The environments retailers face are changing at an ever-faster rate. What is in store for retailing in the future? More than ever, managing changes will be the key to success. Consider the changes of the past 30 years.

The 1960s were a time of high growth in population, income, employment, and profits. Consumers thought in terms of "bigger" and "better." In contrast, the 1970s and the early 1980s brought an energy crisis, inflation, high unemployment, high interest rates, a recession, and, for many people, a loss of confidence in the future.

What was the nature of the 1980s for retailers and their customers? Retailers operated in an environment of decreasing inflation, fluctuating interest rates, and an increasingly global economy. An accelerated information explosion brought about by the personal computer and video technology initiated other changes.

The tenor of the 1990s is still unclear, but continuing adjustment to economic uncertainty seems likely, as do changes in operating philosophy as the intensity of competition continues to accelerate.

## The Globalization of Markets

According to the globalization concept, a firm with a global (i.e., international) orientation considers the world as a few standardized markets, rather than many customized ones, and it attempts to standardize its offering and operations.[2] In a North American context, this is akin to the "nine nations of North America," where markets are defined according to similarities of behaviour and economic conditions rather than national boundaries. As an example, the New England States and the Maritime provinces could form a single market.[3] This trend will be encouraged by the lessening of trade barriers around the world, with major movement in North America and Europe.

### A Single North American Market?

***The Canada–U.S. Free Trade Agreement.***   On January 1, 1989, Canada and the United States started a 10-year process of lowering tariff barriers and liberalizing trade practices. The advent of freer trade with the United States (called the **Free Trade Agreement, FTA**) has been having a major impact on strategies of Canadian retailers in Canada and in the United States.[4] The FTA covers customs, quotas, business travel, and government purchases, and other areas are still to be negotiated. As a result of the FTA, Investment Canada does not require local sourcing (suppliers) and domestic content, but for the next few years will continue to require job creation and Canadian ownership rules.

***How Do Canadian Retailers View the FTA?***   A survey of Canadian independent businesses indicated that in 1988 (just before the agreement came into effect), retailers were mildly positive about the FTA (about 38 percent), few said that it would have a negative impact (7 percent), about 22 percent said it would have no impact, and a very large 33 percent were undecided.[5]

More recently, the FTA (together with the federal value-added sales tax called the GST) has been blamed for the phenomenon of **cross-border shopping** (going to the United States to shop), which has increased the effects of the recession on Canadian retailers, leading to a large number of bankruptcies.

***Implications for Canadian Retailers.***   Canadian retailers will have to improve their competitive strategies to defend their markets in Canada in the face of strong competition from U.S. retailers, both those operating across the border and catering specifically to cross-border shoppers, and those opening stores in Canada.[6] For example, some retailers have been sourcing outside of Canada to be able to maintain and advertise lower prices (e.g., Bata), while Eaton's has been using a "Made in Canada" theme in its advertising.

Another strategy is to form joint ventures or partnerships with U.S. retailers, where each side helps the other penetrate its market. A third strategy is for Canadian department stores to lease departments to U.S. retailers, especially in smaller markets.[7] Finally, although the Canadian retailing industry is heavily concentrated, this size effect is being diluted in a North American market of 280 million customers. Thus, even the large Canadian retailers will see their buying power and merchandise leverage considerably lessened.[8]

On the other side of this picture, U.S. retailers may face a number of problems in penetrating Canadian markets. First, a major characteristic of Canadian markets is that the population density is much lower and more uneven than in the United States, making some location decisions more risky. For the next few years of the accord, the remaining tariffs will pose problems of importing and distributing merchandise (as separate shipments will have to be made to avoid some tariffs). The Canadian requirement of French language labelling will increase the cost of doing business for U.S. retailers (i.e., in terms of translation, printing, smaller runs, and local sourcing). Under the current rules, retailers will not be able to link the computer systems in their Canadian stores to their data processing centres in the United States. Finally, these retailers will have to adjust to different value systems,

*Sears, a U.S. retailer that is part of the Canadian landscape.*

SOURCE: Photo by Sandy McDougall.

legal practices, and taxation requirements.[9] However, as indicated in Retail Highlight 2–1, the U.S. retailers who did enter the Canadian market fared much better than the Canadian retailers who entered the U.S. retail market.

*NAFTA.*   Another agreement is being negotiated by the United States, Canada, and Mexico for a North American Free Trade Agreement (NAFTA), creating an even bigger North American market. Should it be signed, it is not expected to directly impact the domestic retail market as did the FTA because of the large distances involved. However, it will present opportunities for Canadian retailers in large Mexican cities, as well as provide them with a source of lower-cost merchandise for sale in Canadian and U.S. outlets.

### A Single European Market?

On January 1, 1993, the remaining tariff barriers and other national trade practices in the EEC are expected to be progressively eliminated, creating a huge European market. A probable consequence is the formation of huge retailing groups and the entry or expansion of these global retailers into the North American markets, joining the ranks of Marks & Spencer.[10] Whatever opportunities are available in this European market will have to be carefully assessed by Canadian retailers.

---

**Retail Highlight 2–1**

## Canadian versus U.S. Retailers: A Preliminary Scorecard

In the game of scoring in the other's goal, the 16 major U.S. retailers who have entered Canadian markets have a perfect record of success (i.e., a 1.000 batting average), while of the 29 Canadian retailers who have entered U.S. markets, only 8 have been successful (i.e., a .275 batting average). So now, the long-time American successes of Sears, Kmart, and Toys Я Us have been joined by The Gap, Price Club, Costco, and Tiffany, and more will be coming in the future. It has been estimated that, by the year 2000, 25 percent of retail firms in Canada will be headquartered in the United States, and that within the next 10 years, half of all Canadian retailers will fail. In addition, more money is being spent at U.S.-owned retailers in Canada than is spent in the United States itself by Canadian cross-border shoppers.

There are several reasons to explain such a lopsided record, and Canadian retailers must learn their lessons before the game is over:

- One obvious reason is size: U.S. retailers tend to be much larger, serving a market 10 times the size of Canada and benefiting from economies of scale, not only in unit costs but also in terms of operational efficiency (e.g., for many U.S. chains, selling, general, and administrative expenses are a much smaller percentage of revenues than for Canadian retailers).

### A World Market?

All signs seem to point toward a world market for Canadian retailers thinking globally. It is probable that other free trade zones will be established around the world. It is certain that competition will increase, forcing retailers to become better marketers and sharpen their strategies.

# Changing from a Merchandising to a Marketing Orientation

Evidence indicates that retail management's focus will continue to shift from merchandising to marketing. **Merchandising** means that the primary focus of the firm is to have the right merchandise, at the right place, at the right time, in the right quantities, and at the right price. *Marketing* means that all of the retailer's activities support an integrated marketing strategy with a strong consumer focus. This shift does not lessen the importance of the merchandising function within retailing. Rather, it means that merchandising is no longer more important than other functions.

Today, finding the right goods and creatively displaying them no longer ensures that a retailing firm will grow and prosper. Management can no longer simply "mind the store"; it must run the business with a constant eye on the consumer. Historically, retailers have felt that profitability and market share would follow if they presented consumers with the right goods at the right price. Financial systems and business operations under such a philosophy were merely necessary housekeeping chores.

---

*Retail Highlight 2–1 continued*

- Another important reason is the quality of management. American CEOs are more experienced, better educated, more achievement- and risk-oriented, with a stronger work ethic and greater independence. Among U.S. retailers, strategic plans are constantly developed and revised, and managers are fiercely competitive. In addition, in the United States, managers are given more leeway to make decisions according to local market conditions. Conversely, Canadian retailers tend to be very conservative, showing resistance to novel retail concepts and aggressive forays into new markets. Recent failures also show a lack of understanding of U.S. markets, which are very different from the ones they are used to.

- A third critical difference between U.S. and Canadian retailers is the quality of sales personnel and customer service. Americans enter retailing as a profession, and salesclerks are commonly made to feel appreciated and are properly trained in all aspects of selling, which results in a highly motivated sales staff and excellent customer service. In Canada, there is a tendency to see retailing as hiring students or retirees at the minimum wage and putting them on the floor without any training.

Sources: Anne Bokma, "Raking In the Dough," *The Financial Post Magazine,* January 1992, pp. 32–35; John Godfrey, "Retailers Beware, Americans Coming," *The Financial Post,* December 20, 1991, p. 11; Nicholas Hirst, "How to Succeed in U.S. Retailing," *Canadian Business,* October 1991, pp. 77–84.

Today, firms ranging from Zellers to Loblaws are creating new types of retail organizations to meet changing and varying consumer needs. For example, Loblaws has several core stores like Loblaws, Zehrs, or Valu-Mart, discount stores like No Frills, or Econo-mart, convenience stores like Quick Mart, superfood stores like City Farms, or Extra Foods, as well as combination stores like Centres, Super Loblaws, and the Superstores. Dylex has introduced a new concept store for its Fairweather division of women's apparel, built on the Eaton Centre model. These new stores have a grand black and rose marble entrance, with elegant pillars and wide aisles. These new stores try to respond to the challenge of the 1990s and of the FTA, as U.S. companies like Costco, The Gap, and The Limited are entering the Canadian market.[11] Retail Highlight 2–1 provides additional discussion of these issues.

This type of shift has created a major reorganization within the firms. Merchandising experts no longer automatically rise to the top roles in their organizations. These changes have extended managers' planning horizons well beyond one season, which is the standard for a firm with a merchandising orientation.

Today, more and more firms are looking at the long term. They are developing a strategic view of the business and are focusing on such issues as market positioning, changing consumer life-styles, and competitive strategies.

As a result, management is no longer content to respond to competitive pressures simply by changing displays, pricing, layout, or promotion. Instead, it is more prone to re-examine the entire business concept in a search for new growth opportunities. Part of this change has come about as retailers were rudely awakened from a period of rapid growth to find themselves confronted with slow growth, market saturation, stronger competition, and more demanding consumers. Successful retailers today are reorienting their organizations toward:

1. Thinking about the following questions: What business are we in? How are we positioned competitively? Have we tried to be all things to all people? Would we be more successful if we tried to be something specific to someone specific? How can we distinguish ourselves from our competitors in the minds of our target customer? Who is our target customer? Why does it matter?

2. A broader business perspective that examines the impact of each functional specialty on others and strives for excellent, effective business decisions at all levels.

3. Increased financial sophistication and skill in asset management to ensure optimum financial results.

4. Skill in working through people to achieve effective implementation, encourage creativity, and retain valued employees with changed life-style expectations.[12]

Management today is starting to recognize that merchandising genius must be combined with sound management systems, good staff development, and information processing systems to achieve targeted returns on investments. Such people have a willingness to abandon old formulas of success and create new ones that are

*Loblaws creates the Superstore to respond to changing customer needs.*

SOURCE: Courtesy of Loblaws Supermarkets Limited.

more likely to ensure success in today's environment. The new planning equips retailers with methods for determining how and where to improve their business that are more reliable than the planning approaches used in earlier years.

Significant changes in merchandising are also occurring. Many of these trends are highlighted in the following section.

# Merchandising Trends

*Productivity Improvement*

Retailers will continue to seek productivity improvements through an improved merchandise mix, cost reductions, and increased margins.

### Improved Merchandise Mix

Many department stores are reducing the number of marginal lines carried. Department stores are vulnerable in consumable items, health and beauty aids, and various houseware categories because they compete with every discounter, drugstore, and mass merchandising outlet in the city. In specific merchandise categories, fashion areas are where department stores perform best: fashion apparel, accessories, jewellery, and cosmetics. Department stores are dropping lines subject to heavy discounting and low margins. Major appliances, in particular, offer little return relative to their space and inventory costs. Retailers are realizing that consumers have no special inclination to shop for these products at department stores, no matter how favourable a store's image.

### Cost Reductions

Many firms are also focusing on cost reductions as a way to increase productivity. Costs are either fixed or variable. Fixed costs do not vary with the level of sales, while variable costs do, and the latter are easiest to reduce in the short run.

Keys to reducing variable costs include self-service, better use of technology, longer store hours, and making better use of part-time help.[13] The long-term effects of cost reductions lead to increased profit margins and a more effective competitive strategy. Competition is accelerating not only from domestic retailers but also from foreign-based retailers such as Benetton, Laura Ashley, and IKEA.

### Margin Increases

Higher-than-normal prices on low-visibility items or infrequently purchased items are being implemented. Charging for services such as repair or installation is also occurring more frequently. Some firms charge a stiff fee for delivering merchandise, for example. Banks have started to vary their service charges to retail customers based on account balances. Customers with small balances often have to pay a monthly service charge and a cheque-processing fee.

**Merchandise-Assortment Planning**

Retailers are beginning to take a leadership role in identifying the kinds of merchandise that should be added to their assortments. Some drugstores have added auto parts and supplies, since these are sought by many of their mainstream customers. No longer are retailers relying primarily on suppliers to suggest new merchandise lines, particularly as retailers begin to understand more about market segmentation, the role of research in helping to plan product assortments, and the meaning of scanner-generated in-store data on product sales. The examples of Loblaws and Dylex given earlier relate to this concern.

**Space Reduction**

Management is moving aggressively to convert unproductive retail space to other uses. The move is accelerating among department stores, large specialty stores, discount stores, mass merchandisers, and even shopping centres. More productive use of space must be found when land costs, taxes, and rentals become so high that sales productivity drops below a minimum level, often $750 per square metre or so.[14] Conversions or cutbacks to smaller space allow the retailer to save on staff, inventory, and energy. Renting to outsiders in some situations can be more profitable than retailing.

*Sweat Cards, an example of effective space usage.*

SOURCE: Courtesy of Sweat Cards and Begg & Daigle.

*Vertical Merchandising*

The trend in many outlets is also toward **vertical merchandising,** the so-called cube effect, and away from displaying merchandise in low, horizontal formats. Vertical merchandising lowers construction costs and increases space productivity, making smaller stores possible. However, without creativity, vertical merchandising can be boring. Another problem is that management can build up excessive inventory by the use of vertical merchandising. During slack demand and periods of high inventory carrying costs, inventory is likely to be lower. Vertical merchandising can thus make a store look as though it is going out of business.

*Classification Dominance*

**Classification dominance** means displaying and arranging merchandise in such a way that psychologically, the consumer is convinced that the firm has the largest

*Classification dominance is part of Junors' strategy.*

SOURCE: Courtesy of Junors and Begg & Daigle.

assortment of merchandise in that category in the city. Examples of such retailers are Colour Your World, Toys Я Us, and Canadian Tire. Normally, management will display all different sizes and colours of the items for which they want to make a dominance statement. Often, all reserve stock will also be displayed to give a strong statement about the depth of the merchandise available.

Large amounts of space are required for classification dominance. Clearly, management must be careful in selecting the merchandise lines with which it will use this display technique. Management may decide to eliminate some marginal product lines or categories to continue classification dominance.[15]

*Flexible Fixturing*

Many stores today are using flexible, movable, low-cost fixtures, as opposed to high-cost, permanent fixtures. The initial investment in the fixtures is less, and the decor in the store can be easily changed to reflect changing consumer tastes, moods, and seasons. New innovations in flexible fixturing are occurring as management continues to look for ways of reducing construction costs and increasing space productivity.[16]

*Co-Ordinated Graphics*

Accelerated use of self-service to increase store productivity has made in-store consumer information and communications more important than ever. Management is seeking less labour-intensive, less costly, but more effective means of communicating the store image and messages to customers. Graphics play an important role in this effort. Clear, consistent, informative graphics should begin externally with advertising and continue throughout the store. All aspects of communication, including promotional signs, point-of-sale graphics, departmental identification, and institutional messages, are most effective when co-ordinated.

**Signs**

Informative signs are important. Many customers want to inform themselves about merchandise before making a purchase. Salesclerks are often unavailable and may lack technical knowledge about sophisticated products. Careful explanations about product use, warranties, and technical dimensions of the product can be facilitated by the careful use of informative signing.[17]

*Increasing Emphasis on Theatrics*

Retailers also are realizing that not only must they make a major statement in a particular category of merchandise, but they must also present it in a powerful, visual way. Design and layout are thus becoming an increasingly important factor in attracting consumers. With the FTA, upscale retailers should expect the entry or expansion of more U.S. chains with strong designs, such as The Gap or Tiffany, as discussed earlier.

Product demonstrations, lectures by well-known designers, and use of music, art, and other visual means of communication will be an increasingly important part of retail merchandising.

Changes in the external environments facing the firm can also be powerful forces in affecting both marketing strategy and merchandising trends. The next section of this chapter highlights the external forces that are likely to affect retail strategy development and implementation.

# The External Environments

What are some of the specific uncertainties for the next few years? First, economic uncertainty will be a prime issue. This uncertainty means retailers will need to develop multiple strategies depending on which economic forecast they believe. Flexibility will be the key to avoid being trapped by the wrong strategy.

Second, strong price awareness and consumer sensitivity will continue to be major issues. Shoppers will be increasingly price-oriented because of pressures on their incomes, and cross-border shopping is expected to continue, albeit at a slower pace. In addition, innovations such as warehouse retailing and generic-labelled foods will continue to have a marketplace advantage with consumers for this reason.

Third, the level of investment in retailing will have to increase sharply. Land and building costs are up, as are fixture and equipment costs. However, sales in real dollars have been flat in recent years. This will require the investment of large sums of money in fixed assets.

## The Consumer

Consumers will be more careful users of information in their choices of products and services. They will have more of the information they need to make wise choices. Smart retailers will be able to take advantage of this trend by adjusting their offering to specific groups of consumers.

The right information presented correctly will more than ever go a long way toward helping retailers beat the competition. The focus will be on serving the information needs of the consumer whose products needs management wants to satisfy.

Better-educated consumers translate into more demanding and more sophisticated consumers. Highly educated consumers are increasingly confident about shopping in a self-serve environment and will make more sophisticated choices among product options. More and more products, as a result, are likely to move into the commodity arena, as choices are increasingly made more on the basis of features and value added and less on the basis of advertising and packaging.

Also, Canada is an aging society. The average Canadian in 1991 was 32 years old.[18] Consumer values will increasingly reflect middle-aged values. In addition, retailers will no longer be able to ignore the elderly. People over 65 now comprise more than 12 percent of the population, typically are well off financially, and are interested in enjoying their prosperity. Retail Highlight 2–2 discusses some emerging social trends for the 1990s delineated by Faith Popcorn, who defined the *couch potato* group.

## Immigration

A major demographic factor for the 1990s is continuing immigration, the major bulk of net population increase. These immigrants are primarily from Asia (Hong Kong, Philippines, India, Vietnam, and China), Europe (Poland, Britain, and Portugal), Lebanon, and the United States.[19] The five largest ethnic groups in Canada are Germans, Italians, Ukrainians, Native people, and Chinese. About one third of the Canadian population is non-British and non-French. Canada is largely a multicultural society, with varied tastes and needs, and presents many opportunities for retailers.

---

**Retail Highlight 2–2**

# Emerging Social Trends for the 1990s

1. *Cocooning*—A need to protect oneself from a harsh, unpredictable world. Because of this more intense focus on homelife, consumers are reading more, having babies, spending more time with their children, watching more TV, and engaging in other household activities.

2. *Self-expression*—Consumers are seeking items that reflect their individuality and style. The sterile computer age breeds a need to make a personal statement. There is a strong need for self-expression.

3. *Self-gratification*—But not the all-encompassing "buy, buy, buy for me, me, me" mentality of a few years back. Rather, people are choosing small indulgences. So, while yuppies had a yen for little foreign cars and large bank accounts, today's consumers crave imported chocolate, champagne, and Dove Bars.

4. *Grazing*—Involves more than just grabbing a Godiva chocolate here and an espresso there. People are doing everything in short takes. They're eating out of the refrigerator instead

of cooking full meals. They "zap-zap-zap" between TV stations. They read short stories in newspapers or, even trendier, they watch TV news.

5. *A return to tradition*—Religion is back. Proms and weddings are once again spectacular social events. People are returning to the values their parents possessed, such as having a happy family life.

6. *A great emphasis on quality*—Consumers know quality, they want quality, they understand quality. They buy the best. They want guarantees, and they want products that last.

7. *A concern for wellness*—Which should not be confused with fitness. Today, people would rather be in good health and lead long lives than look like models. Because people want to lead longer lives, there's a great deal of fear about aging.

8. *"Cashing out"*—Trading dollars for richer lives by devoting more time to charity work, placing humanity's needs above one's own.

Source: Excerpted from "Popcorn: Trends Last, but Fads Fade Fast," *Marketing News,* March 14, 1988, p. 29. Reprinted with permission of the American Marketing Association.

---

In addition, many of these ethnic groups are concentrated in metropolitan areas. It has been estimated that 37 percent of visible (non-Caucasian and nonaboriginal) minorities live in Toronto, 15 percent in Vancouver, and 13 percent in Montreal. About 50 percent of Canada's visible minority population live in Ontario, 19 percent in British Columbia, and 14 percent in Quebec.[20] This concentration is again favourable to retailers.

**Technology Shifts**    Technology changes will continue to occur at an ever-faster rate. Electronic funds transfer systems will be installed in rising numbers of retail outlets by the end of the decade. These systems will allow consumers to instantly transfer funds from their checking accounts to the accounts of any merchant. **Universal vendor marking (UVM),** an identification system for marking merchandise items at the vendor level, will also continue to make progress in nonfood retailing. Once UVM reaches a very high penetration level in nonfood retailing, major increases in productivity will appear.[21] The use of scanners will also continue to make major inroads into all areas of retailing.

Artificial intelligence expert systems will appear in retailing to make it easier to interact with both customers and suppliers. Such systems will allow management to plan merchandise and store design based on retailer plans, to decide on specific products to be sold based on customer wants, and to do a better job of scheduling staff. Technology of all types will also be more universally available. Technologies such as scanners and electronic data interchange will be easily available even to one- or two-unit shops.

Other new technology advances will include wireless telephones, microwave communications, communication satellites, and fibre optics, all of which are bringing in an era of low-cost, convenient universal communications. These devices are already transforming many forms of retailing as a result of the electronic information links that allow retailers to break out of building walls and shopping malls. Increasingly, the new technology will go directly into households and present images, comparative data, and product descriptions. Electronic bulletin boards will provide the latest information to in-store customers. Similarly, technology will allow shoppers to try on outfits electronically (see how they look on a screen) before deciding on the one to purchase.

Artificial intelligence will also provide devices that can listen, understand, and respond to customer queries. Smart cards (credit cards with a memory chip) will allow retailers to tailor product lines to precise consumer demand since life and family histories of each customer can be recorded on the card.[22]

*Foreign Influences*

As explained in Retail Highlight 2–1, Canadian retail units will increasingly continue to fall into foreign hands, mostly U.S. (accelerated by the FTA), British, and Japanese retailers. Foreigners will also continue to export their merchandising concepts to Canada, as reflected by the proliferation of Price Clubs and Costco warehouse operations, Benetton shops, Bally stores, and similar investments.

*Restructuring*

Mergers, acquisitions, and buyouts will continue because many retailers have prime real estate holdings, limited stock ownership in corporate hands, depressed stock prices, and diversified operations that could be sold on a piece-by-piece basis. Such organizations, even if they can survive takeover attempts, will continue to suffer from lower productivity as a result of management distraction.

*Institutional Forces*

During the past two decades, government has sought to legislate remedies for virtually every issue facing the Canadian public. The consumer and environmental movements of the 1970s brought about a variety of new governmental actions, both at the federal and provincial levels; for example, consumer and corporate affairs and consumer protection agencies. Those agencies have added to the cost of retailing without helping to increase productivity.

Recent trends suggest that Canadians are moving away from **institutional reliance** to self-reliance. Deregulation of the trucking, airline, and banking industries are examples of this change.

Similarly, some Canadians are leaving corporate life, willingly or unwillingly. Self-employment and entrepreneurial activity are accelerating. Educational self-help is growing. As an example, many persons are rebelling against institutionalized medicine; instead, they are seeking to solve their problems through diet and exercise.

*Growth of the Upscale Market*

The population is aging, and a larger share of the wealth will be distributed among fewer people. The result is a growth in the importance of the upscale market, occurring partly because of the increasing number of working women.[23] Other groups identified on the basis of high incomes are *yuppies* (young urban professionals), *muppies* (middle-aged urban professionals), *skoties* (spoiled kids of the 80s), and *woopies* (well-off old people).[24] Merchandise lines such as those offered by Laura Ashley and Holt Renfrew are rapidly growing in importance as a result of the more upscale market opportunities, as are designer furniture outlets, innovative department stores, and specialty stores.

*Continuing Slow Growth*

Retailers can no longer achieve long-term profit growth by simply adding stores. As a result, competition for customers will become very intense. Apparel sales, for example, are expected to increase by only 1 to 2 percent a year.[25] Stores will continue to increase their market share primarily by taking business away from competitors.

*Consumer Resistance to Prices*

The operating costs of retailers are continuing to increase at the same time that consumers are less willing to pay higher prices.[26] Consumer price resistance has led to the growth of cross-border manufacturers' outlet malls and **off-price retailers,** especially apparel stores that sell branded and designer labels at 20 to 40 percent below normal retail prices.

Markdowns are also becoming increasingly frequent. Consumers are witnessing a virtual epidemic of fictitious pricing in which high ''normal'' prices are established, quickly followed in a week or two by 40 to 50 percent markdowns. Sales lose their impact when everyone is having them. Retailers will have to return to strategies based on all elements of the marketing mix, including excellent customer service, not just price.[27]

Another element that complicates the situation for the retailers has been the introduction of the federal Goods and Services Tax (GST), as well as the various provincial taxes for products and services. Since they have been highly unpopular, and they have the effect of increasing the prices at the retail level (at least the perception of the prices by consumers), additional resistance to prices and to shopping in Canada may still be present in the future.

*Holt Renfrew offers attractive, exclusive merchandise lines for the upscale market.*

SOURCE: Courtesy Holt Renfrew.

**Decline in Consumer Loyalty**

Consumers today know that most merchants carry essentially the same brands. The result is that shopping patterns are no longer predictable, and merchandising alone will not be sufficient to retain consumer loyalty, particularly store loyalty.[28]

**Continued Overstoring**

Some experts indicate that most large Canadian markets contain excess retail space, and this problem became worse during the 1991–1992 recession, which saw a large number of retailers go out of business.[29] Still others contend that the problem is not primarily one of overstoring but more of a failure to differentiate one retailer from another in meeting customer needs. In any event, copycat retailing will not suffice in the overcrowded market that will characterize retailing for the decade of the 1990s.

**The Increasing Liability Problem**

The increasing concern over shareholder lawsuits accompanying the wave of merger and acquisition activity in retailing will continue to create a boom in directors' and officers' liability insurance among retailers. Suits brought against retailers include (1) suits made by shareholders on behalf of the corporation, (2) suits made by shareholders on their own behalf, and (3) claims brought by outside individuals or firms. Common charges include:

- Failure to honour employment contracts.
- Manipulation of financial statements.
- Unfair labour practices.[30]
- Violations under the Competition Act.
- Collusion or conspiracy to defraud.
- Improper expenditures.
- Imprudent expansion that results in a loss.
- Conflict of interest.
- Unfair or illegal marketing practices.
- Misleading statements and forms filed with the corresponding Securities Commissions.

# Retailing Strategies for the 1990s[31]

Some trends are becoming evident in retailing strategies as a result of environmental changes. These trends reflect the diversity in retailing and indicate the creativity and innovativeness of merchants as they seek to find a way to meet the needs of consumers in the midst of constant change.

The outlook for the 1990s is for continued consolidation and eventually the establishment of a few national competitors that will dominate each segment of retailing. Existing companies must address these challenges on two fronts: developing merger, acquisition, or restructuring strategies to meet investor expectations; and developing productivity and operations improvement strategies to enhance competitive advantage.

**Enhancing Retail Productivity**

Companies must focus on six major areas of retail productivity improvement to achieve lasting competitive advantage.

### Advanced Merchandising Systems

Point of sale has become as basic to successful retailing as cash registers were in the 1920s. Competition has shifted to the development of item-driven information systems where profitability, inventory status, and rates of sales are known for each stockkeeping unit in the chain.

### Competitive Information and Research

Marketing research is not yet a universally accepted tool, even among major retailers. But companies that systematically study the market through consumer research are discovering gems of competitive information (e.g., unmet needs in terms of style, price point, or size) that can be quickly translated into incremental sales.

### Vendor Communication Systems
The electronic transmission of purchase orders, invoices, and advance shipping notices is being used by leading retailers to make buying and allocation decisions much later in the buying cycle and to dramatically improve in-stock positions as well as inventory turns.

### Value-Added Partnerships
Leading retailers are also working closely with key vendors to create a system of "virtual integration," modeled on the concepts of just-in-time inventory management developed in Japan's manufacturing sector.

### Human Resource Programs
Organizational development is perhaps the most elusive of the six goals. Few retailers have achieved very high levels of employee satisfaction and motivation. In a labour market where hourly rates are rising and the traditional retail labour market (i.e., aged 18 to 24) is shrinking, this is the ultimate weapon.

### Customer Service Programs
Retailers that can establish a sense of loyalty in their customers are also winning big. A lot of customer service is still focused on the basics of merchandising (i.e., right goods/place/time/price).

*Growth Strategies for the 1990s*

Though vital for survival, improved productivity is not enough. Investors have set some demanding financial targets for retailers to meet, such as produce 5 percent growth in real terms, and 10 percent real return on investment to sell for more than their asset value. In a market with too many stores and low, single-digit growth rates, this is no simple task. Successful retailers must therefore take a leaf out of the corporate raider's book and adopt some aggressive strategies to enhance shareholder values.

### Growth through Acquisition
Internally generated growth for most companies is not enough. Prime sites are not readily obtained through purchase of a competitor or acquisition of a package of leases from another retailer that is downsizing operations. The winner in today's market will be alert to opportunities created by restructuring rather than conducting business as usual.

### Leverage the Business
Under today's tax laws, debt is a much more attractive source of financing than equity. If management leaves a lot of cash or "hidden" value on the balance sheet, the firm will eventually become an acquisition candidate.

### Challenge the Asset Base
All companies get comfortable over time, and many get sloppy. Simple improvements in merchandising systems and controls, for example, can have a startling

effect on inventory levels in many cases. Retailers with credit card operations should evaluate third-party options as well as conversion of house cards to affinity cards (Visa or MasterCard in the firm's name).

### Maintain Lean Operations

Investor groups count on a 15 to 20 percent cut in overhead to help finance operations. And in the vast majority of cases, those savings are there for the asking.

### Reward Performance

Perhaps the most powerful change a company can make is to give its employees and key executives meaningful rewards based on performance. The market focuses on cash flow; senior executives should be paid based on their ability to meet or exceed annual cash flows (of course, within reasonable bounds). Performance compensation at the supervisory level can also be a potent force for innovation, if properly applied.

*Characteristics of High-Performance Retailers*

In summary, successful retailers in the future will share several characteristics.

### Attention to Detail

Winners not only do the right big things, they do the little things right.

### Constant Communication with Customers and Employees

Getting close to the customer is more than just a tired expression. Understanding and responding to customer needs requires close continuing contact.

### Market Drive

Progressive retailers will continue to offer strong price/value relationships, including greater value, fashion, and convenience, which will induce customers to spend less time and money at competing outlets.

### Strategic Planning

Successful retailers, as we will see throughout the text, are ones who are committed to a clearly defined purpose and a mission that indicates what they want to be and where they want to go.

### Technological Leadership

Retailers will continue to accelerate their moves to an integrated management information system that will link outlying retail outlets and distribution centres with the headquarters buying and financial functions.

### More Micromarketing

The mass market has shattered into many pieces. "We are a mosaic of minorities . . . all companies will have to do more stratified or tailored or niche marketing."[32]

The fragmentation of markets is resulting in more efforts to reach consumers in-store by putting ads on supermarket loudspeakers, on in-store monitors, on shopping carts, and even in high schools. Retailers will increasingly target messages at the ethnic subgroups and at the elderly. They will continue to experiment with new ways to find out just who it is they want to reach, and they will move beyond the use of demographics and psychographics in identifying customers.

Scanner check-out data are feeding the move to **micromarketing** by providing the types of detailed data required by retailers. The retailer is no longer a passive player but is dictating how little or how much space to give products, demanding a growing list of fees and discounts, and insisting on a partnership role with manufacturers in planning product offerings.

Listening, planning, and technology will be the key priority words for success in the foreseeable future.

# Services Retailing

Services retailing is becoming such an important part of the Canadian economy that we are devoting a separate section of this chapter to the subject. Growth in services retailing exceeds growth in other sectors of the economy. By the year 2000, the service sector of the economy is forecasted to provide four out of every five jobs.[33] Services retailing includes health spas, legal clinics, educational institutions, hair stylists, dental clinics, law firms, and so forth. This list helps to show the diversity that characterizes services retailing.

## *Problems in Services Retailing*

Despite the importance of services retailing to the economy, less attention has been given to the unique problems of services retailers than to those of tangible goods firms. The differences between the two types of retailing pose unique marketing and merchandising problems for services retailers.[34]

### Intangibility
A service cannot be seen, touched, or smelled; it cannot be handled or stored. A service is essentially an intangible product. Because of **intangibility,** services retailers must have the ability to instantly produce a service in order to sell it. This characteristic of services poses unique problems to the services retailer.[35]

### Perishability
Many services are essentially perishable. If a hotel room is empty for an evening, the revenue is lost forever. Tickets to a symphony performance are only good at the time of the performance. Similarly, because of **perishability,** dentists, physicians, attorneys, and beauticians cannot recover revenue lost because of an unfilled schedule.

### Lack of Transportability
The inability to transport services means that services normally must be consumed at the point of production. The services of a physician typically are available only at the physical location of the outlet, for example. House calls are possible but are an inefficient way of service delivery.

### Lack of Standardization
Standardization in service quality is difficult to achieve. Fast-food restaurants, which offer a combination of tangible goods and services, are an exception. A

related problem is the difficulty consumers have in judging the quality of a service. How does one objectively decide which surgeon or dentist is the most qualified, for example?

### Labour Intensity

The labour-intensive nature of services retailing is another factor that prevents such outlets from easily achieving economies of scale. The output of a hair stylist cannot easily be increased, since the service is personally produced and tailored to the needs of each individual client. Services retailers, as a result, have difficulty establishing large market shares, which means that competitors can quickly enter the market.

### Demand Fluctuations

The demand for services also is often more difficult to predict than that for tangible goods. The demand for some services can fluctuate strongly during a month, a day of the week, or even an hour of the day. Management has difficulty forecasting the demand for visitors to museum exhibits, ballet performances, or theme parks such as Canada's Wonderland, for example.

## Planning the Services Offering

Planning the services offering is in many ways similar to planning a tangible goods offering. The question ultimately is one of what people are buying. The *core service* is the primary benefit customers seek from a services firm. *Peripheral services* are secondary benefits sought by customers. The core service for a motel is a clean, comfortable room. Peripheral services could include a swimming pool, cable service, restaurants, or a golf driving range. Management often seeks to integrate core and peripheral services into a coherent competitive strategy.

### Distribution

Distribution is an important aspect of services retailing, even though many services are intangible. As noted above, most services are provided directly by the retailer to the end user, without an intermediary. Still, some indirect channels are used in services retailing. An example is the acceptance of bank credit cards by retailers. Banks extend credit to retail customers who use the bank's credit card. The bank is a third party to any transaction that the customer has with the retail outlet.

### Promotion

Effective use of promotion often is more difficult for services retailers than for tangible goods retailers because services are more difficult for consumers to evaluate than tangible goods.[36] Increasingly, however, services retailers are using a variety of promotional tools and techniques to communicate information. Advertisements for a health spa, for example, often include a pricing schedule in much the same way a person would expect to find price quotations in tangible goods retailing ads. The advertisements also often focus on specific attributes of the service to be performed in an effort to make services more tangible.

### Pricing

Pricing, although a key part of a services retailer's marketing plan, traditionally has been a hush-hush topic. Managers have been reluctant to talk about the prices of their services, and instead have tended to refer to price as "admission" for entertainment events, or a "fee" when using the services of an attorney. Pricing is becoming a more open subject, however, as more and more services firms go aggressively into marketing.

Some services retailers have long used pricing strategies to smooth demand. Resort hotels offer lower prices during the off-season. Airlines offer reduced rates for customers who fly during low demand, "red-eye" periods such as midnight to six A.M. Banks have different fee structures to accommodate various customer segments.

# Critical Contemporary Issues

A text on retailing would be incomplete without a focus on consumerism and other contemporary social issues of importance to retail strategists.

## *Consumerism*

Retailers, in analyzing the economic and social environments and their effects on strategy, would be remiss if they failed to recognize the continuing influence of **consumerism.** *Consumerism is an organized expression of dissatisfaction with selected business practices.* The consumer movement of the 1970s and 1980s is continuing into the 1990s but in a quieter, more mature context.

Many of the issues consumers first rallied around are now being addressed, if not remedied, in retailing. Consumer concerns that still persist, however, include complaints about false or misleading advertising, deceptive price comparisons, and high-pressure selling tactics.

One manifestation of the new consumerism is the increasing number of mandatory bottle and can deposit laws for beverages. The laws mark a continuing fundamental shift in society, away from an energy- and materials-intensive system toward one that is more heavily focused on recycling and the widespread use of the **reduce, reuse, and recycle logo** (reproduced in Exhibit 2–1). Some retailers understandably are unhappy with such trends because of the additional costs involved.

For the foreseeable future, local organizations that can provide direct tangible benefits to consumers will likely be more effective vehicles for change than national groups.

Some persons see a new rise in consumer aggression that will extend the consumerism of the past decades into a new realm. This aggression, they contend, will especially reach those persons with money but little discretionary time. An example of this aggression is defying the smoking bans in airplanes, restaurants, and retail stores.

We also cannot overlook the darker side of consumerism—the era of the consumer as "gyp."[37] Problems range from insurance fraud to supermarket theft. Coupon fraud is another major problem. Coupon fraud by consumers includes redemption of coupons for items not purchased, the purchase of different products sharing the same brand name, or purchase of an item that violates the size, quantity, expiration date, or other terms of the coupon.[38]

**EXHIBIT 2-1**

*The reduce, reuse, and recycle logo*

### Voluntary Responses by Management to Consumer Dissatisfaction

Most retailers would probably agree that providing for customer satisfaction is good business. Thus, retailers in recent years have taken various steps to lessen consumer dissatisfaction.

#### Consumer Advisers

Forward-thinking retailers have appointed consumer advisers to bridge the communication gap between the shopper and management. Such persons make sure that customer complaints and questions are handled quickly and honestly. They represent management to the consumer and the consumer to management. Their job is to keep people happy by giving them straight answers and by allowing management to keep a constant finger on the pulse of the shopper.

#### Corporate Consumer Professionals

Corporate consumer affairs has also become a profession in recent years as retailers have made major investments in professionally trained personnel to more effectively respond to consumer concerns. These persons represent the interests of consumers in corporate councils.

#### Third-Party Arbitration

**Third-party arbitration** is a process by which two parties agree to have an impartial party or panel resolve their difficulty with a final and binding decision. General Motors offers such an option to consumers. In addition to generating consumer goodwill, the programs offer management a way to resolve complaints without litigation. The program also gives merchants protection against irresponsible consumers. Such programs are often sponsored by local Better Business Bureaus.

### Advisory Boards

Consumer **advisory boards** are also experiencing a revival in popularity as retailers seek more effective programs for communicating with consumers. Such boards comprise a cross section of community citizens, including men and women, senior citizens, and representatives of various ethnic groups. The new boards reflect a broadening and maturing of the public interest concept.

## *Quality-of-Life Issues*

Consumerism is concerned with more than the satisfaction of consumer needs in the marketplace, as we observed earlier. Consumers are also becoming increasingly concerned about quality of life in a broader sense. Quality-of-life concerns are evident in consumer protests about endangered wildlife species and vegetation, air and water pollution, beautification, and a host of similar issues.

Consumers clearly expect the retailing community to protect and preserve the environment and our natural resources in addition to operating in an economically efficient manner. Many of the quality-of-life concerns of consumers have culminated in federal and provincial regulations covering such issues as open space, land use, historic preservation, job safety and health, and much more.

Recent polls have indicated that Canadian consumers are becoming more and more environmentally conscious, avoiding products because the packaging is not biodegradable or recyclable. McDonald's has developed a complete recycling program to respond to this new sensitivity to the environment. Many retailers have stopped using material made of chlorofluorocarbons (CFCs), which deplete the ozone layer. Loblaws was one of the first retailers to develop its own line of environmentally friendly products, called the *Green* line.[39]

Consumers have also been pressing in recent years for greater privacy. Consumers are often frustrated by the amount of junk mail and telephone sales calls they receive, especially when the sales call is a prerecorded message. Marketing researchers are experiencing greater difficulties in getting consumers to respond to interviews—consumers are becoming less willing to put up with the annoyances created by the market researchers.

## Future Certainties

Regardless of the changes that are occurring, we can safely make the following observations about the future:

- Retailing will continue to grow in importance as a way of facilitating exchange.
- Retailing, to be successful, must continue to anticipate and respond to changes in the environments.
- Retailing will continue to offer exciting, rewarding, and diverse career opportunities. Job opportunities will continue to abound in promotion, personal selling, distribution, research, and various other dimensions of retailing, including competitor analysis, sales management, and corporate training.

Wouldn't you like to be a part of the phenomenal success of firms such as Club Monaco, Boutique Jacob, or IKEA? Or maybe you want to be on the team helping to rewrite competition in the financial services industries as a result of deregulation, or part of the team that is working to develop a store of the future, or to help make McDonald's more of a world competitor. Perhaps your primary interest is retailing in your hometown, or helping to broaden the public's awareness of the beauty of ballet, or helping to bring more excitement to professional sports. Whatever your interests and career aspirations, retailing can play a vital role in your success. The following chapters should help you understand the dynamic and challenging field of retailing.

# Chapter Highlights

- The trend toward the globalization of markets will create some important challenges to Canadian retailers as they face sharp competition from U.S. and European retailers, and as they take advantage of the opportunities provided by the current Canada–U.S. Free Trade Agreement (FTA), and the coming North American FTA (NAFTA).

- The focus of management will continue to shift from merchandising to marketing as a key to strategy development.

- More and more firms are looking to the long term in developing a strategic view of their business and are focusing on such issues as store positioning, changing consumer life-styles, and unique competitive strategies.

- Numerous changes are also occurring in merchandising as retailers seek to respond to a constantly shifting environment. The key changes include modified merchandise mixes, better merchandise-assortment planning, stringent cost-reduction programmes, increased use of classification dominance, vertical merchandising, flexible fixturing, co-ordinated graphics and informative signing, and more emphasis on theatrics.

- Changes in the external environments are also affecting strategy. Key shifts include stronger price awareness by consumers and less store or brand loyalty, accelerating technology shifts, growth of the upscale market, increasing time pressures on consumers, slow growth in many market segments, and continued overstoring. The increasing liability problem is also impacting retail strategy because of rising insurance costs.

- Retailers are choosing to respond to the changing environments in a variety of ways. The key trends include enhancing retail productivity through information technology, value-added partnerships, and customer service programmes, as well as developing sound growth strategies.

- Services retailing is becoming an important part of the Canadian economy and deserves attention for its unique marketing and merchandising problems: intangibility, perishability, lack of transportability and standardization, labour intensity, and demand fluctuations.

- Greater responsiveness to the social consciousness of society will continue to impact marketing strategies, as will consumerism. Consumer concerns still persist about false or misleading advertising, deceptive price comparisons, and high-pressure selling tactics.

- Management has taken a variety of voluntary steps in helping to alleviate consumer dissatisfaction. The steps include the use of in-store consumer advisers, hiring of corporate consumer professionals, better use of third-party arbitration, and consumer advisory boards.

- Quality-of-life issues continue to be important, as reflected in consumer concerns about air and water pollution, beautification, and a host of similar issues. Consumers clearly expect the retailing community to protect and preserve the environment and its natural resources.

# Key Terms

Advisory boards    50
Classification dominance    36
Consumerism    48
Cross-border shopping    28
EcoLogo    26
Free Trade Agreement (FTA)    28
Green marketing    26
Institutional reliance    41
Intangibility    46

Merchandising    31
Micromarketing    46
Off-price retailers    41
Perishability    46
Reduce, reuse, and recycle logo    48
Third-party arbitration    49
Universal vendor marking (UVM)    40
Vertical merchandising    36

# Discussion Questions

1. What changes are expected in the future relative to store size, layout, and design?

2. What does it mean to say that retail management is shifting its emphasis from a merchandising to a marketing orientation?

3. Summarize the major changes that are projected for the 1990s in the competitive structure of retailing.

4. Highlight the major competitive strategies that are emerging among retailers as keys to success in the 1990s.

5. What are the most common charges against retailers in law suits brought against them by different groups?

6. What are the factors that led to the emergence of consumerism as a major market force?

7. What have been some of the retailer volunteer responses to consumer dissatisfaction?

8. Why should retailers be concerned about quality-of-life issues?

# Application Exercises

1. A major discussion in this chapter relates to the following questions: What are the likely future operating environments? What are some of the specific changes in operations methods likely to be? List these changes. Then interview several retailers in your community and see if they agree. If they believe other things are likely to be as important, ask why they feel this way. You might work with a classmate. Make a table showing your results, and present your findings to the class.

2. Prepare a short questionnaire, one page or so, based on the various trends in the economic and social environments that will affect retailing in the 1990s.

Interview a cross section of retailers in your community to determine the strengths of their beliefs about the likelihood of these trends occurring or continuing in the near future. Prepare a short paper based on your findings.

3. Prepare a short questionnaire to be administered by telephone to a representative group of households in your community. Seek to find out *(a)* the effects of women working outside the home on the household, *(b)* the effects of changing social values on the household, and *(c)* the effects of the inflation and deflation of recent years.

# Suggested Cases

# Endnotes

1. John Oldland, "Lessons to Be Learned from Retailers," *Marketing,* September 14, 1987, p. 28.
2. Theodore Levitt, "The Globalization of Markets," *Harvard Business Review,* May/June 1983, p. 98; see also Michael Porter, *Competitive Advantage* (New York: Free Press), 1985.
3. Joel Garreau, *The Nine Nations of North America* (New York: Avon Books, 1981).
4. Elliott Ettenberg, "Portrait of a Marriage," *Marketing,* October 31, 1988, p. 18.
5. Catherine Swift, "Small Business and the Canada–U.S. Free Trade Agreement," *Journal of Small Business and Entrepreneurship* 5, no. 5 (Summer 1988), pp. 5–10.
6. Barrie McKenna, "U.S. Chain Stores Come Shopping," *The Financial Post,* May 8, 1989, p. 8; and Barbara Aarsteinsen, "California Retailer Gap Looks to Canada to Extend Its Market in Casual Clothing," *Globe and Mail,* March 9, 1989, p. B12.
7. Julie Cohen, "Invasion of the Americans," *Retail Directions,* May/June 1989, pp. 26–31.
8. Ettenberg, "Portrait of a Marriage."
9. Brent Houlden, "Setting Up Shop in Canada," *Retail Directions,* May/June 1989, p. 28.
10. Barbara Aarsteinsen, "British HMV Set to Put New Spin on Record Retailing in Canada," *Globe and Mail,* April 9, 1989, p. B9.
11. Barbara Aarsteinsen, "Ritzy Toronto Store Headlines New Effort to Attract Fairweather Friends," *Globe and Mail, Report on Business,* March 3, 1989, p. B6.
12. Debra J. Cornwall, "Say Good-Bye to the Merchant Mystique," *Business Horizons,* September/October 1984, p. 82. (c) 1984 by the Foundation for the School of Business at Indiana University. Reprinted by permission.
13. Anne Bokma, "Hard Labour," *Retail Directions,* November/December 1988, pp. 20–25.
14. Marian Stinson, "Retailers Facing Escalating Rent Costs, Diminishing Sales," *Globe and Mail, Report on Business,* September 29, 1988, p. B6.
15. For further reading, see "Crowley's Light Motif: A Delicate Balance," *Chain Store Age Executive, General Merchandise Trends,* March 1986, p. 86.
16. Laura Medcalf, "Stores with Style," *Retail Directions,* November/December 1988, pp. 32–41.
17. For further reading, see "Department Stores Score on Price Signs," *Chain Store Age Executive, General Merchandise Trends,* March 1986, p. 18.
18. Statistics Canada, *Census of Canada, 1991* (Ottawa: Information Canada, 1992).
19. "Canada's Family Tree," *The Royal Bank Reporter,* Spring 1992, p. 21.
20. Ibid., p. 9.
21. Serge Fortin, "EDI Efficiency," *Retail Directions,* January/February 1989, pp. 21–22.
22. Bernard Sosnick, "Retailers in an Era of Restructuring," *Retail Control,* March 1989, pp. 19–24.
23. Jo Marney, "Reaching the New Woman of Today," *Marketing,* March 1, 1982, p. 9; Myra Strober and Charles B. Weinberg, "Working Wives and Major Family Expenditures," *Journal of Consumer Research,* December 1977, pp. 141–47; and "Last Year It Was Yuppies—This Year It's Their Parents," *Business Week,* March 19, 1986, pp. 68–72.
24. Jo Marney, "Woopies, Muppies . . . The List Grows," *Marketing,* February 2, 1987, pp. 10–12; Barrie McKenna, "Many Marketers Missing Bets

by Ignoring Over-50s,'' *The Financial Post,* May 15, 1989, p. 21; and Barrie McKenna, ''Ailing Dylex Sees Changing of Guard,'' *The Financial Post,* October 31, 1988, p. 27.

25. Jeremy Main, ''Merchants' Woe, Too Many Stores,'' *Fortune,* May 13, 1985, p. 62; see also Jim Osteroff, ''Updating Present Stores Seen Economizing Trend,'' *Supermarket News,* November 3, 1986, p. 1.

26. ''Rough Times in the Rag Trade,'' *Report on Business Magazine,* October 1988, pp. 158–64.

27. Pat Morden, ''Retailers Rebound from Margins of Terror,'' *Profit,* November 1991, pp. 46–47.

28. ''An Absence of Store Loyalty among Women,'' *Marketing,* August 31, 1987, p. 4.

29. Barbara Wickens, ''Misery at the Malls,'' *Maclean's,* March 23, 1992, pp. 30–31; and Andrew Allentuck, ''Is the Mall Beginning to Pall?'' *Globe and Mail,* May 5, 1992, p. B23.

30. ''Grocery Chains, Unions Attack 'Cut-Rate' Contract,'' *Globe and Mail,* March 29, 1989, p. B13.

31. This section on retailing strategies for the 1990s is reproduced with permission from Thomas R. Rauh, ''Strategies for the 1990s,'' *Discount Merchandiser,* July 1989, pp. 52–54. Copyright ©. All rights reserved.

32. Harriet C. Johnson, ''1990s: Hot Decade for Service Firms,'' *U.S.A. Today,* May 11, 1987, p. 1.

33. David A. Collier, ''Managing a Service Firm: A Different Management Game,'' *National Productivity Review,* Winter 1983–84, p. 36.

34. F. G. Crane, T. K. Clarke, and Steve Ascroft, ''Product Classification and Information Sources Used in Service Selection,'' in *Marketing,* vol. 8, ed. Ronald E. Turner (ASAC, 1987), pp. 21–30; Leonard L. Berry, ''Retail Businesses Are Service Businesses,'' *Journal of Retailing* (Spring 1986), pp. 3–6; and ''When Marketing Services, the Four P's Are Not Enough,'' *Business Horizons,* May–June 1986, pp. 44–50.

35. Gordon H. G. McDougall, ''Products and Services: Some Insight into Consumer Decision Making,'' in *Marketing,* vol. 7, ed. Thomas E. Muller (ASAC, 1986), pp. 212–21.

36. Gordon H. G. McDougall, ''Consumer Preferences for Two Information Sources: Products and Services Compared,'' in *Marketing,* vol. 8 (ASAC, 1987), pp. 1–10.

37. Paul Bernsten, ''Cheating—The New National Past Time?'' *Business,* October–December 1985, p. 24.

38. Marina Strauss, ''Fraudulent Coupon Use Costing Retailers Millions of Dollars,'' *Globe and Mail, Report on Business,* March 22, 1989, p. B13.

39. Gordon H. G. McDougall, ''The Green Movement in Canada: Implications for Marketing Strategy,'' *Journal of International Consumer Marketing* 5, no. 3 (1992); and Emily deNitto, ''. . . As Loblaws Pitches Its Green Line to U.S.,'' *Supermarket News,* August 21, 1989, p. 33.

# 3   ANALYZING THE CANADIAN RETAIL ENVIRONMENT

## Chapter Objectives

After reading this chapter, you should be able to:

1 Describe the major federal regulations affecting retailers.
2 List the key economic indicators that reflect the state of the economy.
3 Evaluate the demographic environment.
4 Discuss how changes in competition affect retailing.
5 Describe trends in technology and their impact on retailing.

## Retailing Capsule

The past decade has brought many changes to the Canadian retail environment. Ten years ago, few stores were open on Sunday. Now, three provinces, Alberta, British Columbia, and Ontario, have wide-open seven-day shopping, while in some other provinces, Sunday shopping is a controversial political and legal issue. And the Competition Act, passed by the federal government in 1986, has a series of measures that directly affects retailers.

In the past decade, the Canadian economic environment has experienced inflation, high unemployment rates, and two recessions, as well as years of strong economic growth. Many Canadians experienced difficult times in the early 1980s when the unemployment rate was 12 percent, the inflation rate was over 12 percent, and interest rates were over 18 percent. The later 1980s saw better times, as employment increased, interest rates decreased, and inflation was around 4 percent. The early 1990s saw a deep recession, high unemployment rates, and a large number of retail bankruptcies. In 1992, unemployment reached 10 percent, real incomes declined, and major Canadian retail chains suffered substantial losses.

The past decade has seen only moderate increases in the total population (less than 1 percent per year). However, some age groups such as the baby boomers (persons born between 1946 and 1966) grew at a far more rapid rate than the overall population. And in the next 10 years, the group called *seniors,* people 65 and over, will grow more rapidly than any other age group.

In the past decade, over 1.7 million women entered the labour force. The overall participation rate in the labour force for married women increased by 6 percent, and today, 6 out of 10 female heads of household with preschool children are in the labour force; 7 out of 10 with school-age kids. Dual-income households are now the norm, not the exception.

In the past decade, technology has had a tremendous impact on retailing. In particular, point-of-purchase scanners allow firms to evaluate tactical decisions on a daily basis and to optimize the merchandising mix.

Today, retailers are faced with many forms of competition that did not exist 10 years ago. Stores within stores, superstores, mixed-use stores, warehouse retailers, and the world's largest shopping mall have created a new competitive environment.

Progressive retailers know that the next decade will bring more change. These retailers constantly monitor the environment so they can anticipate and react to these changes. They develop new strategies to capture opportunities and avoid threats in the retail environment.

The retail strategies to be discussed in Chapter 6 cannot be developed in a vacuum. The strategies must emerge only after an analysis of both the internal and external environments facing the firm. Careful analyses of shifts in the economy, in competitive behaviour, in population demographics, in the legal environment, and in technology are important in order to base planning efforts on realistic assumptions about the future. Consumer responses to economic and social trends are complex and reveal themselves in changing patterns of consumption.

The ability to anticipate and respond to such changes is the key to strategic success in retailing. Forward-thinking managers have established approaches to monitor trends and determine their impact. This chapter discusses the major environmental forces affecting retailers, beginning with the legal environment.

# The Legal Environment

Retailing decisions are affected by the legal environment, which is made up of legislation (federal, provincial, and municipal), government agencies, and various action groups. These laws, agencies, and groups regulate and influence retailers' strategies and tactics. This section introduces you to the federal, provincial, and local regulations, agencies, and groups that can have an impact on strategy and implementation.

## *Legislation Affecting Retailers*

More regulations affecting retailing have been introduced in the past two decades than in the previous 100 years. Devising effective ways to regulate the market-place while sustaining an environment of healthy competition, innovation, and economic growth is a major challenge confronting retailers, the government, and consumers. A description of the major federal legislation affecting retailers is provided in Table 3–1.

In 1986, the federal government enacted the Competition Act—the major legislative act regulating marketing and retailing practices in Canada. The act is designed to protect companies, consumers, and the interests of society. It does this by prohibiting mergers that reduce competition to the detriment of the public. For example, in 1986, Canada Safeway attempted to purchase the supermarket operations of Woodward's in western Canada. The merger was approved by the Competition Bureau (created by the act) only after Safeway agreed to sell 12 Woodward's Food Floor stores in six cities where the acquisition might hurt market competition.[1] As well, the act forbids unfair trade practices such as **predatory pricing, price discrimination, resale price maintenance,** and **exclusive dealing,** and prohibits misleading price advertising. The important sections of the Competition Act that directly affect retailers are shown in Table 3–2 (p. 60), and examples of the types of activities that retailers have been prosecuted for are shown in Retail Highlight 3–1 (p. 61).

At the provincial level, each province has business practices acts that are similar to or extend the federal legislation. For example, all provinces regulate the activities of door-to-door retailers and allow for cooling-off periods ranging from 2 to 10 days, when consumers can cancel contracts with this type of seller. Also, most provinces have consumer protection acts that regulate retailers' activities, including the hours and days a retailer can open. In 1984, the Supreme Court repealed the Lord's Day Act and the provinces were then faced with the Sunday shopping issue.

---

## TABLE 3–1    Major Federal Legislation Affecting Retailers

Trade practices

- *Competition Act:* Encourages competition in the marketplace and benefits consumers by reducing upward pressure on prices, rewarding innovation and initiative, increasing choice and quality of goods offered, and preventing abuses of market power by ensuring that firms compete with each other on a fair basis.
- *Bankruptcy Act* and intellectual property laws (e.g., Copyright Act, Trade-Marks Act, Patents Act and Industrial Design Act, the National Trade Mark and True Labelling Act, and the Canada Business Corporations Act): Make rules for the marketplace that impact on consumers.
- *Tax Rebate Discounting Act:* Protects consumers who use tax-discounting services.
- Other legislation involving trade practices: Broadcasting Act, Canadian Human Rights Act, Income Tax Act, Official Languages Act, Small Loans Act, Employment Equity Act, and Multiculturalism Act.

Health and safety

- *Food and Drugs Act:* Protects consumers from hazards to health and from fraud or misleading representations associated with the sale of foods (partly administered by Health and Welfare Canada).
- *Hazardous Products Act:* Protects the health and safety of consumers by prohibiting or regulating the sale, advertisement, and importation of products considered to be dangerous to the public.

Product standards and grades

- *Consumer Packaging and Labelling Act:* Specifies what product information must be made available to consumers on prepackaged products, and how it must be displayed.
- *Weights and Measures Act:* Sets national standards for fair measure in trade for most measured commodities.
- *Textile Labelling Act:* Requires that information on fibre content and dealer identity be provided on the labels of consumer textile articles.
- *Precious Metals Marking Act:* Protects consumers from false claims for articles containing adulterated or substandard precious metals.

---

SOURCE: "The Marketplace in Transition: Changing Roles for Consumers, Business and Governments?" *Consumer and Corporate Affairs Canada,* Ottawa, 1992.

The controversy led to wide-open seven-day shopping in Alberta, British Columbia, and Ontario, and to some provinces letting each municipality decide the issue. Now, Canadian regulations governing Sunday shopping vary widely across provinces, cities, and even types of stores.

Retailers operating in Quebec need to comply with language requirements for their signs and displays. For example, all outdoor signs must be in French, but within the store, English signs and messages are allowed. Quebec retailers are also governed by regulations concerning advertising to children and roadside advertising.

***Government Agency Activities***    Consumer affairs departments at the federal and provincial level make sure that retailers comply with legislation. They also act as watchdogs for consumers and can act on consumer complaints. In this capacity, these departments ensure that

*Sunday and holiday shopping varies across Canada.*

SOURCE: Photo by James Hertel.

individual consumers receive fair treatment by retailers. For example, the federal Consumer and Corporate Affairs department is considering establishing clear-cut standards for services sold by retailers, such as house-cleaning services. The concern is that consumers may not be able to compare quality among these service sellers because of lack of knowledge and lack of standards.[2]

At the provincial level, the consumer affairs departments will often provide information to consumers as to their rights when buying merchandise. These guides include such things as facts on refunds and exchanges and tips on buying a car.

***Action Group Activities***

Various consumer groups also affect the activities of retailers. On a formal basis, groups such as the Consumers Association of Canada (CAC) lobby governments, manufacturers, and retailers for changes that safeguard and protect consumer interests. As well, the CAC publishes the *Canadian Consumer,* which reports the results of product tests and provides purchasing tips in each bimonthly issue. The

---

**TABLE 3–2    The Competition Act**
Major Sections Affecting Retailers

---

*Mergers:* Section 33 prohibits mergers by which competition is, or is likely to be, lessened to the detriment of, or against, the interest of the public.

*Pricing:* Sections 34 and 35 prohibit a supplier from charging different prices to competitors purchasing like quantities of goods (price discrimination) and prohibit price-cutting that lessens competition (predatory pricing).

*Pricing and advertising:* Section 36 prohibits prices that misrepresent the regular selling price (misleading price advertising). As well, it prohibits advertising activities that misrepresent warranties, guarantees, and testimonials. Provision for double-ticketing (if two prices are shown on a product, the lower price is the price to consumers) and pyramid selling are included in Section 36. Pricing and advertising are also covered under Section 37, which prohibits "bait and switch" selling (offering a product at a low price when very few or none are available for sale) and prohibits selling above the advertised price.

*Pricing:* Section 38 prohibits suppliers from requiring subsequent resellers to offer products at a stipulated price.

*Distribution:* Section 48 prohibits consignment selling if the purpose is to control prices or discriminate between dealers. Exclusive dealing, when retailers agree to handle the products of only one supplier, is prohibited where the result is that competition is, or is likely to be, substantially lessened. Tied selling, where a supplier will sell a line of merchandise only if the retailer also agrees to purchase other merchandise from the supplier, is also prohibited if competition is lessened.

---

Better Business Bureau, which operates branches in 17 Canadian cities, provides a strong voice for consumers who have complaints against specific retailers.

Consumers will band together on an informal basis when they have a common interest or goal. Because retailers are in constant touch with consumers, they often bear the brunt of consumer protests. Retailers have been petitioned and boycotted by citizen groups who have protested Sunday shopping, the selling of war toys, the selling of fur coats, non-union products, and retail bank charges. As a result of numerous consumer complaints about bank service charges, the federal government held hearings on retail banking practices in 1987. On the basis of these hearings, Canadian banks voluntarily agreed to a number of recommendations, including no charges for cash withdrawals.[3]

The Canadian Medical Association has put pressure on drugstores to stop selling cigarettes. This group would like their patients to get their prescriptions filled at pharmacies that do not sell tobacco products.[4]

Consumer concern over environmental issues is reflected in retailer actions. In a recent survey, 80 percent of Canadians expressed a willingness to pay more for environmentally safe products.[5] Retailers such as Loblaws, Becker's Convenience Stores, and The Body Shop have been actively marketing environmentally safe products.

*Industry Codes*    Various industry codes also affect Canadian retailers. This is particularly true in the area of advertising, where broadcast codes and industry guidelines lead to considerable control of advertising. For example, the Canadian Advertising

Retail Highlight 3–1

# Examples of Prosecution of Retailers under Section 36 of the Competition Act

- A Winnipeg sporting goods retailer stated in newspaper advertisements that a discount of "30–40 percent" off the ordinary selling price was available for golf clubs. Investigation revealed that the statements were untrue, and the retailer was fined $2,000.

- A Newfoundland realtor stated in newspaper ads that "over 90 percent of the realtor's listings were sold in 12 days or less." Investigation revealed that the statements were untrue, and the realtor was fined $500.

- A St. Amable (Quebec) retailer, in promoting water purifiers, claimed in brochures that the devices would stop the growth of bacteria and act as a purifying agent. Investigation revealed that the statements were untrue, and the retailer was fined $700.

- An Edmonton retailer, in promoting the sale of meat, claimed in brochures, "Bulk buying at its best," "Reduce impulse buying," and "Hedge against inflation." It was established that there were no savings, and the retailer was fined $6,000.

- A national book retailer stated a regular and a special price for each featured book in newspaper ads and on in-store price tags. Investigation revealed that the quoted regular prices were inflated, and the retailer was fined $25,000.

- An Ontario supermarket chain displayed two (or more) prices on various grocery products. It was established that the products were being sold at the higher of the two prices indicated, and the chain was fined $2,000.

- A department store chain distributed more than a million "scratch and win" cards that gave the impression that consumers had one chance in four of winning a 25 percent discount on merchandise. It was established that over 90 percent of the cards offered only a 10 percent discount, and the chain was fined $100,000.

- A department store chain compared its sale price to its regular price in advertising tires. It was established that the chain had systematically misled the public in misrepresenting the regular price, and it was fined $135,000.

Source: "Misleading Advertising Bulletin," *Consumer and Corporate Affairs Canada,* various issues since 1989.

Foundation has developed the Canadian Code of Advertising Standards, which deals with how products or services, including cosmetics and nonprescription medicines, should be advertised. The foundation also provides guidelines for the use of comparative advertising. Additional broadcast codes administered by other associations provide guidelines about advertising to children and sex-role stereotyping.[6]

*Conclusion*    Various government regulations affect both growth strategies and marketing plans. More than ever, managers must be sensitive to the liabilities they can face from various actions or lack of action. The retailer who is interested in serving the public by providing complete and accurate information and merchandise at fair prices is not likely to encounter difficulties. Legislative remedies are designed to ensure fairness in competitive behaviour and to protect consumers from unscrupulous sellers.

Management needs to develop a positive response to these pressures. Simply put, government regulations are designed to provide consumers with useful and honest information that makes it easier for them to function as rational shoppers.

# The Economic Environment

Retailers need to monitor the economic environment to anticipate the conditions that are likely to occur in the future. This is done by paying close attention to the key economic indicators that reflect the state of the economy. These indicators include the gross domestic product, personal savings rates, unemployment rates, the consumer price index, the prime interest rate, and new housing starts (Table 3–3).

### TABLE 3–3    Key Economic Indicators
Highs and Lows in the Past Decade

Gross domestic product: $702 billion in 1992

- The highest increase was 9.6% in 1984.
- The lowest increase was 1.1% in 1991.

Personal savings rate: 9.2% in 1992

- The highest savings rate was 17.8% in 1982.
- The lowest savings rate was 8.5% in 1988.

Unemployment rate: 10.2% in 1992

- The highest unemployment rate was 11.9% in 1983.
- The lowest unemployment rate was 7.5% in 1989.

Consumer price index: 129.2 in 1992

- The highest increase was 10.9% in 1982.
- The lowest increase was 1.1% in 1992.

Prime interest rate: 6.5% in 1992

- The highest prime rate was 14.0% in 1990.
- The lowest prime rate was 6.5% in 1992.

New housing starts: 180,000 in 1992

- The highest increase was 29.2% in 1983.
- The lowest increase was −29.3% in 1982.

SOURCES: "Report on the Nation," *The Financial Post,* Winter 1989; and *Canada's Business Climate* (Toronto: Toronto Dominion Bank, 1992). Indicators for 1992 are estimates.

In the early 1990s, Canada's economy was in a recession, with high unemployment and reduced consumer expenditures. During that time, retail sales and profits declined and retail bankruptcies increased dramatically. A number of well-known retail chains went out of business during these times (see Retail Highlight 3–2). This period was particularly difficult for Canadian retailers because they faced the introduction of the Goods and Services Tax in 1991, the loss of revenue due to cross-border shopping, and the increase in federal, provincial, and municipal taxes on consumers. In particular, the increased taxes considerably

**Retail Highlight 3–2**

# Retail Casualties of the Recession

Many retailers were unable to survive the ravages of the early 1990s recession and went out of business or closed many of their stores. Among the casualties were:

| Retailer | Stores Closed | Number of Employees | Announced |
|---|---|---|---|
| Beaver Canoe | 20 | 180 | April 1992 |
| Bargain Harold's | 160 | 4,000 | February 1992 |
| Groupe Selection | 100 | 650 | December 1991 |
| Town & Country[1] | 162 | 1,300 | November 1991 |
| Mac's/Mike's Mart[2] | 150 | 750 | June 1992 |
| Marks & Spencer[3] | 25 | 300 | May 1992 |
| Grafton-Fraser[4] | 114 | N/A | December 1991 |
| Maher[5] | 290 | 1,275 | May 1992 |
| Elks[6] | 79 | 700 | January 1991 |
| Ayres[7] | 60 | 750 | December 1991 |
| A&A Records and Tapes[8] | 119 | N/A | January 1991 |

[1]Part of the Dylex chain.

[2]Part of the Silcorp chain.

[3]Forty-two stores remain open in the chain.

[4]Grafton-Fraser is part of the Grafton Group. Stores closed included Madison, Bimini, Jack Fraser (some remained open), and George Richard's Kingsize Clothes.

[5]The footwear chain that was part of the Grafton Group.

[6]The men's wear chain that was part of the Grafton Group.

[7]Operated J. Michael's, Kristy Allan, and Berries chains.

[8]A&A continues to operate 140 stores under new ownership.

Sources: Mark Evans, "Grim Outlook for Retailing," *The Financial Post,* December 12, 1991, p. 5; Barrie McKenna, "Rag Trade Facing Disaster," *Globe and Mail,* May 12, 1992, p. B6; Mark Evans, "Silcorp Shakeup Shuts 150 Stores," *The Financial Post,* June 18, 1992, p. 1; and Mark Evans and Neville Nankivell, "Big Cuts at M&S Canada," *The Financial Post,* May 13, 1991, p. 3.

reduced the spending power of Canadian consumers. In the two years before the recession, 1989 and 1990, total consumer incomes rose by $91.5 billion while government taxes increased by $16.2 billion, leaving consumers with an additional $75.3 billion after taxes. In the two recession years of 1991 and 1992, consumer incomes rose by $36.2 billion while government taxes increased by $22.2 billion, leaving consumers with an additional $13.9 billion after taxes. Real spending by consumers, after inflation, declined by 4 percent in the two recession years.[7]

Many retailers suffered dramatic declines in sales (Sears Canada sales declined $500 million in 1991). However, some retailers were able to implement strategies that led to continued growth in both sales and profits during the turbulent times. For example, Zellers, with its Club Z and ''Lowest Price Is the Law'' strategy, increased its share of the market, its sales, and its profits. Loblaws, with its extensive ''No Name'' and Club Pack merchandise lines, also grew during that time.

Clearly, certain retailers are better positioned than others to respond to changing economic conditions. Through monitoring the economic environment, retailers can take a proactive position and adjust both strategies and tactics to maximize opportunities and minimize threats.

Economic conditions vary considerably across Canada. For example, the Maritimes, particularly Newfoundland, have experienced greater unemployment than most other areas of Canada. As a result, the income rating index for Newfoundland in 1992 was 34 percent below the national average, and the market rating index was 19 percent below the national average (Table 3–4). On the other

TABLE 3–4    **Canadian Markets**
1992

|  | Population (000) | Percent Population Change (1986–92) | Market Rating Index[†] | Income Rating Index[‡] |
|---|---|---|---|---|
| Newfoundland | 573 | .9% | 81 | 66 |
| Prince Edward Island | 133 | 5.1 | 82 | 73 |
| Nova Scotia | 897 | 2.8 | 93 | 83 |
| New Brunswick | 725 | 2.2 | 88 | 76 |
| Quebec | 6,821 | 4.4 | 100 | 92 |
| Ontario | 10,029 | 10.2 | 106 | 114 |
| Manitoba | 1,100 | 3.6 | 86 | 89 |
| Saskatchewan | 1,005 | (.4) | 95 | 85 |
| Alberta | 2,487 | 5.1 | 95 | 101 |
| British Columbia* | 3,303 | 11.7 | 101 | 98 |
| Canada | 27,073 | 7.0% | 100 | 100 |

*Includes Yukon and Northwest Territories.

[†]Market rating index = Retail sales/population.

[‡]Income rating index = Per capita income/population.

SOURCES: *Canadian Markets 1992; The Financial Post,* 1992. Based on estimates.

hand, Ontario often has a favorable economic climate and was 14 percent above the national average on the income rating index and 6 percent above on the market rating index.[8]

# The Demographic Environment

Changing demographics are important because of their impact on retail strategy and responses to competition. Recent changes in the population's age distribution and in the rate of household formation, geographic shifts in the population, and relative income gains among selected market segments all can affect retail strategy.

## *The Changing Age Distribution*

The 20 to 34 age group now constitutes the largest segment of the population and is dominated by baby boomers who are launching careers, establishing families, and developing investment plans. The baby boomers are aging, however, and, by 1996, the largest population segment will be persons 35 to 49 years of age, as shown in Table 3–5. The baby boomers will continue to have major implications for retailers as they move through life. They are responsible for the *echo boom* and will eventually join the *countdown generation* (Retail Highlight 3–3).

The changing age mix of the population will result in different growth rates for various age groups for the next two decades. The three main age segments under 34—children, youths, and young adults—will decline, while the three older age groups—early middle age, late middle age, and retirees—will increase. These shifts will have significant impacts on purchases of many products and services.

In the longer term, the 50-plus age group market will represent about one third of all Canadians and about 40 percent of all households. An important fact is that this population segment will account for about three quarters of all of Canada's population growth in the next 20 years. Proactive retailers should be developing strategies now to capitalize on the future potential of the 50-plus market. Research

TABLE 3–5    **Population Age Distribution**
1976–2006

| Age Group | Thousands | | | | Percent Change | | |
| --- | --- | --- | --- | --- | --- | --- | --- |
| | *1976* | *1986* | *1996* | *2006* | *1976– 1986* | *1986– 1996* | *1996– 2006* |
| Children (0–9) | 3,620 | 3,630 | 3,550 | 2,810 | 0% | (2)% | (21)% |
| Youth (10–19) | 4,620 | 3,730 | 3,710 | 3,610 | (19) | (1) | (3) |
| Young adults (20–34) | 5,750 | 6,930 | 6,280 | 5,870 | 21 | (9) | (7) |
| Early middle age (35–49) | 3,850 | 4,980 | 6,630 | 6,800 | 29 | 33 | 3 |
| Late middle age (50–64) | 3,150 | 3,590 | 4,060 | 5,680 | 14 | 13 | 40 |
| Retirees (65 and over) | 2,000 | 2,730 | 3,580 | 4,280 | 37 | 31 | 20 |
| | 22,990 | 25,590 | 27,810 | 29,050 | 11% | 9% | 4% |

Source: *Marketing Research Handbook 1992*, Statistics Canada, Catalog 63–224.

---

**Retail Highlight 3–3**

---

# The Echo Boom and the Countdown Generation

In 1987, the birthrate in Canada dropped to an all-time low. But that is changing as the baby boomers (those Canadians born between 1946 and 1966) who are now in their early 30s to late 40s are now making the decision to have children (more than one third of the babies born in 1990 were born to women 30 and over). Called the *echo boom,* the birthrate in Canada has been increasing since 1987, and now over 400,000 live births are recorded each year. Opportunities are now available for retailers who target this group. Many couples with new babies change residences, buy cars, and change brands to ones best suited for their babies. They need products such as car seats, playpens, baby foods, and diapers.

The *countdown generation* is at the other end of the age spectrum. The 12 percent of Canadians who expect to retire in the next few years control almost half of the personal wealth in Canada. The group represents about 3 million Canadians, is mature, secure, and relatively rich. The countdown generation is used to saving because of economic hardship in their youth. They have paid off their mortgages and now have considerable wealth, mainly in the value of their homes. This group will provide many opportunities to retailers who can satisfy their needs for experiences (e.g., travel and entertainment) and quality products.

Sources: Hugh Filman, ''Baby Books Benefit from Echo Boom,'' *Marketing,* March 30, 1992, p. 30; Stephen Strauss, ''Baby Boomlet Continues, Statistics Canada Reports,'' *Globe and Mail,* March 3, 1992, pp. A1, A6; and Marina Strauss, ''Retirees Have Big Bucks to Spend,'' *Globe and Mail,* March 17, 1992, p. B7.

---

has shown that these Canadians, who control most of the personal wealth in Canada, are active shoppers with an intense interest in specials. They want to believe they are saving money whenever they spend, and they have a strong value orientation that is based on ''getting your money's worth,'' a reflection of the economic hardship many experienced in their youth.[9] As well, many are travellers. About 400,000 Canadians, aged 65 and older, called *snowbirds,* travel to Florida during the winter.

*Rate of Household Formation*

The rate of household formation has been increasing faster than the growth in population. Between 1976 and 1986, the population grew by 11 percent, while households grew by 29 percent; between 1986 and 1996, it is estimated that the population will grow by 9 percent, while households will grow by 16 percent. Among the reasons for this is a large increase in nonfamily households. The number of one-person households has increased dramatically in the past 10 years, while the number of households with more than four people has declined. Now, over 24 percent of all Canadian households are people who live alone, and 44 percent of all households are nonfamily or single-parent households. These households include singles, widows or widowers, empty nesters, childless and

*The countdown generation will provide many opportunities for Canadian retailers.*

SOURCE: Photo by James Hertel.

unmarried couples, and younger couples planning to have children later. These small households are prime prospects for townhouses, condominiums, kitchen miniappliances, and packaged goods in single servings. SSWDs (single, separated, widowed, and divorced) spend more money on travel and entertainment, save less, and tend to buy more services.

**Population Shifts**    Canadians are a mobile people, with about 1 in 10 moving each year. In the past decade, the populations of the western provinces and Ontario grew more than the national average, while Quebec and the Maritime provinces grew less than the national average. For the 1990s, it is predicted that Ontario will have the fastest-growing population. These population shifts offer opportunities for retailers locating in the faster-growing areas.

Canadians are also moving from rural to urban areas. These concentrated urban areas, called *census metropolitan areas (CMAs)* by Statistics Canada, now hold the majority of the population. About 61 percent of Canadians live in the 25 CMAs, and the three largest markets—Toronto, Montreal, and Vancouver—account for about 32 percent of Canada's population.[10] These large markets provide opportunities for retailers to cater to very specific segments, and stores carrying narrow and deep product lines (e.g., a mystery book store) are found in these locations.

***Skewed Income Distribution***

Income distribution in Canada is very skewed. While the average household income in 1990 was $45,200, 20 percent of households earned less than $18,100 and 20 percent earned more than $66,700. The bottom 20 percent accounted for only 5 percent of the total income earned by all Canadians, while the top 20 percent accounted for 42 percent of the total income earned.[11]

Retailers need to consider the size and spending power of these income groups when making strategic decisions. For example, the Red Apple Apparel Clearance Centre is a chain of stores retailing lower-price men's and women's casual wear to price- and value-conscious shoppers. The stores are located in lower-rental secondary malls and strip centres in nine provinces. On the other hand, Harry Rosen men's wear stores target the upper-income professional man, and one location opened in the heart of downtown Toronto features three levels of shopping, including an entire floor of designer boutiques.

***Regional Differences***

While retailers need to monitor each environmental factor to determine the effect on the firm, additional insights can be gained when two or more factors are examined together. For example, population and personal income per capita together have an important impact on retail sales. This is illustrated in Table 3-6 for the five major regions of Canada. Over the past 10 years, the population of British Columbia grew by 16 percent, more than the national average of 10 percent, but income per capita grew by 72 percent, less than the national average of 96 percent. Retail sales grew by 87 percent, less than the national average of 110 percent. Surprisingly, in the past 10 years, the Maritimes, Quebec, and Ontario outpaced the national average on

**TABLE 3-6   Regional Population, Personal Income, and Retail Sales**

| | **Population** | | **Personal Income per Capita** | | **Retail Sales per Capita** | |
|---|---|---|---|---|---|---|
| | *1992 (000)* | *Percent Change (1982–92)* | *1992* | *Percent Change (1982–92)* | *1992* | *Percent Change (1982–92)* |
| British Columbia | 3,303 | 16% | $18,800 | 72% | $8,700 | 87% |
| Prairies | 4,592 | 6 | 18,300 | 81 | 8,000 | 70 |
| Ontario | 10,029 | 15 | 21,900 | 106 | 9,100 | 119 |
| Quebec | 6,821 | 6 | 17,200 | 100 | 8,600 | 136 |
| Maritimes | 2,328 | 4 | 14,740 | 100 | 7,600 | 126 |
| Canada | 27,073 | 10% | $19,200 | 96% | $8,600 | 110% |

Sources: *Canadian Markets, The Financial Post,* various issues from 1982 to 1992.

retail sales, while British Columbia and the Prairie provinces were below the average, reflecting the impact of both population and income changes. To thoroughly understand the impact of the many environmental factors, retailers combine them to get a complete and accurate picture of changes that are occurring.

# The Competitive Environment

The competitive environment is one of the most important variables for retailers to take into account in developing their strategies.

## *Understanding Competition*

Competition among retailers is a fact of life. The most familiar type is intratype competition. **Intratype competition** is competition between two retailers of the same type, such as two drugstores. Intratype competition is the model most frequently described in basic economics texts. Examples include The Bay, Eaton's, and Woodward's (traditional department stores), Zellers and Woolco (discount department stores), McDonald's and Harvey's (fast-food retailers), and Reitmans and Braemar (women's specialty stores).

A second competitive model is **intertype competition,** which is competition between different types of retail outlets selling the same merchandise. Intertype competition is a common type of retail competition today. For example, Loblaws competes with Sears in many of the nonfood lines sold by Loblaws. The acceptance of scrambled merchandising has allowed similar merchandise to be sold by many different types of retailers. Many convenience products such as chewing gum, candy, magazines, and soft drinks are sold in a wide variety of stores ranging from convenience stores to supermarkets to department stores to drugstores. For example, convenience store chains like Becker's and Mac's have suffered losses and closed stores, due in part to the heightened competition from drugstores who expanded their product lines to include snacks, soft drinks, and easy-to-prepare foods.[12]

**Corporate systems competition** occurs when a single-management ownership links resources, manufacturing capability, and distribution networks. Bata Shoes is an example of corporate systems competition. It manufactures most of its merchandise, handles its own storage and distribution functions, and performs all management activities necessary for the sale of goods and services at the retail level.

Total systems networks can be formed either backward or forward. In **forward integration,** a manufacturer establishes its own wholesale and retail network. Examples are Goodyear and Sherwin Williams. **Backward integration** occurs when a retailer or wholesaler performs some manufacturing functions. Most of the large supermarket chains in Canada have, through various holding companies, engaged in backward integration. For example, Loblaws, part of the Weston empire, has access to numerous products manufactured by Weston-owned companies.

The above types of competition do not exist in isolation. Retail firms in all types of channel structures face competition from retailers in any or all of the other systems. Also, our comments must be regarded only as broad generalizations about the nature of competition and the various types of channel systems because numerous exceptions exist.

*The New Face of Competition*

The competitive structure of retailing is changing radically. The changes are causing a rethinking of the concepts of retail competition and are also causing changes in consumer shopping habits. **Secondary market expansion** (expansion into small markets) is an increasingly attractive move. Thus, firms such as Stedman's, Metropolitan, and Saan typically face less competition, are able to pay lower wages, and face fewer zoning and other restrictions in communities of 50,000 or fewer persons. They provide more viable markets than many of the large metropolitan markets, which are already served by almost every major retailer. As well, many of these communities are located a considerable distance from the U.S. border and are less vulnerable to cross-border shopping.

*Extremes in Establishment Types*

The trend today can be described as diversity in retail outlets. Broad-based merchandising firms such as Canadian Tire and Home Hardware, with their home improvement centres and discount pricing, have made major inroads into the markets of traditional hardware stores. The other high-growth market, at the opposite end of the scale, is the specialty store that carries a deep assortment of a very specialized line, often limited to a concept or "look," as opposed to commodity types. Examples include Radio Shack and Benetton. Their entire operations are programmed to a specific market segment, and they project a sharply defined image as a result.

*Supermarket Retailing*

The supermarket concept, long familiar in the food field, has been adopted by many other types of retailers. The key elements of **supermarket retailing** are (1) self-service and self-selection, (2) large-scale but low-cost physical facilities, (3) a strong price emphasis, (4) simplification and centralization of customer services, and (5) a wide variety and broad assortment of merchandise. This concept has been successful in many lines of trade, including sporting goods (Sporting Life), home improvement (Beaver Lumber), and furniture and housewares (IKEA).

The most recent and probably the most successful use of this concept are giant no-frills warehouse stores such as Price Club and Costco. They have entered the Canadian market and generate annual sales per store of $200 to $300 million. Consumers pay $25 a year to join and shop in large warehouse outlets that carry a limited product selection of groceries, office supplies, appliances, and other merchandise at discount prices. These stores cater to bulk buyers more interested in discounts than in convenience and selection. Canadian retailers have responded by opening their own discount operations, including Loblaws with Fortino's supermarkets, Canadian Tire with its All Out Retail outlets, and Molson with its Aikenhead's home improvement centres.[13]

*Radio Shack, a specialty retailer, focuses on a specific market segment.*

SOURCE: Photo by James Hertel.

**The International Dimension**

Canadian retailers now face new competition on an international basis. It comes in two forms: (1) cross-border shopping, and (2) foreign retailers, primarily from the United States, entering the Canadian market. In an average month in 1992, approximately 5 million same-day car trips were made by Canadians to the United States. It is estimated that over a year, these cross-border shoppers spend between $5 billion and $10 billion in the United States, business lost by Canadian retailers. A variety of strategies have been proposed to combat the sales drain, including "Buy Canadian" campaigns, stricter customs procedures, and departure taxes, but many experts believe the best strategy is to give Canadian consumers what they really want—selection, service, and value.[14]

The list of foreign retailers entering the Canadian market grows each year. Well-known international retailers such as Price Club, HMV, The Gap, Tiffany, Lenscrafter, Pier 1 Imports, IKEA, The Body Shop, Toys Я Us, Kmart, and Woolco have successfully entered the Canadian market. A recent study has predicted that by the year 2000, 25 percent of retail firms in Canada will be headquartered in the United States.[15] Analysts feel that the reasons for the success of foreign retailers in Canada are their experience in highly competitive markets, their high operating efficiency, their clearly defined target markets, and their focus on hiring, training, and motivating salespeople to provide quality customer service.[16]

# The Technology Environment

Changes in technology are affecting virtually every dimension of the retailing outlet. Detailed information that can aid retailers in making decisions ranging from merchandise elimination to credit authorization is now available on a timely basis. This information forms the basis of the **management information system,** the structure necessary to gather, analyze, and distribute information needed by management. The new technology has increased employee productivity, reduced losses due to cash register errors, and lowered losses caused by not having desired inventory in stock to meet customer needs. Other changes include new methods of merchandising presentation ranging from video kiosks to home video shopping through such channels as the Canadian Home Shopping Network.

## *Understanding Point-Of-Sale*

A **point-of-sale (POS)** cash register (or checker terminal) is the key input device for many retailing systems. A POS device records a variety of information at the time a transaction occurs. The information is stored and can be called up at the end of the day or whenever it is needed. The system can reveal which merchandise, styles, and colours of various manufacturers are selling most rapidly. The ability to identify slow- and fast-moving items is a key to good merchandise management.

The use of computers linked to POS terminals allows the retailer to perform a number of activities, including sales reporting, inventory control, and sales forecasting.

### Sales Reporting

One of the most useful retail reports is a daily sales report. This provides an analysis and count of departmental sales dollars and units. Sales analysis reports can also measure the sales performance of individual items by department or category within specified time intervals. Also, a sales activities report can provide a much bigger picture of sales transactions and employee timekeeping activity to help increase sales in selected time periods.

### Inventory Control

Merchandise on hand is another important area of information for retailers. Inventory ties up a large amount of a retail firm's capital, and retailers need to know the composition of the inventory because merchandise outages can result in lost sales. Having too many wrong items will lead to excessive markdowns. Computer-generated reports are a highly efficient way to keep up with inventory and to answer the questions of what to buy, when to buy, how to buy, and from whom to buy.

*Scanning equipment offers major benefits to retailers.*

# Every check out becomes an express lane.

Ask your customers what they hate most about grocery shopping and they will tell you "slow check outs" or "standing in line waiting for a price check". You can often measure a busy day by the number of abandoned carts left in the aisles with meat and produce spoiling. It doesn't have to be that way. Ask Carolyn Shortt, Head Cashier at Fortino's in Stoney Creek, Ontario where we recently installed 14 TEC MA2300-41 POS Master Systems with scanner interface check stand scales.

"There were no start up problems. Our cashiers love them and the customers are really happy. They appreciate the itemized bill and they've even complimented our girls on how fast they get through the check out."

John Theissen, Fortino's Public Relations Director marvelled, "The system went right on line with no hitches and performs better than our highest expectations. Inventory control and price changes are easy, it sure makes our jobs a whole lot easier."

At TEC we couldn't express it any better. So why not check us out.

**TEC**
TOKYO ELECTRIC CANADA LTD.

Head Office: 2 Vulcan Street, Rexdale, Ontario, Canada M9W 1L2 Branch Offices: 625 Erin Square, Unit 613, Winnipeg, Manitoba, Canada R3G 2W1
9-3331 Viking Way, Richmond, B.C., Canada V6V 1X7 Omega Cash Register Ltd., 190 Rockland Road, Ville Mont Royal, P.Q., Canada H3P 2W5

**Reader Service Card Number 34**

Source: Courtesy Tokyo Electric Canada Ltd.

### Sales Forecasting

Inventory data is necessary for forecasting sales. Analysis of previous sales levels can point out trends that can be a clue to future sales levels. Remember, however, that inventory reports can only show trends in past sales and cannot forecast the future. Retailers have to temper sales reports with judgment to make them useful but should not ignore the information and act on gut feeling. In addition, inventory analysis can be used as a tool in merchandise management, and should be viewed as part of a retail reporting system to control the business and improve profitability.

*Item Marking*          Scanning and wanding are the most widely used methods of data entry at the point-of-sale terminal. Scanning has occurred primarily in supermarkets in which bar codes are read by a fixed slot scanner. Wanding has been used primarily in general merchandise retailing. Many items in general merchandise retailing, such as apparel, cannot easily be passed over a fixed slot scanner. Rather, a **wand** is used to capture the information.

### Scanning Technology Used
A variety of merchandise-marking technologies are used as part of scanning/ wanding systems. The most frequently used one is the **universal product code (UPC).** Most persons are familiar with the small, black-and-white bars on supermarket items. These bars are codes that contain information about the product and the manufacturer. These bar codes are passed over a scanner at the check-out counter. The information from the bar codes goes from the scanner into the POS system. Computers can then automatically update the store's inventory, look up the price of the item in question, and print a receipt for the customer. The UPC is the most popular form of general merchandise marking, although many retailers use multiple scanning technologies.

### Potential Benefits to Consumers and Retailers
Tests of UPC scanner systems have revealed the following benefits:

1. Improved accuracy of checking out merchandise.
2. Improved customer satisfaction because of speed, accuracy, quietness, and the detailed shopping tape.
3. Time and labour savings. Some stores report productivity gains of up to 45 percent when item-price marking (no longer necessary since the price is carried in the computer) is eliminated. Even with price marking, other savings make scanner investment worthwhile.
4. Improved inventory and financial control.

### New Data Breakthroughs
Probably scanning's greatest long-term benefit is its ability to generate totally new marketing information. Scanners are providing retailers with:

1. The first-ever accurate reading, item by item, of actual item movement at the point of sale.
2. Overnight, store-by-store readings of consumer buying behaviour.
3. Fast, accurate feedback on test-market experiments.
4. Measurement of the effects of marketing and promotional activity.

*Universal Vendor Marking*

Universal vendor marking (UVM) is a standard vendor-created identification system. The need to mark the items when they are received at the store level can be eliminated largely by the use of such a standardized format. Stores like Price Club, Aikenhead's, and Canadian Tire have begun using vendor marking. The major advantage is the ability of the retailer to handle incoming merchandise through the use of computers and electronic data input.

*Emerging Technologies*

Other changes are occurring in the way technology is used in retailing. These changes involve customer communications, nonstore shopping, and similar activities.

### Videodisc Mail-Order Catalogs

Sears has led the way in experimenting with video catalogs. The retailer has placed some of its catalogs on laser discs for in-home and at-store viewing. The discs contain motion sequences plus colour pictures. Product demonstrations, fashion shows, and footage from Sears TV commercials were part of their experiment. Videodisc use is still limited in retailing today.

### Cable Marketing

Cable marketing recently began in Canada in the late 1980s. The Canadian Home Shopping Network (CHSN) combined traditional merchandising with modern technology to offer consumers a wide variety of products via cable television. While television shopping has grown rapidly in the United States, the initial picture in Canada is less bright. The CHSN has had mixed results in selling merchandise to shoppers by the use of cable television and a toll-free number for ordering the merchandise offered for sale and has just recently made a profit. One major problem for the CHSN is that it is only allowed to show still photographs of the products for sale. This restriction, based on the Canadian Radio-Television and Telecommunications Commission regulations, creates a poor broadcast format for the CHSN.

Cable marketing is also being used by real estate firms to interest potential home buyers in various properties and by automobile traders to sell used cars. Two or more channels in many Canadian communities are devoted to cable marketing shows.

### In-Store Video Sales Aids

Increasingly, retailers are turning to the use of in-store video to provide prerecorded answers to questions frequently asked by customers. The devices help increase productivity because they reduce the need for salespersons to provide basic information. For example, the Atari electronic retail information centre exists in a variety of retail outlets. The device self-activates when customers come near the machine, and it allows customers to have hands-on experience with an Atari computer. The device responds to the customers' button-pushed questions and provides answers by tailoring the video presentation directly to their needs.

Retailers are also experimenting with interactive, electronic in-store couponing. In one form, a kiosk in a supermarket dispenses coupons in 15 to 20 grocery categories that are valid only the same day at the same store. In another form, a kiosk displays nine retailer categories, and after the consumer has selected a category, it displays the names of up to six retailers. The consumer can then select coupons for products from that retailer. One test recorded sales increases of 37 percent for video products.[17]

# Chapter Highlights

- The major federal regulations affecting retailers include acts dealing with trade practices (Competition Act, Bankruptcy Act), health and safety (Food and Drugs Act, Hazardous Products Act), and product standards and grades (Consumer Packaging and Labelling Act, Textile Labelling Act). In particular, the Competition Act is important because it regulates unfair trade practices such as misleading price advertising.

- The economic environment can be understood, in part, by paying close attention to key economic indicators such as interest rates, unemployment rates, and the consumer price index.

- The primary demographic factors of importance to retailers include changing age distribution, rate of household formation, and family relationships; population shifts; skewed income distribution; and regional differences.

- The primary types of competition include intratype competition, intertype competition, and corporate systems competition. The competitive structure of retailing as a whole is undergoing change, including secondary market expansion, extremes in establishment types, supermarket retailing, and the international dimension.

- Changes in technology that have had an impact on retailing include the use of point-of-sale cash registers linked to computers for sales reporting, inventory control, and sales forecasting; scanning technology to improve accuracy and data analysis; and new emerging technologies that offer new ways of shopping.

# Key Terms

Backward integration   69
Corporate systems competition   69
Exclusive dealing   57
Forward integration   69
Intertype competition   69
Intratype competition   69
Management information system   72
Point-of-sale (POS)   72

Predatory pricing   57
Price discrimination   57
Resale price maintenance   57
Secondary market expansion   70
Supermarket retailing   70
Universal product code (UPC)   74
Wand   74

# Discussion Questions

1. What are some retail activities covered by the Competition Act?

2. List four key economic indicators that retailers should monitor. What type of retailer is most likely to be affected by changes in each indicator?

3. Why is competition so intense in retailing today? Does this competitive intensity have an impact on retailers' need to monitor and forecast environmental changes? Explain your answer.

4. Summarize the changes that are occurring in the demographic profile of consumers and households in our society, and the likely impact on retail operations.
5. Summarize the information presented in the text relative to changes in the competitive environment. Explain the impact these changes are having on retailing.

6. What are the advantages of the electronic cash register over mechanical cash registers?
7. What are some of the ways consumers benefit from the installation of POS equipment in a retail store?
8. What are some of the technological advances occurring today that are having an impact on nonstore shopping?

## Application Exercises

1. Visit the managers of two or three of the retail stores in your city. Find out their major problems, if any, with government regulations. Which aspects of the business seem to be most affected? Does the manager think the regulations serve a useful purpose?
2. Develop a sample of fast-food outlets, sit-down restaurants, coffee shops, and supermarkets, and determine which of the outlets are offering breakfast menus. Compare and contrast the offerings and seek to identify the demographic characteristics of the primary customer base.

3. Interview the managers of a large department store, a local outlet of a supermarket chain, and a fast-food store. Determine the type of system (electromechanical cash registers, electronic cash registers, or POS) employed in each. How many terminals are there? Are there any plans to change the type of system currently used? Has this change occurred already? If they plan to change, what type of system will they go to? Why? What savings are associated with the change?

## Suggested Cases

## Endnotes

1. Miriam Cu-Uy-Gam, "Bureau Puts Bite on Some Merger Deals," *The Financial Post,* April 24, 1989, p. 39.
2. "The Marketplace in Transition: Changing Roles for Consumers, Business and Governments?" *Consumer and Corporate Affairs Canada,* Ottawa, 1992.
3. Virginia Galt, "Who's the Boss?" *Report on Business Magazine,* December 1988, pp. 103–9.
4. Joan Breckenridge, "Medical Body Is Targeting Shoppers Drug Mart for Continued Cigarette Sales," *Globe and Mail,* May 27, 1989, pp. A1–A2.
5. Gordon H. G. McDougall, "The Environment and Marketing Strategy: Some Observations," in *Marketing,* vol. 12, ed. Tony Schellinck (Niagara Falls: ASAC, 1991), pp. 192–201.
6. More information on industry guidelines can be obtained from the Canadian Advertising Foundation, Advertising Advisory Board, Advertising Standards Council, the Canadian Association of Broadcasters, and the Canadian Radio-Television and Telecommunications Commission. The Canadian Code of Advertising Standards outlines the major industry codes.

7. Bruce Little, "Bigger Tax Bites Stifle Consumers," *Globe and Mail,* July 6, 1992, pp. B1, B2.

8. *Canadian Markets 1992; The Financial Post,* 1992.

9. Leonard Kubas, "Grey Power," *Retail Directions,* November/December 1988, pp. 10, 11, 30. For more information on retailing to the 50-plus age group, see John Straiton, "Here Are the Goods on the Over-50 Crowd," *Marketing,* December 12, 1988, p. C10; Clayton Sinclair, "The Growing Wave of Seniors' Publications," *Financial Times of Canada,* February 29, 1988, p. 14; Alanna Mitchell, "Seniors' Housing Boom," *The Financial Post,* October 31, 1988, pp. 17, 20; Stan Sutter, "Chasing the Over-50 Market," *Marketing,* April 4, 1988, pp. 25, 28; and Marina Strauss, "Retirees Have Big Bucks to Spend," *Globe and Mail,* March 17, 1992, p. B7.

10. Jill Vardy, "Canada's Population Climbs to 27 Million," *The Financial Post,* April 29, 1992, p. 3.

11. Alan Freeman, "Household Incomes Fall 1.5%," *Globe and Mail,* March 19, 1992, p. A1.

12. John Heinzl, "Becker Posts First Annual Loss," *Globe and Mail,* July 11, 1992, p. B5.

13. Daniel Girard, "The New Retail Giants," *Toronto Star,* February 9, 1992, pp. H1, H4.

14. Mark Evans, "Tax Urged for Shoppers," *The Financial Post,* March 11, 1992, p. 5; and Mark Evans, "Low C$ Takes Bite Out of Cross-Border Shopping," *The Financial Post,* July 15, 1992, p. 3.

15. Anne Bokma, "Raking in the Dough," *The Financial Post Magazine,* January 1992, pp. 32–35.

16. John Godfrey, "Retailers Beware, Americans Coming," *The Financial Post,* December 20, 1991, p. 11.

17. Ken Riddell, "Reaching Consumers In-Store," *Marketing,* July 13, 1992, p. 10.

# 4 UNDERSTANDING THE RETAIL CUSTOMER

## Chapter Objectives

After reading this chapter, you should be able to:

1 Describe the decision-making process of consumers in retail buying.
2 Explain the motives for shopping other than buying.
3 Discuss where consumers buy, how they buy, what they buy, and when they buy.
4 Describe the role of image in consumer buying decisions.
5 Discuss dissatisfied consumers and how to deal with them.

## Retailing Capsule

According to Bryan Robinson, marketing manager at Zellers, the key challenges facing mass retailers today are intense competition, similar low-margin pricing policies, similar product lines, saturation of retail outlets, and lack of market growth.

To remain competitive, Zellers began by gaining a thorough understanding of the consumer. Research indicated that consumers wanted good value (price, quality, and service), convenience, and thank-you's for shopping in a particular store (service). The research also found that customers saw the mass retailers as similar, creating an identity problem. As a result, customer loyalty equalled the best sales price. It was also found that consumers like to be romanced, have fun, and be rewarded.

SOURCE: Illustration by Bill Cox

The prime target market of Zellers is women between the ages of 25 and 55, with a family, who shop frequently for basic clothing and staples, with little discretionary income. These customers often need some credit and are hungry for a bargain, especially in recessionary times.

Zellers decided that it needed to differentiate the store from competition with a program that could not easily be copied. This led to the creation of the Club

*Retailing Capsule continued*

Z membership program. Every time a member makes a purchase at Zellers, the salesperson enters the membership number into the computer, and the member is credited with points based on the amount purchased. This program rewards customer loyalty, is easy to use, is value added, and provides a long-term commitment to Zellers. Television commercials and in-store supports and circulars all contribute to this objective.

In addition to the promotion, Zellers' pricing policy is very competitive, with the slogan: "Zellers . . . Because the Lowest Price Is the Law."

*Zellers, where "the lowest price is the law."*

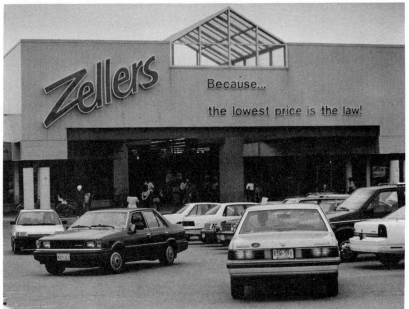

SOURCE: Photo by Sandy McDougall.

It is not surprising that Club Z is one of the most successful customer loyalty programs in North America, with more than 6 million members, and that Zellers is one of the few retailers with growth in revenues and profits during the last recession. More recently, Zellers has introduced a seniors club, a gold card for very frequent buyers, and a travel and auto club. Zellers' brilliant marketing program is based on a thorough understanding of its customers.

Sources: Jo Marney, "Woopies, Muppies . . . the List Grows," *Marketing,* February 2, 1987, p. 10; Carolyn Green, "The 'Law' of Retail," *Marketing,* October 28, 1991, pp. 1, 3; and John Heinzl, "Club Z Leaving Its Mark," *Globe and Mail,* December 6, 1991, p. B1.

Development of retail strategies begins with an understanding of the consumer. An old saying is that "nothing happens until a sale is made." Sales only occur when the retailer understands and responds to how consumers buy, what they buy, where they buy, and when they buy. Retailers must also understand the consumer as a problem solver and seek to develop merchandise offerings to address unmet needs, as Zellers has done. An additional critical dimension is knowing how consumers form images of retail outlets and how to develop merchandising and marketing strategies compatible with the desired image.

# Types of Consumer Decisions

Keep in mind the following points about consumers when studying this chapter:

- *Consumers are problem solvers*. The role of the retailer is to help them solve their buying problems.
- Consumers try to *lower their risk* when buying merchandise by seeking information. They also seek information for reasons other than risk reduction.
- Store choice and merchandise choice depend on variables such as location, image, hours, and price, which are under the influence of the retailer.
- Many other factors, such as store atmosphere and courtesy of salesclerks, affect the in-store behaviour of consumers.

# Motives for Shopping

Consumers shop for reasons other than buying, as shown in Figure 4–1. These reasons can be grouped into personal and social motives. *Personal motives* include role playing, diversion, sensory stimulation, physical activity, and self-gratification. *Social motives* include the desire for social experiences, peer group attraction, status and authority needs, the pleasure of bargaining, and being with others of similar interests. Careful planning by a retailer can influence shoppers to make purchases even when the primary purpose of the trip is social or personal.

## *Personal Motives*

Personal motives result from internal consumer needs that are different from the needs to be fulfilled by purchasing a good or service.

### Role Playing
Consumers often engage in activities that they perceive are associated with their role in life. Familiar roles include those of housewife, student, husband, or father. For example, a husband may perceive that in his role he should purchase only high-quality gifts from prestigious outlets for his wife; or that he should be able to fix things in the house when they break or need adjustment (and proper advice from a well-trained retail clerk may prove invaluable for someone who is not too handy).

### Diversion
Shopping often provides the opportunity to get a break from the daily routine. Simply walking through a shopping centre can allow a person to keep up with the

**FIGURE 4–1**

*Motives for shopping*

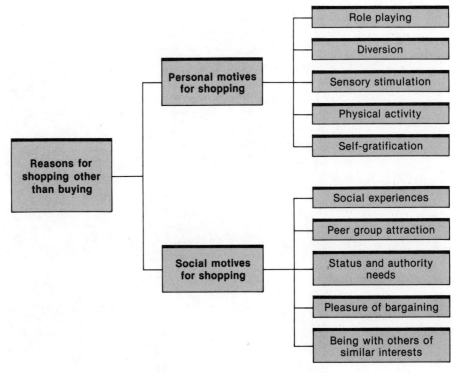

latest trends in fashion, styling, or innovation. Similarly, malls often schedule antique or auto shows in an effort to attract consumers.

Regional shopping malls are popular browsing sites because of their comfortable surroundings and appealing atmosphere. Research has shown that many consumers derive enjoyment from the simple activity of shopping for some types of goods. Stores that carry deep product assortments and unique brands are especially attractive to browsers because of the novelty and stimulation inherent in such outlets. Heavy browsers are more involved with the merchandise, more knowledgeable, and more likely to be opinion leaders than are other consumers.[1]

### Sensory Stimulation

Shoppers often respond favourably to background music, scents, and other types of sensory stimulation as part of the shopping process. Research has shown that customers feel more at ease, spend more time, and shop more often in a store that plays soft background music, compared to no music or loud music.[2]

### Physical Activity

Many people, particularly older people, welcome the opportunity to walk for exercise in a safe, temperature-controlled environment. Thus, some malls have organized walking and health clubs in response to such needs. The malls are opened for walking before the shops are opened for business. Large cities such as Toronto

*Today, malls are designed to satisfy personal and social motives.*

SOURCE: Photo by Betty McDougall.

or Montreal have extensive underground malls, often connected to each other in the downtown areas. Particularly in the winter months, these large malls have often replaced ''Main Street'' as the favourite strolling areas for the whole family or friends.

### Self-Gratification

Shopping can alleviate loneliness or other emotional stress. It has been shown that shopping is often used to compensate for negative moods and to complement positive ones, with the act of shopping displacing cigarettes or chocolate bars.[3]

A recent study showed that young Canadians, in trying to find their identity, tend to shop and buy objects with a high symbolic value, such as clothes or music tapes. This quest for self-gratification by young Canadians could lead to more shopping and buying in the 1990s.[4]

*Social Motives*

Social motives for shopping are also illustrated in Figure 4–1. These motives include the desire for group interaction of one sort or another.

### Social Experiences outside the Home

For many people, shopping has become a social activity outside the home. They take advantage of such opportunities to meet friends or to develop new acquaintances. Some malls feature morning promotions especially designed to serve older persons. Others arrange cooking demonstrations and similar activities.

### Peer Group Attraction

Individuals may shop so as to be with a peer or reference group. Patronage of elite restaurants reflects such behaviour. Similarly, one will often find teenagers at a record shop that offers music styles that appeal to their tastes. Also, some outlets have advisory boards composed of influential people in a city. Local opinion leaders are also often used in advertising and promotion programs.

### Status and Power

Some consumers seek the opportunity to be served and catered to as part of the shopping experience. Such an activity may be one of their primary ways to get attention and respect.

### The Pleasure of Bargaining

Some persons enjoy the opportunity to negotiate over price. They get ego satisfaction as a result of bargaining.

### Communications with Persons of Similar Interests

Interest in a hobby may bring people together. Thus, retailers can provide a focal point for persons with similar interests or backgrounds. Retail computer outlets sponsor hobbyist clubs for this reason.

# A Model of the Consumer Decision Process

The decisions facing shoppers seeking to make a buying decision differ widely and depend on their past experiences with the merchandise to be bought. Many decisions, such as buying a loaf of bread, are routine because consumers have made similar purchases many times before.[5] Other decisions, such as buying an automobile, may be difficult for some consumers because of their lack of experience or the risk involved in making a wrong decision.

When making these more difficult purchases, the consumer normally goes through five decision stages, as shown in Figure 4–2. The stages are (1) problem recognition, (2) search for alternatives, (3) evaluation of alternatives, (4) the purchasing decision, and (5) postpurchase behaviour.

Retailers can influence consumer choices and actions at each stage of the decision process. Such efforts by retailers are key components of their segmentation and positioning strategies.

## Problem Recognition

The decision process begins when the consumer realizes that a difference exists between an existing and a preferred state of affairs.[6] Sometimes, consumers may simply discover that they need to purchase gasoline for their automobile. Other things that may trigger problem recognition are a lack of satisfaction with an existing product or service, a raise, a spouse beginning to work (more money is now available), the need to purchase a gift for someone, or a change in fashions. Retailers can also trigger problem recognition through advertising, in-store displays, or through the creative use of sight, sound, or smell.

**FIGURE 4–2**

*A model of the consumer decision process*

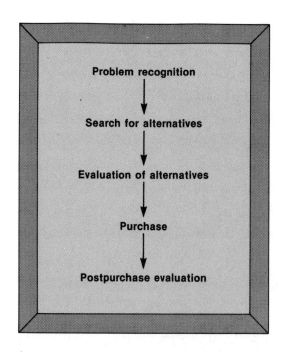

*Search for*
*Alternatives*

The consumer begins to seek and evaluate information after problem recognition occurs. The search may be physical or mental. A mental search means drawing on past experience for information.[7]

The consumer may need up-to-date information about products, prices, stores, or terms of sale. A physical or mental search may be required to obtain the needed information. The search may occur for the merchandise or for the preferred store at which the purchase will be made. Consumers evaluate the store on the basis of factors important to them and choose the outlet that most closely matches these factors.[8]

The retailer can make information available to consumers in a variety of forms to help them in their search. Consumers are normally exposed to (1) marketer-dominated sources, (2) consumer-dominated sources, and (3) neutral sources of information, as shown in Figure 4–3.

### Marketer-Dominated Sources

**Marketer-dominated information sources** include advertising, personal selling, displays, sales promotion, and publicity. The retailer exercises control over their content. Typically, the retailer provides information on price, product features, terms of sale, and where the product may be purchased.

**FIGURE 4–3**

*Sources of consumer*
*information*

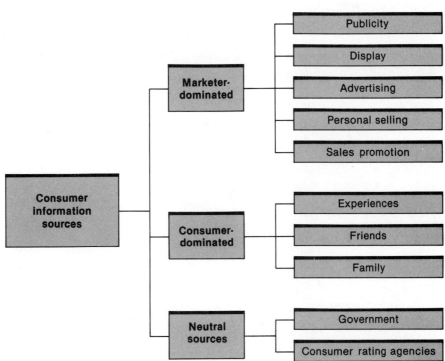

*Sales personnel can provide helpful information for consumers.*

SOURCE: Courtesy Hudson's Bay Company.

### Consumer-Dominated Sources

**Consumer-dominated information sources** include friends, relatives, acquaintances, or others. Consumer-dominated information is normally perceived as trustworthy. Satisfied consumers become especially important since they tend to talk to others about their shopping experiences.

Additional consumer-dominated sources of information are persons who are known and respected by their peers. Consumers are likely to respect information from such individuals. Retailers may therefore be able to utilize such groups as sports leaders, college class presidents, and other socially active persons to convey product and store information. Word-of-mouth information from such persons is likely to be received favourably.

Dissatisfied customers can also have a negative impact on an outlet. They often talk to many people about their bad experiences. Satisfied consumers typically are less vocal. Dissatisfied consumers in positions of influence can have a damaging impact on an outlet because of the large number of people to whom they talk and because they are influential.[9]

### Neutral Sources of Information

**Neutral sources of information** are also likely to be perceived as accurate and trustworthy. The Consumers' Association of Canada is an example of an agency providing neutral information. It publishes the *Canadian Consumer* (in both official languages), which provides independent tests of various products, as well as the annual *Buying Guide*.[10] Federal and provincial consumer protection agencies also provide neutral information. Government agencies, for example, provide information on gasoline consumption for autos and energy efficiency ratings for appliances.

Typically, most information is provided by commercial sources even though consumers may rely more on personal sources. Marketer-dominated sources may serve to create initial awareness, while personal and neutral sources are then used to help evaluate specific outlets or brands of merchandise.

*Evaluation of Alternatives*

After information is acquired, the consumer evaluates the alternatives available and assesses the options involved in a decision. Store and product attributes are used in comparing outlets and merchandise. Examples of these attributes are shown in Table 4–1. Attribute importance varies among consumers. Knowledge of the importance of attributes is critical to management in helping consumers make choices compatible with their personal preferences. Product trial and demonstration, for example, is one way of reducing risk, as shown in Figure 4–4.

When customers evaluate merchandise in terms of want satisfaction, they face six types of risks affecting store and merchandise choice decisions:

- **Performance risk:** The chance that the merchandise purchased may not work properly.
- **Financial risk:** The monetary loss from a wrong decision.
- **Physical risk:** The likelihood that the decision will be injurious to one's health or likely to cause physical injury.
- **Psychological risk:** The probability that the merchandise purchased or store shopped will not be compatible with the consumer's self-image.
- **Social risk:** The likelihood that the merchandise or store will not meet with peer approval.
- **Time loss risk:** The likelihood that the consumer will not be able to get the merchandise adjusted, replaced, or repaired without loss of time and effort.[11]

*The Purchasing Decision*

After evaluating some of the alternatives available, a substantial percentage of shoppers make their final decision while in the store. For example, research has

**TABLE 4–1   Factors Influencing the Choice of Merchandise and the Choice of Retail Outlet**

| Factors Affecting Merchandise Choice | | Factors Affecting Store Choice | |
|---|---|---|---|
| *Product Features* | *Service Features* | *Store Characteristics* | *Employee Characteristics* |
| Fashion | Credit terms | Hours | Knowledge |
| Brands | Installation | Layout | Friendliness |
| Quality | Accessories | Cleanliness | Helpfulness |
| Styles | Delivery | Displays | Courteousness |
| Colours | Layaway | Decor | |
| Assortments | | Image | |

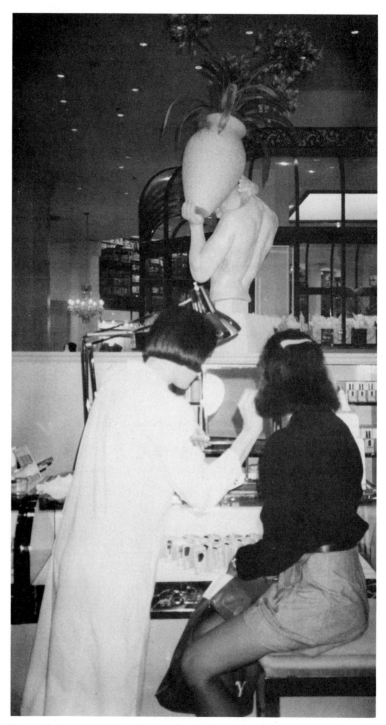

SOURCE: Photo by Betty McDougall.

shown that 80 percent of grocery shoppers make their final buying decision while in the store, and that 60 percent of grocery purchases are unplanned or impulse decisions.[12]

Choosing the store and the merchandise does not end the purchasing process. The consumer has to decide on the method of payment, accessories for the merchandise (such as a camera lens for a camera or a belt for a pair of trousers), whether to purchase an extended warranty, and delivery of bulky merchandise. Retailers often offer a variety of options designed to meet a diverse array of consumer preferences.

*Postpurchase Behaviour*

*Retailers need to reassure consumers after the purchase that they made the right decision.* When making a major purchase, consumers are often afraid that they may have spent their money foolishly. This feeling is called **cognitive dissonance,**[13] and retailers must find ways of reducing this level of dissonance. A follow-up letter from the retailer or a phone call often can help reassure and satisfy the customer. As well, a policy of "Satisfaction Guaranteed or Your Money Back," provides customers with the assurance that stores like Eaton's stand behind their merchandise. The level of consumer satisfaction also influences whether the store and its merchandise will be recommended to a friend. Satisfied customers help to generate stronger customer loyalty, repeat business, reduced vulnerability to price wars, and the ability to command a higher relative price for merchandise without affecting market share, lower marketing costs, and growth in market share.[14]

Retailers need to be sensitive to the uncertainties in the minds of the consumers, then work to alleviate their concerns.

In conclusion, understanding the decision-making process of consumers is essential for retailers because of the implication for strategy development. Retail Highlight 4–1 describes many elements of the consumer decision process discussed in the previous pages. How retailers can influence consumers is detailed in the next section.

# Understanding the Where, How, What, and When of Shopping

Retailers may have the most influence on the behaviour of consumers during the information search and evaluation stages of the decision process. An understanding of the *where, how, what,* and *when* of consumer shopping behaviour can help retailers respond to consumer needs for information during their search and evaluation efforts.

The retailer needs to have the right merchandise at the right place, at the right time, and at the right price and quality to match consumer decisions on where to buy, what to buy, how to buy, and when to buy, as shown in Figure 4–5.

- *Where* means the choice of a downtown location or a shopping centre and the specific store.
- *How* includes decisions on whether to engage in store or nonstore shopping.

---

**Retail Highlight 4–1**

---

# Canadians' Attitudes toward Grocery Shopping Help Segment the Market

A recent study illustrates the difference in behaviour among Canadian grocery shoppers, identifying four basic segments:

- *Bargain hunters* (22 percent): They find it important to get the best prices by shopping for specials and using coupons. They also appreciate the good service they find in traditional supermarkets. They enjoy grocery shopping *and* getting good deals.

- *Do-it-yourself savers* (24 percent): Although their income is high, they like saving money for its own sake. They are not brand or store loyal, and shop around for the best prices. They do not mind such inconveniences as bagging their own groceries and lack of service.

- *Speed demons* (26 percent): They want to get in and out of the supermarket as quickly as possible. They shop often, buying a few needed items and known brands. They prefer fast and convenient service to low prices and store atmosphere. They have the highest per capita grocery expenditures.

- *Leisurely shoppers* (29 percent): They love to shop and browse around the store. Atmosphere and selection are very important to them, and they tend to be brand loyal. Grocery shopping is done in one trip, and location convenience is important.

Source: "Grocery Attitudes of Canadians, 1988," Grocery Products Manufacturers of Canada, Don Mills, Ontario.

---

- *What* includes consumer decisions on merchandise price and quality, whether to purchase store brands or national brands, and criteria used in evaluating merchandise.
- *When* includes decisions on such matters as time of day and day of week to shop.

*Where Do Consumers Shop?*

**Shopping Centres**

Consumers may choose shopping centres because it is easier to take children to these places. Centres may be a good place to meet friends. Better store hours with a wider selection of merchandise may also be available. The controlled climate of a shopping centre often provides a social outing for shoppers who enjoy the festive atmosphere of the centre or simply like to window shop as a way of keeping up with the latest trends in fashion. In 1987, for the first time, Canadians spent more money in the 3,270 shopping centres than in all other retail outlets combined.[15]

**FIGURE 4–5**

*Retailers must match their merchandising to the consumer decision process*

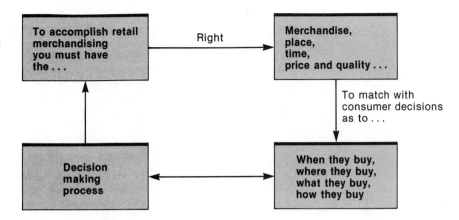

Some people prefer shopping at strip shopping centres as opposed to enclosed malls. Strip centres require less walking and generally involve less hassle. Additionally, access is typically easier than to major enclosed malls.

### Downtown

Some people prefer to shop downtown because of convenient transportation and the availability of nonshopping facilities such as financial institutions. Those who work downtown may find it convenient to shop there. Finally, some consumers, often those with lower incomes and no transportation, live near the downtown area and shop in the outlets closest to their homes.

In most large Canadian cities, the downtown area has seen the opening of *urban centres* like the Eaton's Centres in Calgary, Edmonton, Winnipeg, Toronto, and Montreal, Midtown Plaza in Saskatoon, Pacific Centre in Vancouver, Confederation Court Mall in Charlottetown, Barrington Place in Halifax, Atlantic Place in St. John's, Brunswick Square in Charlottetown, or the underground centres like Les Promenades de la Cathédrale in Montreal, built underneath a church!

### Outshopping

Some consumers go out of town to shop **(outshopping)** because (1) the selection may be better, (2) they may want to get out of town for a visit, including, perhaps, a good meal, (3) they may work out of town and do their shopping after work, and (4) store hours, store personnel, and services such as repair may be better in the other community.

Outshopping (including *cross-border shopping*) activities are particularly important in Canada for a number of unique reasons:[16] (1) the concentration of a large percentage of the Canadian population along the American border, and near some large U.S. cities; (2) the large distance between Canadian cities, particularly on an east-west axis; (3) economic variables such as price and currency differentials, as well as promotional enticements; (4) the lessening of border controls under the Free

Trade Agreement; (5) the severe climatic conditions in Canada, particularly during the winter months; and (6) the tendency to travel south for vacations (Canadian snowbirds). In one study of Maritime consumers, it was estimated that about 88 percent were outshoppers.[17]

With the advent of the Goods and Services Tax (GST), cross-border shopping all across Canada has taken on dramatic proportions, as explained in Retail Highlight 4–2.

### Nonstore Shopping

Catalog and telephone shopping are the primary types of **nonstore shopping,** although in-home, personal selling of merchandise by firms such as Avon or Tupperware is also common. Nonstore shopping is popular because it allows consumers to make purchase decisions at their leisure without leaving home.

These shoppers tend to have higher incomes and higher education. Higher incomes allow them to make more discretionary purchases, and education often widens the opportunity for selling merchandise to these individuals. Because they have more education, nonstore shoppers often see less risk than other consumers in buying in a nonstore setting.[18]

Direct merchants can stress several important factors in nonstore purchases by consumers. Making purchases from their homes is a great convenience to consumers. Good product guarantees are important in assuring consumers that risks in nonstore purchases are not unreasonable. The ease of credit card buying offered by major merchants such as Eaton's is also a major factor in determining purchase decisions.

*Choosing a Store*    If in-store purchases are to be made, consumers make decisions about stores at which to shop after deciding whether to shop downtown or at a shopping centre. The **image** of a retail outlet is important in such a decision.[19] The major attraction characteristics include the type and quality of merchandise and services offered, physical facilities, employees, and other shoppers. For example, consumers may be seeking a particular brand or quality of merchandise, specific services such as credit or delivery, an attractive outlet, courteous employees, and an outlet where consumers with similar life-styles are likely to shop. Other than the characteristics of other shoppers, all of these characteristics are under the direct influence of retailers. Research has shown that quality customer service has a greater effect on sales than any other variable under the control of the retailer.[20]

Research is often necessary to help management develop an understanding of the importance of these characteristics to shoppers. The information may help retailers do a better job of meeting consumer needs. Eaton's, one of Canada's foremost retailers, has done an excellent job in developing a unique position in the minds of consumers by satisfying a specific set of their needs.

There are a number of useful methods for measuring store image—using open-ended questions, semantic differential scales (using bipolar adjectives such as 'helpful/unhelpful'),[21] or a **multiattribute model.** (More details on retail research are provided in Chapter 10.)

# Cross-Border Shopping: Causes and Consequences

Although outshopping has been around for a long time in Canada, the cross-border shopping phenomenon (or explosion) can be traced to two recent events:

- The signing of the Free Trade Agreement with the United States: The FTA took effect on January 1, 1989, and it gave the impression that the border was now open; that is, that tariffs were being eliminated.
- The introduction of the Goods and Services Tax (GST): the GST took effect on January 1, 1991, and it created a public wave of anger.

To the misperception about tariffs and the anger toward the GST, one must add the belief by many Canadians that prices in the United States are much lower than those in Canada. This belief is not true in every case (it is true for about 8 out of 10 items). On the other hand, there are negatives: the costs of driving to the United States, long lines at the border, the obligation to pay the GST and some provincial sales taxes, and problems with warranties.

All of these factors taken together represent a strong motivation to shop in the United States, and U.S. retailers have been very obliging, advertising in Canadian media, staying open on Sundays, posting bilingual signs, and taking Canadian dollars at par. In fact, many retailers in U.S. border towns would not be viable without Canadian shoppers. For example, a study in Plattsburgh, New York, found that 41 percent of retailers depend in major part on the patronage of Quebecers, and would not otherwise be located there.

This is a major problem for Canadian retailers. It has been estimated that about 60 million one-day, cross-border trips were taken in 1991, costing retailers an estimated $10 billion and about 250,000 jobs (already lost or in danger of being lost).

What can retailers do to regain consumer confidence? Surveys show that 62 percent of cross-border shoppers do it because of the lower prices and to beat the GST. Only 3 percent do it because of the variety of goods available, 2 percent because it is a recreational activity (e.g., a shopping vacation, particularly on Sundays when working people have some time for shopping), and 1 percent because of the quality of service or the convenience.

Thus, the main response by retailers has to be: *lower prices*. A study showed that on average, prices were 20 percent higher in Canada than in the United States (this figure will vary with the exchange rate). Partly, these higher prices are due to inefficient distribution systems and higher margins. There is some evidence that Canadian retailers have reduced their prices (some advertise that they will pay the GST) and improved their service. Changes in the distribution system will take longer.

Other responses have come from the federal and provincial governments. The federal government has accelerated the tariff exemptions on many items, particularly electronic products, thus allowing retailers to reduce their prices further. Some provincial governments have eliminated the prohibition of Sunday shopping.

The main lesson of the story is that retailers and governments must listen to consumers and find innovative ways to satisfy their needs. U.S. retailers have benefited from their understanding of consumers and taken advantage of situational factors like the FTA, the GST, the 1991–92 recession, and the higher Canadian dollar.

Sources: Alan Toulin, "Lower Prices Only Way to Stem Border Shopping," *The Financial Post*, February 10, 1992, p. 9; "$10-Billion Loss Cited in Border Shopping," *Globe and Mail*, June 24, 1992, p. B8; Mark Evans, "Shopping Study Faults Mark-Ups," *The Financial Post*, May 15, 1992, p. 9; and Lise Héroux et al., "Do U.S. Bordertown Retailers Adapt Their Marketing Strategies to Accommodate Canadian Shoppers?" unpublished document, S.U.N.Y. Plattsburgh, 1992.

The multiattribute model of consumer choice is one that is frequently used to help retailers understand the importance of various store features to consumers.[22] The model can be applied as follows:

$$As = \sum_{i=1}^{n} B_i W_i$$

where:

As = Attitude toward the store

$B_i$ = Belief by a consumer that a store possesses a particular attribute $i$

$W_i$ = The importance of the attribute $i$ to a consumer

$n$ = Number of attributes $(i)$ important to consumers in their choice of a store.

***Example.*** Assume that the four attributes $(n = 4)$ shown in Table 4–2 are important in the consumer's choice of a store at which to shop. The *belief* about each attribute in store choice is rated on a scale of 1 to 5, with a score of 5 indicating that the store rates high on that attribute and 1 indicating that it rates low. Consumers rate the *importance* of each attribute on a scale of 1 to 5, with 5 reflecting a very important attribute to consumers and 1 a very unimportant one.

As shown in Table 4–2, the importance and belief scores are multiplied for each attribute and summed to develop a measure of the consumer's attitude toward each of the three stores being evaluated. Scores could range from 4 to 100 (5 × 5 × 4), with 4 being the least favourable score and 100 the most favourable.

Store attributes clearly vary in importance to consumers. For example, Store 1 (e.g., a sporting goods store) may offer the widest selection of merchandise and the most qualified salespersons. Store 3 (e.g., a discount store), on the other hand, may offer little, if any, advice and stock only the fastest-moving items. However, its prices are likely to be lower than at other outlets. Store 2 (e.g., a junior department store) rates average on all the attributes.

TABLE 4–2　**The Multiattribute Model of Store Choice**

| Attributes (i) | Importance of Attributes (W_i) | Beliefs (B_i) | | |
|---|---|---|---|---|
| | | Store 1 | Store 2 | Store 3 |
| Low prices | 4 | 1 | 3 | 5 |
| Wide merchandise assortment | 5 | 5 | 3 | 3 |
| Courteous personnel | 2 | 4 | 3 | 2 |
| After-sale service | 4 | 4 | 3 | 1 |
| Attitude toward the store | | 53 | 45 | 43 |

Based on the customer's stated importances in Table 4–2, it is likely that he or she will shop in the first type of store, since the attitude is the highest among the three (i.e., 53 versus 45 and 43). Other types of consumers may express different importances that may lead to different attitudes toward the three stores.

*Understanding Store Image*

The multiattribute model is one way to determine a consumer's image of a retail outlet. Image is the way consumers feel about a store, what people believe to be true about it, and how well those beliefs coincide with what they think it should be like. The image may be accurate, or it may be quite different from reality. Knowing how consumers feel about an outlet is important in developing strategies for attracting them.

### Why Think about Store Image?

The retailer should be concerned about store image because the flow of customer traffic depends on it. Management may have what it thinks is the right merchandise, at the right price, in the right style, and in the desired size, colour, and quality. But it is what the customer thinks of the price, the quality, and the service that is important.

Also important is the impression that customers have of employees. If they like the employees, they are more apt to have favourable impressions of what the store offers.

### How Are Images Formed?

Specific features of a store provide the elements that make up its image. By examining each of the elements, management can determine the importance of these elements to consumers. For example, a study of Canadian grocery shopping habits found an absence of store loyalty. The main factors for choosing a store for grocery shopping were the presence of fresh products, a clean, well-lit, well-stocked store, low prices, friendly service, and name-brand products, in that order.[23] Supermarkets should implement a strategy that creates and delivers a positive image based on these elements.

*Price Policy.   A store's price line influences the way people think of its other aspects.* Therefore, prices must be consistent with the other elements. To illustrate, a supermarket learned that when it installed carpeting, it created a higher price image. Customers felt that prices had gone up even though they had not.

Yet, it isn't always necessary for a store to give the impression that it is a "bargain centre." A low-price policy may create an unfavourable image. Some customers feel that low quality goes with low prices and will not shop at these stores. Yet, other customers like bargain stores. The importance of price varies with a number of factors, including the type of product, family income, and competitive offerings.

Customers usually make up their minds about a store's prices from the store's advertising displays, merchandising practices (such as stocking national brands), and location. They also rely on their impression of the store's pricing policies rather than on actual knowledge.[24]

Two questions that can be helpful in image-building efforts are:

- What price do the customers expect to pay?
- Do the customers consider price as important as quality, convenience, dependability, and selection?

*Merchandise Variety.*    Image improves when customers find a product that they like but don't find in other stores. On the other hand, failure to carry certain items may give a retailer's whole product line a bad name. Similarly, when customers find one product in a store that displeases them, they are apt to become more critical of the rest of the offering. The key is in knowing the preferences of the customers.

*Employees.*    Salespeople and other employees who are seen by customers affect the store's image. A negative impression is formed if the educational level of a store's personnel is considerably above or below the educational level of most of its customers. Whatever group a store appeals to, salespeople should dress and speak in such a way that the customers feel comfortable talking to them. These conversations, even though sometimes brief, determine whether customers regard the store as friendly and helpful or impersonal and uninterested.

A store may get a bad image because salespeople talk to each other rather than stepping up to greet customers. Customers have to ask for help and feel that they are interrupting a private conversation. In the same vein, a quality restaurant may suffer

*Holt Renfrew creates a specific image with merchandise displays.*

Source: Photo by Betty McDougall.

because of a chatty waitstaff. Customers want quiet and decorum when they dine by candlelight.

Employee perceptions of customer service are fundamental to the delivery of quality service and, furthermore, are consistent predictors of sales. If every employee does not perceive that quality service is important, then the employees are unlikely to deliver a quality service response in relating to the customer.[25]

***The Store's Appearance.***   What people see as they pass by the store is another important element in its image. Even people who never enter a store form an impression from its outside appearance. That impression may be the reason they don't break their stride when they go by the store.

Inside the store, the layout and the decor reinforce customers' impressions about the products and salespeople. For example, fixtures that are classic in design usually appeal to older and more conservative groups. Very plain, inexpensive-appearing fixtures help to build an image with young families whose incomes are limited. Low ceilings may make the store more personal, and indirect lighting usually makes the customer think of higher quality. Some colour schemes are more masculine than others.

***Type of Clientele.***   The image that some people have of a store is determined by the type of people who shop there. Some people, for example, think of a shop as one where professional people usually shop. They think of other stores as ones where blue-collar workers usually shop.

***Advertising.***   Advertising tells people whether the store is modern or old-fashioned, low-price or high-price, small or large. It also communicates other things of both a physical and psychological nature.

For example, when printed ads are full of heavy black print, customers get an image of low prices. Conversely, white space often connotes quality. A food store could improve its image by including a personal interest feature in its weekly ad of special prices. The outlet could feature a recipe, perhaps with the picture of the chef who originated it.

Catalogs are also very useful in forming a store's image. Major department stores like Eaton's and The Bay produce beautiful catalogs, particularly during the Christmas season. Birks even produced a "magalog" called "The Spirit of Adventure," with some articles on the theme of an African safari. The objective was to target a high-income, high-education professional and develop a more contemporary image for Birks.[26]

***Changing the Store's Image***

An image is a complex affair, and managers should not try to change a store's image without careful thought and planning. However, if a retailer is dissatisfied with the store image customers seem to have, three questions should be asked:

- What kind of image will best serve the existing market?
- What kind of image does the store have now?
- What changes can be made to improve the image?

A store cannot be all things to all people. In fact, one of the competitive strengths in retailing is that each store can be different. Many stores are successful because they specialize, and their owner-managers build an image around that particular specialty.

### Keeping the Image Sharp

Like the human face, a store's image does not stay bright by itself. Maintaining a store's image—regardless of the type—can be handled in the same way as other management problems. Managers should review the image periodically, just as they periodically review financial statements. They can then find potential trouble spots and correct them before they get out of hand.

### Listen to Customers

Management can ask customers what they like about a store and why they prefer it to others. Their answers give an idea of the strong points in its marketing mix and its image. They can also indicate what products and services should be advertised and promoted.

All customers speak in sales. What they buy or don't buy speaks louder than words. Keeping track of sales by item can help to determine what customers like or don't like.

Customer complaints can help deal with reluctant customers—those who shop only for one or two items that they can't get elsewhere. In most cases, their reluctance is caused by the image they have of the store. Management can change that image only by learning its cause and making adjustments.

Management should also look at competitors. They can do some comparison shopping, with the goal of trying to find out the strong points competitors use to create attractive images.

### Listen to Noncustomers

Management often finds there are more people in their neighbourhood who don't patronize them than who do. Why? Often, only one or two aspects of an operation irritate and keep some people from having a good image of it. Because of a grouchy cashier, for example, such potential customers think poorly of the whole store.

*How Do Consumers Shop?*     The way in which consumers select products and services and the distance they will travel to shop also affect merchandising decisions.

### The Costs of Shopping

Many consumers try to minimize the costs of shopping when making a shopping trip. The costs of shopping are money, time, and energy. *Money costs* are the cost of goods purchased and the cost of travel. *Time costs* include the time spent getting to and from the store(s), getting to and from the car, and paying for merchandise. *Energy costs* include carrying packages, fighting traffic, parking, waiting in line, and various psychological costs, as shown in Table 4–3.

---

## TABLE 4–3   Costs in Shopping and Buying

Cost of merchandise
Other monetary outlays *(money costs)*

1. Parking fees
2. Automobile gasoline and wear and tear
3. Installation
4. Credit
5. Repairs
6. Wrapping
7. Babysitting fees
8. Warranties

Nonmonetary costs *(time costs)*

1. Time away from other activities
2. Waiting in line
3. Comparison of merchandise between stores
4. Comparison of alternative merchandise offerings
5. Travel time

Emotional costs *(energy costs)*

1. Frustration from out-of-stock items
2. Dealing with surly or indifferent sales assistants
3. Bargaining over price and terms of sale
4. Concern over a wrong decision
5. Effects of crowding
6. *Parking + Traffic.*

---

Management can be responsive to these problems by having the proper store hours and by offering shoppers credit, delivery, and similar services.

Consumers are willing to travel farther for specialty goods than for either shopping goods or convenience goods because they believe the satisfaction they obtain from getting exactly what they want more than offsets the cost of the extra effort.

- **Convenience goods** are frequently purchased items for which consumers do not engage in comparison shopping before making a purchase decision.
- **Shopping goods** are products for which consumers make comparisons between various brands in a product class before making a purchase.
- **Specialty goods** are products that consumers know they want and are willing to make a special effort to acquire.

It is not always possible to generalize as to what types of merchandise can be described as convenience, shopping, or specialty goods. Consumers view merchandise differently. What is a shopping good to one consumer may be a convenience good to another. However, typical examples of convenience, shopping, and specialty goods can be identified. Household salt is a convenience good for most shoppers. They will make the purchase at the nearest available outlet. Household durables or appliances are shopping goods for many persons. A lawn mower is an example of such a product. Consumers often do not have strong brand preferences for such an item. As a result, they will compare price, warranties, and various features before making a purchase. Designer label merchandise such as Parachute or Alfred Sung is a specialty good for many shoppers. Similarly, a Rolex watch may be regarded by many shoppers as a specialty good. They will travel considerable distances to purchase the item they want and will not compare alternative merchandise offerings.

Overall, less time is spent today in shopping than in the past. The reasons include (1) advertising, which makes information more easily available; (2) the higher cost of gasoline; (3) the increased number of women who now work outside the home and have less time for shopping; and (4) increasing nonstore alternatives for purchases.[27] Many shoppers do not visit more than two stores even when buying items such as TV sets.

### How Far Are Consumers Willing to Travel?

Most shoppers at a corner food store live within a kilometre of the store. Shoppers usually will travel 10 minutes or so to shop for higher-priced merchandise. Typically, 75 percent of the persons travelling to a large shopping centre live within 15 minutes of the centre. However, shoppers will travel much further to purchase specialty goods.

## What Do Consumers Buy?

*Price and brand are two major attributes that affect consumer purchases.* Price is important because it is often a measure of worth and quality. Brand is often relied on as a measure of quality.[28] Other factors that are important in merchandise choice include open code (freshness) dating, nutritional labelling, unit pricing, shelf displays, shelf location, and coupons.

### Price

Consumers ordinarily do not know the exact price of a merchandise item, but they usually know the price within well-defined ranges.[29] The higher-income consumer usually is less price conscious than the lower-income consumer seeking the same merchandise. The more of a shopper's income that is spent on an item, the greater price awareness there is likely to be. Also, price is not as important to the nondiscount shopper as to the discount shopper.

### Brands

*Know*

Some consumers purchase only well-known brands of manufacturers such as Del Monte. These **national brands** are the brands of a manufacturer such as Procter & Gamble that are sold through a wide variety of retail outlets. Purchasing these brands helps consumers avoid unsatisfactory purchases. But many consumers are now buying *nonbranded* items, as they can save up to 30 to 40 percent when compared to national brands. These nonbranded products, called **generics,** are unbranded merchandise offerings carrying only the designation of the product type on the package. Consumers rely on the reputation of the store as an assurance of quality in buying the items. Many stores such as Sears, Eaton's, Canadian Tire, and Loblaws, sell their own brands. Known as **private brands,** they are brands of merchandise that retailers develop and promote under their own labels.

Private brands have been especially important to department stores and specialty stores in recent years. During much of the previous decade, these outlets had relied heavily on designer labels such as Calvin Klein to develop upscale, somewhat exclusive images. However, as the sales volume of the designer labels levelled off due to the rather exclusive patterns of distribution through department and specialty stores, suppliers began selling the merchandise through mass market outlets. The merchandise thus lost its exclusivity, and in many instances was heavily price discounted. Department and specialty stores, as a defensive strategy, began developing their own private labels to maintain desired margins on the merchandise and to protect the integrity of their image.[30]

### Open Code Dating
**Open code dating** means the consumer can tell the date after which a product should not be used, and food shoppers often use this information. The strongest users tend to be young consumers with higher incomes and higher levels of education who live in the suburbs.

### Nutritional Labelling
**Nutritional labelling** is important for people with allergies, or people on a specific diet. The usage pattern for nutritional labelling is similar to that for open code dating.

### Unit Pricing
**Unit pricing** states prices in such terms as price per litre or gram. Shoppers use this information as a guide to the best buys. Here again, the younger, higher-income consumers are more likely to use the data. Brand switching often occurs when prices are stated on a per unit basis.

### Shelf Displays
Retailers tend to give the most shelf space to merchandise with the highest profit margins. Profits tend to drop, however, if managers shift store displays and layout too often. Point-of-sale materials, even simple signs, can increase item sales by as much as 100 percent. End-of-aisle and special displays can have even larger effects on consumer buying behaviour. Today, with computerized cash registers, managers know exactly how often a product sells. As a result, they often will stock the two or three best-selling brands in each product category. The subject of shelf space allocation is discussed in greater detail in Chapter 12 on layout and merchandise presentation.

### Shelf Location
Shelf location is an important factor in influencing consumer purchase decisions. Consumers are most prone to purchase merchandise displayed at eye level. Merchandise located on the lowest shelves may present difficulties for elderly or infirm consumers, and merchandise on the higher shelves may be difficult for some individuals to reach. The ideal shelf location depends on the consumer. For

example, merchandise directed primarily at children should be on a lower shelf, where they can easily see it.[31]

Shelf location becomes especially critical for **low-involvement** products, since consumers are likely to purchase the first item that catches their attention. Examples include cleaning supplies or paper products. Conversely, consumers are likely to make brand comparisons in a **high-involvement** product class such as salad dressings in which shoppers may compare products on such bases as content or number of calories. Shelf location may be a less critical factor for high-involvement products since customers will be making a more concerted effort to compare alternative offerings.

### Coupons and Other Sales Promotions

**Coupons** can be used to draw new customers to a store and to increase purchases by regular consumers. They can also be used to offset the negative features of a store by drawing customers to a poor location. Coupons can be issued by manufacturers *(manufacturer coupons)* or by retailers *(store coupons)*. Retailers may provide coupons in a variety of ways, the most popular ones being in their weekly advertisements *(in-ad coupons),* on the shelves *(in-store-shelf coupons),* in booklets, or at the cash register (electronically printed coupons). In 1991, of all the coupons distributed, 4 billion were regular (i.e., manufacturers') coupons, and 22 billion were retailers' coupons. Of the 26 billion coupons distributed, 290 million were redeemed, and the average face value was $.58.[32]

Coupon users tend to have slightly higher incomes than the average household and normally have children. They are especially good customers for retailers. Coupons have achieved a high level of acceptance in Canada, and more than three quarters of all retail customers reported using coupons for food, household items, transportation, and dining. More than half reported clipping coupons at least once a week, and over 60 percent of coupon users felt that they were really worth it.[33]

Trading stamps, rebate offers, and similar strategies also can be used to attract new consumers and to retain the loyalty of current customers.

## *When Do Consumers Buy?*

Sunday and 24-hour openings are attractive to many shoppers. Sunday is often the only time some families can shop together, and working wives are more likely to shop in the evenings and on Sunday.

Many retailers do not like Sunday openings or long hours because they feel that costs go up without helping profits. However, consumer preference for these hours and competitive pressures (locally or from cross-border U.S. retailers) are making these openings increasingly common (as provincial governments are forced to allow them).

Retailers may also experience great seasonal variations. Some retailers make one third or more of their annual sales in November and December. Spring dresses sell well just prior to Easter. Picnic supplies sell best in the summer and ski equipment during the fall and early winter.

# Responding to Consumer Dissatisfaction

Consumer complaints are a signal that all is not well in the business. Retailers must make a concerted effort to understand customers' satisfaction and dissatisfaction with their services.[34] Retailers should actively seek feedback from customers—what they like and don't like, how they can be better served, their satisfaction with store policies, and so forth. Unfortunately, too few stores do this.

*It is too simple to say the customer is always right.* Some consumers do not pay their bills. They shoplift, switch price tags, and so forth. Nor is the customer always wrong. Retailers sometimes use bad credit information, make errors in customers' accounts, and sell inferior merchandise.

The level of satisfaction varies with the product category. A nationwide survey of Canadian consumers found that a majority were satisfied with large household appliances. Of those dissatisfied, at least half took some form of action to resolve the problem.[35] For clothing and footwear, they complained about quality, workmanship, and assortment; for groceries, they complained about prices and freshness.[36]

## How Do Consumers View Retailers?

Overall, retailers are rated poorly in communicating with consumers, in being interested in customers, in providing good value for money, and in honesty concerning what they say about merchandise. Chains tend to rate highest in the quality of the job they perform; appliance and automobile repair services rank at the bottom of the list.[37] Also, retailers are often held responsible for the products they distribute and the problems consumers encounter with these products.

What consumers consider a serious product violation depends on the product category and whether it is a quantity, labelling, or quality violation.[38] A recent study provides some indication about the seriousness Canadian consumers attach to each type of violation. The most serious **quantity violations** are for entertainment articles, and the least serious are for fresh fruits and vegetables. The most serious **labelling violations** are for precious metal articles (e.g., gold jewellery), and the least serious are for pet supplies. The most serious **quality violations** are for precious metals and home improvement and automotive products, and the least are for eggs, fresh fruit and vegetables, and other foods and beverages. Finally, quality violations are perceived to be much more serious than quantity violations, which in turn are more serious than labelling violations.

## What's Being Done about Problems?

### Retailer Responses

As noted earlier, freshness dates now appear on many products, nutritional labelling is also being practised, and unit pricing is another aid to the consumer.

Some stores provide in-store consumer consultants, consumer advisory panels, consumer affairs forums, buyer guides, employee training on consumer rights, and signs, sales notices, and applications in languages other than English when appropriate.

### Voluntary Action Groups

Voluntary action groups are organizations sponsored by an industry that are designed to respond to consumer complaints about products or services sold by retailers. The groups also provide needed information to consumers to help them make important buying decisions. However, some studies find a level of scepticism about these voluntary business efforts.[39]

Consumers also need to react responsibly to help avoid unnecessary problems in their capacity as consumers. Consumers are likely to have fewer problems with merchandise when they understand how to operate the items they purchase, if they use proper care in handling the equipment, if they bring defective merchandise to the attention of retailers, if they are aware of their rights as consumers, and if they make comparisons before purchasing. Finally, Better Business Bureaus serve a useful purpose in handling consumer problems at the local level.

*A Philosophy of Action for Management*

Retailers need to be alert to changing attitudes and demands of consumers and to practice better customer relations. The demands of consumers normally are not unrealistic. Customers simply want more, better, and honest information.

Retailers may need to do research from time to time to learn how customers feel about a store and its products. They should take a positive approach in dealing with customers. Most retailers do not want to make money by selling merchandise that may hurt customers or drive them away. Customers simply want such things as better values, labelling, honesty in advertising, and full information on credit terms.

# Chapter Highlights

- Consumers shop for reasons other than buying. These reasons can be grouped into personal and social motives. Personal motives include role playing, diversion, sensory stimulation, physical activity, and self-gratification. Social motives include the desire for social experiences, peer group attraction, status and authority needs, the pleasure of bargaining, and being with others of similar interests. Careful planning by a retailer can influence shoppers to make purchases even when the primary purpose of the trip is social or personal.

- Consumers go through a series of stages in making a purchase decision. The stages, for other than routine purchases, include problem recognition, information search, evaluation, the actual purchase decision, and postpurchase behaviour. Retailers can influence consumer choices and actions at each stage of the decision process.

- Retailers can have the most influence on the behaviour of consumers during the information search and evaluation stage. An understanding of the how, when, where, and what of consumer

shopping and buying behaviour can help retailers be responsive to their needs for information.

- Consumers use consumer-dominated, marketer-dominated, and neutral sources of information in making store and product choices. Marketer-dominated sources include advertising, personal selling, displays, sales promotion, and publicity. Consumer-dominated sources include friends, relatives, acquaintances, or others. Neutral sources include federal and provincial government consumer protection agencies.

- Consumers seek to minimize risks during the purchase evaluation stage. The risks they are seeking to avoid include performance risk, financial risk, physical risk, psychological risk, social risk, and time loss risk.

- Consumers may seek to go to shopping centres, to downtown stores, out of town (outshopping), or out of the country (cross-border shopping), or simply shop from their own homes (nonstore shopping).

- Store image is an important consideration in store selection. It is formed based on information such as price, merchandise variety, employee behaviour and appearance, store appearance, type of clientele, and advertising. Efforts must be made to improve, change, or maintain the store's image.

• Many consumers try to minimize the costs of shopping when making purchase decisions. These costs include money, time, and energy. Actual purchases by consumers are influenced by many factors, including price and brand, shopping aids such as open code dating and unit pricing, shelf displays and shelf locations, coupons, trading stamps, and rebates.

• Retailers also need to be sensitive to consumer concerns that often take the form of consumerism. Efforts at solving consumer dissatisfaction often start with the retailer from whom a purchase was made. In recent years, a variety of retailers have responded by providing in-store consumer consultants, consumer advisory panels, consumer-affairs forums, buyer guides, and employee training on consumer rights.

## Key Terms

Cognitive dissonance   91
Consumer-dominated information sources   88
Convenience goods   101
Coupon   104
Financial risk   89
Generics   102
High involvement   104
Image   94
Labelling violation   105
Low involvement   104
Marketer-dominated information sources   87
Multiattribute model   94
National brands   102
Neutral sources of information   88
Nonstore shopping   94

Nutritional labelling   103
Open code dating   103
Outshopping   93
Performance risk   89
Physical risk   89
Private brands   102
Psychological risk   89
Quality violation   105
Quantity violation   105
Shopping goods   101
Social risk   89
Specialty goods   101
Time loss risk   89
Unit pricing   103

## Discussion Questions

1. Briefly describe each of the stages (steps) of the consumer decision process discussed in the text.

2. What are some of the reasons consumers might prefer to shop downtown? Why do some people prefer to shop in shopping centres?

3. What is the importance of image to the retailer? How does it affect the shopping behaviour of consumers? Think of the two largest department stores in your community. How would you describe their images?

4. How does open code dating and unit pricing information aid consumers in making purchase decisions? Develop a profile of those consumers who are most likely to use these types of shopping information.

5. What are some of the things retailers can do to reduce each of the six types of risks discussed in the chapter?

6. Provide an example of each of the personal and social motives discussed in the chapter as reasons for shopping but not buying.

7. What are some of the things that retailers can do to help consumers minimize the costs of shopping?

8. What are some retailers doing to help consumers buy more effectively?

# Application Exercises

1. Visit a national supermarket in your community, a discount or warehouse grocer food outlet, and a 24-hour type of food store. Prepare a paper that points out the similarities and differences between the three types of stores. Write a brief statement that summarizes your thoughts about the image of each type of outlet. Describe the characteristics of the people you think are most likely to shop at each of the three outlets.

2. Briefly interview 10 to 15 of your fellow students. Find out the latest experience about which they were

dissatisfied with a retail outlet. What action did they take, if any? What was the response of management to the situation if it was called to their attention? Will the situation cause the dissatisfied person not to shop at the outlet again? Write a short paper summarizing their experiences.

3. Investigate the activities that are being undertaken by consumer groups and businesses in your area to help stop consumer dissatisfaction. What roles do voluntary action groups and Better Business Bureaus play in helping to resolve consumer dissatisfaction?

# Suggested Cases

# Endnotes

1. G. H. G. McDougall, ''Shopping Orientations: An Influence on Search Behaviour,'' *1976 Proceedings* (ASAC, 1976), pp. 233–42; T. K. Clarke and F. G. Crane, ''Are Leisure Shoppers Really Different?'' in *Marketing,* vol. 10, ed. Alain d'Astous (ASAC, 1989), pp. 58–65; G. R. Jarboe and C. D. McDaniel, ''A Profile of Browsers in Regional Shopping Malls,'' *Journal of the Academy of Marketing Science* 15 (Spring 1987), pp. 45–52; and C. W. Park, E. S. Iyer, and D. C. Smith, ''The Effects of Situational Factors on In-Store Shopping Behaviour,'' *Journal of Consumer Research* 15 (March 1989), pp. 422–33.

2. E. S. Iyer, ''Unplanned Purchasing: Knowledge of Shopping Environment and Time Pressure,'' *Journal of Retailing* 65 (Spring 1989), pp. 40–57.

3. Corinne Berneman and Roger Heeler, ''Shoppers' Mood and Purchases,'' in *Marketing,* vol. 7, ed. Thomas E. Muller (ASAC, 1986), pp. 152–61.

4. Marina Strauss, ''Young Pleasure Seekers Born to Shop, Study Says,'' *Globe and Mail,* January 27, 1989, p. B6.

5. Michel Laroche, Jerry Rosenblatt, Jacques E. Brisoux, and Robert Shimotakahara, ''Brand Categorization Strategies in RRB Situations: Some Empirical Results,'' in *Advances in Consumer Research,* vol. 10, ed. Richard M. Bagozzi and Alice M. Tybout (Ann Arbor: Association for Consumer Research, 1983), pp. 549–54.

6. R. E. Nisbett and D. E. Kanouse, ''Obesity, Food Deprivation, and Supermarket Shopping Behaviour,'' *Journal of Personality and Social Psychology,* August 1969, p. 290.

7. Peter Thirkell and Harrie Vredenburg, ''Individual and Situational Determinants of Pre-Purchase Information Search: A National Study of Canadian Automobile Buyers,'' in *Marketing,* vol. 3, ed. Michel Laroche (ASAC, 1982), pp. 305–13.

8. R. Neil Maddox, Teresa Moore, Greg McPherson, Carrie Kruitwagen, and Gary Clark, "Business Person's Criteria for Restaurant Selection for Lunch," in *Marketing,* vol. 7, ed. Thomas E. Muller (ASAC, 1986), pp. 201–11.

9. John A. Quelch, Stephen B. Ash, and Mary Jane Grant, "Consumer Satisfaction with Appliances and Personal Care Equipment," in *Marketing,* vol. 1, ed. Vernon J. Jones (ASAC, 1980), pp. 289–97; and W. O. Bearden and R. L. Oliver, "The Role of Public and Private Complaining in Satisfaction with Problem Resolution," *Journal of Consumer Affairs* 19 (Winter 1985), pp. 222–40.

10. René Y. Darmon, Michel Laroche, and John V. Petrof, *Marketing in Canada: A Management Perspective,* 3rd ed. (Toronto: McGraw-Hill Ryerson, 1989), pp. 885–87.

11. M. Dunn, P. E. Murphy, and G. Skelly, "The Influence of Perceived Risk on Brand Preferences in Supermarket Products," *Journal of Retailing* 62 (Summer 1986), pp. 204–16.

12. Jo Marney, "Moment of Decision Is in the Store," *Marketing,* September 27, 1987, pp. 13–14; John Oldland, "Brand Loyalty Reasons Are Changing," *Marketing,* November 23, 1987, p. 9.

13. Leon Festinger, *A Theory of Cognitive Dissonance* (Stanford: Stanford University Press, 1957).

14. L. L. Berry, D. R. Bennett, and C. W. Brown, *Service Quality* (Homewood, Ill.: Dow Jones-Irwin, 1989), p. 29; Gordon McDougall and Terry Levesque, "The Measurement of Service Quality: Some Methodological Issues," in *Marketing, Operations and Human Resources Insight into Services,* ed. Pierre Eiglier and Eric Langeard (Aix, France: Institut d'Administration des Entreprises, 1992), pp. 411–31; and Gaston LeBlanc, "The Determinants of Service Quality in Travel Agencies: An Analysis of Customer Perceptions," in *Marketing,* vol. 11, ed. John Liefeld (ASAC, 1990), pp. 188–96.

15. "The Mall Overtakes Main Street," *Canadian Business,* December 1988, p. 10; and Michael Salter, "Shoppers' Heaven," *Report on Business Magazine,* June 1989, pp. 62–69.

16. N. G. Papadopoulos, Louise Heslop, and Gerry Philips, "A Longitudinal Perspective on Consumer Outshopping," in *Marketing,* vol. 9, ed. Tansu Barker (ASAC, 1988), pp. 58–67; N. G. Papadopoulos, "Consumer Outshopping Research: Review and Extension," *Journal of Retailing,*

Winter 1980, pp. 41–58; and N. G. Papadopoulos, "Consumer Outshopping Research in Canada," in *Marketing,* vol. 4, ed. James D. Forbes (ASAC, 1983), pp. 288–98.

17. Malcolm Smith and Gordon Fullerton, "Outshopping in Maritime Canada: Some Preliminary Research Results," in *Marketing,* vol. 7, ed. Thomas E. Muller (ASAC, 1986), pp. 173–80.

18. George Moschis, Jac Goldstucker, and Thomas J. Stanley, "At-Home Shopping: Will Consumers Let Their Computers Do the Walking?" *Business Horizons,* March–April 1985, pp. 22–29.

19. Nancy J. Church, Michel Laroche, and Jerry Rosenblatt, "Consumer Brand Categorization for Durables with Limited Problem Solving: An Empirical Test and Proposed Extension of the Brisoux-Laroche Model," *Journal of Economic Psychology* 6 (1985), pp. 231–53; and Matt A. Elbeik, "Image Determinants of an Ideal Hospital," in *Marketing,* vol. 7, ed. Thomas E. Muller (ASAC, 1986), pp. 91–100.

20. W. Weitzel, A. Schwarzkopf, and E. G. Peach, "The Influence of Employee Perceptions of Customer Service on Retail Store Sales," *Journal of Retailing* 65 (Spring 1989), pp. 27–39.

21. G. H. G. McDougall and J. N. Fry, "Combining Two Methods of Image Measurement," *Journal of Retailing,* Winter 1974–75, pp. 53–61.

22. Martin Fishbein, "The Relationships between Beliefs, Attitudes and Behaviour," in *Cognitive Consistency,* ed. S. Feldman (New York: Academic Press, 1966), pp. 199–223.

23. "An Absence of Store Loyalty among Women," *Marketing,* August 31, 1987, p. 4.

24. Thomas E. Muller, "Information Load at the Point of Purchase: Extending the Research," in *Marketing,* vol. 3, ed. Michel Laroche (ASAC, 1982), pp. 193–202.

25. Weitzel et al., "The Influence of Employee Perceptions."

26. Ken Riddell, "Birks Gets into Spring with a New 'Magalog,'" *Marketing,* March 14, 1988, p. 1.

27. Judith Marshall, Terry Deutscher, and Bernie Portis, "Convenience Food Purchasing: A Proposed Model," in *Marketing,* vol. 3, ed. Michel Laroche (ASAC, 1982), pp. 144–54.

28. Michel Laroche, Jerry Rosenblatt, Leon Wahler, and Friedhelm Bliemel, "Economic Considerations for Dispensing Pharmacists: The Impact of Price-

Quality Evaluations on Brand Categorization,'' *Journal of Pharmaceutical Marketing and Management* 1, no. 1 (1986), pp. 41–60.

29. Thomas E. Muller, ''In Search of Dr. Weber's K: Market Response to Supermarket Information,'' in *Marketing,* vol. 2, ed. Robert Wyckham (ASAC, 1981), pp. 246–55; and Thomas E. Muller and Kai Kwan Leung, ''Price Awareness in the Supermarket,'' in *Marketing,* vol. 4, ed. James D. Forbes (ASAC, 1983), pp. 238–46.

30. F. Schwadel, ''Complaints Rise about Clothing Quality,'' *The Wall Street Journal,* June 27, 1988, p. 17.

31. A. Swasy, ''More Businesses Put Out Welcome Mat for Children,'' *The Wall Street Journal,* May 31, 1989, p. B1.

32. Ken Riddell, ''Reaching Consumers In-Store,'' *Marketing,* July 13/20, 1992, p. 10; and Ken Riddell, ''Couponers Show Record Year,'' *Marketing,* February 10, 1992, p. 2.

33. Jo Marney, ''Marketing: A Push and Pull Situation,'' *Marketing,* October 3, 1988, pp. 14–16.

34. Judith Langer, ''Upscale Department Stores Often Provide Low-End Service,'' *Marketing News,* March 13, 1987, p. 17.

35. John A. Quelch, Stephen B. Ash, and Mary Jane Grant, ''Consumer Satisfaction with Appliances and Personal Care Equipment,'' in *Marketing,* vol. 1, ed. Vernon J. Jones (ASAC, 1981), pp. 289–97.

36. John D. Claxton and J. R. Brent Ritchie, ''Consumer Prepurchase Shopping Problems: A Focus on the Retailing Component,'' *Journal of Retailing,* Fall 1979, pp. 23–43.

37. Pierre Filiatrault, ''The Automobile Repair Consumption Problem: The Point of View of Producers,'' in *Marketing,* vol. 6, ed. Jean-Charles Chebat (ASAC, 1985), pp. 118–25.

38. Jacques C. Bourgeois and Michel Laroche, ''The Measurement of the Seriousness of Product Violations,'' *Journal of Public Policy and Marketing,* 6 (1987), pp. 1–15; see also John A. Quelch, ''Consumer Attitudes towards Affirmative Disclosure of Nutritional Information in Breakfast Cereal Advertising,'' in *Developments in Canadian Marketing,* ed. Robert D. Tamilia (ASAC, 1979), pp. 93–103.

39. Farouk A. Salem and Asit K. Sarkar, ''Consumer Protection: A Look at Consumer Awareness, Attitudes and Preferences in the Canadian Prairies,'' in *Developments in Canadian Marketing,* ed. Robert D. Tamilia (ASAC, 1979), pp. 116–23.

# 5   SOCIAL INFLUENCES ON THE RETAIL CONSUMER

---

### Chapter Objectives

After reading this chapter, you should be able to:

1 Understand the decision-making process within a family.
2 Understand the role of reference groups and opinion leaders.
3 Explain the influence of social class on retail strategy.
4 Explain the influence of culture and subculture on retail strategy in Canada.
5 Understand the concept of life-style.
6 Describe the role of life-style merchandising in the retail strategy mix.

**Retailing Capsule**

The social influences on retail strategies are often subtle but very real. Consider the following:

• Many Canadian teenagers are compulsive, enthusiastic consumers, searching for self-gratification and pleasure, willing to live their lives to the fullest. They are struggling to find their own identity and use consumption of products for their symbolic value. They ''wear'' products as ''badges'' of the image they want to project to their peers. About 55 percent of teenagers have part-time jobs, and their average income is about $6,000 per year, or $115 per week. They spend about 60 percent of that income weekly and save the rest for larger purchases. In a six-month period, 45 percent of teenagers had bought clothes, and footwear, 17 percent had bought a new stereo, a TV set, or a VCR, 13 percent had bought large gifts, and 11 percent had spent a substantial amount on sports equipment. In terms of shopping habits, in a typical two-week period, 51 percent had shopped in a grocery store, 64 percent in a drugstore, 43 percent in a music store, and 75 percent in a convenience store; in addition, 86 percent had visited a shopping mall and 80 percent a clothing store. Finally, 82 percent of teenagers influence the buying decisions of their families, and their influence is strong.*

As these three examples illustrate, demographics alone are not enough to understand and serve markets. The previous chapter focused on understanding the decision-making process of individual consumers. However, consumers are also influenced by others, including family members, friends and colleagues, other members of their social class, or their cultural or subcultural group (Figure 5–1). This chapter will focus on these influences. Finally, the concept of life-style as a customer's pattern of living has emerged as a major influence on retail merchandising and is covered in the last part of the chapter.

# Family Buying Behaviour

Buying decisions may be influenced by one or several members of a family. Shopping behaviour may involve the husband, the wife, and some of the children. This pattern of influence evolves over time, both in terms of family life cycle and in terms of changing roles within the family.

## *Family Life Cycle*

The concept of **family life cycle** reflects the combined effect of several demographic factors: marital status (legal or common law), age of the adult(s), employment status, and number and age of the children. Although 1 in 10 Canadian couples are living in common law relationships, and 42 percent include children, Statistics

*Retailing Capsule continued*

- Some of the famed baby boomers are becoming homebodies and "cocooning." This social phenomena has been termed the *couch-potato generation*. These professionals are more interested in free time and staying home to enjoy what they have worked for—reading, watching TV, gourmet cooking, and home decoration. Their homes fulfill a desire for security, comfort, and roots, and express their own personalities in the midst of a complex, harsh outside world.[†]

- Recent patterns of immigration to Canada, particularly from Hong Kong, have boosted the Asian population to over 600,000, mostly in Toronto and Vancouver, which have strong, established Chinese communities. Most of the new immigrants are young, they are starting families, and they need to buy houses, major appliances, and cars, which they tend to buy with cash. They are highly educated and have high incomes (the average annual household income for those living in Toronto is $52,800). They are status-conscious and prefer prestige brands like Courvoisier cognac (used as an aperitif). Retailers need to understand what kinds of products they need, and how to appeal to them, in terms of store displays, signs, advertising media and copy, as well as service quality.[‡]

---

[*]*TG Magazine,* reproduced in *Marketing,* November 19, 1990, supplement, p. 2; Marina Strauss, "Young Pleasure Seekers Born to Shop, Study Says," *Globe and Mail,* January 27, 1989, p. B6.

[†]Jo Marney, "Couch-Potato Generation Takes Root," *Marketing,* July 1988, p. 7.

[‡]Don Hogarth, "Marketers Set Sights on Asian-Canadians," *The Financial Post,* September 16, 1991, p. 2; and Barbara Wickens, "Cultural Cross Talk," *Maclean's,* October 25, 1991, p. 42.

**FIGURE 5–1**

*Social influences on the retail consumer*

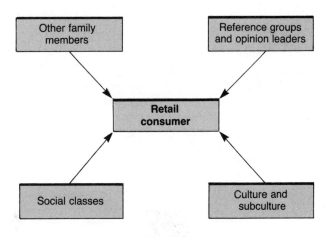

Canada counts these common law couples as families, and in the following discussion, we will use the same convention.[1]

The various stages of a family life cycle are represented in Table 5–1 for the traditional view, and in Figure 5–2 for a modified version that takes into account some more recent family patterns in terms of divorces.

Table 5–1 also provides an indication of financial needs and behavioural patterns at each stage of the family life cycle. As a family passes through some of these stages, their financial resources and needs vary in fairly predictable ways. For instance, the arrival of children for young couples will change their financial situation due to the expenses incurred in terms of housing, appliances, toys, and other child-related costs.

Retail strategies can be based, in part, on the size and location of families in a given stage of the family life cycle. For example, more than 2 million childless couples live in Canada. These are often two-income households with a large disposable income and needs that are very different from other couples of the same age. For retailers, these customers represent an attractive market for fine furniture and appliances, travel, and luxury products.[2] Similarly, other stages or subgroups within a stage (for example, higher income groups) may be targeted by retailers.[3]

*Decision Making within the Family*

For many products such as cars or homes, several family members play a role in the purchase decision. There are four basic types of decisions within a family, as indicated in Table 5–2:[4]

### Wife-Dominant

A decision is said to be a **wife-dominant decision** when the decision to purchase a product is made most of the time by the wife. In the examples in Table 5–2, this is the case for the wife's and children's clothing.

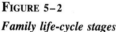

**FIGURE 5–2**

*Family life-cycle stages*

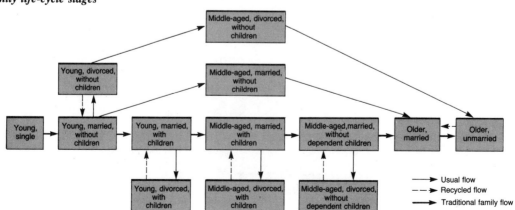

**TABLE 5–1  The Traditional Family Life-Cycle Stages and the Financial Situation and Buying Behaviour at Each Stage**

| | | Young Married Couples | | | Older Married Couples | | | Solitary Survivor | |
|---|---|---|---|---|---|---|---|---|---|
| | | | | | | | No Children Living at Home | | |
| | *Bachelor, Young, Single, Not Living at Home* | *Newly Married, No Children* | *Full Nest I, Youngest Child under Six* | *Full Nest II, Youngest Child Six or Over* | *Full Nest III, with Dependent Children* | *Empty Nest I, Head Working* | *Empty Nest II, Head Retired* | *In Labour Force* | *Retired* |
| *Financial Situation* | Few financial burdens. | Better off financially than they will be in near future. | Home purchasing at peak. Liquid assets low. Dissatisfied with financial position and amount of money saved. | Financial position better. Some wives work. | Financial position still better. More wives work. Some children get jobs. | Home ownership at peak. Most satisfied with financial position and money saved. | Drastic cut in income. Keep home. | Income still good but likely to sell home. | Drastic cut in income. |

**Behaviour with Respect to Marketing Dimensions**

| | *Bachelor, Young, Single, Not Living at Home* | *Newly Married, No Children* | *Full Nest I, Youngest Child under Six* | *Full Nest II, Youngest Child Six or Over* | *Full Nest III, with Dependent Children* | *Empty Nest I, Head Working* | *Empty Nest II, Head Retired* | *In Labour Force* | *Retired* |
|---|---|---|---|---|---|---|---|---|---|
| *General* | Fashion opinion leaders. Recreation-oriented. | Highest purchase rate and highest average purchase of durables. | Interested in new products. Like advertised products. | Less influenced by advertising. Buy larger-sized packages, multiple-unit deals. | Hard to influence with advertising. High average purchase of durables. | Interested in travel, recreation, self-education. Make gifts and contributions. Not interested in new products. | | Special need for attention, affection, and security. | |
| *Specific (Products)* | Basic kitchen equipment, basic furniture, cars, equipment for the mating game, vacations. | Cars, refrigerators, stoves, sensible and durable furniture, vacations. | Washers, dryers, TV, baby food, chest rubs and cough medicine, vitamins, dolls, wagons, sleds, skates. | Many foods, cleaning materials, bicycles, music lessons, pianos. | New, more tasteful furniture, auto, travel, nonnecessary appliances, boats, dental services, magazines. | Vacations, luxuries, home improvements. | Medical appliances, medical care, products that aid health, sleep, and digestion. | Same medical and product needs as other retired group. | |

SOURCE: Adapted from W. D. Wells and G. Gubar, "The Life-Cycle Concept in Marketing Research," *Journal of Marketing Research* 3 (Published by the American Marketing Association, November 1966), p. 362.

---

**TABLE 5–2  Examples of the Four Basic Types of Decision within a Family and Associated Products**

---

| **Wife-Dominant** | **Husband-Dominant** |
|---|---|
| Cleaning products | Life insurance |
| Kitchenware | Other insurance |
| Child's clothing | |
| Wife's clothing | |
| Food | |
| Other furnishings | |
| | |
| **Autonomous** | **Syncratic** |
| Husband's clothing | School |
| Alcoholic beverages | Vacation |
| Garden tools | Housing |
| Housing upkeep | Outside entertainment |
| Appliances | Living room furniture |
| Savings objectives | Children's toys |
| Forms of savings | Television set |
| Car | |
| Nonprescription drugs | |
| Cosmetics | |

---

SOURCE: Adapted from H. L. Davis and B. P. Rigaux, "Perceptions of Marital Roles in Decision Processes," *Journal of Consumer Research,* June 1974, pp. 51–62.

### Husband-Dominant

A decision is said to be a **husband-dominant decision** when the decision is made most of the time by the husband. In Table 5–2, this is the case for life insurance.

### Autonomous

A decision is said to be an **autonomous decision** when the decision is made over time independently by the husband or the wife. Thus, on one occasion, it may be the husband, and on another, the wife. In Table 5–2, this is the case for savings, alcohol, and the husband's clothing. Contrary to the previous two types of decisions, here the retailer should target both spouses in advertising or in-store selling.

### Syncratic

A decision is said to be a **syncratic decision** when the decision is made jointly by both spouses. In Table 5–2, this is the case for vacations, housing, and living-room furniture. As for autonomous decisions, the retailer must make sure that the needs of both spouses are met. For example, in selling living room furniture, the salesperson must interact with both spouses, not just one or the other.

*Role of Children in Decision Making*

There are about 5.5 million children 12 years old and younger in Canada, and these numbers are expected to rise due to a reversal of the birthrate. After reaching a low in 1987, the birthrate has risen to 410,000 births in 1991. This echo boom has led to the launching of new magazines and a renewed interest in marketing baby and children's products such as car seats, playpens, and baby foods.[5]

The previous pattern of decision within the family may be affected by the presence of children. A study on vacation decisions by Canadians found that husbands tended to be more dominant when children were present than in childless couples. However, children's influence on decision making was found to be mainly through alliances with one of the spouses.[6] Another study found that 4 out of 10 times, the children will determine the choice of a restaurant for a family.[7]

In addition to influencing the family decision process, children are also consumers. In one study, the average weekly income of 10-year-olds was found to be $11.[8] These skoties (spoiled kids of the eighties) represent a major market for many retailers of cereal, candy, chewing gum, soft drinks, clothing, toys, and video games (e.g., Nintendo products).

*Role of Teenagers in Decision Making*

With about 3 million teenagers (aged 13 to 19) in Canada, this is another important market for retailers, with an estimated market size of $6 billion. Retail Highlight 5–1 further profiles this segment. Among retailers who have been very successful targeting the teenage market are Benetton, HMV Stores, Roots Natural Footwear, and Château Stores of Canada.[9]

*The Changing Roles of Men and Women*

The last 30 years have seen major changes in the respective roles of men and women within the family, and these changes have important implications for retailers.

First, more women are now working outside the home than at any time in the past; about two thirds of the 10 million women of working age are now in the labour force, and two out of five working women consider themselves career women— that is, they are mostly interested in developing their careers.[10] By contrast to this group, the other working women enter the work force primarily to generate additional income for the family. Different job orientations within the family have been found to lead to different behaviours, as illustrated in Table 5–3. For dual-career and dual-income families, the job orientation is the same for both spouses. In the traditional family, the wife does not work outside the home.

Some implications of these changes for retailers are that shopping is viewed as a chore by working women, and that the emphasis should be on convenience in terms of location and opening hours (evening and Sunday shopping). Another implication is that the additional income puts the family in a higher income group and social group, allowing the purchase of timesaving products and services such as microwave ovens, freezers, convenience foods, and vacation packages. Also, these families spend their time differently and must be reached with different kinds of media (e.g., prime-time television, week-end newspapers, and billboards).[11]

Second, men have reacted in different ways to this new reality. Four distinct types have been identified.[12]

**Progressives (13 percent)**
Progressives are young, educated men, with above-average incomes who are tolerant of their wives' employment. About two thirds do the main food shopping.

---

**Retail Highlight 5–1**

# Understanding the Teen Market

Research conducted by Levi Strauss revealed that teenagers:

- Share similar goals, motivations, and values.
- Are prepared to work hard to succeed in life.
- Struggle between being conformists and innovators.
- Enjoy friendships and music from the 1960s and 1970s the most.
- Feel that growing up in the 1990s is difficult, and worry about time, money, school, life after school, unemployment, and the environment.
- Choose clothes to express themselves and their relationships with peers.
- Want to conserve, preserve, and underconsume, and dislike waste.

- Consider Levi's to be the enduring, classic jeans.

The picture that emerges is that teens, contrary to their parents, are more conservative, less optimistic about the future, and price-sensitive when they are spending their hard-earned money (their average income is $6,000). However, they are brand- and status-conscious and knowledgeable about current social issues (e.g., the environment, AIDS, and drunk driving).

As an example, HMV Stores, selling recorded music, understands that the store environment is essential to attracting teens ("The Medium Is the Message"), and that in order to provide the right kind of service to demanding teens, it uses teenage employees.

Sources: Jo Marney, "Brand Loyalty: A Marketer's Teen Dream," *Marketing*, December 9, 1991, p. 14; Jo Marney, "Teen Loyalty Targeted with a Variety of Promotions," *Marketing*, December 16, 1991, p. 18.

**All Talk, No Action (33 percent)**
Some men have attitudes, but not behaviour, that are similar to the progressives. About 20 percent do the main food shopping.

**Ambivalents (15 percent)**
Because of economic pressures, some men reluctantly accept their wives' employment. About 60 percent do the main food shopping.

**Traditionalists (39 percent)**
Older, less educated men believe that their wives' place is at home.

Some of the implications of these changes for retailers are in terms of targeting both spouses for store loyalty, merchandise selection, pricing, and promotion. In particular, the increase in food shopping by men may affect store layout and placement of impulse products.[13]

**TABLE 5–3   Some Behavioural Differences for Families with Different Job Orientations**

| | *Dual Career* | *Dual Income* | *Traditional* |
|---|---|---|---|
| **Grocery Shopping** | | | |
| Who does it? | Whoever enjoys it | Wife usually | Wife |
| How often? | Once a week or once a month | Once a week or once a month | Once a week |
| When? | No specific day | Same day | Same day |
| Store loyalty | No | Yes | Yes |
| **Household Chores** | | | |
| Cooking | Both spouses | Wife usually | Wife |
| Cleaning and laundry | Both spouses | Wife usually | Wife |
| Housekeeper | Yes | No | No |
| Attitude toward chores | Routine during week to free weekends | Ongoing, but haphazard | Ongoing, but organized |
| **Household Conveniences** | | | |
| Dishwasher and microwave oven | Yes | No | No |
| Freezer | For bulk purchases, extra cooking | For bulk purchases | For garden harvest |
| Attitude toward conveniences | Appreciate time saved | To save money | To save money |
| **Family Finances** | | | |
| Accounts | His, hers, ours | Some pooling | One account |
| Who keeps track? | Household—wife | Wife | Wife |
| Major expenses | Conferences, each spouse contributes | Priorities—family needs | Priorities—spousal territory |
| Budget | Informal, periodic reviews | More formal | More formal |
| Attitude toward money | Can have what we want, "cushions" | Work to get what we want | Have what we need; some wants |
| Credit | Convenience, consolidation of bills | Convenience and instalment buying | Considered dangerous |
| Payment | Pay off each month | Pay interest | Pay interest |
| **Household Durables** | | | |
| Who decides? | Both spouses | Both spouses | |
| Who buys? | Both spouses | Wife, sometimes with husband | Wife |
| Criteria | Timesaving, style, price not a factor, very little shopping around, quality stores | Price major factor, comparison shopping, mid-quality stores | Price major factor, comparison shopping, mid-bargain stores |
| **Life-Style** | | | |
| | Integration of career and family life by both spouses. Affluence allows for conveniences that make both family and individual leisure-time pursuits possible. | Both spouses focus on the family, although the wife usually tends to household and child concerns. Both spouses work to provide needs of family. | The wife's domain is the home; the husband's domain is work. Range of individual and family activities is influenced by sex roles and the earning power of the husband's job. |

Source: Adapted from James W. Hanson and Rosemary Polegato, ''Identifying Dual Career, Dual Income and Traditional Family Segments,'' in *Marketing,* vol. 4, ed. James D. Forbes (Montreal: Administrative Sciences Association of Canada, 1983), pp. 137–39.

# Reference Groups and Opinion Leaders

A **reference group** is any group for which a consumer is a "psychological participant"—that is, with which he or she will identify and accept its norms or judgment. Examples of reference groups are family, relatives, friends, colleagues, professional or religious associations, celebrities, and salespersons.

Retailers can use their knowledge of reference group influences in various ways. For example, they may use recognized members of a group (such as a local celebrity) in their advertisement or in their direct selling, or they may indicate to the customer that members of a certain reference group routinely patronize their store. They may also post letters from or photographs of such persons.

When retailers can identify persons whose product-specific competence is recognized by others (called **opinion leaders**), they can attempt to influence them in a number of ways. These individuals may be consulted when new products are introduced, and they may receive free samples or trial use of a product. The objective is to win over the opinion leader, who through positive word of mouth will generate traffic and sales.

Finally, a good salesperson may act as a reference person for several customers if they have come to trust and depend on such a salesperson. Some customers may be unsure about their purchasing choices, either because they do not have the expertise or do not trust their own judgment. When they find a salesperson who is credible and sincere and has made the right choice for them in the past, they will continue to depend on that person.

# Influence of Social Classes

**Social classes** are divisions of society that are relatively homogeneous and permanent and in which individuals or families often share similar values, life-styles, interests, and types of behaviour. This applies also to shopping behaviour, and as such, is of great importance to retailers, since a large number of studies have found that social class affects the consumption of products, services, the selection of a retail outlet, and the use of credit cards.[14]

In practice, social-class membership is measured using major components such as how prestigious the occupation of the family head is, the area of residence of the family and the type of dwelling (e.g., detached house, or apartment), the source of family income (e.g., salary, investment, or welfare), and/or the level of education.

## *Social Classes in Canada*

A recent study breaks down the Canadian population into four major social classes:[15]

### Upper Classes (11 percent)
The upper classes include self-employed and employed professionals and high-level management. They tend to shop at the better retail outlets, buy high-quality goods and clothing, jewellery, luxury cars, appliances, and furniture. They represent the best market for luxury goods and status symbol products.

### Middle Class (28 percent)

The middle class includes semiprofessionals, technicians, middle managers, supervisors, foremen, and skilled clerical-sales-service. With the working class, they represent the mass market for most goods and services. They tend to shop at department stores and buy good-quality goods, clothing, and furniture. They tend to be price-sensitive while selecting quality items.

### Working Class (41 percent)

The working class includes skilled trade workers, farmers, and semiskilled manual workers and clerical-sales-service. They tend to shop at discount stores and promotional department stores, and they spend less than the middle class on clothing, travel, and services, more on sporting goods and equipment. They tend to prefer national brands.

### Lower Classes (20 percent)

The lower classes include unskilled clerical-sales-service, manual workers, and farm labourers. They tend to spend most of their income on the basic necessities of life, little on luxury products. They purchase second-hand cars and used furniture and less expensive goods and clothes.

Many implications for retailers are based on social-class structure, including merchandise mix, store image, design and layout, pricing, and advertising.

# Influence of Culture and Subculture

Since Canada is a multicultural society, retail customers come from a variety of cultures.

## Culture

As individuals grow up within a cultural group, they learn a set of values, attitudes, traditions, symbols, and characteristic behaviours. In a sense, **culture** affects and shapes many aspects of consumption behaviour, including shopping behaviour. This section deals with the cultural and ethnic groups comprising the Canadian "salad bowl" and their importance to retailers.

In looking at Canadian cultural groups, retailers should recognize that the differences among them stem from a variety of sources, including:

- The system of inherited values, attitudes, symbols, ideas, traditions, and artifacts that are shared by the members of the group. These differences will affect the merchandising mix, the pricing policy, and the promotional strategies of the retailer, depending on the group(s) targeted.
- The dominant religion of the group, which may be confounded by culture, and which may affect some values and attitudes—for example, toward Sunday shopping.

- The dominant language spoken by the group, which may also be confounded by culture, and which may require different promotional or selling strategies—for example, advertising in French or Italian, or using salespeople with certain language skills.

*Cultural Groups
in Canada*

A brief overview of the most significant cultural groups in Canada, and their characteristics of interest to retailers follows.

### English-Canadians

English-Canadians represent the largest group in Canada, with about 12 million people. They are present in all major markets in Canada, although they are not a homogeneous group, with regional differences and differences among those of Scottish descent, Irish descent, and recent immigrants from England.[16] However, as a group, they exhibit consumption and shopping behaviour that is different from that of other groups. Compared to French-Canadians, they consume more frozen

*Retailers in Montreal cater to the second largest cultural group in Canada.*

SOURCE: Photo by Betty McDougall.

vegetables, less beer and wine, more hard liquor, shop at more stores, and purchase furniture more at department or furniture stores than discount stores.[17]

### French-Canadians

French-Canadians represent the second largest market in Canada, with about 7.5 million people, and they account for over $54 billion in retail sales. French-Canadians reside mostly in Quebec, Ontario, and New Brunswick. In many respects, their consumption and shopping behaviour may be vastly different from that of English-Canadians, not only in terms of degree, as illustrated in the previous paragraph, but also in terms of approach. For example, in advertising, they respond better to an emotional approach and react more to the *source* (the spokesperson) of the advertisement, while English-Canadians react more to the (rational) *content* of the message.[18] Retail Highlight 5–2 provides additional characteristics of this major group.

---

**Retail Highlight 5–2**

# How Are French-Canadians Different from English-Canadians?

The 1991 Print Measurement Bureau survey provides fresh evidence of the consumption differences between French- and English-Canadians. Compared to English-Canadians, French-Canadians:

- Are willing to pay premium prices for convenience and premium brands.
- Buy few ''no name'' products but make greater use of cents-off coupons.
- Patronize food warehouses less, and convenience stores and health food outlets more.
- Are less likely to consume tea, diet colas, jam, tuna, cookies, and eggs, but are more likely to consume presweetened cereals, regular colas, instant coffee, and butter.
- Give more importance to personal grooming and fashion, and more frequently visit specialized clothing boutiques.

- Are less likely to use medicated throat lozenges, cold remedies, and nasal sprays.
- Have a higher propensity to drink wine, beer, and smoke cigarettes, but a lower one for hard liquor.
- Are less likely to play golf, jog, garden, go to the movies, and entertain at home.
- Buy more lottery tickets, subscribe to book clubs, and make fewer long-distance phone calls.
- Have more life insurance but fewer credit cards.
- Are less likely to be involved in politics, and more likely to favour the free enterprise system.

Source: François Vary, ''Quebec Consumer Has Unique Buying Habits,'' *Marketing*, March 23, 1992, p. 28.

### German-Canadians

German-Canadians number about 1 million and are mostly concentrated west of Ontario, comprising 14 percent of the population of Kitchener, 13 percent of Regina, and 12 percent of Saskatoon. They maintain their ethnicity through celebrations and rituals, but only 10 percent speak German at home. The four major values of this group are a strong sense of family, the work ethic, a drive for education, and a sense of justice.

### Italian-Canadians

The vast majority of the 700,000 Italian-Canadians are concentrated in the metropolitan areas of Quebec and Ontario. They represent 9 percent of the population of Toronto, 8 percent in St. Catharines-Niagara, 7 percent of Thunder Bay and Windsor, and 5 percent of Montreal.

Italian-Canadians have maintained a strong culture by developing a community with its own stores, cinemas, newspapers, radio stations, and TV programs. About 37 percent speak Italian at home. Their primary relations are with people of their own background, and as their level of affluence increases, they become more status-conscious, want to own their homes, buy new cars, and send their children to university.

A study in Montreal shows very distinct consumption and shopping patterns. For example, 72 percent shop in a large supermarket once or twice a week, and 39 percent shop in a department store.[19]

### Chinese-Canadians

Chinese-Canadians number about 600,000, and more immigrants are expected from Hong Kong as 1997 approaches and Hong Kong reverts back to China. As mentioned earlier, Asian-Canadians have unique behavioural patterns and needs and present interesting opportunities for many retailers. For example, 70 percent of the Chinese in Toronto are exposed to Chinese TV, 78 percent to Chinese newspapers; therefore, retailers advertising in Chinese may get more business from this group. Only 10 percent of the Chinese in Toronto consider themselves truly bilingual.[20]

### Other Significant Groups

Other significant groups are South Asians (500,000), Ukrainians (400,000), Native people (370,000), Dutch (350,000), Jews (245,000), Poles (220,000), Portuguese (200,000), Scandinavians (170,000), and Greeks (140,000).

These groups are being studied to learn more about their consumption and shopping behaviour. What is learned could help retailers to attract more customers belonging to targeted ethnic groups.

### Conclusion on Ethnic Groups in Canada

What can be gathered from this brief discussion is that Canadian retailers must thoroughly understand the ethnic origins of their customers and adjust their strategies accordingly, particularly in the areas of merchandise mix, advertising and sales promotion, store location and design, in-store selling, and pricing.

# Life-Style Merchandising

The concept of consumer life-style has a direct influence on retail merchandising strategies.

## *Life-Style and Psychographics*

**Life-style** is a customer's pattern of living as reflected in the way merchandise is purchased and used. **Psychographics** are the ways of defining and measuring the life-styles of consumers.

Life-style concepts influence almost every dimension of merchandise presentation in retailing. Why has life-style merchandising become so important? We live in an age in which large differences exist in the behaviour of people with similar demographic profiles. This diversity makes it hard to offer merchandise to consumers based only on an analysis of their age, income, and education. Instead, retailers need to know how people (1) spend their time, (2) spend their money, and (3) what they value, so that they can serve the customers better. Market segmentation based on life-style characteristics gives retailers a more realistic picture of the customers they want to serve.

Life-style retailing has grown in importance since the early 1970s. Previously, retailing had been characterized by a sameness in operations. Large retailers such as Sears, Eaton's, and The Bay had few significant differences in strategy. Managers could be shifted from one store to another across the country and would find few differences between the stores.[21]

## *The Marketing Concept*

The marketing concept was developed in the early 1960s by packaged goods firms such as Procter & Gamble as a response to the lack of attention to the needs of consumers in merchandising decisions. The marketing concept involves focusing on consumers' needs and integrating all activities of the store to satisfy the needs identified.

Retailers in the 1960s, even though insisting that "The Customer Is Always Right," often implemented the marketing concept only in the context of day-to-day operations, not in the context of the broader strategic dimensions of the store. Refund policies, hours of operation, and customer service were developed with a consumer focus. Product lines, store location, style of merchandise, and other strategic issues still retained the sameness of earlier years.

## *The Positioning Concept*

The concept of **market positioning** emerged during the early 1970s as the forerunner of contemporary life-style merchandising and as part of an effort to implement the marketing concept. Management began to tailor merchandising strategies to specific consumer segments. The segments to be served were defined, however, largely in terms of demographics such as age, income, and education.

Outlets such as Colour Your World experienced success by market positioning based on demographics, and by offering narrow but deep lines of merchandise to carefully defined consumer segments.

## *Life-Style Merchandising*

Retailers quickly realized that defining consumers in terms of demographics alone was not sufficient for fast growth. The concept of life-style merchandising thus evolved. The new focus was on understanding and responding to the living patterns of customers rather than making merchandising decisions primarily on the basis of consumer demographics; in doing so, retailers integrated all the social dimensions discussed in the first part of the chapter.

## Usefulness of Life-Style Merchandising

Life-style analysis offers retailers (1) an opportunity to develop marketing strategies based on a lifelike portrait of the consumers they are seeking to serve, (2) the ability to partially protect the outlet from direct price competition by developing unique merchandise offerings that attract shoppers for reasons other than price, and (3) the opportunity to better understand the shopping behaviour and merchandise preferences of customers.

Management is simply better able to describe and understand the behaviour of consumers when thinking in terms of life-style. Routinely thinking in terms of the activities, interests, needs, and values of customers can help retailers plan merchandise offerings, price lines, store layout, and promotion programs that are tightly targeted. However, life-style analysis only adds to the demographic, geographic, and socioeconomic information retailers need in serving markets effectively. Life-style analysis is not a substitute for this information. Rather, all the information sources taken together give retailers a richer view of their customers and help them recognize and serve consumer needs.

### What Shapes Life-Styles?

*We are all a product of the society in which we live*. We learn very early such concepts as honesty and the value of money. And these stay with us throughout our lives. These cultural influences, plus individual economic circumstances, produce consumer life-styles—traits, activities, interests, and opinions reflected in shopping behaviour. Individuals can be grouped into distinct market segments based on the similarities of their life-styles.

#### Where Do Life-Styles Come From?
*The life-styles of consumers are rooted in their values*. Values are beliefs or expectations about behaviour shared by a number of individuals and learned from society. Some of these values do not change much over time, while others can change quite rapidly. The major forces shaping consumer values include family, culture, religious institutions, schools, and early lifetime experiences.

### What Do We Know about Changing Cultural and Life-Style Patterns?

There are a number of cultural and life-style trends that have important implications for retailers.

#### The Divorce Rate Remains High
In 1991, there were 1 million single-parent families in Canada, or 14 percent of all families (82 percent were female sole parents). Although the divorce rate has dropped recently, it remains at around 80,000 a year.[22] As a result, the value patterns of today's children are shifting. More children are being raised without

fathers in the home. So, many children now are more likely to learn some of their values from individuals other than family members.

### Parents Are Spending Less Time with Very Young Children
Today, more than 30 percent of preschool children are in day-care centres, a segment of retailing that will continue to grow rapidly.

### People Move More Often than in the Past
As people move away from their families, less influence comes from grandparents and aunts and uncles as part of the extended family. Many of today's young people lack roots and a sense of traditional family values.

### Religion Is Not Important in Many People's Lives
As a consequence, the moral standards of previous years are changing. People are more prone to pursue pleasure and less likely to practice self-denial, although this might be changing as a consequence of the 1991–92 recession.

### Schools Are Becoming More Important in Shaping Values
More young people are staying in high school, and approximately half now go to college. Young people are being exposed to a larger number of different values than in the past and are more willing to experiment and try alternative life-styles.

### Individuals in Different Generations Have Different Experiences
More than 80 percent of consumers today were not alive during the depression of the 1930s. Many have little awareness of World War II. Today's middle-aged people (the baby boom generation) grew up in an era of low-cost credit, plentiful jobs, job security, and loyalty to one's country and parents. Yet, these same people also lived through high inflation and an energy crisis.

On the other hand, teenagers (i.e., their children) have experienced low inflation, a severe recession, and poor employment prospects.

### Family Size Is Small and There Are More Single-Person Households
The small family size of the 1980s (about 3.1 persons) is continuing into the 1990s, and the life-style patterns of these families continue to create new merchandising opportunities. Many of these households have high discretionary income and spend more on restaurants, educational products, and travel services than larger families. Their homes are typically smaller than in the past, and the furnishings also are smaller.

### Single-Person Households Reflect Life-Styles that Are Not Directly Impacted by Family Norms and the Preferences of Other Family Members
In single-person households, activities are on a per person as opposed to a household basis. Products and services for such households are being personalized rather than standardized. Such retail services as health care, personal finance, and insurance are now offered on a per person rather than a per household basis.

### Increasing Emphasis on the Family Is Accompanied by an Increase in Adult-Oriented Life-Styles

More and more adult-oriented programming is available to households through cable television and the networks. The popularity of adult soap operas reflects this trend in society. In addition, the penetration of the VCR and of video stores is making it easier to watch movies at home.

### Yuppies (Young, Urban Professionals) Are Getting Older

In the 1990s, the number of persons aged 35 to 44 will increase rapidly, while persons aged 25 to 34 will actually shrink in numbers by about 20 percent.[23] Such older households typically have two incomes, are well educated, and have the money to spend to support their life-style preferences.

These so-called yuppies are placing more emphasis on their households than they did when they were in their 20s. They are purchasing more expensive home furnishings, quality art, and are major consumers of services. Banks, stockbrokerage houses, and other financial institutions are rejoicing at the opportunity to serve these markets. These consumers are conspicuous in their consumption and are willing to spend heavily to support their life-styles.

*Video stores are catering to changing lifestyle patterns.*

SOURCE: Photo by Sandy McDougall.

## Families Earning More than $50,000 a Year Are Growing at a Rapid Rate (Although They Only Comprise 20 Percent of the Population)

An important number of affluent families include retirees who have earned good pensions during the last 50 years (called the *countdown generation*).[24] Affluent buyers seek products and services that reflect their self-image and are interested in aesthetics as much as performance. From retailers, they seek the highest-quality merchandise that reflects prestige and fashion. They expect high-quality service and expert consultation.

Affluent, dual-income households provide strong markets for luxury products such as satellite dishes, boats, and premium cars.[25] Retailers such as Holt Renfrew are positioned to serve these markets.

## Males and Females in the Household Have Less Clearly Defined Rules

More and more women are buyers of financial services and other male-oriented products. Men are increasingly becoming purchasers of household products, and young adults of both sexes are learning how to manage households and to cope with problems of school and education. Many retail promotions are universal in content and not targeted specifically to either males or females.

## Technology Has Affected Consumer Life-Styles

The development of videocassette players led to the emergence of video outlets that specialize in the rental of movies and VCR equipment. Busy consumers are responding to the opportunity to view films at their convenience in the privacy of their homes, rather than go to movie houses. Microwave ovens have led to changes in the types of foods eaten, and in-home interactive shopping offered through cable services is beginning to redefine how and when consumers shop.

## Not All Consumers Are Affluent

Less affluent consumers, as part of their life-styles, are very responsive to coupons and other promotions. They use generic products, buy at flea markets and garage sales, are willing to accept less service in return for lower prices, and are active in seeking goods that last longer and require less maintenance. Such consumers are responsible for the growth of warehouse outlets for various types of merchandise.

## A Major Shift in Attitudes and Values Has Occurred

In the last few years, there have been some subtle and important shifts in attitudes and values among consumers that will profoundly affect the economy of the 1990s:[26]

- The return to conservative ideals in terms of life, work, love, and family.
- The rejection of the 1980s legacy, particularly conspicuous consumption.
- The demand for real intrinsic value, including product quality and durability.

- The growth of altruism.
- The search for balance and moderation, in particular the search for simplicity and convenience.

These shifts are summarized in Table 5–4.

### More Money to Spend but Less Time to Spend It

The most affluent households typically have two wage earners, which means that they have little time for shopping. As a result, they are willing to pay for timesaving goods, including lawn-care and cleaning services. They also have been responsible for the rapid growth in specialty shops, supermarkets, and downtown department stores. Such consumers also seek high-quality recreation because of the limited amount of time available to them. They are prone to go to fashionable ski resorts, theme restaurants, and expensive golf and tennis resorts, and take "sun and surf" winter vacations (Canadian snowbirds).

*Life-Style Segmentation*

The information used in forming life-style market segments is developed from consumer research. Marketing researchers question consumers about the merchandise they purchase, their media habits, as well as their activities, interests, and opinions.[27] One research study yielded five fashion segments that can provide a key to understanding how **life-style segmentation** can be used in a retail setting.[28] The

TABLE 5–4 **Key Differences between the Values of the 1980s and Those of the 1990s**

| 1980s | 1990s |
| --- | --- |
| New | Old |
| Future | Past |
| Prestige | Comfort |
| Trend | Tradition |
| State of the art | Enduring |
| Fast track | Sure-footed |
| Wealth | Contentment |
| Make-believe | Real |
| Image | Character |
| Leading edge | Heritage |
| Avant-garde | Classic |
| Fitness | Wellness |
| Nutrition | Health |
| Good for you | Feels good |
| High tech | High touch |
| Me | You |

SOURCE: "Torlée Targets Marketing in the 1990s," *Marketing,* December 9, 1991, p. 6.

## An Illustration of Psychographic Segmentation: The Female Clothing Market

*Opinion leaders*. These women shopped most frequently, but placed the least weight on brand, salesperson's evaluation, and store loyalty. They frequently used mail brochures and overseas fashion magazines. This group was willing to pay the most for given items of clothing, and spent the largest percentage of income on clothing purchases. They were younger, more likely to be single, better educated, and more mobile.

*Discontents*. These women bought the least amount of ready-made clothing, being most inclined to do their own sewing. They saw price as very important, had the lowest reasonable price perceptions for an average garment, and were not store loyal. This group was in the lowest family income bracket, and spent the least on clothes.

*Conservatives*. This group spent the lowest percentage of income on clothing. They shopped the least frequently, but were prepared to pay well when they did shop. Fabric and instructions for care were seen as particularly important when buying clothes, and they particularly emphasized the importance of quality and garment care.

*Followers*. These women did not pay much attention to fashion trends, and checked to see what is fashionable only when buying new clothes. They saw brand as important, and were most likely to be store loyal. They were in the average family income bracket, and had the lowest level of education.

*Socializers*. This group saw the type of fabric, price, and the store where purchased as unimportant when buying clothes, but instructions for care as particularly important. They bought virtually all of their clothes ready-made, spent more on clothing than all others, and were in the highest income group. They were older, most inclined to shop at prestige fashion stores, and enjoyed reading local fashion magazines.

Source: Peter Thirkell, "Opinion Leadership and Attitudes toward Fashion of Female Consumers: A Segmentation Study," in *Developments in Canadian Marketing: Proceedings of the Administrative Sciences Association of Canada,* ed. Robert Tamilia (1979), p. 67.

five segments are profiled in Retail Highlight 5–3 as an illustration of the use of life-style analysis in merchandise planning.

### The Effect of Life-Style Merchandising on Marketing Strategies

*Idea-Oriented Presentations.*   Merchandise is often brought together from all areas of the store for its life-style appeal. Life-style merchandising breaks down departmental barriers. This approach allows salespeople to sell primarily to customers with similar life-styles. Management seeks to group merchandise the way customers want to buy it, not the way the store thinks it is easiest to sell. Simply putting dresses into departments labelled better, moderate, and budget can help. Consumers match their life-styles with the departments. Many complementary items are placed together to encourage multiple purchases. For example, all items of sporting equipment may be grouped in one department, women's accessories may be grouped in another, or furniture and accessories may be grouped in a single-room setting. Such efforts break down departmental rigidities, encourage multiple sales, and increase space productivity.

A similar concept is idea-oriented presentations, as shown in Figure 5–3. Increasingly, merchants are using this concept to convey an idea by clustering complementary items to motivate multiple purchases without the extensive involvement of salesclerks. A typical example is the bath shop, where the entire merchandise presentation is idea-oriented. Customers find all items related to the bath brought together from different merchandise categories throughout the store.

***Life-Style Merchandise Classifications.***    One of the trends in merchandising for males is selling to "the better young man," defined as a fashion-aware young man in a college or university, who doesn't have the budget yet for more expensive clothes.

**FIGURE 5–3**

*Leisure-time, active sportswear fits into the physical fitness life-style of the 90s*

SOURCE: Photo by James Hertel.

Some stores have opened separate shops with an updated, traditional flair, giving fashion direction with designer jeans by such names as Sasson.

*Super Specialty Retailing.*    The super specialists include such firms as Toys Я Us. Their exceptional profitability and rapid growth have made them formidable competitors for department/general merchandise stores and small, independent retail operations.

The stores offer a limited assortment of contemporary merchandise aimed at specific segments, typically adults aged 18–35 with an interest in fashion.

Management is centralized, and the organizations are able to respond to market trends almost instantly. Personal service, breadth and depth in merchandise, and the ability to keep pace with fashion trends give these outlets a strong image relative to department stores and independent outlets.

### Serving Customers with Unique Life-Styles

*Information.*    Large retailers in such metropolitan markets as Montreal, Toronto, and Vancouver offer multilingual services to attract and serve foreign tourists. Many of these stores maintain lists of employees with foreign language abilities. Store directions and information pamphlets are sometimes printed in foreign languages. The service is offered free to make shopping easy for tourists.

*Shopping Services.*    Shopping services are becoming increasingly popular with working women (and men). Customers make an initial visit to an outlet and provide retailers with essential measurements and other information needed to help make merchandise selection decisions for the customers. The customers can then call ahead and have several outfits assembled for their approval when they arrive at the store. Such services require creative talent by salespeople but can lead to significant ''plus'' sales for the outlet, as in the example of Brettons in Mississauga.[29]

*Store Hours.*    Longer shopping hours are especially common in suburban areas, where stores may be open late each night of the week and even on Sunday (where it is allowed by law). Increasing numbers of two-income households are likely to demand that retail outlets remain open in the evening and on Sundays to serve the needs of individuals who are unable to shop during ''normal'' store hours.

*Effects on Retail Salespeople.*    Retail salespeople have to identify with both the items being sold and the life-style of the customer buying the items. Even store branches need to be tailored to the life-styles of the customers living in that particular area. For example, the salesperson selling tennis equipment should ideally be an avid tennis player.

*Better Promotion Efforts.*    Life-style merchandising is changing the media mix used by retailers. Life-style programming by various stations that offer sports, middle-of-the road music, or all-news programs represent attempts to reach specific target audiences. Tightly defined media audiences are being sought by retailers today.

*Visual Merchandising.*　Attractively displayed merchandise in harmony with a consumer's life-style increases that consumer's desire to buy. Life-style merchandising based upon this psychology is a highly refined art. Promotional displays are likely to be strong, dramatic, striking, and support the theme of the other promotion efforts.

Creating the artistic environment so essential to life-style merchandising requires a unique blending of lighting, background, and props. All visual merchandising themes should start with what the customer wants and should communicate important merchandise information. These points are discussed in detail in Chapter 12.

# Chapter Highlights

- Retailers must understand how decisions are made within a family, the respective roles of men, women, and children, and the changing needs during different stages of its life cycle.

- Retailers may often use reference groups and opinion leaders such as local celebrities to improve the image of their store and the credibility of their salespersons.

- Social-class distinctions have often been used instinctively by retailers in defining their targets and marketing strategies.

- Most Canadian retailers should be sensitive to the Canadian "salad bowl" and understand the subtleties of attitudes and behaviour of the various subgroups.

- Retailers can more readily meet the needs of customers if they understand how people spend their time and money and what they value. The essence of this type of information is life-style analysis.

- Life-styles are based on the values of people. The forces affecting consumer values are the influence of the family, religious institutions, schools, and early lifetime experiences.

- Retail management philosophies, in meeting the needs of consumers, have evolved gradually over time. Until the 1950s, retailers were supply-oriented. By the 1960s, the marketing concept was introduced as a philosophy of management that required a total consumer orientation in all activities of the firm.

- Positioning as a strategy emerged in the early 1970s. Management began to target its offerings to narrow groups of consumers defined in terms of demographics. By the mid-1970s, life-style merchandising emerged with an emphasis on the activities, interests, and opinions of consumers.

- The latest evolution in marketing strategy is the development of a life-style portfolio of stores owned by a single organization but with each store targeted toward the needs of a different group of consumers.

- Understanding life-style merchandising is the key ingredient in marketing strategy.

# Key Terms

# Discussion Questions

1. What are the major changes occurring within the modern Canadian family, and what impact will these changes have on retailers?

2. Why is it preferable for the backgrounds of salespeople to match the life-styles of the customers they will be serving? How does this relate to the notion of reference group?

3. In what ways does social class affect the kind of strategic decisions retailers must make? Give some specific examples.

4. Select three cultural groups in your community, and describe in detail how local retailers should adjust their strategies to better serve these groups.

5. Summarize changes occurring today in society that are shaping Canadian values, and discuss the resulting effects on consumer behaviour.

6. What is meant by the term *super specialty retailing?* What are some of the operating characteristics of super specialists?

7. What are the things that some retailers are doing now to better serve customers with unique life-styles?

8. Trace the differences in management philosophy between homogeneous retailing, retailing based on the marketing concept, and life-style retailing.

# Application Exercises

1. Examine the range of retail outlets in your community for a specific group of items (e.g., fashion clothes, jewellery, gifts). Either by personal visits or by studying their advertising, group the stores who tend to appeal to a similar clientele. Then define this clientele in terms of age groups, gender, and/or social class. In each case, explain your reasoning.

2. Visit a mall or the central business district and identify as many stores as you can that represent life-style merchandising in action. Discuss whether you feel that the management of the stores you identify needs to be more alert to changes in life-styles.

3. Visit several department and specialty outlets in your area. Describe examples of life-style merchandising you discover in your visits. Relate the strategy to the positioning that you believe management is attempting.

# Suggested Cases

# Endnotes

1. Alanna Mitchell, "Common-Law Households on the Rise," *Globe and Mail,* June 8, 1992, pp. A1–2.

2. Jo Marney, "Woopies, Muppies . . . the List Grows," *Marketing,* February 2, 1987, pp. 10–12.

3. Ibid.

4. Harry L. Davis and Benny P. Rigaux, "Perception of Marital Roles in Decision Processes," *Journal of Consumer Research,* June 1974, pp. 51–62.

5. Hugh Filman, "Baby Books Benefit from Echo Boom," *Marketing,* March 30, 1992, p. 30; and "Canada's Birth Rate Rises for Third Year," *Kitchener-Waterloo Record,* March 31, 1992, pp. A1–2.

6. Pierre Filiatrault and J. R. Brent Ritchie, "Joint Purchasing Decisions: A Comparison of Influence Structure in Family and Couple Decision-Making Units," *Journal of Consumer Research,* September 1980, pp. 131–40.

7. Jo Marney, "Advertising to Children Isn't Kid Stuff," *Marketing,* October 31, 1985, p. 19.

8. Jo Marney, "Woopies."

9. Jo Marney, "New Perspectives on the Teen Market," *Marketing,* June 16, 1986, p. 9; and Lisa Grogen, "Young Money," *The Financial Post,* April 24, 1989, pp. 15, 20.

10. Jo Marney, "Reaching the New Woman of Today," *Marketing,* March 1, 1982, p. 9.

11. Chankon Kim, "Working Wives' Time-Saving Tendencies: Ownership, Convenience Food Consumption, and Meal Purchases," *Journal of Economic Psychology* 10 (1989), pp. 391–409; W. K. Bryant, "Durables and Wives' Employment Yet Again," *Journal of Consumer Research* 15 (June 1988), pp. 37–47; Myra H. Strober and Charles B. Weinberg, "Working Wives and Major Family Expenditures," *Journal of Consumer Research,* December 1977, pp. 141–47; and "Strategies Used by Working and Non-Working Wives to Reduce Time Pressures," *Journal of Consumer Research,* March 1980, pp. 338–48.

12. Jo Marney, "A New Masculine Force Is Emerging in the Marketplace," *Marketing,* April 29, 1985, p. 12.

13. J. Meyers-Levy and D. Maheswaran, "Exploring Differences in Males' and Females' Processing Strategies," *Journal of Consumer Research* 18 (June 1991), pp. 63–70; and R. Neil Maddox, "The Importance of Males in Supermarket Traffic and Sales," in *Marketing,* vol. 3, ed. Michel Laroche (ASAC, 1982), pp. 137–43.

14. Pierre Martineau, "Social Class and Spending Behaviour," *Journal of Marketing,* October 1958, pp. 121–30; L. H. Mathews and J. W. Slokum, Jr., "Social Class and Commercial Bank Credit Card Usage," *Journal of Marketing,* January 1969, p. 73; and Susan M. Clarke, F. G. Crane, and T. K. Clarke, "Social Class and Adolescent Buying Behaviours," in *Marketing,* vol. 7, ed. Thomas E. Muller (ASAC, 1986), pp. 309–16.

15. Gurprit S. Kindra, Michel Laroche, and Thomas E. Muller, *Consumer Behaviour in Canada* (Toronto: Nelson Canada, 1989), Chapter 9.

16. Carl Lawrence, Stanley J. Shapiro, and Shaheen Lalji, "Ethnic Markets—A Canadian Perspective," *Journal of the Academy of Marketing Science,* Summer 1986, pp. 7–16.

17. Charles M. Schaninger, Jacques Bourgeois, and W. Christian Buss, "French-English Canadian Subcultural Differences," *Journal of Marketing,* Spring 1985, pp. 82–92; Annamma Joy, Chankon Kim, and Michel Laroche, "Ethnicity as a Factor Influencing Use of Financial Services," *International Journal of Bank Marketing* 9 (1991), pp. 10–16.

18. Robert D. Tamilia, "A Cross-Cultural Study of Source Effects in a Canadian Advertising Situation," in *Marketing,* eds. Jacques M. Boisvert and Ron Savitt (ASAC, 1978), pp. 250–56.

19. "Montreal Ethnics Focus of New Study," *Marketing,* March 5, 1984, pp. 12–13.

20. Stan Sutter, "Advertisers Missing Out," *Marketing,* October 20, 1986, pp. 22–23.

21. Jagdish N. Sheth, "Marketing Megatrends," *Journal of Consumer Marketing* 1, no. 1 (Summer 1983), pp. 5–13.

22. Alanna Mitchell, "Affair with Divorce Shows Signs of Cooling," *Globe and Mail,* March 23, 1992, pp. A1–2.

23. Jim McElgunn, "Foot Puts Boot to Current 'Life-Cycle' Trends," *Marketing,* June 15, 1992, p. 7.

24. Marina Strauss, "Retirees Will Have Big Bucks to Spend," *Globe and Mail,* March 17, 1992, p. B7.

25. "Affluentials: The Class Mass Market," *Marketing Communications,* December 1983, pp. 17–21.

26. "Torlée Targets Marketing in the 1990s," *Marketing,* December 9, 1991, p. 6.

27. Russell Haley, "Benefit Segments: Backwards and Forwards," *Journal of Advertising Research,* February/March 1984, pp. 5–22.

28. Peter Thirkell, "Opinion Leadership and Attitudes towards Fashion of Female Consumers: A Segmentation Study," in *Developments in Canadian Marketing,* ed. Robert D. Tamilia (ASAC, 1979), pp. 66–67.

29. Rona Maynard, "Satisfaction Guaranteed," *Report on Business Magazine,* January 1988, p. 58.

# II DEVELOPING THE RETAIL STRATEGY

In Part II, the conceptual, financial, and organizational aspects of the retail strategy are systematically developed. Chapter 6 deals with strategic planning as a method of defining the objectives of the firm and deciding how to compete. To compete successfully, retailers need to understand how to finance and organize a business, which is the topic of Chapter 7. Franchising as a means of owning and operating a retail firm is examined in detail in Chapter 8. Chapter 9 discusses the critical issues in the recruitment, selection, training, and motivation of retail employees. Knowledge of markets is essential to strategy development, and the retail research methods used to obtain this knowledge are covered in Chapter 10.

# 6 STRATEGIC RETAIL MANAGEMENT

## Chapter Objectives

After reading this chapter, you should be able to:

1 List the steps involved in strategic retail planning.
2 Understand the concept of an organization's mission statement.
3 Evaluate the issues involved in a situation analysis.
4 Discuss the factors involved in deciding on markets in which to compete.
5 Review the components of retail positioning strategy.
6 Describe several strategic options available to retailers.
7 Discuss the issues involved in evaluating and controlling retail operations.

**Retailing Capsule**

The battle for leadership in the $750 million music retail industry has led to brutal competition since HMV entered the arena. In 1991, A&A Records and Tapes filed for bankruptcy (it has since been reborn under new ownership), and Discus Music World closed many unprofitable stores; since then, many independent music retailers have gone out of business. HMV, part of a massive British conglomerate, opened its first Canadian store in 1987, but the intense competition really began with the launching of its flagship Toronto store in 1991. By the end of 1991, HMV's 51 stores sold more than $100 million in CDs, cassettes, and videos, closing in fast on the market leader, Sam the Record Man, which sold about $135 million in its 140 stores.

The Canadian music retailing industry has experienced dramatic changes in the past few years—the shift from records to CDs and cassettes, changing demographics—yet many retailers sold their product with little innovative marketing or customer service.

HMV shook up the industry by pursuing an aggressive strategy that included the following elements:

- *Location:* Many stores were located in upscale shopping centres across Canada on very favourable terms (shopping centre developers were keen to have HMV during the hard economic times).
- *Atmosphere:* From the displays, to banks of video screens, to "listening posts" where customers can play the latest hits, to in-store concerts, HMV provided a new experience for shoppers.
- *Customer service:* A helpful, knowledgeable staff, many of whom were hired from the competition.
- *Selection:* A wide and targeted selection provided by store managers who can decide what titles to carry in their particular store.
- *Prices:* On average, higher prices than other chains like Sam's because HMV decided that customers would be willing to pay something extra for helpful staff and a broad selection.

The strategy led to increased sales of over 50 percent in the past year, profit increases of over 100 percent, and second place behind Sam's in the industry. HMV's objective is to be the number one retailer in the near future.

Sam the Record Man's future strategy involves expanding the size of its present outlets and maintaining its large selection of CDs, cassettes, and video movies. A&A, under new ownership, is attempting to stay in the game with deep price discounting. This low-price strategy may work in the short term, but industry experts feel that A&A needs greater margins to survive.

The success of any of the three strategies—HMV's service-oriented approach, the selection approach at Sam's, the price approach at A&A—will

*HMV's strategy has led to increased sales and profits.*

SOURCE: Courtesy HMV Canada.

depend on how well each of the competitors implements its plan and meets the needs of customers. In a highly competitive market, a well-designed and executed strategic plan is essential for survival.

Sources: Mathew Ingram, ''The Battle for the Music-Sales Market,'' *Financial Times,* November 4, 1991, pp. 1, 12; Mark Evans, ''Music Retail War Could Take Heavy Toll,'' *The Financial Post,* November 11, 1991, p. 9; and ''At A&A Records and Tapes, You're a Homebody,'' *Canadian Business,* May 1992, p. 15.

**Strategic planning** includes defining the overall mission or purpose of the company, deciding on objectives that management wants to achieve, and developing a plan to achieve these objectives. HMV evaluated the retail music industry in Canada and identified strategies that would allow the firm to prosper and grow. The strategies are being implemented through pricing, promotion, and physical facility plans in order to accomplish the overall mission of the firm.

Figure 6–1 illustrates the steps involved in strategic planning. The plan begins with a statement of the mission or purpose of the organization. Objectives that management wants to achieve are then established. A situation analysis of internal strengths and weaknesses and external threats and opportunities is then undertaken to help management decide on the best way to carry out the organization's mission and to achieve its objectives. Markets in which to compete must be selected and resources needed to compete must be obtained. A positioning strategy that outlines how the organization will compete in serving the needs of chosen markets is

**FIGURE 6–1**

*Strategic planning*

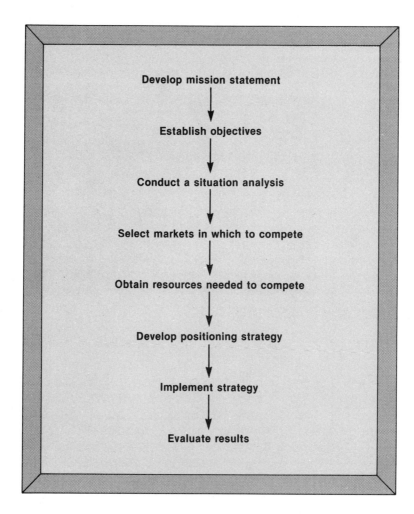

Develop mission statement

↓

Establish objectives

↓

Conduct a situation analysis

↓

Select markets in which to compete

↓

Obtain resources needed to compete

↓

Develop positioning strategy

↓

Implement strategy

↓

Evaluate results

developed. An important aspect of the positioning strategy is determining how the retailer will develop and exploit its competitive advantage. The strategy must then be implemented. Finally, results must be measured and evaluated to ensure that the strategy is working.

# Defining the Mission or Purpose of the Organization

Management begins the planning process by identifying the organization's mission or purpose. The **mission statement** describes what the firm plans to accomplish in the markets in which it will compete for customers it wants to serve. Figure 6–2 outlines the ingredients of a mission statement. Ideally, the mission statement indicates the types of products and/or services to be offered, the markets to be served, and how the firm plans to compete. The character of the organization and its key activities are readily evident. The mission statement provides a clear sense of direction for the organization and distinguishes the firm from all others.

Retail Highlight 6–1 provides examples of Canadian retailers' mission and goal statements as presented in their annual reports. Most of these retailers have prepared more detailed mission statements that are provided to employees within the firm.

Mission statements often reflect an organization's values or corporate culture. **Corporate culture** establishes the values of greatest importance to the organization. These are values on which emphasis is constantly placed. Often, these values reflect the personal goals of top management. A firm's values are often stated in the company motto, as shown in the following examples:

- *McDonald's:* "QSCV—Quality, Service, Convenience, and Value." This slogan is emphasized to all employees as they are brought into the organization.
- *Eaton's:* "Satisfaction Guaranteed or Your Money Refunded." This motto has been a policy of Eaton's since its beginning over 120 years ago.

FIGURE 6–2

*Ingredients of a mission statement*

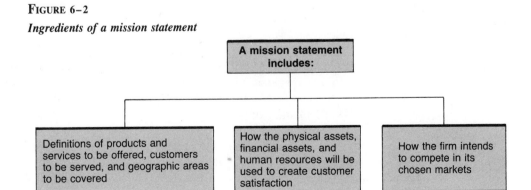

Retail Highlight 6–1

# Canadian Retailers' Mission and Goal Statements

Many retailers today are focusing on customer satisfaction as their primary goal. Listed below are mission statements from a number of Canadian retailers. Which retailers seem to have adopted a mission of customer satisfaction?

- *Mark's Work Wearhouse* provides quality name-brand, private, and captive label products competitively priced and supported by active sales promotion. The stores are easily accessible, one-stop retail outlets offering a complete range of workwear, casual wear, and related apparel.

  The company's mission is to be a mature and stable enterprise, with a nationwide reputation for:

  1. Being the most customer-sensitive, customer-responsive, customer-driven specialty retail organization in Canada.
  2. Having a people-oriented work environment where people are allowed the greatest possible freedom to carry out their responsibilities, to own what they do, to have fun, and to earn fair financial rewards.
  3. Achieving an annual 4 percent after-tax profit on sales by fiscal 1995, thus providing a worthwhile financial return to investors and lenders through the successes that flow from being customer-driven and people-oriented.

- *Loblaw Companies Ltd.* Providing our customers with the best possible service is a goal which unites employees at all levels. If we serve our customers well, they will reward us with their patronage and loyalty, the cornerstone upon which we can build and maintain a profitable company.
- *Computer Innovations'* mission is to be Canada's leading integrator of small computer-based products and services.

# Setting Objectives

Management's task, after agreeing on the mission statement, is to establish objectives. **Objectives** are statements of results to be achieved. Objectives may include profitability, sales volume, market share, or expansion results that the firm wants to accomplish.

Management normally sets both long-term and short-term objectives. One- or two-year time frames for achieving specific targets are considered short term. Long-term objectives are less specific than short-term targets and reflect the strategic dimensions of the firm. Retailing is too dynamic to establish specific targets much beyond five years.

Good objectives are measurable, are specific as to time, and indicate the priorities for the organization. To illustrate, Southam Inc. has set an objective of an annual return on sales of 8 percent for Coles Book Stores, one of its divisions.[1] Examples of well-stated and poorly stated objectives appear in Table 6–1.

---

*Retail Highlight continued*

- *Sears Canada Inc.'s* mission is to excel by satisfying our customers and to have them say that "Sears is a great place to shop." To meet that goal, Sears is increasingly a customer-driven company. Sears and its team of employees are committed to exceeding customer expectations for value, quality product, and superior service.

- *Canadian Tire* is an integrated supplier of automotive products and services and home and leisure products through a network of associate dealers across Canada. The corporation provides a variety of marketing, merchandising, administrative, and ancillary services to its associate dealers, as well as financial services to both associate dealers and their customers.

  The company's agenda for the future, a program of continuous improvement in every aspect of its operations, is enabling the corporation to meet and exceed customers' demands for value, service, and selection in a very competitive marketplace.

- *Pennington's* mission is to excel in understanding and responding to the needs of our most valued asset—our customer.

- *Le Château's* mission has always been to deliver the most wanted fashions to our stores at a moderate price so as to encourage customer purchasing even in poor economic conditions.

- *Dylex's* goal is to be the Canadian retail industry's most efficient and strategically managed player; to be dominant in each of the markets that we serve; and to be financially independent.

- *Hudson's Bay Company* aims to develop its human and material resources and capitalize on its experience in merchandising to anticipate and satisfy the needs of customers for goods and services they seek at fair prices, and thereby earn a satisfactory return for its shareholders.

Sources: Mark's Work Wearhouse, Loblaw Companies Ltd., Computer Innovations, Sears Canada Inc., Canadian Tire, Pennington's, Le Château, Dylex, and Hudson's Bay Company, Annual Reports, 1991 and 1992.

---

# Conducting a Situation Analysis

Once objectives are set, management must decide on a plan for achieving them within the context of the firm's mission. This plan is based on an analysis of strengths and weaknesses of the organization and threats and opportunities in the environment. This assessment of internal strengths and weaknesses and external threats and opportunities is referred to as a **situation analysis,** popularly known as a SWOT analysis (strengths, weaknesses, opportunities, and threats).

**Internal factors** are those variables largely under the control of store management. Such factors include financial resources, physical assets (for example, buildings, or display fixtures), management skills, sales force composition, merchandise lines carried, the reputation of the firm with customers, and employee attitudes towards the company. The questions the retailer wants to answer are shown in Table 6–2.

*Pennington's
understands and
responds to
customers' needs.*

SOURCE: Courtesy Pennington's.

**External factors** are those over which store management has very little or no control. The external environments on which management focuses—legal, economic, social, competitive, and technological—were discussed in Chapter 3. Management examines trends in these environments and determines whether the trends pose threats or opportunities, or have no relevance for the organization.

The result of the situation analysis suggests markets in which to compete. Management may "stay the course" and make only minor adjustments in strategy. In other instances, major changes may be made in markets served and in strategies for serving new markets. In the recession period in the early 1990s, many Canadian retailers made major changes to their strategies to reflect the harsh economic times. For example, the Oshawa Group, which operates Food City and supplies IGA stores, has reduced operating expenses by restructuring its stores, warehouses, and

---

**TABLE 6–1    Examples of Well-Stated and Poorly Stated Objectives**

| *Examples of Well-Stated Objectives* | *Examples of Poorly Stated Objectives* |
|---|---|
| Our objective is to increase market share from 15 percent to 18 percent in 1994 by increasing promotional expenditures 15 percent. | Our objective in 1994 is to increase promotional expenditures. |
| Our objective for 1994 is to earn after-tax profits of $5 million. | Our objective is to maximize profits. |
| Our objective is to open three new units by 1994 in each of the following provinces where the chain presently has no units: Nova Scotia, New Brunswick, and Prince Edward Island. | Our objective is to expand by adding units to the chain. |

---

**TABLE 6–2    SWOT Appraisal**

**Internal Appraisal**
Strengths

- What is the firm's present position?
- What is the firm good at?
- What major resources/expertise exist?

Weaknesses

- What is the firm's present position?
- What are the major problems faced?
- What is the firm poor at doing?
- What major resources/expertise deficiencies exist?

**External Appraisal**
Opportunities

- In what areas could success be achieved?
- What favourable environmental trends exist?
- How are markets developing?

Threats

- Where is performance likely to suffer?
- What unfortunate environmental trends exist?
- How are competitors behaving and developing?

SOURCE: Nigel Piercy, "Analyzing Corporate Mission: Improving Retail Strategy," *Retail and Distribution Management,* March/April 1983, p. 35.

---

offices. As well, it is expanding its Price Choppers stores—standard-sized supermarkets that offer limited selections of groceries, fresh meat, and produce at lower prices. The Oshawa Group hopes to win back consumers who have cut back spending, shop more often in the United States, and seek bargains in discount warehouse–style stores.[2]

# Deciding on Markets in Which to Compete

**Market segments** are the groupings of consumers based on homogeneous responses to merchandise offerings. Segment descriptors reflect the ways in which market segments can be described.

Typical descriptors based on demographics (age, income, occupation, etc.) are the most frequently used ways of segmenting markets. Psychographics (the activities, interests, and opinions of consumers) are often used to supplement demographic data.

**Target markets** are the segments that management decides to serve. Market positioning is how management plans to compete in target markets that appeal to the firm. Let us briefly use the Harvey's restaurant chain to show the relationships between segmentation, targeting, and positioning in strategy development before we discuss each concept in more detail.

Based on age and income segmentation variables, Harvey's target market is adults 18+—specifically, adults 18 to 24 who are on the go and have a comfortable disposable income level. Harvey's mission statement, which establishes its positioning, is "to be the first choice for every quick service dining occasion through prompt, friendly, and customized service; the best-tasting food; generous portions; and clean and attractive restaurants. In all of this we must exceed customer expectations of value." The blend of some of the retailing mix variables in support of this positioning strategy is as follows:

1. *Product variable:* Charbroiled and topped with the customer's choice of fresh garnishes. Alternative menu selections include a Light Choice menu and a Children's Programme.
2. *Price variable:* Competitive (parity to market leaders).
3. *Presentation variable:* Warm, friendly atmosphere with a selection of seating packages to accommodate a variety of customer groups.
4. *Promotion variable:* Continuity through Pennyfries campaign to deliver best taste, best value positioning. Customers may select specialty sandwiches and receive fries for a penny.
5. *Personal selling variable:* Staff trained to serve customers efficiently in a friendly and courteous manner.
6. *Customer service variable:* Exceed customer expectations or money refunded.

You can probably better understand segmentation, targeting, and positioning if you think about how the McDonald's, Wendy's, Burger King, and A&W chains compete against Harvey's by choosing different market targets and positioning strategies.

## *Segmenting Markets*

### Requirements of Segmentation
The market segments selected by management must be:

1. Measurable—Is the segment measurable and identifiable?
2. Accessible—Will focusing marketing efforts on a particular market segment have a positive impact on eliciting desired responses?

3. Economically viable—Is the segmentation variable shared by enough potential customers to justify the expense and effort of focusing marketing efforts on that segment?

4. Stable—Are the consumer characteristics stable indicators of market potential?

In strategy development, consumers can be viewed in one of three ways, depending on the product or service offered:

1. Similarity—All consumers are viewed as basically similar. Although difference such as age, income, needs, and preference exist among them, these differences are not thought to be important influences on the purchase of the firm's specific product class. A standard product will essentially satisfy most consumers.

2. Differences/similarities—Consumer differences and similarities are important sources of influence on market demand. These differences and similarities facilitate the grouping of consumers in aggregates and appealing to these aggregates on common bases.

3. Uniqueness—All consumers are somewhat different. The differences among them make a standardized offering unacceptable. Market offerings must be tailored specifically to the needs of a very narrowly defined group of consumers.

## Target Market Selection

No single best way exists for selecting market segments in which to compete. The market grid (Table 6–3) is commonly used as a first step in deciding on such targets. The grid is developed based on the want-satisfying needs of the segment that management can satisfy. Often, management begins by looking at the market in terms of both the size and consumer segments to which it might appeal. Table 6–3 shows how a new retailer might first view the segments it wants to serve.

Next, management zeros in on the possible identified targets and applies a final set of screening criteria to help select targets. A number of variables are normally evaluated for each target to determine the ones most compatible with the organization's resources and skills. Typical criteria are shown in Table 6–4. They include the growth potential of each likely target market, the investment needed to compete, and the strength of the competition. The possible market targets are evaluated by deciding (1) on each screening factor's importance to management and (2) how each possible target ranks on each factor. Multiplying importance by attractiveness yields a score for each factor. The sum of factor scores for each possible target allows management to objectively evaluate each target on the basis of previously identified criteria. This lets management select targets for further development of marketing strategies. Dylex, the retail specialty chain, has used segmentation to cover many targets in the Canadian market (Retail Highlight 6–2).

Once retailers have chosen markets in which to compete, a plan must be developed for attracting targeted consumers. The basis for such planning is a thorough understanding of those consumers—their behaviour, values, motives, and

**TABLE 6–3   Market Grid Example for the Offerings of a New Supermarket**

| Young single professional | Middle-income household with children at home | Low-income, older shopper and limited education | Customer segments / Offering |
|---|---|---|---|
| | | | 24-hour opening |
| | | | Generics |
| | | | Cheque cashing |
| | | | In-store bakery |
| | | | Delicatessen department |
| | | | Frequent sales or specials |
| | | | Unit pricing |
| | | | Helpful personnel |
| | | | Strong nonfood department |

**TABLE 6–4   Market Alternatives Profile Analysis**

| *Critical Market Factors* | *Importance to Management* | × | *Attractiveness of the Market Based on the Factor Evaluated* | = | *Weighted Score* |
|---|---|---|---|---|---|
| Future growth potential | 2 | | 1 | | 2 |
| Present size | 6 | | 4 | | 24 |
| Investment required | 5 | | 6 | | 30 |
| Strength of competition | 4 | | 5 | | 20 |
| Ability to meet the needs of the market | 1 | | 3 | | 3 |
| Profit potential | 3 | | 2 | | 6 |
| TOTAL SCORE | | | | | 85 |

NOTE: A 1 denotes most Important to Management or most Attractive to Management. The lower the total score, the more attractive the market alternative is to management.

expectations. Especially important is an understanding of the decision process customers go through in making merchandise and store choice decisions. Because of the importance of this topic, we devoted Chapter 4 to the consumer as problem solver and Chapter 5 to the social characteristics and living patterns of customers. Knowledge of consumer behaviour helps retailers better understand consumers' merchandise and store preferences and their shopping behaviour.

# Dylex: Segmenting the Retail Market

Dylex, a Canadian specialty chain, has over 1,300 stores throughout North America. Its stores target various consumer segments based on sex, age, income, and life-styles to achieve sales in excess of $1.8 billion annually.

| Target Markets | Stores | Overall Positioning | Number of Outlets | Average Size (sq. metres) |
|---|---|---|---|---|
| Women (young) | La Senza | Fashionable lingerie | 15 | 200 |
| Women (middle to higher income) | Braemar, Braemar Petites | Selected sportswear, dresses, coats | 71 | 340 |
| Women (higher income) | Fairweather | Fashionable | 132 | 530 |
| Women (economy) | Suzy Shier, L.A. Express | Value-priced fashion | 221 | 250 |
| Men (young) | Steel | Fashionable clothing | 106 | 200 |
| Men (professional) | Harry Rosen | Quality apparel | 26 | 930 |
| Men (business) | Tip Top Tailors | Medium prices | 185 | 370 |
| Unisex (young) | Thrifty's | Casual wear | 142 | 230 |
| Family (economy) | BiWay | Low cost housewares and clothing | 261 | 830 |
| Family (economy) | Drug World | Discount products and prescription drugs | 9 | 2,100 |
| Family (middle income) | Club Monaco | Quality casual wear | 47 | 210 |

Source: Dylex, Annual Report, 1991.

## Obtaining Resources Needed to Compete

As part of the planning process, retailers must evaluate the alternatives for owning a business as well as avenues for entering a retail business. For example, a retail firm can be operated as a sole proprietorship, a partnership, or a corporation. To enter retailing, a person can start his or her own business, buy an existing business, or become part of a franchise operation. Such issues are the topics for Chapters 7 and 8. Chapter 7 focuses on different forms of ownership, issues in buying a retail business, determining capital needed for a new business and sources of needed funds, and issues related to organization structure. Because franchising is one of the fastest growing segments in retailing today, a separate chapter, Chapter 8, is devoted to a discussion of franchising as a retail business concept.

Store location, a crucial element of retail planning, is the topic of Chapter 11. For example, Peoples Jewellers, with over 280 stores in Canada, recognizes that Canadians now prefer to shop in malls, particularly suburban malls, for many products including jewellery. As demographics change and customer preferences for store locations drift, Peoples Jewellers is closing stores in locations that no longer meet customer needs and opening new stores in preferred locations in smaller cities. This is an important component of its strategy.[3]

Human resources are just as vital to the success of a retail operation as are financial resources and physical facilities. As will be shown in Chapter 9, the human resources plan must be consistent with the overall strategy of the retail organization. Human resources management also involves a variety of issues such as recruiting, selecting, training, compensating, and motivating personnel, and it is essential that these activities be managed effectively and efficiently.

# Developing a Positioning Strategy

After target markets are selected and the necessary resources are obtained, a positioning strategy is developed. **Positioning** is the design and implementation of a retail mix to create an image of the retailer in the customer's mind relative to its competitors.[4]

One example of positioning is Zellers, the discount department store chain. Zellers is positioned to appeal to budget-minded customers by assuring them of the lowest price. Zellers focuses directly on this position with its slogan: "The Lowest Price Is the Law." A profile of Zellers is provided in Retail Highlight 6–3.

The importance of developing a positioning strategy must be stressed, especially in an era when competition in retailing is fierce. The critical nature of positioning is indicated in the following quote:

> In an era of cutthroat retail competition, few if any strategic responses are more critical to a retailer than positioning: identifying—and then occupying—an available position in the market. . . . Occupying an available position involves selling the store, not just the merchandise. A store becomes the "brand" with all marketing variables— merchandise mix, ambience, personnel, advertising, pricing policy—coordinated to reinforce what the firm stands for, why it exists. In brief, occupying a position requires that the retailer's *reason for being* is clearly and powerfully defined in the prospective customer's mind and in the mind of management and personnel. An effective positioning strategy can contribute greatly to a retailer's success. In a cluttered marketplace, the well-positioned retailer is distinctive; it is a first-choice outlet.[5]

The positioning strategy involves the use of retailing mix variables. The **retailing mix** consists of all variables that can be used as part of a positioning strategy for competing in chosen markets. As shown in Figure 6–3, the retailing mix variables include product, price, presentation, promotion, personal selling, and

*Zellers is positioned to appeal to budget-minded customers.*

SOURCE: Courtesy Hudson's Bay Company.

customer services. Issues related to retailing mix variables are included in Chapters 11 to 18 of the text.

The Gap, a popular and profitable specialty clothing chain, will be used to illustrate how marketing mix variables play a critical role in positioning efforts within target markets. The Gap has over 1,200 stores in the United States and has entered the Canadian market, targeting consumers with a simple yet powerful positioning strategy — good style, good quality, and good value. The blend of some of the retailing mix variables in support of this position strategy are:

- *Product:* The Gap designs its own clothes with a focus on simplicity. New collections hit the stores about every eight weeks, and unpopular designs are marked down and quickly sold off.

---

**Retail Highlight 6–3**

---

# Zellers Profile

Zellers is the leading national chain of discount department stores. It targets the budget-minded customer with the assurance of the lowest price. Excellent values are offered in both national and private brand merchandise, and these are communicated aggressively with frequent advertising in both print and electronic media. Zellers is further distinguished by Club Z, its frequent buyer program. Zellers is able to compete successfully in its competitive retail segment by operating with a very low expense rate.

Zellers stores are characterized by self-service and a central check-out counter. Zellers markets its own credit card and accepts those of the major banks. Merchandising and sales promotion are centrally directed. Zellers operates 272 stores across Canada, mainly in shopping malls. The typical store is 6,000 square metres in size.

Source: Hudson's Bay Company, *Annual Report,* 1991.

---

- *Price:* Strict quality control procedures and using manufacturers in 40 countries ensure high quality, low costs, and a very good price for customers.
- *Presentation:* Merchandise is displayed to emphasize the deep assortment of colours, and is laid out on tables and shelves where it can be easily touched.
- *Promotion:* Advertising for The Gap has been striking, including the ''Individuals of Style'' campaign, a series of black-and-white photos of personalities from Miles Davis to k.d. lang. The message communicates an individual sense of style.
- *Personal selling:* Sales staff receive no commissions, but constant contests are run to motivate the staff to provide quality service.
- *Customer services:* The Gap accepts all credit cards.[6]

## Strategy Implementation

A sound strategy is no guarantee of success if it cannot be well executed. To implement a firm's desired positioning effectively, every aspect of the store must be focused on the target market. Merchandising must be single-minded; displays must appeal to the target market; advertising must talk to it; personnel must have empathy for it; and customer service must be designed with the target customer in mind.

**FIGURE 6–3**

*Variables of the
retailing mix and
types of decisions*

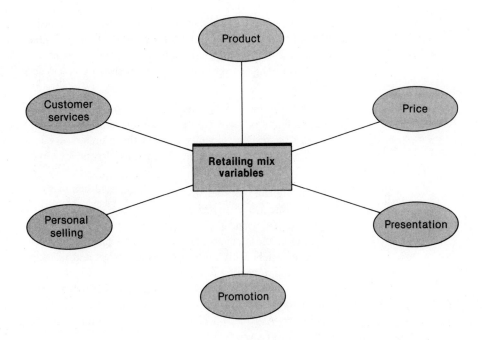

| Variable | Types of Decisions |
|---|---|
| Product | Merchandise lines (width, depth, assortment) |
| | Brand lines (national, store, generic) |
| | Supplier selection |
| | Inventory levels |
| Price | Pricing policy (above, at, below the market) |
| | Price levels |
| | Price adjustments |
| Presentation | Store design |
| | Store layout |
| | Merchandise presentation |
| Promotion | Advertising budget, copy, and media |
| | Sales promotions |
| | Publicity and public relations |
| Personal selling | Sales force size, training, and compensation |
| | Motivation of staff |
| Customer services | Support services |
| | Credit policies |
| | Return  policies |

The purpose of this section is to show how retailing mix variables can be blended to implement a store's positioning strategy. Three major strategy options are discussed: market penetration, market development, and productivity improvement. The range of options within each strategy is shown in Figure 6–4.

*Market Penetration*

Retailers following a strategy of **market penetration** seek a differential advantage over competition by a strong market presence that borders on saturation. Such a strategy is designed to increase (1) the number of customers, (2) the quantity purchased by customers, and (3) purchase frequency.

### Increasing the Number of Customers

Using strategies designed to increase the number of customers is one way of increasing sales and profitability. Adding stores and modifying in-store offerings can lead to more customers. Woodward's has changed its merchandise mix to be more consistent with western Canadian tastes and its merchandise price points to levels more appealing to the middle-class family. Sobey's is adding new stores in Atlantic Canada to increase its dominant position in the market. Sobey's also is remodeling existing stores—making them brighter and larger—to attract more customers. As well, a penetration strategy could include the use of the retailing mix variables to ensure:

1. The lowest price lines and the lowest prices within the market area.
2. Extensive width and depth of consumer goods such as health and beauty aids and housewares.
3. Aggregate convenience including location, parking, hours, and ease of purchase; features such as supermarketlike front ends, total merchandise display, wide aisles, easy-to-see-and-locate merchandise groups, shopping carts, and, usually, a single display floor.

### Increasing the Quantity Purchased

Improving the store layout and merchandise presentation can help to create an atmosphere that is conducive to more spending. As part of a five-year, $200 million facelift, Kmart Canada has widened its aisles, brightened its floor space, broadened its merchandising mix to include more brand-name merchandise, and expanded customer services—from food courts to bank machines to hair salons—to get more customers into the stores and to increase the quantity purchased.[7]

### Increasing Purchase Frequency

Toy supermarkets such as Toys Я Us, the U.S. chain with 29 stores in Canada, have been quite successful in implementing strategies designed to increase purchase frequency. The keys to the success of these firms include (1) a complete selection of toys year-round; (2) customer awareness that if a toy is bought at such outlets at Christmas, there will be a good selection after Christmas to accommodate returns; (3) stable, year-round lines, plus merchandise categories

**FIGURE 6–4**

*Retail strategy options*

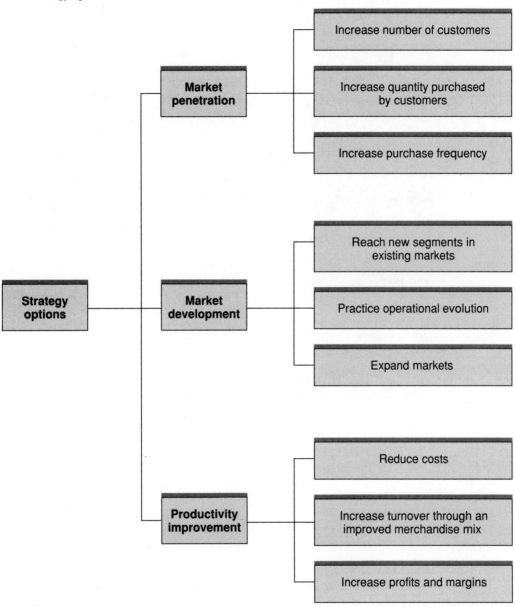

with seasonal appeal in spring and summer, such as juvenile furniture, bicycles, gym sets, and family pools; (4) a huge inventory; (5) low prices; (6) minimum service; and (7) wide aisles.[8]

*Kmart Canada's strategy includes expanding customer services — such as the Eatery Express.*

SOURCE: Courtesy Kmart Canada.

Basically, these firms offer items that sell year-round. Toys in the low- to medium-price ranges, often with strong licensed-character affiliations such as the Smurfs and Care Bears, provide sales day in and day out. High-impulse items like peg boards, die-cast toys, and hobby kits lead to high customer traffic. The firms capitalize not only on birthdays and Christmas but also on other holidays and special occasions like Valentine's Day, Easter, Halloween, and the back-to-school period.

## Market Development

A strategy of **market development** focuses either on attracting new market segments or on completely changing the customer base. Market development normally involves bolder strategy shifts, more capital, and greater risk than a market penetration strategy. Examples of market development efforts include (1) reaching new segments, (2) operational evolution, and (3) market expansion.

### Reaching New Segments

Fast-food restaurants provide a good example of the strategy of attracting new segments in existing markets. McDonald's, through the years, has added chicken, breakfast items, and more recently, salads and pizza to its menu. This helps attract consumers who are looking for something nonfried, less filling, with lower calories, and more nutritious than many traditional fast-food offerings. Harvey's has broadened its product line to include sandwiches to attract new segments. McDonald's also seeks to reach new segments by opening restaurants in unique, nontraditional sites including hospitals, subway and train stations, and tourist areas. In the Toronto SkyDome, McDonald's has four outlets, including one seating 600 people.

### Operational Evolution

**Operational evolution** means changing competitive strategy over time by focusing on a new target market and developing a business concept different from the existing one. This strategy is different from that of increasing the customer base as previously discussed because it involves changing, rather than adding customers to, the customer base.

Fairweather, a women's clothing retail chain in the Dylex group, provides an example of operational evolution. Fairweather had been targeting the fashion-conscious teenage market with less than satisfactory results. Market research indicated that the chain was attracting women in their mid-20s as well as the teenage market. The decision was made to focus on the older, more affluent segment. The next step was staff training, to ensure that the new direction was understood. Then an aggressive marketing campaign and customer-driven merchandising strategies were implemented to communicate this new position to consumers. As well, store managers were encouraged to blend the merchandise mix to suit local customer preferences. The result was an increase in sales of 40 percent.[9]

### Market Expansion

An effective strategy for many retailers is to expand on a geographic basis. The basic premise is that if the store concept works in one locale, it should work in another. Franchise retailers have successfully used geographic expansion for many years. Probably one of the most interesting and well-documented franchise expansions was the McDonald's Canada expansion to Moscow.

*Productivity Improvement*

The strategy of **productivity improvement** focuses on improved earnings through cost reductions, increased turnover through an improved merchandise mix, and increased prices and margins. Productivity improvement often occurs in firms in the mature or declining phases of their life cycles. During these stages, strategies requiring major infusions of cash are not acceptable to management. Rather, the emphasis is on squeezing as much profit as possible from the operation. The strategy is more a refinement of existing strategies than a dramatic new way of doing business. Le Château, a clothing chain with 174 stores in Canada, improved productivity through reducing overheads and returned the company to profitability.[10]

### Cost Reductions

Some retailers concentrate on cost reductions as a competitive weapon in increasing productivity. A key to such a strategy often is to increase self-service to hold down labour costs. Reducing store hours, making better use of part-time help, and cutting back on customer services are other actions that can be taken to reduce costs.

Provigo, a large Canadian wholesale and retail organization (retail operations include Provigo, LEOB, and Intermarché), focuses on a sophisticated information technology system to achieve significant cost reductions in its distribution system. Information obtained from the company's point-of-sale scanners in their supermar-

**TABLE 6-5   Evaluating Competitive Strategy**

**Merchandising Plan**

1. What is the growth pattern of existing merchandise lines?
2. Is the merchandise line portfolio balanced? Should merchandise lines be added or deleted?
3. Should product line breadth or depth be modified?
4. What is the strength of the individual brands carried?
5. Are the merchandise lines properly positioned against the competition and in support of the marketing plan?
6. Does the firm have an adequate open-to-buy plan?
7. Are adequate inventory controls in place?

**Pricing Plan**

1. What are the profit margins on the merchandise lines carried? Are they increasing or decreasing? How do they compare to those of competition?
2. Are the pricing policies, including price lines (at, equal to, or above the competition), appropriate for each target market?
3. Does pricing have a primary or secondary role in the marketing plan?
4. Is a realistic system for planned markdowns in place?

**Advertising and Sales Promotion Plan**

1. Are the objectives for advertising and sales promotion clearly stated? Do they support the marketing plan?
2. Is the media mix supportive of the marketing plan?
3. Are budgets adequate to accomplish the objectives? How are budgets established?
4. Are the creative strategies compatible with the marketing plan?
5. Does the firm have weekly, monthly, and seasonal plans for such activities in place?

**Distribution and Sales Support Plan**

1. Are customer service levels such as on warranties and repairs satisfactory? What weaknesses exist?
2. Are mail and telephone sales programs compatible with the overall marketing plan?
3. Are the after-sales delivery programs, if any, compatible with the marketing plan?
4. Are the credit programs offered cost effective? Should credit options be added or deleted?
5. Is the breadth and intensity of market coverage satisfactory for a firm with branches or multiple outlets?

**Financial Plan**

1. Is a profit analysis possible, including a break-even analysis and analysis of ROI and leverage?
2. What are the profit margins by merchandise line? Are they increasing or decreasing? How do they compare to those of the competition? Compare with trade statistics where possible.
3. Does the firm have a sound accounting and information system?
4. What are the trends in such indicators as return on assets, earnings per share, and net profits?

**Physical Facilities Plan**

1. Is adequate emphasis placed on space productivity?
2. Is flexible fixturing used whenever possible?
3. Does signing provide adequate information to shoppers?
4. Do the atmospherics support the other elements of the marketing plan?
5. Is merchandise arranged for easy cross-selling whenever possible?
6. Is lighting appropriate for each area?

**The Retail Information System**

1. Does the merchandise information system provide the information needed for key operating decisions?
2. Is a sound, competitive shopping system in place?
3. Is someone in the firm responsible for evaluating environmental trends that can affect the continuing success of the firm?
4. Are the financial and merchandising ratios of the firm regularly compared to comparable trade statistics?

**Human Resources Plan**

1. Does the firm have the talent to execute its marketing strategies?
2. Is the firm adequately staffed?
3. Are the firm's selection and recruiting efforts and training programs adequate?
4. Are the firm's pay scales adequate? Are opportunities for promotion available? Are performance appraisals and feedback occurring?
5. If several outlets exist, are personnel decisions centralized or decentralized?
6. Are disciplinary procedures in place?
7. Do union/management relations receive adequate attention?

kets allows the firm to measure the contribution of individual products to profitability. Provigo uses information technology to achieve productivity improvements through reducing costs and improving the merchandise mix. As well, the company processes virtually all its orders with suppliers through electronic data interchange, resulting in significant cost savings.[11]

### Improved Merchandise Mix

Most stores attempt to improve productivity by increasing their turnover through a better merchandise mix. The key is to ensure that the new merchandise satisfies the needs of the target market while maintaining the store's desired position. Mark's Work Wearhouse encourages in-store product managers and product category coordinators to introduce new items into the product assortment on a test basis. By using local knowledge of customer needs, this ongoing testing allows Mark's to respond quickly to changing market demands. Video chains such as Jumbo Video have broadened their merchandising mix to include games and laser disk rentals.

### Price and Margin Increases

Price and margin increases can be a key element in productivity-based strategies. Higher-than-normal prices may be possible on low-visibility items or infrequently purchased products. Charging for services such as delivery or installation may also be feasible. Many furniture retailers charge a fee for delivery of merchandise. Adding high-margin items to the merchandise mix, as is done by superstores, is a further dimension of such a strategy. Banks have also started to vary service charges to retail customers based on account balances.

# Evaluating and Controlling Operations

Once a strategy is implemented, managers need feedback on the performance of the new strategy. Some types of information are needed on a routine, ongoing basis to help management determine whether objectives are being met. Chapter 19 focuses on several types of control systems that help management assess the success of operations.

The effectiveness of the long-term competitive strategy of the firm, however, must also be evaluated periodically. Such an evaluation covers all elements of the plan, as shown in Table 6–5. This type of evaluation guarantees that the firm's plan does not degenerate into fragmented, ad hoc efforts that are not in harmony with the overall competitive strategy of the business. Management can also use the process to decide what changes, if any, should be made in the future to ensure that the combination of retailing mix variables supports the firm's strategy.

# Chapter Highlights

- The steps involved in strategic planning are (1) develop a mission statement, (2) establish objectives, (3) conduct a situation analysis, (4) select markets in which to compete, (5) obtain resources needed to compete, (6) develop a positioning strategy, (7) implement the strategy, and (8) evaluate the results.

- The beginning point in developing a strategic plan is identification of the organization's mission or purpose. The mission statement tells what the firm intends to do and how it plans to do it. The mission statement often reflects the firm's values or corporate culture.

- The retailer's plan for achieving objectives within the context of the mission statement is based on an analysis of the strengths and weaknesses of the organization and threats and opportunities in the environment. Such an analysis is called a situation analysis.

- The situation analysis helps store management identify markets in which to compete. The markets that management decides to serve are referred to as target markets.

- The factors involved in deciding on markets in which to compete include segmentation (and the preparation of a marketing grid) and screening criteria (such as future growth potential and strength of competition).

- The retailer must develop a positioning strategy. The positioning strategy is a plan of action that outlines how the organization will compete in chosen markets and how it will differentiate itself from other organizations competing for the same customers. The positioning strategy is developed through a combination of retailing mix variables. These variables include product, price, presentation, promotion, personal selling, and customer services.

- A sound strategy is no guarantee of success if it cannot be implemented successfully. The retailing mix variables must be blended appropriately in implementing a store's positioning strategy.

- Three strategy options available to retailers include market penetration, market development, and productivity improvement. Market penetration includes strategies designed to increase (1) the number of customers, (2) the quantity purchased by customers, and (3) purchase frequency. Market development strategies focus on attracting new market segments, completely changing the customer base (operational evolution), or market expansion. A strategy of productivity improvement focuses on improved earnings through cost reductions, increased turnover through an improved merchandise mix, and increased prices and margins.

- Once a strategy is implemented, managers need feedback on how the organization is performing based on its strategy. Some types of information are needed on a routine, ongoing basis to help management determine whether objectives are being met. However, the effectiveness of the long-term competitive strategy of the firm must also be evaluated periodically.

# Key Terms

Corporate culture    145
External factors    148
Internal factors    147
Market development    160
Market penetration    158
Market segments    150
Mission statement    145
Objectives    146

Operational evolution    161
Positioning    154
Productivity improvement    161
Retailing mix    154
Situation analysis    147
Strategic planning    144
Target markets    150

# Discussion Questions

1. Indicate the steps involved in developing a strategic plan.

2. What is meant by an organization's mission statement? What does this statement normally include?

3. What is the difference between long-term and short-term objectives?

4. What is a situation analysis? Which factors are evaluated in such an analysis?

5. What is the ultimate value and use of a situation analysis?

6. What are the four requirements for market segmentation?

7. Explain the relationships between target markets, positioning strategy, and the retailing mix.

8. Discuss each of the following strategy options: market penetration, market development, and productivity improvement.

# Application Exercises

1. Mission statements of a number of Canadian retailers are included in the text. Visit your library and find mission statements of other retail operations from their annual reports.

2. Visit several different types of retail stores in your community and ask store managers to define the store's positioning strategy. Which of the three major strategic options are they following?

3. Select at least three fast-food operations in your community. Indicate each firm's target market and positioning strategy and discuss how the elements of the retailing mix are combined in implementing the positioning strategy.

# Suggested Cases

1. Videofile    565
10. The Perfect Pace    585
11. Diego's    590
12. The Undercover Agency    597
13. Donna Holtom    602

14. Woodward's Department Stores: Holiday Travel    610
15. West Coast Furniture    613
16. Eaton Centre (Edmonton)    615

# Endnotes

1. Southam Inc., Annual Report, 1991.
2. Marina Strauss, "Oshawa Group Pins Hope on Price Chopper," *Globe and Mail*, June 6, 1992, p. B7.
3. Peoples Jewellers Ltd., Annual Report, 1991.
4. David A. Aaker and J. Gary Shansby, "Positioning Your Product," *Business Horizons*, May–June 1982, pp. 56–62; and George Lucas and Larry Gresham, "How to Position for Retailing Success," *Business*, April–June 1989, pp. 3–12.
5. Leonard L. Berry, "Retailing Positioning Strategies for the 1980s," *Business Horizons*, November–December 1982, p. 45.
6. Russell Mitchell, "The Gap," *Business Week*, March 9, 1992, pp. 58–64; and Mario Shao and Laura Zinn, "Everybody's Falling into the Gap," *Business Week*, September 23, 1991, p. 36.
7. James Pollock, "Kmart Continues Repositioning with Latest Store Redesigns," *Marketing*, July 6, 1992, p. 9.
8. "Founder Lazarus Is a Reason Toys Я Us Dominates Its Industry," *Wall Street Journal*, November 21, 1985, p. 1.
9. Mark Evans, "The Tricky Art of Changing Formats," *The Financial Post*, January 13, 1992, p. 3; and Dylex, Annual Report, 1991.
10. Alan D. Gray, "An Internal Reno for a Crumbling Chateau," *Financial Times*, February 6, 1989, p. 14; and Le Château, Annual Report, 1991.
11. Provigo, Annual Report, 1992.

# 7   FINANCING AND ORGANIZING THE RETAIL FIRM

## Chapter Objectives

After reading this chapter, you should be able to:

1 Describe the risks and advantages of ownership.
2 Explain the differences between a sole proprietorship, a partnership, and a corporation.
3 Define issues in buying a retail business.
4 Discuss the importance of planning in starting a business.
5 Estimate the operating capital needed for a new business and the sources of the funds.
6 Explain how to organize for profits.

**Retailing Capsule**

For many years, Terry and Janet Fullerton wanted to start their own business—something where they could stay at home, raise their children, and be challenged. Mrs. Fullerton identified an opportunity for a day-care facility when she was swamped with enquiries after she placed a small notice on a supermarket bulletin board offering to take care of one or two children. The couple started Wee Watch Day Care Systems, which provides private child care. The irony of the situation is that their retail business is now so successful that they are in the office full time and have hired a nanny to care for their children. However, as Mr. Fullerton has commented, "It's a good thing we like what we are doing—we're working more than ever before, but we're enjoying it more." Now, Wee Watch, headquartered in Markham, Ontario, is a franchise operation with 35 franchises and revenues exceeding $6 million annually.

Jim Treliving, an RCMP officer working in Edmonton, wanted to find a business that would allow him to relocate to British Columbia. He was impressed with a local pizza chain, Boston Pizza International, where he and his partner would eat when on late-night duty. He convinced the owner to let him open a franchise in Penticton, British Columbia. Within 10 years, he had 10 outlets in the province. Today, along with three partners, he controls the 83-outlet chain, and he has moved the head office to Vancouver. As Mr. Treliving notes, "I'm still enjoying the beautiful weather of B.C., which is what I wanted in the first place. Cold weather lit a fire under me."

These are just two of the thousands of stories of Canadians who wanted to be their own bosses and who started retail businesses. While not everyone succeeds, many people take up the challenge because they are seeking the independence and feeling of dignity that goes with being your own boss.

Sources: Barbara Aarsteinsen, "Converts to Self-Employment Diverse," *Globe and Mail*, September 5, 1988, p. C13; and John Southerst, "Agents of Change," *Profit*, June 1992, pp. 38–43.

Many people dream of owning their own business in spite of the long hours, the financial risks, and the fiercely competitive nature of retailing. They can get started in many ways. Examples include starting a business and operating as an independent organization; banding together with other retailers or wholesalers to have more power in buying goods but still operating as an independent business; becoming a franchisor; or becoming a franchisee. (Franchising is discussed in the next chapter.)

A successful retail venture depends not only on successful marketing strategies, but also on the legal form of the organization, access to the types of capital needed, and the right internal organization. Additionally, the aspiring retailer needs to do a

*Owning your own business is the dream of many Canadians.*

SOURCE: Photo by James Hertel.

careful assessment of the personal attributes necessary for success. All of these issues are explored in this chapter.

Over 1 million people are employed in retailing in Canada. Two thirds of retail firms have less than four employees, and 90 percent are single-unit establishments. Clearly, most retail businesses are small by any standard. Persons who want one day to manage a family business or open a business may decide to start their retail career by working in a small firm. Better and more specialized training is normally available in a chain organization.

Chains are usually larger than independent firms and, because they have two or more units, they may achieve economies of scale. Specialized functions such as finance, accounting, buying, and legal services can be handled in one central location for all of the stores.

# The Advantages of Ownership

Retailing offers more opportunities for ownership than virtually any other type of business. Read the newspaper on almost any day and you will probably find several retail businesses for sale. Also, many suppliers and bankers will loan the funds to help people open their own firms; however, they will probably want to see a cash flow plan, as discussed later in this chapter, and will need to understand the organization's planned business strategy.

Most retailing is local in nature, so independent retailers can often compete successfully with large national firms. Store trading areas are small and the outlets are viewed as part of the local neighbourhood. At the local level, small retailers can do things that a national firm cannot do. Most national firms do not vary their operations from town to town. Consequently, local merchants can offer unique merchandise lines, more specialized services, and more personal attention than are normally available from chain store merchants.

# The Risks of Ownership

Going-out-of-business signs are a part of every community, although few people voluntarily go out of business. But aspiring entrepreneurs should not be discouraged from starting their own businesses if they are willing to take risks, because the rewards can be large.

### Early Failure Is Likely

The first five years are the toughest for the business owner. Of the businesses that fail, more than 50 percent fail in the first five years.[1] For example, one study showed that between 1978 and 1986, over 58,000 retail firms ceased operation in Canada. On the other hand, over 90,000 retail firms started up during the same time.[2]

### What Are the Causes of Failure?

The most common reasons for failure are incompetence, unbalanced experience, lack of experience in the line, and a lack of managerial experience. Failure because of neglect, fraud, or disaster is unusual.[3] The early 1990s saw an increase in business and retail failures due to the harsh economic climate. In 1991, there were 13,500 business bankruptcies in Canada, most of them in the retail sector. A total of 28,000 jobs were lost in retailing during that year.[4]

Systematic differences exist between businesses that survive for three years and those that fail. The surviving businesses are more likely to use business plans, to get started with higher levels of capital, and to use professional advisers. Similarly, the owners of successful businesses are more likely to have college degrees and to run their businesses full time, as opposed to hiring professional managers.

# Starting a New Business

People interested in opening a new business can form a sole proprietorship, a partnership, or a corporation. The advantages and disadvantages of each form of business are shown in Table 7–1. Management may also decide to purchase an

TABLE 7–1    **The Advantages and Disadvantages of Forms of Business Ownership**

|  | *Sole Proprietorship* | *Partnership* | *Corporation* |
|---|---|---|---|
| Advantages | Easy to organize | Easy to organize | Limited financial liability |
|  | Easy to dissolve | Greater capital availability | Easier to raise capital |
|  | Owner keeps all profits | Combined management experience | Specialized management skills |
|  | Preferential government treatment |  | Easier to transfer ownership |
| Disadvantages | Unlimited financial liability | Unlimited liability | Complex government regulations |
|  | Difficult to raise capital | Dividend authority | Expensive to organize |
|  | Limited life of firm | Hard to dissolve | Various tax disadvantages |
|  | The business is based on the heartbeat of one individual |  | Lack of personal involvement |
|  | Limited by owner's skills |  |  |

existing business instead of starting a new one. The forms of business are the same whether starting a new business or buying an existing firm.

## Sole Proprietorship

The **sole proprietorship** is the most common form of ownership today. Everything belongs to the owner.

Being the sole owner of a business has several advantages. Such a business is the easiest to start, as less paperwork is necessary and fewer restrictions exist other than for inspection or licensing. As well, the owner is the boss, the owner keeps all the profits, and the owner decides on the goods to be sold, store hours, and so forth. The owner can go out of business very quickly, often simply by locking the door and hanging a sign in the window that says "Closed." In addition, because both the federal and provincial governments view small businesses as important to Canada's economy, certain financial aid and consulting programs may be available to small retailers.

Disadvantages also exist. For example:

1. The full risk of loss is borne by the owner, who can be forced to pay business debts out of personal assets.
2. The firm has limited borrowing power.
3. Qualified people may be hesitant about working for the firm.
4. Such a business can probably offer fewer fringe benefits to employees than could larger employers.
5. No one is legally able to make business decisions except the owner.

## Partnership

A **partnership** exists when two or more people jointly own a retail business. Partnerships can take various forms. For example, in a *general partnership,* the partners share all of the responsibilities and benefits of the partnership, including profits and management authority. *Limited partners* are persons whose input is

*Starting a new business can take many forms in retailing.*

SOURCE: Photo by Betty McDougall.

limited to one area of the business. For example, a lawyer may be a limited partner. The liability of limited partners is restricted to their investment.

*Silent partners* likewise have limited liability. They are not active in the business but are willing to allow their names to be used as one of the partners. Often, these partners are well known in the community and the use of their names is an asset to the firm. *Secret partners* do not allow their names to be used. They do not always have limited liabilities.

The disadvantages of partnerships, as shown in Table 7–1, make them less popular than other forms of organization, and the problems can be complicated when a firm has several partners. Partnerships often cease to exist when one of the partners becomes incapable of continuing in the business. Likewise, the unlimited liability for the debts of the business can be a drawback, as can the fact that the actions of any one partner are binding on the others.

Consequently, the articles for a partnership are very important. They need to carefully spell out the roles of the partners, the ways for a partner to get out of the business, and what happens when one of the partners dies or becomes disabled.

*Corporation*

A **corporation** is a separate legal entity apart from the owners. Thus, liability is limited to the amount that each individual stockholder has invested in the firm. Since management is separate from ownership, it may be easier for a corporation to attract strong managerial talent. It may also be easier to raise capital, either by issuing stock or through loans. Since corporations are often large and have greater earning power than single proprietorships, they have easier access to borrowing money at favourable rates.

Again, some disadvantages exist. For example, earnings are taxed more heavily. Corporate earnings are taxed as well as dividends to stockholders.

Corporations may be either private or public. **Private corporations** are those owned by a few people (a maximum of 50 shareholders is allowed), often a family, and persons outside the corporation cannot buy the stock on the open market. The stock does not have a known market value and does not vary widely in price. **Public corporations** are those in which the stock of the firm can be purchased on the open market. Normally, only larger retailers are public corporations.

Incorporating is relatively easy to do and can be done under the Federal Canada Business Corporations Act or under a Provincial Corporations Act. A corporation can be established by a single individual or two or more individuals. The individual or group is issued a corporate charter, which is a contract between the provincial or federal government and the person or group. The corporate charter allows the business to operate. The advice or counsel of a lawyer should be sought on the details for such an arrangement.

Two of the most important factors in deciding on the form of ownership are the liability of the owners and tax considerations. In general, only corporations provide for limited liability with respect to debts incurred by the business. With respect to taxes, knowledge of the Canadian tax system and the tax laws relating to personal income and corporate income should be obtained before making the decision. The advice of an accountant should be sought on tax matters.

# Buying a Retail Business

A person may decide to buy an existing business instead of starting a new one. Buying a retail business is a complex process. The potential buyer needs the help of professionals such as accountants, bankers, brokers, and lawyers on specific issues.

*Deciding on the Type of Retailing*

The type of retailing depends on the personal characteristics of the potential buyer, including his or her personality, interests, experiences, and skills. The amount of financing available may also determine the type of business that can be purchased. The growth potential is also important. Information on the future prospects of the business can be developed by talking with executives in trade associations, bankers, suppliers, and others knowledgeable about the business.

*Identifying Potential Stores*

Newspaper classified ads are a source of possible leads. Prospective buyers can also place "business wanted" ads in the newspaper. Persons specializing in buying and selling retail firms often can provide valuable assistance. The potential buyer needs to remember, however, that the broker represents the seller and gets a commission based on the sales price.

Other potential sources of leads are suppliers, distributors, trade publications, and trade associations. Occasionally, accountants or other management consultants may also be able to identify a business that is for sale.

*Evaluating the Business Opportunity*

The potential buyer needs to determine the reasons why a business is for sale. Old age, poor health, and pending bankruptcy are reasons that can easily be spotted. Other less obvious reasons include excessive competition, problems with creditors, excess accounts receivable, or a pending lease loss.

### Assessing Earnings Potential

The potential buyer should look at past profits, sales, and expenses. Operating ratios should be compared with industry data provided by such sources as the Retail Council of Canada and Dun & Bradstreet before making an offer for a business.[5] In particular, key performance measures such as those for profitability, productivity, and financial management, as shown in Table 7–2, should be examined; if possible, these measures should be compared with those for similar businesses. An independent accountant who specializes in retailing may need to analyze the profit and loss performance of the business over the past three to five years. The buyer should be wary of a seller who will not provide background information, including financial statements, income tax returns, purchases, and bank deposits.

A detailed analysis will sometimes indicate a business is not profitable. The potential owner must then make an assessment about whether it is possible to earn a profit from the business. Perhaps the person has better management skills or is willing to invest more time and energy than the current owner, or has identified industry trends that make the business attractive in the near-term future.

### Evaluating the Assets

The assets of the business should also be carefully considered. Independent appraisers should determine the dollar value of the inventory and its age, style, condition, and quality. Is the inventory compatible with the trading area of the store? How much inventory would have to be liquidated at a loss? What is the market value of the furniture and fixtures? Will they have to be replaced? Are the fixtures compatible with the business?

Accounts receivable should also be studied to determine their age, the credit standing of some of the larger customers, and the success of the firm in collecting past due accounts. Are too many of the credit customers slow in paying their bills? Would customers be lost if stricter credit requirements were established? Similarly, what is the condition of accounts payable? Are any lawsuits pending against the retailer?

TABLE 7–2  **Selected Key Performance Measures**

**Profitability**
Net profit after tax to net sales—measures amount of net profit produced by each dollar of sales
Net profit after tax to total assets—measures return on all invested funds
Net profit after tax to net worth/invested—measures return on net equity invested

**Productivity**
Space:
  Sales per square metre of selling area—measures sales generated through a store
  Gross margin per square metre of selling area—measures gross margin dollars generated by use of space
  Transactions per square metre of selling area—measures traffic per square metre

Inventory:
  Gross margin percent—indicator of gross profit level
  Gross margin return on inventory—measures the relationship between investment in inventory and gross margin generated by that margin
  Inventory turnover (times) —used to determine how effectively managers utilize their investment in inventory

Personnel:
  Sales per selling employee—measures staff levels relative to volume
  Gross margin per employee—measures gross profit generated per employee

Accounts receivable:
  Days outstanding in receivables—measures quality of credit management

Total assets:
  Net sales to total assets (times) —used to evaluate how effectively managers use their assets

**Financial Management**
Leverage:
  Total assets to net worth (times) —the relationship between how much a firm owes to how much the firm owns

Liquidity:
  Current ratio (times) —indicator of liquidity
  Quick ratio (times) —indicator of liquidity

The potential buyer should also determine if the lease is transferable. Also, what are the terms of the lease and how much time is left on the lease? Will mailing lists and customer lists be included as part of the sale? Is the business name included as part of the sale?

Finally, the potential buyer should check to determine whether the business has a good reputation and a satisfied clientele. Do the potential customers have a unique attachment to the present owner such that they might not continue to shop at the outlet if it is sold? Finally, any sales agreement should include a provision that keeps the seller from opening a similar business within the same market for a specified period of time.

# The Characteristics Needed for Success as an Owner/ Manager[6]

Not all persons can succeed as owners of retail businesses. Retail owner/managers need to be highly motivated to succeed. They need great energy and commitment and need to be prepared to overcome a lot of obstacles. In the face of setbacks, they need to be able to "pick themselves up, dust themselves off, and start over again."

## *What Characteristics Are Essential to Success in Retailing?*

This section discusses factors that may be helpful in deciding whether to open a retail business. In reviewing the factors, it is important to remember:

1. Not all successful people possess all of these characteristics in the same measure. An individual may be strong in some and not so strong in others. The more of them a person possesses, however, the more likely he or she is to succeed in retailing.
2. Many of the characteristics can be acquired if one sets out to do so with purpose.

### Risk-Taking
It may come as a surprise, but successful entrepreneurs prefer to take moderate rather than big risks. Moderate risks are defined as situations where the chances of winning are neither so small as to be a gamble nor so large that winning is assured. Remember, though, that every business has an element of risk. If it didn't, everybody would be in it.

### Dealing with Failure
The successful retailer can handle failure and setbacks. It is how successful retailers handle failure and not whether they have experienced failure that counts.

### Self-Confidence
The type of self-confidence useful in retailing is not necessarily being the life and soul of the party. Rather, the retailer needs to be self-reliant and trusting in his or her ability when the going gets tough. Successful executives do not trust luck, nor do they believe that their own success or the success of others is due to luck.

### Persistence and Determination
Persistence, determination, and the desire to overcome hurdles, solve problems, and complete the job are extremely important.

### Setting Objectives
Successful retail owners set clear goals and objectives. What does this mean? A world of difference exists between setting out to sell more merchandise this year,

and setting out to increase sales by 5 percent by the end of three months or 7 percent by the end of six months. Having clear objectives helps to concentrate effort and to achieve goals.

### Attitude about Feedback

Some people look for feedback on how well they are doing, while others prefer not to know. Successful retailers are continuously looking for feedback. They are as much, or more, interested in competing against their own standards as they are in competing against other people.

### Using Initiative and Taking Personal Responsibility

The successful retailer is likely to get frustrated if meetings or discussions drag on. More important, if the opportunity arises, they tend to take over running meetings and organizing activities of people. These are some of the characteristics of the successful retailer who likes to take on personal responsibility and who takes the initiative to solve a problem or provide leadership.

### Using Resources and Services

While the retailer is self-reliant and likes to take charge, successful retailers are also good at knowing when they need help. Thus, self-reliance is important but not to the exclusion of other sources of advice.

### Living with Uncertainty

One of the characteristics of ownership is risk; it also takes time to start a business. Both of these factors mean that the person who succeeds in retailing must be able to live with uncertainty and commit to something that, after a lot of effort, may not bear fruit for a couple of years.

### Drive and Energy

Successful retailers are generally recognized as having a high amount of energy and drive and as possessing a capacity to work long hours. Before considering starting and managing a retail business, the potential owner should examine critically the single overall factor more crucial to the business than any other—his or her set of personal characteristics. It is difficult to be realistic in a self-appraisal. However, the following guidelines might be of some help:

- What can the potential owner offer? Is the person prepared for life-style changes and a greater commitment to work?
- Can the person initially accept a lower standard of living?
- Can the person accept shorter leisure hours and make greater demands on his or her family?
- What is the person's state of health? Will it stand up to the heavy stresses of business and longer working hours?

# The Importance of Planning[7]

In beginning the new business, proper planning is the most important ingredient in success. As stated earlier, over half of all retail firms fail in their first five years. Effective planning will do more than anything else to help you avoid becoming a part of this alarming failure rate. Success and planning go together. The owner/manager should:

1. Plan together with partners/associates.
2. Make performance expectations clear to everyone.
3. Provide for feedback on progress to keep plans on track.
4. Make plans goal-oriented rather than activity-oriented.
5. Remember that hard work is vital to success, but this should be accompanied by efficient work.

## *Professionals Who Can Help Make It Go*

The retailer can improve the chances for success by securing the services of these professionals: lawyer, accountant, banker, insurance specialist, and other professional consultants. In planning the business, some basic questions also need to be considered:

- Why am I entering retailing?
- What business am I entering?
- What goods or services will I sell?
- What is my market and who is my consumer?
- Who is my competition?
- Can I compete successfully with my competition?
- What is my sales strategy?
- What marketing methods will I use?
- How much money is required?
- Where will the money come from?
- What technical and management skills do I need?
- Can I make just as much money working for someone else?

Answering the above questions honestly and objectively will help ensure that the new businessperson is well on the way to building a successful business plan.

## *The Business Plan*

A quality business plan can be important in many ways:

1. A business plan provides the retailer with a path to follow. It sets out goals and steps that allow the retailer to be in better control of steering the firm in the desired direction.
2. A business plan allows one's banker, accountant, lawyer, and insurance agent to know clearly what the business is trying to do. A plan will give them insight into the situation so that they can be of greater assistance to the business.

3. A business plan can help the owner communicate better with the staff, suppliers, and others about operations and objectives of the business.

4. A business plan can help the owner develop better management skills and abilities. It can help management consider competitive conditions, promotional opportunities, and what situations are most advantageous to the new business. In short, a business plan will help the owner to make sound business judgments.

There are no set requirements as to the contents of the plan. The contents depend on the type and size of the business being started. The most important consideration is the quality of the plan, not its length. The plan should include all aspects of the proposed business. Any possible problem areas in starting the venture should be listed with possible methods of dealing with them. Bankers would rather know the problems before the business is started than down the road where possible solutions may be limited. In fact, most major Canadian banks, including the Royal Bank and the Bank of Montreal, provide information on how to start a new business and how to prepare a business plan. Suggested contents for a business plan are provided in Table 7–3. Each plan will be different and subject to variations of this list, but these suggestions will at least help to get a plan started.[8]

## Operating Capital Needed

After the business plan is developed, sources of capital must be obtained. The nature of retailing affects the types of capital needed. The main thing to do is avoid an early shortage of funds. Therefore, retailers need to begin by estimating the capital needed to open a business. Many have a tendency to underestimate the needed opening capital.

Retailers need to plan for two categories of costs: (1) *opening costs,* which are one-time costs such as the cost of fixturing and decorating; and (2) *operating expenses,* which are the estimated ongoing expenses of running the business for a designated time period. Examples of both these costs are shown in Table 7–4.

### Developing a Cash Flow Forecast

Cash flow projections are helpful in planning for the opening and preparing for unforeseen difficulties, and they are a necessity when approaching a bank about loans.

A cash flow forecast is designed to predict when cash will be received by the firm and when payments need to be made. Cash inflow and outflow vary by type of retailer, especially for those that are seasonal and stock merchandise based on varying seasonal sales levels.

Management can use a cash budget, as shown in Table 7–5, to help estimate cash flow. Negative cash flow (when outlays exceed income) should be funded with the initial capital developed for the new venture. Retailers can base the projections on experience, an estimate published in trade magazines, and on information from their banker. A retailer should ideally know approximately what the operating costs and the cash inflow will be before opening the business. A person should have

---

**TABLE 7–3   Contents for a Business Plan**

---

1. A summary of the mission of the retail firm—a few paragraphs on what the owner is doing, and the plans for the future.
2. A paragraph each on the retail industry in the community as a whole, the company, and its products or services.
3. Market research and analysis:
   a. Consumers.
   b. Market size and trends.
   c. Competition.
   d. Estimated market share and sales.
4. Marketing plan:
   a. Overall marketing strategy.
   b. Merchandise and services.
   c. Pricing.
   d. Sales tactics.
   e. Advertising and promotion.
5. Management team:
   a. Organization.
   b. Key management personnel—who are they and what will they do?
   c. Ownership and compensation.
   d. Board of directors.
   e. Any supporting services.
6. The financial plan (you may need accounting help):
   a. Profit and loss forecasts.
   b. Pro forma cash flow analysis.
   c. Pro forma balance sheets.
7. Proposed company offering:
   a. Desired financing.
   b. Capitalization.
   c. Use of funds.
8. Overall schedule of activities for the next three years.

---

**TABLE 7–4   Opening Costs and Operating Expenses for a Typical Retail Business**

---

| *Opening Costs* | *Operating Expenses* |
|---|---|
| Inventory | Rent (including one month's deposit) |
| Fixtures and equipment | Taxes, licenses, and permits |
| Leasehold improvements (wiring, plumbing, lighting, air conditioning) | Advertising and promotion |
| | Legal and accounting fees |
| Security system | Wages (including owner's) |
| Exterior sign | Utilities |
| | Supplies |
| | Depreciation |
| | Insurance |
| | Maintenance and repair |
| | Auto expenses |
| | Miscellaneous |

---

TABLE 7–5   **Projected Cash Flow Budget for a Jewellery Firm for Three Months Ending December 19—**

|  | *October* | *November* | *December* |
|---|---|---|---|
| Anticipated cash receipts: |  |  |  |
| Cash sales | $53,000 | $58,000 | $66,000 |
| Payment for credit sales | 2,000 | 4,000 | 4,500 |
| Other income | — | — | — |
| Total receipts | 55,000 | 62,000 | 70,500 |
| Anticipated payments: | — | — | — |
| Cost of merchandise | 27,500 | 31,000 | 32,250 |
| Payroll | 20,000 | 21,000 | 21,500 |
| Promotion | 4,000 | 4,500 | 6,000 |
| Sales commissions | 1,200 | 1,300 | 1,600 |
| Loans to be repaid | 1,500 | 1,500 | 1,500 |
| Maintenance | — | 100 | 300 |
| Utilities | 600 | 600 | 700 |
| Outside accounting and legal fees | 400 | 2,000 | 1,300 |
| Total | 55,200 | 62,000 | 65,150 |
| Expected surplus at end of month | (200) | — | 5,350 |
| Desired cash operating balance | 2,000 | 2,000 | — |
| Short-term loan needed | 2,000 | 2,000 | — |
| Cash available | — | — | 5,350 |

enough money to cover all expenses for about six months. Management should be conservative if it is uncertain about how much money is needed. It should borrow too much rather than too little, in order to avoid having to come back later for additional funds.

As shown in Table 7–5, anticipated cash sales for a jewellery firm in the first three months of operation are $53,000, $58,000 and $66,000 per month. Average monthly sales based on a sales forecast of $750,000 are $62,500 ($750,000 divided by 12). Management expects a $200 loss at the end of the first month, to break even at the end of the second month, and to show a profit at the end of December. December is traditionally a very strong month for jewellery sales. Conceivably, the business could lose funds during the early part of the following year, since 30 percent or more of the jewellery sales typically are made the last three months of the year.

***Sources of Funds***   One way to illustrate how merchants can get the capital they need is by the use of a scenario. Suppose that the daughter of the owner of Jackson's jewellery store decides to go into business. She has worked for the family business for 10 years, in addition to part-time and summer work. She wants to be on her own, and her father has given his blessing. Using the logic suggested earlier in the chapter, young Jackson computes that she will need the following capital:

| | |
|---|---|
| Operating expenses for six months | $175,000 |
| Opening costs (fixtures, equipment, leasehold, improvements) | 50,000 |
| | $225,000 |

## Equity

Over the years, Jackson has saved and inherited enough to "comfortably" cover 45 percent of her capital needs. Thus, she needs an additional $123,750 ($225,000 × .55).

## Suppliers

Jackson's projected annual sales are $750,000. Assume a markup of 50 percent on retail and two merchandise turns per year. Retail markup is the difference between the invoice cost and the retail price. Merchandise turns are the number of times the average inventory is sold and replaced in a given time period. The computations are as follows:

$$\frac{\text{Projected annual sales} \times \text{Percent markup}}{\text{Number of turns}} = \frac{\$750,000 \times .50}{2} = \$187,500,$$

which is the total cost of inventory for 6 months.

The $187,500 must be financed. With terms of 30 days in payment (invoice must be paid within 30 days to maintain a good credit rating), with no discount for early payment, Jackson can probably get financing for one sixth (or 17 percent) of the inventory needed for one turnover period. A turnover period is six months (30 days is one sixth of the six-month turnover period based on two turns per year). Thus, the amount financed by suppliers will be:

$$\$187,500 \times .17 = \$31,875.$$

Thus, Jackson still needs $91,875 additional capital ($123,750 − $31,875 = $91,875).

## Financial Institutions and Government

With her relatively healthy equity investment, Jackson would probably have success in securing loans from banks to assist in financing inventory and accounts receivable as well as some fixed assets. The Federal Business Development Bank is a source of government funds, as is the Small Business Office of the Ministry of Industry, Trade and Technology, which has developed a loan guarantee plan. At the provincial level, a number of provinces have established small business development departments that may also provide assistance.

To continue the scenario, assume that Jackson secured her permanent capital needs. Her jewellery store has been in operation for some time. She has brought in additional partners as owners; she has increased her sales; her receivables have grown; and she needs more financing.

Jackson can generate her capital needs to meet these new obligations either from internal or external sources. The major way to generate capital inside the firm is from profitable operations. Her external sources of capital have been discussed above, except that once the business is profitable, she may be able to issue stock or perhaps bonds if the business is a corporation.

# Organizing

Decisions must also be made on how the retail firm will be organized. Most merchants are all-arounders. They do all jobs as the need arises, or assign tasks to various employees on a random, nonspecialized basis. Small merchants don't think of setting up distinct functions and lines for the flow of authority, nor do they select specialists to handle each function. As a store grows, however, specialization becomes necessary.

## *Basic Organization Principles*

Before discussing organization structure, certain management principles must be taken into consideration in organizing the firm. Four organization principles are important here. They are:

1. Specialization of labour.
2. Departmentalization.
3. Span of control.
4. Unity of command.

These four principles are reflected in the organization chart of the retail firm.

### Specialization

Modern business organizations are built on the concept of **specialization.** More and better work is performed at less cost when it is done by specialists than when it is done by employees who shift from one job to another and who continually improvise.

Specialization is of two kinds: tasks and people. Specialization of tasks narrows a person's activities to a specific area. For example, various billing procedures may be assigned to a particular employee who can quickly become proficient at this specialty. This can increase productivity because the employee becomes very efficient at this activity.

Specialization of people does not involve simplifying the job but developing a person to perform a certain job better than someone else can. Training and experience improve the quality and quantity of the particular type of work. For example, customer service personnel can focus on becoming experts at handling customer complaints. In smaller retail stores, most of the specialization is of the second type, but in larger stores there is a need for narrow task specialization. For example, certain records must be kept, and certain phases of merchandise handling must be done by a well-trained person.

### Departmentalization

Management will probably find that it can use **departmentalization** where jobs are grouped into categories such as the following (each requiring a certain combination of skills for good performance):

- Merchandising—including buying and managing inventory for different groups of merchandise.
- Direct and general selling and adjustments—customer contact.
- Sales promotion—largely concerning advertising and display.
- Accounting and finance—records, correspondence, cash handling, insurance, and perhaps credit.
- Store operation—problems having to do with building, equipment, and safety measures.
- Merchandise handling—receiving, marking, storing, and delivering.
- Personnel—employment, training, employee benefits, and personnel records.

Recognizing the many functions to be performed in the firm doesn't mean a specialist is necessary for each of them. Management can combine and delegate some functions. But management should look ahead and have an organization plan that provides for various specialized positions when they are needed.

### Span of Control

**Span-of-control** addresses the question of how many subordinates should report to a supervisor. Generally, a supervisor's span of control should be small because an individual can work effectively with only a limited number of people at one time. Span of control, however, depends on factors such as the competence of the supervisor and subordinates, the nature of the functions to be performed, and the physical location of the persons involved.

### Unity of Command

The **unity-of-command** concept involves a series of superior/subordinate relationships. This concept states that any employee should be supervised by only one person. Thus, an employee should receive decision-making power from and report to only one supervisor. An unbroken chain of command should exist from top to bottom. Otherwise, frustration and confusion will occur.

*How to Organize for Profitable Operations*

The two functions that probably will be organized first are *merchandising* and *operations,* or store management. Such an organization would look like the one illustrated in Figure 7–1.

The *merchandise manager* is responsible for buying and selling. As well, the manager supervises and/or prepares merchandise budgets, handles advertising,

**FIGURE 7–1**

*The simplest organization*

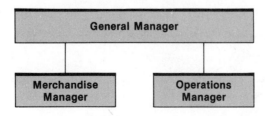

displays, and other promotions, and is responsible for inventory planning and control.

The *operations manager* is responsible for building upkeep, delivery, stockroom(s), service, supplies, equipment purchasing, and similar activities.

As a store continues to grow in size, specialization of labour occurs. The organization structure may begin to look like the one in Figure 7–2. After merchandise and operations managers, the next managers who would be added are financial, promotion, and personnel managers. The financial manager, or controller, handles the finances of the firm and probably has an accounting background. The organizational structure in Figure 7–2 is typical of many department stores.

## *Organizing in the Branching Era*

The typical organization plan, illustrated in Figure 7–2, gives the merchandising manager responsibility for both buying and selling. But in the late 1940s, shopping centres were developed, and downtown stores ''branched'' to the shopping centres. The merchandise manager became responsible not only for buying and selling merchandise in the downtown (main) store but also in the branches. This situation proved to be difficult. One merchandise manager could not be responsible for buying, supervising sales, and general management of the main store and the branch stores as well. So, a trend developed during this branching era to separate the buying and selling functions.

### Separation of Buying and Selling

There are arguments for and against the separation of the buying and selling responsibilities in an organization. Those opposing the separation of the two functions argue that:

1. The buyer must have contact with consumers to be able to interpret their needs.
2. Those who buy merchandise should also be responsible for selling it.
3. It is easier to pinpoint merchandising successes and failures when the two functions are combined.

**FIGURE 7–2**

*Five function organizational plan*

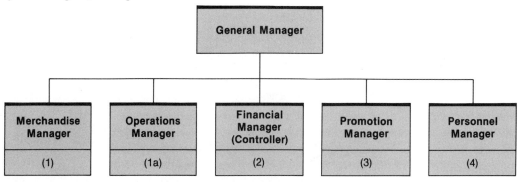

Those who favour the separation of the two functions argue that:

1. If the two functions are combined, buying is likely to have more importance than selling.
2. Buying and selling require two different types of job skills.
3. With technology, reports, and the like, it is not necessary for the two functions to be combined.
4. Salespeople can be shifted more easily when the two functions are separate.

The arguments against separating the buying and selling functions do not seem as strong as the counterarguments. The branch store problem seems to demand separation. Thus, the trend is to separate the two. Figure 7–3 shows a department store that is organized for the separation of buying and selling. The general merchandise manager is responsible for buying, and the vice president for branch stores is responsible for selling.

**FIGURE 7–3**

*Organization for separation of buying and selling*

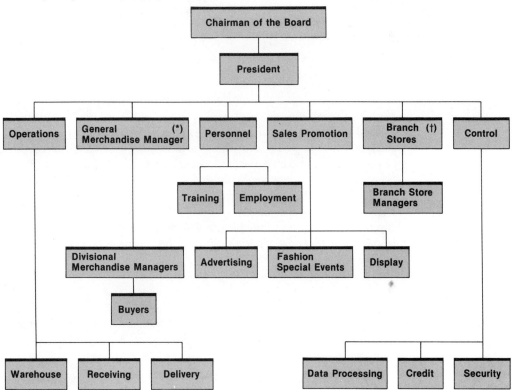

*Buying functions.
†Selling functions.

Retail Highlight 7–1

# Mr. Sam's Thoughts on Organizing

Sam Walton, who died in 1992, built the world's largest retail chain, Wal-Mart, with more than 2,000 stores and sales of over $55 billion. Recognized as one of the best and brightest retailers ever, he offered these thoughts on organizing a retail firm:

- Keep your ear to the ground. Managers and buyers should spend most of their time in stores seeing what customers are or are not buying.
- Push responsibility and authority down. As companies (like Wal-Mart) get bigger, it becomes more important to shift responsibility and authority toward the front lines, toward that department manager who is stocking the shelves and talking to the customer.
- Force ideas to bubble up. Encourage store employees to push their ideas up through the system.
- Stay lean and fight bureaucracy. If you are not serving the customer or supporting the folks who do, Wal-Mart doesn't need you.

Wal-Mart also has a profit-sharing plan that all employees can participate in. Sam Walton felt this was critical to Wal-Mart's success because the salespeople feel that they are part of the company and treat customers better than salespeople in other stores do.

Source: "Sam Walton in His Own Words," *Fortune,* June 29, 1992, pp. 98–106.

Food stores could have faced the same conflict, but their expansion history actually solved their problems. Rather than branching, these companies expanded as chain store organizations. No main stores exist in a chain organization. Buying and selling are always separated. Many Canadian retailers, including Loblaws, have buyers who focus on maximizing the rate of return on shelf space investment.[9] Using computer analysis, Loblaws' buyers know the volume and rate of return that competitive products are delivering to a store. More recently, a new buyer/seller relationship is evolving where the buyer works very closely with the seller to develop a mutually beneficial partnership. Called *reverse marketing,* it reflects the proactive stance taken by many buyers today.[10]

### Chain Store Organization

Certain features of a chain should be explained, since major differences exist between a chain organization and a branch store arrangement. Some of the differences are as follows:

1. In a chain, responsibility is more centralized in the headquarters, or home office.
2. More divisions exist in a chain organization, such as real estate, transportation, warehousing, public relations, and legal divisions.

3. The chain organization has tighter supervision of store activities.

4. The chain probably has more reports for control purposes.

For some thoughts on organizing from the individual who built the world's largest retail chain, see Retail Highlight 7–1.

**Recent Trends in Organizing**

With the intense competitive pressures facing Canadian retailers, some have changed their organization structures to better respond to the needs of required or local markets. For example, a number of chains, including Dylex and the Hudson's Bay Company, have moved to greater centralized buying in order to achieve greater economies of scale and buying power. At the same time, these chains are providing more flexibility for individual store managers to select a merchandise mix that reflects local market needs. The link between buying and selling is provided by sophisticated computer information systems that allow managers to identify merchandise sales trends at the store, regional, and national levels.[11]

# Chapter Highlights

- The main risk of ownership of a retail business is the possibility of failure, but the main benefit is the independence of being your own boss. The important traits for success as a retail owner/manager include self-confidence, willingness to take risks, persistence and determination, initiative, a high level of drive and energy, and the ability to live with uncertainty. The most common reasons for failure in retailing are management incompetence, unbalanced experience, and the lack of experience in the line of trade. Failure because of neglect, fraud, or disaster is unusual.

- Retailers have the choice of forming a new business as a sole proprietorship, a partnership, or a corporation. Also, they can operate as an independent firm or become part of a marketing system. The major differences between a sole proprietorship, a partnership, and a corporation are in terms of organization (sole proprietorships are easiest to organize), ability to raise capital (partnerships and corporations have greater access to capital), and financial liability (corporations have limited financial liability).

- Many persons enter retailing by buying an existing business. Such persons have to decide on the type of business they want to buy based on their interests, skills, and experience as well as the financing they can arrange. Available opportunities for buying

a business can be discovered by working with business brokers and realtors, by studying newspaper ads, and by contacts with trade sources. In making the decision on whether to buy a business, the potential buyer should determine the reasons the business is for sale, whether a profit is being earned, the operating ratios of the business as compared to industry averages, and the worth of the business assets.

- Proper planning is the most important ingredient for success in starting a business. The business plan includes setting clear performance objectives, measuring progress towards achieving the objectives, and addressing basic questions in preparing the plan.

- Capital is needed for two categories of cost in starting a business: (1) opening costs, which are one-time costs; and (2) operating expenses, which are the estimated ongoing expenses of running the business. Sources of cash include owners' equity, the credit available from suppliers, loans from financial institutions and governments, and the sale of stock.

- Basic organizational principles are specialization of labour, departmentalization, span-of-control, and unity of command. The two functions that probably will be organized first in a retail store are merchandising and operations.

## Key Terms

Corporation    172
Departmentalization    182
Partnership    170
Private corporation    172
Public corporation    172

Sole proprietorship    170
Span of control    183
Specialization    182
Unity of command    183

## Discussion Questions

1. Why are the risks of business ownership so high today?

2. What are the major causes of retail business failure?

3. Evaluate the three forms of business ownership (sole proprietorship, partnership, and corporation) in terms of the strengths and weaknesses of each.

4. What is the difference between the following: general partnership, limited partner, silent partner, and secret partner?

5. What is the difference between a public corporation and a private corporation?

6. How does a retailer determine the amount of capital needed?

7. Describe the various sources of capital that are available to a retailer opening a new retail operation.

8. Discuss the following four principles of organization: specialization of labour, departmentalization, span of control, and unity of command.

## Application Exercises

1. Visit four independent retail firms in your community that have opened in the last five years. Identify the factors that prompted their owner/managers to go into their businesses, the backgrounds of the owners prior to entering their businesses, the biggest mistakes the owners have made thus far, and the advice the owner/managers would offer to individuals contemplating opening a new retail business. Write a brief essay that summarizes your findings.

2. Review the material in the chapter on the characteristics essential for success. Interview three people employed in retailing—an owner/manager, a manager, and a clerk—and ask them to what extent they agree with each of the characteristics. Write a brief report that summarizes your findings.

3. Talk to three buyers in retail stores in your community. Ask for their views on the separation of the buying and selling responsibilities within a retail organization. Prepare a brief report on your findings.

## Suggested Cases

# Endnotes

1. David A. Whyte, "Interest Rates as a Factor in Small Business Failures," *Journal of Small Business—Canada* 2, Winter 1984/85, pp. 44–66.

2. Russell M. Knight, "Business Growth and Job Creation in Canada 1978–1986," *Journal of Small Business and Entrepreneurship* 6, Fall 1988, pp. 29–39.

3. See *The Canadian Business Failure Rate,* Dun and Bradstreet, various years, since 1985. For further reading on small-business failures in Canada, see: A. Bakr Ibrahim, "Is Franchising the Answer to Small Business Failure Rate? An Empirical Study," *Journal of Small Business and Entrepreneurship* 3, Fall 1985, pp. 48–54; and A. Bakr Ibrahim and W. Ellis, "An Empirical Investigation of Causes of Failure in Small Business and Strategies to Reduce It," *Journal of Small Business and Entrepreneurship* 4, Spring 1987, pp. 18–24.

4. Alan Toulin, "Ottawa Attacked over Record Bankruptcies," *The Financial Post,* February 5, 1992, p. 3; and *Canadian Economic Observer,* Statistics Canada, Catalog 11–010, May 1992.

5. See, for example, *Canadian Business Financial Ratios,* Dun and Bradstreet.

6. Adapted from Dennis Moynihan, *A Business of Your Own* (Irish Productivity Center, 1984).

7. Adapted from K. Mark Weaver, "The Importance of Planning," in *How to Start a Successful New Business* (Tuscaloosa, Ala.: West Alabama Chamber of Commerce, undated).

8. For further insights on preparing a retail plan, see John C. Williams and John A. Torella, *Strategic Retail Marketing* (Toronto: Retail Council of Canada, 1984).

9. John Oldland, "Beware of New Breed of Buyer," *Marketing,* June 5, 1989, p. 14.

10. Michiel R. Leenders and David L. Blenkhorn, *Reverse Marketing: The New Buyer-Supplier Relationship* (New York: Free Press, 1988).

11. Dylex, Annual Report, 1991; and Hudson's Bay Company, Annual Report, 1991.

# 8    FRANCHISING

---

## Chapter Objectives

After reading this chapter, you should be able to:

1 Discuss the importance of franchising in the Canadian economy.
2 Evaluate the advantages and disadvantages of becoming a franchisee.
3 Describe the basic types of franchise arrangements.
4 List the types of costs involved in becoming a franchisee.
5 Evaluate franchise opportunities.
6 Explain the items contained in a typical franchise contract.
7 Discuss the trends and outlook for franchising.

**Retailing Capsule**

In 1978, Adrienne Stringer founded Molly Maid Home Care Services Ltd. in Toronto for $15,000. Her concept was simple: Offer customers a professional cleaning job for a reasonable price. Two-person teams in uniforms, including maids' caps, were trained to clean houses in an efficient manner. One year later, Ms. Stringer was overwhelmed by the demand (sales had reached $80,000), imitators were rapidly entering the market, and she felt that she didn't have the resources or the business expertise to expand the business.

Enter Jim McKenzie, an experienced business executive, who wanted to start a business catering to the working woman. He had tried one franchise, buying the Canadian rights to a U.S. chain of hairdressing salons, but it had failed. He contacted Ms. Stringer when she was considering selling the business, and they struck a deal designed to make Molly Maid a household name throughout Canada.

Since then, Molly Maid has been franchised across Canada, and Stringer and McKenzie have extended the venture to the United States and the United Kingdom. Annual sales exceed $28 million, with $15 million of the total generated by the over 160 franchisees in Canada. One of the reasons for their success is that the market is growing rapidly. In over 60 percent of all families with children, both parents are working outside the home, a dramatic increase in the past 15 years. Working parents are willing to pay for a clean house so they can have more time for other activities. In fact, 80 percent of Molly Maid's customers are dual-wage families, and 90 percent have household incomes above $30,000 per year.

The current market for house-cleaning services in Canada is estimated to be worth $100 million a year. But high growth is not the only reason for Molly

*(continued on next page)*

A **franchise contract** is a legal document that enables a firm (the **franchisor**) to expand by allowing an independent business person (the **franchisee**) to use the franchisor's operating methods, financing systems, trademarks, and products in return for the payment of a fee. Franchisors may sell products, sell or lease equipment, or even sell or rent the site and premises.

Franchising is one of the fastest-growing segments of retailing in Canada and accounts for about 35 percent of all retail sales. Experts predict continued growth in new franchises and sales.[1]

Franchises exist in virtually every line of trade today, including lawn care, maid services, baby-sitters, dentists, tutors, funeral homes, dating services, skin care centres, and legal offices, among many others. About 1,300 franchising companies are operating in Canada today, with over 50,000 outlets across the country. Surprisingly, even though many of the best-known franchises are the foreign giants—McDonald's, Burger King, Kentucky Fried Chicken—nearly 75 percent

*Retailing Capsule continued*

Maid's success. A number of home-cleaning franchises have folded, and the next largest franchise—Mini Maid—is only doing half the business of Molly Maid. Molly Maid has tried to ensure its continuing success by carefully selecting the franchisees and providing them with extensive training. New franchisees spend a week in training, followed by regular seminars that cover all aspects of the business, including employee supervision and customer relations. In addition, field supervisors provide franchisees with advice and reassurance.

Molly Maid also excels at promotion. For example, *Canadian Living* magazine ran a contest, and the grand prize was a year's free cleaning by Molly Maid. More than 16,000 readers entered, eight times the average for these competitions. And, after the company cleaned its 1 millionth home, it hung 500,000 "Thanks a Million" doorhangers in prime locations.

A Molly Maid franchise now costs $11,000, with start-up costs an additional $3,000. The franchisee pays a royalty fee of 6 percent of sales and an advertising fee of 2 percent of sales. The average sales per franchise are between $100,000 and $150,000 each year, and the average franchisee nets $30,000. The biggest problem is to attract and keep maids, and Molly Maid is doing its best with a newsletter, the occasional freebie, and weekly wages of $150 to $250. Molly Maid appears to be a well run franchise where both the franchisor and franchisees are happy—key ingredients for future prosperity.

Source: Based on an article by Rona Maynard, "Mop Your Way to Millions," *Report on Business,* September 1987, pp. 38–44.

of all franchises in Canada were started in Canada. From Shoppers Drug Mart to Canadian Tire, from Provi-Soir to Tim Horton Donuts, from Becker's to Beaver Lumber, numerous franchises are owned and operated by Canadians.[2]

Franchising has become a powerful force partly because economic factors have made growth through company-owned units difficult for many businesses. Therefore, by emphasizing independent ownership, franchising provides an effective method of overcoming such problems as shortage of capital, high interest rates, and finding and hiring competent employees.

# Advantages of Becoming a Franchisee

A number of advantages exist for franchisees as part of a franchising program. The advantages include training programs that teach the retailer how to operate the business. Also, such programs allow individuals to enter a business with no previous experience. Less cash may be required to enter the business, since the franchisor is often willing to provide credit to a prospective franchisee.

The purchasing power of the franchisor can result in lower costs and higher gross profits for the franchisee. The franchisee also benefits from the national advertising and promotion by the franchisor, which exceeds the advertising of

*McDonald's, one of the most successful franchise operations in the world.*

Source: Photo by James Hertel.

conventional independent businesses. Additionally, up-to-date merchandise assistance, displays, and other materials are prepared by the franchisor and distributed to franchisees.

An equally important advantage is the program of research and development that is designed to improve the product or service. Firms such as Wendy's and McDonald's have regular, ongoing programs of research designed to identify new menu additions to help increase the sales base. Franchisees may also have access to a variety of fringe benefits such as dental plans at lower rates than are available to independent retailers.

The franchisor can also provide advice for handling special problems. Help is available in site selection, record-keeping, taxes, and other issues. As a result, around 90 percent of all franchises succeed in Canada, whereas around 80 percent of all new small businesses fail. However, these statistics are somewhat misleading, as the top 20 franchise operations account for over 80 percent of the business. More than 50 percent of Canadian franchisors have been in business for less than five years and most of these for less than two years. While the well-established franchises have excellent track records, some of the newer companies may not be as successful.[3] Oversaturation is also a problem in the franchise area. Two of the hot franchises of the 1980s—fast-food restaurants and quick printing shops—declined during the early 90s, and some went bankrupt due to the recession and over-saturation.[4]

## Disadvantages of Becoming a Franchisee

Disadvantages to franchising do exist. A major problem is the high cost of the franchise. Many franchisees feel they have to pay too much for supplies, fees, and other arrangements. In some cases, franchisees have found that they could purchase their supplies for less and have more favourable credit and payment terms if they dealt directly with a supplier rather than the franchisor.[5]

Also, the franchisee gives up flexibility in return for the right to a franchise. Operations are handled centrally at the corporate office, and standard policies apply to all outlets. Individuals who want to run a business their own way would probably find a franchise unsuitable because of the inflexible nature of franchise operations. The rigidity that results from centralized operations can also be detrimental to franchisees who face unusual local market conditions.

Decisions on how profits are to be shared between the franchisor and the franchisee typically favour the franchisor because of its financial strength. However, the major complaint typically is the nature of the contract itself. Often, franchisees do not understand the document. They also have problems in terminating a franchise, as the conditions of termination also typically favour the franchisor.

Another problem is that the overall franchise may get into trouble, creating problems for both the franchisor and the franchisee. Burger King, faced with intense competition in the fast-food business, tried a strategy of discounting and coupon promotions to hold market share during the 1991–92 recession, but these tactics led to reduced profits for the franchisees. As well, the franchise had internal problems, including rapid management turnover and erratic advertising. The result was that Burger King was reduced from 202 to 172 stores in Canada within two years. Franchise agreements were cancelled, franchisees sued Burger King, and one franchisee withdrew 15 restaurants from the chain.[6]

### The Franchisor's Perspective

From the franchisor's perspective, the primary advantage in franchising is the opportunity to enjoy rapid expansion without decreasing the ownership or working capital of the company. Even a large firm like Beaver Lumber, owned by The Molson Companies, decided that it could gain greater market share without stretching its financial resources by franchising stores. It began franchising in 1977, and of over 200 Beaver Lumber outlets today, over 60 percent are franchised.

However, one of the serious problems facing franchisors is finding management with the ambition and incentive to make a franchise a success. Still, the franchise system is often better than hiring employee/managers, since the franchisee has a financial investment in the outlet and can benefit directly from its profits.

## Types of Franchises

Franchises are of two basic types. The first is **product** and **trade-name franchising** such as used by automobile dealers and gasoline outlets. The second is **business format franchising,** in which firms that have developed a unique method of performing a service or of doing business decide to expand by selling the rights to use the concept.

*Product and Trade-Name Franchising*

Product and trade-name franchising began as an independent sales relationship between a supplier and a dealer where the dealer acquired some of the identity of the supplier. Franchised dealers concentrate on one company's product line and to some extent identify their business with that company. Typical of this segment of franchising are automobile and truck dealers (Ford, Chrysler, General Motors), gasoline service stations (Petro Canada, Sunoco), and soft drink bottlers (Pepsi Cola). This type of franchise dominates the field, accounting for over one half of all franchise sales in Canada. For strategic reasons, Coca Cola began buying back its franchisees in Canada in 1986, and now only 3 percent of its sales are accounted for by franchisees.[7] Recently, Pepsi Cola Canada also began buying back its franchises.

*Business Format Franchising*

Business format franchising is characterized by an ongoing business relationship between the franchisor and the franchisee that includes not only the product, service, and trademark, but the entire business format. Such franchises include a marketing strategy and plan, operating manuals and standards, quality control, and continuing two-way communications. Restaurants (Smitty's Family Restaurants), nonfood retailing (Color Your World, Cyclepath), personal and business services (Uniglobe), rental services (Rent-A-Wreck, Jumbo Video), real estate services (Re/Max), and a long list of other service businesses fall into the category of business format franchising. Business format franchising has been responsible for much of the growth of franchising in Canada and will probably continue to offer excellent opportunities. The top 10 Canadian business format franchises are presented in Table 8–1.

---

**TABLE 8–1    Top Ten Canadian Business Format Franchises**

| Rank | Franchise | Type of Business | Gross Revenue | Number of Franchises |
|---|---|---|---|---|
| 1 | Shoppers Drug Mart | Pharmacy | $2,356,000,000 | 612* |
| 2 | McDonald's | Fast food | 1,500,000,000 | 302* |
| 3 | Beaver Lumber | Building materials | 902,000,000 | 123* |
| 4 | Goodyear Tire Centre | Automotive service | 695,534,000 | 18* |
| 5 | Kentucky Fried Chicken | Fast food | 500,000,000 | 767 |
| 6 | Provi-Soir | Convenience stores | 500,000,000 | 233* |
| 7 | Re/Max | Real estate | 490,200,000 | 362 |
| 8 | Marlin Travel | Travel agency | 400,000,000 | 100* |
| 9 | Becker's | Convenience stores | 313,000,000 | 80* |
| 10 | Century 21 | Real estate | 269,100,000 | 424 |

*In addition, the franchisor also operates its own outlets.

SOURCE: "Canada's Top 75 Franchises," *Financial Times of Canada,* June 6, 1988; and "Fast-Growing Franchises," *Canadian Business,* June 1989, pp. 18–19.

# Elements of an Ideal Franchise Programme

Successful franchises have a number of characteristics (shown in Table 8–2) that are also appropriate to the services field, a rapidly growing area of business format franchising. An important ingredient for a franchising programme is a line of merchandise with high gross margins. High margins are needed to cover the annual franchise fee, operating expenses, and profits. As an example, personal services have sufficient gross margins to make franchising a good operating vehicle. A major advantage of a franchising programme is the ability to quickly expand a store network with limited capital.

# Forms of Franchise Arrangements

Product and trade-name franchises and business format franchises can assume a variety of forms. The franchisor may sell individual franchises to persons who will develop each one. Alternatively, franchisors may sell **master franchises,** or **area-development franchises.**

Master franchisees buy the rights to an extensive geographic area but do not build and operate franchises. Rather, they divide the area into segments and sell the rights within the territory to individual franchisees. Franchisors often are attracted to the master franchise concept because it is easier for corporate management to work with one large franchisee than many small ones. Persons granted such franchises have substantial financial strength, which increases their likelihood of success.

A second alternative is the area-development franchise. The franchisees purchase a large territory and open a large number of shops themselves.

## *Franchising Formats*

Franchises can assume a variety of formats. In **mobile franchises,** business is done from a mobile vehicle. Snap-On Tools of Canada is an example of this type of

---

**TABLE 8–2    Elements of an Ideal Franchise Programme**

*High gross margin*—In order for the franchisee to be able to afford a high franchise fee (which the franchisor needs), it is necessary to operate on a high gross margin percentage. This explains the widespread application of franchising in the food and service industries.

*In-store value added*—Franchising works best in those product categories where the product is at least partially processed in the store. Such environments require constant on-site supervision—a chronic problem for company-owned stores using a hired manager. Owners simply are willing to work harder over longer hours.

*Secret processes*—Concepts, formulas, or products that the franchise can't duplicate without joining the franchise program.

*Real estate profits*—The franchisor uses income from ownership of property as a significant revenue source.

*Simplicity*—The most successful franchises have been those that operate on automatic pilot. All the key decisions have been thought through, and the owner merely implements the decisions.

SOURCE: Philip D. White and Albert D. Bates, "Franchising Will Remain Retailing Fixture, but Its Salad Days Have Long Since Gone," *Marketing News,* February 17, 1984, p. 14. Reprinted by permission.

franchise. **Distributorships** include systems where franchisees maintain warehouse stocks to supply other franchisees. The distributor takes title to the goods and provides services to other customers.

**Co-ownership** and **comanagement franchises** are those in which the franchisor has an ownership interest in the operation. One example is the Travelodge motel system. **Service franchises** are those in which franchisors license persons to dispense a service under a trade name. H&R Block, First Choice Haircutters, Kwick Kopy Printing, and Weed Man are examples of this type of franchise.

# The Costs of Franchising

Typically, a franchisee agrees to sell a product or service under contract and to follow the franchisor's formula. The franchisor is normally paid an initial fee for the right to operate at a particular location and a franchise fee based on monthly sales. The various costs involved in becoming a franchisee can include the initial cost, the franchise fee, opening costs, working capital, premises expenses, site evaluation fees, royalties and service fees, and promotion charges. Each cost is briefly described below.

- *Initial costs:* Franchisees typically must pay an initial sum for the right to operate under the terms and conditions of the franchise. The amount may be only a down payment, with the remainder financed by the franchisor or from other financing sources.
- *Franchise fee:* The right to use the trademark, license, service mark, or other operating procedures of the franchise.
- *Opening costs:* Payments for equipment, inventory, and fixtures.
- *Working capital:* The operating expenses needed until the business breaks even.
- *Premises costs:* The costs of building, remodeling, and decorating.
- *Site evaluation fee:* The charge by the franchisor to determine the market potential at alternative sites.
- *Royalties:* A continuing service charge or payment based on monthly gross sales. In return for the charge, the franchisor provides such services as product research, management advice, accounting services, inventory records, and similar activities.
- *Promotion costs:* A percentage of gross sales, normally 1 or 2 percent, to support local advertising and promotion.

Typical franchise fees are structured as follows:

- *Becker's:* Franchisees pay a $25,000 franchise fee and require $125,000 in start-up costs. They also pay a 5 percent royalty on gross sales. Financing assistance is available from the parent company.

- *Wendy's:* To be considered seriously for a franchise, an individual needs between $600,000 and $800,000 to start the business. These funds allow the franchisee to lease or buy the land, the building, and the equipment, purchase supplies, and hire employees. Franchisees are charged a $35,000 franchise fee for technical assistance, for each restaurant. Franchisees pay 4 percent of gross sales as royalties and a further 4 percent for advertising.
- *McDonald's:* Franchisees invest, on average, $700,000 to open a new outlet. The money pays for the equipment within the store and entitles the franchisees to a 20-year operating license. Additionally, the franchisee pays fees generally totalling about 11.5 percent of annual gross sales in return for services that include training for management and crews, operating assistance, marketing, financial advice, and menu research.
- *College Pro Painters:* There is no franchise fee, and the start-up costs are estimated at $2,000 to $3,000. The royalty fee ranges between 14 and 17 percent of gross sales. All College Pro franchisees start out as university or college students.
- *Print Three:* Franchisees pay a franchise fee of $42,000, and the minimum start-up fee is $130,000. They are required to pay up to 6 percent of gross sales for royalty fees and 3 percent for advertising. The franchisor will help with financing.

## Identifying Franchise Opportunities

Franchise opportunities are easy to identify. Choosing the right one is difficult. Intense competition exists among franchisors in attracting interested franchisees, and advertisements for franchise opportunities are common in many newspapers. Both *The Financial Post* and the *Financial Times of Canada* have an advertising section devoted to franchise opportunities ranging from travel agencies to submarine sandwich shops to total body care retail concepts. Various publications also provide information on available franchises. The *Franchise Annual* contains listings of Canadian franchise opportunities.[8] *The Rating Guide to Franchises* rates a number of franchises, including some Canadian operations.[9] Each franchise is rated on six criteria: industry experience, franchising experience, financial strength, training and services, fees and royalties, and satisfied franchisees. Each criterion receives a rating of from one to four stars. Business fairs are also held at which franchisors try to attract franchisees.

## Evaluating the Franchise and the Franchise Company

Potential franchisees should consider carefully all factors before buying a franchise, including examining such legal aspects as existing legislation and the terms of the franchise contract and evaluating the franchisor and its product or service.

*Provincial Legislation*

Alberta is the only province in Canada that has regulations governing franchising companies.[10] The Alberta Franchise Act is designed to protect potential franchisees by requiring the franchisor to provide complete disclosure of all the facts relating to the franchise being offered. A prospectus must be filed with the Alberta Securities Commission outlining the franchisor's financial capabilities, the history of the franchise company, and its principals. Potential franchisees in Alberta are entitled to a copy of the prospectus. Because most Canadian franchisees are not protected by specific legislation, individuals considering buying a franchise should proceed with caution, and a lawyer should be consulted before any franchise purchase is made.

*Evaluating the Company*

The franchising company should have a good credit rating, a strong financial position, and a favourable reputation in the business community. The firm also should have been in business for a sufficient period of time to demonstrate expertise and the ability of its products or services to prosper in a competitive environment. The local and national offices of the Better Business Bureau should be contacted to determine if there have been complaints about the franchise company and, if so, how they were resolved. Also, the Canadian Franchise Association and the appropriate provincial Ministry of Consumer Affairs should be contacted about the reputation of the company and its product.[11] Various books and other information sources are also available to help guide the potential franchisee through the evaluation process.[12]

*Evaluating the Product or Service*

Interested buyers should make sure the product or service has been tested in the marketplace before signing a franchise agreement. An independent investigation to determine the likelihood for the franchise's success in a local market is also in order. Equally important is an evaluation of the product warranties as part of the franchise agreement. The prospective buyer should understand the terms and conditions of the warranty, who is issuing the warranty, and the reputation of the company for keeping its promises. The buyer should also determine the legitimacy of claimed trademarks, service marks, trade names, and copyrights.

*Understanding the Franchise Contract*

The franchise contract varies by franchisor. The contract is a legal document that specifies the rights and responsibilities of the franchisor. The advice of a lawyer should be sought before signing the document. The critical areas to be considered in deciding whether to sign a franchise agreement include the nature of the company, the product, the territory, the contract, and assistance available.

All franchise contracts contain a variety of provisions to which the franchisee must agree. For example, the franchisee typically must agree to abide by the operating hours established by the franchisor. The franchisee often must also agree to use a standardized accounting system, follow companywide personnel policies, carry a minimum level of insurance, use supplies approved by the franchisor, and follow the pricing policies established by the franchisor.

The franchisor often retains the right to require the franchisee to periodically remodel his or her establishment(s) and to allow the franchisor to conduct unscheduled inspections. Territorial restrictions are typically stated in the contract agreement, and provisions for expanding into additional territories are carefully stated.

Some contracts impose sales quotas that are designed to ensure that the franchisee vigorously pursues sales opportunities in the territory. Most contracts also prohibit a franchisee from operating competing businesses and prohibit an individual whose franchise has been terminated from opening a similar type of business for a specified period of time.

Most franchise contracts cover a minimum period of 15 years. They typically contain provisions for termination and renewal of the contract, the franchisee's right to sell or transfer the business, and a provision for arbitration of disputes between the franchisor and the franchisee.

### Termination

Franchise contracts typically contain a provision for cancellation by either party upon 30 to 60 days' notice. Normally, franchises can only be terminated when the franchisee fails to meet the conditions of the franchise contract, including minimum payments required, sales quotas, and the need to keep the premises in good condition.

### Renewal

The franchisor can refuse to renew the contract of any franchisee who does not fully comply with the terms of the contract, including maintaining required quality standards. Termination provisions give the franchisor substantial power over franchisees.

### Transferring a Franchise

The franchisee normally does not have the right to sell or transfer the franchise to a third party without the concurrence of the franchisor. However, sale or transfer to a third party typically is not a problem.

### Buy-Back Provisions

The franchisor often has the option to purchase a franchise unit or the inventory if the franchisee decides to sell. The buy-back provision is an advantage to the franchisee because it can provide a ready sale for the outlet.

Deciding on the price for the sale is often not easy. Some franchisors will offer a price that will only cover the value of the building and the equipment and will not consider payment for goodwill. Goodwill is the price set for the intangible assets of a business, including its future earning power and its condition at the time of the sale. Franchisors often maintain that the goodwill of the business is reflected in the trademark or trade name.

### Arbitration Provisions

**Arbitration** is the settlement of a dispute by a person or persons chosen to hear both sides and come to a decision. Arbitration may be used to settle disputes between franchisors and franchisees. It is faster and less expensive than litigation and, in Canada, most problems are settled by arbitration, not by the courts.[13]

*Franchisee Associations*

Some franchisees have established **franchisee associations** to represent individual owners in dealing with the franchisor. The purpose of joining together is to allow the franchisees to accomplish common goals and to exert greater power over the franchisor in resolving issues that are of concern to the individual franchisees. The franchisees as a group can also support needed legislation, exchange ideas, and generally work to strengthen their position relative to the franchisor.

# Trends and Outlook

All trends indicate that franchising will continue to expand, creating great opportunities for existing and new businesses, developing new entrepreneurs, new jobs, new products, and new services. With long-term prospects for franchising extremely bright, growing numbers of smaller companies, operating in local or regional markets, are turning to franchising for new ways to distribute their goods and services. These new small franchising companies quickly react to changing market conditions and seek out new services and merchandising alternatives to broaden store appeal and attract greater patronage. Franchising is the most popular method of business expansion and, in the past few years, average annual franchise sales growth has exceeded 15 percent, compared to 7.4 percent for the gross national product and 7.7 percent for overall retail sales growth.[14] Most of the fastest-growing franchises in Canada are retail operations, as shown in Table 8–3.

Continuing economic improvement, stable prices, a slower-growing population, and increased competition for market share are turning many companies, both large and small, to franchising. Franchising can enable these firms to cover existing markets or penetrate new markets at minimal cost.

With the rising costs of construction, marketing, and training, and with franchising enlarging its share of retail and service sales, there may be an increased trend toward multiunit ownership by franchisees and the increased granting of rights to develop large regional areas. Stepped-up activity may also occur with larger franchisors acquiring existing chains for expansion instead of developing new, individual franchises.

Two new trends in franchising that are growing in popularity are *branchising* and *piggybacking*.[15]

Branchising is the conversion of company-owned stores to franchise operations. The advantages for the retailer are influx of capital when franchisees buy the store, reduced inventory costs, and a more motivated store manager. The main disadvantage is the possibility of reduced profits per store to the franchisor. One Canadian company, the Agnew Group, which owns about 350 Agnew, Aggies, and Ashton shoe chains, is branchising most of its stores. The Agnew Group has found that branchising seems to be a winning formula for boosting sales and improving productivity. On average, after stores have been franchised, sales have increased by about 25 percent in a year and annual costs have dropped by 5 to 10 percent. Two

TABLE 8–3    **Top Twenty Fastest-Growing Franchises\***

| Rank | Franchise | Franchise Sales | | Number of Canadian Franchises | | Number of Foreign Franchises | Franchising Since | |
|---|---|---|---|---|---|---|---|---|
| | | Percent Change (1988–87) | $000 (1988) | 1988 | 1987 | | In Canada | In the United States |
| 1 | Print Three (printing) | 100.0 | 30,000 | 78 | 54 | 25 | 1982 | 1987 |
| 2 | Yellow Submarine Deli (fast food) | 100.0 | 10,000 | 73 | 57 | 0 | 1986 | N.A. |
| 3 | Beaver Lumber (building materials) | 64.0 | 597,000 | 123 | 116 | 0 | 1977 | N.A. |
| 4 | Scooter Photo (photo finishing) | 62.5 | 26,000 | 168 | 105 | 0 | 1968 | N.A. |
| 5 | Alimentation Couche-Tard (convenience stores) | 59.1 | 175,000 | 117 | 42 | 0 | 1985 | N.A. |
| 6 | Uniclean Systems (cleaning) | 47.5 | 885 | 84 | 58 | 15 | 1981 | 1987 |
| 7 | Triple A Student Painters (painting) | 45.1 | 7,400 | 140 | 100 | 300 | 1982 | 1985 |
| 8 | Fabri-Zone Cleaning Systems (cleaning) | 37.5 | 5,500 | 75 | 60 | 16 | 1984 | 1985 |
| 9 | Weed Man (lawn care) | 35.0 | 27,000 | 96 | 80 | 3 | 1976 | 1985 |
| 10 | Tim Horton Donuts (fast food bakery) | 33.3 | 240,000 | 396 | 341 | 0 | 1964 | N.A. |
| 11 | Treats (fast food bakery) | 31.6 | 17,500 | 103 | 83 | 20 | 1979 | 1987 |
| 12 | Second Cup (food, retail) | 30.9 | 33,653 | 125 | 108 | 0 | 1979 | N.A. |
| 13 | Groupe Jean Coutu (pharmacy) | 30.3 | 680,000 | 139 | 104 | 4 | 1973 | 1987 |
| 14 | Uniglobe Travel (Int'l) (travel agency) | 29.7 | 830,000 | 124 | 99 | 502 | 1980 | 1981 |
| 15 | Hartco Enterprises (computers) | 29.5 | 149,800 | 85 | 62 | 0 | 1980 | N.A. |
| 16 | Magicuts (hair care) | 28.3 | 25,225 | 147 | 126 | 20 | 1982 | 1984 |
| 17 | First Choice Haircutters (hair care) | 27.5 | 24,600 | 143 | 115 | 49 | 1982 | 1982 |
| 18 | Arby's (fast food) | 27.3 | 56,000 | 86 | 71 | 2,000 | 1982 | 1964 |
| 19 | Panhandler Group (gifts and novelties) | 24.3 | 22,556 | 76 | 68 | 0 | 1975 | N.A. |
| 20 | Mike's Restaurant (restaurant) | 24.1 | 72,000 | 106 | 91 | 0 | 1969 | N.A. |

\*Based on percentage increase in total franchise sales.

SOURCE: "Fastest Growing Franchises," *Canadian Business*, June 1989, pp. 18–19.

other Canadian retailers, Consumers Distributing and Angelo Retail Corporation, are branchising most of their stores.

Piggybacking is a concept that puts two different franchise operations under the same roof. The idea is to find a combination where consumers shop for two different types of product at different times of the day and during different seasons. For

*Tim Horton Donuts, one of the fastest-growing franchises in Canada.*

SOURCE: Photo by James Hertel.

example, combining doughnut and ice cream franchises may lead to a more balanced and profitable operation. Burger King is experimenting with video rental franchises within its restaurants.[16]

Franchised restaurants of all types will continue to be a popular sector of franchising. Casual theme restaurants designed to reflect a particular life-style or mood are finding increased acceptance in franchising, while restaurant franchisors associated with the popular fast-food concept will continue to show the greatest sales growth. Restaurant franchisors are moving toward more diversified menus, including salad bars, fish, and poultry, as personal health concerns influence increased consumption of such food items. The shift to ethnic foods is also increasing.

Business and personal services franchises in particular are expected to continue to rise significantly for the next few years. Companies will need additional business and management consulting services to provide innovative marketing ideas geared to a better-educated and more affluent consumer in highly segmented markets. The trend toward specialized contract services is expected to continue, boosting such business areas as maid services (Molly Maid), repair and home remodeling (Triple A Student Painters), temporary help (Kelly Services), carpet cleaning (Uniclean Systems), lawn care (Weed Man), and various maintenance and cleaning services (Roto Static International).

Because 70 percent of economic growth is in the service sector, franchises that add an element of service will have an advantage. In particular, opportunities exist for franchising in the home renovations area, from window installation to roofing.[17]

In summary, major changes are in progress in the economy as a whole. As we move into the mid 1990s, creativity and imagination in the treatment of goods and services will be richly rewarded. Education, computer usage, and the ability to work with and manage people will be profitably utilized by new emerging businesses. All these developments suggest that franchising will be the leading method of doing business in the 1990s.

# Chapter Highlights

- Franchising is a way of doing business that allows an independent businessperson (the franchisee) to use another firm's (the franchisor's) operating methods, financing systems, trademarks, and products in return for payment of a fee.

- Franchising is one of the fastest-growing segments of retailing in Canada and accounts for about 35 percent of retail sales. Experts predict continued growth in new franchises and sales. About 1,300 franchising companies are operating in Canada today, with over 50,000 outlets across the country.

- The overriding advantage of a franchising program is the ability to quickly expand a company with limited capital. Another advantage of franchising is the training programs that are available, which allow an individual to enter a business with no experience. The franchisee can also benefit from the purchasing power of the franchisor. Equally important are the programs of research and development that many franchisors have established to improve their product or service.

- A major disadvantage of a franchise is the high initial fee. The franchisee also gives up some flexibility in return for the right to purchase a franchise. Complaints may arise over the nature of the franchise contract.

- Franchises are of two basic types: product and trade-name franchises such as automobile dealers and gasoline outlets, and business format franchising, in which firms that have developed a unique method of

performing a service or of doing business sell the concept to others.

- Franchisors may grant individual franchises to businesspersons. Alternatively, they may sell master franchises. Some persons purchase area-development franchises, which give them rights to an extensive territory in which they develop a large number of outlets.

- The various costs involved in becoming a franchise can include the initial cost, the franchise fee, opening costs, working capital, premise expenses, site evaluation fees, royalties and service fees, and promotion charges.

- Evaluating franchise opportunities includes determining the credit rating, financial position, and reputation of the franchisor. As well, the product or service offered should be market tested and the franchise concept should be thoroughly understood.

- The typical franchise contract gives the franchisee the right to sell a product or service under an arrangement that requires the individual to follow the franchisor's formula. The franchisor is usually paid an initial fee for the right to operate at a particular location and a franchise fee based on monthly sales.

- Trends indicate that franchising will continue to expand, creating great opportunities for new businesses, jobs, products, and services.

# Key Terms

## Discussion Questions

1. What are the differences between product and trade-name franchising, and business format franchising?

2. Discuss the ingredients of an ideal franchise programme. What are the types of franchises that appear to be suited to the elements of such a programme?

3. Write a brief essay on the cost elements that are typically included as part of a franchising contract.

4. What are the issues a prospective franchisee should evaluate in deciding whether to purchase a franchise?

5. What are the ingredients of a typical franchise contract?

6. Highlight the advantages and disadvantages of becoming a franchisee and of franchising as a way of doing business.

7. What are the legal restrictions on franchising?

8. Discuss the trends and outlook for franchising.

## Application Exercises

1. Review the various sources cited in the endnotes to the chapter (the sources can probably be found in your local library) and try to establish the initial opening costs for the following types of franchises: A national food franchise such as Tim Horton Donuts, a personal services franchise such as Weed Man, a retail cosmetics franchise such as Faces, and a car rental business such as Rent-A-Wreck.

2. Talk to the owner/managers of three fast-food franchises in your community, and write an essay outlining the primary advantages and disadvantages they see in being franchisees.

3. Interview the owner of a local automobile agency (an example of a product and trade-name franchise) and the owner of a services franchise. What are the similarities and differences between the two types of franchises? Which type franchise is likely to generate the greatest loyalty to the franchisor?

## Suggested Cases

11. Diego's    590

17. The Maaco Franchise    617

## Endnotes

1. Bruce Gates, ''Predictability Breeds Profitability,'' *The Financial Post,* March 20, 1992, p. 11.

2. Carolyn Leitch, ''What You Should Look For,'' *The Financial Post,* June 13, 1988, p. 35; and

Bruce Gates, "Many Routes to Pick in Franchise Forest," *The Financial Post,* June 13, 1988, p. 35.

3. Ibid.

4. Gates, "Predictability Breeds Profitability."

5. Andrew Tausz, "Franchises Cushion Ex-Managers," *Globe and Mail,* April 14, 1992, p. B24.

6. John Heinzl, "Burger King Makes It His Way, Right Away," *Globe and Mail,* April 17, 1992, p. B1.

7. Coca Cola Beverages, Annual Report, 1991.

8. *The 1988 Franchise Annual* (St. Catharines, Ontario: Info Press, Inc., 1988).

9. Dennis L. Foster, *The Rating Guide to Franchises* (New York: Facts on File Publications, 1988).

10. Tausz, "Franchises Cushion Ex-Managers."

11. Taylor Gilbert, David Thomson, and Peter Dabbikeh, *Franchising in Canada 1992,* 2nd ed. (Toronto: CCH Canadian Limited, 1992). For more information on evaluating franchises, see "Franchising 1992," *Financial Times,* March 16, 1992, Special Supplement; and Jennifer Low, "Avoiding Franchise Fly-by-Nights," *Profit,* July/August 1991, p. 44.

12. Douglas Queen, *Low-Risk Franchising: The Canadian Guide to Buying and Running a Successful Franchise Business* (Toronto: McGraw-Hill Ryerson, 1991); and Canadian Franchise Association, *Invest before Investing* (monograph), 1990.

13. Bruce Gates, "Arbitration, Mediation Keys to Settling Disputes," *The Financial Post,* March 20, 1992, p. 14.

14. Stan Brown, "Should You Franchise?" *Retail Directions,* November/December 1988, p. 17.

15. Terry Brodie, "New Directions for the Company Store," *Financial Times of Canada,* June 6, 1988, p. A3.

16. K. Charise Clark, "The Future of Franchising," *Profit,* March 1992, p. 59.

17. "Experts Provide Franchising Advice," *Financial Times,* March 16, 1992, Special Supplement.

# 9   MANAGING THE RETAIL EMPLOYEE

---

## Chapter Objectives

After reading this chapter, you should be able to:

1 Understand the importance and content of personnel policies.
2 Discuss how to determine needed job skills and abilities.
3 Discuss how to recruit applicants.
4 Explain how to select employees.
5 Discuss the need to train employees.
6 Describe the essentials of an employee pay plan.
7 Explain how to plan employee benefits.
8 Describe an employee performance appraisal system.
9 Discuss the issues involved in employee motivation and job enrichment.
10 Discuss problems associated with shoplifting and employee theft and measures retailers can take to detect and prevent such behaviours.

**Retailing Capsule**

According to a recent Angus Reid poll, 56 percent of Canadians said they had not had a recent shopping experience where the customer service was excellent, and 30 percent said the service was so bad, they swore never to return to that store. About 18 percent blamed rude employees, and 11 percent fingered slow service or a long wait. On the other hand, many Canadians indicate that they like to shop in the United States because of the excellent service they receive. There is more to good customer service than a smiling and polite salesperson. A large part of excellent customer service is a highly trained and competent staff. Consider the following examples.

- Much of the success of British-owned HMV can be credited to its president, Paul Alofs, who runs what he calls "superstores with a soul." According to Alofs, Canadian retailers tend to overlook the importance of their most obvious asset: their employees. This, in turn, explains the generally poor customer service tradition in Canada. "I go to the Young Presidents' organization and the Retail Council of Canada and they say the customer is number one . . . but if you ask them what their incentive programs are like, or how much they spend on training and development, they answer, 'Well, what does that have to do with customer service?' " At HMV, all staff, from clerks to managers, are paid above the industry norm, and HMV spends "more than all of our competitors put together times five" on staff training and development. Store managers earn 10 to 20 percent above competition, and last Christmas they received higher bonuses than the senior management team and the board of HMV received for the entire year. Says Alofs: "We put our money where our mouth is. It's not us taking the glory and us taking the money."

- According to Dacia Moss of Holt Renfrew, providing information about gourmet foods to customers is as much a part of the game as is making sure the right products are available, and that function rests mainly with the staff. However, it is difficult to get qualified help in gourmet food stores these days, unless one is willing to properly train them. "There are many people who have lived elsewhere, who are widely travelled and 'widely eaten,' so to speak, and who would lose confidence in a shop if the staff is not well-versed in the world of gourmet foods."

- In the field of retail jewellery, you hear a similar story: According to a jewellery manager, "No matter how well you watch your cash flow, manage your inventory or make your store attractive to customers, you'll lose business if you don't work to develop your salespeople. In a high-service business such as jewellery retailing, contact between the salesperson and the customer makes or breaks the bond between your

*Retailing Capsule continued*

store and your clientele. However, many jewellers still don't recognize how important that connection is. A retailer who is doing a poor job of developing employees' potential will see a high turnover rate among salespeople, combined with a general lack of motivation and bad customer relations. Employees will be more interested in coffee breaks and quitting time and less interested in taking care of customers.''

*Salespeople are critical to a specialty store like Birks.*

SOURCE: Photo by Betty McDougall.

Sources: Anne Bokma, ''Raking in the Dough: Canadian Retailers Are Folding, while Foreigners Flourish,'' *The Financial Post Magazine,* January 1992, pp. 32–35; ''Retailers Add Insult to Injury,'' *Profit,* September 1991, p. 48; Colin Wright, ''Consumers Will Scrimp on Basics to Afford Luxury,'' *Marketing,* June 28, 1982, p. F6; and Richard Outcalt, ''Human Assets,'' *Canadian Jeweller,* April 1987, p. 12.

The unique success of well-known retail outlets such as HMV, Holt Renfrew, or Birks depends to a substantial degree on the skills, motivation, and dedication of their employees. Employees should not be regarded as throwaway assets. All dimensions of the human resources plan, ranging from selection and placement to pay and performance appraisal, should be structured to allow employees to feel they are a vital part of the organization. Sensitivity to the issues inherent in employee motivation and job enrichment are also important in progressive organizations.

The human resources environment has become increasingly volatile in recent years as a result of such issues as testing for illegal drug use, concern about AIDS, undocumented foreign workers, growing labour shortages for hourly employees, concerns over child care, and the impact of mergers, acquisitions, restructuring, and the Canada–U.S. Free Trade Agreement on human resources.

All managers need to understand and appreciate the importance of good personnel policies in the recruiting, training, and compensation of employees in addition to organizational issues. Understanding the goals and values of employees can also be of great benefit in avoiding unnecessary conflicts in the enterprise.

The development of a human resources plan in helping to implement competitive strategy is thus becoming increasingly important in retailing. One reason is that the age of growth through expansion seems to be almost over for many firms. More emphasis is being placed on market share management and improving productivity through better use of people, current assets, and facilities.

Both of these avenues for growth put stress on human resources personnel because of the labour-intensive nature of retailing. The payroll/sales ratio runs to as much as 25 percent in the higher-price/better-service stores such as Holt Renfrew. The specialty store is the most labour-intensive type of retailer, with payroll ratios as high as 30 percent.

Success in maintaining a results-oriented focus in the organization depends on defining or enforcing performance standards at each level in the organization. Specific performance measures are needed not only for the entire organization but for each line of business and each functional area. Normally, multiple measures are needed. Some measures are objective, while others are necessarily somewhat subjective and include employee morale, customer satisfaction, and employee-management relations.

The focus should always be on achievement, producing results by using the full array of rewards and punishments outlined in this chapter. Intense people orientation, constantly reinforced, is the key to getting everyone in the organization committed to the goals to be achieved. The key element is making champions out of people who turn in winning performances. Firms such as Disney (see Retail Highlight 9–1) refer to employees as *cast members,* and McDonald's uses the term *crew members*. They all seek out reasons and opportunities to reward good performance.

# Good Employees Are a Major Part of the Retail Offering

Everyone who is employed by Disney, from dishwasher to monorail operator, begins with three days of training and indoctrination at Disney University.

Disney never hires an employee for a job. The "actors" are "cast" in a "role" to perform in a "show." Sometimes the show is called Walt Disney World, sometimes Disneyland, sometimes The Disney Store, etc. Their main purpose is to look after the "guests." Disney has never had customers.

Every cast member is provided with a "costume," not a uniform. That way a guest shouldn't have to ask, "Do you work here?" Each cast member is told not to hesitate getting a new costume if the old one gets dirty. Cast members do not work the floor, they are "onstage" and the stock rooms, etc. are "backstage."

There is almost always one cast member designated to be the "greeter." The greeter position is a very important one. His or her role is to greet all guests as they enter and as they leave, thanking each of them for "visiting our store," not for shopping. The greeter sets the tone for the guest's visit and also acts as a small deterrent to shoplifting since people are less likely to shoplift if they have been recognized by someone when they entered the store.

The words *no* and *I don't know* are not usually part of the Disney script. Everything should be positive. Instead of "I don't know," cast members should say, "I'll find out." Instead of "We don't have any . . ." cast members should say, "We are out of . . ." Instead of saying, "That item won't be available until . . ." cast members try to say, "That item will be available on . . ." Any response to the guests should be phrased in a positive manner if at all possible.

The Disney Store does not have stuffed animals, it has "plush" animals. A Disney Store cast member always points with an open palm, not the index finger, because when you point with the index finger, four fingers are pointing back at you. Also, when you were younger and your mother pointed at you, you knew you were in trouble.

The Disney show is several things. It's the entire experience created by the environment, the merchandise, the attractions, and the music, but most importantly, it is the people. The cast members have a certain look which includes style of hair, makeup, name tags, all of which are part of the Disney script.

Source: Prepared by Donald Smith, a cast member at The Disney Store, a Division of Walt Disney Enterprises.

# The Job Description and Job Analysis[1]

A manager looking for someone to fill a job should spell out in a job description exactly what he or she wants. Imagine an owner/manager advertising for a "salesclerk." What should the applicant be able to do? Just tally sales receipts accurately? Keep a customer list and occasionally promote products? Run the store while the manager is away? The job of salesclerk means different things to different people. Retailers should determine what skills are needed for the job, what skills an applicant can get by with, and what kind of training should be given to the employee.

Good *job descriptions* and *job specifications* are excellent tools, but they will not, by themselves, ensure the best possible selection and assignment of employees to jobs, nor will they ensure that employees will be trained and paid properly. If good job descriptions and clear job specifications exist, however, selection, training, and salary decisions will be much easier, and better.[2] Job descriptions and job specifications are written from a *job analysis*.

## *Job Analysis*

**Job analysis** is a method of obtaining important facts about a job. Specifically, the job analysis obtains answers to four major questions that the job description and job specification require:

1. *What* physical and mental tasks does the worker accomplish?
2. *How* does the person do the job? Here, the methods used and the equipment involved are explored.
3. *Why* is the job done? This is a brief explanation of the purpose and responsibilities of the job that will help relate the job to other jobs.
4. What *qualifications* are needed for this job? Here are listed the job knowledge, skills, and personal characteristics required of a worker.

A job analysis thus provides a summary of job (1) duties and responsibilities, (2) relationships to other jobs, (3) knowledge and skills, and (4) working conditions of an unusual nature.

### Conducting a Job Analysis

An easy way to begin a job analysis is to think about the various duties, responsibilities, and qualifications required for the position and jot them down on a note pad. The ingredients of a job analysis outline for a sales manager are shown in Exhibit 9–1. Management should chat with the job supervisor or a person who now holds the job to fill in the details about the job.

When conducting a job analysis, it is important to describe the job and the requirements of the job rather than the employee performing it. (The present employee may be overqualified or underqualified for the job, or simply have characteristics irrelevant for the job.)

It is also a good idea to keep in mind the ultimate goals of job analysis: to simplify and improve employee recruitment, training, and development, and to evaluate jobs for the determination of salary and wage rates.

### Using the Job Analysis

After a job analysis has been conducted, it is possible to write a job description and job specification from the analysis. A **job description** is that part of a job analysis that describes the content and responsibilities of the job and how the job ties in with other jobs in the firm. The **job specification** is that part of a job analysis that describes the personal qualifications required of an employee to do the job.

**EXHIBIT 9-1**

*Job analysis outline for a sales manager*

**Duties**
Assist customers with purchases
Develop expertise of staff
Achieve sales goals
Schedule hours and assign work to subordinates
Complete performance reviews on time
Present merchandise
Manage inventory
Open and close store
Provide floor supervision

**Education**
University or college graduate

**Relationships**
Report to store manager daily
Meet daily with subordinates

**Knowledge/Skills**
Transaction entry
Merchandising and operating procedures
Selling skills and product knowledge
Sales analysis knowledge
Knowledge of company's human resources standards and procedures
Performance review skills
Merchandise program knowledge
Inventory control procedures
Employee training
Supervisory skills

**Physical Requirements**
Capable of basic manual skills
Able to work on feet all day

**On-the-Job Hazards/Working Conditions**
No danger if safety rules and regulations are followed.

SOURCE: Sears Canada.

**FIGURE 9-1**

*Relationship among job analysis, job description, and job specification*

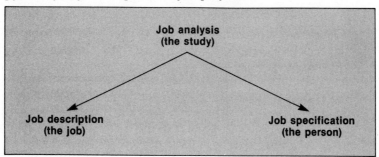

Figure 9-1 demonstrates the relationship of job analysis to job description and job specification.

In addition to their usefulness in explaining duties and responsibilities to applicants, job descriptions and job specifications can help with:

*Considerable product knowledge is required for many retail positions.*

SOURCE: Photo by James Hertel.

- *Recruiting:* Job descriptions and specifications make it easier to write advertisements or notices announcing the job opening or explaining the job to an employment agency.
- *Interviewing applicants:* Since a job description provides a written record of the duties and requirements of a particular job, and a job specification provides the qualifications needed for the job, they can be very helpful in planning an interview, especially as guidelines for asking the applicant questions about his or her abilities.
- *Training and development of new employees:* Having the duties of each job clearly defined can provide a basis for determining what knowledge and skills should be taught to new employees and can help to plan training so that *(a)* important skills are learned first and *(b)* the training is comprehensive.

- *Coordination:* Job descriptions, when they are available, can ensure that people know what is expected of them and that their activities are coordinated.
- *Setting wage rates and salaries of employees:* By providing a perspective of the relative amounts of work required and qualifications needed for different positions, fairer wage rates and salaries may be established.
- *Employee relations:* The information about the job in the description can ensure that fewer misunderstandings will occur about the respective duties and responsibilities of various jobs.

*Job Description*

A job description is a summary of the important facts about a particular job. It states in a concise, clear way, the information obtained in a job analysis. A fully adequate job description should be outlined on less than one page. For instance, a job description for a buyer at Sears Canada could be written as in Exhibit 9–2.

*Job Specification*

A job specification, like a job description, is written from the job analysis and describes those personal requirements that should be expected of anyone who is placed on the job, as well as any unusual or hazardous environmental conditions that the job holder must be prepared to accept. A job specification thus describes the type of employee required for successful performance of the job. One way to prepare a job specification is shown in Exhibit 9–3

**Exhibit 9–2**

*Job description for a buyer*

**JOB DESCRIPTION**

JOB TITLE:   Buyer                                    Date:_____

**Statement of the Job**

Develops a marketing plan and advocates what is best for the company—item by item, line by line—and brings forth those recommendations to the company via the department/group marketing plan.

**Major Duties**

1. Makes recommendations on items and/or lines. This includes private label/national brand or combination, selling plan, item price by geographic region, vendor, inventory investment, and assortment and depth by store volume.
2. Purchases goods as agreed to in the marketing plan.
3. Ensures that sales personnel and customers understand the value of the product line.

**Relationships**

The buyer works with other buyers and store managers in preparing the group marketing plan. The buyer works with vendors to obtain merchandise and store personnel to market merchandise.

Source: Sears Canada.

**EXHIBIT 9–3**

*Job specification for a sales manager*

---

### JOB SPECIFICATION

JOB TITLE:   Sales Manager                              Date:_____

**Education:** (List only what is really necessary for the job; e.g., high school, college, trade school, or other special training.)

University or community college graduate.

**Experience:** (The amount of previous and related experience that a new employee should have.)

None specifically.

**Knowledge/Skills:** (List the specific knowledge and skills that the job may require.)

Must know how to:
- Enter customer transactions.
- Work within the merchandising and operating procedures. [The list would include the elements listed in the job analysis in Exhibit 9–1.]

**Physical and Mental Requirements:** (Mention any special physical or mental abilities required for the job; e.g., 20/20 eyesight, availability for irregular work hours, ability to work under time pressure, etc.)

Must have a good personality and be able to lead and motivate people.

---

SOURCE: Sears Canada.

# Recruiting Applicants

When the owner-manager knows the kind of skills needed in a new employee, he or she is ready to contact sources that can help recruit job applicants. Application forms help screen and select the best candidates.

## Sources of Candidates

In each province, there is an employment service with several Canada Employment Centres. All are affiliated with the federal department of Employment and Immigration Canada, which operates a computerized, nationwide job databank. Local Canada Employment Centres are ready to help businesses with their hiring problems. A retailer should be as specific as possible about the skills required for a job, and notify the Canada Employment Centre, which will post the notice of a job opening, with its requirements, on its bulletin board. All interested applicants are interviewed by a Centre counsellor, and if the assessment is positive, a referral is made to the retailer.

*Private employment agencies* can also help in recruitment. However, the employee or the employer must pay a fee to the private agency for its services.

Another method of recruiting is a Help Wanted sign in the front window. But there are drawbacks to this method: Many unqualified applicants may inquire about the job, and a retailer cannot interview an applicant and wait on a customer at the same time.

*Newspaper advertisements* are another source of applicants. They reach a large group of job seekers, and retailers can screen these people at their convenience. But a retailer should think twice before listing the store's phone number in the ad—he or she may end up on the phone all day instead of dealing with customers.

Job applicants are also readily available from schools. The local high school may have a distributive education department, where the students work in the store part time while learning about selling and merchandising in school. Many part-time students stay with the store after they finish school.

Retailers may also find applicants from a variety of informal sources (e.g., friends, neighbours, customers, suppliers, or present employees), local associations such as the Chamber of Commerce, or service clubs.

A combination of the many sources for job applicants may serve best. The important thing is to find the right applicant with the correct skills for the job, whatever the source.

*Developing Application Forms*

Some method of screening applicants and selecting the best one for the position is needed. The application form is a tool that can be used to make the tasks of interviewing and selecting easier. An example is shown in Exhibit 9–4. The form should have blank spaces for all the facts needed as a basis for judging the applicant. Retailers will want a fairly complete application so they can get sufficient information. However, the form should be kept as simple as possible.

The retailer must not abuse the information from the application in hiring. The Canadian Human Rights Act prohibits discrimination in employment based on race, national or ethnic origin, religion, age, sex, marital status, family status, disability, and conviction for which a pardon has been granted.[3] This act applies to all departments and agencies of the federal government, all Crown corporations, and businesses under federal jurisdiction. The act is administered by the **Canadian Human Rights Commission** and a tribunal with broad powers to order an end of the discriminatory practice, require some financial compensation for the victim, or develop and implement an affirmative action program (Section 15). This last application of the act has been strengthened by the Constitution Act of 1982, especially the Charter of Rights and Freedoms.

In areas not under federal jurisdiction, which includes most retailers, protection is given by provincial human rights laws, which are similar in contents and remedies to the federal law.

The list of laws related to employment practices is provided in Table 9–1, and they are compared in Table 9–2.

# Selecting Employees

The next step is to select employees through job interviews.

*The Job Interview*

The objective of the job interview is to find out as much information as possible about the applicants' work background. The major task is to get the applicants to talk about themselves, their skills, and their work habits. The best way to go about this is to ask each applicant specific questions, such as "What did you do on your last job? How did you do it? Why was it done?" Questions that have no relationship

**EXHIBIT 9–4**

*Employee application form*

## APPLICATION FOR EMPLOYMENT

Name: _____ Date: _____
         Last             First          Middle

Present address: _____ Social insurance no.: _____

Telephone number: _____ Driver's license no.: _____

Indicate dates you attended school:

Elementary from _____ to _____

High school from _____ to _____

College from _____ to _____

Other (specify type and dates) _____

Can you be bonded? _____ If yes, in what job? _____

Do you have any physical limitations that preclude you from performing certain kinds of work? _____

If yes, describe each and specify work restrictions: _____

List below all present and past employment, beginning with most recent (include military service, if relevant):

| Name and address of company | From Mo/Yr | To Mo/Yr | Name of supervisor | Reason for leaving | Weekly salary | Describe the work you did |
|---|---|---|---|---|---|---|
|  |  |  |  |  |  |  |
|  |  |  |  |  |  |  |
|  |  |  |  |  |  |  |
|  |  |  |  |  |  |  |
|  |  |  |  |  |  |  |
|  |  |  |  |  |  |  |
|  |  |  |  |  |  |  |

May we contact the employers listed above? _____ If no, indicate which ones you do not wish us to contact:

Remarks: _____

## TABLE 9–1    Major Laws Related to Employment Practices in Canada and the Provinces

**Federal Regulation**
Canada Labour Code
Canadian Human Rights Act
Fair Wages and Hours of Labour Act
Holidays Act
Employment Act
Multiculturalism Act

**Alberta**
The Employment Standards Act
The Child Welfare Act
Individual's Rights Protection Act
Industrial Wages Security Act

**British Columbia**
Employment Standards Act
Human Rights Act

**Manitoba**
Employment Standards Act
Payment of Wages Act
Remembrance Day Act
Vacations with Pay Act
Wages Recovery Act

**New Brunswick**
Days of Rest Act
Employment Standards Act
Minimum Employment Standards Act
Minimum Wage Act
Vacation Pay Act

**Newfoundland**
Child Welfare Act
Labour Standards Act
Newfoundland Human Rights Code

**Nova Scotia**
Labour Standards Code

**Ontario**
Employment Standards Act
One Day's Rest in Seven Act
Industrial Standards Act

**P.E.I.**
Labour Act
Minimum Age of Employment Act

**Quebec**
An Act Representing Labour Standards
Charter of Human Rights and Freedoms
Civil Code
Manpower Vocational Training and Qualification Act
National Holiday Act

**Saskatchewan**
Labour Standards Act
Wages Recovery Act

**Northwest Territories**
Fair Practices Ordinance
Labour Standards Ordinance
Wages Recovery Ordinance

**Yukon**
Employment Standards Act

SOURCE: Adapted from Shimon L. Dolan and Randall S. Schuler, *Personnel and Human Resource Management in Canada,* (St. Paul, Minn.: West Publishing, 1987), pp. 590–92.

to the ability of a person to do the job in question cannot be considered in making a hiring decision.

As the interviews go along, evaluate the applicants' replies. Do they know what they are talking about? Are they evasive or unskilled in the job tasks? Can they account for discrepancies?

When conducting an interview, the following guidelines can be helpful:

- *Describe the job in as much detail as is reasonably possible:* Give descriptions of typical situations that might arise and ask the applicant how

# TABLE 9–2  A Comparison of Antidiscrimination Laws in Canada and in the Provinces

| Jurisdiction | Federal | British Columbia | Alberta | Saskatchewan | Manitoba | Ontario | Quebec | New Brunswick | Prince Edward Island | Nova Scotia | Newfoundland | Northwest Territories | Yukon |
|---|---|---|---|---|---|---|---|---|---|---|---|---|---|
| Race | ● | ● | ● | ● | ● | ● | ● | ● | ● | ● | ● | ● | ● |
| National or ethnic origin[1] | ● | | | | ● | ● | ● | ● | ● | ● | ● | | ●* |
| Ancestry | | ● | ● | ● | ● | | ● | | | | | ● | ● |
| Nationality[7] | | | | ● | ● | | | | | | ● | | |
| Based on association[8] | | | | | | | | | | ● | | | ● |
| Place of origin | | ● | ● | ● | | ● | ● | | | | ● | | |
| Colour | ● | ● | ● | ● | ● | ● | ● | ● | ● | ● | ● | ● | ● |
| Religion | ● | ● | | ● | ● | | ● | ● | ● | ● | ● | | ● |
| Creed[2] | | | ● | ● | ● | ● | | | | ● | ● | ● | ● |
| Age | ● | ● (45–65) | ● (18+) | ● (18–65) | ● | ● (18–65) | ● | ● (19+) | ● | ● (40+) | ● (19–65) | | ● |
| Sex[6] | ● | ● | | ● | ●**** | ● | ● | ● | ● | ● | ● | ● | ● |
| Pregnancy or childbirth[6] | ● | | ● | ● | ● | ● | ● | | | | | | ● |
| Marital status[3] | ● | ● | ● | ● | | ● | ● | ● | ● | ● | ● | | ● |
| Family status[3] | ● | | | | ● | ● | ● | | | | | ● | ● |
| Pardoned offence | ● | | | | | ● | ● | | | | ● | | |
| Record of criminal conviction | | ● | | | | | ● | | | | | | ● |
| Physical handicap or disability | ● | ● | ● | ● | ● | ● | ● | ● | ● | ● | ● | ● | ● |
| Mental handicap or disability | ● | ● | ● | ● | ● | ● | ● | ● | ● | ● | ● | ● | ● |
| Dependence on alcohol or drug[9] | ● | | | | | | ● | | | | | | |
| Place of residence | | | | | | | | | | | | ● | |
| Political belief | | ● | | | ● | | ● | | ● | | ● | | ●** |
| Assignment, attachment or seizure of pay[4] | | | | | | | | | | | ● | | |
| Source of income | | | | | ● | | | | | | | | |
| Social condition[4] | | | | | | | ● | | | | | | |
| Language | | | | | | | ● | | | | | | |
| Social origin[4] | | | | | | | | | | | ● | | |
| Sexual orientation[5] | | | | | ● | | ● | ● | | | | | ● |
| Harassment[5] | ● | | | | ●*** | ● | ● | | | | ● | | ● |

[1]New Brunswick includes only "national origin."

[2]Creed usually means religious beliefs.

[3]Quebec uses the term *civil status*.

[4]In Quebec's charter, "social condition" may include assignment, attachment or seizure of pay and social origin.

[5]The federal, Ontario, Quebec and Yukon statutes ban harassment on all proscribed grounds. Ontario and Newfoundland also ban sexual solicitation.

[6]Sex includes ground of pregnancy. Pregnancy or childbirth is included within ground of sex. Based on policy for B.C., N.B., P.E.I., Nova Scotia, Newfoundland, Northwest Territories, Supreme Court of Canada has held that sex includes sexual harassment.

[7]Ontario's Code includes only "citizenship."

[8]Association with individuals determined by prohibited grounds of discrimination.

[9]Based on the policy for British Columbia, Saskatchewan, Manitoba and P.E.I.

*Includes linguistic background.

**Includes political activity or political association

***Does not include sexual orientation.

****Includes gender determined characteristics.

SOURCE: Canadian Human Rights Commission, 1992.

220

he or she would handle it: What would you say to a customer with a complaint? What colour blouse would you recommend to complement a red plaid skirt? The interviewer shouldn't expect responses to be expert, but training could make them so. Do not be discouraged or discouraging. Offer praise such as, "That is a good way to go about it. If we hire you, we can teach you several other ways to handle situations such as that."

A detailed description lets the applicant know the expectations from the earliest stage. It also lets the applicant make a realistic personal judgment as to his or her ability to fill the job.

- *Discuss the pluses and the minuses of the job:* No job is without its minuses. If they are known initially, they are less likely to become obstacles later. If the person is expected to work nights, weekends, or holidays, say so. Disclosure can prevent many misunderstandings later.
- *Explain the compensation plan:* What is the salary? What fringe benefits are offered? What holidays are allowed? What is the vacation policy?
- *Weigh all factors in reaching a decision:* Of all the factors mentioned above, no single one is overriding. Perhaps the most important characteristics to look for are common sense, an ability to communicate with people, and a sense of personal responsibility. The interviewer's personal judgment will be needed to decide whether the applicant has these characteristics.

***Making the Selection***

When the interviews are over, the applicants should be asked to check back later if the interviewers are interested in the applicant. The interviewers should never commit themselves until they have talked with all likely applicants.

Next, the interviewers should *verify the information obtained.* Previous employers are usually the best sources. Sometimes, previous employers will give out information over the telephone that they might hesitate to put on paper for fear of being sued. But it is usually best to request a written reply.

To help ensure a prompt reply, retailers should ask previous employers a few specific questions about the applicant that can be answered with a yes-or-no checkmark, or with a very short answer. For example: How long did the employee work for you? Was his or her work poor, average, or excellent? Why did the employee leave your employment?

After the retailers have verified the information on all the applicants, they are ready to make the selection. The right employee can help the firm make money. The wrong employee will cost the firm much wasted time and materials, and may even drive away customers.

# The Need to Train Employees[4]

The next step is to train employees. Sales training programs will be covered in Chapter 16, so this section will discuss the evolving nature of sales training in the context of the human resources plan.

In the past, sales training programs have been related to the hiring sequence and perhaps to retraining. Today, with the evolution of retail systems, the complexity of the environment, and the need to improve the delivery of customer service, old ideas of integrating an employee into the retail operation are no longer useful. In addition, the situation is complicated by the different educational or cultural backgrounds of employees.

Today, employees must deal with complicated automated systems, and retailing requires candidates with high intellectual qualities for a successful training program. These kinds of candidates are difficult to find even during recessions. Once found and selected, they must be given a customized training programme covering all aspects of modern retail operations. Retail Highlight 9–2 illustrates how important training employees is to excellent customer service.

An additional complication in today's environment is the changing demographic and cultural profile of the market, providing a pool of candidates who are culturally different from past employees and from current customers. Again, the

---

**Retail Highlight 9–2**

# Masterminding Success by Training and Good Customer Service

One important strategy for independents to beat large, often impersonal chain stores is by emphasizing *product knowledge*—that is, knowing just about all there is to know about products, related goods and services, and how they are used. To provide it requires commitment, a trained staff, and low turnover. Jonathan Levy, co-owner of the 10 Toronto-area Mastermind stores, which sell educational toys and computer and science wares, knows that salespeople have to know what's appropriate for children of different ages and interests. But sales also depend on his staff giving out reliable, on-the-spot, easy-to-understand information.

*Training is a priority.* Levy holds regular seminars, bringing in suppliers "to transplant as much product knowledge as possible from the source to the end-user of the knowledge." But just to be sure, he has built in a fail-safe system. When

store employees can't answer a customer's question, they can call any of three designated "experts," one for books, one for science, or Levy for other subjects. The experts work in the combined head office and warehouse, and Levy says that the trio respond to three or four calls a day from each store.

Reaching out to customers after the sale keeps the information flowing and sparks interest in new purchases. Three times a year, Levy publishes a newsletter that goes out to 20,000 customers, containing news, product reviews, and children's activities. "It's a way to reach out and touch our customers, to keep them informed about what we're doing," says Levy. What the newsletter also does is educate consumers (who are easier to sell to) *and* reinforce employee knowledge (ongoing training).

Source: Marlene Cartash, "Catching a Falling Store," *Profit,* December 1990, pp. 27–28.

training programme must try to bridge these gaps. Otherwise, the retailer should anticipate customer service perception problems.

# Developing an Employee Pay Plan[5]

*Pay administration* may be another term for something management is already doing but has not bothered to name. Or, perhaps the organization has not been paying employees according to any system, but waiting until unrest shows up to make pay adjustments—using payroll dollars to put out fires, so to speak.

A formal pay plan, one that lets employees know where they stand and where they can go as far as salary is concerned, will not solve all employee-relations problems. It will, however, remove one of those areas of doubt and rumour that may keep the work force anxious, unhappy, less loyal, and more mobile.

What is the advantage of a formal pay plan for the firm? In business, it is good people who can make the difference between success and failure. Many people like a mystery, but not when it is how their pay is determined. Employees working under a pay plan they know and understand can see that it is fair and uniform, and that pay is not set by whim. They know what to expect and can plan accordingly. In the long run, such a plan can help to (1) recruit, (2) keep, and (3) motivate employees, and (4) build a solid foundation for a successful business.

## Types of Salary Plans

A formal pay plan does not have to be complex nor cost a lot of time and money. Formal does not mean complex. In fact, the more elaborate the plan is, the more difficult it is to put into practice, communicate, and carry out.

The foremost concern in setting up a formal pay administration plan is to get the acceptance, understanding, and support of management and supervisory employees. A well-defined, thoroughly discussed, and properly understood plan is a prerequisite for success.

The steps in setting up a pay plan are (1) define the jobs as discussed earlier in the chapter, (2) evaluate the jobs, (3) price the jobs, (4) install the plan, (5) communicate the plan to employees, and (6) appraise employee performance under the plan.

### Job Evaluation and Compensation

The question of how much to pay an employee in a particular position is an important but complicated matter. If management offers too little pay for a particular position, the good employee will leave to perform the same work elsewhere and only the less motivated, less able employee will remain for the lower pay. On the other hand, management has very little to gain by paying an employee far more than what is being paid in other organizations for the same work.

*Job Evaluation.*   **Job evaluation** is a method of ranking jobs to aid in determining proper **compensation.** Figure 9–2 can now be used to demonstrate the relationship of the four basic personnel management tools: job analysis, job specification, job description, and job evaluation. Thus, a job evaluation is obtained by evaluating

**FIGURE 9–2**

*Relationship of job evaluation with respect to the other three management tools*

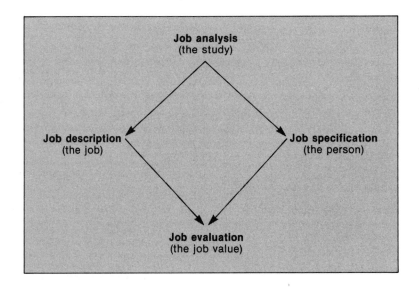

both the responsibilities from a job description and the items on a job specification. The reason for job evaluation is to establish a fair method of compensating employees for their work.

*Compensation.*    In determining pay rates, it is important to take several principles into consideration:

- Equal pay for equal work. This is a very important principle that is gaining acceptance by legislators in the federal and provincial level. The federal government and some provincial governments (such as Ontario) have some form of pay equity regulations. More initiatives are expected in the future.
- Higher pay for work requiring more knowledge, skill, or physical exertion.
- Reasonable pay in comparison to pay for similar work in other organizations.
- Overqualified employees are not paid more (or much more) than a qualified employee in the same position.
- After several years, very little or no extra pay for the length of time an employee has remained with the firm.
- Total earnings reflect, in some way, the employee's contribution to the organization.
- As much as possible, pay scales are known to employees.
- Fairness in application of these principles.

One general but fairly effective rule of thumb to follow when determining salaries and wage rates is to pay the most important nonsupervisory job as well as or somewhat better than the job receives elsewhere and to do the same for the least important full-time job. Rates for all other jobs can then be set in a reasonable way, in between. Job descriptions are often helpful in finding similar positions in other businesses with which to compare pay rates.

Management can obtain information on *competitive salaries* from various sources, including:

- Local surveys conducted by nearby business associations and organizations.
- Informal contacts, such as meetings with other owners/managers in social, civic, or community functions. Usually this information is useful only to get a general feel of things, since competitors may not wish to disclose salaries of jobs, and noncompetitive companies may be different from your firm.
- Industry meetings and conventions.
- Job advertisements in local newspapers and trade journals.
- National surveys, if they are available.

It is not always possible to compare salaries with pay rates in other businesses. This is especially true if some of the jobs in a business are not standard or common jobs.

***Methods of Job Evaluation.***   Another way to establish salaries and pay rates for jobs is to evaluate the worth of the job to the business, so that more important jobs receive more pay. In this way, management is able to take into consideration all but one of the principles of salary administration discussed earlier. This principle concerns providing a reasonable pay level, in comparison to pay for similar work in other organizations.

There are two different ways to evaluate jobs. They are:

1. Ranking—comparing a job against a job.
2. Classification—comparing the jobs with the aid of a scale.

These two methods are described in detail in the next sections.

**The Rank Method of Job Evaluation**

**Job ranking,** possibly with the aid of job descriptions, is the simpler and usually more practical way to evaluate jobs. The most valuable and complex job is assigned the rank of 1, the job that is second in complexity and importance is assigned the rank of 2, and so on until all jobs have been assigned a number. Jobs that are equal in importance may be assigned the same number. If management uses this method, it knows that the higher the job's position on the list—that is, the lower its number—the more important the job is to the business, and it can assign pay levels accordingly.

In creating new jobs, management can place them into their proper places in the ranking.

***Examples.***   Suppose that a restaurant owner/manager who is looking for an assistant manager, a cook's helper, and a dishwasher has the situation indicated in

Table 9–3. In this case, the assistant manager should be paid more than a cook but less than a manager, somewhere between $25,000 and $30,000 a year. A cook's helper seems to fit in the range of less than $8.00 per hour but more than $5.50 per hour. The dishwasher, being the least important job, would receive the minimum wage or only a little above it.

*The Classification Method of Job Evaluation*

In the **job classification** method, jobs are evaluated and rated on two scales:

- The *complexity* of the various responsibilities and qualifications that are required on the job and their respective importance to good performance.
- The *length of time* the respective responsibility and qualification are utilized during the average day.

For each responsibility and qualification, two rating numbers are assigned—one for the complexity and importance of the job, and the other one for the length of time during which it is used. For instance, if knowledge of computer programming is required on a job, it may receive a 7 for responsibility and qualification; but if that knowledge is required only a few hours out of each week, it may receive a 2 for length of time. These two numbers can then be multiplied and averaged with all other qualifications and responsibilities of that job, to provide a classification number. Large numbers indicate the more difficult and important positions. The method of evaluating jobs based on classification is a complex one that is beyond the scope of this book.

In general, a planned pay structure makes it possible to tie individual rates of pay to job performance and contribution to company goals. Table 9–4 shows the most frequently used retail sales pay plans.

A *straight salary* is most likely to be paid in a small store in which employees have a variety of responsibilities other than selling. This pay plan also avoids the temptation for employees to engage in "pressure" selling. The drawback of the plan is that it does not provide an incentive for extra effort, which may lower employee motivation.

**TABLE 9–3   Application of Job Ranking**

| Job Rank | Job Title | Salary or Wage Rate |
|---|---|---|
| 1 | Manager | $30,000 to $35,000 per year |
| 2 | Assistant manager | ? |
| 3 | Cook 1 | $24,000 to $26,000 per year |
| 4 | Cook 2 | $8.00 to $8.50 per hour |
| 5 | Head waiter/waitress | $7.50 to $8.00 per hour |
| 6 | Cook's helper | ? |
| 7 | Waiter/waitress | Minimum wage plus tips averaging $5.50 per hour |
| 8 | Dishwasher | ? |

A *salary plus commission* is the most frequently administered plan in retailing, primarily because it emphasizes both selling and customer service. It provides an extra incentive for "plus sales" and also provides a stable income for employees.

The *quota plus bonus plan* provides for the payment of a bonus as a varying percentage of sales achieved above a quota established for each category of merchandise. The pay plan allows unique sales incentives to be established by category of merchandise/tasks, does not encourage overly aggressive selling, and does provide a stable income during periods of slow sales. The disadvantages are that the plan can be misunderstood by employees and must be changed to reflect changes in the merchandise mix by season.

The *straight commission* pay plan provides a strong financial incentive for outstanding salespersons and thus is likely to attract strong sales personnel. The disadvantage is that the arrangement can promote overly aggressive pressure selling that can antagonize customers. Employees may also be prone to focus excessive attention on high-cost goods, creating ill will and tension between salespersons.

## Installing the Plan

At this point, employers have a general pay plan, but they do not, of course, pay in general—they pay each employee individually. They must consider how the plan will be administered to provide for individual pay increases.

There are several approaches for administering the pay increase feature of the plan:

- **Merit increases,** granted to recognize performance and contribution.
- **Promotional increases,** given to employees assigned different jobs in higher pay levels.
- **Tenure increases,** given to employees for time worked with the company.
- **General increases,** granted to employees to maintain real earnings as required by economic factors and in order to keep pay competitive.

These approaches are the most common, but there are many variations.[6] Most annual increases are made for cost of living, tenure, or employment market reasons. Obviously, employers might use several, all, or combinations of the various increase methods.

Employers should document salary increases for each employee and record the reasons for them.

## Updating the Plan

To keep the pay administration plan updated, the employer should review it at least annually. Adjustments should be made where necessary, and supervisory personnel should be retained in using the plan. This is not the kind of plan that can be set up and then forgotten.

During the annual review, the owner/managers should ask themselves these important questions: Is the plan working? Are they getting the kind of employees they want or are they just making do? What is the turnover rate? Do employees seem to care about the business? What matters is how the plan helps employers achieve the objectives of the business.

**TABLE 9–4    Strengths and Weaknesses of Selected Forms of Retail Salesperson Compensation Plans**

| Method of Payment | Formula | Advantages | Disadvantages |
|---|---|---|---|
| Straight salary | Amount of pay established in advance for a defined pay period. | Definite and easy for employees to understand<br>Generally best for smaller stores<br>Minimizes temptation to use "pressure" selling<br>Encourages more conscientious and careful work<br>Provides easier managerial control<br>Good for inexperienced/new employees<br>Simplifies payroll<br>Provides a definite income to employees<br>Fair | Inflexible<br>Provides no financial incentive for extra effort<br>Compensation does not fluctuate in proportion to sales volume<br>Lack of incentives could promote laziness<br>Strong supervision often required<br>No opportunity to earn extra income |
| Salary plus commission | Guaranteed minimum salary plus a small additional percentage based on amount of sales | Easy for employees to understand<br>Emphasizes selling and customer service<br>Stable income assured when volume is low<br>Provides financial incentive for extra effort<br>Incentives easily controlled by management<br>Good opportunity to earn extra income<br>Less managerial supervision necessary | Small incentives could be ineffective<br>Even ineffective salespersons receive commissions<br>Increases departmental selling costs<br>Poor salespersons could lose customers with "pressure" selling |

# Planning Employee Benefits[7]

Employee benefits costs have greatly affected business expenses and profits since the establishment during the First World War of the Workers' Compensation Board of Ontario. However, very few people could benefit from these programmes, and in 1927, the Old Age Pension programme was instituted by the federal government. Unemployment Insurance was a result of the Great Depression and instituted into law in the 1940s. The Canada Pension Plan (1966) and the Quebec Pension Plan are mandatory for all employees. Health insurance is covered under the Canada Health Act (1984) and some provincial health plans. Other benefits are covered under the Pension Benefits Standards Act and the Old Age Security Act. Benefits-pay costs as a percentage of direct compensation grew from 24 percent in 1964 to 31 percent in 1984.[8]

**TABLE 9–4**   *Continued*

| Method of Payment | Formula | Advantages | Disadvantages |
|---|---|---|---|
| Quota plus bonus plan | Varying percentages of sales are paid for different levels of sales achieved above the quotas set for each category of merchandise | Effective in smaller establishments<br>Good incentives for special sales/tasks<br>Encourages competitive spirit<br>Stable income assured when volume is low<br>Does not overly promote "pressure" selling<br>Very flexible for managerial use<br>Automatic check against overstaffing of store<br>Ensures prompt service to customers<br>Less managerial supervision necessary | Not as easily understood by employees<br>Sales returns could cause withheld bonuses, thus ill feelings<br>Setting rates for quota bonuses is a delicate task<br>Quota could be difficult to set from past sales<br>Bonuses must be changed often for seasonal goods<br>Unattainable bonuses destroy incentive |
| Straight commission | Salary is based entirely as a percentage of sales. The percentage is typically higher for the most profitable merchandise. | Provides *strong* incentives to salespersons<br>Easy for employees to understand<br>Attracts better salespersons<br>Guarantees planned selling cost for store<br>Easy to operate by management<br>Drawing account to ensure a definite income per pay period could be established by management to offset some disadvantages of this method (when necessary, pay is charged against future commissions) | Employees *must* be well trained and supervised<br>No assured income<br>Factors beyond salesperson's control could substantially diminish earnings<br>Too uncertain for average retail salesperson<br>"Pressure" selling strongly encouraged<br>Customers could be antagonized<br>Focus generally on high-cost goods<br>Senior salespersons take high-cost goods, leaving juniors with low-cost goods<br>Ill will and tension level between salespersons |

**Employee compensation** includes wages or salary, commissions, incentives, overtime, and benefits. **Benefits** include holidays and paid vacations, unemployment insurance, Canada/Quebec pension, health care, company pensions, welfare benefits (life insurance, supplementary health, dental plan), disability payments, and services like credit unions, product or service discounts, legal assistance, travel clubs, education subsidies, profit-sharing plans, and food services.

After productivity, employee compensation is the most difficult employee relations issue for management. Employee benefits can help develop a stable and productive work force, but employers must have effective cost and administrative controls. Legally required benefits (e.g., Canada Pension, unemployment insurance) can be managed with minimal difficulty by keeping records, submitting forms to the proper authorities, and paying for the required coverage. But when choosing and managing other types of benefits, employers should get professional advice in planning and setting up programs.

As the benefits cost increases as a percentage of total compensation, the direct pay cost percentage decreases. Employers cannot recognize outstanding achievement with direct pay increases because funds for direct pay are diminishing as benefits spending gets bigger. As a result, unfortunately, the compensation differential between the mediocre employee and the outstanding achiever is narrowing. Managers need to recognize the advantages, limitations, and cost impact that employee benefits have on business operations and net profit.

Analyzing benefits costs can be accomplished by grouping them into the following categories:

- Legally required benefits (Canada/Quebec pension plan, health insurance, unemployment insurance).
- Private pensions.
- Group insurance.
- Supplementary insurance.
- Payment for time not worked.
- Employee services such as day care.
- Perquisites such as employee discounts or free merchandise.

Many employers now pay for most, if not all, of the employees' life, medical, and disability insurance. The rapid escalation of benefits cost, as compared to direct pay compensation, has caused managers to become more diligent in controlling these costs and in getting better employee relations.

## Selecting Employee Benefits

Benefits should be designed with the help of an individual who is a competent planner and manager. Employers need an approach that allows them to offer employee benefits designed to meet the company's and the employees' needs. For example, employees who are older and no longer have the responsibility of a family will have different requirements from the employees who have families. Also, employees whose spouses are covered by another employer's plan might be considered to minimize double coverage.

## Employee Performance Appraisal

Many retail employees are under a merit increase pay system, though most of their pay increase may result from other factors. This approach involves periodic review and appraisal of how well employees perform their assigned duties. An effective employee appraisal plan (1) achieves better two-way communications between the manager and the employee, (2) relates pay to work performance and results,

(3) provides a standardized approach to evaluating performance, and (4) helps employees see how they can improve by explaining job responsibilities and expectations.

Such a performance review helps not only the employee whose work is being appraised, but also the manager doing the appraisal to gain insight into the organization. An open exchange between employee and manager can show the manager where improvements in equipment, procedures, or other factors might improve employee performance. Managers should try to foster a climate in which employees can discuss progress and problems informally at any time throughout the year.

Again, to get the best results, it is a good idea to use standardized forms of appraisal. A typical form includes job performance factors such as results achieved; quality of performance; volume of work; effectiveness in working with others in the store; effectiveness in dealing with customers, suppliers, and so on; initiative; job knowledge; and dependability.

Employers can design their own forms, using examples in books on personnel administration, if necessary. The forms should be tailored to the jobs and should follow from job analyses as discussed earlier.

# Employee Relations and Personnel Policies[9]

There are many ways to manage people. The manager can be strict and rigidly enforce rules. Communications can be one way from boss to employee. The job might get done but with fairly high turnover, absenteeism, and low morale.

Or the owner can make an extra effort to be a "nice guy" to everyone on the payroll. This management style may lead to reduced adherence to the rules, and employees may argue when they are asked to do work they do not like. Controlling the daily operation of the business may become more and more difficult. The business may survive, but only with much lower profits than if the owner followed more competent personnel policies.

But there is another way in which employees can feel a part of the firm, where manager and employees can communicate effectively with each other, where rules are fair and flexible yet enforced with positive discipline. The job gets done efficiently and profitably, and the business does well.

Large companies have a separate personnel department. Most managers of a small firm view this personnel function as just part of the general job of running a business. It is good practice, though, to think of the personnel function as a distinct and separate part of management responsibilities—only then are personnel responsibilities likely to get the priorities they deserve.

The human resources function is generally considered to include all those policies and administrative procedures necessary to satisfy the needs of employees. Not necessarily in priority order, these include:

1. Administrative personnel procedures.
2. Supervisory practices based on human relations and competent delegation.

3. Positive discipline.
4. Grievance prevention and grievance handling.
5. A system of communications.
6. Adherence to all governmental rules and regulations pertaining to the personnel function.

*Administrative Personnel Procedures*

Favourable employee relations require competent handling of the administrative aspects of the personnel function. These include the management of:

1. Work hours.
2. The physical working environment.
   *a.* Facilities.
   *b.* Equipment.
3. Payroll procedures.
4. Benefit procedures, including insurance matters, and vacation and holiday schedules.

*Supervisory Practices and the Personnel Function*

If an employee's job satisfies his or her needs, the employee responds more favourably to the job. Such employees tend to take their responsibilities seriously, act positively for the firm, and are absent from work only rarely. The key point is that when a job satisfies needs, the employee may bring greater commitment to the job.

There are five factors that generally cause a deep commitment to job performance for most employees. These are:

1. *The work itself:* To what extent does the employee see the work as meaningful and worthwhile?
2. *Achievement:* How much opportunity is there for the employee to accomplish tasks that are seen as a reasonable challenge?
3. *Responsibility:* To what extent does the employee have assignments and the authority necessary to take care of a significant function of the organization?
4. *Recognition:* To what extent is the employee aware of how highly other people value the contributions made by the employee?
5. *Advancement:* How much opportunity is there for the employee to assume greater responsibilities in the firm?

These five factors tend to satisfy certain critical needs of individuals:

1. The feeling of *being accepted* as part of the firm's work team.
2. *Feeling important*—that the employee's strengths, capabilities, and contributions are known and valued highly.
3. The chance to *continue to grow* and become a more fully functioning person.

If the kinds of needs just described are met by paying attention to the five factors listed, management will have taken significant steps toward gaining the full commitment of employees to job performance. To do this, several practical strategies can be used:

- Establishing confidence and trust with employees through open communication and the development of sensitivity to employee needs.
- Allowing employees participation in decision making that directly affects them.
- Helping employees set their own work methods and work goals as much as possible.
- Praising and rewarding good work as clearly and promptly as inadequate performance is mentioned.
- Restructuring jobs to be challenging and interesting by giving increased responsibilities and independence to those who want it and who can handle it.

## *Positive Discipline*

The word *discipline* carries with it many negative meanings. It is often used as a synonym for punishment. Yet discipline is also used to refer to the spirit that exists in a successful ball team where team members are willing to consider the needs of the team as more important than their own.

Positive discipline in a retail firm is an atmosphere of mutual trust and common purpose in which all employees understand the company rules as well as the objectives, and do everything possible to support them.

Any disciplinary programme requires, as its base, that all of the employees have a clear understanding of exactly what is expected of them. This is why a concise set of rules and standards must exist that is fair, clear, realistic, and communicated. Once the standards and rules are known by all employees, discipline can be enforced equitably and fairly.

A good set of rules need not be more than one page, but it can prove essential to the success of a business. A few guidelines for establishing a climate of positive discipline are:

1. There must be rules and standards that are communicated clearly and administered fairly, and these must be reasonable. In addition, employees should be consulted when rules are set.
2. Rules should be communicated so they are known and understood by all employees. An employee manual can help with communicating rules. While a rule or a standard is in force, employees are expected to adhere to it. Even though rules exist, people should know that if a personal problem or a unique situation makes the rule exceptionally harsh, the rule may be modified or an exception granted.
3. There should be no favourites, and privileges should be granted only when they can also be granted to other employees in similar circumstances. This means that it must be possible to explain to other employees, who request a similar privilege with less justification, why the privilege cannot be extended to them in their particular situation.

4. Employees must be aware that they can and should voice dissatisfaction with any rules or standards they consider unreasonable, as well as with working conditions they feel hazardous, discomforting, or burdensome.

5. Employees should understand the consequences of breaking a rule without permission. Large companies have disciplinary procedures for minor violations that could apply equally well in small companies. They usually call for one or two friendly reminders. If the problem continues, there is a formal, verbal warning, then a written warning, and if the employee persists in violating rules, there would be a suspension and/or dismissal. In violations of more serious rules, fewer steps would be used. It is not easy to communicate this procedure, since it should not be so firm that it can be expressed in writing. If it is made clear to employees who violate a rule at the first reminder, the procedure soon becomes understood by all.

6. There should be an appeals procedure for employees who feel that management has made an unfair decision. At the very least, the employee should be aware that management is willing to reconsider a decision at a later time.

7. There should be recognition for good performance, reliability, and loyalty. Negative comments, when they are necessary, will be accepted as helpful if employees also receive feedback when things go well.

## *Grievance Prevention and Handling*

No matter how good the atmosphere of positive discipline in a business, rules are bound to be broken by some people from time to time. In those situations, corrective action is sometimes necessary. In some rare cases, the violation may be so severe that serious penalties are necessary. If an employee is caught in the act of stealing or deliberately destroys company property, summary dismissal may be necessary. In all other severe cases, a corrective interview is needed to determine the reasons for the problem and to establish what penalty, if any, is appropriate. Such an interview should include all, or most, of the following steps:

1. Outlining the problem to the employee, including an explanation of the rule or procedure that was broken.

2. Allowing the employee to explain his or her side of the story. This step will often bring out problems that need to be resolved to avoid rule violations in the future.

3. Exploring with the employee what should be done to prevent a recurrence of the problem.

4. Reaching agreement with the employee on the corrective action that should be taken.

Even in the best environment, though, employees will occasionally feel unhappy about something. They may not get paid on time, or may feel that the room is too hot, too cold, or too dark. They may feel that they deserve a merit increase, or that someone has hurt their feelings. When this happens, good personnel policies require that employees know how they can express their dissatisfaction and obtain some consideration.

A *written grievance procedure,* known to employees, can be very helpful in creating a positive atmosphere. It informs employees how they can obtain a hearing on their problems, and it ensures that the owner/manager becomes aware that the problem exists. When employees know that someone will listen to them, grievances are less serious; hearing a complaint carefully often is half the job of resolving it.

A good grievance procedure begins with the manager making it a point to actively look for signs of possible sources of dissatisfaction and to notice changes in employee behaviour that signal that a problem may exist. This often makes it possible to handle a situation when it is still easy to resolve.

# Job Enrichment

Too many companies today treat employees as throwaway assets. The average annual turnover rate among restaurant workers, for example, is 250 percent, while management turnover is about 50 percent. Many employees leave within 30 days of employment, wasting whatever training they have been given.[10] The retail investment is too high to take such an approach. Forward-thinking managers view the employee as a total person. They are concerned with what the employee does during working hours and during time off the job. They try to help employees get more education, sharpen job skills, and participate in worthwhile nonjob activities.

Keeping employees satisfied at work is more than a matter of salary. Employees want to feel they belong and that the company cares about them as total human beings. Careful attention to these needs will contribute to higher employee productivity and a lower turnover rate.[11]

Motivation and job enrichment cannot be separated. **Motivation** is normally related to work policies and supervisor attitudes. Motivated employees will devote their best efforts to company goals. As a result, management is recognizing the benefits of flexibility in work schedules, enrichment programs, and building employee motivation. Yesterday's human resources solutions don't work with today's life-styles. Programmes such as flex time, job sharing, on-site day care, and quality circles have emerged in retailing in recent years as management has sought ways to increase productivity and enrich the job by reducing worker stress at home and at work.

## Flex Time

**Flex time** is a system by which workers can arrive and depart on a variable schedule. Flex-time programmes contribute to improved employee morale, a greater sense of employee responsibility, less stress, and reduced turnover. Retailers with flex-time programmes include Sears and the Bank of Montreal.

## Job Sharing

**Job sharing** occurs when two workers voluntarily hold joint responsibility for what was formerly one position. In effect, two permanent, part-time positions result from what was one full-time position. Job sharing differs from work sharing. **Work sharing** usually occurs in organizations during economic recessions where all employees are required to cut back on their work hours and are paid accordingly. Job sharing is a way to retain valuable employees who no longer want to work full time. Management has found that the enthusiasm and productivity in such programs is high. This practice is particularly prevalent among large department stores such as Woodward's and Eaton's.[12]

*Child and People Care Programmes*

Young children pose a special problem for working parents. About 57 percent of all single mothers with preschool children are now in the work force. There is a growing recognition in Canada about the value of providing good day-care services, with the increased assistance of governments.

Some companies, such as the Bank of Montreal, provide **people care programmes.** They give their employees paid time off, called "people care days," to deal with personal matters such as taking a driving test, applying for a mortgage, or doing volunteer work in the community.[13]

*Employee Assistance Programmes*

Drug abuse and alcohol are two of the most obvious areas in which employers can provide counselling and assistance. Other programmes include scholarships for children of employees and encouraging community volunteer work.

# Controlling Shoplifting and Employee Theft

An important part of merchandise management is controlling for merchandise shortages. Merchandise shortages are caused by a variety of factors—poor paperwork controls, human error, computer glitches, vendor theft, shoplifters, and dishonest employees. In one survey, retailers attributed approximately 83 percent of inventory shrinkage to employee theft and customer shoplifting, and 17 percent to poor paperwork control. It has been estimated that Canadian retailers lost $2 billion in 1991 (over $6 million a day) to shoplifters, paperwork errors, and employee theft. This represents 1.8 percent of total retail sales, and is greater than the total profits of the retail sector in 1991.[14] Because the greatest percentage of merchandise losses is due to shoplifting and employee theft, the following sections will focus on these two areas, including how they occur and what actions can be taken to control and prevent them.

*Shoplifting*

Shoplifting is the largest monetary crime in the nation. It affects retailers' profits, so plans should be made to control shoplifting.[15]

**Controlling Shoplifting**
Time and money are better spent in preventing shoplifting than in prosecuting the offenders. There are several areas where retailers can take actions to control shoplifting.

***Educate Employees.***    Retailers know that salespeople are the first line of defense against shoplifting. However, some salespeople hesitate to get involved because of their fear of a possible confrontation. However, management can do a number of things to use salespeople more effectively as a way of controlling shoplifting. Here are five key points:[16]

1. *Create awareness and concern:* Managers must communicate their concern about shoplifting and keep employees constantly aware of the problem. For example, shoplifting and its effects should be discussed periodically at staff meetings.

2. *Provide employee training:* Salespeople will respond to shoplifting only when they feel comfortable in doing so. Thus, they need to be taught to recognize shoplifters and how to respond to the situation. Retail Highlight 9–3 provides some practical advice on how to recognize shoplifters.

3. *Motivate salespeople to get involved:* Store managers should remind salespeople that shoplifters cost them personally. Salespeople must be

---

**Retail Highlight 9–3**

# How to Recognize Shoplifters

Be on the lookout for customers carrying concealment devices such as bulky packages, large pocketbooks, baby carriages, or an oversized arm sling.

Be on the lookout for shoppers walking with unnatural steps—they may be concealing items between their legs.

Employees should be alert to groups of shoppers who enter the store together, then break up and go in different directions. A customer who attempts to monopolize a salesperson's time may be covering for an associate stealing elsewhere in the store. A gang member may start an argument with store personnel or other gang members or may feign a fainting spell to draw attention, giving a cohort the opportunity to steal merchandise from another part of the store.

Shoplifters do not like crowds. They keep a sharp eye out for other customers or store personnel. Quick, nervous glances may be a giveaway.

Sales help should remember that ordinary customers want attention; shoplifters do not. When busy with one customer, the salesperson should acknowledge waiting customers with polite remarks such as, "I'll be with you in a minute." This pleases legitimate customers—and makes a shoplifter feel uneasy.

Salespeople should watch for a customer who handles a lot of merchandise, but takes an unusually long time to make a decision. They should watch for customers lingering in one area, loitering near stockrooms or other restricted areas, or wandering aimlessly through the store. They should try to be alert to customers who consistently shop during hours when staff is low.

aware that shoplifting affects their pay cheque and benefits (averaging $1,500 per employee per year in many stores). Shoplifting makes the salesperson's job more difficult and diverts time from customers who are buying merchandise.

4. *Support the salesperson:* Salespeople need to know they are not alone in controlling shoplifting. Management needs to support salespeople's efforts by giving them the tools and devices they need to detect shoplifters and by providing backup assistance when needed.

5. *Show appreciation:* Salespeople need positive feedback; they need to know that their efforts are meaningful and recognized by management. Salespeople should be provided with periodic information on progress being made toward controlling shoplifting. Individual performance should be recognized by certificates of merit, monetary awards, notations on personnel evaluations, and similar means.

***Plan Store Layout with Deterrence in Mind.***    Retailers should maintain adequate lighting in all areas of the store and keep protruding "wings" and end displays low. In addition, display cases should be set in broken sequences and, if possible, run for short lengths with spaces in between. Small items of high value (e.g., film, cameras, small appliances) should be kept behind a counter or in a locked case with a salesclerk on duty. Display counters should be kept neat; it is easier to determine if an item is missing if the display area is orderly. If fire regulations permit, all exits not to be used by customers should be locked. Noisy alarms should be attached to unlocked exits. Unused check-out aisles should be closed and blocked off.

***Use Protective Personnel and Equipment.***    Protective devices may be expensive, but shoplifting is more expensive. Table 9–5 presents information related to retail

---

**TABLE 9–5    Shrinkage Control Devices**

| *Devices by Frequency of Use* | *Devices Judged to Be Most Effective* | *Devices Judged to Be Least Effective* |
|---|---|---|
| Mirrors | Electronic tags | Mirrors |
| Limited-access areas | Guards | Visible TV cameras |
| Lock-and-chain devices | Point-of-sale systems | Guards |
| Guards | Observation booths | Observation booths |
| Point-of-sale systems | Visible TV Cameras | Concealed TV cameras |
| Observation booths | Fitting-room attendants | Lock-and-chain devices |
| Electronic tags | Limited-access areas | Fitting-room attendants |
| Visible TV cameras | Lock-and-chain devices | Limited-access areas |
| Concealed TV cameras | Concealed TV cameras | Point-of-sale systems |
| Fitting-room attendants | Mirrors | Electronic tags |

Source: *6th Annual Study of Security and Loss Prevention Procedures in Retailing 1984* (New York: National Mass Retailing Institute and Arthur Young, 1984), p. 18.

use of shrinkage control devices. The table shows frequency of use of selected devices as well as the effectiveness of the devices according to retailers.

Electronic tags are judged by retailers to be the most effective protective device. Retailers using such devices, however, should be sure that salespeople and cashiers are diligent in their use. If an employee forgets to remove the tag and the customer is falsely accused, the retailer could be held liable.[17]

Guards are also considered by retailers to be powerful visual deterrents to shoplifters. While mirrors are the most frequently used device, they are judged by retailers to be the least effective. The nearest runner-up in lack of effectiveness is visible TV cameras.

Finally, audible and subaudible messages may be used. In particular, some retailers have had some success using subliminal messages such as ''Do not steal.''[18]

### Apprehending, Arresting, and Prosecuting Shoplifters

To make legal charges stick, retailers must be able to:

1. See the person take or conceal the merchandise.
2. Identify the merchandise as belonging to the store.
3. Testify that it was taken with the intent to steal.
4. Prove the merchandise was not paid for.

If retailers are unable to meet all four criteria, they leave themselves open to countercharges of false arrest. False arrest need not mean police arrest: Simply preventing a person from conducting normal activities can be deemed false arrest. Furthermore, any physical contact, even a light touch on the arm, may be considered unnecessary and may be used against the retailer in court.

It is wisest to apprehend shoplifters outside the store. The retailer has a better case if it can be demonstrated that the shoplifter left the store with stolen merchandise. Outside apprehension also eliminates unpleasant scenes that might disrupt normal store operation. However, retailers may prefer to apprehend a shoplifter if the merchandise involved is of considerable value or if the thief is likely to elude store personnel outside the store premises. In either case, one recommended procedure is for store employees to identify themselves, then say ''I believe you have some merchandise you have forgotten to pay for. Would you mind coming with me to straighten things out?''

Some organizations have control files on shoplifters who have been caught. The local retail merchants' association can supply information about the services available in the area.

Prosecution is in order if the shoplifter is violent, lacks proper identification, appears to be under the influence of alcohol or other drugs, or appears to be a professional.

*Employee Theft*     Employee theft is a major problem facing retailers. One study revealed that the large majority of dishonest employees steal only occasionally. The study also found that 10.6 percent of dishonest employees steal at a weekly frequency or more and that these individuals are responsible for nearly 79 percent of total theft incidents.[19]

Another study among managers of mass merchandise, department, and specialty stores revealed that apprehensions of female employees are slightly more prevalent (54 percent) than those of male employees (46 percent). Retailers apprehend young-adult employees more frequently than other age groups. This same study found that more than 60 percent of all reported employee apprehensions were attributed to cashiers (45 percent) and selling floor personnel (17 percent).[20]

### How Do Employees Steal?

Statistics emphasize discount abuse as the leading form of retail theft by employees. Most frequently, employees will purchase merchandise for friends and relatives who are not eligible for a discount. The amounts of merchandise purchased often exceed limits set by company policy. Employees may purchase merchandise at a discount and then have it returned by a friend for full value.[21] Employees also steal using a variety of other means. Some employee theft may be carried out in collusion with customers (who are acquaintances), or with a vendor. Theft of merchandise and cash can also occur.

Because of the magnitude of the problem, retailers must establish prevention and detection procedures for controlling employee theft.

### Controlling Employee Theft

Some of the ideas discussed earlier for controlling shoplifting, such as use of guards and detection devices like mirrors and TV cameras, also serve to detect and prevent employee theft. This section looks at some of the measures retailers are taking specifically to control employee theft.

Obviously, the greatest deterrent to internal theft is to hire honest people. Traditionally, retailers have used the polygraph in employee screening. Now, however, they are turning to written honesty tests and better background checks because of some controversy surrounding the use of polygraph tests. Some retailers are using the Reed report, which consists of 90 psychologically oriented questions whose yes/no answers classify a person as prone or not prone to theft. In addition to the use of these honesty tests, security experts stress that retailers must also implement drug testing. Such tests are needed because of the growing incidence of internal theft resulting from drug use.

Another way to cut employee theft is to run awareness programmes. Such programmes show how employees can hurt themselves by stealing. Through awareness programmes, management points out the store's policy on dealing with employee theft and how important honesty is to job security and to a good reference when an employee changes jobs. Letting employees know that management cares about them is an effective way to prevent theft.

Peer pressure and use of a reward system can be effective. For such a system to work, however, management must assure employees that confidences will be respected and anonymity ensured—that their efforts in helping catch employee thieves will not place them in danger of termination, retaliation, lawsuits, or reputation as a "snitch."[22]

Other deterrents to internal thievery include use of (1) employee identification badges; (2) restriction on employee movement within the store before, during, and after selling hours; (3) regular internal audits; (4) surprise internal audits; and (5) tight controls over petty cash, accounts receivable, payroll, and inventory.

# Chapter Highlights

- Staffing a store with the right people is a critical part of the strategic plan for a retailer. Staffing needs vary depending on the type of merchandise carried, services the store will offer, the image management wants to project to customers, and the way in which the firm wants to compete.

- The initial step in developing a human resources plan for the firm is to develop good job descriptions and job specifications. These are written after a job analysis has been undertaken to obtain important facts about the job. The job description provides the content and responsibilities of the job and how it ties in with other jobs. The job specification describes the personal qualifications required to do the job.

- Recruiting—attracting the right people—is a critical element of the plan. Recruits may be sought either inside or outside the firm. Specific guidelines exist that management must follow in administering selection tests and in otherwise screening employees.

- Simply hiring the right people is not enough. Training is often necessary for new employees and should be offered as an ongoing part of the personnel program.

- Employees need to know about their rights and responsibilities within the firm, the history of the firm, and specific information about their job responsibilities. Sales personnel may also need training in technical dimensions of the merchandise for which they will be responsible.

- An equitable employee pay plan is a further important component of a personnel plan and can contribute to

higher employee productivity and satisfaction. A wage survey within the surrounding area can determine the wages paid for comparable jobs. Retailers should make sure that employees understand how they will be evaluated for pay increases or promotions and how the pay plan was developed and will be administered. Closely related to the pay plan is establishing the level and type of employee benefits to be paid.

- Employee performance appraisals also need to occur on a regular basis; normally, employees are appraised annually. Standardized forms should be developed for this purpose. Ratings by supervisors should be discussed with the employees and suggestions should be given as to how the employees can improve their performance.

- Employee motivation and job enrichment are also important elements of the personnel plan. Management must recognize that employees have needs such as the desire for recognition and achievement, which cannot be satisfied by money alone.

- Shoplifting is a very large monetary crime in Canada. Retailers, however, can take a number of actions to detect and prevent shoplifting.

- Employee theft is also a major problem retailers face. Because of the magnitude of the problem, retailers must establish prevention and detection procedures for controlling internal theft.

# Key Terms

Benefits    229
Canadian Human Rights Commission    217
Compensation    223

Employee compensation    229
Flex time    235
General (salary) increases    227

# Discussion Questions

1. What are the key federal and provincial laws that affect recruiting, selection, and compensation of employees? What are the likely effects as a result of these regulations?

2. Assume you are the manager of a men's clothing outlet located close to a major university campus. What would be the basic elements of a training program for the outlet? How would your program likely differ from the type of training that might be offered to new employees who have been hired by Sears?

3. Briefly describe the steps that must be carried out in developing a formal compensation plan.

4. What is likely to be the most effective method for compensating *(a)* a retail salesperson, *(b)* an accountant, and *(c)* a department buyer?

5. Why should retail management institute an employee performance appraisal plan? What might be some of the performance factors that are evaluated?

6. Why should an employee grievance procedure and a procedure for handling disciplinary matters be established, even in the absence of a union?

7. What are some of the things retail management can do to provide greater job enrichment and enhance motivation among employees?

8. What are the various types of shoplifters? What can retail managers do to control shoplifting? What can retail managers do to control employee theft?

# Application Exercises

1. Devise a format and interview at least five people who have worked in the retailing industry in some capacity. Determine each individual's honest views on wages, working conditions, superior-subordinate relationships, and so on. Prepare a report for class discussion on what you have discovered.

2. Select several different retail companies (differing in organizational arrangement, number of stores and sales volume, and product line) and make an appointment with the executive responsible for the personnel functions. Describe the employment process of each (include selection, training, and benefits, including compensation) and draw comparisons among the group. See if you can explain the differences in apparent effectiveness of the programmes. See if you can get the executives to discuss affirmative action.

3. Arrange through your college or university placement office to have a few minutes with several of the recruiters coming to campus to interview people for retailing companies. Structure a questionnaire to administer to each recruiter to find out what he or she is looking for in a student; how the interview on campus enters into the selection process; what kinds of questions are asked of the interviewee; what the recruiter expects the interviewee to know about the company; what variables are considered in evaluating the student; and what the subsequent steps are in the employment process.

# Suggested Cases

# Endnotes

1. The material on job analysis, job descriptions, and job specifications is reproduced, with modifications, from *Job Analysis, Job Specifications, and Job Descriptions, a Self-Instructional Booklet,* No. 1020 (Washington, D.C.: U.S. Small Business Administration).

2. This material is reproduced, with modifications, from Walter E. Green, "Staffing Your Store," *Management Aid,* No. 5.007 (Washington, D.C.: U.S. Small Business Administration).

3. *Canadian Human Rights Act,* paragraph 2, subsection (a); see also William B. Werther, Jr., Keith Davis, Hermann F. Schwind, Hari Das, and Frederick C. Miner, Jr., *Canadian Personnel Management and Human Resources* (Toronto: McGraw-Hill Ryerson, 1985), Chapter 3.

4. "Training Programs Must Reflect Today's Environment," *Chain Store Age Executive,* June 1989, pp. 60–61.

5. This material is condensed from Jean F. Scolland, "Setting Up a Pay System," *Management Aid,* No. 5.006 (Washington, D.C.: U.S. Small Business Administration).

6. See, for example, "Incentive Pay Is Catching On," *Chain Store Age Executive,* January 1986, p. 9.

7. This material is condensed from John B. Hannah, "Changing Employee Benefits," *Management Aid,* No. 5.008 (Washington, D.C.: U.S. Small Business Administration).

8. The material on employee relations and personnel policies is reproduced, with modifications, from *Employee Relations and Personnel Policies,* Self-Instructional Booklet, no. 12 (Washington, D.C.: U.S. Small Business Administration); see also, *Managing People, Retailing's Prime Resource* (Toronto: Retail Council of Canada, 1988).

9. Shimon L. Dolan and Randall S. Schuler, *Personnel and Human Resource Management in Canada* (St. Paul, Minn.: West Publishing, 1987), Chapter 11.

10. Brian Bremner, "Among Restaurateurs, It's Dog Eat Dog," *Business Week,* January 9, 1989, p. 86.

11. Julia R. Galosy, "Teaching Managers to Motivate: When Theory Isn't Enough," *Professional Trainer,* Spring 1984, p. 10.

12. Dolan and Schuler, *Personnel and Human Resource Management,* p. 145.

13. Brian Brennan, "Employers Try to Show They Care," *Kitchener-Waterloo Record,* July 9, 1992, p. E8.

14. Erik Heinrich, "Canadian Retailers Pummelled by Theft," *The Financial Post,* May 13, 1992, p. 6; see also, *Retail Shrinkage = Profit Erosion: How to Shore Up the Dike* (Toronto: Retail Council of Canada, 1988); and Barbara Aarsteinsen, "Shoplifting, Worker Theft Cost $2 Million a Day, Retailers' Survey Finds," *Globe and Mail,* May 3, 1989, pp. 1–2.

15. "The Juvenile Shoplifter," *The Marketing Mix* 19, no. 1 (Winter–Spring 1986), p. 1.

16. "Five Key Steps to Reducing Shoplifting," *Shrinkage Control,* September 1985, pp. 1–2; see also, *Shrinkage Survey* (Toronto: Retail Council of Canada, 1985).

17. "More Deterrents to Theft," *Stores,* June 1989, p. 63.

18. "New Study Supports Use of Subliminal Messages to Deter Retail Theft," *Shrinkage Control,* September 1985, p. 3.

19. "Facts Continue to Show that Shoplifting Exceeds Employee Theft," *Shrinkage Control,* September 1987, p. 1.

20. "EAS: Prime Deterrent to Thieves," *Stores,* June 1989, p. 59.

21. "Number One Form of Employee Theft," *Shrinkage Control,* March 1986, p. 7.

22. "Employee Pilfering Rockets in Some Industries, Which Toughens Controls," *The Wall Street Journal,* January 28, 1986, p. 1.

# 10 RETAILING RESEARCH

## Chapter Objectives

After reading this chapter, you should be able to:

1 Discuss the issues involved in gathering, analyzing, and presenting data for retail decision making.
2 Highlight the types of internal and external secondary data useful to retail managers.
3 Identify sources of secondary data for retail managers.
4 Describe the primary data collection process.

---

### Retailing Capsule

A major component of the success of retailers is making correct decisions based on the best information available. Properly conducted research provides valuable information to retailers. Consider the following examples:

- Research can help the retailer find answers to questions such as: How is store loyalty created? How does the use of smell (e.g., freshly baked goods) or music affect the customer's impression of the store? How many shoppers make their final decisions while in the store? (Answer: Over 80%.)

- Research can assist in determining merchandise selection and pricing. For example, customer brand loyalty continues to decline. Sixty percent of grocery shoppers think that generics are just as good as manufacturers' brands, and they would pass up their preferred brand in favour of a cheaper one. In addition, 1 in 10 shoppers regularly patronizes discount "club" stores such as Price Club or Costco, and 38 percent of these shoppers have household incomes of $50,000 and over.

*Fairweather used research to reposition its stores.*

SOURCE: Courtesy Fairweather.

*(continued on next page)*

A strategic plan can be no better than the information on which it is based.[1] In today's highly competitive environment, the need for better information is essential to the success of retail strategy. Retail managers need information on consumer market trends, competitive actions, and customer perceptions of each element of the firm's and competitors' retail strategies.

*Retailing Capsule continued*

- Research is also useful in finding out who are the retailer's customers. For example, until it conducted some research, Fairweather, a fashion retailer catering to the fickle teenage market, did not realize that it was also attracting women in their mid-20s. This surprising information prompted management to focus on this older and more affluent target market.
- Research can also help check the complex system of hotel services. For example, consultants with formal training in the hospitality industry posed as guests and tested every feature of the service, from wake-up calls to cleanliness. The resulting 200-page report provided a comparison of the hotel against its competitors, and included examples of $250 rooms where no one changed the sheets!
- Finally, planned research helps retailers generate sales on a continuing basis. For example, Brettons, a Canadian-owned chain of fashion stores, has a great reputation for service and follow-up thanks to an effective information system. With it, the staff keeps a record of every customer's favourite designer, sizes, and clothing needs. The salesclerks routinely call customers one week after a purchase to ask, for instance, "How was the dress you bought last week?"

These examples illustrate the many uses of research by the modern retail firm. It is clear that research plays a role in helping retailers understand customer behaviour and evaluate the quality of service.

Sources: Jo Marney, "Moment of Decision Is in the Store," *Marketing,* September 28, 1987, pp. 13–14; Jo Marney, "On Retail Success in the '80s," *Marketing,* February 15, 1982, pp. 15–16; Marina Strauss, "Brand Loyalty Losing Impact with Shoppers," *Globe and Mail,* April 14, 1992, p. B8; Mark Evans, "The Tricky Art of Changing Formats," *The Financial Post,* January 13, 1992, p. 3; Rona Maynard, "Satisfaction Guaranteed," *Report on Business Magazine,* January 1988, pp. 58–64.

# Types of Information Needed

Retail managers need information to add to their intuition and experience as they make decisions within the firm's external and internal environments. The **external environment** consists of the political, social, technological, and economic forces surrounding the organization. The **internal environment** consists of forces at work within the organization. *Internal information* is information generated within the retail business. *External information* is information about outside factors that may affect the business on a regular basis. As shown in Table 10–1, the key external factors on which information may be needed include technological trends, legislative trends, work force availability, and the actions of potential competitors. Examples of internal information include financial resources, company strengths and weaknesses, and merchandise quality.

---

TABLE 10–1    **Examples of Internal and External Environments Affecting Retail Decision Making**

---

| *External Environments* | *Internal Environments* |
|---|---|
| Technological trends | Company strengths and weaknesses |
| Environmental trends | Financial resources |
| Economic trends | Capacity utilization |
| Social issues | Quality control |
| Life-styles | |
| Regulation | |
| Pressure groups | |
| Industry growth rate | |
| Potential competitors | |
| Legislation | |
| Work force availability | |

---

Information needs vary widely within an organization because of the various responsibilities of managers. The level of detail needed in data analysis, the frequency of data use, the need for updating, and the source and uses of data differ depending on the purpose of the activity. A chief executive officer needs one type of data when making high-risk, strategic decisions, while lower-level management requires different kinds of data to make detailed, practical, policy-based decisions. Some examples are as follows:

- *Monitoring sales by merchandise type:* Data is needed frequently and is available from internal sales records. The data can be used to decide which types of merchandise to reorder.

- *Monitoring the sales levels of retail salespeople:* Such data is evaluated often on a monthly basis to determine whether salespeople are meeting their quotas.

- *Evaluating the actual percentage of markdowns and expenses:* This is compared to the objectives established at the beginning of the year.

- *Obtaining information on demographic and life-style trends, forecasts of interest rates and inflation, and likely technological changes* that will affect the firm. Such data can be used in planning new store locations, repositioning the firm, and planning expansion into new markets.

## Issues in Gathering and Analyzing Data

Management gathers and analyzes data to help avoid surprises, to develop benchmarks for objective evaluation, and to identify opportunities that might not otherwise be available. Any time a firm begins research, management must decide (1) what data is needed, (2) what priorities should be established, and (3) what indicators should be monitored. Similarly, management must decide how data will be analyzed and how the resulting information will be presented. The overall process for gathering data and transforming it into useful information occurs in the context of a retail decision support system.

## The Retail Decision Support System

A **retail decision support system** is the structure of people, equipment, and procedures to gather, analyze, and distribute the data that management needs for decision making. Depending on the size of the retail firm, such a system may vary from very informal to very formal and structured. The important point is that the firm must have an ongoing procedure to provide simple statistics, to allow for statistical analyses to be undertaken, to develop new products and services, and to measure advertising effectiveness.[2] In addition, the availability of inexpensive microcomputers and the development of accompanying software can provide retailers, whatever their size, with tools that were once available only to large firms.[3] Retail Highlight 10–1 describes in detail how a small chain developed a system to improve the effectiveness of its retailing mix.

The components of a retail decision support system, shown in Figure 10–1, include (1) secondary data, (2) data generated through a merchandise information system, and (3) primary data.

**Secondary data** are existing data that have been previously collected for other purposes, but may help answer some management problems. Secondary data may be either internal or external to the firm. **Internal data** help management systematically determine what's going on in the firm. Examples include records of customer complaints, reports on out-of-stock items, analysis of customer charge accounts, information from warranty cards, and observations of customer traffic flow in a store. **External data** are gathered by groups or organizations and made available to the retail firm. Examples include census data from Statistics Canada, data from syndicated services such as A. C. Nielsen, and trade association data.

**Merchandise information systems (MIS)** are computer-based systems that provide retail managers with better and faster information on their merchandising activities. The system can provide a series of reports that allows retailers to find quick answers to issues such as establishing seasonal plans, measuring performance against plans, order management, vendor analysis, price revisions, and sales promotion evaluation.

**Primary data** collection occurs when the firm must collect data because neither internal nor external sources can supply the data the firm needs. Examples include analysis of the firm's image, the effectiveness of promotion, and competitors' merchandise assortments.

## *Secondary Data Sources*[4]

**Internal Data**

Internal data are probably the least expensive type of data. Some data generation, such as sales by merchandise line, can be provided on a daily basis, while other data may be collected only periodically.

Retail Highlight 10–1

# Improving Effectiveness with an "Accountable" System

Perfect Portions, a chain of 11 southwestern Ontario frozen-food retail stores, is enjoying dramatically increased sales on a much leaner marketing budget thanks to an "accountable" system developed by consultant Tri-Media Marketing & Publicity. The idea behind the system is to analyse promotion, product, and purchase data to fine-tune the firm's marketing mix.

First, using in-store questionnaires, Tri-Media asked 1,500 customers where they saw their most recent Perfect Portions ad. Tri-Media director Albert Iannantuono discovered that flyers and newspaper ads were the most effective media, so all other media, including radio, were dropped, generating important savings in promotional spending. The effectiveness of the flyer program led to the launch of a newsletter to promote sales items and offer new product information and recipes. This newsletter generated chainwide sales increases. The in-store survey also revealed that the average shopper patronized a Perfect Portions store every two weeks, so all specials were harmonized to last two weeks.

Tri-Media also introduced a coupon coding system to evaluate the effectiveness of the various media. Based on the coupon tally, more customers redeemed flyer coupons than newspaper ones, suggesting a 60–40 mix of coupons to be produced in favour of flyers.

Next, the stores' electronic cash registers were replaced by point-of-sale computer systems linking registers with PCs and forwarding individual store information to the head office in Welland for analysis and interpretation. By using a Lotus spreadsheet covering 2,000 products and sales variables, owner André Champagne knows the traffic count by the hour, the number of featured items sold, and what other products were also sold at the same time. "From the data, we try to figure out why a customer bought something." For example, after a flyer offered a 1.4 kg box of chicken fingers for $.99 with every box purchased at the regular price of $17.99, sales went up 1,300 percent. Comparisons with other promotions indicated that customers respond more to "buy one, get one at a special price" offers than straight discounts. In addition, the system revealed that, excluding chicken fingers, sales per customer almost doubled during the special.

Source: Jennifer Low, "Results-Based Promotions Help Retailer Beat Cross-Border Blues," *Profit,* September 1991, pp. 47–48.

As shown in Figure 10–2, internal data can be developed from (1) customer feedback, (2) salespersons, (3) an analysis of customer charge accounts, (4) consumer panels, and (5) financial records.

*Customer Feedback.*   Customer feedback can include information obtained based on product returns, warranty cards, coupon redemptions, or customer service records. Customer correspondence such as complaint letters can also provide useful information on product quality and service problems.

As an example, Sears keeps track of the appliance purchases made by each of its customers as well as the service and maintenance calls on each appliance. This

FIGURE 10–1

*The components of a
retail decision support
system*

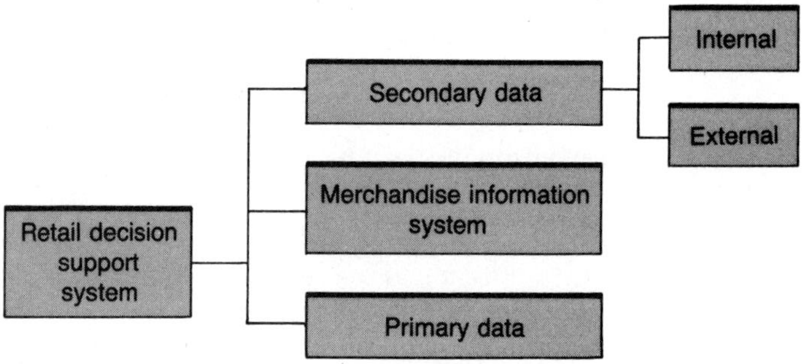

FIGURE 10–2

*Examples of internal
information sources*

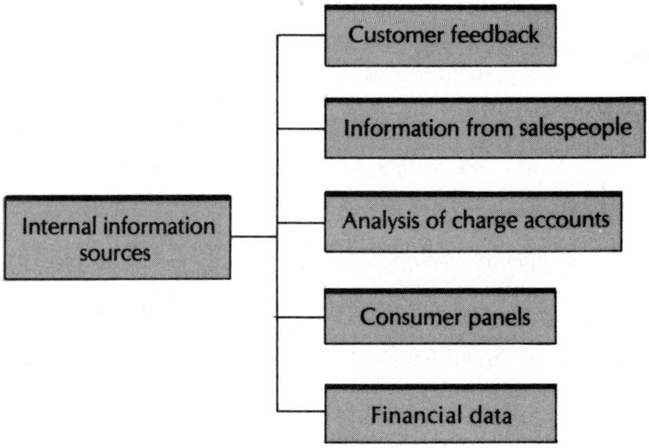

practice has given Sears a powerful marketing tool that helps boost service revenue and win customer goodwill. The firm also has been able to use the feedback from its retail customers to reach such targeted groups as appliance buyers, gardening enthusiasts, and mothers-to-be.[5]

***Information from Salespersons.***    Salespersons have the closest continuing contact with customers. They are in the best position to recognize shifts and trends in consumer demand. Salespersons can be especially important in providing information on missed sales opportunities because of merchandise that was out of stock or that the firm does not carry.

Many retailers require salespeople to complete "want slips" each time a customer requests merchandise the retailer does not stock. Managers also have regular meetings, some even daily, with salespeople to generate suggestions, criticisms, and feedback from clerks, all of which is not easily communicated by a written system.[6]

***Analysis of Charge Accounts.***    Retailers who maintain their own credit systems have a highly valuable source of information. These records can form the basis of consumer surveys to determine why some accounts are relatively inactive while others are very active. Lists of customers can also be used to test special mailings or merchandise and to track consumer purchases over time. Plotting the addresses of credit card holders is also an inexpensive way of estimating a store's trading area.

***Consumer Panels.***    Retailers sometimes assemble **panels** of consumers to elicit information for making better merchandising decisions. The following are two common types of consumer panels:

*Continuous-Purchase Record Panel.*    Such panels consist of groups of consumers who record their purchases of particular types or brands of products on a continuing basis. The panels provide valuable information on any changes that may be taking place in consumer purchasing of products and brands.

*Consumer Advisory Panel.*    A selected group of consumers can be used by the retailer to give its opinion on a variety of matters, ranging from possible new products that the store should consider carrying to store services and policies and advertising copy. With respect to merchandise assortment planning, the consumer advisory panel can be a good source of ideas for decisions regarding product additions or deletions.

***Financial Data.***    Financial data can reveal a wealth of useful information. Such information can include sales trends over time by merchandise lines, profitability by merchandise lines and departments, frequency of maintained markup by merchandise line, and information on merchandise turnover. Other valuable information can be obtained on vendors, such as which vendor is offering the best financial terms, the relative popularity of selected brand names by vendor, the frequency of unfilled orders, or orders that have been incorrectly filled.

### External Data

Information published by external sources helps management determine what is going on outside the firm. As shown in Figure 10–3, information is available from (1) syndicated services; (2) government reports; (3) guides, indexes, and directories; (4) trade associations; and (5) computerized searches.

***Syndicated Services.***    **Syndicated services** specialize in collecting and selling either financial or market information to clients.

**FIGURE 10–3**

*External sources of information*

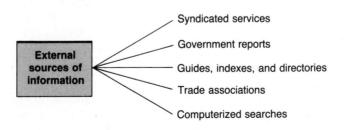

- Syndicated services
- Government reports
- Guides, indexes, and directories
- Trade associations
- Computerized searches

---

**TABLE 10-2    Typical Secondary Sources of External Information**

---

**Statistics Canada**
1. Census of Canada: Conducted every five years, it contains detailed information on population by census tract, enumeration area, and census subdivision.
2. *Reports on Commerce, Construction, Finances, and Prices:* Covers the retail trade.
3. *Reports on Employment, Unemployment, and Labour Income.*
4. Income tax data: Can be obtained by forward sortation area (FSA, first three digits of postal codes).
5. *Market Research Handbook:* Published yearly.

**Other Government Sources**
1. Consumer and Corporate Affairs: Conducts studies on consumer problems and regulations; publishes the *Misleading Advertising Bulletin.*
2. Economic Council of Canada: Publishes an Annual Report and ad hoc studies.
3. Public Archives of Canada: Provides information on machine-readable format.
4. Federal Royal Commission Reports.
5. Provincial Governments: References are listed in the ProFile Index.

**Syndicated Commercial Information**
1. Financial data: *The Financial Post,* Moody's, Dun & Bradstreet, and Standard & Poor's.
2. Market data: Store audit panels (Nielsen's Retail Index Services), consumer panels (Market Facts of Canada, International Surveys, Dialogue Canada), various market reports (Maclean Hunter Research Bureau), and market data (*The Financial Post* Survey of Markets).

**Other Published Sources**
1. Trade and Professional Associations: *Supermarketing, Progressive Grocer,* and *Journal of Retailing.*
2. Indexes and Directories: *Canadian Periodical Index, Business Periodical Index, Canadian Trade Index, Fraser's Canadian Trade Directory,* and *Canadian Directory of Shopping Centres.*
3. *Handbook of Canadian Consumer Markets.*

---

SOURCE: Compiled from René Y. Darmon, Michel Laroche, and K. Lee McGown, *Marketing Research in Canada* (Toronto: Gage, 1989), Chapter 5.

---

*Financial Data.* The major suppliers of financial data are shown in Table 10-2. For example, Dun & Bradstreet provides average operating ratios of various companies. *The Financial Post* annually publishes its Survey of Markets, and the *Globe and Mail Report on Business* publishes the Top 1,000 Companies in Canada.

*Market Data.* Such information may be in the form of store audits, warehouse withdrawal services, or consumer purchase panels. One of the most widely known firms providing such information is the A. C. Nielsen Company. Nielsen-type data on product movement is tracked by Sears to determine which merchandise is most popular with various consumer market segments.[7]

A promising new source of syndicated information is emerging from advances in electronic scanning of purchased items at the check-out counter. The advances have been greater in the supermarket than in other sectors of retailing. Today, more than 90 percent of dry groceries are marked with the universal product code (UPC), as well as more than 85 percent of the merchandise stocked by deep-discount stores.[8] Products equipped with the familiar bar code, when passed over a laser beam scanner, allow management to capture detailed information far more quickly than was possible before the bar-coding system was developed. The data captured include brands and sizes of products purchased, prices paid, and frequency of purchase. Such information on product movement can help management quickly drop slow-moving items and increase shelf space allocated to more popular items.

Some firms have developed systems that allow product purchases to be identified with specific households. Retailers are able to determine differences in product sales by household characteristics. Product promotions can then be targeted to households that have been shown to be the best markets for the items. Systems like these offer several benefits:

- Automatic purchase recording is more accurate than the conventional research techniques of keeping a diary or interviewing consumers.
- Response rates are high since respondents' work is simplified. This makes the data more representative of the population.
- Perhaps the greatest advantage is that a kind of information is provided that has hitherto been unavailable—what people *didn't* buy. Researchers know what alternatives were open to the consumer in the scanner stores. What is bought can be related both to previous history and to those alternatives.

Scanner-store panels may soon be taking over as the usual form of manually tracking product sales auditing. It will be possible to track very small markets and to change item specifications retrospectively. Two developments may be available within the next few years:

1. Data will automatically be transmitted by telephone line to the computers analyzing the figures, then on to the retailer for use by the salesclerks.[9] This will make data available according to the clients' needs—weekly, daily, or even hourly. It will be truly continuous data. The collection of in-store information about promotions, stockouts, facings, and so forth will become a normal part of a store's own requirements.
2. Instead of predetermined regions, users will be able to specify their own area requirements in relation to sales regions, climatic regions, or income characteristics. They will also be able to pick out groupings of towns or districts for tests.

Other new services also promise retailers greater insight into the hearts and minds of consumers. During the past decade, new research tools, such as the categories developed by Compusearch, Goldfarb, VALS (Stanford), or Thompson, Lightstone, have been introduced to track changes in consumer attitudes and life-styles. Retail Highlight 10–2 provides a summary of Compusearch services.

## Retail Highlight 10-2

# Compusearch Services

- *Consumer lists:* Compusearch maintains Canada's largest and most detailed national consumer database, with over 7.5 million names to choose from, using selection variables such as age, sex, life-style clusters, language preference, new movers, house values, and product-buying behaviour.
- *Demographic/Geographic data:* This information includes consumer expenditure estimates for over 1,000 product and service categories. All data are linked to postal and census geography for site location and local marketing programs.
- *Marketing databases:* Micromarketing requires extensive location or distribution data such as name and address of a store, trade area

definitions, and information on competitor sites. Compusearch can integrate client proprietary location data into all of its systems and provide data on shopping centres, financial institutions, grocery stores, and so on.
- *Segmentation systems:* Compusearch has developed a geodemographic neighbourhood classification system called Lifestyles, with 70 clusters.
- *Media analysis:* Compusearch has created systems to match the distribution of a product with the audience distribution of a magazine, newspaper, TV, or radio program. One such example is the Television Spending Index, developed with A. C. Nielsen and Harris Media Systems.

Source: *Canadian Markets 1992,* The Financial Post Publications, 1992.

These methods track shifts in consumer life-styles and are providing information about consumer behaviour that has made it easier to implement market segmentation strategies based on life-styles, as described in Chapter 5.[10] The emphasis on these services is on the "nonrational, emotional aspects of decision making, as well as the kind of information that can be obtained from such techniques as trade-off modelling and conjoint analysis. The services have emerged as retailers began to realize that there is more to understanding the consumer than just demographics and turned to life-style and psychographic information to 'explain some of the things that previously weren't explainable' by demographic analysis."[11]

*Government Reports.*[12]  Provincial and federal governments maintain detailed information on many aspects of the economy that can be useful to management. Among the censuses conducted by Statistics Canada are the Census of Canada, as well as surveys covering many areas, including retail trade. Examples of these publications of interest to retailers are *Family Expenditures in Canada, Retail Trade, Operating Results* (various categories), and *Direct Selling in Canada.* Results of these and other studies are available in virtually every library. The *Marketing Research Handbook* also contains such information in capsule form, including average sales per square metre for various categories of retailers.

Provincial agencies typically publish similar information at the provincial level.

***Guides, Indexes, and Directories.***    Other valuable sources of external information include guides, indexes, and directories. Examples of such information are also shown in Table 10–2. Guides such as the *Canadian Periodical Index* provide complete references by subject matter to articles in a wide array of journals. Specialized indexes such as *The Financial Post Index* or the *New York Times Index* provide information for those specialized sources only and are available as computerized databases. Finally, the *Canadian Trade Index* is an index for information on specific companies and industries, particularly useful to exporters.

Directories are often helpful in identifying diverse sources of information. For example, the *Fraser's Canadian Trade Directory* is organized by industrial sectors. Other directories such as the *Canadian Directory of Shopping Centres* provide detailed information on shopping centres of various sizes and regions of Canada.

***Trade Associations.***    Most retailers belong to trade groups that collect and publish data for association members. For example, the Grocery Products Manufacturers of Canada published a research report entitled *Grocery Attitudes of Canadians* based on research conducted by Dialogue Canada.[13] Such information can be useful for comparing the retailer's performance to industry averages. Associations may also publish annual industry forecasts that can be used as guides to firms making their own forecasts. As well, the Retail Council of Canada is an association that actively promotes the interests of retailers to governments, the public, and manufacturers.

***Computerized Searches.***    The amount of new information generated each year is multiplying so quickly that keeping up-to-date in a specialized field can be difficult. New journals are started each year, specialized reports appear, and information of interest is published in literally thousands of often obscure publications. Organizations specializing in abstracting, storing, and retrieving such information by subject area are thus often the starting point in information development by management. These computerized databases often contain thousands of items by subject that are available for quick retrieval. Organizations may subscribe to the specialized services for an annual fee or may pay a research firm a fee to retrieve information on a project-by-project basis.

### Strengths and Weaknesses of Secondary Data
Secondary data can be gathered quickly and inexpensively, although using it can present problems. Some data—for example, a survey on attitudes toward the environment—may become out-of-date, as such attitudes may rapidly evolve in response to external events (e.g., an oil spill, or illegal dumping of chemicals).

Another problem is a lack of standardized reporting units. One organization may define the west as British Columbia, the Yukon, and the Northwest Territories, while another may say the region also includes Alberta. Both organizations use the west as the unit for reporting, but the information is not comparable. Similarly, various organizations may use different breaking points in reporting information by age or income.

Another issue is the accuracy and objectivity used in collecting the data. Management should go to the source of external data whenever possible. This reduces the possibilities for errors made in publishing the information. Management also needs to know the magnitude of sampling errors and possible nonsampling errors. Were the persons gathering the data qualified to do so? What was the motive for gathering the data? A chamber of commerce, for example, might present only positive information about a community. Similarly, advocacy groups such as the Canadian Pharmaceutical Association tend to publish only information favourable to their causes.

*Merchandise Information Systems*

Recall from Figure 10–1 that secondary data is only one of three elements in a retail decision support system. Another ingredient is the merchandise information system. Merchandise information systems (MIS) are used to improve merchandise information gathering and analysis. Such a system is based on information available from both internal and external sources, such as merchandise vendors. It produces a series of computerized reports that can answer questions about merchandise classifications available in a store, in the branches of a department store, or in the outlets of a large chain. At the heart of this information breakthrough are electronic point-of-sale systems and in-store computers. This equipment began appearing in retail outlets during the early 1970s. Industry experts proclaimed then that it would quickly become an integral part of information gathering and processing for virtually all store operations. Change was slower than expected, though, because available software packages could not handle such broad applications as inventory control, cash management, and accounts payable. With improved software, the dream is becoming a reality in the 1990s. Retailing has entered the era of the professional manager who relies heavily on information. Still, entrepreneurial flair and creativity will probably always remain an essential ingredient of retail management success, as was illustrated in Retail Highlight 10–1.[14]

### The Ingredients of a Merchandise Information System

One of the primary emphases in systems development today is on improved merchandise reporting. No single "right" system is applicable to all types of retailing. However, the concepts underlying such systems are basically the same for many retail sectors, especially in nonfood retailing.[15]

Agreeing on merchandising objectives is the first step in developing a merchandise information system. A typical objective is to facilitate planning and decision making at all levels to increase gross margins, reduce markdown, and optimize inventory turnover.

A processing system includes all activities associated with the ordering, receiving, handling, and distribution of merchandise from the time the decision to buy is made until the items are available for sale in the store.

An information reporting system allows management to establish a record of sales and merchandise on hand and on order at multiple selling and nonselling locations. The information is available by store, merchandise, division, department, and class, as well as by vendor, style, colour, size, price, and perhaps other merchandise assortment characteristics.

Not all information can be generated internally. Management may need to collect original, or primary, data to help in making such decisions. Primary data are required, for example, in studying store image and determining the price elasticity for various merchandise categories. Thus, the third component of the retail decision system shown in Figure 10–1 is primary data.

*Primary Data Collection*

When management cannot find what it needs to know from any existing source, it must generate firsthand information. For example, among the research projects Sears conducts at the corporate level are studies of credit, public relations, and home installations. Similarly, Eaton's corporate research department conducts economic research to track economic trends and help evaluate sales trends, and consumer research to determine consumer attitudes and buying habits. Large retailers such as Sears and Eaton's conduct new-product research with the same vigour as manufacturers do. Advertising is also subject to the same intensive scrutiny.[16]

In this section, the focus is on primary data-gathering activities. Primary data collection can take many forms: observation, exploratory research, surveys, or experimentation.

### Observation

**Observation** can be an accurate method of collecting certain information. Competitors, for example, will not volunteer information on their prices, in-store displays, and other promotional efforts. Observing competitors is the only way to collect such information. Also, observation may be the least expensive way to collect certain types of data.

Methods of observation can be classified according to four dimensions: (1) natural or contrived situation, (2) open or disguised observation, (3) structured or unstructured observation, and (4) direct or indirect observation (human or mechanical observation).

*Natural versus Contrived Situation.* Natural observation occurs when management records the normal shopping behaviour of consumers without intervening in the shopping process. A *natural situation* for data collecting occurs when researchers observe the characteristics of individuals who enter or leave a retail outlet in a specified time period.

A *contrived situation* occurs when management observes the reaction of salespersons in an artificially created stressful situation. Thus, management might send an individual disguised as a shopper to pose a particularly difficult problem for a salesclerk to see how the person will react.

***Open versus Disguised Observation.***   An example of *open observation* is a supervisor observing the sales presentation of a retail salesperson to a prospective customer. *Disguised observation* occurs when researchers act as salespeople and mingle with the shoppers to observe how they handle merchandise, move up and down aisles, and generally react to various in-store displays.

***Structured or Unstructured Observation.***   *Structured observation* occurs when an individual is given a checklist or questionnaire to use in observing behaviour or a situation. For example, management might have a checklist for evaluating the cleanliness of company-owned gasoline service stations. Similarly, management might have a checklist to determine whether employees are adhering to dress codes. *Unstructured observation* occurs when an individual is told to observe a particular situation and record whatever is of interest.

***Direct versus Indirect Observation.***   Using mechanical counters to identify the volume of traffic moving past a location is one of the most frequent uses of *indirect observation* by management. Using cameras to record shopping patterns within a store for later analysis by management is a similar example. *Direct observation* would involve the use of humans to record the same information.

***An Example of Structured, Direct Observation.***   Shopping the competition is a time-honoured dimension of the retailers' marketing intelligence system. Merchants tend to look at six elements when shopping competitor stores: (1) shifts and emphasis in merchandise classifications, (2) stock content, (3) display and presentation, (4) pricing, (5) traffic patterns, and (6) service.[17] Most competing stores today carry basically the same merchandise. Management thus needs to check the competition and find out what everybody else is doing that might be different. Retailers can be quite aggressive in their competitor shopping programs. As one individual observed, "Hit or Miss will do anything, as long as it's legal, to get a leg up on the competition. . . . We'll buy merchandise at a competitor if we can't recognize the source. We'll do whatever it takes to find out who a resource is and what a direction is. We're there to find out."[18]

### Exploratory Research

Management may not be able to carefully specify the problem about which it is concerned. In such situations, exploratory research is needed to help define the problem. **Exploratory research** is characterized by flexibility in design and the absence of a formal research structure. Management, in seeking to more carefully define a problem, may obtain some qualitative information from three major sources by:[19]

1. Evaluating data either internal or external to the firm. Internally, there may be reports and sales analyses that may assist the manager in more clearly defining the problem. Externally, some secondary sources may contain information bearing on the situation faced by the manager—for example, trade publications may explain that consumers are becoming

more environmentally conscious and that they may avoid buying certain types of products.

2. Talking to knowledgeable people about the issue. These may include some suppliers, other retailers, and even customers. The retailer may even ask 8 to 12 suppliers, customers, or noncustomers to meet around a table to talk informally about the issue, with the assistance of a trained interviewer. This is called a **focus group,** and it is often used because it is a quick and inexpensive way to obtain qualitative information.[20]

3. Observing the behaviour of consumers who may be making purchase decisions. If necessary, this may be followed by an in-depth interview, using a trained interviewer, to ascertain some of the reasons for the behaviour.

Once the problem has been defined, a formal research design may be necessary to collect the data on which to base a decision. Such efforts may involve survey research or experimental designs for determining the presence of cause-and-effect relationships.

*Survey Research*    **Survey research** often includes the collection of information on the opinions or perceptions of persons in a market segment of interest to management. The process can be quite complex. For example, developing a questionnaire, normally the first step in survey research, is an art one can best learn by experience. Many different decisions have to be made. Survey research is probably the most frequently used method of data collection by management. The major steps in survey research must answer the following questions:[21]

- *Objectives:* What are the objectives of the survey?
- *Questionnaire:* What information should be collected to meet these objectives?
- *Sample:* From whom will the information be obtained?
- *Survey method and organization:* How will the information actually be collected?
- *Analysis and reporting:* How should the data be prepared for analysis, analyzed, and the findings be reported?

### Questionnaire Development

The **questionnaire** used for the survey must respond as closely as possible to the information needed by the retail manager. In developing a questionnaire, a number of decisions must be made:

*Question Format.*    Questions can be either **open-ended,** in which the respondents are simply asked to give their opinions without a formal response structure, or *close-ended,* in which response choices are prespecified.

*Open-Ended Questions.*    An example of an open-ended question is:

What is it that you like most about shopping at Loblaws? _____

_____

*Close-Ended Questions.*   Close-ended questions may use one of five popular formats:

- *Dichotomous:* Asks for yes or no answers. For example:

  Do you shop at Eaton's at least once a month?

  Yes _____     No _____

- *Multiple choice:* Allows a respondent to choose from among several predetermined answers. For example:

  Which of the following stores do you shop most often for your shoes?

  | | | | |
  |---|---|---|---|
  | Bata | _____ | Kinney | _____ |
  | Ingledew's | _____ | Other | _____ |

- *Likert scale:* Allows respondents to express their level of agreement or disagreement with various statements. For example:

  Canadian Tire offers the best selection of bicycles in this city.

  | Strongly Disagree | Disagree | Neither Agree Nor Disagree | Agree | Strongly Agree |
  |---|---|---|---|---|
  | _____ | _____ | _____ | _____ | _____ |

- *Semantic differential scale:* Allows the respondents to select the point representing the direction and intensity of their feelings between two bipolar words. For example:

  How would you describe Harvey's Restaurants?

  | Clean | __ __ __ __ __ __ __ | Dirty |
  |---|---|---|
  | Friendly | __ __ __ __ __ __ __ | Unfriendly |

- *Importance scale:* Allows the respondents to indicate the level of importance they attach to an attribute. For example:

  When I go grocery shopping, free parking is:

  | Extremely Important | Very Important | Somewhat Important | Not Very Important | Not at All Important |
  |---|---|---|---|---|
  | 1 | 2 | 3 | 4 | 5 |

**Number of Questions.**   The number of questions to be included in a questionnaire is often a function of the type of data collection that will be used: few if by telephone, more if by mail, and even more if by personal interview. In addition, for a questionnaire dealing with a "fun" subject (like cars), more questions may be added.

**Content of the Questions.**   Only questions for which one may expect relatively accurate answers should be asked. A question that will elicit inaccurate answers is: How many times did you go to a restaurant last year? For most people, the answer would be extremely difficult to estimate. In addition, sensitive issues involving age, income, or personal matters should be avoided or worded carefully. For example, instead of asking:

What is your age? _____

it is better to ask:

In which age category do you fall?
15–25     25–35     35–45     45–55     55–65
_____   _____   _____   _____   _____

***Order of the Questions.***   Order the questions logically, avoid biasing the answers, and make the questionnaire easy to answer. The first questions should be simple, just to make the respondent feel at ease. Questions should be placed so that the answer to one does not influence the answer to a subsequent one. Open-ended questions are usually placed toward the end, as are classification questions about age, income, and education.

### Sample Selection

Sampling is also often a major part of both survey and experimental research. The **sample** chosen can be either nonprobability or probability.

***Nonprobability Samples.***   *Nonprobability samples* are chosen in such a way that each unit does not have a known chance of selection, and thus they cannot be evaluated using standard statistical techniques. Nonprobability samples do not allow management to make the assumption that the sample is representative of the overall population.

The most common nonprobability sample is a **convenience sample.** Researchers, when using convenience samples, simply talk to the most readily available individuals. Convenience samples are often used in the preliminary testing of a questionnaire to make sure that respondents understand and can answer all the questions.

***Probability Samples.***   **Probability samples** are those in which each sampling unit has a known chance of selection, and it has been selected using a random procedure. Probability samples allow researchers to select samples in such a way that the results of the findings are representative of the group in which management is interested.

A simple **random sample,** a special type of probability sampling, is selected so that each sampling unit has an equal chance of selection. For example, a researcher who was going to choose a sample from the telephone directory would first have to number each telephone listing in the directory and then select the sample from the list of household numbers using a standard table of random numbers (found in any statistics book).

A **systematic sample** is often chosen when researchers want a probability sample because it is simpler to generate (i.e., you do not need to refer to a table of random numbers). In systematic sampling, researchers choose a random beginning—for example, the 4th listed number in the telephone directory—and then choose every *n*th number thereafter. Thus, if management decided on a 10 percent sample, the first telephone number chosen would be the 4th, the second one the 14th, the third the 24th, and so forth.

Using **area sampling** is often a useful way for retailers to obtain a representative sample of the trading area for the store (which may not be possible or feasible with the telephone directory, for example). First, the retailer defines the trading area on a map; next, some blocs are randomly selected (for example, census tracts or enumeration areas); third, some streets are randomly selected; and finally, houses or apartments are either systematically or randomly selected. Questionnaires are then distributed or administered door to door to the selected addresses.

### Data Collection

The next step is a decision on how the data is to be collected. The four primary methods of contact with respondents are (1) personal interviews, (2) telephone interviews, (3) mailed questionnaires, and (4) computer interviews. Personal interviews can be conducted either at the respondents' homes or in central locations such as shopping malls. Each of the four methods of contact has unique strengths and weaknesses, as shown in Table 10–3. Management weighs these strengths and weaknesses in choosing the method most suited to its needs.

*Personal Interviews.*   Personal interviews are expensive and time-consuming but allow interviewers to get more information than do the other methods. Personal interviews often are the only way to collect data if researchers need to demonstrate merchandise or to use visual aids.

*Telephone Interviews.*   Telephone interviewing is the quickest of the four methods. However, the amount of time the respondents are willing to spend on the telephone often is limited, the questioning process must be kept simple, and the use of visual aids is not possible.

---

TABLE 10–3   **Strengths and Weaknesses of the Most Frequent Means of Respondent Contact**

| *Issues* | *Mail* | *Telephone* | *Personal* | *Computer* |
|---|---|---|---|---|
| Cost per subject | Low | Low | High | Low |
| Amount of time required | Large | Small | Medium | Small |
| Response rate | Low | High | High | Low |
| Ability to collect complex data | Good | Poor | Good | Poor |
| Control over response | Poor | Good | Good | Good |

*Mailed Questionnaires.*    Mailing questionnaires, the slowest of the four methods, is the least expensive. A major drawback, however, is the lack of control over who responds to the questionnaire. Researchers may want responses from adult males over 18 years of age. A mailed survey gives researchers no assurance that such an individual actually responds to the questionnaire. Response rates are also low, often less than 20 percent.

*Computer Interviews.*    Computer technology also has made possible in-store survey research by means of electronic push-button questionnaires for a fraction of the cost and time of personal interviews in malls or households (see Exhibit 10–1 for one such example). This technology allows management to measure consumer perceptions of retail service performance, store image, and advertising effectiveness. The equipment is positioned in a prominent location in an outlet. Signs invite customers to express their viewpoints on the issues of interest to management. The machine can tabulate customer responses by count, computer averages, and cross tabulations. The result can be a fairly sophisticated analysis of the data.

### Field Work
Careful control over the persons involved in data collection is necessary. **Field work** researchers must guard against cheating and ensure that sampling instructions

**EXHIBIT 10–1**

*Example of a push-button questionnaire*

are followed and callbacks, if necessary, are made according to a predetermined plan. Essentially management wants to be sure that the most representative set of data possible is collected.

Even in the best of circumstances, some potential respondents will refuse to co-operate and others will not be at home. Plans must be made for substituting for such persons. Careful training of interviewers is necessary to minimize the biases that can enter the data-collection process because of the interviewer's attitudes, preconceived notions about the research findings, or the degree of care with which field workers conduct the interviews.

**Experimental Methods**

Some issues on which management wants information may not be resolved easily by survey research. Experimental research may be the only way to answer such questions as: What is the effect of a reduction in price on sales levels? Which of several advertising themes is most preferred by customers? Which of several package designs is the most effective in stimulating sales?

**Experimental designs** allow management to infer cause-and-effect relationships in variables of interest. Thus, management seeks to rule out explanations for changes in a variable such as sales (a dependent variable to be explained) other than those caused by changes in such variables as price or advertising (independent variables). For example, field experiment can answer the question: How does a small retailer measure the profitability of a couponing promotion?[22]

Ruling out alternative explanations for change in a dependent variable such as sales is important to management. Unless other explanations can be eliminated, management might mistakenly assume that a 10 percent reduction in the price of a carton of soft drinks would increase sales from 20 to 25 units per week. Part of the five-unit change, however, might be caused by unusually hot weather during the week of the research. Such a possibility must be evaluated if management wants to determine whether the increase in sales is due either in whole or in part to the reduction in price. Establishing cause-and-effect relationships is quite difficult because of the possibility of intervening variables.

Retailers can use a before/after experimental design with a control group to measure the reaction of demand to price changes in a product. In the research design shown in Table 10–4, the retailer selects two stores that are matched in terms of

**TABLE 10-4     A Research Design**

| Measurement | Before/After with Control | |
| --- | --- | --- |
| | *Test Group (Store 1)* | *Control Group (Store 2)* |
| Measurement of sales before price change (sales) | Yes (10) | Yes (10) |
| Price reduction of 10 percent | Yes | No |
| Measurement of sales after price reduction of 10 percent (sales) | Yes (20) | Yes (15) |

customer profiles, management, policies, store size, and other features so that they are as similar as possible. Unit sales in both stores are then determined for the product of interest. Since the stores are matched, the level of sales should be the same—10 units in each outlet. The price level for the product in Store 1 is reduced by 10 percent and left unchanged in Store 2. At the end of the specified period of time, sales are measured in both stores. As noted, sales increased from 10 units to 20 units for the store in which the price was reduced. However, sales also increased from 10 units to 15 units in the store for which the price was not reduced. This five-unit increase was due to various forces beyond the control of management and probably would also have occurred in Store 1 even without the reduction in price. The net effect of the price reduction was five units: $20 - 15 = 5$.[23]

In another example, an unobtrusive field experiment in four supermarkets found that price elasticity differed sharply between stockup (i.e., frequently consumed) and nonstockup (i.e., perishable or infrequently consumed) items. The first group of items showed much higher price elasticity than the second one.[24]

# Test Markets

Regional or national retail chains test products or store concepts on a limited basis to help decide whether to make changes in the merchandise mix, decor, store layout, or similar variables. Management may test colour schemes, price points, or menu variations before introducing the changes in all outlets—for example, McDonald's testing its pizza in Montreal, prior to a national rollout (in Canada and then in the United States).

**Test marketing** assumes that the results obtained from the test cities can be projected to the national market, which may be questionable if the test cities collectively are not representative of Canada. For example, would success of the McDonald's pizza in Montreal guarantee success in Toronto, Winnipeg, Calgary, Vancouver, or Halifax?

However, retailers may learn more about customers reactions to the new concept (leading to improvements), and they can pretest alternative strategies such as pricing or promotion (using several cities, with one set of alternatives per city).

Nevertheless, test marketing is difficult, risky, and expensive in Canada because of the diversity of life-styles and geographic cultures.

# Ethics and the Use of Information

Ethics should always be the foremost issue when management is collecting and utilizing research-based information. Some of the ethical issues involve the question of confidentiality of the respondents, the use of surveys as a disguised means of selling, misrepresentation of results, and truthfulness in advertising.[25]

In addition to the moral aspects of questionable behaviour, adverse publicity will almost always affect the profits of the firm.

# Chapter Highlights

- The transition from a merchandising to a marketing orientation increases the need for quality information ranging from data on consumer market trends and competitive actions to market share measurement and measurement of consumer perceptions.

- The components of a retail decision support system include secondary data, data generated through a merchandise information system, and primary data.

- Internal information is probably the least expensive source of data and can be developed from customer feedback, by feedback from salespeople, by analysis of charge accounts, by the use of consumer panels, and by analysis of internal financial data.

- Frequently used external sources of information include information available from syndicated services, government reports, guides, indexes and directories, trade associations, and computerized bibliographic searches. One of the most promising sources of syndicated information is emerging as a result of the rapid advances in electronic scanning of items purchased at the check-out counter.

- A merchandise information system is an integral part of the ongoing data-gathering and analysis

efforts by management. Such a system is developed based on information obtained both internally and from such external sources as vendors. The typical components of a merchandise information system include the planning system, the processing system, and the information reporting system.

- Primary data collection can take many forms, including observation, exploratory research, survey research, and experimental research.

- Observational approaches to data collection can be natural or contrived, open or disguised, structured or unstructured, and direct or indirect (human or mechanical).

- Survey research is the collection of information on the opinions or perceptions of market segments of interest to management. The process includes questionnaire development, sample selection, data collection, and field work.

- Experimental methods allow management to make inferences about cause-and-effect relationships in data. Such efforts can be especially important in pricing decisions, in shelf-space allocation decisions, and in merchandise-mix decisions.

# Key Terms

# Discussion Questions

1. What is the difference between primary and secondary data?

2. What are the various stages and decision areas involved in developing an effective merchandise information system?

3. What are some internal secondary sources of information available to retailers?

4. What external secondary sources are available to retailers?

5. How does exploratory research differ from survey and experimental research?

6. Define probability sample, nonprobability sample, convenience sample, judgment sample, and random sample.

7. Discuss the advantages and disadvantages of telephone interviews, personal interviews, mailed questionnaires, and computer interviews as methods of contact with respondents.

8. Explain the differences among the five most popular types of close-ended questions. Under what conditions should each one be used?

# Application Exercises

1. Visit the library and list all of the indexes or directories. Note the kinds of information contained in each. Project this exercise into the future and predict how you might use each index or directory in a specific kind of work with a retailing company.

2. Work with your university or college bookstore (or some other retailer with whom you or your instructor have a good relationship) and identify a "problem" the outlet experiences. Define the problem; devise a questionnaire to seek answers (assuming it is a problem for which a survey may be helpful) or an observation sheet for in-store research; collect and analyze your data; write up your findings; and present conclusions to the retailer.

3. Interview a retailer in each of the major kinds of businesses, such as grocery, clothing, and department stores. Determine the image that person perceives of retailing as a career opportunity. Summarize the perceptions; generalize your findings; present conclusions and recommendations.

# Suggested Cases

5. Canadian Population, Household, and Retail Sales Trends    574
9. York Furniture Company    583
10. The Perfect Pace    585
11. Diego's    590
12. The Undercover Agency    597
20. The Gourmet Palace    624

# Endnotes

1. David B. Montgomery and Charles B. Weinberg, "Toward Strategic Intelligence Systems," *Journal of Marketing,* Fall 1979, p. 41; and Leonard Lodish, "A Marketing Decision Support System for Retailers," *Marketing Science,* Winter 1982, pp. 31–56.

2. John D. C. Little and James J. Findley, "Blueprint for a Revolution," *Marketing Communications,* March 1984, pp. C-5–C-7.

3. Serge Fortin, "EDI Efficiency," *Retail Directions,* January/February 1989, pp. 21–22.

4. For more details, see René Y. Darmon, Michel Laroche, and K. Lee McGown, *Marketing Research in Canada* (Toronto: Gage, 1989), Chapter 5.

5. "Business Is Turning Data into a Potent Strategic Weapon," *Business Week,* August 22, 1983, pp. 92–98.

6. See, for example, "Sales Force Feedback: The Inside Source of Marketing Information," *Small Business Report,* October 1983, pp. 19–21.

7. For further reading, see Peter Nulty, "The Bar-Coding of America," *Fortune,* December 27, 1982, pp. 98–99; and Ellen Hackney, "Universal Product Code," *Hardware Retailing,* April 1984, pp. 65–80.

8. "Scanner Data Being Used More for Marketing," *Marketing,* March 14, 1988, p. 41.

9. Serge Fortin, "EDI Efficiency"; and Laurence N. Gold, "Support the Sales Staff with Scanning Data," *Marketing News,* April 10, 1989, pp. 2, 5.

10. D'Arcy Masius Benton & Bowles Canada, "How to Define Target Audience Segments," *Marketing,* June 20, 1988.

11. Jordan J. Louviere and Richard D. Johnson, "Reliability and Validity of the Brand-Anchored Conjoint Approach to Measuring Retailer Images," *Journal of Retailing* 66, no. 4 (Winter 1990), pp. 359–82; and "Polishing New Research Tools for the Future," *Advertising Age,* October 18, 1982, p. M-26.

12. For additional reading, see William J. Klocke, "Don't Overlook Secondary Data When Researching Retail Markets," *Marketing News,* May 14, 1982, p. 17.

13. Grocery Products Manufacturers of Canada, *Grocery Attitudes of Canadians, 1988* (Don Mills, Ontario).

14. For further reading, see D. Walters and C. A. Rands, "Computers in Retailing," *International Journal of Physical Distribution and Materials Management* 13, no. 4 (1983), pp. 3–12; "Management Information Systems (MIS)," *Small Business Report,* April 1982, pp. 11–15; and William Andres, "The Business of Retailing and Management Information Systems," *Computers and People,* April 1979, pp. 7–10.

15. "Shopping for a Computer System," *Retail Directions,* March/April 1989, pp. 38–40.

16. "Research Helps Sears Optimize Impact from Ads," *Marketing News,* December 26, 1980, p. 7.

17. Jules Abend, "Busman's Holiday," *Stores,* July 1982, p. 34.

18. Ibid., p. 37.

19. Darmon, Laroche, and McGown, *Marketing Research in Canada,* pp. 95–98, 101.

20. Suanne Kelman, "Consumers on the Couch," *Report on Business Magazine,* February 1991, pp. 50–53.

21. Ibid., pp. 150–58.

22. Randall G. Chapman, "Assessing the Profitability of Retailer Couponing with a Low-Cost Field Experiment," *Journal of Retailing* 62, no. 1 (Spring 1986), pp. 19–40.

23. For further reading, see Randy L. Allen, "Effective Decisions Need Market Research," *Chain Store Age Executive, General Merchandise Edition,* April 1984, pp. 106–8.

24. David S. Litvack, Roger J. Calantone, and Paul R. Warshaw, "An Examination of Short-Term Retail Grocery Price Effects," *Journal of Retailing* 61, no. 3 (Fall 1985), pp. 9–25.

25. Darmon, Laroche, and McGown, *Marketing Research in Canada,* pp. 461–69.

# P A R T

# III DESIGNING THE RETAILING MIX

In Part III, the various decisions on the major variables of the retailing mix are discussed. The key issues in retail location decisions are covered in Chapter 11. Store design, layout, and merchandise presentation decisions are covered in Chapter 12. Merchandise and expense planning decisions are the focus of Chapter 13. Buying, handling, and inventory management decisions are explained in Chapter 14. Determining retail prices is the topic of Chapter 15. In order to successfully promote their products or services, retailers need to help their employees develop the keys to successful selling (Chapter 16); design effective programs in retail advertising, sales promotion, and publicity (Chapter 17); and instill in their employees a customer-focused culture (Chapter 18).

# 11   MAKING RETAIL LOCATION DECISIONS

---

## Chapter Objectives

After reading this chapter, you should be able to:

1 Explain the strategic dimensions of the location decision.
2 Explain how to make the market selection.
3 Explain how to evaluate a trade area.
4 Determine the volume of business that can be done in a trading area.
5 Explain how to analyse and evaluate a site.

**Retailing Capsule**

How difficult and complex retail location decisions are can be illustrated by the following cases:

- The merchants in Montreal's downtown shopping area have had a great deal to worry about in the past few years. They first had to survive the tough competition from new downtown malls (e.g., Place Montreal Trust, and Les Promenades de la Cathédrale), then had to witness the sudden shutdown of Simpsons' downtown store. Their fears were that, with four big shopping malls opening within a five-block area, there would not be enough business to go around.

  Initially, most merchants claimed that their business was as good or better than before. Observers of the retail scene agree that, although some stores succumb to competition, it is a well-accepted principle that more variety attracts more customers. For this reason, downtown department stores usually cluster in the same area of that city.

  However, a combination of factors has created havoc in the retail scene: The 1991–92 recession, the Canada–U.S. Free Trade Agreement, and the federal Goods and Services Tax (GST) have not only reduced customers' purchasing power (i.e., an economic factor), but also accelerated shopping in the United States (i.e., cross-border shopping, a competitive factor), with stores only 45 minutes from the city (i.e., a location factor). This situation has forced the closing of many stores.

- Leonard Kubas, a noted retail consultant, has observed that the Toronto Eaton Centre has become a major tourist attraction, and that contrary to some predictions, and until the 1991–92 recession hit, surrounding streets did not suffer an absence of pedestrians and an abundance of bankrupt stores. Instead, the chains went into the mall, and the more specialized and innovative stores remained at street level attracting spillover customers from the mall. However, since 1991, a similar although not as dramatic situation as in Montreal has happened, due to similar factors, including cross-border shopping, with many stores closing or hurting financially.

- The West Edmonton Mall, dubbed the "eighth wonder of the world," has exerted an enormous power of attraction on Americans and Canadians, all the way to Japanese tourists. However, it has also created major problems for downtown Edmonton merchants, who saw business drop dramatically after the mall opened in 1981. With facilities such as an indoor ice palace, a zoo, public aquariums, a 360-room hotel, a 35,000-square-metre indoor amusement park, a 42,000-square-metre indoor water park, and a 1-hectare miniature golf course, it has been a major attraction, although its novelty has declined over time. The West Edmonton Mall has 800 tenants, including nine anchors (Canadian Tire, IKEA, Zellers, Sears, Eaton's, Woodward's Book Store, The Bay, Ashbrooks, and Brettons), a total leasable area of more than 350,000 square metres, and a market population of 4.7 million!

*Retailing Capsule continued*

*The West Edmonton Mall, the world's largest fun, fashion, and entertainment centre.*

Source: Courtesy the West Edmonton Mall.

During the last recession, economic factors hurt the profitability of the mall but cross-border shopping has not, since Edmonton is too far from the U.S. border. In 1992, its American sister, called the Mall of America, opened in Minnesota, further eroding the West Edmonton Mall's base of American and Japanese tourists. With its planned expansion, the Mall of America may take the title of largest shopping mall in the Guiness Book of Records, again diminishing the power of attraction of the West Edmonton Mall.

Sources: Adapted from Jay Bryan, "Downtown in the Doldrums?" *The Montreal Gazette,* February 11, 1989, p. G1; Robert Melnbardis, "The Decline and Fall of Montreal," *Financial Times of Canada,* December 23, 1991, pp. 8–10; *Canadian Directory of Shopping Centres, 1992* (Toronto: Maclean Hunter Limited), pp. 158–60; and Miro Cernetig, "A Wonder Wobbles," *Report on Business,* December 14, 1992, p. B18.

These examples illustrate the importance of location decisions for retailers, and how these decisions are affected by the economic situation and the competition. Building the right type of store in the right location is the key to serving a carefully targeted market.

Location decisions are essential elements of the competitive strategy of any retail organization. Outlets such as Canadian Tire can succeed in a stand-alone location. Other firms such as Eaton's seem to function best as an anchor tenant in a major shopping centre. Small specialty firms, lacking the ability to attract customers on their own, often choose a high-traffic location in a shopping mall.

We cannot overemphasize the importance of a carefully developed location strategy. Such a strategy is the spacial expression of a retailer's goals. Location decisions must be made in the context of the demographics of the target market segments, the patronage behaviour of consumers within the segments, the geographic dimensions of demand, and all other dimensions of the marketing program.

The selection process begins with an assessment of the firm's strategy, followed by (1) market selection decisions, (2) trade area analysis, and (3) site selection. Choice of location in essence determines how goods and services are made available to the customer. Even small differences in location can have a major impact on profitability and market share because location affects both the number of customers attracted to the outlet and the resulting level of retail sales.

# Strategic Decisions in Selecting a Location

Differences in competitive strategy can result in different location objectives even for firms with similar types of merchandise. For example, discount stores, specialty retailers, and chain department stores sell clothing and may even feature the same national brands. Still, each firm may be targeting a different market segment, as reflected in their location strategies. Firms such as Kmart are likely to be freestanding. Major department stores will serve as anchor tenants in shopping centres, and may also locate in the downtown section of major metropolitan areas.

Competition among firms offering similar merchandise and shopping experiences occurs primarily on the basis of location and price. Consumers, in choosing between highly similar outlets, are likely to shop at the most conveniently located outlet offering the best prices. The result is that firms such as gasoline stations are likely to be tightly clustered. Frequently, such outlets will be located on all four quadrants of a major high-traffic artery. Supermarkets are another example of a type of retailing with interchangeable merchandise. Grocery outlets also rely on convenience of location, and price competition is likely to occur among such outlets in a narrowly defined area.

Thus, key strategic decisions in retail location relate to the type of market coverage and the type of goods sold.

*Type of Market Coverage*

Three primary strategies are possible: (1) regional dominance (primarily for large retail outlets), (2) market saturation, and (3) emphasis on smaller towns and communities. These decisions are important even when a retailer is opening an initial outlet because they indicate the path of greatest growth over the years.

### Regional Dominance

The retailer may decide to become the dominant retailer in a particular geographic area rather than locate the same number of outlets over a much wider geographic area. Examples of regionally dominant retailers include Sobey's in the Maritimes, Provigo in Quebec, Loblaws in Ontario, Safeway in Manitoba, Alberta, and British Columbia, and Co-op in Saskatchewan.

The advantages of **regional dominance** include:

1. Lower costs of distribution because merchandise can be shipped to all the stores from a central warehouse.
2. Easier personnel supervision.
3. The ability to better understand customer needs.
4. The likelihood of a strong reputation in the area.
5. Better economies in sales promotion since the outlets are concentrated in one region.

### Market Saturation

The strategy of **market saturation** is similar to regional dominance. However, saturation is often limited to a single metropolitan market such as Toronto, Montreal, Vancouver, Calgary, or Halifax, where the population base is large. The advantages are the same in both instances. Regional dominance simply occurs on a larger scale than a single metropolitan market.

### Smaller Communities

Why are smaller communities so popular in location decisions today? One reason is that building codes make it easier to build in smaller communities. Also, costs are lower and competition isn't as strong.

Secondary markets—communities of less than 50,000—present some advantages to retailers: (1) these communities often welcome new business, such as pulp mills and sawmills in Grande Prairie (Alberta), tourism in Whistler (B.C.), and an auto plant in Bromont (Quebec);[1] (2) the quality of life is often higher; (3) wage rates are lower; (4) unions are less of an issue; (5) the markets are easier to serve; and (6) competition is often less intense.

Some retail chains such as Stedman's and Metropolitan operate primarily in small towns—less than 50,000 population—as these companies feel that they can more effectively serve these markets. For example, the Metropolitan chain operates over 450 chains across Canada under various names (e.g., Metropolitan, Greenberg, and Red Apple Clearance Centre) mainly in secondary markets.

*Type of Goods
Sold*

*Know*

Merchandise can be classified as convenience, shopping, or specialty goods based on customer buying habits. Stores can be classified in the same way as shown in Table 11–1. Understanding how consumers perceive merchandise and stores can help in evaluating the importance of location.

### Convenience Goods

*Convenience goods* are often purchased on the basis of impulse at outlets such as 7-Eleven and Mac's Milk. The volume of traffic passing a site is thus the most important factor in selecting a site at which to sell convenience goods. Some convenience goods outlets such as card shops are often located close to major department stores in shopping malls and depend on the department stores to attract traffic for them.

### Shopping Goods

*Don't need*

Consumers purchasing *shopping goods* prefer to compare the offerings of several stores before making a buying decision. A store such as Classics Bookstores is an example of a shopping goods outlet. Thus, consumers will travel farther in

**TABLE 11–1    Matrix of Consumer Goods and Stores**

| | | Stores | | |
|---|---|---|---|---|
| | | *Convenience* | *Shopping* | *Specialty* |
| **Goods** | *Convenience* | Consumers prefer to buy the most readily available brand and product at the most accessible store. <br><br> 1 | Consumers are indifferent to the brand or product they buy, but shop among different stores in order to secure better retail service and/or lower retail prices. <br> 4 | Consumers prefer to trade at a specific store, but are indifferent to the brand or product purchased. <br><br> 7 |
| | *Shopping* | Consumers select a brand from the assortment carried by the most accessible store. <br><br><br> 2 | Consumers make comparisons among both retail-controlled factors and factors associated with the product (brand). <br><br> 5 | Consumers prefer to trade at a certain store, but are uncertain as to which product they wish to buy and examine the store's assortment for the best purchase. <br> 8 |
| | *Specialty* | Consumers purchase their favoured brand from the most accessible store that has the item in stock. <br><br> 3 | Consumers have strong preference with respect to the brand, but shop among a number of stores to secure the best retail service or price for this brand. <br> 6 | Consumers have preference for both a particular store and a specific brand. <br><br><br> 9 |

SOURCE: Yoram Wind, *Product Policy: Concepts, Methods, and Strategy* (Reading, Mass.: Addison-Wesley Publishing, 1982), p. 71.

*Many convenience goods are sold through stores like 7-Eleven with locations in high-traffic areas.*

SOURCE: Photo by Sandy McDougall.

purchasing shopping goods than convenience goods but will not make a special effort to reach an outlet if others are more easily accessible.

### Specialty Goods

*Specialty goods* are items for which consumers will make a special effort to purchase a particular brand or shop at a given store. Such outlets generate their own traffic. As a result, retailers of such merchandise can choose a somewhat isolated site relative to outlets offering shopping goods or convenience goods.

For example, if management offers shopping goods—items such as men's and women's clothing, major appliances, or expensive jewellery—the best location is near other stores carrying shopping goods. Conversely, locating a shopping goods store in a convenience goods area or centre is not recommended.

On the other hand, with the advent of the regional shopping centre, shopping goods outlets may now be found co-existing easily under the same roof. In this situation, it is still important to be located in a section of the shopping complex that is in keeping with what management is selling. For example, a pet store should not be located immediately adjacent to a restaurant or a dress shop. Management would want to locate a gift shop near department stores, theatres, restaurants—in short, any place where lines of patrons may form, giving potential customers several minutes to look in the gift shop's display windows.

**The Process of Selecting a Retail Location**

The location strategy for the firm ultimately reflects both growth and expansion objectives. Developing the location plan after making such decisions requires a careful study of potential markets. Assessment of markets begins with choices among regions or metropolitan areas that appear to offer the greatest market potential in meeting the firm's growth objectives. Such a process is known as *market selection*.

Choices must then be made within the regions or the cities chosen. Considerable variation within such areas can occur because of the geographic configuration of the area, housing patterns, or land use. Analysis of the different subareas of a city is known as *trading area analysis*. Finally, *site analysis and evaluation* decisions must be made. At this point, management assesses the cost of land and development, traffic flows, ingress and egress, and similar issues in making specific site choices.

Thus, selection of a retail location typically follows a three-step process, as indicated in Figure 11–1:

Step 1: Market analysis.

Step 2: Trading area analysis.

Step 3: Site analysis and evaluation.

It must be clear that every step is a refinement of the previous one, and that the process is not necessarily linear. The remainder of the chapter will be devoted to detailing these three steps.

# Making the Market Selection

In making the market selection, management evaluates the economic base of targeted regions, the level of competition, size, and socioeconomic characteristics of the population, and the overall potential of the area, as shown in Table 11–2.

**Factors to Consider in Market Selection**

**Population Characteristics**

For example, a retailer needs to study the number of people in the population and their education, income, age, and family composition, as well as probable population increases in the area. Census data are a useful source of such information and are available for all markets in the yearly publication *Canadian Markets*. For example, the detailed listing on Moose Jaw indicates a 1992 population of 38,100, a per capita income of $16,600 (14 percent below national average), and total retail sales of $300 million (on a per capita basis, 8 percent below national average).[2]

**FIGURE 11–1**

*The three-step process of selecting a retail location*

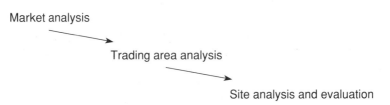

*Step 1*

---

### TABLE 11-2   Factors to Consider in Market Selection

**Population Characteristics**
  Total size
  Age and income distributions
  Growth trends
  Education levels
  Occupation distribution and trends

**Competitive Characteristics**
  Saturation level
  Number and size of competitors
  Geographic coverage
  Competitive growth trends

**Labour Characteristics**
  Availability of:
    Management
    Clerical
    Skilled
  Wage levels
  Unions
  Training

**Economic Characteristics**
  Number and type of industries
  Dominant industry
  Growth projections
  Financial base

**Supply Source Characteristics**
  Delivery time
  Delivery costs
  Availability and reliability
  Storage facilities

**Location Characteristics**
  Number and type of locations
  Costs
  Accessibility to customers
  Accessibility to transportation
  Owning/leasing options
  Utility adequacy

**Promotion Characteristics**
  Type of media coverage
  Media overlap
  Costs

**Regulation Characteristics**
  Taxes
  Licensing
  Zoning restrictions
  Local ordinances

---

### Labour Availability

Management talent is most readily available in larger areas, but is more expensive, as is clerical help.[3] In smaller communities, local management talent may not be available, and outsiders may not want to move to the area. However, clerical labour is less likely to be a problem.

### Distribution Problems

Distribution problems include the timing and frequency of delivery schedules to the store and the reliability of delivery, as well as the distance between the store and the company-owned or the distributor's warehouses.

### Media Mix Issues

Media mix issues include the availability of newspapers, radio stations, and television coverage of the market. Also, good production facilities are needed to help ensure high-quality commercials.

### Types of Industries in the Area

Large manufacturing plants with highly skilled union workers provide better market potential than small plants using unskilled labour and paying low wages. However, unionized firms are more subject to strikes that can hurt retail sales.

Service organizations such as hospitals and government offices provide a stable economic base but pay low wage rates. Retailers ideally seek a community with a balanced economic base. They also seek a community with a history of growth and aggressiveness in seeking new industries. They tend to avoid a community with a history of labour problems or that is losing population.

### Competition

Who are the likely competitors? Are any national retailers located in the area? How long have they been present? Can the market support another retailer without taking too much business from competition and inviting retaliation?

### Availability of Locations

Does the community have several shopping centres with vacancies? Does the downtown area look "alive"? Are plans under way to revitalize downtown? Is land available at reasonable prices for building a stand-alone location? During a recession (as in 1991–92), vacancy rates tend to be high, forcing rents down and providing better choices.

### Regulations

Can a business license to operate be obtained, and how much will it cost? Can the firm be open on Sundays? Is the community aggressively seeking new retailers?

*Index of Retail Saturation*

Not on test

One of the more commonly used measures of market attractiveness is the *Index of Retail Saturation (IRS)*. The index is based on the assumption that if a market A has a low level of **retail saturation,** the likelihood of success is higher than would otherwise be the case. The calculation of the IRS can be made with the following formula, and Exhibit 11–1 provides a concrete example of the use of the formula.

$$\text{Index of Retail Saturation}_A = \frac{\text{Demand}}{\text{Square metres of retail selling space}}$$

Thus, for market 1:

$$\text{IRS}_1 = \frac{C_1 \times RE_1}{RF_1}$$

where

$\text{IRS}_1$ = Index of retail saturation for market 1
$C_1$ = Number of consumers in market 1
$RE_1$ = Retail expenditures per consumer in market 1
$RF_1$ = Retail facilities in market 1

Census data, which are published every five years, can provide information on the number of potential customers within a trading area. Statistics Canada reports expenditure data by product category for households by income level. The

**EXHIBIT 11–1**

*Evaluating the*
*saturation for*
*women's clothing*
*stores in Fredericton*

Teresa Juppe, the owner of a small chain of women's clothing stores, is interested in opening a new store in Fredericton, New Brunswick, and she is concerned about the women's clothing store retail saturation in this market. Through some research, she has been able to gather the following information:

- The 115,600 consumers in Fredericton spend an average of $207.61 per year in clothing stores.
- There are numerous clothing stores serving Fredericton with a total of 10,000 square metres of selling area.

This information allows her to calculate an index of retail saturation for women's clothing stores in this market:

$$\text{IRS} = \frac{115,600 \times 207.61}{10,000} = \frac{24,000,000}{10,000} = \$240$$

The revenue of $240 per square metre of selling area measured against the revenue per square metre necessary to break even provides her with the measure of saturation in Fredericton. The $240 figure is also useful in evaluating relative opportunities in different market areas.[4]

number of competitors within the trading area can be determined by counting them, although selling areas would have to be estimated. Another very useful source is *Canadian Markets,* published annually.

# Trade Area Analysis

Trade area analysis occurs after management agrees on a specific geographic region or a general area of a city as a possible retail location.

## *Understanding Trade Areas*

Retail sales forecast accuracy depends on the ability to estimate the trade area for an outlet. The **trading area** is the geographic region from which a store primarily attracts its customers, and it is further subdivided into two major parts: the **primary trading area,** which includes the majority of the store's customers, living within a certain range of the store and having the highest per capita sales; and the **secondary trading area,** which includes almost all of the customers situated outside the primary area (the rest is called the *fringe trading area*). For example, for the Sahili Centre Mall in Kamloops, the primary area includes 62,000 customers within 5 minutes driving range, and the secondary area includes 68,000 customers within 25 minutes.[5]

A variety of factors determines trading area size, including:

1. The price of the good at one place compared to its price at another place.
2. The number of inhabitants concentrated in various places.
3. The density and distribution of the population.
4. The income and social structures of the population.
5. The proximity of other shopping opportunities.

What does this all mean for students of retailing? It means that the more highly specialized a product or service being offered, the larger the trading area must be before the service can be supported.

## *Population Characteristics*

We mentioned earlier the importance of population in market selection. An analysis of population characteristics is even more critical when evaluating a trading area. Management needs to understand such features as the population profile of the trading area, population density, and growth trends. The population of a trading area may not change over time, for example, but the characteristics of the people in the area may change dramatically. Some older, inner-city areas in recent years have experienced the return of young urban professionals (yuppies). Similarly, minorities can become the dominant force in a trading area and can change its suitability for a particular type of retailing.

Such variables as sex, occupation, education, and age are also important, as are family size and family life cycle. An outlet selling lawn supplies would be interested in the number of single family homes in the vicinity. On the other hand, retailers seeking suitable sites for a day-care centre would be more interested in the number of families with preschool children.

## *Evaluating a Trade Area*

Retailers differ from manufacturers because they have to be close to their target market, since consumers typically shop at the nearest retail outlet that will meet their needs. Techniques for measuring a trade area range from a simple "seat of the pants" approach to complex mathematical models.

### Information from Existing Stores

Retailers with existing stores have an advantage over a person seeking to open an outlet for the first time. Experienced retailers can use information they have obtained about their existing stores in making decisions about a planned new store. If the new store is similar to the old one, the sales generated will likely be similar. But retailers must, of course, make sure that the stores are alike in all key respects.

### License Plate Analysis

One of the most common methods of measuring trading areas for comparable stores is auto license plate analysis. The retailer determines the addresses from public records of the vehicles in the parking lot of an existing store or one similar to the planned outlet. By plotting these locations on a map, it is possible to get a feel for the general nature of the trading area. This information can be used in planning for additional stores.

### Cheque Clearance

Cheque clearance data, when available, may also be used to determine a store's trading area. Some stores such as supermarkets (e.g., Provigo) provide their customers with a privilege card that allows them to pay by cheque. Plotting the addresses from the customers' cheques makes it possible to determine the characteristics of the trading area for an existing store. However, this is based on the assumption that the distributions of cash customers and cheque-paying customers are basically the same.

### Credit Records

Credit records can be analyzed to determine the trading area of an existing store. A sample of charge accounts is selected and customer addresses are plotted on a map. Of course, this is only possible if the retailer has developed a credit-granting procedure.

### Customer Spotting

Customer spotting is a technique used for determining the location of target customers. Target customers must first be defined, say by income group or profession. Next, a mailing list of these types of customers within a defined region may be purchased from mailing lists suppliers (such as direct marketing companies, or research companies such as Compusearch). Then the home addresses of the target customers are spotted on a map and a circle is drawn to define the primary trading area for the outlet.

### Driving Time Analysis

Driving time analysis can also be used to define a trading area by determining how far customers are willing to travel to reach an outlet. Trading areas typically are measured in terms of time instead of distance because of problems of congestion and physical barriers. A rule of thumb is that customers will travel no more than five minutes to reach a convenience outlet. Three fourths of the customers of a large regional shopping centre normally will drive 15 minutes to reach the centre. Of course, the West Edmonton Mall is a major exception since it attracts people from the United States and even Japan!

### Customer Survey

A good way to determine a trading area is to conduct or sponsor a customer survey. The survey can be done by mail, telephone, or by personal interview, and each method has its good and bad points, as was explained in Chapter 10. The interviews can be conducted at the store if they are personal interviews. Alternatively, a sample of respondents can be chosen from customer records and called on the phone or mailed a questionnaire. Retailers may also be able to participate in surveys sponsored by the local chamber of commerce or a similar organization, or buy into an omnibus survey.

   The customer survey can provide information on where people shop for items similar to the planned merchandise offering. For example, if a store interviews its own customers, the addresses can be plotted on a map to measure the store's trading area. Also, retailers can do a survey of noncustomers and establish trading areas for competitors.

   Drawing circles with a radius of 1, 2, and 5 kilometres makes it possible to see how far most customers travel to shop at the outlet. If a retailer is planning the first store, the information for an outlet similar to the planned one can be plotted.

   A customer survey can provide other useful information as well. Such information might include (1) *demographics* (e.g., age, occupation, number of children); (2) *shopping habits* (e.g., type of store preferred, how often consumers shop, and area of town preferred); (3) *purchasing patterns* (e.g., who does the family buying); and (4) *media habits* (e.g., radio, TV, and newspaper habits).

## Reilly's Law of Retail Gravitation[6]

Retail **gravity models** are an improvement over other methods of trading area analysis. They are based on both population size and distance or driving time as the key variables in the models.

Reilly's Law is the oldest of the trading area models.[7] The model, as described in Exhibit 11–2, allows the calculation of a breaking point in retail trade between two communities.

These breaking points can be calculated between several cities and, when joined together, form a set of trading area boundaries for a community, as shown in Figure 11–2 for four smaller cities around city *a*.

The formula can be modified in several ways, including the substitution of driving time for distance, and square metres of retail floor space for population.

Reilly's Law works satisfactorily in rural areas where distance has a major impact on the choice of a community at which to shop. Breaking points do not exist in metropolitan areas, however, because consumers typically have several shopping choices available within the distance that they are willing to travel.

**EXHIBIT 11–2**

*Reilly's Law*

According to Reilly's Law, the breaking point in retail trade between two cities *a* and *b* is calculated as follows:

$$D_b = \frac{D}{1 + \sqrt{\dfrac{P_a}{P_b}}}$$

where

$P_a$, $P_b$ = Population sizes of centres *a* and *b* (*b* is the smaller city)
$D_b$ = Breaking point distance of trade to centre *b*
$D$ = Distance between centres *a* and *b*

*Example:* In applying the formula, assume the following information:

$P_a$ = 97,000 population, and *a* is Kelowna
$P_b$ = 41,000 population, and *b* is Penticton
$D$ = 65 kilometres

$$D_b = \frac{65}{1 + \sqrt{\dfrac{97,000}{41,000}}} = \frac{65}{1 + 1.54} = 25.6 \text{ kilometres}$$

The breaking point between Kelowna and Penticton is thus 25.6 kilometres from Penticton (and 39.4 kilometres from Kelowna).

**FIGURE 11–2**

*The breaking points between city* **a** *and each of four smaller cities help define the boundaries of the trading area for a store in city* **a**

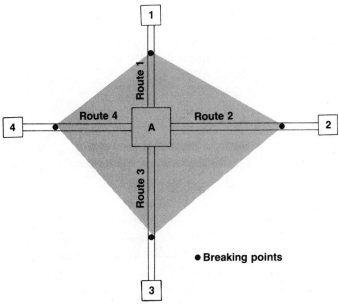

• **Breaking points**

In essence, Reilly's Law states that the size of a trading area increases as population density decreases. For example, people may travel several kilometres to shop at a small rural village. However, the same persons would only be willing to travel a few blocks in a major metropolitan area. Further, the use of Reilly's Law is appropriate only for communities of roughly similar size. Also, trade areas vary by type of goods sought, a reality not reflected in Reilly's model. Patronage is also assumed to be linearly related to time or distance from the consumer's household.

*The Huff Model*    A model developed by David Huff helps overcome the limitations of Reilly's model. For example, Huff's models are premised on the assumption that the likelihood of consumer patronage increases with the size of a centre. Thus, consumers are willing to travel greater distances when additional merchandise is available at a central location. The probability of patronage is also assumed to be linearly related to time or distance from the consumer's household.

The formal expression of the model is as follows:[8]

$$P(C_{ij}) = \frac{\dfrac{S_j}{T_{ij}^{\lambda}}}{\displaystyle\sum_{j=1}^{n} \dfrac{S_j}{T_{ij}^{\lambda}}}$$

where

$P(C_{ij})$ = Probability of a consumer at a given point of origin $i$ travelling to a given shopping centre $j$

$S_j$ = Square metres of selling space devoted to the sale of a particular class of goods at shopping centre $j$

$T_{ij}$ = Travel time involved in getting from a customer's travel base $i$ to shopping centre $j$

$\lambda$ = A parameter (Lambda) estimated empirically to reflect the effect of travel time on the various kinds of shopping trips

The most frequently used method of estimating $\lambda$ is a computer programme developed by Huff and Blue.[9] After estimating $\lambda$, management can determine the trading area of a shopping centre for any product class. The steps involved are as follows:

1. Divide the area surrounding a shopping centre into small statistical units within a constructed grid. Such units are represented by $i$ in the model.
2. Determine the square metres of retail selling space of all shopping centres $(j)$ included within the area of analysis.
3. Ascertain the travel time involved in getting from each statistical unit $i$ to each of the specified shopping centres $j$.
4. Calculate the probability of consumers in each of the statistical units going to each shopping centre for a given product purchase, using the above formula.
5. Map the trading area for the shopping centre by drawing lines connecting all statistical units having the same probabilities.

A concrete example of the application of the Huff model is given in Exhibit 11–3.

Still, the Huff model has its weaknesses. It assumes that consumers with comparable demographic characteristics will exhibit similar retail patronage behaviour. Huff's model includes all potential retail centres in the system although all centres might not be patronized. Recent research has shown that allowing consumers to specify their choice set of shopping centres, as opposed to an arbitrarily imposed set in the traditional Huff model, substantially improves the performance of the model and can be used for predictive and explanatory purposes.

***How Much Business Can Be Done in the Trading Area?***

Retailers need five sets of data to help estimate the amount of sales available in a trading area: (1) number of people in the trading area; (2) average household income; (3) amount of money spent each year by the households on the type of goods sold by the firm—that is, groceries, drugs, or apparel; (4) total market potential; and (5) share of the total market potential management can expect to get.

The number of people in a trading area can be obtained from an analysis of Statistics Canada census data, available in almost any library, as noted above. The

**EXHIBIT 11–3**

*A numerical application of the Huff model*

Teresa Juppe, the owner of a women's clothing store, is interested in opening a new store in one of the three major shopping centres (Thorncliffe, Westmount, and Eaton Plaza) serving the West Park residential area, a high-income community. After doing some research, she has been able to ascertain the following facts:

Square metres of selling space devoted to the sale of women's clothing at each shopping centre:

$S_1 = 1,000$ m$^2$ for Thorncliffe Shopping Mall
$S_2 = 1,500$ m$^2$ for Westmount Shopping Centre
$S_3 = 2,000$ m$^2$ for Eaton Plaza

Travel time in getting from a customer's home in West Park to each shopping centre:

$T_{i1} = 2$ km from West Park to Thorncliffe Shopping Mall
$T_{i2} = 3$ km from West Park to Westmount Shopping Centre
$T_{i3} = 4$ km from West Park to Eaton Plaza
$\lambda = 2$

Probability of a consumer from West Park travelling to each shopping centre:

$$P(C_{i1}) = \frac{\dfrac{1,000}{2^2}}{\dfrac{1,000}{2^2} + \dfrac{1,500}{3^2} + \dfrac{2,000}{4^2}} = \frac{250}{250 + 167 + 125} = .46, \text{ for Thorncliffe}$$

Similarly:

$P(C_{i2}) = .31$, for Westmount
$P(C_{i3}) = .23$, for Eaton Plaza

One can easily verify that $.46 + .31 + .23 = 1.00$.

From this information, one can deduce that Teresa would have a potential 46 percent of West Park residents if she located in Thorncliffe, compared to 31 percent for Westmount and 23 percent for Eaton Plaza.

If the population of West Park is 100,000 residents, and the average per capita sales of women's clothing is $240, each centre would generate in women's clothing sales:

Thorncliffe:   $100,000 \times \$240 \times 0.46 = \$11,040,000$
Westmount:   $100,000 \times \$240 \times 0.31 = \$7,440,000$
Eaton Plaza:   $100,000 \times \$240 \times 0.23 = \$5,520,000$

Next, Teresa must estimate the share of these total sales that she could realistically expect, given the competition already there for each centre. By multiplying these market shares by the total sales, she will get an estimate of the sales from West Park residents in each location to be compared to the costs of opening a store in each centre. Of course, if each centre draws customers from other areas, the same calculations should be made and aggregated into total expected sales for each location.

data are reported by **census tracts** (small areas with 2,500 to 8,000 people) for all cities with a population of 50,000 or more. There are over 5,000 census tracts in Canada, and these can be used for large shopping centre location decisions. A finer breakdown can be obtained by using **enumeration areas,** which contain 100 to 200 households. There are about 40,000 enumeration areas in Canada, which are very useful for small store location decisions. Finally, distances can be entered into the analysis by using the **universal transverse mercator (UTM)** system, which gives the coordinates of every possible location in Canada, including the centre of the enumeration areas.[10]

The average household income in each census tract is published by Statistics Canada every five years. Information about the amount of money spent each year on various types of merchandise can be found in Statistics Canada publications on family expenditures.[11]

Multiplying average annual household income by the number of families in the trading area yields total sales potential. Multiplying total sales potential by the percentage of the average annual household income spent on each type of goods (for example, groceries) yields total sales potential by type of goods.

Retailers then decide on the amount of the available sales potential they can get. One way to do this is by plotting competitors in the trading area on a map and trying to establish the sales levels of each. Indicators may be the number of check-out counters, number of employees, square metres, and industry trade averages for sales per square metre. Retailers must also decide on the amount of business they need to make a profit. Then, they decide on whether and how much business they can take from the competition. Table 11–3 shows this five-step process.

# Site Analysis and Evaluation

Site analysis and evaluation is the third and final step in the selection of a retail location. The retailer has three basic choices for a site: a shopping centre, the central business district (the downtown shopping area), or a solo (or stand-alone) location. Even within these types, there are more categories to choose from. The

**TABLE 11–3    Estimating Annual Sales in a Retail Store's Trading Area**

| | *(1)* | | *(2)* | | *(3)* | | *(4)* | | *(5)* |
|---|---|---|---|---|---|---|---|---|---|
| Method: | Number of households in a census tract in retail trading area | × | Median annual income of the households in the census tract | × | Proportion of a household's annual income spent on type of items sold by store | × | Proportion of money spent on item that will be spent in this store | = | Proposed store sales revenue from census tract |
| Census tracts in trading area: | | | | | | | | | |
| 354XX | 6,500 | × | $10,000 | × | .20* | × | .10† | = | $1,300,000 |
| 354XY | 8,500 | × | 8,000 | × | .15 | × | .15 | = | 1,530,000 |
| Total projected annual sales | | | | | | | | | $2,830,000 |

*The proportion of .20 means that 20 percent of the typical household's annual income of $10,000 is spent on merchandise sold by this store.
†The proportion of .10 means that management anticipates that 10 percent of the total merchandise purchased in this census tract will be purchased at this specific store.

following sections describe the different types of locations and provide criteria for selecting a particular site. Table 11–4 gives an overview of the strengths and weaknesses of the basic choices.

*Shopping Centres*    Shopping centres are a geographic cluster of retail stores collectively handling an assortment of varied goods that satisfy one or more categories of the merchandise wants of consumers within convenient driving time of the centre. Shopping centres with a mix of stores that meet a very large variety of needs are said to have a **balanced tenancy.** These are the traditional and original shopping centres.

In recent years, other types of shopping centres have emerged by catering to more narrow needs (e.g., only food, clothing, or home decoration). Retail Highlight 11–1 explains the nature of shopping centres in Canada.

**What Are Shopping Centre Strengths and Weaknesses?**
The strengths of shopping centres are (1) balanced tenant mix for the traditional type, depth of assortment in the category for most of the others; (2) common store hours; (3) centrewide promotions; (4) controlled climate; (5) few parking problems; (6) longer store hours; and (7) a pleasant environment for attracting shoppers.

Small shopping centre stores can take advantage of the traffic-drawing ability of large, mass merchandisers or outlets with national reputations. Often, people will shop in the small shops even though they came to the shopping centre primarily to shop at the large, mass merchandisers.

TABLE 11–4    **Strengths and Weaknesses of Selected Location Alternatives**

| *Type of Location* | *Strengths* | *Weaknesses* |
|---|---|---|
| Regional shopping centre | Large number of stores<br>Drawing power of large anchor stores<br>Parking availability<br>Balanced tenant mix | Occupancy costs<br>Some inflexibility (i.e., store hours, merchandise sold) |
| Community shopping centre | Operating costs<br>Shopping convenience<br>Shared promotions | Poor tenant mix<br>Facility condition<br>High vacancy rate |
| Neighbourhood shopping centre | Shopping convenience<br>Very low operating costs<br>Distance from customer | Few tenants<br>Susceptible to competition<br>Facility condition |
| Central business district | Mass transit<br>Urban development<br>Business/work traffic generates exposure<br>Rent costs | Parking<br>Limited shopping hours<br>Facility condition<br>Suburban shift<br>Rent costs (exclusive sections) |
| Solo location | Lack of close competition<br>Lower rent<br>More space for expansion<br>Greater flexibility | Harder to attract customers<br>Probably have to build instead of rent<br>Higher promotion costs |

## Retail Highlight 11–1

# Shopping Centres: Are They the New Town Centres?

The recession of the early 1990s has challenged the notion that shopping centres can be compared to the ancient city square, a meeting place for people to socialize and be seen. Consider the following examples:

- When it opened its doors in 1975, the TransCanada Mall in Calgary was a shiny example of modern consumerism. It seemed ideally located at a major intersection, dominating an established neighbourhood where no competing malls would likely be built. It obviously was not enough of an attraction for the nearby residents, and the mall was torn down to be replaced by a strip shopping centre of food and convenience stores, all facing the street.

- In downtown Halifax, along Spring Garden Road, there are several "ghost malls." According to Geri Shepard, manager of Bayer's Road Shopping Centre, "Spring Garden Road was a wonderful pedestrian place bounded by parks. It was a residential neighbourhood with seniors, young families, and university students. The developers saw that traffic and translated it into shopping centre traffic. But it would not work. . . . The empty

malls are huge statues for the ego that built them."

What these examples illustrate is that the success of shopping centres is not only a function of traffic or competition, but it must correctly account for the needs of the population and develop a competitive advantage beyond location. For example, industry analysts have pointed out that:

- Middle-aged couples, many juggling children and two jobs, found that they had less time and inclination to browse through the malls.

- The *mix* of retailers is the second most important factor after location, particularly for customers who do not want to go through several malls to find an item.

- Malls must provide more services—for example, day care for children and medical offices for seniors.

- Some developers have increased the *density* of nearby population by adding office towers, hotels, and car showrooms at mall locations.

The success of a mall as a popular town centre will depend on how well it meets the needs of the population.

Sources: Barbara Wickens, "Misery at the Malls," *Maclean's*, March 23, 1992, pp. 30–31; and Andrew Allentuck, "Is the Mall Beginning to Pall?" *Globe and Mail*, May 5, 1992, p. B23.

But shopping centres also have weaknesses. The primary problems centre around what the individual merchant can and cannot do. Specifically, tenants face restrictions on (1) what can be sold and (2) store hours. Also, the policies of the centre are often dictated by the large **anchor tenant(s).** Finally, rent will be higher than in a stand-alone location.

*A shopping centre can create a stimulating environment.*

SOURCE: Photo by Betty McDougall.

## What Are the Choices?[12]

Whether a retailer can get into a shopping centre depends on the market and management. A small shopping centre may need only one children's shoe store, for example, while a regional centre may expect enough business for several.

In order to find tenants whose line of goods will meet the needs of the market to be reached, the developer-owner first signs prestige merchants as lead tenants. Then, other types of stores are selected that will complement each other. This bolsters the centre's competitive strength against other centres, as well as supplying the market area's needs. However, many malls in Canada tend to have the same types of tenants, especially the large chains such as Eaton's or the specialty chains such as Dylex. This may adversely affect new entries with this kind of sameness and favour new malls with a special flavour.

To finance a centre, the developer needs major leases from companies with strong credit ratings. Lenders favour tenant rosters that include the triple-A ratings of national chains. When most spaces are filled, a developer may choose small outlets to help fill the remaining vacancies.

However, a person who is considering a shopping centre for a first-store venture may have trouble. Financial backing and merchandising experience may be unproven. The problem is to convince the developer that the new store has a reasonable chance of success and will help the tenant mix.

## Factors to Consider in a Shopping Centre Choice

Suppose that the owner-developer of a shopping centre asks a retailer to be a tenant. In considering the offer, the retailer needs to investigate what he or she can do in the centre. What rules will affect the operation? In exchange for following the rules, what will the centre do for the firm?

Even more important, the trading area, the location of competition, and the location of available space need to be considered. These factors help to determine how much business can be done in the centre.

***The Centre's Location.***    In examining the centre's location, look for answers to questions such as these:[13]

1. Can the store hold old customers and attract new ones?
2. Does the centre offer the best sales volume potential for the kind of merchandise to be sold?
3. Can management benefit enough from the centre's access to a market? If so, can it offer the appeal that will make the centre's customers come to the store?

A retailer should make an analysis of the market the developer expects to reach. In this respect, money for professional help is well spent, especially when the research indicates that the centre is not right for the type of firm planned.

***Store Space.***    Determine where the space will be. The location within a centre is important. Does the store need to be in the main flow of customers as they pass between the stores with the greatest "customer pull"? What will be the nature of the adjacent stores? What will be their effect on sales of the planned firm?

***Amount of Space.***   Using their experience, retailers should determine the amount of space needed to handle the sales volume expected. The amount of space will also determine the rent to be paid.

***Total Rent.***   Most shopping centre leases are negotiated either on a percentage basis or on a fixed fee per square metre. The contents of a lease will be covered later in the chapter.

Rental expenses may begin with a minimum guarantee that is equal to a percentage of gross sales. While this is typically between 5 and 7 percent of gross sales for nonanchor tenants, it varies by type or size of business and other factors. For anchor tenants, this percentage is usually lower.

Alternatively, fixed annual rents in most Canadian shopping centres tend to average between $100 and $200 per square metre, and may go higher in some instances; for example, in the West Edmonton Mall, the average annual rent can go as high as $350 per square metre.[14]

Other charges are assessed in addition to the minimum guarantee or the monthly rent. A retailer may have to pay dues to the centre's merchants association and for maintenance of common areas.

Rent, then, should be considered in terms of *total* rent. If total rent is more than the present rent in an existing location, the space in the centre will have to draw enough additional sales to justify the added cost.

***Finishing Out.***   Generally, the developer furnishes only the bare space in a new centre. The retailer does the finishing out at his or her own expense. For example, a retailer pays for lighting fixtures, counter shelves, painting, and floor coverings. In addition, heating and cooling units may have to be installed.

Some developers help tenants plan store fronts, exterior signs, and interior colour schemes. They provide this service to ensure store fronts that add to the centre's image rather than detracting from it.

### Types of Shopping Centres

Because **planned shopping centres** are built around a major tenant, centres are classified, in part, according to the leading tenant. The classification includes three types: neighbourhood, community, and regional. The typical characteristics of these are described in Table 11–5.

***Neighbourhood Shopping Centre.***   Statistics Canada defines a **neighbourhood shopping centre** as one with 5–15 stores, and that offers free parking.[15] The supermarket or the drugstore is the leading tenant in a neighbourhood centre. This type is the smallest in size among shopping centres, with few stores, and it caters

---
TABLE 11–5    **Description of the Three Types of Shopping Centres**

|  | *Neighbourhood* | *Community* | *Regional* |
|---|---|---|---|
| Number of stores | 5–15 | 16–30 | More than 30 |
| Leading tenant | Supermarket or drugstore | Variety or junior department store | At least one full-line department store |
| Typical leasable space | 5,000 m$^2$ | 10,000 m$^2$ | 20,000 m$^2$ |
| Typical site area | 1.6 hectare | 4 hectares | 12 hectares |
| Minimum trade population | 7,500 to 25,000 | 25,000 to 75,000 | 75,000 or more |

---

to the convenience needs of a neighbourhood. For example, Westsyde Shopping Centre in Kamloops is anchored by Coopers, has 11 stores, a gross leasable retail area of about 5,200 m$^2$, a primary population of 7,000, and a secondary population of 25,000.[16]

***Community Shopping Centre.***    Statistics Canada defines a **community shopping centre** as one with 16–30 stores, and that offers free parking.[17] Variety or junior department stores are the leading tenants in the next bigger type—the community centre. Such centres include some specialty shops, wider price ranges, greater style assortments, and more impulse-sale items. For example, County Fair Mall in Summerside (P.E.I.) is anchored by Zellers and Sobey's, has 24 stores, a gross leasable retail area of about 14,000 m$^2$, and a population base of 65,000.[18]

***Regional Shopping Centre.***    Statistics Canada defines a **regional shopping centre** as one with more than 30 stores, and that offers free parking.[19] The department store, with its prestige, is the leader in the regional centre—the largest type of shopping centre. When a retailer finds that a second or third department store is also locating in such a centre, he or she will know the site has been selected to draw from the widest possible market area. The smaller tenants are picked to offer a range of goods and services approaching the appeal once found only downtown. The biggest regional shopping centre is the West Edmonton Mall described at the beginning of the chapter. A more typical regional shopping centre is the Fredericton Mall, with four anchors, 60 tenants, a gross leasable area of 21,500 m$^2$, and a market population of 120,000.[20] Retail Highlight 11–2 provides some interesting facts about shopping malls in Canada.

When considering locating in a mall, retailers should weigh the benefits against the costs. At the outset, it may be difficult to measure savings such as the elimination of store fronts against costs. For example, the cost of heating and air conditioning may be higher in the enclosed mall. In an enclosed mall centre, tenant groupings include drugstores and supermarkets in a separate building at the edge of the parking area. Relatively high-priced women's goods stores tend to cluster

**Retail Highlight 11–2**

# Shopping Malls in Canada

Major malls have been built in most regions of Canada, but nowhere to the extent of Edmonton, which, on a per capita basis, has *four times* the national average of per capita square metres of mall retail area. The top eight metropolitan areas in Canada are:

| Metropolitan Area | Number | Leasable Area (000 $m^2$) | Area Per Capita ($m^2$) |
|---|---|---|---|
| Edmonton | 9 | 874 | 1.03 |
| Quebec City | 5 | 418 | 0.66 |
| Calgary | 7 | 446 | 0.60 |
| Hamilton | 5 | 335 | 0.56 |
| Ottawa | 5 | 353 | 0.52 |
| Vancouver | 12 | 800 | 0.50 |
| Toronto | 19 | 1,571 | 0.41 |
| Winnipeg | 3 | 251 | 0.30 |
| Total Canada | 103 | 7,435 | 0.28 |

Of Canada's 103 malls, 34 can be called *super regional malls,* with more than 75,000 $m^2$ and three department stores. Almost half (47) were built in the 1970s, and 21 were added in the 1980s. It remains to be seen if the 1990s, which started with a severe recession, will see a resurgence of mall construction.

Source: Bruce Little, "Amazing Facts," *Globe and Mail*, January 18, 1992, p. B19.

together. Service and repair shops are located where customers have direct access from the parking lot for quick in-and-out pickup of goods.

*Other Types of Shopping Areas*

### The Mega-Multi-Mall[21]
It has been suggested that the West Edmonton Mall is a new kind of retail institution. While regional malls were designed and managed to satisfy a major purpose—that is, shopping—the mega-multi-mall is a multifunctional centre where several needs, in addition to shopping, can be satisfied (e.g., entertainment, recreation, eating, drinking, socializing, working, and sightseeing).

### Urban Arterial Developments
**Urban arterial developments** are often found in an older part of the city. The sites were initially developed to provide good locations on busy streets for shoppers.

Typical examples include home repair centres, appliance stores, automobile repair shops, and office equipment firms, which serve either a commercial or a consumer market.

Highway-oriented strip developments occur on the outskirts of major cities and are characterized by such facilities as motels and restaurants.

### Specialized Functional Areas

**Specialized functional areas** are largely self-defining. Entertainment districts offering theatres, restaurants, bars, and similar facilities characterize these developments. "Old towns" in Montreal and Vancouver are examples. Medical districts around large hospitals also fit this description, as do streets known for their high-class fashion stores or art galleries, such as Sherbrooke Street in Montreal.

### Life-Style Clusters

**Life-style clusters** or "festival" markets include Le Faubourg in Montreal, a collection of food stalls, specialty shops, and restaurants in an old warehouse building. Often, these enterprises are the result of young entrepreneurial merchants who fill an indoor marketplace with boutiques selling items ranging from towels and hats to strawberry-scented soaps. Ultrasmall retailers are a fixture in many such operations. Many of the urban centres built by developers as part of a commercial building offer local neighbourhood customers (including the office crowd) and tourists a new experience.

### Off-Price and Factory Outlet Centres

Off-price centres consist of merchants selling merchandise at a minimum of 25 percent off normal prices—for example, Super Carnival. These centres do not compete directly for the Kmart or Zellers clientele in that the former offer high-quality merchandise at reduced prices.

**Factory outlet centres** are occupied by manufacturers selling directly to the public. Vanity Fair, Burlington, and Bally are examples. The factory outlet is the low end of the off-price branded field. Complete centres devoted to factory outlets have become a permanent fixture in many areas because they combine two of the key draws that lure shoppers: *perceived value* and *one-stop shopping*. Add to that plenty of parking space, fast-food restaurants, a movie theatre, and a recreation store with blinking electronic games, and you have a sure winner.

### Power Strip Centres

**Power strip,** or destination, **centres** are a hot new development. They are typically anchored by what are known as destination-oriented retailers or superstores. The most frequently represented power centre anchor tenants, in descending frequency, are: toy/children's superstore, off-price apparel outlet, soft lines promotional department store, discount department store, consumer electronic superstore, deep-discount drugstore, or a consumer-oriented home improvement outlet.

In essence, a power centre is an oversized strip centre. Typically, it has the drawing power of a regional shopping centre. Everything is visible from the street, and consumers can drive directly to where they want to go. Such centres have smaller acquisition, building, and maintenance costs than regional malls. Additionally, the developers achieve a greater merchandise depth than the typical strip centre. The strongest candidates for power centres are national, regional, and local retailers with a strong presence and name recognition. A strong value image is also important.

*A Downtown Location*    **Central business district** (downtown) locations also offer several advantages:

1. Rents are lower than in many shopping centres.
2. Public transportation may be more readily available.
3. The locations are usually close to large office complexes that employ many people.

*A downtown location has advantages for many retailers.*

SOURCE: Photo by Betty McDougall.

*Drug World chooses solo locations because of its wide merchandise assortment and customer loyalty.*

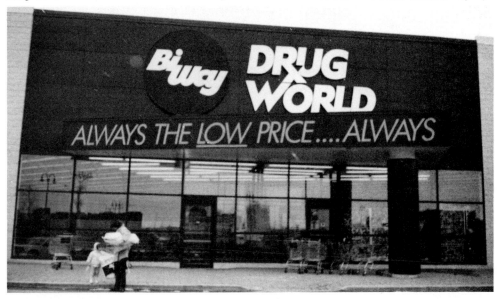

SOURCE: Courtesy BiWay.

However, disadvantages can exist. They include the following:

1. Downtown stores are often not open in the evening.
2. Crime rates may be higher.
3. Traffic congestion is bad.
4. Downtown areas are sometimes decaying and run-down.

*A Solo Location*     Statistics Canada defines a **solo location** (also called an on-street or stand-alone location) as a store or outlet located in a residential neighbourhood, commercial section, or major traffic arterial that is not in a shopping plaza or other type of shopping mall.[22] Organizations such as Canadian Tire and Drug World often choose solo locations.

Solo locations in heavily travelled areas have several advantages including:

- The lack of close competition.
- Lower rent.
- More space for parking and expansion.
- Greater flexibility in store hours and other methods of operation.

But disadvantages also exist. For example:

- Such stores may have difficulty attracting consumers because comparison shopping is not easy.

- Advertising costs are often higher than if the firm were in a shopping centre with other stores that advertise together.
- The retailer will probably have to build its own store, rather than finding one available to rent.

The most successful stores in on-street locations are those with strong customer loyalty and a wide assortment of national-brand merchandise from which consumers can choose. After deciding on an acceptable general location, a retailer then assesses the economic potential of the trading area to determine whether it can support the planned store.

## Making the Choice

Ultimately, the choice of a location depends on the retailer's strategy for growth. The choice also depends on the market to be served, the characteristics of the customers who will be shopping at the outlet, the image of the firm, the current or projected competitive position of the retailer, and the growth objectives and capabilities of the firm.

A 100 percent satisfactory location rarely exists. Ideally, management can find a location with easy accessibility, high traffic flow, at a reasonable price, and in a desirable shopping environment. Exhibit 11–4 provides a checklist of specific site evaluation criteria.

Accessibility is affected by physical barriers such as rivers, ease of ingress (i.e., going in) and egress (i.e., going out or exiting) from the site, traffic congestion, and road conditions. As a generalization, the higher the volume of traffic, the higher the level of potential sales. However, the composition of traffic is also important. A high volume of commercial or truck traffic, for example, is not desirable. Similarly, a high volume of pedestrian traffic with little time for browsing is also not desirable.

**Exhibit 11–4**

*Evaluation checklist*

**Zoning**
  Type
  Surrounding zoning patterns
  Likelihood of getting changes if needed

**Utilities**
  Water, sewer, gas
  Adequacy
  Cost
  Location of lines

**Accessibility**
  Quality of ingress and egress
  Traffic volume and flow
  Public transportation availability

**Land use**
  Vacancies
  Terrain
  Parking availability
  Building patterns
  Amenities

**Growth Potential**
  Trends in income
  Trends in number and mix of population
  Trends—building permits issued
  Location pattern of competitive businesses

The amount of parking needed depends on frequency of vehicle turnover, type of merchandise sold, and peak parking requirements. However, peak parking should be evaluated in a "normal" period, as opposed to a heavy shopping period such as Christmas. Otherwise, the retailer will find excess parking spaces sitting vacant most of the year.

**Traffic counts** can be of critical importance in evaluating the suitability of a site. The general objective of a traffic count is to count the passing traffic—both pedestrian and vehicular—that would constitute potential customers who would probably be attracted into the store.[23] Data from traffic counts should not only show how many people pass by but generally indicate what kinds of people they are. Analysis of the characteristics of the passing traffic frequently reveals patterns and variations not readily apparent from casual observation.

In order to determine what proportion of the passing traffic represents potential shoppers, some of the pedestrians should be interviewed about the origin of their trip, their destination, and the stores in which they plan to shop. This sort of information can provide a good estimate of the number of potential customers. The season, month, week, day, and hour all have an effect on a traffic survey. For example, during summer, there is generally an increased flow of traffic on the shady side of the street. During a holiday period, such as the month before Christmas or the week before Easter, traffic is denser than normal. The patronage of a store varies by day of the week, too, as store traffic usually increases during the latter part of the week. In some communities, on factory paydays and days when government cheques are received, certain locations experience heavier-than-normal traffic.

Management also has to decide whether it wants to locate in proximity to the competition. Locating in proximity to competitors can encourage comparison shopping. Some areas of a community, for example, have a concentration of automobile dealers or furniture outlets for that reason.

### Rating Sites

Alternative sites can be evaluated after management decides on (1) the *importance* of selected factors in choosing a site and (2) the *attractiveness* of the site based on the factors identified as important. Multiplying importance by attractiveness, as shown in Table 11–6, yields a weighted score for each factor. The total score for each site allows management to compare and rank alternative sites more objectively.

*Other Factors to Consider*

Most first-time business owners have no idea how effective a strong merchants' association can be in promoting and maintaining the business in a given area. Management should always find out about the merchants' association. The presence of an effective association can strengthen the business and save management money through group advertising programs, group insurance plans, and collective security measures.

A strong merchants' association can accomplish through group strength what an individual store owner could not even dream of. Some associations have induced

## TABLE 11–6    Rating Sheet for Sites

| Factor | Importance* | Attractiveness[†] Ranking of Site | Weighted Score |
|---|---|---|---|
| Growth potential | 2 | 2 | 4 |
| Rental conditions | 6 | 4 | 24 |
| Investment required | 5 | 5 | 25 |
| Strength of competition | 1 | 1 | 1 |
| Ability to serve target | 3 | 6 | 18 |
| Profit potential | 4 | 3 | 12 |
| Total Score for Site | | | 84 |

*1 is most important to the owner/manager.
[†]For the site considered, 1 is most attractive to the owner/manager.

city planners to add highway exits near their shopping centres. Others have lobbied for (and received) funds from cities to remodel their shopping centres, including extension of parking lots, resurfacing of buildings, and installation of better lighting.

Merchants' associations can be particularly effective at organizing store promotions around common themes or events and during holiday seasons. The collective draw from these promotions is usually several times that which a single retailer could have mustered.

### Responsiveness of the Landlord

Directly related to the appearance of a retail location is the responsiveness of the landlord to the individual merchant's needs. Unfortunately, some landlords of retail business properties actually hinder the operation of their tenants' businesses. They are, in fact, responsible for the demise of their properties. Retail Highlight 11–3 provides examples of effective landlords.

By restricting the placement and size of signs, by forgoing or ignoring needed maintenance and repairs, by renting adjacent retail spaces to incompatible—or worse, directly competing—businesses, landlords may cripple a retailer's attempts to increase business.

Sometimes landlords lack the funds to maintain their properties. Rather than continuing to invest in their holdings by maintaining a proper appearance for their buildings and supporting their tenants, they try to squeeze the property for whatever they can get.

In addition to speaking with current tenants, management should talk to previous tenants of the possible locations. Find out what businesses they were in and why they left. Did they fail or just move? What support or hindrances did the landlord provide? If the opportunity presented itself, would they be retail tenants of this landlord again?

### Leases

A lease is a legal contract that conveys property from the landlord to the tenant for a specified period of time in return for an agreed-on fee. Leases can take several

## Retail Highlight 11-3

# For Effective Landlords, a Lease Agreement Is a Partnership

For a landlord, a good tenant is a steady source of revenue, particularly when the lease agreement includes a percentage of sales and when the economy is faltering. It is, thus, extremely important for the landlord to help current and potential tenants succeed. Some examples help illustrate the benefits of this proactive approach:

- When Confed Realty Services bought the Eaton Centre mall in downtown Edmonton from Triple Five Corp. for $1, the mall was doing very poorly and tenants were asking for rent concessions. Sandy McNair, a proprietor and manager of the mall, knew that rent concessions would not increase sales, which is what was needed to make the mall profitable. He used the amount of money that would have gone into rent concessions to invest in a program that produced impressive results. Some of the elements were (1) a complete interior renovation of the mall to make it more appealing to customers; (2) an ongoing program to advise retailers on improving their operations, including window displays and store designs (using consultants paid by Confed); (3) the Eaton Centre Retail Management Institute, taught by professional consultants (again paid by

Confed), which gave an eight-week course on customer service, salesmanship, time management, and human resources; (4) a customer-loyalty program developed, run, and financed by Confed that served as a database for marketing, providing useful information to retailers about their customers and serving as a basis for targeted promotions.

- Trilea Centre, a Toronto-based shopping mall operator, has devised a program to allow aspiring retailers to test market their ideas while lowering their financial risk. For the last two years, several of its malls have been renting small carts by the week (for as little as $300 a week), or a 10-square-metre shop by the month. By comparison, renting a space in a shopping centre would require an investment of about $200,000, with a five-year lease. In addition, mall managers give basic advice, and some malls such as the Lougheed Mall in Burnaby run workshops to first-time retailers. The program has been very successful in helping miniretailers gain valuable experience and go on to lease full-fledged quarters once they are convinced that their ideas are profitable.

Sources: John Southerst, "The Reinvention of Retail," *Canadian Business,* August 1992, pp. 26–31; and Jerry Zeidenberg, "Malls Give Entrepreneurs a Chance to Test Market," *Globe and Mail,* December 23, 1991, p. B4.

forms. Under a **fixed-payment lease,** the landlord charges the tenant a fixed amount each month. In a **variable-payment lease,** the retailer pays a guaranteed minimum rent plus a specified percentage of sales. The minimum rent typically covers the landlord's expenses such as taxes, insurance, and maintenance. The percentage of sales component of the rent allows the landlord to share in the profits the retailer makes as a result of being in a choice location.

The rent to be paid is determined by several factors. The primary factor is the sales per square metre that can be generated at the site. Retailers with high sales per square metre typically pay a lower percentage rent than retailers with lower sales per square metre. Outlets with high sales per square metre generate higher volumes of customer traffic and, as a result, are able to negotiate lower percentage rents because they are more desirable tenants.

### Other Considerations for Retail Site Decisions

Other considerations have varying importance in choosing a retail location, depending on the line of business. While they certainly do not cover all possibilities, the following questions may help in choosing a retail location:

1. How much retail, office, storage, or workroom space is needed?
2. Is parking space available and adequate?
3. Does the business require special lighting, heating, or cooling, or other installations?
4. Will the advertising expenses be much higher if management chooses a relatively remote location?
5. Is the area served by public transportation?
6. Can the area serve as a source of supply of employees?
7. Is there adequate fire and police protection?
8. Will sanitation or utility supply be a problem?
9. Is exterior lighting in the area adequate to attract evening shoppers and make them feel safe?
10. Are customer restroom facilities available?
11. Is the store easily accessible?
12. Does the store have awnings or decks to provide shelter during bad weather?
13. Will crime insurance be prohibitively expensive?
14. Will space be needed for pickup or delivery?
15. Is the trade area heavily dependent on seasonal business?
16. Is the location convenient to where employees will live?
17. Do target customers live nearby?
18. Is the population density of the area sufficient?

***Consider the Future***

Management should look ahead. Try to picture the situation 10 years from now. Try to determine whether the general area can support the firm as the business expands. Also, management must consider whether a site that fills its present needs will allow for future expansion. If management has to move a second time and the distance is too far, the firm is apt to lose a majority of its customers.

***Relocate for Growth?***

Sometimes an owner/manager should consider relocating even though the need for doing so is not apparent—the present space may seem adequate, and customers are being served without undue complaints.

If a facility has become a competitive liability, moving to another building may be the most economical way to become competitive again. For example, if a new, high-quality shopping centre in a downtown area is expected to attract a lot of traffic away from street merchants, the owner of a retail store situated in an old building should seriously consider relocating inside the centre.

The company that prospers is the one whose owner/manager chooses the best possible site and remains there only until factors indicate that the present location's benefits no longer outweigh the advantages to be gained by moving.

## Chapter Highlights

- Location is a key factor in the retailing mix. Retailers should consider such a decision as carefully as pricing, promotion, and other elements of the marketing mix.

- Key strategic decisions in retail location relate to the desired type of market coverage and the type of goods sold. The process of selecting a retail location goes from market analysis to trade area analysis and site analysis and evaluation.

- Key factors in making the market selection include its size, composition of the population, labour market, closeness to the source of merchandise supply, media mix available, economic base of the community, existing and probable future competition, availability of store sites, and local, provincial, and federal regulations.

- Trade area analysis is done once the market has been selected. Retailers can employ a variety of techniques in assessing the size of the probable trading area (primary and secondary). These techniques include a study of existing stores, license plate or cheque clearance analysis, an analysis of credit records, consumer spotting, driving time analysis, gravity models, and conducting a customer survey to help them understand customer shopping behaviour.

- After establishing the size of the trading area, management then has to determine the amount of business that can be done in the trading area. The amount of business is a function of the number of people in the trading area, the average household income, the amount of money spent each year by households on the type of goods sold by the firm, the total market potential available, and the share of the total market that management expects to attract.

- Choosing a site in a trade area is the final step in selecting a retail location. Retailers can decide on a shopping centre, a downtown, or a solo location. The retailer has the choice of locating in a neighbourhood centre, a community centre, a regional centre, or one of the other new types (mega-multi-malls, urban arterial developments, specialized functional areas, life-style clusters, off-price and factory outlet centres, and power strip centres).

- Choosing a specific site also involves assessing the adequacy and potential of vehicular or passenger traffic passing a site, the ability of the site to intercept traffic en route from one place to another, the nature of adjacent stores, type of goods sold, and adequacy of parking.

- Finally, there are a number of other factors to consider, including the responsiveness of the landlord and the contents of the lease agreement.

## Key Terms

## Discussion Questions

1. Explain why regional dominance, market saturation, and emphasis on smaller towns and communities are seen today as the three best location strategies.

2. What do you consider to be the important factors in selecting a site for a fast-food outlet? How do these contrast, if at all, with your notion of the key factors for the location of an outlet selling stereo components?

3. In deciding whether to locate in a particular shopping centre, what are the factors (questions) the retailer needs to consider?

4. Distinguish among the following: neighbourhood shopping centres, community shopping centres, and regional shopping centres.

5. What factors have led to the decline of downtown areas as desirable locations for many retail outlets? What can downtown areas do to better compete with suburban shopping centres?

6. Distinguish among the following techniques used by retailers to determine the size of a trading area: license plate analysis, cheque clearance analysis, gravity models, credit records analysis, and customer surveys.

7. What are the various types of information a retailer needs to estimate the amount of likely sales within a trading area? What are some of the sources from which this information can be obtained?

8. Why is information about a retail store's target market an essential factor to consider when conducting a pedestrian traffic count?

## Application Exercises

1. Devise a questionnaire to obtain the following information for the shopping centre at which a sample of consumers most frequently shop:
   *a.* Distance travelled to the shopping centre.
   *b.* Number of visits per week/month.
   *c.* Items usually purchased at this shopping centre.
   *d.* Factors most liked about the shopping centre.
   *e.* Dominant reason for shopping at the centre.
   *f.* Opinion about the prices of the merchandise.
   *g.* Opinion about the quality of the merchandise.
   *h.* Opinion about the selection of the merchandise.
   *i.* Opinion about the salespeople.
   *j.* Opinion about the convenience of the location.
   *k.* Amount spent here on the average per week/month.

   Expand this questionnaire to obtain similar information about the second most frequented shopping centre. Using the data obtained from your questionnaire, do an analysis to isolate the factors that determine the choice of shopping centres. Which factors are the most important? Which are the least important? Are greater dollar amounts spent at the shopping centre visited most frequently? What meaning does this have for the retailer? What are the similarities and differences in the reasons given for the shopping centre visited most and secondmost?

2. A topic of interest in many cities is the future of the central business district (CBD). If you are in a city that has gone through a downtown revitalization programme, arrange to have interviews with the public servants (and volunteers) who were responsible for getting the project going. Describe it; indicate the views of success; and indicate future directions. If you are not in such a

situation, search the current literature for examples of cities that have undergone downtown revitalization. Contact their chambers of commerce for information and indicate some of the national efforts along these lines.

3. Prepare a location and site analysis for a good-quality cafeteria for your local community (other types of service retailers or tangible goods establishments may be used) based on the information in the text. Assume that the cafeteria is a regional chain, with excellent regional recognition and acceptance, but that it is not in your community. Prices are higher than fast-food outlets but lower than service restaurants of comparable quality food.

# Suggested Cases

# Endnotes

1. Bernard Simon, "Good Times Have Arrived in Some Surprising Places," *The Financial Post,* May 15, 1989, p. 17.
2. *Canadian Markets, 1992* (Toronto: The Financial Post Information Service, 1991), p. 23.
3. Anne Bokma, "Hard Labour," *Retail Directions,* November/December 1988, pp. 20–25.
4. *Canadian Markets, 1992;* and Bernard LaLonde, "The Logistics of Retail Location," in *Fall American Marketing Association Proceedings,* (Chicago: American Marketing Association, 1961), p. 572.
5. *Canadian Directory of Shopping Centres, 1992.*
6. William J. Reilly, *Methods for the Study of Retail Relationships,* research monograph No. 4, University of Texas Bulletin No. 2944 (Austin: University of Texas Press, 1929).
7. See also P. Peter Yannopoulos, "Salient Factors in Shopping Centre Choice," in *Marketing,* vol. 12, ed. Tony Schellinck (Montreal: ASAC, 1991), pp. 294–302; Adam Finn and Jordan Louviere,

"Shopping-Centre Patronage Models," *Journal of Business Research* 21 (1990), pp. 259–75; Hiro Matsusaki, "The Estimation of Retail Trading Areas by Using a Probabilistic Gravity Model: An Evaluation from a Cross-Cultural Perspective," in *Marketing,* vol. 1, ed. Vernon J. Jones (ASAC, 1980), pp. 248–57; and George H. Haines, Jr., Leonard S. Simon, and Marcus Alexis, "Maximum Likelihood Estimation of Central-City Food Trading Areas," *Journal of Marketing Research* 9, no. 2 (May 1972), pp. 154–59.
8. David L. Huff, "A Probabilistic Analysis of Shopping Centre Trade Areas," *Land Economics* 39. Copyright © 1963 by the Board of Regents of the University of Wisconsin System, p. 86.
9. David L. Huff and Larry Blue, *A Programmed Solution for Estimating Retail Sales Potential* (Lawrence, Kansas: Center for Regional Studies, 1966).
10. Ronald E. Turner, "Marketing Applications of the 1981 Census Data," in *Marketing,* vol. 6, ed. Jean-Charles Chebat (ASAC, 1985), pp. 335–42.

11. Statistics Canada, *Family Expenditures in Canada,* Cat. 62–555 (Ottawa: Information Canada).

12. J. Ross McKeever, "Factors to Consider in a Shopping Centre Location," *Small Marketers Aid,* No. 143 (Washington, D.C.: Small Business Administration); see also, Eric Peterson, "Site Selection," *Stores,* July 1986; and "Firm Anchors Secure Small Centre Financing," *Chain Store Age Executive,* September 1986.

13. An interesting approach can be found in Finn and Louviere, "Shopping-Centre Patronage Models."

14. *Canadian Directory of Shopping Centres, 1992,* pp. 158–160.

15. Statistics Canada, *Sales per Selling Area of Independent Retailers,* Cat. 61–522 (Ottawa: Information Canada, 1986), Appendix I.

16. *Canadian Directory of Shopping Centres, 1992.*

17. Statistics Canada, *Sales per Selling Area of Independent Retailers.*

18. *Canadian Directory of Shopping Centres, 1992.*

19. Statistics Canada, *Sales per Selling Area of Independent Retailers.*

20. "Festival Market Places: Entertaining the Shopper," *Chain Store Age Executive,* October 1985, pp. 51–57; and *Canadian Directory of Shopping Centres, 1992.*

21. Adam Finn and John Rigby, "West Edmonton Mall: Consumer Combined-Purpose Trips and the Birth of the Mega-Multi-Mall," *Canadian Journal of Administrative Sciences* 9 (June 1992), pp. 134–45.

22. Statistics Canada, *Sales per Selling Area of Independent Retailers.*

23. James R. Lowry, *Using a Traffic Study to Select a Retail Site* (Washington, D.C.: Small Business Administration).

# 12  STORE DESIGN, STORE LAYOUT, AND MERCHANDISE PRESENTATION

## Chapter Objectives

After reading this chapter, you should be able to:

1  Discuss the main dimensions of exterior and interior store design.
2  Describe typical store layout arrangements.
3  Explain how to allocate space to selling departments and nonselling activities.
4  Explain how to measure selling-space productivity.
5  Evaluate factors to consider in locating selling departments and sales-supporting activities within the store.
6  Describe the essentials of merchandise presentation.

The importance of store design, store layout, and merchandise presentation is illustrated in the following examples:

- *Kmart:* Kmart is reorganizing its departments, widening its aisles, and brightening its floor space to target single mothers and families. Refurbishing includes revamping the in-store lunch counter and offering foods reflecting the mix available in the food court of a shopping mall. More floor space is devoted to ladies' and men's wear, jewellery, cosmetics, and home fashions. Outfitted with "power aisles and power walls" that will display a broader variety of merchandise, the new-look outlets will have about 32 percent more retail space than the chain's traditional stores and feature an expanded range of brand-name goods and customer services—from food courts and bank machines to hair salons. Some departments will be equipped with electronic buttons that shoppers can press to alert staff when they need assistance. And check-out counters are being equipped with the latest in price-scanning technology.

- *Fairweather:* The Fairweather chain has completely changed its image and moved to a new upscale look. It has spent over $1 million on its new spacious design for its flagship store in the Toronto Eaton Centre. The new design incorporates more mirrors, extra-large fitting rooms, redesigned cash areas, and a broad marble aisle directly down the centre of the store leading to a series of distinct boutiques, recreating the prestige environment of an upscale department store. Good design not only creates customer space, it shows the merchandise to best advantage. Fairweather management knows that the more elegant the store is, the more attractive the merchandise will seem.

- *Décor Décarie:* Old Décarie Square in Montreal has flipped its roof, to be replaced with Décor Décarie, a sunny new shopping centre that has everything for the home, including the kitchen sink. What was a dreary retail hodgepodge has been transformed through skillful, airy renovations by Michelangelo Panzini and interior work into a focused design concept that is accessible to consumers and professional designers. The spiffy new look includes a soaring skylight atrium and some postmodern accents, and it readily signals the function of this massive building. A visit to Décor Décarie is a wonderful day outing, particularly during the winter doldrums.

As these examples illustrate, innovative retailers take great care in the design and layout of their stores and the presentation of their merchandise. This chapter focuses on these decision areas. The end goals are to show how effective layout and presentations can lead not only to increased sales levels but also to greater space productivity.

Store layout and design and merchandise presentation are critical elements of a firm's positioning strategy. At times, firms may need to redesign their stores' interiors and exteriors as part of a new image projection for the organization.

*(continued on next page)*

*Retailing Capsule continued*

*Kmart is redesigning its stores to include "power aisles and power walls."*

SOURCE: Courtesy Kmart.

Sources: James Pollock, "Kmart Continues Repositioning with Latest Store Redesigns," *Marketing,* July 6, 1992, p. 6; John Heinzl, "Kmart Powers Up for the 90s," *Globe and Mail,* October 21, 1991, p. B1; Anne Bokma, "Makeover Magic," *Retail Directions,* May/June 1989, pp. 34–37; and Annabelle King, "Décor Décarie Has It All under One Roof," *The Montreal Gazette,* February 16, 1989, p. F–3.

Ideally, an effective design creates a store that invites customers to shop, makes them feel comfortable, helps them find the merchandise, and increases their satisfaction. The major goal of store design and layout and merchandise presentation is to get the shopper into the store to spend as much money as possible on a given shopping trip. In many instances, identical merchandise can be found in directly competing stores. Thus, it is very important for any given store to create a general atmosphere and specific presentations that will trigger buying decisions on its own sales floor rather than that of competitors.

*Black's, with a new store design and layout for the 1990s.*

SOURCE: Courtesy of Black Photo Corporation.

## Creating the Physical Environment

In order to more easily discuss the important physical environment of a store, a few terms should be defined:

- **Store planning** includes exterior and interior building design, the allocation of space to departments, and the arrangement and location of departments within the store.
- **Store design** refers to the style or atmosphere of a store that helps project an image to the market. Store design elements include such exterior factors as the store front and window displays and such interior factors as colours, lighting, flooring, and fixtures.
- **Store layout** involves planning the internal arrangement of departments—both selling and sales supporting—and deciding on the amount of space for each department.

Figure 12–1 shows the relationships among these three terms.

# Store Design

## *Store Design: A Critical Element in Positioning Strategy*

Store design is an important image-creating element and should begin with an understanding of the preferences, desires, and expectations of the store's target market. For example, store design for warehouse food stores, whose target segment is price-conscious shoppers, would feature tile floors, harsh lighting, and limited in-store signing. Similarly, a design using bold colours, flashing lights, and eye-popping displays might be very appropriate for a store targeting young people, but inappropriate for a store focusing on older, conservative shoppers.

Demographic characteristics such as income and age are not the only variables of the target market to affect store design. Increasingly, store design is influenced by the life-styles of target customers. A store that specializes in tennis equipment could reflect the life-style of its intended clientele by using murals with large photographs of tennis courts and famous tennis players.

Retailers must also constantly monitor changes occurring in the external environment and alter store design to be responsive to such changes. Retailers must use store design as a competitive weapon, appealing to the changing life-styles of their target shoppers. For example, retail store design is being affected by the changing buying roles of men and women. With women becoming bigger buyers of hardware and automotive products, some hardware and auto-parts stores are changing their store design to shed their "macho" image. When a stores changes its target market, repositioning requires changes in store design as well.

**FIGURE 12–1**

*The store planning process*

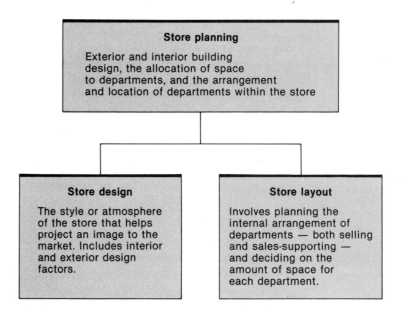

*Design and Store Image*

In developing an image for the store, the design should answer five fundamental questions:[1]

1. Can the concept and merchandise being sold in your store be explained in one or two sentences?
2. Will the customer distinguish your store from the competition?
3. Can you explain the concepts of your competitors that appeal to customers?
4. Will your name, logo, and store design reflect the image that you want to project?
5. Will your store design still look good two or five years from now?

Store design is a reflection of two elements: (1) the exterior design and (2) the interior design, which includes everything within the store—walls, floor, ceiling, lighting fixtures, colours, scents, and sounds. The exterior and interior designs should be in harmony with the store's merchandise and customers.

*Exterior Design*

Store designers indicate that many retailers make the mistake of concentrating only on the inside of the store and fail to give adequate attention to the exterior of the building. However, a store's exterior is a most important aspect of image creation, as illustrated in Retail Highlight 12–1.

The building's architecture, entrances, display windows, and signs are some of the image-creating elements related to exterior design.

### Architecture and Entrances

A store's architecture can create image impressions in a number of ways. The architectural design may reflect the nature of the products sold in the store. A restaurant emphasizing Mexican dishes may use yellow and green colours with adobe-style walls and Mexican decorations (e.g., sombreros or piñatas).

The store's architectural style may also reflect the size of the store. For example, a huge food store may design a building on the model of a French market, with a large curved glass ceiling and big columns to give a feeling of space and scale.

A store's entrance should provide for easy entry into the store. However, some designers may also see entrances as a transition zone—for example, using corridors leading to courtyards—in order to ease the customer into a busy or large area.

Finally, some designers emphasize the importance of consistency between the exterior and interior design elements, in order to carry through the same theme associated with the design.

### Display Windows

Window-shopping is often very important for many types of retailers, and window displays should primarily be used to attract the attention and interest of customers, enticing them into the store.

Window displays were downplayed during the 1970s and early 1980s because of increased cost cutting and energy consciousness among retailers. Also, during

Retail Highlight 12–1

# Importance of Exterior Design:
# The First Canadian Optical Experience

When moving to a larger location, First Canadian Optical, which sells designer eyeglasses, decided to redesign the store. With such fashionable merchandise and well-to-do customers, president Bob Karir knew that a unique environment must be created. "Most optical stores look like dispensaries with their big mirrors and poor lighting. Lighting is especially important in an optical store, and poor lighting makes eyeglasses appear unattractive to customers." That problem was solved with the placement of wall-mounted indirect halogen lights, covered by shades in the shape of pyramids.

The most unusual feature of the new store is the bright red storefront, with its seven closed-in window displays ranging in height from 2 to 4 feet.

Each is framed to look like a portrait, and the displays themselves are imaginative works of art produced by a free-lance window dresser. They vary from the conservative—"serious" eyeglasses hanging from a banker's lamp with leather-bound books—to the whimsical—wild, red and violet frames on top of a bunch of eggs. The storefront has a fairly narrow entrance that leads to the reception area.

Karir is convinced that the new store design has made all the difference. "We have much more traffic in the store than we've ever had before. The store is so strong in the front everybody wants to come in and have a look."

Source: Jack Fraser, "Makeover Magic," *Retail Directions*, May/June 1989, pp. 36–37.

this period, emphasis was placed on building stores in malls; thus, attention was focused more on interior merchandise presentations than on window displays.

Today, however, there is a renewed interest in store window displays, especially among department stores and higher-priced retailers and in cities where walking and window-shopping are still in style. Window displays may be used to enhance store image, to expose would-be shoppers to new products, or to introduce a new season.

Retailers put much effort in designing window displays for Christmas, since for many of them this is the best selling period of the year. Properly decorated Christmas windows will put the customers into the right mood, bring back childhood memories, break down their inhibitions, and put them into the spirit of giving. For Eaton's, Christmas represents the largest decorating expenditure and is the responsibility of a special committee that works 12 months to plan and order for the upcoming season.[2]

Much art is involved in developing window displays. Principles of good design—balance, proportion, and harmony—are all essential. Errors retailers sometimes make are using too much or too little merchandise, inappropriate props and lighting, or simply not changing a display frequently enough, with the result

*The exterior design contributes to the overall image of the store.*

SOURCE: Courtesy Marks & Spencer and Begg & Daigle.

that it loses its special significance. The ideal is to change the window displays about 15 to 20 times a year.[3]

Management can evaluate the results of window displays by counting the number of people who (1) pass the window in a certain period, (2) glance at the window, (3) stop at the window, and (4) enter the store after looking at the window display.

### Signs

The creative use of an easy-to-read outdoor sign serves the purpose of identifying the store and providing some information about it. The sign can also be an important factor in creating a favourable image for the store. Some retailers have developed distinctive signs that are widely recognized by consumers. An example is McDonald's with its golden arches.

Many cities, however, have zoning laws that require both sign permits and design approval.

***Interior Design***    Within the store, consumers respond not only to the products or services being offered but also to their surroundings. Environmental factors can affect a shopper's

*Good display windows attract shoppers.*

SOURCE: Photo by James Hertel.

desire to shop or not shop at the store and the amount of time spent in the store. The internal environment can also influence the customer's desire or willingness to explore the environment and to communicate with salespeople. Thus, retailers must consider the psychological effects of their outlets on consumer purchasing behaviour. Fast-food restaurants do this by utilizing hard chairs and fast-tempo music to encourage rapid turnover during lunch times.

As has been observed: "A subtle dimension of in-store customer shopping behaviour is the environment of the space itself. Retail space—that is, the proximate environment that surrounds the retail shopper—is never neutral. The retail store is a bundle of cues, messages, and suggestions which communicate to shoppers. Retail store designers, planners, and merchandisers shape space, but that space in turn affects and shapes customer behaviour. The retail store . . . create[s] moods, activates intentions, and generally affects customer reactions."[4]

Some retailers view the interior of their stores as a stage in a theatre and realize that theatrical elements can be used to influence customer behaviour. They feel the customer should be entertained and excited. This principle is illustrated in Retail Highlight 12–2.

Many fast-food outlets are undergoing interior design changes as a way of attracting customers in an intensely competitive environment. Many feel that a more upscale design will attract a broader range of customers. Customers will see less plastic, metal, and bright primary colours. Typically, operators are now aiming for subtler lighting and are using pastel colours, marble, mirrors, brass, wood, and greenery to create a warm, earthy environment.[5] Other Canadian store designers use state-of-the-art fixtures as well as borrow some European flavour, particularly in designing fashion stores where the trend is to use sophisticated mannequins, "invisible" fixturing, and showing "less than more" in terms of merchandise.[6]

The store's interior design should be based on an understanding of the customer and how design contributes to the strategy for reaching the target market. This is a very important decision, and the selection of a store designer should be done with a great deal of care.[7]

A store's interior design includes everything within the store walls that can be used to create store atmosphere. These elements include floor, wall, and ceiling materials; lighting; fixtures; colours; scents; and sounds. The following sections of this chapter focus on colour, lighting, and sound as store image-creating variables.

---

**Retail Highlight 12–2**

## Alive and Well and Doing Well

Alive and Well is a women's fashion outlet in Markham, Ontario, that is making money and having fun doing it. "In this business, you don't get talked about by being ordinary. If retail is theatre, then we have a 750-square-metre stage," says owner Donald Cooper. At Alive and Well, he has created an environment that treats customers as if they were guests in his home. Each customer is offered a complimentary drink and is encouraged to take it along while browsing.

The store is laid out in a way that reflects customer life-styles. There is Easy Street for casual wear, Fit Life for exercise wear, Best Dressed for career women, Beach Life, Mega Accessories, and

Zelda's Country Store (Cooper threw in the country store at the last minute to give Alive and Well some warmth). The store is equipped with a children's play area and a changing room for babies, stocked with complimentary diapers.

Massage chairs dot the store for those customers wanting to take a breather. "Most retailers, through the layout of their stores, do not encourage customers to spend a lot of time in the shops, but at Alive and Well, customers spend an average of one hour." Twenty-five change rooms line the store, each equipped with four hooks, a shelf, and a mirror, which lets a customer check out her appearance privately.

Source: Stephen Forbes, "This Retailer Is Alive and Well," *Marketing,* October 15, 1990, pp. 15, 17.

## Colours

The use of colours should be done with a great deal of thought, since colours often create an atmosphere for the store. For example, a children's store needs primary bright colours. A bookstore needs soothing and reflective colours. Traditional menswear is best set with country club colours (like forest green) and young women's wear in a pastel environment.[8]

Research has determined that colour can affect store and merchandise image and customer shopping behaviour. People, regardless of colour preferences, are physically drawn to warm colours such as red and yellow. Thus, warm colours (red and particularly yellow) are good colour choices for drawing customers into a retail store, department, or display area. Warm colours are appropriate for store windows and entrances as well as for buying situations associated with impulse purchases. Think of "red tag sales" or "red dot specials," for example. Cool colours (such as blue and green) are appropriate where customer deliberations over the purchase decision are necessary.[9]

Background colours for product presentations are also a major concern for retailers. For example, the colours white, pink, yellow, and blue should not be used in the toddler department. Those are the colours of most of the merchandise; thus, the garments would merely "fade into the walls." Sometimes, the colour that is used to show off the product should be related to the final use of the product. Fine jewellery, for example, may look dramatic against bold colour backgrounds, but it is most often seen against flesh tones. On the other hand, costume jewellery is best presented against a vivid background.

## Lighting

Lighting can be used to spotlight merchandise and to impact customer shopping behaviour. Some supermarket retailers have chosen to make the produce area dark and then put light on the merchandise to make it stand out. Others, however, feel that customers are not comfortable in a dark area and thus are moving away from the overall dark, theatrical effect while still focusing light onto the product.

## Sound

Music has been found to have an impact on shopping behaviour. Research has found that shoppers spend less time in a store when music is played loudly.[10] A 30 percent increase in supermarket sales was experienced when the store played slow music compared to fast music. Also, in a restaurant, customers spent more time at their tables, consumed more alcoholic beverages, but ate no more food when slow music was played compared to fast music.[11] These improvements in sales were attributed to customers spending more time in the outlet, usually because they moved at a slower pace. Of interest is that a significant number of these customers, after they left, did not recall that music was being played. The implication is that shopping behaviour was altered by the music without customers' awareness.

# Store Layout

Store layout is a very important element of store planning. Layout not only affects customer movement in the store but also influences the way merchandise is displayed. The following elements are part of layout planning:

1. The overall arrangement of the store.
2. Allocation of space to selling departments and sales-supporting activities.
3. Evaluation of space productivity.
4. Location of selling departments and sales-supporting activities within the store.

## *Arrangement of the Store*

Typical layout arrangements are the grid, the free-flow or open plan, and the boutique concept. Let's look first at the grid layout.

### Grid Layout

In a **grid layout,** merchandise is displayed in straight, parallel lines, with secondary aisles at right angles to these. An example is shown in Figure 12–2. A supermarket typically uses a grid layout.

The grid arrangement is more for store efficiency than customer convenience, since the layout tends to hinder movement. Customer flow is guided more by the layout of the aisles and fixtures than by the buyer's desire for merchandise. For example, 80 to 90 percent of all customers shopping in a supermarket with a grid layout pass the produce, meat, and dairy counters. Fewer shoppers pass other displays, because the grid forces the customers to the sides and back of the supermarket.

In department stores, a grid layout on the main floor usually forces traffic down the main aisles. Thus, shoppers are less likely to be exposed to items along the walls. Shopping goods (highly demanded merchandise) should be placed along the walls, and convenience goods should be displayed in the main part of the store. Customer traffic then is drawn to otherwise slow-moving areas.

### Free-Flow Layout

In a **free-flow layout,** merchandise and fixtures are grouped into patterns that allow an unstructured flow of customer traffic, as shown in Figure 12–3. The free-flow pattern is designed for customer convenience and exposure to merchandise. Free-flow designs let customers move in any direction and wander freely, thus encouraging browsing and impulse purchasing. The layout, however, is more costly and uses space less efficiently than the grid layout.

### Boutique Layout

A variation of the free-flow layout is the **boutique layout,** where merchandise classifications are grouped so that each classification has its own "shop" within the store, as shown in Figure 12–4. The boutique concept is an outgrowth of life-style merchandising wherein a classification is aimed at a specific life-style segment,

**Figure 12–2**

*Grid layout*

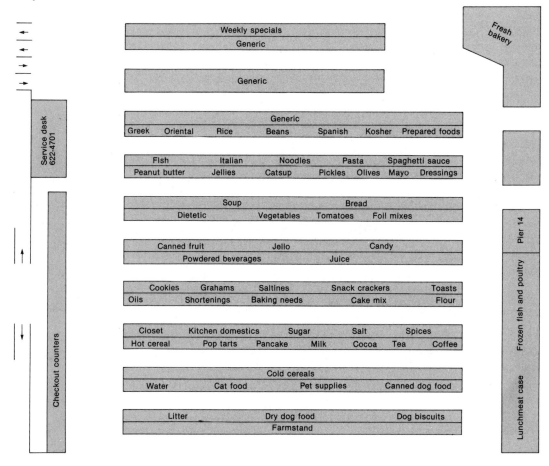

often featuring merchandise from a single designer or company, as shown in Exhibit 12–1 on page 323.

Each shop has its own identity, including colour schemes, styles, and atmosphere. Even though greater flexibility is possible with this arrangement, construction costs and security costs are higher. As a result, the concept is used in high-status department stores and other outlets where the sale of higher-priced merchandise allows absorption of the increased costs. However, some discounters are experimenting with the store-within-the-store concept.

*Allocation of Space*

Dividing total space between selling and sales-supporting (e.g., storage) areas is the first step in space allocation. In general, the larger a store, the higher its ratio of sales-supporting space to selling space. As a general rule, retailers, other than

**FIGURE 12-3**

*Free-flow layout*

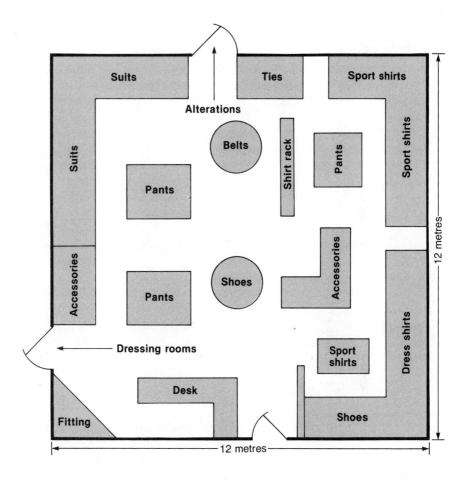

specialty or fashion outlets, devote as much space to the sales area as possible. However, the amount of sales space varies by size and type of store. In a very large department store, selling space may account for roughly 65 percent of total space. Jewellery stores need almost no sales-supporting space. A home improvement centre, however, may use more space for warehousing and storage than for selling. A warehouse-type store will put all its inventory on the selling floor. This practice seems to have sparked a trend in the industry, and more and more stores are using a larger proportion of their space for selling. For example, a regular Canadian Tire store devotes just 40 percent of its space to selling, while Canadian Tire's warehouse concept has 80 percent of its space accessible to customers.[12]

The amount of space allocated to nonselling areas may be affected by the advent of electronic data interchange (EDI) and greater UPC vendor marketing. With EDI and UPC, merchandise moves more quickly and accurately through the

**FIGURE 12–4**

*Boutique layout*

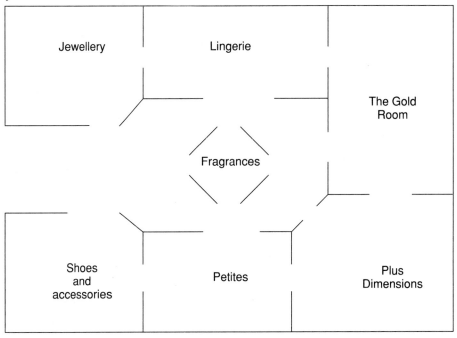

distribution channel, with smaller quantities arriving at the store more frequently. Since large "cushion" stocks will not be required, backrooms can be greatly reduced in size, and greater use will be made of store space by merchandising.

Management can use three basic methods for allocating selling space:

1. Industry averages by type of merchandise.
2. Sales productivity of product lines.
3. The build-up (model stock) method.

**Industry Averages**

Management can use the national average percentage of selling space that a particular merchandise line occupies in a certain type of store. For example, assume that the health and beauty aids department accounts for 4 percent of total selling space as an average in a superstore. Thus, in a superstore with 3,400 square metres of selling space, management would set aside 136 square metres for the health and beauty aids department (3,400 × .04 = 136).

**Sales Productivity Method**

Sales productivity is measured by sales per square metre of selling space. Assume that planned sales for health and beauty aids amount to $136,000. If the national average sales per square metre for this department is $1,000, then management

**EXHIBIT 12–1**

*A boutique layout featuring merchandise from a single designer*

SOURCE: Photo by James Hertel.

would allocate 136 square metres to the department ($136,000/$1,000 = 136). Table 12–1 gives an idea of the average sales per square metre for various types of stores.

### Build-Up (Model Stock) Method

Let us use a ladies' blouse department to illustrate this space allocation method. The build-up method would proceed as follows:

1. What is the ideal stock balance necessary to achieve expected sales volume? The merchant, based on past experience, may believe that sales of $30,000 per year are obtainable. Trade sources indicate that in the price line planned, three turns per year are realistic. Within the price-line structure, the average price of a blouse is $15. Given these assumptions, approximately 666 blouses will be needed as a normal offering during each turnover period ($30,000/3 = $10,000 in merchandise; $10,000/$15 = 666 blouses). Normally, 666 blouses must be in stock. However, the merchandise planner may vary from this number during high- and low-sales-volume months. Under this method, planning ties merchandise needs to actual seasonal variations rather than yearly averages. For example, Mother's Day might be the yearly peak sales period and should be considered in layout planning.

2. How much merchandise should be kept on display, and how much should be kept in reserve stock? How many of the 666 blouses should actually be displayed? Ideally, 100 percent should be on display, because

---

**TABLE 12–1    Average Sales per Square Metre for Selected Types of Stores**

| *Type of Store* | *Average Sales per $m^2$ ($)* |
| --- | --- |
| Pharmacies | 5,356 |
| Camera and photographic supply stores | 5,193 |
| Jewellery stores | 5,016 |
| Appliance, television, radio, and stereo stores | 4,810 |
| Supermarkets | 4,567 |
| Sporting goods stores | 4,264 |
| Grocery stores | 4,043 |
| Record and tape stores | 4,041 |
| Shoe stores | 3,142 |
| Men's clothing stores | 3,128 |
| Women's clothing stores | 2,900 |
| Book and stationery stores | 2,729 |
| Florist shops | 2,465 |
| Toy and hobby stores | 2,370 |
| Pet stores | 2,118 |
| Children's clothing stores | 1,997 |

SOURCE: Statistics Canada, *Market Research Handbook,* January 1992, Table 3–22.
Reproduced with the permission of the Minister of Supply and Services Canada, 1992.

goods do not sell if they are not seen. Since this is not realistic, and since the decision is arbitrary, assume that two thirds of the stock—approximately 444 blouses—will be displayed, and one third will be in reserve.

3. What is the best method of displaying the merchandise? This decision depends on the merchandise display equipment available and the affordable opportunities for display. Let's decide that we will hang the less expensive blouses on circular steel racks that have a glass top for display purposes. The most expensive blouses will be displayed in glass cases where they can be accessorized with jewellery, scarves, and other small items. Reserve stock will be stored in drawers beneath the display cases. Only one of each style will be displayed.

4. How many display racks and cases are necessary to display the items? The physical size and capacity of the fixtures must be determined to answer this question. Scale models of fixtures are often placed on floor plans to assist in the layout-planning process.

5. What is the best way to handle the reserve stock? We have already determined that the reserve stock for the expensive blouses will be maintained under the display cases. Space can be allocated for the remaining items in special storage fixtures on the selling floor or in a stock area as close to the selling area as possible.

6. What service requirements are necessary for the department? Fitting rooms and a point-of-sale terminal or register will be needed. Likewise, depending on the nature of the operation, space for packaging may be required. Finally, all departments need aisles.

7. What are the total space requirements? The total space needs can be determined in steps 4, 5, and 6.

## Evaluation of Space Use

Good use of space involves more than creating an aesthetically pleasing environment, although such a goal is important. Effective use of space can also translate into additional dollars of profit. Thus, retailers must evaluate whether store space is being used in the most effective way. Management can use a variety of measures to evaluate space utilization. The gross margin per square metre method is discussed below to illustrate one method retailers can employ.

To determine whether a department can "afford" the space it occupies, the gross margin per square metre of the department should be measured. Big-ticket items may ring up more sales than lower-priced goods, yet the ratio of gross margin to square feet may be smaller for high-priced merchandise.

As shown in Table 12–2, three calculations are involved in evaluating space utilization by the gross margin per square metre method. Sales per square metre less cost of merchandise sold per square metre yields the gross margin per square metre figure.

With this gross margin per square metre figure, departments of varying sizes selling different types of goods can be compared. Gross margin per square metre

---
### TABLE 12–2    Calculating Gross Margin per Square Metre
---

Three calculations are involved in figuring gross margin per square metre:

1. $\dfrac{\text{Total sales}}{\text{Total square metres}}$ = Sales per square metre

2. $\dfrac{\text{Cost of merchandise sold}}{\text{Total square metres}}$ = Cost of merchandise sold per square metre

3. Sales per square metre − Cost of merchandise = Gross margin per square metre
   sold per square metre

**Example**

|  | Department A | Department B |
|---|---|---|
| Sales | $ 50,000 | $ 70,000 |
| Cost of merchandise sold | $ 30,000 | $ 35,000 |
| Square metres of space | 50 m$^2$ | 70 m$^2$ |
| Sales per square metre | $    1,000 | $    1,000 |
| Cost of merchandise sold per m$^2$ | 600 | 500 |
| Gross margin per square metre | $      400 | $      500 |

can show management which departments are doing well, which are not, which might improve if expanded, and which can be reduced in space allotment.

For example, based on the calculations shown in Table 12–2, management might be tempted to decrease the selling space allocated to department A and increase the selling space devoted to department B. However, the decision to reallocate space is not a simple one. Advertising and selling costs may rise when selling space is increased. After the reallocation, the merchandise mix may change, which can result in either higher or lower gross margins. Management thus needs to simulate the likely changes in the three variables used in the calculations as a result of possible shifts in space allocation and determine whether reallocations are likely to increase the overall profitability of the firm.

An evaluation of space utilization may not only lead to a reallocation of space among selling departments; some stores are converting unproductive retail space to other uses.

## Locating Departments and Activities

Management must decide where to locate selling and sales-supporting activities within the store. Several guidelines are available to retailers to aid in making these decisions.

### Locating Selling Departments

The convenience of customers and the effect on profitability are the primary concerns of management in locating selling departments within the store. With these factors in mind, the following suggestions are offered:

- *Rent-paying capacity:* The department with the highest sales per square metre is best able to pay a high rent. Thus, this department should be placed in the most valuable, highly travelled area of the store. If a number of departments are equally good, the decision should be made based on the gross margins of the merchandise.

- *Impulse versus demand shopping:* **Impulse merchandise** is bought on the basis of unplanned, spur-of-the-moment decisions. Departments containing impulse merchandise normally get the best locations in the store. **Demand merchandise** is purchased as a result of a customer coming into the store to buy that particular item. Departments containing demand merchandise can be located in less valuable space because customers will hunt for these items.

- *Replacement frequency:* Certain goods, such as health and beauty aids, are frequently purchased, low-cost items. Customers want to buy them as conveniently as possible, so the department should be placed in an easily accessible location.

- *Related departments:* Similar items of merchandise should be displayed close together. In a superstore, for example, all household items—paper products, detergents, and kitchen gadgets—should be placed together, so customers will make combination purchases. Similarly, the men's furnishings department—shirts, ties, and underwear—should be placed near the suit department in a department store. A customer wanting a new suit often needs a matching shirt and tie as well. Combination selling is easier when related items are close together. Location of related goods is even more important in a self-service store because no salesperson is around to help the customer.

- *Seasonal variations:* Items in some departments are big sellers only a few months or weeks of the year. Toys and summer furniture are examples. Management might decide to place these departments next to each other. When toys expand at Christmas, extra space can be taken temporarily from summer furniture, and vice versa.

- *Size of departments:* Management may also want to place very small departments in some of the more valuable spaces to help them be seen. A very large department could use a less desirable location in the store because its size will contribute to its visibility.

- *Merchandise characteristics:* In a supermarket, bakery products (especially bread) should be near the check-out counter. Customers avoid crushing these items in the carts by selecting bakery products at the end of their shopping. Products such as lettuce are usually displayed along a wall to allow more space and to better handle wiring for cooling.

- *Shopping considerations:* Items such as suits and dresses are often tried on and fitted. They can be placed in less valuable locations away from heavy traffic. Also, they are demand, not impulse, items and can be placed in out-of-the-way areas, since shoppers will make an effort to find them.

- *New, developing, or underdeveloped departments:* Assume management has added a new department such as more ''nonfoods'' in a superstore. Management may want to give more valuable space to the new department to increase sales by exposing more customers to the items.

### Locating Sales-Supporting Activities

Sales-supporting activities such as credit departments can be thought of in several ways:

- Activities that must be located in a specific part of the store: Receiving and marketing areas should be located near the dock area, usually at the back of the store.
- Activities that serve the store only: Such activities are office space and personal services for employees of the store. These departments can be located in the least valuable, out-of-the-way places.
- Activities that relate directly to selling: Cutting areas for fresh meat need to be close to the refrigerators. Both refrigeration and cutting need to be close to the display cases. Drapery workrooms in department stores need to be close to the drapery department.
- Activities with direct customer contact: In a supermarket, customers often want to check parcels, cash a personal cheque, or ask for information about an item. Credit departments and layaway services are needed in department stores. Such activities can be located in out-of-the-way places to help increase customer movement in the store.

## Merchandise Presentation

Merchandise displays are part of the so-called silent language of communication. They can be used to excite, entertain, and educate consumers. If effectively used, they can have a profound influence on consumer behaviour, as illustrated in Retail Highlight 12–3.

Often, entire courses are devoted to the technical aspects of merchandise display. Because of space limitations, however, we must limit our discussion and will provide a brief overview of the following topics: principles of display, interior displays, and shelf-space allocation.

### Principles of Display

Customers in a retail store stop at some merchandise displays, move quickly past some, and smile at others. Shoppers are professional display watchers and know what they like. However, customers usually do not consciously judge displays. So the job of the retail manager is to ''prejudge'' for the purchaser. Managers need to be clever and creative enough to affect behaviour by display. Displays should attract attention and excite and stimulate customers. An illustration of such a display is seen in Exhibit 12–2.

---

**Retail Highlight 12–3**

# Someplace Special

Someplace Special is owned by Canada Safeway. This truly different store, the first of its kind in Canada, opened in October 1987 in West Vancouver. The store offers a number of unique products and services, never offered before in a supermarket, from a complete in-home catering service to a department specializing in imported labels and specialty foods. For example, fresh sushi is available daily, and the store will "search the world" for any food item requested by a customer.

According to Bruce Nicoll, division manager, "While other food retailers are building giant mega-stores that offer little service and a ware-house-like shopping environment, we are striving to make shopping more enjoyable for our customers by offering new products and services in attractive new stores designed to complement the neighbourhood in which they are located." The store has a skylight, a brass-and-oak trimmed decor, a European-style deli with more than 100 international cheeses, a flower shop with professional florists, a full-service butcher shop, and a seafood department with 45 varieties of fresh seafood from around the world. All of these elements combine to present the merchandise in a very appealing environment.

Source: "B.C. Store for Special Tastes," *Canadian Grocer,* November 1987, p. 10.

---

In spite of the basically artistic and creative flair needed for display, some principles do exist.[13] The following basic principles have been developed from years of experience.

1. Displays should be built around fast-moving, "hot" items.
2. Goods purchased largely on impulse should be given ample amounts of display space.
3. Displays should be kept simple. Management should not try to cram them with too many items.
4. Displays should be timely and feature seasonal goods.
5. Colour attracts attention, sets the right tone, and affects the sense of the display.
6. Use motion. It attracts attention.
7. Most good displays have a theme or story to tell.
8. Show goods in use.
9. Proper lighting and props are essential to an effective display.[14]
10. Guide the shopper's eye where you want it to go.

*Interior Displays*    Interior displays can take a variety of forms, depending on the type of merchandise and image to be projected by the firm. While space does not permit an in-depth

**Exhibit 12–2**

*Displays attract customer attention*

Source: Photo by James Hertel.

discussion of the principles of interior display, we do offer several guidelines for planning the effective arrangement of merchandise in departments.

Consider the following suggestions regarding interior merchandise display:[15]

- Place items so that choices can readily be made by customers. For example, group merchandise by sizes.

- Place items in such a way that ensemble (or related-item) selling is easy. For example, in a gourmet food department, all Chinese food components should be together. In a women's accessories department, handbags, gloves, and neckwear should be together to help the customer complete an outfit.

- Place items in a department so that trading up or getting the customer to want a better-quality, higher-priced item is possible. For example, place the good, better, and best brands of coffee next to each other so customers can compare them. Information labels on the package help customers compare items displayed next to each other.

- Place merchandise in such a way that it stresses the wide assortments (choice of sizes, brands, colours, and prices) available.
- Place larger sizes and heavy, bulky goods near the floor.
- If the firm carries competing brands in various sizes, give relatively little horizontal space to each item and make use of vertical space for the different sizes and colours. This arrangement exposes customers to a greater variety of products as they move through the store.
- Avoid locating impulse goods directly across the aisle from demand items that most customers are looking for. The impulse items may not be seen at all.
- Make use of vertical space through tiers and step-ups, but be careful to avoid displays much above eye level or at floor level. The area of vertical vision is limited.
- Place items in a department so that inventory counting (control) and general stockkeeping is easier.
- Finally, make the displays as attractive as possible.

*Shelf-Space Allocation*

A very important merchandise presentation issue is determining the amount of space that should be allocated on shelves to individual brands or items in a product category. This amount of space is called *facings*. A number of rules have been devised for allocating facings to competing brands. One rule frequently stressed by major consumer goods manufacturers is that shelf space should equal market share. Thus, a brand with 20 percent market share in a category takes 20 percent of shelf space.

For a retailer, however, this rule makes little sense. It takes no account of the profit margins or direct costs associated with each item. Some retailers, therefore, allocate space according to gross margin. Other retailers apply the concept of *direct product profit (DPP)*. DPP is the remainder when the direct costs of ordering, receiving, stocking, displaying, selling, and transporting a product are subtracted from gross margin. The problem is that many retail management accounting systems are not sophisticated enough to be able to assign these costs directly to items. However, where this is achievable, more space should be allocated to brands/items with greater DPP. Computer applications for shelf-space allocations are becoming more widespread. With the aid of software such as Lotus 1-2-3, and the greater affordability of computers (particularly personal computers), retailers can determine optimum formulas for deciding how much shelf space each item should be allotted.[16]

A particularly thorny problem is how to assign space to new products. Some manufacturers, having conducted test markets, are able to recommend facings levels. The new-item problem is simpler for a line extension. A new flavour of potato chips, for example, is invariably located with existing products in single-carton quantities until increased sales demand otherwise. In the case of a completely new category, facings can only be provided by creating new space or by destocking one or more lines from another category. Some firms tackle the new-item problem by allocating a special display to the item until demand has stabilized at a predictable level of trial and repurchase.

# Chapter Highlights

- Store layout and design and merchandise presentation are important aspects of a firm's positioning strategy. The major goal of store design and layout and merchandise presentation is to get the shopper into the store to spend as much money as possible on a given shopping trip.

- Store design is a reflection of two elements: the interior design and the exterior design. Both should be in harmony with the store's merchandise and customers. Exterior design includes the building's architecture and entrances, display windows and signs. Today, there is a renewed interest in window displays, especially among department stores and higher-priced retailers and in cities where walking and window-shopping are in style. Window displays can be used to enhance store image, to expose shoppers to new products, or to introduce a new season.

- Some retailers view the interior of the store as a theatre and realize that theatrical elements can be used to influence customer behaviour. Interior design includes everything within the store walls that can be used to create an atmosphere, such as colours, lighting, and sound.

- Store layout is a very important part of store planning. One aspect of store layout is the arrangement of the store. Typical arrangements are the grid layout, the free-flow or open plan, and the boutique concept.

- Another element of store layout is space allocation. Dividing total space between selling and sales-supporting areas is the first step in space allocation. Management can use three basic methods

for allocating selling space: industry averages by type of merchandise, sales productivity of product lines, and the build-up (model stock) method.

- Effective use of space can translate into additional dollars of profit. Thus, retailers must evaluate whether store space is being used in the most effective way. The gross margin per square metre method is one method retailers may use.

- Management must decide where to locate selling and sales-supporting activities within the store. Several guidelines are available to aid in making these decisions.

- Merchandise displays can be used to excite, entertain, and educate consumers. If effectively used, they can have a profound influence on consumer behaviour. In spite of the basically artistic and creative flair needed for merchandise display, some guidelines and principles do exist.

- Interior displays can take a variety of forms, depending on the type of merchandise and image to be projected by the firm. A number of guidelines to the use of interior merchandise displays are offered.

- An important aspect of merchandise display is determining the amount of space that should be allocated to individual brands or items in a product category. Some retailers allocate shelf space according to gross margin; others use the concept of direct product profit. Some retailers use computer software packages to determine optimum formulas for deciding how much shelf space each item should be allocated.

# Key Terms

Boutique layout     319
Demand merchandise     327
Free-flow layout     319
Grid layout     319

Impulse merchandise     327
Store design     311
Store layout     311
Store planning     311

# Discussion Questions

1. Define store planning, store design, and store layout.

2. What are the decision areas that comprise layout planning?

3. Compare the following layout arrangements: the grid layout, the free-flow or open plan, and the boutique concept.

4. Describe the three methods retailers can use for allocating selling space in a store among the various departments.

5. Explain the gross margin per square metre method of evaluating space use.

6. What various factors do retailers need to consider in deciding where to locate selling departments and sales-supporting activities within the total store space?

7. Discuss the guidelines retailers can use for the interior display of merchandise.

8. What information can retailers use in making shelf-space allocation decisions?

# Application Exercises

1. Select three different types of stores (e.g., a traditional department store, a discount department store, and a specialty apparel shop) and carefully observe their displays, fixturing, appearance—all the elements that make up the interior design of the stores. Write a report describing differences between the stores and how these differences relate to image projection and market segmentation.

2. Visit the following types of stores: a multilevel department store, a supermarket, a national chain such as Sears, a national specialty chain outlet, and a discount department store. Describe the overall arrangement of the stores (e.g., grid, free-flow, or boutique). Evaluate the layout of each store and comment on the impact of each layout on the general image of the outlet. What changes, if any, would you suggest, and why?

3. Visit several department stores and interview store management. Determine the method(s) used to allocate selling space to the various departments and how management evaluates space use. Based on what you learned in the chapter, evaluate the location of selling departments and sales-supporting activities within each store.

# Suggested Cases

# Endnotes

1. Anthony J. Stokan, "Design: The Silent Salesperson," *Retail Directions,* May/June 1989, pp. 45–55.

2. Linda Haist, "Creating Christmas Cheer," *Retail Directions,* May/June 1989, pp. 39–42.

3. Stokan, "Design," p. 46.

4. Rom J. Markin, Charles M. Lillis, and Chem L. Narayana, "Social Psychological Significance of Store Space," *Journal of Retailing,* Spring 1976, p. 43.

5. Trish Hall, "At Fast-Food Restaurants, Plastic Is Out, and Marble, Brass, and Greenhouses Are In," *The Wall Street Journal,* December 2, 1985, p. 33.

6. Laura Medcalf, "Stores with Style," *Retail Directions,* November/December 1988, pp. 32–41.

7. Elizabeth Garel, "How to Select a Store Designer," *Retail Directions,* January/February 1989, pp. 25–28.

8. Stokan, "Design."

9. J. Bellizzi, A. Crowley, and R. W. Hasty, "The Effects of Colour on Store Design," *Journal of Retailing* 59 (September 1983), p. 43.

10. P. C. Smith and R. Curnow, "Arousal Hypotheses and the Effects of Music on Purchasing Behaviour," *Journal of Applied Psychology* 50, no. 3 (1966), pp. 255–56.

11. R. E. Millian, "The Influence of Background Music on the Behaviour of Restaurant Patrons,"

*Journal of Consumer Research* 13 (September 1986), pp. 286–89; and R. E. Millian, "Using Background Music to Affect the Behaviour of Supermarket Shoppers," *Journal of Marketing* 46 (Summer 1982), pp. 86–91.

12. Andy Willis, "Canadian Tire Goes Flat for Investors," *Financial Times,* June 1, 1992, p. 1.

13. Charles Schefler, "Effective Presentation—the Art and Science of Merchandising," *Retail Merchandising,* October 1987, p. 5.

14. "Lighting the Way to the Customer's Attention— and Price," *Retail Merchandising,* October 1987, p. 6; and Lee Carpenter, "Eight Sure Ways to Drive Customers Out of Your Store," *Retail Merchandising,* October 1987, p. 3.

15. Schefler, "Effective Presentation."

16. Susan Zimmerman, "Computerized Shelf-Space Management Works Wonders," *Supermarket News,* November 24, 1986, p. 18; and "Space-Managing Program Offered Auto Aftermarket," *Marketing News,* October 24, 1986, p. 31.

# 13 MERCHANDISE AND EXPENSE PLANNING

---

## Chapter Objectives

After reading this chapter, you should be able to:

1 Define merchandise management.
2 Explain how merchandise strategies can be implemented to obtain a competitive advantage.
3 Prepare a merchandise budget.
4 Describe expense planning.

## Retailing Capsule

A good example of a company with a compelling competitive advantage is Toys Я Us, the toy supermarket chain operating in Canada, the United States, and Japan. The chain is a warehouse-style operation with over 250 outlets "filled with thousands of competitively priced products from animals (the stuffed kind) to zoos (miniature, that is)." The company strives for assortment dominance. It does this by carrying the widest and deepest selection of toys of any toy retailer. Toys Я Us wants the market to be convinced that if an item is not in one of its stores, it won't be found anywhere.

Toys Я Us sells three things—selection, stock, and price. The firm differentiates itself primarily by offering a dominant assortment of merchandise at the best price in the market.

The typical store is 4,500 square metres of selling and sales-supporting space. The preferred site for stores is in freestanding locations some distance from busy shopping centres. The overall strategy of Toys Я Us has helped the company to become a leader in its field, the ultimate goal in retailing.

High-performance retailers such as Toys Я Us are credited with having a "compelling competitive advantage." Also consider Dylex, with its portfolio of businesses targeting specific market segments. Then there is Shoppers Drug Mart, with its "Everything You Want in a Drugstore" strategy that commits the retailer to carrying an extensive product assortment to satisfy customer needs.

Each of these companies, differing in strategic approach, has carefully positioned itself to achieve a competitive advantage, which is the topic of this part of the text. In this chapter, we begin our discussion of competitive advantage by addressing merchandise and expense planning.

Merchandise is the logical place to begin a discussion about competitive advantage in the marketplace, because without merchandise (or some offering), a retail establishment cannot exist. In addition to the merchandise planning process, this chapter also includes a discussion of expense planning, because the planning processes are interrelated and their purposes are similar.

# Merchandise Management

Canadian Tire is recognized as a leader in merchandise planning and management in the field of automotive products and services and home and leisure products. Ninety percent of all adults in Canada shop at Canadian Tire stores. We are thus using that firm's concept of strategic planning within which merchandise management fits as an illustration.[1]

*Toys Я Us differentiates itself through selection, stock, and price.*

SOURCE: Photo by James Hertel.

### Merchandise Management— The Management of Change

Canadian Tire manages change through its strategic planning process. Management must recognize change and identify it in a way that is compatible with the firm's merchandising strategies. In the future, Canadian Tire plans to build on the strength of its core business to expand into related areas.

Part of Canadian Tire's corporate philosophy is based on providing value as defined by the customer. Management believes that customers look for the following four elements in deciding where to shop:

1. *Dominance:* Having the best assortment possible in the merchandise categories carried in the stores.
2. *Quality:* Having quality not only in the merchandise but also in the management, service, and shopping environment.

3. *Convenience:* Respecting customers' time; making it easy to shop.
4. *Price:* Striving for competitive prices and defining what that means to customers.

Canadian Tire's merchandising philosophy is based on these elements of customer value. An integral part of its merchandising process consists of continually working with vendors to increase the number of proprietary products offered. Today, there are more than 12,000 Motomaster automotive and 5,000 Mastercraft home and hand tool products exclusively available through Canadian Tire stores. As well, the company has introduced the SMART program—Strategic Merchandising and Retail Techniques—that includes product assortment planning.

Recently, Canadian Tire introduced a new merchandise line targeted at the consumer who wants to do major home improvements. Approximately 500 square metres of retail space was devoted to a new line of products that included floor and ceramic tiles, exterior doors, wallpaper, bathroom and light fixtures, and window blinds and shades. Colours and graphics were used to convey Canadian Tire's value position in home decorating. As well, the overall retail space in the stores was rearranged to ensure there would be no noticeable loss of floor area devoted to the main lines of automotive and hardware products.[2]

Progressive retailers like Canadian Tire recognize the importance of identifying merchandise trends and responding to them quickly. Retailers must be extremely alert to the particular phase of the merchandise trend so that inventories can be adjusted accordingly. In fact, merchandise planning is managing change, particularly meeting the changing needs (value changes) of customers, and interpreting the trends and adapting to the volatile elements of customer value (see Retail Highlight 13–1).

A large part of this chapter is directed toward the merchandise plan at the department or classification level. The departmental buyer usually prepares six-month merchandise plans within the bounds of the firm's corporate mission and strategic plan. The technical nature of the plan, however, may cause students as well as practitioners to lose sight of the big picture. We make this point to remind you of the strategic perspective that underlies merchandise planning.

The merchandise plan would be referred to as the *product plan* in perhaps all nonretailing companies. We may at times use the *product* designation, but tradition dictates the use of *merchandise* plan or planning. Practising retailers do not speak of *product planning* as they prepare their plans. Still, **merchandise management** is the management of the product component of the marketing mix, and the key to successful merchandising is to ensure that the customer is offered the right merchandise, at the right price, at the right time, and in the right quantities (the five "rights" of merchandising).

*Merchandising Strategies: Capitalizing on the Momentum of Change*

The following examples illustrate retailing efforts to understand, anticipate, and capitalize on the momentum of change through the implementation of individual merchandising strategies. Our focus here is on brand strategy and licensing.

**Private-Label versus National-Brand Strategy**
One of the most difficult problems facing merchants today is the optimal balance between private and national brands and, in some instances, generics. **Private**

---

**Retail Highlight 13–1**

---

# Listen to the Consumer or Go Broke

According to retail expert Phillip Lichsztral, Canadian retailers who don't get back on the selling floor to see what consumers want will fail. Among the points he makes are:

- Consumers are smarter and more educated about what they want and how they want to be served. Retailers must get back on the selling floor at key shopping times each week to see what customers want versus what buyers want to sell them.

- Customers are looking for location, a good quality/price ratio, durability, and uniqueness. Destination retailers such as Toys Я Us and Club Price are having a big impact on retailing in Canada because they offer customers what they want.

- Retailers should work with suppliers on electronic data interchange so that stocks can be automatically replenished.

- Retailers need an excellent merchandising system. They need to gain more detailed knowledge about when to take markdowns. Even a small chain can't be effectively managed without a proper data-processing facility.

- Develop database information on customers. Call your customers when new lines come in or when a product complementary to something they bought earlier arrives.

Source: "Listen to the Customer or Go Broke," *Marketing*, March 23, 1992, p. 19.

---

**brands** (or **private labels**) are owned by a retailer (e.g., Canadian Tire's Mastercraft tools). *National brands,* often called *manufacturer brands,* are owned by a manufacturer and can be sold to whomever the owner desires (e.g., Procter & Gamble's Tide laundry detergent). The issue is not limited to the general merchandise sector of retailing. The grocery and drug trades have struggled with such decisions for many years. In all merchandise categories and lines of trade, the position of the ideal mix is critical. Additionally, the drug and grocery trade face the *generic* program issues. Generics are unbranded merchandise offerings that carry only the designation of the product type on the package—for example, "salt."

One retailer who has aggressively used a blend of generic, private, and national brands is Loblaws. To differentiate itself from its competitors, Loblaws has introduced over 1,500 "no name" and 400 President's Choice store-branded products. As well, it has introduced the Teddy's Choice line and the environmentally friendly Green line. This merchandising strategy allows Loblaws to offer customers a product assortment that cannot be duplicated by competitors. Loblaws' executives believe that these products provide their customers with a powerful combination of excellent quality and low price. The President's Choice line now accounts for $1.5 billion in sales or 20 percent of Loblaws' revenues. The trend

The *"President's Choice"* store brands provide Loblaws' customers with a unique product offering.

SOURCE: Courtesy of Loblaws Supermarkets Limited.

indicates that each year, sales of Loblaws' brands are increasing at the expense of national brands.[3]

Retailers promote private-label programs to (1) defend themselves against off-price and outlet-store competition; (2) offer an alternative, as the upscale catalog companies feature virtually all competitive national labels; (3) guarantee some market exclusivity; (4) achieve a degree of control over merchandising programs; and (5) protect their profit margins.

In deciding on the best mix of national, private, and generic brands to carry, the retailer should consider a number of factors. National brands are well known and are usually supported by advertising. Additionally, consumers usually regard national brands as superior to either private or generic brands in terms of reliability and quality. Private brands generate higher margins for retailers, offer economic benefits to consumers because they are usually cheaper than national brands, and may assist in developing store loyalty. Private brands do require the retailer to invest time and money and could damage the store's image if the brand is viewed by consumers as having poor quality. For the retailer, generics share some of the same risks as private brands but they appeal to price-conscious customers. Generics can help to create a strong competitive price image for a retailer.

The competition for shelf space for national versus private and generic brands has been referred to as the "battle of the brands." The battle is very intense in Canada, where department stores (e.g., Eaton's, Sears), supermarkets (e.g., Loblaws, Safeway), and specialty chains (e.g., Canadian Tire, Home Hardware) have considerable buying power. These large retail chains are developing and stocking more private brands at the expense of national brands. Whether this trend will continue depends, in part, on the merchandise preferences of the target customers these chains are serving.

### Licensing as a Merchandising Strategy

**Licensing** is a strategic tool of marketing in which the *licenser* or owner of a "property" (the concept to be marketed) joins with a licensee (the manufacturer of the licensed product) and attempts to sell to retail buyers who offer the goods through retail organizations. Licensing is an important retail merchandising strategy.

Licensing is gaining widespread acceptance as a merchandising strategy among retailers because it provides the opportunity to capture a market whose customer is younger, richer, better educated, and willing to pay more than the average consumer for what he or she wants. The challenge for the merchant strategist is to choose the right licensees, weed out the weak ones, and cut back on those that are always popular but may, from time to time, lose momentum.

When considering licensing as a merchandising strategy, retailers must evaluate the opportunity in terms of the partnership that must evolve. The licensee who offers the property must be strong, have a good product, and provide sufficient advertising and marketing effort for the offering. The Esprit line of clothing is an example of licensing that has been profitable for both the licenser and the licensee. In fact, it has been so successful that Esprit is also opening its own retail outlets in Canada and around the world.

Sears has established an exclusive licensing arrangement with McDonald's. McKids clothing is sold through Sears; the merchandise mix covers infant through size 7 and consists of playwear in skirts, shorts, tops, accessories, and shoes.

### Summary

The goals of this initial part of the chapter have been threefold: (1) to place merchandise management within the context of strategic planning; (2) to introduce

FIGURE 13–1

*The merchandise mix*

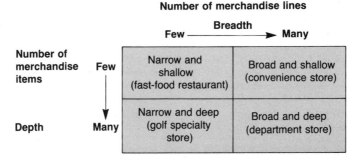

merchandising as a concept integral to managing change; and (3) to provide real-world evidence of various ways that merchandise strategies, especially brand and licensing, are being implemented. The next section will assist you in understanding merchandise management at the store level, with particular emphasis on the mechanics of planning and control. Our focus thus far has been at the level of strategy formation.

## The Mechanics of Merchandise Planning

This section of the chapter focuses on the planning component of merchandise management. The other element of the total management process is control. The control aspect is addressed in Chapter 18 as a part of the evaluation of performance. **Merchandise planning** includes those activities that are needed to ensure a balance between inventories and sales. Control efforts provide information on how effective the planning has been.

## Essential Terms

A review of certain terms is necessary here. A **product** is simply a tangible object, service, or idea, such as a dress or a dress-cleaning service. A **merchandise line** refers to a group of products that are closely related because they are intended for the same end use (dishwashers), are used together (knives and forks), or are sold to the same customer group (children's footwear). Two important decisions the retailer makes are the breadth and depth of the merchandising lines carried by the store. **Breadth** ( or **width**) is the number of different merchandising lines carried. **Depth** is the number of items that are carried in a single merchandise line. Breadth and depth, illustrated in Figure 13–1, define the merchandise mix, which is the total of all the merchandise lines.

*Kinney's offers a relatively narrow but deep merchandise mix.*

Source: Photo by James Hertel.

Assortment means the range of choices (selection) available for any given merchandise line. Assortment can also be defined as the number of **stockkeeping units (SKUs)** in a category. For example, a 1-kilogram package of Nabob coffee is one SKU; a 500 g bag of Maxwell House coffee is another SKU. However, do not confuse the number of items with an SKU. In other words, a food store might have 100 packages of the 1-kg Nabob coffee, but this represents only one SKU.

Merchandise (or inventory) turnover is the number of times the average inventory of an item (or SKU) is sold, usually in annual terms. Turnover can be computed on a dollar basis in either cost or retail dollars. Turnover can also be calculated in units.

*Width and depth can be connected through displays.*

SOURCE: Courtesy Drug World.

The major focus of this section is merchandise assortment planning, the purpose of which is to maintain *stock balance*—a balance between inventories and sales. Figure 13–2 is a diagram of the merchandise planning process. Reference will be made to this diagram throughout most of this chapter.

*Stock Balance*

Retailers can consider merchandise assortment in three different ways: width, depth, or dollar planning. Let's assume that we are planning for the men's sport shirt assortment in the furnishings department of a department store.[4]

**Ways to Look at Stock Balance**

The three aspects of stock balance as shown in Figure 13–2 are: (1) width or breadth, point 5; (2) depth, point 6; and (3) total dollars, point 4.

*Width.*     Width (breadth) of merchandise assortment refers to the assortment factors necessary to meet the demands of the market and to meet competition. Decisions must be made on the number of brands, sizes, colours, and the like. In our example for shirts, the following might be a planning process in terms of width:

**FIGURE 13-2**

*How to understand the merchandise planning process*

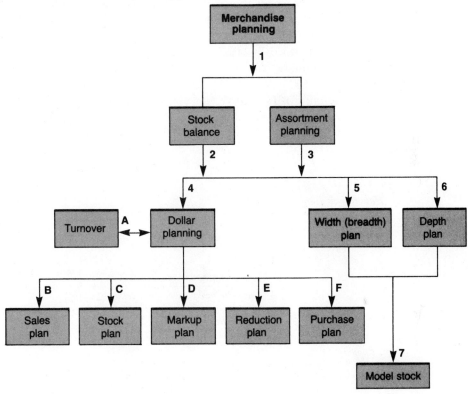

| Brand (Arrow, Forsyth, Manhattan) | 3 SKUs |
| Sizes (small, medium, large, and X-large) | $\times$<br>4 = 12 SKUs |
| Prices ($25.95; $35.95) | $\times$<br>2 = 24 SKUs |
| Colours (white, grey, blue) | $\times$<br>3 = 72 SKUs |
| Fabric (knit, woven) | $\times$<br>2 = 144 SKUs |

Thus, we see that there are 144 stockkeeping units (SKUs) necessary to meet customers' wants and the offerings of competition.

***Depth.*** The next question is: How many units of merchandise do we need to support our expected sales of each assortment factor? This decision must be based on expectations of the sales importance for each assortment factor. For example, how many small Arrow shirts, at $25.95, in blue knit do we expect to sell? Such decisions involve the art of merchandising. Knowledge of the customer market, the segment appealed to, the image of the store and/or department, and other factors all enter into this subjective decision.

Only experience in planning the composition of stock will give retailers confidence in this activity.

***Dollar Planning of Inventory.***    Assume that 1,000 shirts are needed for the ideal stock level. This number, however, does not tell the manager how many dollars need to be invested in stock at any one time. Thus, the total dollar investment in

**FIGURE 13–3**

*How to calculate stock turnover*

**Based on dollars**

 **Turnover at retail**

$$Turnover = \frac{Retail\ sales\ (\$100,000)}{Average\ inventory\ in\ retail\ dollars\ (\$25,000)} = 4\ times$$

How to calculate average retail inventory

| Add together | Begining of year | $30,000 |
| all available | +Midyear | 20,000 |
| inventory figures | +End of year | 25,000 |
| and divide by the | =Total | $75,000 |
| number of counts, e.g., ⟶ | Average = $75,000 ÷ 3 = $25,000 | |

 **Turnover at cost**

$$Turnover = \frac{Cost\ of\ sales\ (\$60,000)}{Average\ inventory\ at\ cost\ (\$15,000)} = 4\ times$$

How to calculate cost of sales:

| See what | Begining inventory | $18,000 |
| was available; | +Purchases | 67,000 |
| add purchases; | =Total dollars available | $85,000 |
| subtract what is left; then | −Ending inventory | 25,000 |
| see what moved out—all at cost ⟶ | =Cost of goods sold | $60,000 |

**Based on units**

$$Turnover = \frac{Number\ of\ units\ sold\ (3,200)}{Average\ inventory\ in\ units\ (800)} \div 4\ times$$

inventory is the final way to look at stock balance.[5] Here, merchandise turnover comes into play.

Figure 13–3 shows how to calculate turnover. For turnover goals to be meaningful, they must be based on merchandise groupings that are as much alike as possible. Planning on the basis of large, diverse merchandise groupings is unwise. Also, it is impossible to tell whether a particular turnover figure is good or bad unless it is compared to something. The retailer can compare turnover rates to average rates for various merchandise classifications or to the firm's own rates for past periods. The goal, however, is to have a turnover rate that is fast enough to give the retailer a good return on money invested in inventory, but not so fast that the retailer is always out of stock. (See Retail Highlight 13–2 for examples of turnover rates for various retailers.)

Figure 13–4 recaps what has been discussed thus far in the chapter. Students should understand this material before proceeding to the next section, which discusses how to set up a merchandise budget.

***The Merchandise Budget***

This section of the chapter focuses on merchandise planning in total dollars. Later sections look at planning in terms of width and depth.

### Approaches to Merchandise Planning

Traditionally, merchandise planning has been structured around either a bottom-up or a top-down approach. The bottom-up approach starts with estimates at the classification level. These estimates are then combined into a departmental

---

**Retail Highlight 13–2**

# Turnover Rates of Selected Canadian Retailers

|                                    | *Annual Turnover Rate* |
|------------------------------------|:----------------------:|
| Food stores                        | 15.4                   |
| Florists                           | 10.6                   |
| Women's clothing                   | 5.6                    |
| Drugstores                         | 5.3                    |
| Department stores                  | 5.0                    |
| Book and stationery stores         | 5.0                    |
| Men's clothing                     | 4.8                    |
| Furniture and appliance stores     | 4.7                    |
| Jewellery stores                   | 2.2                    |

Source: Dun & Bradstreet of Canada, Key Business Rates Canada Corporations, 1990.

**FIGURE 13–4**

**How to look at stock balance**

| Ways to Look at Stock Balance | Examples | Things to Consider in Assortment Planning |
|---|---|---|
| Width (or breadth) | Number of brands, sizes, colours. | What customers want. What competitors offer. |
| Depth | How many units are needed to support expected sales of each size, etc. | The sales importance of each size. |
| Total dollars | How many dollars are inventory? | Look at turnover. *a.* Fast enough to get good return. *b.* Not so fast that out-of-stocks occur. |

merchandise budget and finally into a total company plan. The **merchandise budget** is a plan of how much to buy in dollars per month based on profitability goals. The top-down approach starts with a gross dollar figure established by top management. This dollar figure is then allocated to the various merchandise classifications. A third method of merchandise planning is the interactive approach. Interactive means that management sets broad guidelines, and the buying staff then follows the bottom-up approach with reviews by management. The interactive approach results in the most accurate merchandise plan.

**Items Included in the Merchandise Budget**

The following items affect profit return and are included in the merchandise budget:

1. Sales (Figure 13–2, point 4B).
2. Stock/inventory (Figure 13–2, point 4C).
3. Reductions (Figure 13–2, point 4E).
4. Purchases (Figure 13–2, point 4F).

Figure 13–5 presents a diagram of these profit factors. References will be made to this diagram as each of these factors is discussed in more detail.

*Sales Planning.*   The beginning point in developing a merchandise budget is the sales plan. Note from Figure 13–5 that sales are first planned by season and then by month. In discussing sales planning by season and month, let's assume we are planning a merchandise budget for sporting goods.

*Planning by Season.*   A *season* is the typical planning period in retailing, especially for fashion merchandise. Assume that the merchandise budget is being planned for the 1994 spring season (February, March, April, May, June, and July). The retailer would start planning in November 1993. The factors the retailer needs to consider in developing this seasonal plan are given in Figure 13–6.

**FIGURE 13-5**

*Schematic diagram of merchandise budget*

| | Components to Be Budgeted | | | | | |
| | Sales | | Stock | Reductions | | Purchases |
| | Season | Month | | Season | Month | |
|---|---|---|---|---|---|---|
| Quantitative (factual) data | | | | | | |
| Qualitative (subjective) data: trends and environmental factors | | | | | | |

**FIGURE 13-6**

*Diagram of the sales budget for 1994*

| | Sales | |
| | Season | By Month |
|---|---|---|
| Information available for planning | 1. Sales for spring 1993.<br>2. Recent trends in sales.<br>3. Check trend against. | 1. Sales percentages by month, 1993.<br>2. Check distribution against published trade data. |
| Judgment applied in certain issues | 1. Factors outside the store such as new competition.<br>2. Internal conditions such as more space available. | 1. Factors outside the store such as new competition.<br>2. Internal conditions such as more space available. |

In planning seasonal sales, the retailer begins by looking at last year's sales for the same period. Assume sales were $15,000 for the spring of 1993. Too many retailers at this point merely use the past period's figure as their sales forecast for the planning period. However, recent sales trends should be considered. For example, if sales for the 1993 fall season have been running about 5 percent ahead of fall 1992 and this trend is expected to continue, the retailer would project spring 1994 sales to be $15,750 ($15,000 × 1.05 = $15,750).

But the retailer cannot stop here. Now one must look at *forces outside the firm* that will have an impact on the sales forecast. For example, the retailer's projections would be affected if a new sporting goods store opened next door, carrying similar assortments (especially if this new store were part of a national chain with excellent management), or a major manufacturer in the community were planning a large expansion. Next, the retailer must look at *internal conditions* that might affect the sales forecast. Moving sporting goods to a more valuable location within the store is an example of an internal condition.

Exact numbers cannot be placed on all of these external and internal factors. Retailers must, however, use judgment and incorporate all factors into the sales forecast. Assume that the retailer has decided sales should increase by 10 percent. The sales plan for the 1994 spring season is now $16,500 (15,000 × 1.10 = $16,500).

*Planning by Month.*    The planned seasonal sales must now be divided into monthly sales. Figure 13–6 presents those factors that must be considered.

Again, the starting point is spring 1993. Assume the following sales distribution by month for this season: February, 10 percent; March, 20 percent; April, 15 percent; May, 15 percent; June, 30 percent; and July, 10 percent. Further assume that the retailer has considered all internal and external factors that would affect this distribution and has decided that no adjustments need to be made. Based on this breakdown, the season's sales plan by month for spring 1994 would look like that in Figure 13–7.

**Stock Planning.**    The next step in developing the merchandise budget is to plan stock (inventory) levels by month. In planning monthly stock needed to support monthly sales, several different techniques can be used, depending upon the characteristics of the merchandise. For example, the **week's supply method** is a good approach to planning stock levels for staple goods. The formula is:

BOM inventory = Average weekly sales × Number of weeks of stock needed

With this method, the number of desired stock turns (for example, 10 turns per year) is divided into the stock turnover period (for example, 52 weeks) to determine the number of weeks of stock that should be on hand at the beginning of a selling period (in this example, 5.2 weeks' supply).

With the **percentage deviation method,** the actual stock on hand during any

**FIGURE 13–7**

*Spring sales plan for 1994*

| Month | Percent of Total Season's Business in 1993 | × | Season's Sales Forecast | = | Planned Sales for Months of 1994 Season |
|---|---|---|---|---|---|
| February | 10 | | $16,500 | | $ 1,650 |
| March | 20 | | 16,500 | | 3,300 |
| April | 15 | | 16,500 | | 2,475 |
| May | 15 | | 16,500 | | 2,475 |
| June | 30 | | 16,500 | | 4,950 |
| July | 10 | | 16,500 | | 1,650 |
| Total | 100 | | | | $16,500 |

**FIGURE 13–8**

*Diagram of inventory budget for 1994 (by month)*

| Concrete information available for planning | 1. Stock-to-sales ratios based on past history |
|---|---|
| | 2. Trade stock-to-sales ratios or your own performance |
| Judgment applied to planning | 1. Compare actual turnover with turnover goal |

month varies from average planned monthly stock by only half of the month's variation from average estimated monthly sales. The formula is:

$$\text{BOM inventory} = \text{Average inventory} \times \frac{1}{2}\left(1 + \frac{\text{Planned sales for the month}}{\text{Average monthly sales}}\right)$$

This method is typically used for high-turnover classification. The **basic stock method** is often used for style goods with annual turnover of less than six times. The formula is:

$$\text{BOM inventory} = \text{Planned sales for month} + \text{Average stock} - \text{Average monthly sales}$$

The **stock-to-sales ratio method** is used to plan monthly stock levels for fashion merchandise and for highly seasonal merchandise. The formula is:

$$\text{BOM inventory} = \text{Planned monthly sales} \times \text{Stock-to-sales ratio}$$

### Critique of Methods

Stock-to-sales ratios are based on the planned inventory turnover for the classification in question. The weeks' supply, percentage deviation, and basic stock methods utilize average sales. The stock-to-sales method uses a ratio of stock to sales for a particular month to determine inventory levels. All of the methods fail to consider such factors as net margin contributions, perishability, fashion influences or style obsolescence, lead time needed before a new order can be received, and the effect that an out-of-stock condition can have on regular customers' store preference patterns.

Returning to the example, the stock-to-sales ratio method could be used for sporting goods. Figure 13–8 is a guide to planning monthly inventory levels.[6]

To determine beginning-of-the-month (BOM) inventory, the retailer multiplies the month's planned sales figure by the month's stock-to-sales ratio figure. For example, as shown in Figure 13–7, planned sales for February are $1,650. If the retailer knows from past experience and industry trade data that 4.7 times more dollars in inventory than planned sales are needed, the beginning-of-the-month inventory for February would be $7,755 ($1,650 × 4.7 = $7,755). The 4.7 figure is the stock-to-sales ratio figure for the month of February.[7]

To figure the average stock-to-sales ratio, divide the turnover figure into 12 (the number of months in a year). For example:

| If Turnover Is: | Divide Turnover into 12 (number of months in year) | Then Average Stock-to-Sales Ratio Is |
|---|---|---|
| 4.0 | 12 ÷  4.0 = | 3.0 |
| 2.5 | 12 ÷  2.5 = | 4.8 |
| 30.0 | 12 ÷ 30.0 = | .4 |

As one can see, the *lower* the turnover rate, the *higher* the stock-to-sales ratio.

Figure 13–9 provides information on needed monthly BOM stock for spring 1994, using planned monthly sales for spring 1994 from Figure 13–7 and the monthly stock-to-sales ratios for past years. In reality, the retailer would use judgment in deciding whether to use last year's monthly stock-to-sales figures or whether any conditions exist that would require them to be changed.

The end-of-the-month (EOM) inventory for a particular month would be the BOM inventory for the following month. For example, as shown in Figure 13–9, the BOM inventory for February is $7,755. The EOM inventory for February would be $13,860, which is also the BOM inventory for March.

***Reductions Planning.***    Reductions are anything other than sales that reduce inventory value.

*Employee discounts* are reductions. If an item sells for $100, and employees receive a 20 percent discount, the employee pays $80. The $80 is recorded as a sale. The $20 reduces the inventory dollar amount but is *not* a sale. It is an employee discount—a reduction.

*Shortages (shrinkage)* are reductions. A shoplifter takes a $500 watch from a jewellery department. Inventory is reduced by $500 just as if it were a sale. But no revenues come from shoplifting. If a salesperson steals another watch (internal pilferage), the results are the same. A $1,000 watch is received into stock and marked at $500 because of a clerical error. Fewer inventory dollars are in stock than the retailer thinks.

*Markdowns* are reductions. Markdowns are the only type of reductions we will focus on.[8] For example, assume a $50 tennis racket does not sell during the season

**FIGURE 13–9**

***BOM stock for spring 1994***

| Month | Planned Sales | × | Stock-to-Sales Ratio | = | Planned BOM Stock |
|---|---|---|---|---|---|
| February | $ 1,650 | | 4.7 | | $  7,755 |
| March | 3,300 | | 4.2 | | 13,860 |
| April | 2,475 | | 4.3 | | 10,640 |
| May | 2,475 | | 4.4 | | 10,890 |
| June | 4,950 | | 3.4 | | 16,830 |
| July | 1,650 | | 6.9 | | 11,385 |
| Total | $16,500 | | | | $ 71,360 |

and is marked down to $30. The $20 markdown is counted as a reduction of inventory and only $30 is counted as a sale.

Why plan reductions as a part of the merchandise budget? Note from Figure 13–9 that a planned BOM stock of $13,860 for March is needed to support March sales of $3,300 (with a 4.2 stock-to-sales ratio). However, suppose that the retailer's reductions during February amount to approximately $5,000. The EOM inventory in February (BOM for March) is $5,000 less than if no reductions had been taken. Reductions must be planned and accounted for so the retailer will have sufficient BOM inventory to make planned sales.

Assume that reductions for the spring season in the department are planned at 8 percent, or $1,320 ($16,500 seasonal sales × .08). Figure 13–9 could be used to allocate the reductions by month (e.g., February would be $1,650 × .08 or $132 and March would be $3,300 × .08 or $264). Reductions normally vary by month.

***Planned Purchases.***    Up to this point, the retailer has determined planned (1) sales, (2) stock, and (3) reductions. The next step in developing the merchandise budget is to plan the dollar amount of purchases on a monthly basis. Planned purchases are figured as follows:

| | |
|---|---|
| We *need* dollars of purchases to | Make sure we have enough retail EOM inventory to ''be in business'' the following month. |
| | Make sure we have enough to cover our sales plan. |
| | Take care of our planned reductions. |
| We *have* dollars to contribute to the above needs in the form of | Retail BOM inventory. |

Stated more concretely:

Planned purchases = Planned EOM stock + Planned sales + Planned reductions − Planned BOM stock

To calculate planned purchases for March, look at Figure 13–9 to get the needed information.

| Planned purchases = $10,640 | EOM March or BOM April | (Figure 13–9) |
|---|---|---|
| +3,300 | Planned sales, March | (Figure 13–9) |
| + 264 | Planned reductions, March | (see above) |
| = $14,204 | Dollar *needs*, March | |
| −13,860 | BOM March—what you *have* | (Figure 13–9) |
| = $ 344 | | |

One additional point. Purchases are planned in terms of *retail* dollars. However, when buying merchandise, the buyer must think in terms of the *cost* of merchandise. Thus, it is necessary to convert the planned purchase figure at retail to a cost figure. This conversion process will be explained in detail in Chapter 15. At this point, simply remember: To convert retail dollars to cost dollars, multiply retail dollars by the complement of the initial retail markup. For example, assume that planned purchases for a given month are $1,000 at retail, and that the planned initial markup is 40 percent of retail. To convert retail dollars to cost dollars, multiply $1,000 by 60 percent, the complement of the planned initial markup (100 percent − 40 percent = 60 percent). Thus, planned purchases at cost would be $600 ($1,000 × .60 = $600).

We have now worked through the dollar merchandise planning process.[9] Figure 13–10 is a planning form for a typical six-month merchandise plan that includes all the factors just discussed. However, as Figure 13–2 shows, the retailer still needs to plan the width and depth factors of stock balance (points 5 and 6). The following sections of the chapter describe how to plan these parts of the merchandise budget.

## Planning Width and Depth of Assortments

Now that the retailer knows how much to spend for stock, a decision still must be made on (1) what to spend the dollars for (width) and (2) in what amounts (depth). The goal here is to set up a **model stock plan** (Figure 13–2, point 7). A model stock plan is the retailer's best prediction of the assortment needed to satisfy customers.

### The Width Plan

Figure 13–11 is a model stock plan for a sweaters classification in a sporting goods department. Assume that only two customer-attracting features are important—synthetic and natural fibres. Even though the illustration is simple, it shows that to offer customers only *one* sweater in each assortment *width* factor (in both synthetic and natural fibres), 270 sweaters (2 × 5 × 3 × 3 × 3) are needed (column 1 of Figure 13–11).

### The Depth Plan

The depth plan involves deciding how many sweaters are needed in each of the five assortment factors (Figure 13–11). Assume that 800 are needed for one turnover period. (If turnover is to be 3, then 800 sweaters are needed for 4 months—12 months divided by 3 is 4.) Also remember that the retailer is planning dollars at the same time as assortments. Thus, the amount of dollars will affect support.

If the retailer believes that 90 percent of sales will be in synthetic fibres, then 720 sweaters will be needed (800 × .90 = 720). Following Figure 13–11, one sees that the retailer will have 144 of size A, 58 in colour A, 29 at price point A, and 14 in design A.

*The Art of Planning.*    The foregoing illustration of the formulation of the width and depth (model stock in units) appears to be a rather routine approach to planning. In fact, the decisions as to the percentage relationships among the various

**FIGURE 13–10**

*Six-month merchandising plan*

| Six-Month Merchandising Plan | | Department name _____ Department no. _____ | | | | | | |
|---|---|---|---|---|---|---|---|---|
| | | | | | Plan (this year) | | Actual (last year) | |
| | | Stock turnover | | | | | | |
| | | Workroom costs | | | | | | |
| | | Etc. | | | | | | |
| Spring 19— | | Feb. | Mar. | Apr. | May | June | July | Season Total |
| Fall 19— | | Aug. | Sep. | Oct. | Nov. | Dec. | Jan. | |
| Sales | Last year | | | | | | | |
| | Plan | 1,650 | 3,300 | 2,475 | 2,475 | 4,950 | 1,650 | 16,500 |
| | Percent of increase | | | | | | | |
| | Revised | | | | | | | |
| | Actual | | | | | | | |
| Retail Stock (BOM) | Last year | | | | | | | |
| | Plan | 7,755 | 13,860 | 10,640 | 10,840 | 16,830 | 11,385 | 71,360 |
| | Revised | | | | | | | |
| | Actual | | | | | | | |
| Markdowns | Last year | | | | | | | |
| | Plan (dollars) | 132 | 264 | 198 | 198 | 396 | 132 | 1,320 |
| | Plan (percent) | | | | | | | |
| | Revised | | | | | | | |
| | Actual | | | | | | | |
| Retail Purchases | Last year | | | | | | | |
| | Plan | 344 | | | | | | |
| | Revised | | | | | | | |
| | Actual | | | | | | | |
| Percent of Initial Markup | Last year | | | | | | | |
| | Plan | | | | | | | |
| | Revised | | | | | | | |
| | Actual | | | | | | | |

**FIGURE 13–11 *Model stock of sweaters***

**Column 1**                                          **Column 2**

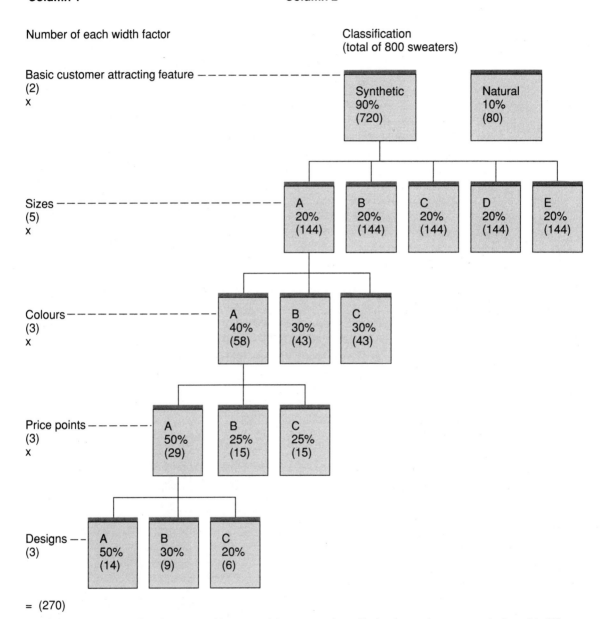

NOTE: The percentage in each factor is the expected importance of that assortment factor. Numbers in parentheses represent the share of the 800-sweater total; for example, 90% × 800 = 720; 20% × 720 = 144, and so on.

assortment factors are based on many complex factors relating to store objectives and to the merchandising art of retailing. Obviously, in planning the assortment width factors, the entire merchandising philosophy and strategic posture of management assume critical importance. The factors would be significantly different for a classification in a unit of Eaton's than for the same classification in a Kmart outlet. The Eaton's merchandiser would consider the most unusual styles and fashion colours. Also, price points would greatly exceed those of Kmart.

In other words, the total image management wants the store to project and the strategy assumed to accomplish the store's objectives affect decisions on width factors and the relative importance of each. Certainly the target market of the store affects planning decisions, as do environmental conditions of the planning period. For example, as technological advances in textile fibres allowed more vibrant colourfast materials to enter the menswear industry, the width of offerings was expanded. The technology was, of course, a response to changing life-styles, which dictated a more fashion-conscious male market for sportswear in general; also, changing styles of living and utilization of time for such activities as tennis and golf were reflected in sportswear offerings.

We have focused on the *how to,* rather than the *what* and *why,* because of the artistic and creative nature of merchandising, the immense variability among differing types of merchandise classifications, and, especially, because of the virtual impossibility of teaching the *art* of merchandising. Our major concern is that you appreciate how the operating and creative aspects of merchandise planning relate to each other.

# Expense Planning

The final section of this chapter introduces expense planning and ties it to the analysis of merchandise planning because of the close relationship and process of the two acts of budgeting. Expenses need to be forecast for a specific period, just as the retailer makes predictions for the merchandise budget. The main purpose of merchandise budgeting is to maintain a balance between inventories and sales. The main purpose of expense budgeting is to balance planned expenses with planned income. Effective management of expenses can have a profound effect on profits.

## *Expense Classification*

Essential to the process of expense management is a system of expense classification. Ideally, the retailing industry should adopt a uniform method of expense classification, but this is not likely to happen. Philosophies differ, organizations are diverse in size, and merchandise varies. Major trade associations do, however, attempt standardization. The three major classifications are natural, functional, and expense centre.

### Natural
Examples of expenses under a natural classification include:

- Labour.
- Advertising and promotion.

- Store supply.
- Store occupancy (rent and utilities).
- Equipment depreciation or rental cost.
- Maintenance and repair.
- All other store expenses.

The natural system is appropriate for small retail stores where management is in continuous contact with all the operations and is involved with few transactions.

### Functional

The functional system identifies the *purpose* of an expense, whereas the natural classification system focuses on its *nature*. The main functions are:

- Administration.
- Occupancy.
- Promotion.
- Buying.
- Selling.

Medium-sized stores, in particular, can benefit from a combination of the natural and functional systems.

### Expense Centre Accounting

Expense centre accounting is a development of the mid-1950s. The appropriate natural expenses become a part of the expense centre approach to classification. Examples include:

- Credit and collection (expense centre).
- Payroll.
- Services purchased.
- Bad debts.
- Equipment costs.
- All others.

*Allocation of Expenses and Budgeting*

The allocation of store expenses to various departments or classifications is critical if management is to know the profitability of specific subdivisions. Why isn't gross margin an adequate measure of operating effectiveness for a department or, for that matter, for the store? The reason is that departments with identical sales and margins may have different operating costs. For this reason, as many expenses as possible should be charged to a specific department.

The technical issue of expense allocation procedures is not addressed here. Our purpose, instead, is to stress that expense management is as important as merchandise management. Just as the retailer must plan for necessary merchandise, management must also plan for required expenditures. Expenses must be forecast for a specific period. The principal connection between the two budgets is that both are based on planned sales. The expense budget period coincides with the planning cycle of the merchandise budget.

Realistically, small stores seldom have even informal expense budgets, just as they seldom have formal merchandise plans. To the unsophisticated small retailer, expense management simply means "cut expenses."

Any merchant, however, regardless of size, is capable of utilizing trade associations, buying offices, vendors, noncompeting retailers, trade papers, and informed accountants as sources of the expense information needed for planning. The reasons for not planning expenses appear to be excuses rather than realistic impediments.

The major purpose of merchandise management is to maintain a healthy balance between investments in merchandise inventories and planned sales. The major purpose of expense management is to balance planned income and planned expenses. Income, or maintained markup, must cover operating expenses and profit.

## Chapter Highlights

- Merchandising management is the management of the product component of the marketing mix. The key to successful merchandising is to ensure that the customer is offered the right merchandise, at the right price, at the right place, at the right time, and in the right quantities (the five "rights" of merchandising).

- Two of the merchandising strategies retailers use to gain a competitive advantage are branding (private-label versus national) strategies and licensing strategies.

- Licensing is gaining widespread acceptance as a merchandising strategy among retailers because it provides the opportunity to capture a market whose customers are younger, richer, better educated, and willing to pay more than average consumers.

- One of the more difficult problems facing merchants is the optimal balance between national, private, and generic brands. The question affects most types of retailing.

- Preparing a merchandise budget is a challenging and important task. It includes ways to look at stock balance (width, breadth, and total dollars).

- Merchandise planning can be structured around either a bottom-up or a top-down approach, and perhaps best by the interactive approach.

- The following items affect profitability and are included in the merchandise budget: (1) sales, (2) inventory or stock, (3) reductions, and (4) purchases.

- The main purpose of expense budgeting is to balance planned expenses with planned income. The three major expense classification systems are (1) natural, (2) functional, and (3) expense centre.

## Key Terms

Basic stock method   351
Breadth   342
Depth   342
Licensing   341
Merchandise budget   348

Merchandise line   342
Merchandise management   338
Merchandise planning   342
Model stock plan   354
Percentage deviation method   351

# Discussion Questions

1. By using examples, distinguish among the following: product, product line, variety, and assortment.
2. Describe the three points that go together in planning stock balance.
3. Explain merchandise turnover; indicate how it is useful in planning total dollars in inventory.
4. What factors must a retailer consider in deciding how many dollars to spend on inventory?
5. Discuss the following: sales planning, stock planning, and reductions planning.
6. Explain the relationship between stock-to-sales ratios and turnover. How are stock-to-sales ratios used as a guide to stock planning in the merchandise budget?
7. How does a retailer plan purchases? Give an example of the process.
8. Explain the difference in the purposes of merchandise budgeting and expense budgeting.

# Problems

1. If net sales for the season (6 months) are $48,000, and the average retail stock for the season is $21,000, what is the annual stock-turnover rate?
2. If cost of goods sold for the first four months of operation is $127,000, and average stock at cost for this same time period is $68,000, what is the annual stock-turnover rate?
3. Given the following figures, what is the stock-turnover rate for the season?

|  | Retail Stock on Hand | Monthly Net Sales |
|---|---|---|
| Opening inventory | $16,000 |  |
| End of:   1st month | 16,450 | $7,500 |
| 2nd month | 16,000 | 6,900 |
| 3rd month | 17,260 | 7,250 |
| 4th month | 16,690 | 6,840 |
| 5th month | 15,980 | 6,620 |
| 6th month | 16,620 | 7,180 |

4. What is average stock if the stock-turnover rate is 4 and net sales are $36,000?

5. What is cost of goods sold if the stock-turnover rate is 2.5 and the average stock at cost is $8,700?
6. A new department shows the following figures for the first three months of operation: net sales, $150,000; average retail stock, $160,000. If business continues at the same rate, what will the stock-turnover rate be for the year?
7. Last year a certain department had net sales of $21,000 and a stock-turnover rate of 2.5. A stock-turnover rate of 3 is desired for the year ahead. If sales volume remains the same, how much must the average inventory be reduced (a) in dollar amount and (b) in percentage?
8. A certain department had net sales for the year of $71,250. The stock at the beginning of the year is $22,500 at cost and $37,500 at retail. A stock count in July showed the inventory at cost as $23,750 and at retail as $36,250. End-of-year inventories are $25,000 at cost and $38,750 at retail. Purchases at cost during the year amounted to $48,750. What is the stock-turnover rate (a) at cost and (b) at retail?
9. Given the following information for the month of July, calculate planned purchases:

| | |
|---|---|
| Planned sales for the month | $43,000 |
| Planned BOM inventory | 60,250 |
| Planned reductions for the month | 1,200 |
| Planned EOM inventory | 58,000 |

10. Given the following information for the month of October, calculate planned purchases:

| | |
|---|---|
| Planned sales for the month | $198,000 |
| Planned EOM inventory | 240,000 |
| Stock-to-sales ratio for the month of October | 1.2 |
| Planned reductions for the month | 3,860 |

11. Given the following figures, calculate planned purchases for January:

| | |
|---|---|
| Stock on hand—January 1 | $36,470 |
| Planned stock on hand—February 1 | 38,220 |
| Planned sales for January | 21,760 |
| Planned reductions for January | 410 |

# Application Exercises

1. Contact a local buyer of a line of merchandise that interests you. If possible, do a full six-month merchandise plan for a specific merchandise classification. Utilize the text format for your process of planning. You will need to get information from the buyer. If such information is not available from the store, you may have to make certain assumptions to come up with your planned purchases.

2. Attention is given in the text to formal merchandise planning. Select some stores and find out how they handle this function. How much planning do they do? What levels of sophistication do they achieve? Does the degree differ by merchandise lines? See if you can develop some generalizations from your investigations.

3. Visit two competing supermarkets and list the SKUs in one product category (e.g., laundry detergents). Analyze the lists and prepare a short paper on the two supermarkets' apparent merchandising strategies.

# Suggested Cases

# Endnotes

1. Information on Canadian Tire was obtained from various *Annual Reports* from 1989; and Barbara Aarsteinsen, "Canadian Tire Expecting Retail Growth, Eyeing New Ventures," *Globe and Mail,* February 17, 1988, p. B11.

2. Canadian Tire, Annual Report, 1991.

3. Loblaw Companies Ltd., *Annual Report,* 1987; and George Weston Ltd., *Annual Report,* 1987.

4. The men's furnishings department would include all shirts, ties, underwear, and so on—the planning can be in terms of classifications, or subdepartmental units, or for a small department; but for illustration,

we will look at the sport shirt classification only, as we are illustrating a procedure.

5. Obviously, dollars invested in inventory relate to width and support. In fact, the dollars planned become the controlling decision. How many dollars the retailer has will determine investment in SKUs. But planning width, depth, and dollars do not guarantee the optimal stock. Many of the questions about how well the planning is being carried out will be answered in Chapter 19.

6. Stock-to-sales ratios designate the amount of inventory necessary to support sales for a particular period of time (e.g., a month). This discussion assumes a going concern with last year's figures available. In a budget process for a new store, estimates/projections based on trade figures and/or experience are particularly valuable.

7. Readers may wonder why 4.7 times more dollars of inventory than sales are needed. This relates to the support factor. An example can help illustrate this point. If customers were individually predictable—that is, if retailers needed only one jacket to satisfy each customer's demand—then retailers might get by with a one-to-one ratio. But people want to select from many colours, designs, fabrics, and so on. Thus, retailers need many more SKUs to support planned sales. The more fashion-oriented (or the less stable) the merchandise, the more stock is needed to support sales.

8. The planning of employee discounts and shortages is rather predictable, differing from markdowns. Retailers estimate the former based on historical data. Seldom will employee discounts and shortages vary from year to year in percentage terms as related to sales.

9. Chapter 19 discusses setting up a control system (open to buy) to measure how well the plan is working. Readers may want to look at that part of the book now.

# 14   BUYING, HANDLING, AND INVENTORY MANAGEMENT

---

## Chapter Objectives

After reading this chapter, you should be able to:

1 Identify factors influencing the buying cycle.

2 Calculate desired inventory levels.

3 Describe alternatives in the selection of merchandise suppliers.

4 Explain how retailers negotiate prices, discounts, datings, and transportation charges.

5 Evaluate issues related to the management of physical handling activities.

6 Describe activities involved in the receiving and checking of merchandise.

7 Discuss the key issues in inventory records management.

**Retailing Capsule**

The buying decision—what merchandise to offer a target market—is of critical importance to the retailer. The right decision can lead to satisfied customers and profits for the firm. The wrong decision can lead to inventory write-offs, losses, and even bankruptcy.

The buying decision is particularly difficult when it comes to new products. In these cases, the buyer has no previous sales results to help with the decision. What criteria do buyers use when considering whether or not to accept a new product? In a study of over 250 Canadian nonfood retail chain buyers such as Sears, Shoppers Drug Mart, Canadian Tire, Eaton's, and The Bay, the major criteria used in decisions to accept new products were identified. In order of importance, the top 10 criteria were:

- Expected profit contribution.
- Supplier's ability to fill repeat orders quickly.
- Product quality.
- Retailer or dealer markup.
- Product's meeting government regulations.
- Competitive price.
- Supplier's known track record.
- Potential market volume.
- Manufacturer's initial supply capabilities.
- Product's fitting new trends in the market.

Not surprisingly, expected profit contribution tops the list. What is interesting is the second criterion—the ability to fill repeat orders quickly. The buyer knows that the key to profitability for many new products is repeat sales, which require more stock. In many instances, the buyer will work closely with the supplier, build repeats into the order contract, and provide the supplier with a forecast. In some cases, the buyer will ask the supplier to have inventory on hand, and the buyer will share the financial risk.

Source: Peter M. Banting and David L. Blenkhorn, "The Mind of the Retail Buyer," *Management Decisions* 26, no. 6 (1988), pp. 29–36.

Retail buyers can be viewed as investment specialists. In their function, they invest at wholesale (cost) and plan to earn a profit on their investments (retail). Retail buyers can be responsible for millions of dollars in merchandise. They must be able to forecast demand for the merchandise, negotiate with vendors on a variety of issues such as price and transportation, and work as partners with the vendors to maximize the sale of the merchandise to the benefit of both the retailer and the vendor. This chapter begins with a discussion on the roles of the buyer and vendor in retail success and the responsibilities of the retailer in establishing strong vendor relationships.

# Personal Traits Needed for Buying

Because the responsibilities of the buyer are many and varied, buyers need certain qualifications. The following are some of the abilities a successful buyer must have:

> Buyers must be merchandise *specialists*. They should be able to recognize quality, judge workmanship, and have knowledge regarding materials, colour, and design. Although buyers should be able to appreciate the aesthetic appeal of merchandise, they must be prudent enough to buy what they think will sell rather than what might be in good taste in their opinion. . . . Experience plus a natural talent will aid buyers.
>
> Buyers must learn how to be traders. The profit margin of their departments will be bigger if they can negotiate low purchasing prices and take advantage of vendor volume discounts as well. . . .
>
> Buyers should be good managers. . . . Too often buyers get bogged down in paperwork or become too involved in the details of running their department. The ability to delegate authority . . . should be developed early in their careers. Otherwise they will soon find themselves on a treadmill leading nowhere.
>
> A successful buyer must exhibit an uncommon amount of drive and a will to succeed. Buying is a highly competitive and exhausting job. Although the rewards are many, some persons cannot take the daily strain of meeting people, bargaining with vendors, placating customers, and pleasing superiors. Buyers are more subject to ''ups and downs'' than are persons in many other lines of endeavor. Buyers must be firm and decisive because quick decisions are part of their everyday lives.[1]

# The Buying Function[2]

The buyer is the operating manager in the merchandising division. This chapter focuses on the buying responsibility of this person. (The selling function is discussed in Chapter 16.)

## Goals of Good Buying

For people not acquainted with retailing, the work of a buyer may seem to be a relatively simple one—finding and purchasing the needed merchandise at a good price. But there is more to buying than bargaining with vendors. Not only are there other functions to consider, but good buying involves buying the right merchandise for customers, at the best price, in the right quantity, of the right quality, and from vendors who will be reliable and provide other valuable services. Many considerations are involved in doing this thoroughly and competently. These are all described in the buying cycle (Figure 14–1).

The process of buying involves four major steps. They are:

1. *Determining needs:* The buyer must determine for each line of merchandise what will be needed until the next time the line is reviewed. Determining *what* is needed involves, for some items, merely looking at inventory and past sales. For other lines, it concerns risky decisions— *which* styles to select and *how much* of each to buy.

*The buying function is particularly important with perishables to ensure freshness and avoid spoilage.*

SOURCE: Photo by James Hertel.

2. *Selecting the supplier:* After determining the merchandise needs, the buyer must find a vendor(s) who can supply the merchandise. Some merchandise can be bought only from one vendor; in this case, the only decision to be made is whether to carry the line. For most merchandise lines, several suppliers are available. In these instances, the buyer must evaluate prices as well as services in terms of reasonable and reliable delivery, adjustment of problems, and help in emergencies and in other matters such as credit terms, spaced deliveries, and inventory management assistance. For a retailer like Canadian Tire, supplier selection is a major task, as the company deals with more than 4,000 Canadian and international suppliers.

3. *Negotiating the purchase:* This crucial third step involves not only the purchase price but also quantities, delivery dates, single or multiple shipment deliveries, freight and packing expenses, guarantees on the quality of the merchandise, promotion and advertising allowances, special offers on slightly damaged materials or sellouts, and so forth.

4. *Following up:* Finally, to improve service, the buyer must review the relationship with each vendor from time to time to determine if changes should be made. If necessary, a search for alternate or new suppliers should take place.

**Determining Needs**

Different types of merchandise require different techniques to determine what is needed. Therefore, it is important to recognize whether the various merchandise lines in the store are primarily *staples, seasonal items, style items,* or *perishable items.*

**FIGURE 14–1**

*The buying cycle*

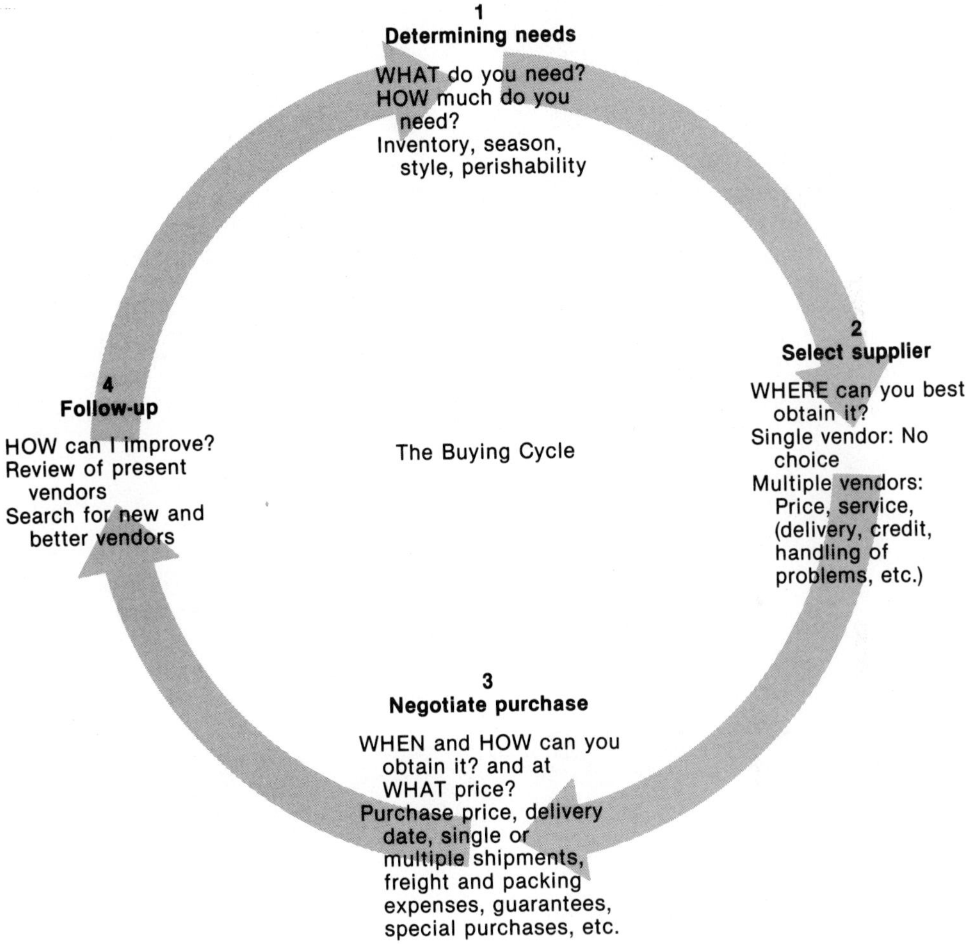

**1**
**Determining needs**

WHAT do you need?
HOW much do you
    need?
Inventory, season,
    style, perishability

**2**
**Select supplier**

WHERE can you best
    obtain it?
Single vendor: No
    choice
Multiple vendors:
    Price, service,
    (delivery, credit,
    handling of
    problems, etc.)

**4**
**Follow-up**

HOW can I improve?
Review of present
    vendors
Search for new and
    better vendors

The Buying Cycle

**3**
**Negotiate purchase**

WHEN and HOW can you
    obtain it? and at
    WHAT price?
Purchase price, delivery
    date, single or
    multiple shipments,
    freight and packing
    expenses, guarantees,
    special purchases, etc.

Most businesses carry some merchandise in each of these categories. Effective management of the buying function means planning the buying program and record-keeping with the differences between these merchandise categories in mind.

The goal in each case, whether the merchandise is primarily staple, seasonal, style-oriented, or perishable, is to establish or maintain inventory at the lowest possible level and still have a sufficient variety of colours, sizes, or models available from which customers can choose. Such a practice will minimize losses due to obsolescence and spoilage, while freeing capital that may be put to other worthwhile uses.

*Forecasting Sales*   **Staples**

**Staple** or semistaple **merchandise** is generally in demand year-round, with little change in model or style. Basic appliances, hardware, housewares, books, linens, and basic clothing items like underwear and pyjamas fall into this category. The staples in the store, even if the store carries primarily in-style or seasonal merchandise, not only bring extra profits but also serve as an incentive, bringing customers into the store who may then purchase some of the primary merchandise. Department stores such as Eaton's and The Bay have a large portion of their sales in staple or semistaple items.

The important characteristic of staples is steady usage, enabling the buyer to order more of them whenever needed. Deciding how much to buy, therefore, concerns primarily:

1. *Sales trends:* If records are available that show how much of each staple was sold during the past two or three months, and also how much of the same staple sold during the same period in the previous year, the buyer knows whether the item has increased in popularity or has remained the same. The buyer can then decide on inventory levels based on this information.
2. *Profitability:* Items that bring a better return on investment in space and capital are the more desirable items to buy.
3. *Discounts:* These are usually available with quantity purchases.

The combination of these factors provides a general indicator of needs in staple merchandise.

**Seasonal Merchandise**

**Seasonal merchandise,** as implied, is in demand only at certain times of the year. Obvious examples include sleds, snow tires, bathing suits, toys, sunglasses, lawn equipment, holiday greeting cards, and patio furniture. Although some seasonal items can be secured during peak demand to replenish inventory, many are unavailable or cannot be obtained quickly enough at this time. Therefore, such merchandise is best bought well in advance of the season. Most clothing stores in Canada would have some seasonal component to their merchandise mix, reflecting the different clothes worn in the four seasons.

Because seasonal items are fast moving in season and slow moving or stagnant during the off-season, it is important to maintain the stock to satisfy this on-off movement. Determining needs for seasonal items (predicting, forecasting) relies heavily on *knowing* what customer demand for that item or merchandise line was in the past. One method of knowing previous customer demand on seasonal items is by maintaining a month-by-month tally of units sold, either by dollar value or volume count. These records then can be examined on a yearly basis, enabling the buyer to clearly see selling trends and make buying decisions accordingly.

One method of maintaining records is to use a separate sheet index card or computer record for *each* merchandise *item, group of items,* or *entire line.* In the example shown in Table 14–1, note that in 1993, most of the sales on this item took

**TABLE 14–1   Merchandise Item Record**

| Merchandise item: _____ | Sales Record | | | | |
|---|---|---|---|---|---|
| | *1993* | *1994* | *1995* | *1996* | *1997* |
| January | 0 | | | | |
| February | $   50 | | | | |
| March | 700 | | | | |
| April | 2,200 | | | | |
| May | 1,000 | | | | |
| June | 300 | | | | |
| July through December | 0 | | | | |
| Total sales | $ 4250 | | | | |
| Total units: | | | | | |
| Bought | 300 | | | | |
| Remaining and sold below cost | 20 | | | | |

place in April; at the end of the season, the 20 remaining items in inventory had to be sold below cost.

Where orders cannot be placed during the season, or where suppliers could delay shipments, good forecasting is very important to help predict what quantity of each item will be needed for the season. Predictions can also include plans for a preseason sale that would entice customers to buy from the store rather than competitors. The forecast can also consider any end-of-season sales. If such late sales events are profitable, it may not be difficult to decide what quantities are needed. If such sales are not profitable, then the buyer has to estimate much more carefully so as not to be left with a large stock of slow-moving or dead merchandise.

Unfortunately, there is no foolproof method of accurately predicting future sales. Usually, though, good prediction of future sales can be made from consideration of:

- Past experience with the movement of the merchandise.
- Records of previous sales.
- Length of the season.
- Planned selling price.
- Planned advertising and promotion effort, including sales.
- The extent to which there is an increase or decrease in competition.
- Predictions of consumer buying from trade journals.

These factors together can give a fairly good idea of the quantity of each item likely to sell during the upcoming season.

### Style and Perishable Items

Items of style include such merchandise as ladies' apparel, men's apparel, and sportswear. Stylish items are usually more expensive than staples and seasonals.

Because the demand for any particular style tends to increase rapidly, then drop off rapidly, overbuying can have a disastrous effect on profits.

Le Château, a specialty clothing chain with over 150 stores in Canada, has an interesting approach to forecasting and purchasing fashion merchandise. Using a reporting system that provides fast information on inventory and style performance, the company can identify and react quickly to trends in clothing style and colour. It then manufactures more of the items in its Montreal-based facility and uses the information in the design and buying of the next season's collections.[3]

Perishable merchandise has similar characteristics. If management buys more than can be sold, some of it will begin to spoil and bring only a fraction of the normal price.

In the case of items with which management has experienced previous difficulties, one option is to plot the progress of different styles to see how they usually behave. A few examples of such graphs are shown in Figure 14–2. They can help to predict how much to buy and also when to buy.

When plotting graphs, it is important to note all special, significant events such as sales in the store and those of major competitors. These events also have to be planned or predicted and kept in mind when forecasting merchandise needs. These

*Fashion items are difficult to forecast accurately, and management must react quickly to trends in clothing style and colour.*

**FIGURE 14–2**

*Sales of different styles*

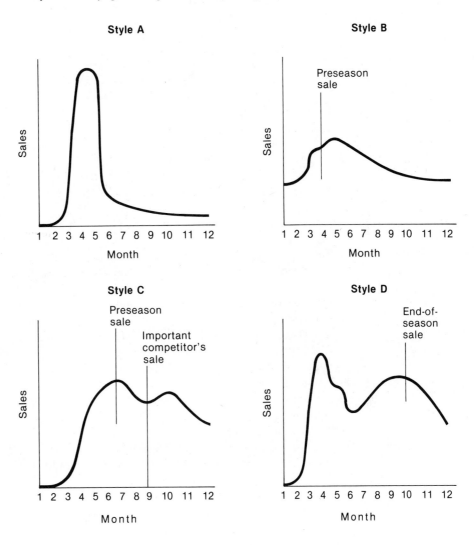

graphs may not predict sales very accurately, but they usually will narrow the amount of buying error.

**Establishing Buying Guidelines**

Determining the amount of stock that should be ordered is an important decision. In some cases, product shelf life may be the deciding factor. For example, delivery of muffins to a food store is immediate. The grocer gives the order directly to the bakery truck driver, and the driver fills the order in minutes. If the grocer stocked more than a two days' supply of muffins, the muffins would lose their freshness and the grocer would lose customers.

There are many other factors to consider in addition to shelf life. Take the case of the retailer who may require two weeks to receive delivery from suppliers on most items. On an emergency basis, the retailer may be able to replenish inventory more promptly, but only by forfeiting quantity discounts or incurring extra delivery charges. For most items, it is better to accept normal delivery, taking full advantage of all available discounts and minimizing freight charges.

The length of time between order placement and receipt of goods is called **lead time.** If the lead time is two weeks, would it be sufficient to establish a minimum inventory level of two weeks' supply? Probably not. If no order were placed until the supply of a certain item reached two weeks, there would probably be just enough stock on hand to cover expected sales until the order arrived. However, if anything went wrong (and it usually does), there would be a stockout before the order was received. An unexpectedly large request from a customer might not be filled because of insufficient inventory. A strike, shipping delays, manufacturing problems, or unforeseen weather conditions could seriously delay the arrival of the merchandise so that the stockout could last for several weeks. Therefore, most businesses maintain a **safety stock** as protection against such occurrences. For many Canadian retailers who purchase merchandise from the Far East, lead times may be measured in months, not weeks. In these cases, the purchase of seasonal merchandise could be made up to six months before it is expected to go on sale.

The size of the safety stock will depend on the number and extent of the factors that could interrupt deliveries. Suitable guidelines have to be based on experience in the industry.

Additionally, many items require a basic stock, an amount sufficient to accommodate regular sales, offering customers a reasonable assortment of merchandise from which their selection can be made.

Assume that the lead time for a particular item is two weeks. The safety stock that the business wishes to maintain is four weeks' supply. Additionally, a one-week basic stock is required. The desired inventory level would be established as the sum of these factors:

|  | |
|---|---|
| Lead time | 2 weeks |
| + Safety stock | 4 weeks |
| + Basic stock | 1 week |
| = Inventory level | 7 weeks |

### When to Buy?

The **order point** is the amount of inventory below which the quantity available should not fall or the item will be out of stock before the next shipment arrives. For example, if a camera shop wishes to maintain an eight-week supply of film as safety stock, with a lead time of two weeks, and average sales of a particular film type at 50 rolls per week, the order point is 500 ($50 \times 10$ rolls). When inventory drops below 500 rolls, more film should be ordered.

## How Much to Buy?

The quantity of film to purchase depends on the usual time between orders, called the **order interval** (in the film example, assume the order interval is two weeks). In this way, sufficient supplies are maintained so that inventories between orders average out to the desired level.

A stock equal to expected sales during the camera shop's two-week order interval should be added to the order point to determine the **order ceiling.**

$$\text{Order ceiling} = \text{Order point} + \text{Order interval sales}$$
$$\text{Order ceiling} = 500 + (50 \times 2)$$
$$\text{Order ceiling} = 600$$

An order quantity can then be determined as follows, assuming 450 rolls are on hand:

$$\text{Order quantity} = \text{Order ceiling} - \text{Stock on hand}$$
$$\text{Order quantity} = 600 - 450$$
$$\text{Order quantity} = 150 \text{ rolls}$$

If an order for 50 rolls had already been placed but had not yet been received, the present order should be *reduced* by the 50 rolls on order. The new order would then be 100 (150 − 50) rolls.

## Review

Let us review the steps involved in establishing order quantities, using a hardware store as an example. The store wants to maintain a basic tool stock equal to one week's sales and a safety stock of one week's sales for saws. Average weekly sales are three saws. Lead time for order placement and delivery is two weeks. Orders are placed every four weeks.

A desirable inventory level, or order point, is then calculated as follows:

|  |  |
|---|---|
| Lead time | 2 weeks |
| + Basic stock | 1 week |
| + Safety stock | 1 week |
| = Order point | 4 weeks or 12 (4 × 3) saws |

Whenever the supply of any tool drops to a four weeks' supply or below (i.e., 12 saws), an order should be placed.

To determine the order quantity, management must first calculate the order ceiling:

|  |  |
|---|---|
| Order point | 4 weeks |
| + Order interval | 4 weeks |
| = Order ceiling | 8 weeks or 24 (8 × 3) saws |

Assume that an order is being prepared for saws. Average weekly sales are 3 saws, and the stock on hand is 10 saws. This is below the order point of 12 (4 × 3) saws.

The order quantity would then be calculated as follows:

|  |  |
|---|---|
| Order ceiling | 24 |
| − Stock on hand | 10 |
| = Order quantity | 14 |

The hardware store should order 14 saws. If any are already on order, the outstanding order quantity should be subtracted.

## Selection of Suppliers

The first step in supplier selection is to obtain a list of those to consider. Awareness of available suppliers and their services will place the buyer in a position to choose the best one.

Sources of information concerning suppliers are plentiful. They include:

1. *Salespeople:* Salespeople of existing suppliers often provide excellent information concerning possible sources of supply. Many are well informed about alternative sources of noncompeting lines, and they can often suggest new services and new products. Since they call on many different businesses, salespeople are also a good source of information concerning merchandise selection of similar stores in different parts of their territories. All of this information is available to alert, open-minded buyers who know how to obtain it without devoting too much time to the vendor representatives who call on them.

2. *Trade magazines:* General and specialized trade journals often contain advertisements placed by suppliers and articles that provide clues to desirable new sources. For example, the *Canadian Grocer* carries ads for new supermarket products.

3. *Business contacts:* Often, customers or other business contacts may be able to provide useful information concerning potential suppliers.

4. *Trade exhibits:* These provide an excellent opportunity to see a variety of new products and compare similar products of different manufacturers. A host of trade shows are held in Canada, focusing on a range of products from grocery items to children's fashion wear to hardware, housewares, and home improvements.

5. *Yellow Pages:* The Yellow Pages in the telephone directory contain listings of local suppliers.

### How to Make Market Contacts

**Vendor Contacts**

Vendor contact may begin through catalogs and price lists. These documents are available to all potential retailers. Another source of vendor contact is the sales representative who calls on the retailer. In such lines as groceries and drugs, where item turnover is very fast, salespersons may call on the retailer almost weekly. For fashion lines, the representative will call on a seasonal basis.

Another source of vendor contact is a central market, a place where a large number of suppliers concentrate. Because of the close proximity of the United States, many Canadian retailers will visit central markets such as New York City for women's fashion goods and High Point, North Carolina, for furniture.

### Selecting the Supplier

Factors to be considered in determining the best supplier are price and discounts, quality, reliability, services, and accessibility.

1. *Price* is the most important consideration in the selection of a supplier, provided that quality and service are equivalent to that of other vendors. Price has many dimensions since it includes quantity discounts, special allowances, the chance to buy special lots, seconds, or sellouts, and dating of invoices.

2. *Quality,* and assurance of consistent quality, is almost as important as price and closely linked to it. Obviously, in selecting a supplier, buyers want to be certain that they will rarely, if ever, receive a poor-quality shipment.

3. *Reliability* of delivery from a supplier is important, as unreliable delivery can create problems of stockout, resulting in lost sales. In addition, slow or unreliable delivery also requires the buyer to maintain larger average inventories, which results in increased carrying costs. A good supplier will be reliable when the store has a sudden emergency and needs some quick supplies and will protect the store when there are shortages of material due to a strike or disaster.

4. *Services* suppliers might provide are many and include spaced deliveries, allowing the buyer to purchase (but not take delivery of) a larger quantity than the store can immediately handle, thus giving the advantage of quantity discounts; recycling of packaging to reduce overall freight and packing expenses; providing advertising and promotional materials and displays to help promote merchandise; and giveaways such as literature and bags for the customers.

5. *Accessibility* is another factor on which suppliers should be judged. It is often important to personally contact the supplier concerning special problems that may arise. A supplier that is difficult to contact is clearly not as desirable as one that is easy to reach.

Keeping these factors in mind can help to (1) avoid mistakes in selecting suppliers, (2) compare vendors competing for the retailers' business, and (3) provide a firm foundation for thorough negotiations.

### Getting the Best Price from Vendors

*Group Buying.*    **Group** (or co-operative) **buying** is the joint purchase of goods by a number of noncompeting, nonaligned stores such as independent hardware stores in different areas of a province. By combining their orders into one large order, the stores hope to get lower prices. These group arrangements can be beneficial in other ways, too, because the noncompeting buyers can share knowledge about markets, fashion trends, and so forth.

There are disadvantages to group buying. Members of the group give up some of their individuality, which they may not want to do. Fashion merchants, particularly, find co-operative buying difficult because they feel their customers are unique.[4]

In Canada, buying groups have been formed by independent sporting good stores (Sports Distributors of Canada), grocery and convenience stores (Distribution Canada), and drugstores (Drug Trading Company). For many of these independents, the buying groups provide the opportunity for volume discounts and are an important source of merchandise and marketing information.[5]

*Central Buying.*    **Central buying** is most often practiced by chains such as Canadian Tire. As branch-store organizations grow in size, central buying is also logical for them. Central buying means that one person handles the buying of goods for all stores in the firm.

In firms where central buying occurs, most of the authority for buying lies outside any one retail outlet. In some firms, store managers are given limited authority to purchase locally produced items. For example, in a food store, locally grown produce might be bought by the local store instead of by the central buyer.

One of the major recommendations of a study on cross-border shopping was that Canadian retailers should band together in buying groups to increase their clout with manufacturers. The study found that grocery retailers have buying groups that have resulted in a very efficient distribution system.[6] Retail Highlight 14–1 provides a summary of the study.

Because they order in such large quantities, central buyers hope to get favourable prices. Technology is important in central buying, as the buyer must have adequate and rapid information from individual stores. Canadian Tire is in the forefront of Canadian retailers who use technology to improve buying practices (see Retail Highlight 14–2).

*Committee Buying.*    **Committee buying** is a version of central buying. It is a way to achieve the savings of central buying while having more than one person share the buying responsibility. This type of buying is common in firms such as hardware stores that sell staples.

*Consignment.*    In **consignment,** suppliers guarantee the sale of items and will take merchandise back if it does not sell. University and college bookstores often purchase textbooks on this basis. The retailer assumes no risk in such an

Retail Highlight 14–1

# What Makes Canadian Prices High

A six-month, $400,000 study on cross-border shopping concluded that an inefficient distribution system results in higher prices for consumer goods in Canada, relative to the United States. The study focused on products that show marked price differences and are most often shopped across the border—clothing, appliances, bedding and linen, electronics, hardware, footwear, groceries, lumber and building products, sporting goods, and toys.

The study tracked 49 products as they moved from the manufacturer to store shelves on both sides of the border. It found that prices in 40 of the 49 products were an average of 21 percent higher in Canada. For example, the retail markup on a medium-priced men's dress shirt imported from Korea is $34.80, while a U.S. retailer takes a U.S. $23.30 markup.

Three of the areas that lead to higher retail prices in Canada are:

- Canadian wholesalers are considerably smaller than their U.S. counterparts, which reduces their bargaining power with manufacturers. The problem is made worse by the high number of multinational subsidiaries that are forced to buy from their foreign parents at unfavourable terms.

- U.S.-made goods often pass through an additional level of distribution once they arrive in Canada, whereas U.S. manufacturers typically sell directly to major U.S. retailers.

- Manufacturers often charge more for identical goods that enter the Canadian distribution system because, for example, they face higher costs of doing business here or consider the domestic market less strategically important.

Among the recommendations contained in the report is the development of closer partnerships between suppliers and retailers to eliminate layers of bureaucracy and, as a result, lower costs. As well, the system should be examined to see if there can be more efficient ways to operate using fewer middlemen.

Sources: John Heinzl, "What Makes Canadian Prices High?" *Globe and Mail,* May 15, 1992, p. B6; and Mark Evans, "Shopping Study Faults Mark-Ups," *The Financial Post,* May 15, 1992, p. 9.

arrangement. Merchandise from an unknown supplier or a high-risk item might require such an arrangement. If a buyer has overspent the assigned budget, consignment can be attractive. But the buyer must be aware that most vendors would not offer consignment if the goods could be sold any other way.

*Leased Departments.*    If retailers do not have the skills to operate a specialized area, they may choose to **lease departments.** Shoe, camera, jewellery, and optical departments, as well as beauty salons and restaurants, are often operated under lease arrangements. By leasing to an expert, the retailer can provide customers with specialized items without fear of failure caused by inexperience.

Retail Highlight 14–2

# Technology Improves the Buying Process

Progressive retailers such as Canadian Tire, Eaton's, and Sears Canada are linking both stores and vendors into a computer system that allows for buying and ordering without sending paper through the mail or Fax machines. Called electronic data interchange (EDI), companies can trade and "talk" electronically; they can exchange business documents such as cheques, invoices, and purchase orders for different transactions via computer on standard forms.

Canadian Tire has installed or converted more than 130 vendors to its EDI system. The benefits of EDI include (1) more efficient order processing, (2) saving time preparing and delivering purchase orders, and (3) reducing invoice errors.

Canadian Tire has more than 420 associate stores that can select and stock more than 44,000 items through EDI. With EDI, Canadian Tire has (1) reduced its inventory safety stock (saving five days' lead time), (2) almost completely eliminated paper handling in its buying transactions, and (3) allowed buyers to take action immediately if there is a problem.

The EDI project leader for Canadian Tire has stated that EDI is a prerequisite for retailers, and that success in the 1990s will depend on how you do it, not whether. EDI facilitates Canadian Tire's

Quick Response Strategy (a program to ensure faster delivery, reduce administrative expenses, and turn inventory faster), and for an initial investment of 1.9 percent of sales, and an annual cost of .28 percent of sales, it is realizing a saving of 5.1 percent of sales.

Eaton's has used EDI to cut inventory and improve customer service. For example, Eaton's just carries samples of mattresses on the floor and holds no inventories. Eaton's mattress suppliers, such as Bedford Furniture, Simmons, and Serta, are linked to Eaton's through EDI. When an Eaton's salesperson sells a mattress, the order is electronically sent to the supplier and moved right into manufacturing. Orders arriving by 7 A.M. are ready by the end of the day.

Everything—from the individual item to the carton it's packed in—gets bar-coded. Input at Eaton's warehouse records receipt of the goods and indicates which store or truck they're destined for. It also triggers an inventory update and alerts accounts payable. When it's time for payment—there's no cheque issued. The money is simply put in the client's account on the correct date. There are no invoices, no bills of lading, no shipment notices, no receipt notices. When the supplier gets the order, nothing has to be rekeyed.

Sources: Serge Fortier, "EDI Efficiency" *Retail Directions*, January/February 1989, pp. 21–22; and "EDI or Die," *Issues for Canada's Future*, June 1992.

*Negotiations*    A good relationship between buyer and vendor may be one of the most important assets of the retail business. If a strong, friendly, yet professional, relationship exists with suppliers, negotiations can go smoothly. Of course, bargaining with vendors does not begin until the buyer is sure that the items are truly what are needed for the store.

The buyer should be prepared to sacrifice something during a negotiation. Then the buyer can ask the supplier, "What are you willing to give up?" Remember, the

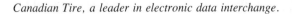

*Retail Highlight 14–2 continued*

*Canadian Tire, a leader in electronic data interchange.*

Source: Photo by Sandy McDougall.

buyer is trying to get the best deal, while the vendor is trying to hold the price up to protect profits.

Buyers normally attempt to negotiate on the following elements: cost (list) price of the items, discounts and datings, and transportation charges.

### Cost Price (List Price)

Suppliers typically provide retailers with a price list of the merchandise available for sale. These list prices form the starting point for negotiations. While some suppliers are flexible in the negotiating process, other suppliers will not negotiate price.

### Discounts

Even though identical list prices may be offered by various vendors, they may offer different discounts and different provisions as to who will be responsible for paying transportation charges. An understanding of these purchase terms is necessary to negotiate the best price.

***Trade.***   A **trade discount** is a reduction off the seller's list price and is granted to a retailer who performs functions normally the responsibility of the seller.

A trade discount may be offered as a single percentage or as a series of percentages off list price. If the list price on a sport shirt is $14.95, with a trade discount of 40 percent, the trade discount will be $5.98 ($14.95 × .40), and the retailer will pay $8.97 ($14.95 − $5.98). The same buyer might be offered a similar sport shirt from another manufacturer at a list price of $14.95 less 30 percent, 10 percent, and 5 percent. The three discounts (30 percent, 10 percent, and 5 percent) offered by the manufacturer could be for advertising support, transportation charges, and other promotional activities. The net price in this case would be computed as follows:

$$
\begin{array}{rl}
\text{List price} = & \$14.95 \\
- & \underline{4.48} \quad (\$14.95 \times 0.30) \\
= & 10.47 \\
- & \underline{1.05} \quad (\$10.47 \times 0.10) \\
= & 9.42 \\
- & 0.47 \quad (\$9.42 \times 0.05) \\
\text{Net price} = & \$\ 8.95
\end{array}
$$

An alternative way of calculating the net price in the example above is to use the *complement* of the discount percentages. In this case, the net price would be calculated as: $14.95 × .70 × .90 × .95 = $8.95.

***Quantity.***   A **quantity discount** is a reduction in unit cost based on the size of the order. Such discounts may be noncumulative, meaning the reduction is based on each order, or cumulative, meaning the reduction is computed over the sum of purchases for a specified period of time.

When deciding whether a quantity discount is worthwhile, the buyer must compare the money saved with the extra inventory carrying cost.

To determine the *value* of a quantity discount, use the following steps:

1. Determine the savings from the quantity discount.
2. Determine how much extra merchandise the store would have to carry in inventory, and for how long.
3. Multiply the average extra stock by the carrying charge (which is usually 20 to 25 percent) to obtain the additional cost of carrying the extra stock for a year.
4. Determine the additional carrying costs for the period of time it will take to sell off the extra stock.

5. Compare the savings from the quantity discount with the cost of carrying the extra inventory and decide whether it is worthwhile to buy the larger quantity.

For example, if the buyer can save $500 by taking an extra $6,000 of merchandise into stock, and if it will take six months to sell off the extra stock, the calculations are as shown below:

$$\text{Cost savings (discount)} = \$500$$

*Extra* inventory would be $6,000 in the beginning and zero six months later; therefore:

$$\text{Average extra inventory} = \$3,000$$
$$\text{Carrying costs of average extra inventory} = \$3,000 \times 25\% \times 1/2 \text{ year}$$
$$= \$750 \times 1/2 = \$375$$
$$\text{Actual savings} = \text{Cost savings} - \text{Carrying costs}$$
$$= \$500 - \$375 = \$125$$

Since the real savings from taking the discount would be only $125, this deal is worthwhile only if the store can sell off the extra inventory in six months without getting stuck with any hard-to-sell merchandise.

*Seasonal.*    A **seasonal discount** is a special discount given to retailers who place orders for seasonal merchandise in advance of the normal buying period.

*Promotional Allowance.*    Vendors offer a **promotional allowance** to retailers as compensation for money spent in advertising particular items. This discount may also be given for preferred window- and interior-display space for the vendor's products. One form of promotional allowance is co-op advertising. A manufacturer will pay for up to 50 percent of a retailer's advertising costs for ads that promote the manufacturer's products. For example, appliance manufacturers will allow a retailer an allowance of up to 50 percent if the retailer devotes at least 50 percent of the space or time in the ads to the manufacturer's products.

*Cash.*    A premium is often granted by the vendor for cash payment prior to the time that the entire bill must be paid. The three components of the cash-discount terms are (1) a percentage discount, (2) a period in which the discount may be taken, and (3) the net credit period, which indicates when the full amount of the invoice is due. A **cash discount** stated as 2/10, n/30, means that the retailer must pay the invoice within 10 days to take advantage of the discount of 2 percent. The full amount is due in 30 days.

A cash discount may be taken in addition to a trade or another type of discount. Returning to the earlier example, assume an $895 net bill for 100 sport shirts and that the invoice is dated May 22. The retailer has 10 days to take the discount. Payment is due June 1 (nine days in May and one in June). If the invoice is paid within this time, the retailer will remit $877 instead of $895 ($895 × .02 = $18; $895 − 18 = $877). If the retailer does not discount the invoice, the bill must be paid in full by June 21.

The 2 percent in the example represents an annual interest rate of 36 percent. Why? The full invoice payment is due in 30 days. Since the 2 percent cash discount can be taken if the invoice is paid within 10 days, the discount is allowed for paying the bill 20 days earlier than necessary. Since there are 18 20-day periods in the year (using 360 days as a year), this comes to 36 percent annually (18 × 2 percent).

### Datings

The agreement between vendor and retailer as to the time the discount date will begin is known as *dating*.

*Cash Datings.*    Technically, if the terms call for immediate payment, the process is known as **cash dating** and includes COD (cash on delivery) or CWO (cash with order). Cash datings do not involve discounts.

There are two reasons a negotiation may include cash terms. First, the seller may have a cash flow problem and may insist on cash on delivery (or with the order) to meet the bills incurred in the processing or distribution of the goods. Second, the retail buyer's credit rating may be such that the seller will deal with the firm only on a cash basis. In periods of tight money, retailers who must pay cash for orders may place themselves in a difficult cash flow position. Retailers who are faced with COD or CWO terms should examine the supplier's reasons. They may be a symptom of much more serious problems in the future—for example, the vendor may be in financial trouble.

*Future Datings.*    There are four main types of **future datings:** end-of-month, date-of-invoice, receipt-of-goods, and extra dating.

- *End of Month (EOM):* If an invoice carries EOM dating, the cash and net discount periods begin on the first day of the following month rather than on the invoice date.
- *Date of Invoice (DOI):* DOI, or ordinary dating, is self-explanatory. Prepayments begin with the invoice date, and both the cash discount and the net amount are due within the specified number of days from the invoice date.
- *Receipt of Goods (ROG):* With ROG datings, the time allowed for discounts and for payment of the net amount of the invoice begins with the date the goods are received at the buyer's place of business.
- *Extra:* Extra datings allow the retailer extra time to take the cash discount.

### Transportation Charges

The final aspect of negotiation relates to who will bear the responsibility for shipping costs. The most favourable terms for the retailer are *FOB (free-on-board) destination*. In this arrangement, the seller pays the freight to the destination and is responsible for damage or loss in transit. A more common shipping term is *FOB origin*, which means the vendor delivers the merchandise to the carrier, and the retailer pays for the freight.

Small retailers typically do not have the power to bargain with a vendor on discounts or the transportation charges. On the other hand, large retailers may be able to obtain price concessions from the supplier by bargaining on discounts even though the list price of the merchandise does not change.

# Follow-Up

The last step in the buying cycle is follow-up. Follow-up consists of continuous checking to find more desirable suppliers, merchandise, and buying and merchandise control practices.

Finding better suppliers can be accomplished only by getting to know existing suppliers and being alert to information sources on new ones who may come into the market. Improving merchandise selection is a matter of merchandise management, as discussed in Chapter 13. Better buying practices evolve from experimentation with improved methods whenever a problem appears.

Lastly, maintaining good merchandise control practices, as described below, will ensure success while operating within the buying cycle.

Two tasks remain to ensure success while operating within the buying system. The first is to develop an effective merchandise handling system; the second is to design a good inventory management system. Each is discussed in turn.

# Merchandise Handling

An effective merchandise distribution system in a multiunit retail organization can be an important element of competitive strategy and can have a positive impact on profitability. The first part of this section focuses on **merchandise distribution**—getting merchandise from consolidation warehouses/distribution centres to the individual stores. The second section focuses on the physical handling aspect of merchandise management, including the receiving, checking, and marking of goods.

## Merchandise Distribution in Multiunit Organizations

Some multiunit retailers operate under a system whereby merchandise is shipped from vendors directly to the individual stores in the chain. Many chain operations, however, employ a merchandise distribution system involving the use of consolidation warehouses or distribution centres. Merchandise is shipped from vendors to the retail chain's distribution centre(s) and from there is redirected to the individual store units. Many of these centres are computerized and highly automated, using the most recent innovations in merchandise handling and moving equipment.

Multiunit retailers such as Canadian Tire are also using a new distribution approach called *cross-docking*. With cross-docking, designated products on incoming trailers to Canadian Tire's main distribution centre are immediately loaded onto scheduled outbound trucks taking shipments to the individual stores. Cross-docking effectively reduces handling costs by eliminating the typical storage and retrieval of goods.[7]

*Distribution centres* provide advantages of better inventory control, quicker reordering of merchandise, and rapid movement of merchandise, so as to increase turnover and margins at the stores. Central warehouses allow management to take advantage of the discounts offered by vendors for buying in larger quantities. Such facilities also simplify the accounts payable process, since fewer purchase orders need to be paid. Vendors also pay more attention to large bulk orders that are moving to a central point.

*Physical Handling Activities*

As noted, **physical handling** involves receiving, checking, and marking merchandise. While these activities are often performed in distribution centres, the following sections focus on these activities as performed in the retail store.

### The Receiving Activity

**Receiving** is that phase of physical handling in which the retailer takes possession of the goods and then moves them to the next phase of the process. Certain operations are necessary as part of the receiving function. When the goods reach the store, packing cartons must be inspected for damages. After the cartons are opened, individual packages in the cartons must also be inspected for damages. A receiving record, an essential part of the procedure, must also be prepared. This record normally includes date and hour of arrival, weight, form of transportation, number of cartons, receiving number, invoice number, condition of packages, delivery charges, name of deliverer, amount of invoice, and department ordering the goods.

The receiving department's layout depends on the system used in handling the items received. Four methods are widely used: stationary tables, portable tables, bins, and mechanical conveyor belts or roller conveyors.

The following ideas can help improve the effectiveness of the receiving department:

1. Plan for the straight-line movement of all materials with as little backtracking as possible.
2. Plan the movement of all materials through the shortest possible distance and with the fewest possible motions.
3. Plan for maximum machine operation and minimum hand operation.
4. Determine the most efficient methods for performing operations.
5. Pay careful attention to working conditions.
6. Practice careful selection and training of personnel.
7. Maintain adequate supervision.
8. Have sufficient equipment.
9. Purchase standby equipment.
10. Maintain enough records for adequate control.

### The Checking Activity

**Checking** means matching the store buyer's purchase order with the supplier's invoice (bill), opening the packages, removing the items, sorting them, and comparing the quality and quantity of the shipment with what was ordered. Let us focus on the activities of quality and quantity checking.

*Quality Checking.*    The decision to check or not to check for quality resides with the buyer. When quality checking is considered to be important, the responsibility is assumed by the buying staff. Remember—buyers are merchandise specialists; checkers are not.

*Quantity Checking.*    The two basic methods of quantity checking are:

1. The **direct check:** The shipment is checked against the vendor's invoice. The goods under this system cannot be checked until the invoice arrives. This method can result in items accumulating in the checking area if invoices have not arrived.
2. The **blind check:** This system is designed to avoid carelessness and merchandise accumulation problems associated with the direct check. The checker lists the items and quantities received without the invoice in hand. The system is slower than the direct check, because the list prepared by the checker must then be compared to the invoice.

### The Marking Activity

**Marking** is putting information on the goods or on merchandise containers to assist customers and to aid the store in the control functions.

Various methods are used for establishing the price information to be marked on the goods. One common method is **preretailing.** Under this system, the buyer places the retail price on the store's copy of the purchase order at the time it is written. The buyer may also **retail the invoice.** In this practice, the buyer places a retail price on the copy of the invoice in the receiving room.

Goods can be marked either within the store or by a vendor. In **source marking,** the vendor rather than the retailer marks the merchandise. Source marking involves the use of codes such as the universal product code (UPC). This technology was discussed in detail in Chapter 3. The remainder of the chapter discusses various aspects of the inventory management system.

## Recording Inventory[8]

To manage inventory successfully, management should maintain accurate and up-to-date records of sales and stock on hand for every item. Inventory records tell you what you have. Sales records tell you what you need. Inventory records are used for making the following decisions: (1) purchases for inventory replenishment, (2) scrapping or clearing of obsolete items that are no longer in demand, and (3) addition of new items to inventory.

### Electronic Data Processing

While some retailers may use a manual inventory control system, with the advent of inexpensive microcomputers and software packages, the vast majority of retailers use some form of electronic data processing system. Some retailers may use an outside processing service, but most retailers use their own computer system. The system records all transactions and keeps a continuous record of changes in inventory. The system also prepares a sales summary. This information is needed for determining the adequacy of inventories and for order preparation. The sales summary can be compared periodically with stock on hand so that items that are not showing sufficient sales activity can be cleared through price reductions, scrapped, or otherwise disposed of. In this way, space and dollars invested in inventory are available for more active and potentially more profitable items.

*Physical Inventory*

A physical inventory should be taken periodically to be sure that the actual quantities on hand equal those shown on the inventory records. The inventory records must then be adjusted to reflect any difference between physical inventory and "book" inventory, the quantities shown on the inventory records. The actual quantity of each item on hand must be counted and compared with that shown on the inventory records. Necessary adjustments should be made immediately.

Differences between book and physical inventory arise for many reasons. The most easily understood, of course, is pilferage. Any business naturally wants to maintain an inventory control system to detect this situation as early as possible.

Other reasons for inventory shortages are somewhat more subtle but equally damaging, if not worse. For example, if receiving procedures are faulty, a receiving clerk may not be counting actual quantities received and comparing them with those on the vendor's packing list or invoice. If the quantity actually received is less than that invoiced to the store, management is paying for the difference.

Merchandise may be sold to customers without being billed to them, through oversight or carelessness. In these cases, management will take a loss equal to its cost of the product and also lose the profit that should have been earned on the sale.

Clerks may be accepting customer returns of merchandise that are no longer salable because of damage, stains, or packing defects. Management may be ignoring opportunities to return merchandise to vendors when it arrives in a condition unfit for resale.

Any of these factors can result in inventory shortages. While most businesses take careful steps to guard against theft, relatively few adopt serious procedures for protection from inventory shortages caused by such factors as poor receiving procedures, poor billing procedures, and merchandise damage.

# Chapter Highlights

- The buying cycle consists of determining needs, selecting suppliers, negotiating purchases, and following up after the purchase. Buyers face different problems depending on whether the merchandise bought is primarily staples, or seasonal, style, or perishable items. The goal in each instance is to establish or maintain inventory at the lowest level and

still have a sufficient assortment from which customers can choose.

- The primary factors influencing the level of staples to be purchased include sales trends, profitability on various items, and discounts available. One way to establish buying levels for style and perishable items is to plot the sales of different styles in the past to see how they typically behave and use the resulting information as a guide in future purchasing decisions.

- A variety of factors determine desired inventory levels and when stock should be ordered. Product shelf life may be the determining factor for some items. The length of time between order placement and receipt of goods is also important. Most businesses maintain a safety or cushion stock as a protection against variation in demand and delivery.

- Merchandise suppliers can be identified by using salespeople, trade magazines, business contacts, trade exhibits, and the Yellow Pages. Factors to be considered in determining the best supplier include prices and discounts, quality, reliability, services, and accessibility.

- The physical handling process involves receiving, checking, and marking merchandise. Receiving is that phase of the physical handling process that involves taking possession of the goods and then moving them to the next phase of the process. Checking means matching the store buyer's purchase order with the supplier's invoice, opening the packages and removing the items, sorting them, and comparing the quality and quantity of the shipment with what was ordered. Marking is putting information on the goods or on merchandise containers.

- Successful inventory management requires retailers to maintain an accurate and up-to-date record of sales and stock on hand for every item they sell. A physical inventory should be taken periodically to be sure that the actual quantities on hand equal those shown on the inventory records.

# Key Terms

Blind check    385
Cash datings    382
Cash discount    381
Central buying    376
Checking    384
Committee buying    376
Consignment    376
Direct check    385
Future datings    382
Group buying    376
Lead time    372
Leased departments    377
Marking    385
Merchandise distribution    383
Order ceiling    373

Order interval    373
Order point    372
Physical handling    384
Preretailing    385
Promotional allowance    381
Quantity discount    380
Receiving    384
Retail the invoice    385
Safety stock    372
Seasonal discount    381
Seasonal merchandise    368
Source marking    385
Staple merchandise    368
Trade discount    380

# Discussion Questions

1. Discuss the roles and responsibilities of a buyer.
2. Discuss each element of the buying cycle.
3. Describe the different methods of buying.
4. Explain the types of discounts available to retailers.
5. Explain the types of datings available to retailers.
6. What are the most favourable transportation terms for the retailer? Explain your answer.
7. Explain the two methods of quantity checking.
8. What factors determine the desired inventory level for various types of merchandise?

# Problems

1. A manufacturer of tables offers terms of 2/20, n/60. A furniture store places an order for a dozen tables at $27 each and receives an invoice dated July 2. The invoice is paid August 10. Failure to obtain the discount is equivalent to paying what annual rate of interest? (Use 360 days as a year.)

2. An invoice dated June 5 in the amount of $1,800, with terms of 3/10, n/30 EOM, and a trade discount of 20 percent, arrives with the merchandise on June 8. The invoice is paid July 2. What amount is due the vendor?

3. An invoice dated January 3 in the amount of $12,200, with terms of 2/10, n/30 ROG, and a trade discount of 10, 5, and 2 percent, arrives with the merchandise on January 10. The invoice is paid January 30. What amount is due the vendor?

4. A manufacturer of women's blouses quotes terms of 2/20, n/30, and grants retailers trade discounts of 10 and 5 percent. The list price of a blouse is $140 per dozen. A retailer receives an invoice dated July 7 for eight dozen of these blouses. The invoice is paid July 10. What is *(a)* the net cost per blouse and *(b)* the net amount of the cash discount taken?

5. A manufacturer of women's skirts quotes terms of 2/10, n/30 EOM, and grants retailers trade discounts of 10, 5, and 2 percent. The list price of the skirts is $360 per dozen. A retailer receives an invoice dated September 16 for 10 dozen of these skirts. The invoice is paid October 2. What is the net cost per skirt to the retailer?

# Application Exercises

1. To clarify the relationships between the buyer and the supplier, the text approaches the subject from the retail point of view. It may be valuable to approach the subject from the other point of view. Make contacts with local suppliers (wholesalers, agents, or local manufacturers who sell to retailers), and see what they attempt to do to strengthen relationships with their customers. What problems do they incur in these relationships? What efforts do they make to improve the relationships?

2. Select a product line in which you are particularly interested. Identify merchants in your area who handle this line. Set up interviews after you have devised a questionnaire to determine how important the merchants believe relationships with suppliers are. Administer the questionnaire to the managers of the stores. Attempt to find out how these managers implement their philosophy of relationships with vendors. If you can get measurements of the various stores' success, see whether you can attribute some of that success to the programmes for vendor relationships you discover. This will be a difficult project, but attempting to carry it out will be a beneficial experience, regardless of the outcome.

3. In interviews with retailers with whom you establish good rapport, attempt to find out: *(a)* what special problems have been encountered with vendors; *(b)* what kinds of special concessions are offered to the retailers; *(c)* whether any particular plans have been effective in improving relations; and *(d)* why vendors are dropped.

# Suggested Cases

# Endnotes

1. Ralph D. Skipp, Jr., *Retail Merchandising: Principles and Application* (Boston: Houghton Mifflin, 1976), pp. 12–14.

2. The material on the buying function is based, with modifications, on *Business Basics: Retail Buying Function,* Self-Instructional Booklet No. 1010 (Washington, D.C.: U.S. Small Business Administration); for further reading, see Daniel Bello, "Retailer Buying Strategies at Merchandise Marts," in *1986 American Marketing Association Educators Proceedings,* ed. Terry Shrimp et al. (Chicago: American Marketing Association, 1986), pp. 178–81.

3. Château Stores of Canada, Annual Report, 1992.

4. For more on the pros and cons of group buying, see Kenneth G. Hardy and Allan J. Magrath, "Buying Groups: Clout for Small Businesses," *Harvard Business Review,* September–October 1987, pp. 16–24.

5. Cara Kuryllowricz, "Strength in Numbers," *Retail Directions,* July/August 1989, pp. 29–32.

6. John Heinzl, "What Makes Canadian Prices High?" *Globe and Mail,* May 15, 1992, p. B6.

7. Canadian Tire, Annual Report, 1991.

8. The material on inventory management is based, with modifications, on *Inventory Management Wholesale/Retail,* Self-Instructional Booklet No. 1011 (Washington, D.C.: U.S. Small Business Administration).

# C H A P T E R

# 15 RETAIL PRICING STRATEGY

## Chapter Objectives

After reading this chapter, you should be able to:

1 Explain how external factors affect the setting of retail prices.
2 Describe the store policies that affect pricing decisions.
3 Discuss the kinds of price changes that may be made after the original pricing decision.
4 Understand a simple way to handle the arithmetic of pricing.

## Retailing Capsule

One of the most successful books published in Canada was the first edition of *The Canadian Encyclopedia,* a three volume set that provided comprehensive information on Canada. Mel Hurtig, the owner of Hurtig Publishers, was responsible for this massive work. He began planning for the second edition shortly after the first edition was published in 1985.

The second edition of *The Canadian Encyclopedia* cost $8.5 million to produce, and a sales target of 150,000 copies was set. Approximately $750,000 was spent to advertise and promote the second edition, which was launched in the fall of 1988. The marketing plan was as follows:

- Extensive prepublication promotion to all bookstores in Canada (this activity was started in 1987).
- An introductory retail price of $175, later to increase to $225.
- A rebate to customers who had purchased the first edition. They could trade in the first edition and receive a $50 credit on the second edition, reducing the price to $125.
- Varying discounts to retailers, depending on the volume purchased. Coles, one of the leading book retailers in Canada, ordered 20,000 copies and received a 55 percent discount (Coles' cost was $78.75 per set). Small booksellers who ordered less than five copies received a 30 percent discount (the cost to these retailers was $122.50 per set).

Mel Hurtig had expected that some retailers would offer the book at less than the recommended retail price of $175, but he was not prepared for what happened. Coles deep-discounted the book to $99, a retail price that was less than the small bookstores could buy the book for from Hurtig. W. H. Smith, another large chain, quickly followed suit, and the result was the two chains sold a large number of copies of *The Canadian Encyclopedia* during the Christmas season and also brought extra traffic into their stores.

However, the small independent bookstores were extremely angry and began returning their copies to Hurtig. All told, Mr. Hurtig estimated that the returns from the small booksellers cost the company $475,000. The book was still profitable but less so than expected. Since that time, Mel Hurtig went on to publish *The Junior Encyclopedia of Canada,* but only 30,000 copies of the 100,000 printed were sold. In 1991, due to a number of factors, his publishing company was sold to another Canadian publisher.

Setting retail prices is an important issue, where the actions of the manufacturer and competitive retailers must be considered. For Mel Hurtig, there were long-term consequences to short-term actions.

*(continued on next page)*

*Retailing Capsule continued*

*Pricing the new* Canadian Encyclopedia *proved to be a difficult task.*

SOURCE: Photo by James Hertel.

Sources: Tamsim Carlisle, ''Hurtig Unbowed by Discount Damage,'' *The Financial Post Daily,* September 24, 1988, p. 6; William French, ''Shock Waves Continue after Coles Prices Cuts,'' *Globe and Mail,* November 8, 1988, p. A23; Diana Shepard, ''A Million-Dollar Promotion and Satisfaction Guaranteed,'' *Quill and Quire,* July 1987, p. 48; Diana Shepard, ''Coles Discounting Shocks Industry,'' *Quill and Quire,* November 1988, p. 4; and Mel Hurtig, ''Deep Discounting: Learning Lessons the Hard Way,'' *Quill and Quire,* November 1988, p. 30.

The difficulties experienced by Mel Hurtig illustrate the critical importance of price in retailing strategy. Pricing decisions must be compatible with the overall marketing strategy of the firm.

Discussions of retail price often centre on the techniques for establishing prices, the legal constraints on price, and the meaning of psychological pricing, at-the-market pricing, and similar terms. Strategic issues, however, are of equal importance, because pricing is part of the retailing mix available to management. Pricing can also be of strategic importance in deciding how to compete. For example, target goals can be achieved through both margin and turnover management. Competitive strategy thus guides the establishment of overall price policies for the firm.

Pricing is clearly the most visible result of planning, at least from the customer's viewpoint. Also, pricing strongly influences the image of the retail outlet. Consumers can readily understand the merchandising strategy of Zellers, with its slogan, "The Lowest Price Is the Law."

A retail pricing plan should start from explicitly defined objectives. For example, management must decide whether financial goals will be achieved by higher margins on merchandise and thus perhaps lower turnover, or lower margins and higher turnover. Various trade-offs are in order in such decisions. For example, if management's objectives are short-run profit maximization, pricing should maximize cash flow. A policy of strengthening market position, on the other hand, probably would call for prices that were not above those of the market leader.

The absence of a distinct pricing policy often reflects a lack of strategic focus. For example, traditional department stores are being squeezed from both above and below their traditional market segments. They are being squeezed by discount chains such as Zellers and by specialty chains such as Fairweather and Reitmans. In response, Eaton's has emphasized its everyday prices to be as good as or better than its competitors'—including their sale prices. Eaton's uses the slogan "Why Wait For Sales" to focus on its competitive prices.

## Factors Affecting Retail Pricing

In setting the right price, the retailer must first consider those factors that affect the pricing decision. The retailer may not have set up these conditions—they may be the result of things the retailer or manager did in the past. But at the time of pricing, the factors still exist.

Such factors include (1) type of goods carried, (2) store image, (3) level of profit desired, (4) level of customer demand, (5) level of competition, (6) supplier policies, (7) economic conditions, and (8) government regulations.

### *Type of Goods*

Pricing decisions depend on whether the products offered by the retailer are primarily convenience, shopping, or specialty goods.

- If products are viewed by consumers as convenience goods, prices are usually about the same in all stores. Consumers do not feel it is worth their time to shop around for a better price (or quality) for convenience goods since the savings are likely not to be worth the extra effort of comparison shopping. The retailer has only a little latitude in the pricing of these goods.

- A retailer has more leeway in setting prices for shopping goods. These are items consumers carefully compare for price and quality differences before making a purchase decision.
- The retailer has the greatest latitude in pricing specialty goods. Specialty items are products consumers know they want and are willing to make an effort to acquire, and price is not particularly important.

One retailer who is attempting to move shopping goods to specialty goods in the eyes of its customers is Pennington's. This retailer, with over 160 Pennington's and Liz Porter stores in Canada, targets larger-sized women with fashion merchandise that is styled for their special needs. By offering unique fashions that are targeted to a particular segment, Pennington's is seeking to create specialty items, where price is less important than the product or service to the customer.[1]

### Store Image

Retailers must be familiar with their customers if they want to achieve profitable pricing. Customers may come to a store because of its quality image or because of its reputation for low prices. In the quality stores, customers expect to pay more but also expect more service and a better environment (atmosphere). These extras cost money, and prices must cover them. The retailer's value equation in this context (''what I pay for what I get'') must not be out of balance. The retailer cannot survive for long by charging high prices but offering lower-quality merchandise and mediocre service in an unimaginative atmosphere.

### Profit Desired

Prices must be high enough to cover *all* costs of doing business. This includes the original cost of the goods plus the expenses of doing business. Prices also must provide the level of profit the retailer wishes to earn. (This point is discussed further in the section The Arithmetic of Retail Pricing.) High prices do not necessarily mean high profits because the firm may have a high overhead or may have to discount merchandise to sell it.

### Customer Demand

Retailers must consider consumer reactions to different prices. In general, consumers will purchase more of a product at a lower price than at a higher price. Thus, the retailer needs to understand the effects of different price levels on consumer demand. Known as **price elasticity,** or the elasticity of demand, it is the ratio of the percentage change in the quantity demanded to a percentage change in price:

$$\text{Price elasticity} = \frac{\text{Percent change in quantity demanded}}{\text{Percent change in price}}$$

Elastic demand is a situation where the change in price strongly influences the quantity demanded (consumers are sensitive to price changes). For example,

*Liz Porter offers
unique fashions
targeted to specific
segments.*

SOURCE: Courtesy Pennington's.

demand for many convenience products like soap and toothpaste is elastic; consumers will stock up on these items at a lower price. Inelastic demand is a situation where the change in price has little influence on the quantity demanded (consumers are relatively insensitive to price changes). For example, total demand for gasoline tends to be inelastic because consumers typically do not increase or decrease their driving if the price of gasoline decreases or increases. Retailers should understand which products are sensitive, or not, to price changes (Retail Highlight 15–1).

***Level of
Competition***

The degree of competition in the market will greatly affect pricing decisions. If little competition exists, pricing decisions are easier than if there is a great deal of competition. For example, a retailer with an "exclusive" on a brand in a market can probably price with greater freedom.

In addition, competitors' actions in the pricing area must be monitored. A good retailer is aware of prices being charged by competitive outlets. A word of caution is in order, however. To focus too much on the competition means you're relying on them to do their marketing job right.

When competition is severe, retailers must run efficient operations, as their prices need to reflect the competitive nature of the market. The entry of the giant U.S. warehouse clubs, Price Club and Costco, to the Canadian market created tremendous competition in the grocery trade and the home improvement business. In its first year in Canada, Price Club generated sales of over $1 billion with its

---

**Retail Highlight 15–1**

---

# Sam Walton on Price Elasticity

Sam Walton, called America's most successful merchant, built the Wal-Mart chain into a retail dynasty, based on a number of simple but powerful concepts such as price elasticity. In his own words, talking about his early days in retailing: "Here's the simple lesson we learned—which others were learning at the same time and which eventually changed the way retailers sell and customers buy all across America. Say I bought an item for 80 cents. I found that by pricing it at a dollar I could sell three times more of it than by pricing it at $1.20. I might have made only half the profit per item, but because I was selling three times as many, the overall profit was much greater."

Source: "Sam Walton in His Own Words," *Fortune,* June 29, 1992, p. 100.

---

no-frills warehouse stores. Canadian supermarket chains have responded by opening up their own warehouse-type outlets (Loblaws), matching Price Club's prices (Loeb, IGA), and modifying the merchandise selection in existing outlets (Oshawa Group).[2] It has been predicted that some supermarket chains will not survive in this highly competitive environment.[3]

**Supplier Policies**

Suppliers will often suggest prices to retailers. If the retailer depends heavily on a particular supplier, then the supplier may have some influence over price decisions. However, as noted in Chapter 3, the Competition Act prohibits suppliers from requiring retailers to offer products at stipulated prices.

**Economic Conditions**

Retailers must be conscious of economic conditions and their impact on pricing decisions. During periods of inflation, increases in prices are expected (though not welcomed) by consumers. In times of recession, as Canada experienced in the early 1990s, prices often go down. For example, during 1992, the consumer price index increased by only 1 percent, one of the lowest increases in 30 years. Prices of many grocery products actually decreased during that period. Part of the decrease was due to the extensive price-cutting that many retailers were using just to remain in business or to meet competitive prices (see Retail Highlight 15–2).

In addition, the retailer must be aware of any voluntary or required governmental price controls that can limit price decisions. Clearly, changing and uncertain economic conditions make pricing complex.

**Government Regulations**

Retailers are restricted from certain kinds of pricing actions, most of which are covered by the federal Competition Act. Chapter 3 presented a full discussion of the legal impacts on pricing.

**Retail Highlight 15–2**

# The Pressure on Retail Prices

During the early 1990s, a number of factors led to what retail analysts are calling a "revolution" in Canadian retailing. Consider the following:

- Canadians are becoming more price-conscious, due in part to the recession.
- The Free Trade Agreement is forcing Canadian manufacturers to meet a continental price or perish. Canadian manufacturers have become more competitive, and Canadian retailers are reaping the benefits through lower prices.
- Cross-border shopping, diverting up to $10 billion away from Canadian retailers, has forced them to use aggressive price-cutting to regain this lost business.
- New, low-cost retail formats like Aikenhead's, Toys Я Us, Price Club, and factory outlets are very popular with consumers.

Analysts are predicting that to survive, retailers, particularly Canada's major department store chains, will have to operate on permanently lower margins. Future success will depend on better inventory controls, lower operating costs, and more focused merchandising strategies. One analyst noted that traditional department store chains have typically operated with a 40 percent gross margin on sales. Mass merchandisers like Zellers and Kmart operate in the 33 to 36 percent range, and supermarkets are between 20 and 25 percent. But warehouse-type stores have gross margins of 20 percent and Price Club has 12 percent. That's the competition.

Source: Giles Gherson, "Now the Good News: Much Lower Retail Prices," *Financial Times,* August 3, 1992, pp. 1, 4.

One government regulation that had a major impact on retailers was the federal government's introduction of the Goods and Services Tax (GST) in January 1991. The GST, at 7 percent, coupled with the recession, dealt a heavy blow to Canadian retailers. Total retail sales declined dramatically in the first three months after the introduction of the GST. A number of retailers also felt that the GST led to the significant increase in cross-border shopping.

Retailers faced an interesting pricing decision when the GST was introduced. Should they include the GST in their price or add it on at the cash register? While most retailers decided to add it on at the cash register, some, like Woolco, included it in their price and advertised their prices as "GST included."

The factors discussed thus far affect the pricing decision but are factors over which the retailer has little—and in some cases no—control. The following section focuses on store factors that impact the retailer's pricing decisions. These are store policies (guidelines for action) that management supports and that can be adjusted.

## Store Policies Affecting Retail Pricing

Retailers must make decisions regarding their pricing policy in terms of (1) the desired price level, (2) price flexibility, (3) private-brand and generic merchandise, (4) customer psychology, (5) trade-in allowances, (6) price lining and single-price policy, and (7) leader pricing.

*Price-Level Policy*

The pricing decision is affected by the retailer's policy on the price level desired. The three choices are: (1) **at the market pricing,** (2) **below the competition pricing,** and (3) **above the competition pricing.**

### Pricing at the Market Level

Most retailers are competitive pricers. The prices they offer are roughly the same as their competitors. When following such a policy, the retailer tries to make the store different in ways other than price. This is called *nonprice competition.* Supermarkets, for example, try to be competitive on prices with other supermarkets and the warehouse outlets. But they may try to make themselves different, particularly against the warehouse outlets, by carrying more brands, carrying higher-quality private brands, having a better produce section, and offering different services.

A department store such as Eaton's is typically a competitive, at-the-market pricer. Management attempts to meet discount store prices on identical merchandise. However, extra services may be offered by the department store that the discount store does not offer—for example, clothing alterations or delivery. If alterations or delivery are offered, then the department store will charge for these extra services, and the total product price may be higher.

When a retailer like Eaton's adopts an everyday low-pricing strategy, it can benefit if it gains the trust of consumers who believe that the store does offer competitive prices. However, to gain this trust, the merchant must have competitive prices on merchandise that customers can compare with those of the competition. If retailers advertise a low-pricing strategy but have higher prices than the competition, the consumer's trust is lost.

### Pricing below the Competition

Off-price retailers, warehouse giants such as Price Club and Loblaws' No Frills, or other low-margin, high-turnover retailers, typically price below the competition. Since this pricing strategy reduces the profit margin per sale, a firm needs to increase its sales and reduce costs by:

1. Obtaining the best prices possible for the merchandise.
2. Locating the business in an inexpensive location or facility.
3. Closely controlling inventory.
4. Limiting the lines to fast-moving items.
5. Designing advertising to concentrate on price specials.
6. Offering no or limited services.

Below-competition pricing is a difficult pricing policy to carry out and maintain because every cost component must constantly be monitored and consistently

*Loblaws' No Frills warehouse stores typically price below the competition.*

SOURCE: Courtesy of Loblaws Supermarkets Limited.

adjusted. It also exposes firms to pricing wars, as grocery retailers in Canada have experienced. The consequences are better prices for consumers but retail casualties.

One firm that competes primarily on a price basis is Zellers. While Zellers has Club Z, a customer loyalty programme in which members collect points based on purchases that can be redeemed for merchandise, its main strategy is to emphasize price—and it does so by spending over \$20 million annually on television advertising and sending out over 6 million weekly circulars to more than half the households in Canada. [4] During the recession in the early 1990s, Zellers' sales and operating profit increased.

### Pricing above the Competition

Some firms can price above the competition for a number of reasons: (1) they carry unique (exclusive) merchandise; (2) they cater to customers who are not price-conscious and want the highest quality and/or style goods; (3) they offer convenience of location and time (convenience stores); (4) they provide many unusual services; (5) they take greater risks on credit terms; or (6) they have a prestige image customers are willing to pay for. Birks, the jewellery retailer, is an example of a merchant with above the competition pricing.

*One-Price versus Variable-Price Policy*

The majority of retail firms in Canada offer goods at one take-it-or-leave-it price. Bargaining with customers is unusual. In other countries, such as Mexico and Italy, varying prices with "haggling" is expected. In Canada, some stores selling big-ticket items such as automobiles, appliances, and furniture do not follow a one-price policy. Bargaining occurs over the price paid for the product. If this practice is usual and expected, consumers may form a negative view of retailers who do not engage in this bargaining process. However, many consumers appear to favour one price when it comes to buying automobiles (see Retail Highlight 15–3).

Certain advantages exist in a store with a one-price policy. Customers do not expect to bargain, so salespersons and customers save time. Salespeople are not under pressure to reduce prices. Of course, self-service would not work where there is bargaining.

Retailers can follow a variable price policy even when they do not negotiate with consumers on the price itself. Negotiating over whether to charge for delivery and installation, and varying the price of warranties, can all result in a variable price policy.

*Private-Brand Policy*

Many retailers such as Sears, Eaton's, Canadian Tire, The Bay, and Loblaws have their own private brands. Private brands (often called distributor brands) are owned by the retail firm, whereas national brands are owned by manufacturers. A private brand may be carried only by the owner or someone the owner allows. A manufacturer's brand may be carried by anyone who buys from the manufacturer of the brand. President's Choice is a private brand of coffee owned by Loblaws. Maxwell House is a manufacturer's brand owned by General Foods.

*Exclusive merchandise allows the opportunity to price above the competition.*

SOURCE: Photo by Betty McDougall.

If private brands are featured, the retailer may offer them at below the prices charged for national brands and still make a good profit. This is possible because the retailer can pay less for the private-brand merchandise than for a comparable manufacturer's brand. Consequently, the merchant has more freedom in pricing private-brand items.

---

**Retail Highlight 15–3**

---

# Car Buyers Favour No-Dicker Prices

Norman Hébert, Jr., president of the Park Avenue Group of automobile dealerships in Montreal, has put an end to bargaining over prices for his cars. Go into any of his six outlets and the price that hangs on a tag on the rear-view mirror is the price you, or anyone else, will pay. Mr. Hébert is picking up on a trend that is sweeping the United States—the switch to no-dicker sticker prices.

The idea is to offer "fair but equitable" prices. The prices are slightly below market, but the drop in margins is compensated for by the increase in volume. While one-price selling may not be the answer for everyone, it is working for Mr. Hébert:

- Customers in after-sale interviews have given it a 95 percent favourable rating.

- The percentage of shoppers who come back for a second visit has risen to 30 percent from 20 percent. As a rule of thumb, two thirds of those who visit a second time become buyers.

Retail experts feel that everyday low and honest pricing is the right spot to be in for the 1990s. They point out that consumers want to believe they are going to get the best price without having to spend three or four hours in a showroom haggling. While no one is certain if the trend will last, a one-price policy is being favourably received by many car buyers.

Source: Timothy Pritchard, "Car Buyers Favour No-Dicker Prices," *Globe and Mail*, June 8, 1992, pp. B1, B4.

---

Department stores, grocery chains, and some specialty retailers are increasingly turning to private-brand merchandise as a source of competitive advantage, especially in the face of the challenges posed by off-price retailers. Private brands such as Mastercraft at Canadian Tire and President's Choice at Loblaws are not subject to the price-cutting that may occur with national brands.

*Generic Merchandise Policy*

The question of generic merchandise and pricing is important. For example, if a supermarket offers generic paper products, the identification might read *paper napkins*. Customers may be willing to accept lower quality in some types of goods in return for lower prices. They rely on the reputation of the store and figure, "If my supermarket has generics for sale, they must be OK for the price." More profits may be made on generics than on private brands, even though generics are priced lower. Generics are strongest in low-involvement merchandise such as paper products and other staples.

Loblaws pioneered no-name generic brands in Canada in 1978 and, at one time during the early 1980s, offered 1,500 no-name products. As the Canadian economy improved in the mid 1980s, consumers began switching back to brand names. Then Loblaws began introducing its own private label, President's Choice, in many product categories. As the economy declined in 1990, Loblaws began to reemphasize its generic no-name products and introduced Club Pack, products at reduced prices for large sizes. During 1991, at the height of the recession, sales of generics surged and represented almost 50 percent of Loblaws' private-brand sales. This private-brand strategy offers four potential benefits for Loblaws: (1) to meet price-cutting with no-name and Club Pack; (2) to avoid the price-cutting that often occurs with national brands with President's Choice; (3) to position Loblaws as a store that offers consumers more variety (no-name, Club Pack, President's Choice, Green); and (4) to gain greater control over distribution by selling more retailer brands (both private and generic).

## *Psychological Pricing*

A retailer can price merchandise too low. A blouse might not sell at $20, but marked up to $27, it might. The reason for this phenomenon is that, for some goods, customers believe that price reflects quality (or value).[5] This situation may occur when the consumer has difficulty judging the quality of the product (e.g., fashion merchandise).

Odd price endings are believed by many to have psychological value. Odd endings ($10.98 instead of $11.00) seem lower than even-ending prices. Some retailers, however, prefer the even endings, wanting the extra markup, even if it is only a few pennies. Many transactions of a few cents can be important over time.

## *Trade-In Allowance Policy*

Trade-in allowances are similar to varying price policies discussed earlier. In certain merchandise lines (e.g., automobiles, tires, and batteries), customers expect trade-ins. If the customers are good bargainers, the retailer may actually take a lower price than desired. Thus, retailers who have a trade-in policy should plan their original prices very carefully.

## *Price-Lining Policy*

Retailers practising **price lining** feature products at a limited number of prices, reflecting varying merchandise quality. A price-lining strategy can be implemented either in the context of rigid **price points** or by the use of **price zones.** Using suits as an example, the merchant might establish a limited number of price points to indicate quality difference between merchandise. The "good" suits might be priced at $175, the "better" suits at $225, and the "best" suits at $300. Alternatively, the retailer may decide to use price zones instead of rigid price points. For example, prices for good suits might fall between $175 and $200.

Price lining offers certain advantages. For example, some customers become confused and cannot make up their minds when they see too many prices. Price lining makes shopping easier for consumers, since there are fewer prices to consider. The merchant can offer a greater assortment of depth and width with fewer price points. In addition, inventories can be controlled more easily.

With price lining, the salesperson can more easily become familiar with the merchandise. And it is much easier to explain differences between the merchandise when it is carefully planned and priced to show differences. In addition, the retail buyer may reduce the number of suppliers needed to provide merchandise in specific retail price ranges.

Certain disadvantages do exist in price lining. The retailer may feel hemmed in by the price line and lose some flexibility. Also, selection may be limited. If wholesale prices rise and fall rapidly, it may be difficult to maintain rigid price points. This is a reason for the use of price zones.

*Single-Price Policy*

Small specialty stores may have **single-price policies.** A "$10.00 tie store" or a "$24.95 budget dress store" are such examples. Clearly, with this policy, the variety of offerings is limited. Also, fewer assortments are possible. The real strength of this policy is being able to target a specific customer group. These customers know what to expect in the store.

Recently, stores have appeared where every product in the store is sold for $1 or $2. Appealing to price-conscious consumers during difficult economic times, retailers like Buck or Two Stores and Dollar Bill are among Canada's fastest-growing retailers. Offering thousands of items like health and beauty-care products, candy, toys, stationery, cleaning supplies, and kitchen gadgets, these new single-price stores have total sales estimated at over $250 million annually.[6]

*Leader-Pricing Policy*

Some retailers use leader pricing with selected product categories. A less-than-normal markup or margin on an item is taken to increase store traffic. Some call this **loss-leader pricing.** The loss implies loss of the normal amount of markup or margin.

In using leader pricing, the retailer is trying to attract customers to the store who will also purchase items carrying normal profit margins. If customers only buy the leaders (called *cherry picking*), the retailer is in trouble. Retailers often limit the quantity of leader items that can be bought at one time.

Supermarkets and mass merchandisers often use loss leaders. Typically, however, leader pricing does not occur for all items. The best price leaders are items that are (1) well-known and widely used, (2) priced low enough to attract numerous buyers, and (3) not usually bought in large quantities and stored. Grocery items that have proved to be good leaders are coffee, toilet tissue, and dishwashing liquid.

# Pricing Adjustments

In practice, retailers may raise or lower prices after the original pricing decisions have been made. These pricing adjustments may be (1) additional markups (markons) or (2) markdowns.

*Additional Markups*

In inflationary periods, additional markups may be needed. Such adjustments are made when the retailer's costs are increasing.

*Markdowns*

A **markdown** is a reduction in the original selling price of an item. Most retailers take some markdowns, since this is the most widely used way of moving items that do not sell at the original price. Other things a retailer might do instead of taking a markdown are to (1) give additional promotion, better display, or a more visible store position to an item; (2) store the item until the next selling season; (3) mark the item up (discussed in Psychological Pricing); or (4) give the goods to charity.

One of the most famous retail department store organizations in the United States is Filene's Basement in Boston. This firm made its name through its widely known ''automatic markdown policy.'' The policy operates as follows: When an item has been in the store for 12 days, it is marked down to 75 percent of list; after 6 more days, it is reduced to 50 percent; when 6 more days pass, it is reduced to 25 percent; and after 30 days, it is given to charity. Very little merchandise is given to charity.

*Markdowns can create activity.*

Source: Photo by James Hertel.

Markdowns are also used for promotional reasons. The goods may not be slow moving, but markdowns create more activity. The next sections of this chapter present illustrations of how smart merchants *plan* certain amounts of markdowns in order to protect profits.

Markdowns should be handled with care. If an item is marked down too often, the customer may come to view the markdown as the "normal" price and will not buy the item at the "regular" price. Consumers normally do not expect large markdowns on luxury items. Customers may question product quality if prices are slashed too much. Seasonal, perishable, and obsolete stock are exceptions. Further, excessive markdowns should be avoided. If markdowns are too high, the retailer should find out the need for such markdowns. The causes can come from buying, selling, or pricing errors. A plan should be worked out to correct the errors once they have been determined.

## The Arithmetic of Retail Pricing

This section presents a simple plan to help you understand the arithmetic of pricing. Every retailer is faced with pricing issues. Even though retailers may use crutches such as markup equivalent tables (see Table 15–1), it is important to understand the relationships discussed here.

### Concepts of Retail Price

Price can be looked at as shown in Table 15–2. The **original retail price** ($1,020 in Table 15–2) is the first price at which an item (or a group of items) is offered for sale. The **sales retail price** ($1,000) is the final selling price, the amount the customer paid. Before the item was sold, a reduction or markdown ($20) occurred. (In a classification of merchandise, reductions also include employee discounts and shortages or shrinkage. See the section Reductions Planning in Chapter 13 for a review of these concepts.)

### Concepts of Markup

The figures in Table 15–3 show the various ways to look at markup. **Initial markup** is the difference between the cost of the merchandise and the original retail price ($1,020 − $800 = $220). Initial markup as a percentage of the original retail price is 21.6 percent ($220/$1,020). The concept of initial markup is used when planning a total classification or department (as discussed in Chapter 13).

**Maintained markup,** shown in Table 15–4, is the difference between invoice cost and sales retail price ($1,000 − $800 = $200). In percentage terms, maintained markup is related to sales retail ($200/$1,000 = 20 percent).

Maintained markup covers operating expenses and provides the retailer with a profit. Maintained markup and initial markup differ by the $20 reduction. For purposes of the present discussion, maintained markup can be considered the same as gross margin.

### Planning Required Initial Markup

Initial goals for margins are essential, as are plans for sales and reductions. Assume that management has forecast sales of a merchandise line at $100,000, no

## TABLE 15–1    Markup Table

To use this table, find the desired percentage in the left-hand column. Multiply the cost of the article by the corresponding percentage in the Markup Percent of Cost column. The result, added to the cost, gives the correct selling price.

| Markup Percent of Retail Price | Markup Percent of Cost | Markup Percent of Retail Price | Markup Percent of Cost | Markup Percent of Retail Price | Markup Percent of Cost |
|---|---|---|---|---|---|
| 4.8 | 5.0 | 18.5 | 22.7 | 33.3 | 50.0 |
| 5.0 | 5.3 | 19.0 | 23.5 | 34.0 | 51.5 |
| 6.0 | 6.4 | 20.0 | 25.0 | 35.0 | 53.9 |
| 7.0 | 7.5 | 21.0 | 26.6 | 35.5 | 55.0 |
| 8.0 | 8.7 | 22.0 | 28.2 | 36.0 | 56.3 |
| 9.0 | 10.0 | 22.5 | 29.0 | 37.0 | 58.8 |
| 10.0 | 11.1 | 23.0 | 29.9 | 37.5 | 60.0 |
| 10.7 | 12.0 | 23.1 | 30.0 | 38.0 | 61.3 |
| 11.0 | 12.4 | 24.0 | 31.6 | 39.0 | 64.0 |
| 11.1 | 12.5 | 25.0 | 33.0 | 39.5 | 64.0 |
| 12.0 | 13.6 | 26.0 | 35.0 | 40.0 | 66.7 |
| 12.5 | 14.3 | 27.0 | 37.0 | 41.0 | 70.0 |
| 13.0 | 15.0 | 27.3 | 37.5 | 42.0 | 72.4 |
| 14.0 | 16.3 | 28.0 | 39.0 | 42.8 | 75.0 |
| 15.0 | 17.7 | 28.5 | 40.0 | 44.4 | 80.0 |
| 16.0 | 19.1 | 29.0 | 40.9 | 46.1 | 85.0 |
| 16.7 | 20.0 | 30.0 | 42.9 | 47.5 | 90.0 |
| 17.0 | 20.5 | 31.0 | 45.0 | 48.7 | 95.0 |
| 17.5 | 21.2 | 32.0 | 47.1 | 50.0 | 100.0 |
| 18.0 | 22.0 | | | | |

SOURCE: *Expenses in Retail Business,* a publication of NCR Corporation, Dayton, Ohio.

## TABLE 15–2    The Concept of Sales Retail

| | |
|---|---|
| Original retail price | $1,020 |
| Less reductions | 20 |
| Sales retail price | $1,000 |

## TABLE 15–3    The Concept of Initial Markup

| | |
|---|---|
| Original retail price | $1,020 |
| Less invoice cost | 800 |
| Initial markup | $ 220 |

## TABLE 15–4    The Concept of Maintained Markup

| | |
|---|---|
| Original retail price | $1,020 |
| Less planned reductions | 20 |
| Sales retail price | 1,000 |
| Less invoice cost | 800 |
| Maintained markup | $ 200 |

reductions, expenses of $15,000, and a profit return of 5 percent of sales, or $5,000. The result is maintained markup of $20,000, or 20 percent. On the other hand, assume that management expects reductions such as markdowns and employee discounts to be 2 percent of sales, or $2,000. A planned initial markup of $22,000, or 21.6 percent ($22,000/$102,000), is necessary to maintain a markup of $20,000, or 20 percent (20,000/$100,000). This type of planning requires management to consider all elements that can affect profit. For the formula-oriented, the relationships discussed above can be shown as:

$$\text{Initial markup percentage} = \frac{\text{Expenses} + \text{Profit} + \text{Reductions}}{\text{Sales retail price} + \text{Reductions}}$$

$$\text{Maintained markup percentage} = \frac{\text{Expenses} + \text{Profit}}{\text{Sales retail price}}$$

A retailer cannot expect to have a uniform initial markup policy. That kind of policy would suggest that every item brought into a department will carry the same initial markup. Too many external factors and store policies exist for a uniform markup to make sense, as noted in the first part of this chapter. As one example, retailers should consider consumers' sensitivity to prices (price elasticity of demand) when setting markups. When consumers are very sensitive to price, retailers should consider lower markups. When consumers are less sensitive to price, retailers should consider higher markups.

The planned initial markup figure becomes a good check. Actual performance in markup during an operating period can be checked against what has been planned.

### Computations

Every merchandiser needs practice in computing some routine relationships among cost, initial markup, and original retail price. There is no need to memorize formulas, though we will present formulas for readers who like them. Simply remember that *Cost + Initial markup = Original retail price*.

***Given Cost and Retail.***    A colour television costs the retailer $500. The original price charged is $800. What is the initial markup in dollars and percent computed on both cost and retail bases?

The difference between retail and cost is $300 ($800 − $500). Based on cost, the markup would be $300/$500 = 60 percent. Based on retail, the markup is 37.5 percent ($300/$800). Remember that markup percentage on cost = $ markup/ $ cost, and markup percentage on retail = $ markup/$ retail.

***Conversion of Markup on Retail to Markup on Cost.***    In working with pricing, the buyer is often confronted with the problem of converting a markup on retail to a markup on cost. If the buyer thinks in terms of cost and the vendor quotes in terms of retail price, the buyer needs to know how to make the switch. As noted earlier, conversion tables do exist (see Table 15–1).

Assume that a supplier quotes an initial markup of 42 percent on retail. What is the same markup on cost? The formula is shown below:

$$\text{Markup percentage on cost} = \frac{\text{Markup percentage on retail}}{100 \text{ percent} - \text{Markup percentage on retail}}$$

If the retail markup is 42 percent, then retail is 100 percent and cost must be 58 percent. So, markup as a percentage of cost is .42/.58 = .72, or 72 percent. In other words, 42 percent markup on retail is the same as 72 percent on cost. Clearly, markup on cost will always be larger than markup on retail because the cost base is smaller than the retail base.

***Conversion of Markup on Cost to Markup on Retail.***    Suppose a vendor quotes an initial markup of 60 percent on cost. What is the equivalent markup on retail? Use the following formula:

$$\text{Markup percentage on retail} = \frac{\text{Markup percentage on cost}}{100 \text{ percent } + \text{ Markup percentage on cost}}$$

If the cost markup is 60 percent, then cost must be 100 percent, and retail has to be 160 percent. So, markup on retail base is .60/1.60 = 37.5 percent. Or, 60 percent markup on cost is the same as 37.5 percent on retail.

***Other Relationships.***    The following examples and results provide additional types of relationships the merchant will face.

1. A chair costs a retailer $420. If a markup of 40 percent of retail is desired, what should the retail price be? If 60 percent = $420, then 100 percent = 420/.60, or $700, the retail price needed to achieve the desired markup of 40 percent on retail.

    *Formula:* Whenever the retail price is to be calculated and the dollar cost and markup percentage on retail are known, the problem can be solved with the following:

$$\$ \text{ Retail} = \frac{\$ \text{ Cost}}{100 \text{ percent } - \text{ Markup percentage on retail}}$$

2. A dryer retails for $300. The markup is 28 percent of cost. What was the cost of the dryer? If 128 percent = $300, then 100 percent = $300/1.28, or $234.37, the cost that is needed to achieve the desired markup of 28 percent on cost.

    *Formula:* Whenever the cost price is to be calculated and the dollar retail and markup percentage on cost are known, the problem can be solved as follows:

$$\$ \text{ Cost} = \frac{\$ \text{ Retail}}{100 \text{ percent } + \text{ Markup percentage on cost}}$$

3. A retailer prices a sport jacket so that the markup amounts to $36. This is 45 percent of retail. What are the cost and retail figures? If 45 percent = $36, then 100 percent = $36/.45, or $80. If retail is $80 and markup is $36, then cost is $80 − $36 = $44.

*Formula:* Whenever the dollar markup and the markup percentage on retail are known, the retail price can be determined as follows:

$$\$ \text{ Retail} = \frac{\$ \text{ Retail markup}}{\text{Markup percentage on retail}}$$

## Other Factors Affecting Retail Prices

Other factors can affect pricing decisions, in addition to those discussed earlier.

### Distributor Allowances

A television manufacturer such as RCA may give special promotional allowances to distributors to help expand the sales of its television sets. Similarly, these **distributor allowances** became widespread when the stereo equipment business entered the maturity stage of its life cycle in the late 1970s. A shakeout occurred as the manufacturers battled to maintain market share by offering distributor discounts and extended payment plans to encourage dealers to buy more stock. These situations allow retailers to lower prices to stimulate sales.

### Consumer Rebates

**Consumer rebates** are a common practice when manufacturers want to increase the sale of slow-moving merchandise. Rebates are a financial transaction by the manufacturer with the consumer and are separate from the original purchase. Rebates of $400 to $1,000 on some automobiles have been common in recent years. Technically, rebates do not affect the initial retail markup since they are given by the manufacturer. However, retailers may also lower their markup to further stimulate sales. Rebates, if sizable, are often accepted as a down payment by retailers on the item to be purchased.

### Consumer Pressures

Consumer pressures for unit pricing, individual item pricing, and similar consumer shopping aids also affect pricing practices at the retail level. For example, some provinces now require retailers to price-mark each item instead of marking only the shelf. Such a requirement adds to the retailers' cost structure. This situation has occurred because of scanning technology that allows retailers to "read" the price from universal product codes instead of manually entering the price into the cash register. Similarly, activist consumer groups often publish market basket prices of competing stores, especially for food, in efforts to force down prices.

### Consumer Price Perceptions

Consumer price perceptions include price knowledge, the importance of price, and the sensitivity to discounts.

#### Price Knowledge
Consumers' responses to price levels and price changes can also influence what is bought. Consumers seldom have a high level of absolute price knowledge.

Consumer price perceptions tend to be imprecise about exact amounts, though reliable within well-defined ranges. Similarly, price-conscious shoppers perceive prices more accurately than less price-conscious shoppers. The number of stores shopped and frequency of shopping trips also affect price-perception accuracy.

### The Importance of Price

Not surprisingly, prices are often not as important to the nondiscount shopper as to the discount shopper. Thus, management can appeal either to the discount shopper with low prices or to the nondiscount shopper through service-related store attributes.

Consumers have ranges of acceptable prices for products: Prices outside the acceptable range—whether too low or too high —are objectionable. Demand provides not only an upper constraint on pricing decisions—pricing at what the market will bear—but also a lower constraint. Cost-plus pricing may thus lead to a pricing error even if the price satisfies the cost and competition requirements. Optional price ranges are a function of market demand. Below certain price points, which vary widely from category to category, there is no elasticity of demand. Lowering prices further does not have the classic effect of adding sales.

Research has shown that when buyers are given a range of prices, they are likely to choose the middle-priced item. Retailers thus can influence the choice of products that are perceived as middle prices. In particular, retailers who use price lists or price catalogs can influence the price perceptions of consumers this way.

In judging prices, customers who find it difficult to compare the prices of individual items generalize from the overall price image of a store. Price images tend to be relatively stable, even in the face of special promotions. Management should thus consider not only the pricing of individual items but also the need for a favourable overall price image. A store may not need to place low prices on every item to have a low-price image; only certain key items need to be priced lower than expected.

### Sensitivity to Discounts

Retailers need to understand consumer sensitivity to price discounts: A price discount of less than 10 percent appears to have only a limited effect on consumer response. One study of Canadian consumers' reactions to retail price-offs found that consumers thought the "best deal in town" was more likely when substantial savings were announced (for example, 50 percent off), and depended on the particular store doing the advertising (for example, a discount store).[7]

Price discounts are also used to generate store traffic. Studies have shown that retail price promotions are effective in increasing the sales of complementary products.[8] Through the use of scanner data, retailers are gaining a better understanding of the impact of price promotions on sales of product lines within the store and store profitability.[9]

## *Variations in the Service Mix*

Increasingly, retailers are competing in certain lines of business on a price and nonprice basis at the same time. For example, some gasoline service stations have full-service pumps that sell gasoline for about 1 cent per litre more than other gasoline stations in the same chain that have self-service pumps. Some furniture outlets are also following a similar approach by charging for delivery and installation.

*Cash Discounts*

Cash discounts can be profitable if retailers have (1) a high proportion of credit sales, (2) a high proportion of credit customers who are willing to pay by cash or cheque as a result of a discount, and (3) large-ticket items or large-volume purchases.

A variation of cash discounts is offered by Canadian Tire. If customers pay cash or use a Canadian Tire credit card for payment, the customers receive Canadian Tire "store money" in proportion to their purchases. The store money can be used to purchase merchandise at Canadian Tire stores. This tactic encourages customers to pay cash instead of using a Visa or MasterCard credit card, draws traffic to the stores, and provides an incentive for customers to return to the store and spend their Canadian Tire store money.

*Frequent-Shopper Discounts*

Some retailers are experimenting with frequent-shopper discounts, much like the frequent-flyer programmes offered by the airlines, to generate greater sales volume and customer loyalty. Shoppers' cumulative purchases are tracked throughout the year, and bonuses are offered after shoppers reach a specified dollar volume of purchase. Additional bonuses are sometimes given to stimulate shopping on slow days or to clear out slow-moving merchandise. Zellers, the discount department store chain, launched Club Z, a frequent-buyer programme, in 1986. It now has over 6 million members, and Club Z is one of the most successful customer loyalty programmes in North America.[10] Sears Canada also has a large customer loyalty programme, with over 4 million members in its Sears Club. In an interesting twist on customer loyalty programmes, the Loyalty Management Group started the Air Miles co-op programme. Consumers join the programme and accumulate points when they purchase goods and services from retailers who participate in the programme. The points can be used for air travel on several airlines, including Air Canada. Sears Canada, along with other retailers (including a supermarket chain and a bank), are participating in the programme.[11]

## Chapter Highlights

- A variety of external factors affect retail pricing decisions. The factors include the type of goods carried, the type of store at which the merchandise is sold, the level of profit desired, the level of customer demand, the market structure, supplier policies, economic conditions, and government regulations.

- Primary government regulations affecting retail pricing decisions include the Competition Act and the Goods and Services Tax (GST).

- Retail pricing decisions are affected by the retailer's policy on the price level desired. The three pricing choices are (1) at the market, (2) below the competition, and (3) above the competition.

- The majority of retail firms in Canada offer goods at one "take it or leave it" price. Some stores—for example, appliance dealers—however, do not follow a one-price policy.

- Many retailers have their own private brands. Alternatively, manufacturers may develop different brands for sale to different retailers. Additionally, some retailers sell no-name (generic) merchandise.

- Some retailers use leader pricing with selected product categories. The best price-leader items are (1) well known and widely used, (2) priced low enough to attract numerous buyers, (3) not usually bought in large quantities and stored.

- In practice, retailers may raise or lower their prices after the original pricing decisions have been made. These pricing adjustments may be in the form of additional markups or markdowns.

- A variety of factors can affect pricing decisions in addition to markups and markdowns. These factors include distributor allowances, consumer rebates, and consumer pressure.

- Retailers often face indirect price competition. The most frequent means of pursuing a policy of indirect price competition include multiple distribution by vendors, variations in the service mix, and offering price discounts for cash payment.

# Key Terms

| | | | |
|---|---|---|---|
| Above the competition pricing | 398 | Markdown | 404 |
| At the market pricing | 398 | Original retail price | 406 |
| Below the competition pricing | 398 | Price elasticity | 394 |
| Consumer rebates | 410 | Price lining | 403 |
| Distributor allowances | 410 | Price points | 403 |
| Initial markup | 406 | Price zones | 403 |
| Loss-leader pricing | 404 | Sales retail price | 406 |
| Maintained markup | 406 | Single-price policy | 404 |

# Discussion Questions

1. Why is pricing such a vitally important part of the retail planning process?

2. What external factors affect the prices a retailer charges? Discuss each of these factors.

3. Discuss the possible price level policies available to the retailer. Give an example of a type of retail organization that follows each of the policy options.

4. How can a retailer offer private brands and generics at below the competition price and still make a good profit?

5. Illustrate price lining and evaluate the policy.

6. Discuss the concept of a leader-pricing policy. What are the characteristics of products that are good price leaders?

7. Explain the kinds of pricing adjustments that may be made after the original price decision has been made.

8. Define original retail price, sales retail, initial markup, and maintained markup.

# Problems

1. If markup on cost is 36 percent, what is the equivalent markup on retail?

2. If markup on cost is 44 percent, what is the equivalent markup on retail?

3. If markup on retail is 18 percent, what is the equivalent markup on cost?

4. If markup on retail is 41 percent, what is the equivalent markup on cost?

5. A suit costs a retailer $36.80. If a markup of 43 percent on cost is required, what must the retail price be?

6. A lamp is marked up $168. This is a 61 percent markup on retail. What is *(a)* the cost and *(b)* the retail price?

7. The retail price of a ring is $7,800. If the markup on retail is 78 percent, what is the cost of the ring to the retailer?

8. The retail price of a picture is $48.50. If the markup on cost is 38 percent, what is the cost of the picture to the retailer?

9. Men's wallets may be purchased from a manufacturer for $300 per dozen. If the wallets are marked up 28 percent on cost, what retail price will be set per wallet?

10. Women's scarves may be purchased from a manufacturer at $81.60 per dozen. If the scarves are marked up 16 percent on retail, what is the retail price of each scarf?

11. What is the *(a)* initial markup percent and *(b)* the maintained markup percent in a department that has the following planned figures: expenses, $7,200; profit, $4,500; sales, $28,000; employee discounts, $450; markdowns, $1,200; and shortages, $225?

12. Sales of $85,000 were planned in a department in which expenses were established at $26,000; shortages, $2,200; and employee discounts, $600. If a profit of 6 percent of sales is desired, what initial markup percent should be planned?

13. Department Z has taken $600 in markdowns to date. Net sales to date are $22,000. What is the markdown percentage to date?

# Application Exercises

1. Devise a questionnaire to get consumer reaction to raising the price of goods already on display. Also question consumer reaction to the fact that UPC codes allow supermarkets to change prices immediately even if old stock is still on the shelves. Do consumers feel these practices are fair or unfair? Why? Allow room for individual consumer comments on your questionnaire.

2. Assume that you are a management trainee for a major supermarket chain. Select a market basket of products that are available in all stores and easily comparable (for example, no private brands), and compare prices (including specials) in a conventional supermarket, a warehouse-type outlet, and a convenience store (a Mac's Milk). Keep your record over a period of time, present your data in an organized format, and draw conclusions about the pricing philosophy of the different types of food operations.

3. Health and beauty aids are carried in many different kinds of retail establishments—for example, conventional drugstores, supermarkets, discount drugstores, and department stores. Often, each type of establishment promises lower prices, better assortments, and so on, to establish a differential advantage. List selected items available in each store and group stores by type. Compare and contrast the items among the various types of stores. See what you find to be the "real" strategy of the competing stores in the market. Why is the lowest-priced store able to price as indicated? What are the specials? Are they similar for all stores?

# Suggested Cases

# Endnotes

1. Pennington's, Annual Report, 1991.
2. Daniel Girard, "The New Retail Giants," *Toronto Star,* February 9, 1992, pp. H1, H4.
3. Marina Strauss, "Warehouse Outlets Create Turf Wars," *Globe and Mail,* May 11, 1992.
4. John Heinzl, "Club Z Leaving Its Mark," *Globe and Mail,* December 6, 1991, pp. B1, B4.
5. For more information on the price-quality issue, see Valarie A. Zeithaml, "Consumer Perceptions of Price, Quality, and Value: A Means-End Model and Synthesis of Evidence," *Journal of Marketing,* July 1988, pp. 2–22; Kent B. Monroe and William B. Dodds, "A Research Program for Establishing the Validity of the Price-Quality Relationship," *Journal of the Academy of Marketing Science,* Spring 1988, pp. 151–68; Eitan Gerstner, "Do Higher Prices Signal Higher Quality?" *Journal of Marketing Research,* May 1985, pp. 209–15; Loren V. Geistfeld, "The Price-Quality Relationship Revisited," *Journal of Consumer Affairs,* Winter 1982, pp. 334–46; and Benny Rigaux-Bricmont, "Influences of Brand Name and Packaging on Perceived Quality," in *Advances in Consumers Research,* vol. 9, ed. Andrew A. Mitchell (Ann Arbor, Mich.: Association for Consumer Research, 1982), pp. 472–77.
6. Mark Evans, "Dollar Stores Buck Retail Downtrend," *The Financial Post,* July 30, 1992, p. 11.
7. Joseph N. Fry and Gordon H. G. McDougall, "Consumer Appraisal of Retail Price Advertisements," *Journal of Marketing,* July 1974, pp. 64–67. For more on retail price promotions, see John Liefeld and Louise A. Heslop, "Reference Prices and Deception in Newspaper Advertising," *Journal of Consumer Research,* March 1985, pp. 868–76; and Abhijit Biswas and Edward A. Blair, "Contextual Effects of Reference Prices in Retail Advertisements," *Journal of Marketing,* July 1991, pp. 1–12.
8. Rockney G. Walters, "Assessing the Impact of Retail Price Promotions on Product Substitution, Complementary Purchase, and Interstore Sales Displacement," *Journal of Marketing,* April 1991, pp. 17–28.
9. Francis J. Mulhern and Robert P. Leone, "Implicit Price Bundling of Retail Products: A Multiproduct Approach to Maximizing Store Profitability," *Journal of Marketing,* October 1991, pp. 63–76.
10. Heinzl, "Club Z Leaving Its Mark."
11. Stan Sutler, "Sears' New 'Club' Spots Outline Air Miles Tie-In," *Marketing,* May 4, 1992, p. 16.

# 16   KEYS TO SUCCESSFUL RETAIL SELLING

---

### Chapter Objectives

After reading this chapter, you should be able to:

1 Describe the types of selling needed in retailing.
2 Understand the steps in the selling process.
3 Describe ways to increase sales force productivity.
4 Understand the need for sales training programmes.
5 Understand how to help people in buying.
6 Understand the opportunities for motivating retail salespersons.

**Retailing Capsule**

"As I paid for my Egg McMuffin, the teenager behind the counter smiled and said, 'Thank you for coming.' When I got back to the office around noon, I returned a call to my dentist. His answering machine responded: 'We are out to lunch. Call back after 1:30.'

"What a contrast in service! Getting my teeth cleaned costs a lot more than an Egg McMuffin, but the dentist's machine can't be bothered to thank me for calling. After all, I'm only a customer. Then, there is the salesman who has just sold me a $15,000 car but can't seem to locate the title. When I inquire about it, he tells *me* to call *him* tomorrow. Why can't he say something like, 'I'm sorry about the mix-up. I'll look into it and call you in the morning'?

"Many retailers seem to have forgotten about serving the customer. The good news, of course, is that there are some fine salespeople out there who make buying a pleasure. They know how to make you feel comfortable when you spend your money—a sure sign of being a pro. Pros know that investing money and time in a customer is far cheaper than finding a new one. For instance, the other day I stopped by the local Sears to buy a lawn mower, only to discover that I no longer had a Sears credit card. I'd let the card lapse: There was no way I could take the new mower home with me. Fortunately, the manager did the next best thing, overlooking a couple of rules in the process. He had me reapply for credit and agreed to deliver the mower to my home gratis once the application was approved."

Source: Michael C. Ramundo, "How the Pros Hang In There," *Sales & Marketing Management,* August 1987, p. 10.

A high-quality sales force can generate "plus" sales for a retail outlet. Consumers are increasingly frustrated over the poor quality of service they receive in retail outlets. One way to create strong customer loyalty is by offering a superior quality sales force as a complement to good merchandise and strong price/value relationships. Creative selling differs dramatically from the image of the huckster salesclerk that too many people have in their mind when they think of retail sales.

To the customer, the salesperson often is the business. The salesperson is the only person with whom the customer has contact. The salesperson encourages the customer to buy or, through a hostile or indifferent attitude, drives the customer away—forever. Salespersons can act as sales *preventers* instead of sales facilitators by their rudeness or indifference.[1]

# Building Sales and Profit

Salespeople can help build a business for greater sales and profit. They can:

- Sell skillfully to realize maximum sales and profit from each customer attracted to the firm.

- Provide customers with useful selling suggestions that will build sales and improve customer satisfaction.
- Ensure that customers' needs are met so that returns are held to a minimum.
- Develop a loyal following of customers who will return to the store and send their friends.
- Follow store policies and procedures so that losses through billing oversights, failure to secure credit approvals, and acceptance of bad checks are held to a minimum.

Personal selling in retailing is essentially matching customers' needs with the retailer's merchandise and services. In general, the more skillfully this match is made, the better the personal selling. If salespeople make a good match, not only is a sale made, but a satisfied customer is developed (or maintained), as Retail Highlight 16–1 illustrates. Thus, a long-term, profitable relationship can be established. Figure 16–1 illustrates this process.

In retailing, the top producers far outsell the average. The more top producers in a store, the more profitable it will be. Retailers cannot expect salespeople to become top producers by accident. There is no magic wand to wave or button to push to make this happen. However, there are a number of positive actions retailers can make to attract people with potential and, once hired, develop that potential so that maximum performance is achieved.

---

**Retail Highlight 16–1**

# Finding the Right Merchandise Is Not Always Easy

It was an impossible request. One of Jan Dawe's regulars was begging her to find a certain pin-striped jacket made by American designer Donna Karan, an item last seen on Barbra Streisand in the March issue of *Us* magazine. Dawe, who manages the designer sportswear department at Holt Renfrew's flagship store in Toronto, did some research. Alas, the jacket for Streisand was one of a kind. Undaunted, Dawe found an equally attractive Karan blazer. The customer approved.

This is just one example of what makes Jan Dawe an excellent salesperson. Lynn Joliffe, Holt Renfrew's general manager, says: "Jan exemplifies what good service should be. She is sincere, hospitable, and truly wants to assist customers."

To Holt Renfrew's emphasis on superior service, Jan Dawe adds her own rule: "Never high-pressure sell. Never put something on a customer that does not look right on her. Give the customer your undivided attention—you can't just stare off into a corner."

Source: Jared Mitchell, "I Can Sell You Anything," *Report on Business Magazine*, June 1992, pp. 48–9.

**FIGURE 16–1**

*Matching customer needs with retailer merchandise and services*

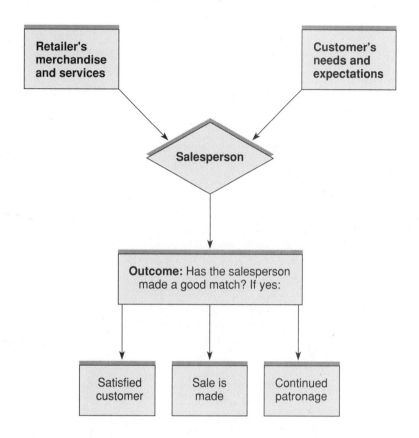

# Basic Decisions

Retailers must first make a number of basic decisions regarding their sales force.

## Self-Service or Full Service?

The key to a good sales force is creating the right interaction between (1) the merchandise, (2) the customer, and (3) the salesperson. Some items such as groceries can be sold by self-service. A fully staffed store is needed when selling items such as expensive fashions. A third possibility is a combination of self-service and full staffing. This is the policy of most stores.

## When Are Salespersons Needed?

A salesperson is needed when:

1. Customers have little knowledge about the product they plan to buy.
2. Price negotiation is likely, as when buying a car.
3. The product is complex—for example, VCR equipment.

The sales force represents the store. In many respects, the image projected by salespersons is one of the most important elements of the retail operation. But far too often, the key role of the retail salesperson is not acknowledged.

*What Are the Types of Retail Selling?*

Several types of selling occur in retailing. A different type of person and different skill levels are needed for each type.[2]

### Transaction Processing

The easiest selling task is **transaction processing.** Employees simply serve as check-out clerks or cashiers and do little selling, as shown in Figure 16–2. Typical examples are personnel in warehouse clubs or supermarkets.

### Routine Selling

**Routine selling** involves more product knowledge and a better approach to the sales task. Often, people in routine selling are involved in the sale of nontechnical items such as clothing. These salespeople assist the shopper in buying by giving them confidence in their judgment and answering simple questions.

Personnel involved in routine sales should also be trained in the techniques of suggestion selling, as shown in Figure 16–3 and discussed later in this chapter. For example, a salesperson might suggest a shirt and tie to go with the suit a customer is trying. They should then be monitored closely by superiors to make sure they practice the concepts they have learned. Such techniques may increase sales by 10 percent or more, and additional sales are almost pure profit, since they add little, if anything, to the cost structure of the firm. Retailers such as McDonald's consistently practice suggestion selling when the salesperson asks: "Would you like french fries or a Coke with your order?"

### Sales Consultant

**Creative selling** requires the use of salespeople who have complete information about product lines, product uses, and technical features. These people are often called sales consultants and may, for example, work as interior designers in a furniture store. Creative selling occurs when the product is highly personalized.

**FIGURE 16–2    *Transaction processing***

SOURCE: Courtesy Price Club.

**FIGURE 16–3**

*Suggestion selling requires product knowledge and good selling skills*

Source: Courtesy Town and Country/Photo by James Hertel.

Regardless of the type of selling involved, salespeople have a key role in the communications plan for a firm. Many extra sales can be made by creative sales efforts. The cost of retail selling is high, in spite of the low wages paid to sales personnel, and these costs must be offset by high productivity. A well-trained sales force can be a major advantage for a firm. Competing firms may duplicate price cuts and promotion but may have difficulty in developing a quality sales force. The main differences in the three types of selling are summarized in Table 16–1.

*An Overview of Personal Selling*

A basic concept in retail sales is that a sale must first occur in the mind of the buyer. The job of the salesperson is to lead the customer into a buying situation. A successful salesperson should think of selling as a process consisting of the steps shown in Table 16–2.

**TABLE 16–1    Types of Personal Selling in Retailing**

| Criteria for Comparison | Transaction Processing | Routine Selling | Sales Consultant |
|---|---|---|---|
| Purpose | Assist at check-out counter | Suggestion selling | Creative selling |
| Training required | Clerical training | Sales training | In-depth product knowledge |
| Source of sales | Impulse purchases | Maintain sales volume plus "add on" accessories | Creation of new sales volume |
| Type of products | Simple convenience items | Standardized with new options | Complex and customized |
| Primary activity | Order processing | Suggestion selling | Creative problem solving |

**TABLE 16–2    The Selling Process**

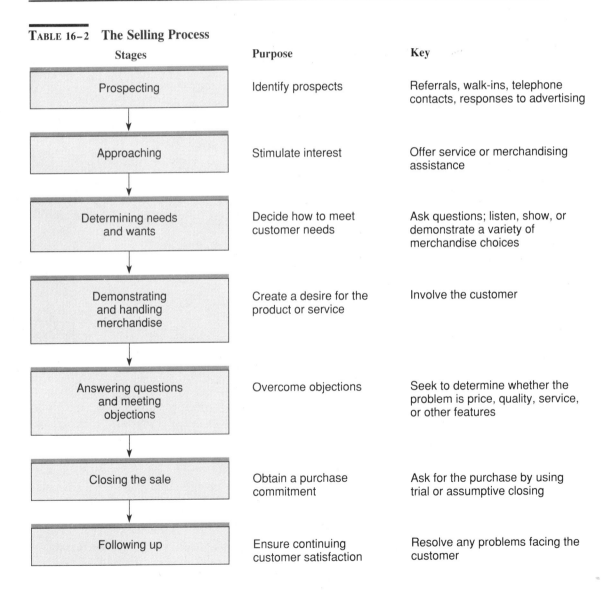

| Stages | Purpose | Key |
|---|---|---|
| Prospecting | Identify prospects | Referrals, walk-ins, telephone contacts, responses to advertising |
| Approaching | Stimulate interest | Offer service or merchandising assistance |
| Determining needs and wants | Decide how to meet customer needs | Ask questions; listen, show, or demonstrate a variety of merchandise choices |
| Demonstrating and handling merchandise | Create a desire for the product or service | Involve the customer |
| Answering questions and meeting objections | Overcome objections | Seek to determine whether the problem is price, quality, service, or other features |
| Closing the sale | Obtain a purchase commitment | Ask for the purchase by using trial or assumptive closing |
| Following up | Ensure continuing customer satisfaction | Resolve any problems facing the customer |

### Prospecting

**Prospecting** involves identifying and qualifying possible customers. Promotional, telephone, and direct-mail programmes often attract potential customers to the firm. Likewise, word of mouth can be effective when satisfied customers refer friends to the store.

Salespeople should try to know as much about their customers as possible before approaching them. This may seem difficult at first, but the concept of market segmentation discussed earlier may aid in identifying customers. The type of promotion programme featured by the store is also a key. For example, most customers shopping at Zellers expect good price/value relationships and normally buy on the basis of price. These customers are often presold on products through national-brand advertising and do not expect many services. On the other hand, the customers of an exclusive store such as Birks expect personalized attention, a high level of product knowledge by the salesperson, and a wide variety of services.

Some firms keep lists of their good customers' likes and dislikes, measurements, and past purchases, as illustrated in Retail Highlight 16–2 about Harry Rosen stores. Salespersons in such stores often call their customers when a new shipment of merchandise arrives.

### Approaching the Customer

The initial approach is crucial in getting the sale. When approaching the customer, the salesperson should quickly (1) gain the customer's attention, (2) create interest, and (3) make a smooth transition into a presentation. Various approaches to

---

**Retail Highlight 16–2**

---

# Generating Sales through Good Customer Service

According to Harry Rosen, CEO of the menswear chain of the same name, good service means more than having someone friendly standing by your elbow, ready to do your bidding; it's also knowing about the product and individual customer needs. And, adds Rosen, "It's imparting knowledge to the customer so that he can make an informed decision on his purchases."

In order to provide this level of service, all 24 Harry Rosen stores across Canada have been linked with a computer database. "Whenever a customer returns to one of our stores," says company president Bob Humphrey, "a sales associate can call up his name on a computer terminal and receive a detailed accounting of all his past purchases. In this way, we can ensure that our customer's wardrobe is kept well-rounded, that no duplications are made, and that he can always get the proper size and fit."

Source: Leslie C. Smith, "Dressing Up Customer Service," *Globe and Mail*, June 11, 1992, p. D1.

customers are possible. Commonly used approaches are (1) the service approach, and (2) the merchandise approach.

***The Service Approach.***    The **service approach** (''May I help you?'') is weak if a customer is simply browsing. The customer is given an opportunity to quickly say ''No.'' It is better to approach by saying, ''Hi, if you need my help, let me know.''[3] However, the service greeting is useful when the customer (1) has apparently made a selection, (2) clearly needs a salesperson to explain something about the merchandise, or (3) needs someone to ring up a sale. Above all, sales personnel should always make the customer feel welcome. The customer needs to know that the salesperson is willing to serve him or her, and that the salesperson is knowledgeable about the merchandise.

***The Merchandise Approach.***    When using the **merchandise approach,** the salesperson waits until a potential customer seems to have decided on an item before approaching the individual. The salesperson then begins talking to the customer about the merchandise without asking whether the person would like to be waited on, making a statement about the merchandise such as: ''The style you are looking at is very popular this year.''

Table 16–3 outlines 12 basic types of customers that salespeople are likely to meet in their day-to-day activities. The information in the table describes their characteristics and how to respond to their behaviour and actions.

### Determining Customers' Needs and Wants

Salespeople should quickly discover the customers' needs and wants after the greeting. Good listening skills are the key. Once the salesperson has the customers' attention and understands their needs, the salesperson can quickly move them into the interest and desire stage and on to the buying stage. Motives for buying generally are either emotional or rational.

One way to develop information on customer needs and desires is to ask the customer about his or her planned use for the merchandise. This knowledge will help the salesperson better understand the buying problem and how the merchandise can help solve the problem. Such information can also provide insight into the price, styles, and colours that a customer may prefer.

Good listening is more than giving the other person a chance to talk—it means giving the person your undivided attention. Getting a prospect to talk is important because it is the only way to find out the person's special problems, interests, and needs. Then, when making the sales presentation, the salesperson is in a position to stress the things that are important to the prospect and to talk specifically about the situation.

Knowing the *importance* of listening and actually doing it are two different things. Many salespeople keep planning what to say next instead of listening. A salesperson who is wrapped up in the sales pitch cannot hear the prospect. A good listener concentrates on what is being said. A good salesperson learns the attitudes

## TABLE 16–3    Recognizing Customers of All Types

| | Customer | | | Salesperson |
|---|---|---|---|---|
| *Basic Types* | *Basic Characteristic* | *Secondary Characteristics* | *Other Characteristics* | *What to Say or Do* |
| Arguer | Takes issue with each statement of salesperson | Disbelieves claims; tries to catch salesperson in error | Cautious; slow to decide | Demonstrate; show product knowledge; use "yes, but . . ." |
| Chip on shoulder | Definitely in a bad mood | Indignation; angry at slight provocation | Acts as if being deliberately baited | Avoid argument; stick to basic facts; show good assortment |
| Decisive | Knows what is wanted | Customer confident his or her choice is right | Not interested in another opinion—respects salesperson's brevity | Win sales—not argument; sell self; tactfully inject opinion |
| Doubting Thomas | Doesn't trust sales talk | Hates to be managed | Arrives at decision cautiously | Back up merchandise statements by manufacturers' tags, labels; demonstrate merchandise; let customer handle merchandise |
| Fact finder | Interested in factual information—detailed | Alert to salespersons' errors in description | Looks for actual tags and labels | Emphasize label and manufacturers' facts; volunteer care information |
| Hesitant | Ill at ease—sensitive | Shopping at unaccustomed price range | Unsure of own judgment | Make customer comfortable; use friendliness and respect |
| Impulsive | Quick to decide or select | Impatience | Liable to break off sale abruptly | Close rapidly; avoid oversell, overtalk; note key points |
| Look around | Little ability to make own decisions | Anxious—fearful of making a mistake | Wants salesperson's aid in decision—wants adviser—wants to do right thing | Emphasize merits of product and service, zeroing in on customer-expressed need and doubts |
| Procrastinator | "I'll wait 'til tomorrow" | Lacks confidence in own judgment | Insecure | Reinforce customer's judgment |
| Silent | Not talking—but thinking! | Appears indifferent but truly listening | Appears nonchalant | Ask direct questions—straightforward approach; watch for buying signals |
| Think it over | Refers to desire, but needs to consult someone else | Looking for another adviser | Not sure of own uncertainty | Get agreement on small points; draw out opinions; use points agreed on for close |

SOURCE: From C. Winston Borgen, *Learning Experiences in Retailing* (Santa Monica, Calif.: Goodyear Publishing, 1976), p. 293. Copyright © Goodyear Publishing Company, Reprinted by permission.

*Good listening skills are key to discovering customer needs and wants.*

SOURCE: Courtesy St. Clair Paint & Wallpaper.

and problems the customers have. Learning what is important to the individual may be important in selling to the individual.

By visualizing the person's problems, the salesperson can better understand them. Eye contact is important. The salesperson should make a special effort to be attentive, not letting the mind wander to other subjects. To keep the prospects talking, salespeople should acknowledge that they are listening by prompting with nods, or commenting with "I see" or "I understand." Asking a question now and then helps. Salespeople should not worry about what to say next. If they listen carefully, their next move will usually be obvious. It is not easy to be a good listener, but it is important. Top salespeople listen to a prospect, show that they understand, and remember what is said.[4]

### Demonstrating and Handling Merchandise
Good listening helps determine which merchandise to show the customer and which features of the merchandise will help solve the buying problems the customer faces.

Good salespeople have a mental outline they follow when presenting the merchandise. This mental outline differs from a canned sales presentation in which the salesperson repeats exactly the same statements to each customer. The salesperson is free to deviate from a fixed statement but still keeps key points from the outline in mind as a checklist. A mental guide should include the following points:

- *Begin with the strongest features of the product:* These features might be price, durability, performance, and so forth.
- *Obtain agreement on small points:* This helps the salesperson establish rapport with the customer.
- *Point out the benefits of ownership to the customer:* Salespersons should try to identify with the customer in making these points.
- *Demonstrate the product:* A demonstration helps the customer make a decision based on seeing the product in action.
- *Let the customer try the product:* Good salespersons get the customer involved as much as possible. The involvement pushes the customer toward the sale.

Other useful techniques include testimonials of customers who have used the product, discussion of research results, and discussion of product guarantees and case histories.

### Answering Questions and Meeting Objections

Customers may object to a point during the sales process. When that occurs, the salespersons should try to find the real reason for the objection, which may be price, quality of the product, service available, or various other reasons. Salespersons should try to get the customer to see the situation in a different way. They should acknowledge that they can understand why the customer holds a particular view. But they also should try to provide information that can overcome the objection. For example, an objection to a high price might be overcome by pointing out that the purchase is really an investment. Also, salespersons might point out that the price of the product has not gone up any more than other items the consumer has recently purchased.

Above all, salespersons should consider a customer's question as an opportunity to provide more information about the product or service. They should welcome objections as providing a way for overcoming obstacles to a sale. The key to handling objections is *timing,* as explained in Exhibit 16–1.

### Transition to the Close

Salespersons often have a problem with the close. Too often, they simply wait for shoppers to buy instead of trying to close the sale. The customers often give signals to alert salespeople that a buying decision is at hand. Such signals may include questions about the use of the item, delivery, or payment. Facial expressions may also indicate that the customer is close to the buying stage. More frequently, it's up to the salesperson to bring up the closing question.

**EXHIBIT 16–1**

*Overcoming objections*

Knowing *when* to answer an objection is almost as important as being able to answer it.

Timing is crucial! In general, it's wise to answer as many objections as you can *before* the prospect brings them up.

Putting the answers to objections into the sales talk saves time. But more important, when a salesperson, rather than the prospect, mentions an objection, the issue seems less important. It also makes the customer feel you're not trying to hide anything.

Sometimes a customer may hesitate to bring up a particular objection because he doesn't want to embarrass you. You can save the day by getting it out in the open, showing the customer you understand his or her concerns.

Another reason for discussing as many obvious objections as possible is that you avoid an argument. If the prospect brings up an objection, you may have to prove he's wrong in order to make the sale. That's a situation to avoid if you possibly can.

On the other hand, what if the customer *does* bring up an objection before you get to it? If you can give a satisfactory reply without taking attention away from your sales point—answer it immediately.

Sometimes you should delay your answer to a customer's objection. For example, you may not even need to answer if there's a good chance the objection will diminish in importance as you continue your presentation.

It's also best to delay answering if you would seem to be flatly contradicting the prospect. Rather than do this, wait and let the answer become clear as you proceed with your presentation. This gives the prospect a chance to save face.

There are some objections that it's best not to answer at all. If the prospect's statement is simply an excuse, or a malicious remark, don't bother trying to answer. This will only put you on the defensive.

Having good answers to objections and presenting them to the customer's satisfaction is important. But so is timing. Choosing the right time and the right way to handle objections keeps you in control of the selling process.

SOURCE: *On the Upbeat,* June 1982, pp. 11–13.

*Trial Closes.*[5]   An easy way to do this is through trial closes. A **trial close** is a question that is asked to determine the prospect's readiness to buy. An example of such a question is: "Are you satisfied that our product will help you reduce your maintenance costs?" If the answer is negative, the salesperson can reemphasize how the product reduces maintenance costs or can ask the prospect to be more specific about the cause of his or her doubt.

*Seeking Agreement.*   If the prospect agrees with the salesperson on a series of points, it becomes difficult to say no when the salesperson asks for the order. However, the prospect who disagrees on a number of points will probably defend this position by also saying no when the salesperson asks for the order.

The salesperson should **seek agreement** on a number of points such as:

- "Don't you think the self-defrosting feature of this refrigerator is a real convenience, Mr. Baker?"
- "You probably need a larger refrigerator than your present one, don't you?"

The salesperson probably knows the points to which the prospect will agree. The idea is to summarize them and ask them consecutively to establish a pattern of agreement, one that will make it difficult for the prospect to say no when the salesperson asks for the order.

Above all, salespersons should:

- Not make exaggerated claims.
- Use honest facts and figures to back up the claims they do make.
- Demonstrate and prove their points whenever possible.
- Use solid, legitimate testimonials that the prospect can check.
- Not promise what they cannot deliver.
- Back promises in writing and in performance.
- Show sincere interest in every customer's problems.
- Consistently and conscientiously put the customer's interest ahead of their own.[6]

Salespersons should not be pressed to act too quickly or make exaggerated claims because of potential legal consequences. Five categories of careless statements with potential legal consequences are (1) creation of unintended warranties, (2) dilution of the effectiveness of existing warranties, (3) disparagement of competitive offerings, (4) misrepresentation of the firm's own offerings, and (5) unjustified interference with business relationships.[7]

Table 16–4 summarizes the critical skills needed and common errors to avoid in the personal selling process.

***Benefit Summary.*** Another effective transition is the **benefit summary,** a statement that summarizes **product benefits,** such as the following:

> Ms. Perkins, I think you'll find that the Brand X washer has everything you're looking for. A partial load cycle saves you water, energy, and money. Temperature controls protect your fabrics. And Brand X's reputation for quality assures you that this machine will operate dependably for a long time with little or no maintenance.

Product benefits will be discussed later in this chapter.

---

**TABLE 16–4    Critical Skills and Common Errors in Personal Selling**

**Critical Skills**
Good listening to establish needs and to develop basic information
Demonstrating how a product or service can meet an identified need
Establishing rapport with customers
Skillfully handling objections or negative attitudes
Summarizing benefits and actions required in closing the sale

**Common Errors**
Talking instead of listening
Not seeking critical information from a customer by failing to ask crucial questions
Failing to match customers' needs with product benefits
Failing to handle objections
Not knowing how or when to close the sale

### Closing the Sale

Now let us look at the most vital factor in the selling process—closing the sale. All previous steps have been taken with one purpose in mind—to close the sale, to get the prospect to buy. A variety of techniques can be used to close the sale, as shown in Table 16–5. The best approach often depends upon the salesperson's individual selling style, the prospect, the product or service that is offered, and the salesperson's earlier success in convincing the prospect of the advantages of the product and the benefits that it offers.

**TABLE 16–5   Salesperson Perceptions of Closing-Tactic Effectiveness**

| Closing Tactic | Mean Scale Value* |
| --- | --- |
| *Summary:* Restate major points or benefits and ask for the order. | 4.2 |
| *Comparison:* Compare product features with those of a well-known rival, then ask for the order. | 4.0 |
| *Multiple choice:* Reduce alternative offerings to two or three choices, then ask which one the prospect prefers. | 3.4 |
| *Assumptive:* Conduct oneself as if the prospect has decided to buy. | 3.4 |
| *Ask for the order:* In a straightforward manner, ask for the order. | 3.2 |
| *Report:* Describe situation where another prospect had a similar problem and benefited from the offerings, then ask for the order. | 3.1 |
| *Close on an objection:* Answer an important objection, then ask for the order. | 3.1 |
| *Counselling:* Advise the prospect to order an item, based on the sales representative's role as a counsellor or expert. | 2.8 |
| *Contingency:* Ask the prospect if he or she will order if a contingency is provided for by the sales representative. | 2.7 |
| *Major point/minor point:* Ask closing questions, then immediately ask questions on minor points. Agreement on minor points is taken as suggestive of making an order. | 2.6 |
| *Contract:* Fill out a contract and hand to prospect for signature. | 2.5 |
| *Continuous affirmation:* Seek agreement on minor points, then ask for the order. | 2.5 |
| *Emotional:* Show an emotional value of purchasing the product, then ask for order. | 2.4 |
| *Single obstacle:* Get prospect to agree that only one obstacle prevents a purchase; remove obstacle and ask for the order. | 2.3 |
| *Balance sheet:* Make T-account and write reasons for purchasing in the left row and reasons for not purchasing in the right. Ask for the order. | 2.1 |
| *Buy now:* Raise anxiety by pointing out that delay by the prospect in placing an order may result in increased prices, out of stock conditions, or some other problem. Ask for the order. | 2.0 |
| *Complimentary:* Compliment prospect on the wisdom of making an order. | 2.0 |
| *Concession:* Give in to the prospect on one or more points in order to close the sale. Ask for the order. | 1.6 |

*Scored on a 5-point scale ranging from very effective (5) to very ineffective (1).
SOURCE: Robin Peterson, ''Sales Representative Perceptions on Various Widely Used Closing Tactics,'' in *Educators Proceedings,* eds. Gary Frazier et al. (Chicago: American Marketing Association, 1988), p. 221.

*Direct Close.*    The **direct close** assumes that the prospect is ready to buy. In closing, the salesperson asks a direct question such as the following:

- ''We can deliver your sofa next week. What is the address we should ship to?''
- ''You want this in green, don't you?''
- ''Will this be cash or charge?''
- ''Would you like to put this on a budget plan?''

*Assumptive Close.*    The **assumptive close** is a modification of the direct close. The salesperson assumes that the prospect is ready to buy, but asks less direct questions, such as:

- ''Which colour do you prefer, red or green?''
- ''Which model do you prefer, the standard or the deluxe?''
- ''Have you decided where you would like the machine installed?''
- ''Shall I call an electrician to arrange for the installation?''

*Open-Ended Close.*    In the **open-ended close,** the salesperson asks open-ended questions that imply readiness to buy, such as:

- ''How soon will you need the sofa?''
- ''When should I arrange for installation?''

The prospect's answer to these questions leads to an easy close. If the prospect needs the sofa in three weeks, the salesperson can respond, ''Then I'll need an order right away, to assure you of delivery on time.''

*Action Close.*    In an **action close,** the salesperson takes some positive step toward clinching the order, such as:

- ''I'll write up the order right now, and as soon as you sign it, we can deliver.''
- ''I'll call the warehouse and see if they can ship immediately.''

*Urgency Close.*    In the **urgency close,** the salesperson advises the prospect of some compelling reason for ordering immediately, such as:

- ''That's a pretty tight schedule. I'll have to get an answer from you very quickly if we are going to be able to meet it.''
- ''That item has been very popular, and right now our inventory is running pretty low.''
- ''Our special price on this product ends the 15th of the month.''

### Dealing with Delay

Not all closing attempts are immediately successful. The prospect may delay, unable to make a decision. If so, the salesperson should ask the reason for the delay. The reason will often help the salesperson plan the next course of action in reestablishing the presentation of the product or service.

For example, the prospect might say: "I think I'll stick with my present machine a while longer." If the salesperson has properly qualified the prospect earlier, he or she might respond: "But didn't you say that repair costs were running awfully high? Isn't it worth a few dollars to know that you will save on maintenance costs and not have to worry about a breakdown at a critical time?"

### Choosing the Closing Technique

The choice of the closing technique will depend on the salesperson, the salesperson's style, the customer, and the facts. Regardless of the technique chosen, the most important thing to remember is to pursue some closing technique and not avoid this critical step.

### Following Up

Salespeople should make sure that the merchandise is delivered on time, that it arrives in good condition, and that installation, if needed, is satisfactory. The salesperson should take this opportunity to try to sell the customer an extended warranty, for example, if this was not done initially.

Above all, salespeople should think back over the sale to determine what they learned that will help them in their future sales efforts. Also, they should think about why some sales were not made and what might have been done to overcome the lack of a sale. Salespersons should always seek to identify ways of achieving future sales by satisfying their customers, as the Retail Highlight 16–3 demonstrates.

## What Can Be Done to Increase Sales Force Productivity?

Developing a strong retail sales force is not a matter of luck. Training is needed. Adequate incentives must exist to motivate personnel to high levels of performance. And supervision is necessary. Above all, management of the sales force means planning for increased sales. With selling expenses around 8 percent of sales, and assuming pretax profits of 4 percent, a 10 percent increase or decrease in the selling expense ratio can affect pretax profits as much as 20 percent! Also, selling costs are the most flexible payroll expense item in the short run.

The level of selling expense varies by store. The expense even varies by department because of differences in merchandise and customer services needed. Regardless, the goal should always be to hold down selling costs without reducing sales.

### What Are the Ways of Increasing Sales Productivity?

The percent of selling time can be increased. How? One way is to avoid overscheduling employees and knowing how many salespersons are needed at a

**Retail Highlight 16–3**

# Following Up Is Showing Customers that You Care

Stan Rich gave up his coal-mining job to become a car salesman at Halifax's Colonial Honda. During his first 18 months, he moved 150 automobiles, a phenomenal achievement during a recession. According to Rich, the key to his success is by showing customers that you care about their needs. Before hitting the sales floor each day, Rich consults index cards to see which of his previous customers he is scheduled to telephone. "How is the car?" he'll ask them in his Cape Breton drawl one week after they have driven away a new Prelude, Accord, or Civic. He'll do the same thing in a month's time, then in three months' time, and every six months after that, trouble-shooting where necessary but always reminding customers that Stan Rich cares.

Source: Jared Mitchell, "I Can Sell You Anything," *Report on Business Magazine,* June 1992, p. 50.

given time. Management should consider having less overtime and more part-time personnel. They should avoid having too few personnel available at periods such as lunchtime and think about split schedules to cover these busy periods. Also, salespersons should be used for selling only. Such tasks as wrapping and shelf stocking can be done by nonselling personnel.

*Better Employee Selection*

Finding good salespeople is a problem for both large and small retailers. What retailers fail to realize is that much of the problem is of their own making. They may not define clearly what they mean by "good" salespeople or specify what qualities they are seeking.

An effective way to avoid this problem is to use *job descriptions,* as discussed in Chapter 9. A job description is a written statement, often no longer than one or two paragraphs, spelling out the requirements for a particular job. For example, the job description for a retail sales position in a sporting goods store might appear as Exhibit 16–2.

The job description forces the retailer to be more explicit about what a job requires and provides a guide for appraising the capabilities of prospective employees. For example, since the job discussed above emphasizes big-ticket items, the retailer should look for people who have this kind of experience. There are many instances of salespeople who can do an excellent job on low-unit-value merchandise but have trouble closing sales on the big-ticket items. Job specifications help to avoid such problems.

*Sales Training*

Many people wonder why training salespeople is necessary, since their turnover is often so high. But effective training can increase employee sales levels, lead to

**Exhibit 16-2**

*Job description for retail sales of sporting goods*

---

*Type of job:* Retail sales of sporting goods.

*Requirements of the job:* This job involves mainly in-store sales of a full line of sporting goods ranging from items of low-unit value (such as golf balls) up to higher-priced merchandise (such as complete sets of golf clubs and skiing equipment). The emphasis is on big-ticket items. Telephone follow-up selling is expected, and there is occasional stock work.

---

better morale, and produce higher job satisfaction and lower job turnover. Training or retraining gives employees more knowledge about the items they sell and may make them feel more a part of the firm. Much training occurs on the job for the purpose of skills enhancement.

Retailers should budget dollars for training just as they budget dollars for hiring staff members, since training is a way to increase sales. Most people really want to succeed, but no one can succeed without adequate training. Customers will show their appreciation by increased levels of buying. And add-on sales as a result of employee training are almost pure profit, since they add little or nothing to expenses.

Unfortunately, when the word *training* is mentioned, the retailer typically associates it with formalized programmes conducted by large department stores and national chains. A good example is the Eaton's Professional Selling Skills (EPSS) seminar. However, sales training by smaller retailers does not have to be a formal and structured programme. Actually, any conscious effort the retailer makes to improve the basic skills needed for effective retail selling is a form of sales training.

Some of the frequently used retail sales training methods are (1) role playing, (2) sales meetings, and (3) seminars.

## Role Playing

**Role playing** is an excellent method for developing a salesperson's skills at learning customer needs. In role playing, one person plays the part of the customer, while the other plays the part of the salesperson. Next time around, they reverse the roles. Role playing enables salespeople to see various sales situations from the customer's point of view. The skill necessary to quickly size up customers (learn about their needs) is rapidly sharpened through role playing.

## Sales Meetings

Knowledge of the merchandise and service can be improved with regularly scheduled sales meetings. Sales meetings offer an excellent opportunity to discuss the features of new products, changes in store policies, new merchandising strategies, or other matters relating to the store's merchandise and services. Sales meetings do not have to be formal and precisely scheduled events. Instead, they can be conducted right on the sales floor during slack periods or shortly before the store opens for business.

What is important is that management holds the meetings regularly and frequently (once per week at a minimum) and each has a specific theme or focus. For example, at one meeting, management might discuss the features of a new line of products the store is now carrying and how to introduce them to the customer. The next meeting might focus on changes in the store's merchandise return policy. At another meeting, management might talk about the sales strategies for the upcoming inventory clearance sale. If meetings are held regularly, management may be pleasantly surprised at how much better informed salespeople will be about the store's merchandise and service offerings.

### Seminars

Training aimed at improving the ability to convince customers that a store's merchandise and service offering are superior is perhaps the most difficult. Some people believe that an individual either has this skill naturally or does not, and hence, training makes little difference. While there may be some truth in this position (people do differ in their natural communication abilities), training can still make a difference. Training can range from encouraging salespeople to take a formal course in salesmanship, to informal *sales seminars* organized by the store. These seminars may be no more elaborate than sitting down with salespeople for half an hour over a cup of coffee and discussing ways that merchandise and service offerings can be better communicated to customers.

If conducted informally (but regularly), these sessions may foster a constructive interchange of ideas about selling. For example, a salesperson may have developed a good argument that can be used successfully to close a sale when it looks as if the customer is ready to walk out.

*What Should Training Include?*

Sales training should include:

- *Information about the company and its products:* Who started the company? How long has it been in business? What lines of merchandise are sold? What are their main characteristics, uses, and so on?
- *Expectations of the salesperson:* A training programme should outline such things as dress code, job skills expected, goals to be met, and how performance will be measured.
- *Basic training in selling techniques:* Will the personnel need special technical skills? Management should also help employees to understand their nonselling duties.
- *The company's promotion and fringe benefit policies:* Management should explain promotion opportunities. Does the company pay for education for the employees? What are the sick leave and annual leave policies? What benefits such as health and life insurance does the company provide?
- *Training in telephone selling:* Salespersons may call a list of regular and preferred customers when new merchandise arrives.

*Teaching Selling*
*Skills*[8]

Teaching selling skills consists of the following three steps:

1. *Customer communications:* Developing a courteous approach to greeting customers and discussing their buying needs. This permits the salesperson to assist customers in their product selection and to describe products in terms that show how they fulfill the customers' buying needs.
2. *Feature-benefit relationship:* Understanding the reasons why customers buy, relating products or services to those reasons, and describing the products or services to the customers accordingly.
3. *Suggestion selling:* Using customers' original purchase requests to develop suggestions for related or additional sales in which the customers might be interested.

### Customer Communications

Customer relations is the foundation of a successful selling effort, not simply because a courteous approach to selling is "nice," but because it can build sales and profit. In small businesses, it is particularly important because the customers of small retailers generally expect more personal service than they find in a major department or discount store. The personal service could be advice on the colour, quality, or use of certain products. Or it might be just a friendly greeting and the customers' confidence that comes with knowing that they are buying from people who are interested in them and their business, as Retail Highlight 16–4 demonstrates.

---

**Retail Highlight 16–4**

## Showing Customers that They Are Important

Of all the 24 Walters Jewellers stores, the one in Barrie, Ontario, is the best, thanks to Karen MacPherson's selling skills. Once, when a necklace that a customer had brought in for repair failed to return from the factory a few days before an important wedding, MacPherson took the customer to the jewellery case and asked her to pick out a piece she could borrow for the big day. The woman chose a gold piece valued at $2,000. A few days after the wedding, she came back to say that she'd received so many compliments about it that she'd decided to buy it.

Another time, MacPherson took 15 minutes to explain diamonds to a customer who admitted he knew nothing about gems. When he went to another jewellery store and started using the information to ask detailed questions, the saleswoman said she did not have a clue to what he was talking about. When he told her he had just received a crash course in diamonds at Walters, the clerk sniffed, "We don't do things like that here." This superior attitude was more than enough to persuade the man to hightail it back to MacPherson and buy a ring.

Source: Jared Mitchell, "I Can Sell You Anything," *Report on Business Magazine,* June 1992, p. 48.

The salesperson should try to know as much about the customer's buying interest as possible. This is done by asking questions such as:

- "Are you looking for a fall or a winter coat?"
- "How long has your daughter been playing tennis?"
- "How often do you need a power saw?"

The answers to these questions will help the salesperson direct the customer to the right product—perhaps the winter coat, the expert model tennis racket, or the most durable saw. The salesperson will be performing a service for the customer by matching the customer's needs to the right product and will be increasing the chances of closing the sale.

As in the hiring interview, the most effective questions are those that cannot be answered yes or no. Instead, the salesperson should try to use open-ended questions that require a more complete answer. These are usually questions that begin with why, what, how, or offer a choice for the customer to make.

Even an apparently negative response can be useful. The customer who likes the style of a skirt but dislikes the colour can be shown another skirt in a colour she may prefer. The customer who objects to the price of an appliance can be shown a lower-priced model or can be shown how the particular appliance justifies the apparently high price. Unless the salesperson is aware of the customer's objections, nothing can be done to overcome them.

Salespeople are responsible for *selling* products and services. Customers have no responsibility to buy them. It is up to the salesperson to find out what the customer wants and match a product or service to those wants.

### Feature-Benefit Relationship

Whenever a salesperson describes the product or service to a customer, it should be described in terms of the **feature-benefit relationship.** Features and benefits are defined as follows:

- A *feature* is any tangible or intangible characteristic of a product or service.
- A *product benefit* is the customer's basic buying motive that is fulfilled by the feature.

For example, a salesperson says, "These all-leather hiking boots have waterproof seams. They are our highest-priced line, but the leather will last a long time, look good, and keep you dry even on wet trails." The salesperson mentioned two features, "all leather" and "waterproof seams." The benefits that the owner can expect to derive from these features were also mentioned as follows:

- "Last a long time." Although they are higher priced, they represent value because they won't have to be replaced frequently.
- "Look good." People want things that they wear to look good.
- "Keep you dry." People are naturally interested in comfort and in preserving their health.

People's buying motives vary widely. In fact, several people buying the same product might be looking for altogether different benefits. One man buys an expensive suit because of the status it confers upon him. Another man buys the same suit because its superior tailoring will make it more durable and long-lasting. A third buys it because he likes the styling.

The following are some typical benefits, as noted in Table 16–6, that people seek from the things they buy:

- *Safety:* The desire to protect their lives and property.
- *Economy:* Not just in the initial purchase price but in long-run savings through less frequent replacement or, in the case of certain products, lower maintenance and operating costs.
- *Status:* People buy things to be recognized. The woman buying an evening dress may consider the designer's name all-important. A 12-year-old boy might consider the brand of blue jeans or the autograph on a baseball bat to be equally important.
- *Health:* People buy exercise equipment, athletic equipment, and outerwear because they wish to preserve their health.
- *Pleasure:* People attend theatres, go to athletic events, eat at restaurants, and buy books and objects of art because they expect to derive personal pleasure from these pursuits.
- *Convenience:* People buy many things to make the routine chores of life easier. For example, the cook buys a cake mix because it is far more convenient than mixing the individual basic ingredients.

The list could go on indefinitely. The important question to consider is the customer benefits that are provided by the goods or services to be sold. Knowing these benefits, salespeople can describe products to customers in terms of the benefits that the customers can derive from them. Relatively few customers are interested in the technical or design details of a product. Customers are primarily interested in what the product will do for them. The principal reason for a salesperson to describe features of a product or service is to prove the benefits that the person can expect from it. For example, a salesperson might describe insulating material to a customer as follows: "This insulating material creates a thermal

**TABLE 16–6  Types of Buying Motives**

| Rational | Emotional |
|---|---|
| Price | Life-style image |
| Convenience | Adventure and excitement |
| Warranties | Pleasure |
| After-the-sale service | "Keeping up with the Joneses" |
| Economy | Good provider for family |
| Length of service | Pride |
| Health and safety | Fantasy fulfillment |
| Quality | Status |

barrier.'' Impressive words, perhaps, but the statement tells the customer little or nothing about the reasons for buying.

### Suggestion Selling

In **suggestion selling,** the salesperson tries to build upon the customer's initial request in order to sell additional or related merchandise. For example, the salesperson might suggest that a woman buy two blouses to take advantage of a weekend special. If a man buys a dress shirt, the salesperson should suggest a complementary tie. With a tablecloth, a salesperson might suggest napkins that go well with it. With a stereo receiver, a skilled salesperson could suggest a pair of speakers matched to the output of the receiver.

The opportunities for suggestion selling are endless. Frequently, the benefit that a customer might derive from one product could be used to develop suggestions for others. Young parents buying one safety product for a baby would be interested in seeing others. Or the man who buys a designer necktie for status reasons could be persuaded to buy a belt, shirt, or eyeglass frames from the same designer.

Even a ''no sale'' or a return can become a sales opportunity through suggestion selling. The customer who is looking for a shirt to buy as a gift may not find the right shirt but could be persuaded to buy something else, perhaps a necktie or a sweater. The man who returns a raincoat because it doesn't fit properly still needs a raincoat and could be sold one if the salesperson takes advantage of the opportunity for a suggestion sale.

### Involvement and Feedback[9]

When training people in sales skills, it is relatively easy to get their involvement and the feedback needed to evaluate their progress to better shape the training needed. Instead of telling salespeople how you would sell a certain product, ask them how they would do it, and what they would say to a customer.

After the trainer hears their presentations, he or she can explain any other features that should have been mentioned and any other benefits that are important. Then let the person try again, perhaps reviewing the basic technique of features and benefits if necessary.

Similarly, management can list a number of products that the store offers and have the salesperson write down a related product that he or she would suggest to every customer. In so doing, management will be gaining the trainee's active involvement and securing necessary feedback so it can see where review or correction is necessary. Management will also learn the employee's strengths and weaknesses so it can supervise more effectively.

*Criteria for Successful Training*

Regardless of the training method used, there are two key elements for success: trainee participation and feedback.

### Trainee Participation

The training process should directly involve the trainee. Listening to a person talk has little value. Few can absorb it. The passive role of reader or listener is seldom helpful in understanding and remembering. Reading a book or hearing a speech is fine for entertainment or intellectual stimulation, but these activities are seldom effective in a training environment. People learn by doing things. When new personnel are taught how to prepare an invoice or credit memo, it is not enough to tell them how or show them how. It is far more important to have them do it.

### Feedback

Feedback is what is learned by testing the employee's understanding of the facts that are being taught. It permits the trainer to measure the employee's progress at each step. Through feedback, management can recognize problems when they arise. Through early recognition of misunderstandings, management can correct the problems as soon as possible so that training can progress.

Feedback helps direct training efforts, since management then knows those things that give the employee particular difficulty, such as arithmetic or trade terminology. In the remainder of the training effort, management can then be particularly careful and painstaking in teaching anything that involves trade terminology or arithmetic skills.

## *Job Orientation*

A job description and a job specification can simplify the process of providing an orientation or introducing a new employee into the business. An orientation will make the new employee feel at ease and better able to begin work. It is important to note, however, that a job orientation only explains the job to the employee and does not train him or her to do it. A typical job orientation checklist is shown in Exhibit 16–3.

After the period of formal job training and orientation is completed, management still faces the task of helping the salesperson perform successfully. One way to do this is a programme of **management by objectives** that helps the person work to achieve tangible goals.

**EXHIBIT 16–3**

*Job orientation checklist*

□ Explain:
  □ Company purpose
  □ Company image
  □ Kind of clients catered to

□ Introduce to other employees and positions
□ Explain relationship between new employee's position and other positions

□ Tour the building:
  □ Working areas
  □ Management office
  □ Rest facilities

  □ Records
  □ Employee locker room or closet
  □ Other relevant areas

□ Explain facilities and equipment

□ Review the duties and responsibilities of the job from the job description

□ Introduce to emergency equipment and safety procedures

□ Questions and answers

# Chapter Highlights

- The trend today is toward more self-service. Improved signing, displays, packaging, and store layouts all make self-service possible. But retailers still need salespersons to answer customers' questions about the technical dimensions of products, to reassure customers about items of fashion apparel, and to help customers fit items such as shoes.

- The key to a good sales force is the right interaction between the merchandise, the customer, and the salesperson. A salesperson is needed when customers have little knowledge about the merchandise they plan to buy, when price negotiation is likely, and when the product is complex.

- The easiest type of selling is transaction processing. This means that employees simply serve as check-out clerks or cashiers and do little selling. Routine selling involves more product knowledge and a better approach to the sales task. Creative selling requires the use of creative sales skills by salespersons who need complete information about product lines, product uses, and technical features.

- The job of the salesperson is to lead the customer to a buying situation. Successful salespersons normally think of selling as a process consisting of the following steps: prospecting (preapproaching), approaching, determining needs and wants, demonstrating and handling merchandise, answering questions and meeting objections, closing, and following up.

- The most vital step in the selling process is closing the sale. Techniques include direct, assumptive, open-ended, action, and urgency closes.

- Developing a strong sales force is not a matter of luck. Training is needed; adequate incentives must exist to motivate personnel to high levels of performance; and supervision is necessary. Above all, management of the sales force means planning for increased sales. Sales per person can be increased by: better employee selection, training, and supervision; improved departmental layout; more self-selection by customers; streamlining sales processing; improved merchandising and promotion; making sure salespersons are fully knowledgeable about the products they're selling; and following up where necessary after the sale (for example, with the service department).

# Key Terms

Action close   431
Assumptive close   431
Benefit summary   429
Creative selling   420
Direct close   431
Feature-benefit relationship   437
Management by objectives   440
Merchandise approach   424
Open-ended close   431
Product benefit   429

Prospecting   423
Role playing   434
Routine selling   420
Seek agreement   428
Service approach   424
Suggestion selling   439
Transaction processing   420
Trial close   428
Urgency close   431

# Discussion Questions

1. What are the various types of retail selling? How do the skills required vary by type of selling? What is the difference between the service approach and the merchandise approach?

2. Under what conditions is the presence of sales personnel most essential in a retail store?

3. What are the various ways a salesperson can determine customer needs and wants?

4. Comment on the following statement: The best way for a salesperson to deal with a customer objection is simply to ignore it and continue with the sales presentation.

5. In closing a sale, how does an assumptive close differ from a close that might be used during a special sale event?

6. Why is sales force productivity so important? How can it be increased?

7. Why are self-selection and self-service becoming more common in retailing?

8. Assume that you have been asked by a retail store manager to describe what an effective sales training programme should include and what sales training methods can be used. How would you respond?

## Application Exercises

1. Visit with the personnel manager of the leading department store in your community and discuss briefly its training programmes for salespeople. Find out its major problems with sales personnel. Do the same thing with the manager of a fast-food franchise. Be prepared to discuss the differences you find.

2. Interview 10 to 15 of your fellow students and find out their overall impressions of salespersons in your community. Are they satisfied? If yes, why? If not, why not? Get their thoughts on what can be done to improve the quality of service in retail outlets. Now, talk to several of your friends who have worked or are working as part-time salespersons. Prepare a report based on their experiences. Get them to talk about their reactions to most customers in the stores where they work, their likes and dislikes about their jobs, and what could be done to make their jobs easier.

3. Visit three new-car dealers in your community and act as a serious buyer. Develop a list of questions ahead of time about such things as miles per gallon of the auto, service requirements, and warranty and safety features. Compare and contrast the results you get in talking to the different salespersons about each of these points. Find out if they have what you consider the needed knowledge for selling the product. Do they conduct themselves in the way you would expect from persons who are selling items valued at $10,000 to $20,000? If not, make suggestions for improving their quality of service to customers.

## Suggested Cases

## Endnotes

1. "Tuning into the Time Efficiency Factor," *Chain Store Age,* General Merchandise Edition, February 1984, p. 149.

2. This material, including Figure 16–1, is adapted from Bert Rosenbloom, *Improving Personal Selling* (Washington, D.C.: Small Business Administration), pp. 1–3.

3. Marlene Cartash, "Catch a Falling Store," *Profit,* December 1990, p. 22.

4. *On the Up-Beat,* no. 7A, 1980, pp. 12 and 13.

5. The material on closing the sale is adapted from *Marketing Strategy,* self-instructional booklet No. 1009 (Washington, D.C.: Small Business Administration).

6. *On the Up-Beat,* p. 23.

7. K. A. Boedecker and F. W. Morgan, "Managing the Salesperson—Prospect/Customer Interaction: Potential Legal Consequences of Salespersons' Statements," in *Enhancing Knowledge Development in Marketing,* eds. Paul Bloom et al. (Chicago: American Marketing Association, 1989), p. 307.

8. This material is adapted from *Managing Retail Salespeople,* self-instructional booklet No. 1019 (Washington, D.C.: Small Business Administration).

9. The material on involvement and feedback and criteria for successful training and job orientation is adapted from *Job Analysis, Job Specifications, and Job Descriptions,* self-instructional booklet No. 120 (Washington, D.C.: Small Business Administration).

# 17 RETAIL ADVERTISING, SALES PROMOTION, AND PUBLICITY

---

### Chapter Objectives

After reading this chapter, you should be able to:

1 Understand the requirements for good promotion plans.
2 Explain how to establish and allocate an advertising budget.
3 Describe the available media options.
4 Understand how to determine the effectiveness of media.
5 Explain how to measure the results of advertising.
6 Determine when to use an advertising agency.
7 Understand the essentials of a good advertisement.
8 Describe the role of sales promotion and publicity for the retail firm.

## Retailing Capsule

Advertising and sales promotion are an integral part of the marketing strategy of many successful retailers. Consider the following example:

Mega Movies, a Vancouver video chain, is anticipating that fewer consumers will want to rent videos, its principal source of income. "People have more and more choices through taping, cable, pay-per-view, and satellite," says vice-president Rob Thornton. "And the solution is to get consumers to buy videos to build their own libraries." Through an aggressive campaign of advertising, pricing, and promotion, video sales have reached 23 percent of revenues at Mega Movies' 24 stores in B.C. and Alberta (the Canadian average for the industry is 4 percent). To sell videos, says Thornton, the price has to be right (e.g., old classics and Disney children's movies that list for $26.99 are sold for $19.99). Shaving margins requires selling large volumes, and that's where creative marketing comes in. In 1991, $1 million—about 6 percent of revenues—was spent on direct-mail promotion, contest giveaways, and print and radio advertising. For Disney's release of *101 Dalmatians,* 850,000 full-colour flyers were mailed, and a full-page colour ad appeared in the *Vancouver Sun* and *Province* newspapers, highlighting their special-offer prices. To promote the heroines' run from the law in the movie *Thelma and Louise,* Mega Movies held an in-store draw for a trip to Mexico. And at Christmas, the chain again adopted a direct-mail strategy, sending out 650,000 gift video catalogs. The other side to discount marketing is selling other movies at full price. "We have to give customers other reasons to come here." For that purpose, the number of video titles for sale at each store was increased from 300 to 1,200, to give movie buffs greater selection.

Source: John Southerst, "Agents of Change," *Profit,* June 1992, p. 42.

This example illustrates the role of advertising and other forms of promotion in conveying the retailer's strategy to a target market. Retailers use promotion as a major source of communication with consumers. Promotion includes the creative use of advertising, sales promotion, and publicity in providing information to customers. The purposes of communication may be to inform the consumers of short-term price promotions, to help establish and maintain the desired image, or a variety of other tasks. The processes of developing promotion plans, establishing budgets, and evaluating the effectiveness of promotions are critical issues in the success of any retail firm. Retailers such as Mega Movies are constantly seeking new and creative ways of communicating with the consumer.

Promotion is an integral part of a firm's total merchandise process. If promotion efforts are not in harmony with decisions on pricing and other elements of the retail mix, the outlet will project a confusing and distorted image. Developing and maintaining store identity thus becomes the cornerstone of most retailers' promotion plans. Think about the successful positioning strategies the following retailers promoted through their campaigns:

- Zellers: "Where the Lowest Price Is the Law."
- Sears: "Your Money's Worth . . . and More."
- Goodyear: "From Tune Ups to Tires, Goodyear Takes You Home."
- Kentucky Fried Chicken: "We Do Chicken Right."
- McDonald's: "You Deserve a Break Today."
- Wendy's: "Where's the Beef?"
- Red Lobster: "For the Seafood Lover in You."

A sound promotion plan can be developed only in the context of the firm's marketing strategies. All promotion efforts should seek to tap the buying motivations of the target market groups selected by management. Sophisticated retailers develop promotion plans similar to those of leading nonretail firms. Each element of the retail plan should be supportive of the targeting and positioning of the firm. For example, media choice is affected by target market selection. Radio station audiences can be segmented by their appeal to teenagers, ethnic groups, or car drivers. Similarly, magazines can be chosen to reach boaters, hunters, tennis players, or the prospective bride. University or college newspapers are appropriate for reaching students.

Promotion objectives may be either strategic or tactical. *Strategic objectives* are long term, broad based, and designed to support the overall competitive strategy of the retailer by developing and maintaining a favourable identity or image. *Tactical objectives* are short run and designed to achieve specific, measurable goals that support the strategic objectives—for example, to liquidate last year's inventory and launch a new line.

## Understanding Communication

As individuals, we communicate in different ways. Retailers similarly have a variety of ways of communicating with consumers. One role of retail communications is to *inform,* by providing information on store hours, brands carried, services available, and so forth. Another role of retail communications is to *persuade* individuals to do a variety of things—for example, to make a merchandise purchase during a reduced price sale.

To be effective, these communications must mean the same thing to both the sender (the retailer) and the receiver (the target market). The **source** in the communication process is the originator of the message, normally the retailer. The **message** is the idea to be transmitted. The message must be right for the audience and for the purpose of the promotion. A careful analysis of the target audience will help the retailer understand how the ideas can be most effectively communicated to achieve the desired effect.

The next decision after message content selection is how to *transmit* the message in a communicable form. The message can be transmitted by such media as radio, television, newspaper, direct mail, or other means of message transmission. Market segmentation plays a particularly important role in this process because segmentation ensures that the message is targeted at a relatively homogeneous audience.

Developing the **promotion plan** requires starting with the goals of the firm. Retailers must decide (1) who they want to reach, (2) the message they want to get across, and (3) when and how often their message should reach the audience. Answers to the following questions can help in making such decisions:[1]

- What quality of merchandise do I sell?
- What kind of usage do I want to project?
- How do I compare with competition?
- What customer services do I offer?
- Who are my customers?
- What are their tastes?
- What are their income levels?
- Why do they buy from me?

Retailers cannot be all things to all people. They must segment their messages, markets, and merchandise. Understanding the customer is the key in all such decisions.[2] Sears' strategy, for example, makes its pitch to one family member at a time, informing dad of a new electronic tool, or trying to convince mom or the kids that Sears' apparel is fashionable. Sears carefully targets individual niches with product-oriented ads that allow the firm to make very specific statements, sometimes using moods or techniques that might not seem appropriate in its total store ads.[3]

Some people define promotion to include advertising, personal selling, and displaying merchandise. Personal selling was discussed in Chapter 16, and display and layout were explained in Chapter 12. We define promotion in this chapter as also including mass media advertising, publicity, and sales promotions such as coupons, contests, and premium offers.

# Advertising Goals and Budget

The basic goals of advertising can include:

- Communicating the total character or image of the store.
- Getting consumer acceptance for individual groups of merchandise.
- Generating a strong flow of traffic.
- Selling goods directly.

These goals can be combined with merchandising and store image objectives into the following framework:[4]

*How* much to spend ———→ Advertising budget

*What* to advertise ———→ Merchandise

*When* to advertise ———→ Timing

*Where* to say it ———→ Media

*How* to say it ———→ Copy

*Whom* to reach ———→ Audience

*How* to provide balance ——→ Planning

Communicating the total character of the store is known as **institutional advertising,** and the corresponding advertising campaign is called an *image campaign*. Neither specific merchandise nor prices are featured; rather, institutional advertising is designed to enhance the image of the outlet and to communicate targeting and positioning strategies to consumers. *Direct response advertising,* in contrast, induces consumers to take a specific action such as purchase particular merchandise, increase the volume of store traffic, or participate in some type of contest or giveaway. The corresponding advertising campaign is called an **event campaign.** The advertisement in Figure 17–1 is part of an image campaign, while the one in Figure 17–2 is part of an event campaign.

## *How to Set an Advertising Budget*

### Why Have an Advertising Budget?

A budget helps retailers plan their promotions. This step alone can go a long way toward better campaigns. Why? There are at least three reasons: (1) a budget forces retailers to set goals so they can measure the success of the promotions; (2) retailers are required to choose from a variety of options; and (3) budgets are more likely to result in well-planned ads.

### What Should Be in the Budget?[5]

Promotion is a completely controllable expense, and the function of the budget is to control expenditures. By comparing the budget with actual financial reports coming from business activities of the firm, it is possible to compare planned activities with actual events. This can be done through monthly tabulation, as shown in Table 17–1 (on p. 451). With this record, danger signals flash when the budget is becoming overextended. The accounts listed in Table 17–1 are not comprehensive; they serve only as examples.

What retailers would like to invest in advertising and what they can afford are seldom the same. Spending too much is obviously an extravagance, but spending too little can be just as bad in terms of lost sales and reduced visibility. Costs must be tied to results. It is necessary to be prepared to evaluate goals and assess capabilities and a budget will help do this.

The budget can help retailers choose and assess the amount of advertising and its timing. The budget also will serve as a benchmark for next year's plan.

**FIGURE 17–1**

*Institutional advertising in action*

**FIGURE 17–2**
*Event advertising*

SOURCE: Courtesy of Sears Canada.

***Methods of Establishing a Budget[6]***

There are three basic methods of establishing an advertising budget: (1) percentage of sales or profits, (2) unit of sales, and (3) objective and task. Management needs to use judgment and caution in deciding on any method or methods. The first two methods are naive in the sense that sales, in effect, help determine the advertising budget, while logically it should be the other way around. The third method is more in keeping with the logic that advertising affects sales, but it is more difficult to apply.

### Percentage of Sales or Profits

A widely used method of establishing an advertising budget is to base it on a percentage of actual sales. Advertising is as much a business expense as the cost of labour and should be related to the quantity of goods sold for a certain period.

The *percentage-of-sales method* avoids some of the problems that result from using profits as a base. For instance, if profits in a period are low, it might not be the fault of sales or advertising. But if retailers base the advertising budget on profits, they will automatically reduce the advertising allotment when profits are down. There is no way around it: 2 percent of $10,000 is less than 2 percent of $15,000.

If profits are down for other reasons, a cut in the advertising budget may very well lead to further losses in sales and profits. This, in turn, will lead to further reductions in advertising investment, and so on.

**TABLE 17–1    Promotion Budget**

| | Month | | Year to Date | |
|---|---|---|---|---|
| *Account* | *Budget* | *Actual* | *Budget* | *Actual* |
| **Media** | | | | |
| Newspaper | | | | |
| Radio | | | | |
| TV | | | | |
| Literature | | | | |
| Other | | | | |
| **Promotions** | | | | |
| Exhibits | | | | |
| Displays | | | | |
| Contests | | | | |
| **Advertising expense** | | | | |
| Salaries | | | | |
| Supplies | | | | |
| Stationery | | | | |
| Travel | | | | |
| Postage | | | | |
| Subscriptions | | | | |
| Entertainment | | | | |
| Dues | | | | |
| Totals | | | | |

In the short run, it may be possible to make small additions to profit by cutting advertising expenses. But such a policy could lead to a long-term deterioration of profits. By using the percentage-of-sales method, it is possible to keep advertising in a consistent relationship with sales volume. Sales volume is what advertising should be primarily affecting. Of course, gross margin, especially over the long run, should also show an increase if advertising outlays are being properly applied.

***How High Should the Percentage Be?***    The choice of a percentage-of-sales figure can be based on what other similar retailers are spending. This can be done since these percentages are fairly consistent within a given category of business. The information can be found in trade magazines such as *Marketing,* association publications, and reports published by financial institutions such as Dun & Bradstreet. It can also be purchased from companies such as Elliott Research (and its subsidiary, Media Measurement).

Table 17–2 presents some of the retailers that are among the top 100 companies in advertising spending.

Knowing the ratio for a particular industry helps retailers put their spending into a competitive perspective. Then, depending on the situation, retailers can decide to advertise more than or less than the competition. For example, compare Kmart Canada and Woodward Stores, both in terms of advertising expenditures and

TABLE 17–2   **Some Canadian Retailers that Advertise Heavily**

| Rank in 1991* | Retailer | Spending (000) | Revenues (000) | Spending/Revenues (percent)† |
|---|---|---|---|---|
| 3 | Sears Canada | $73,719 | $ 4,089,200 | 1.8% |
| 6 | Eaton's of Canada | 46,570 | N/A | N/A |
| 11 | Cineplex Odeon | 37,912 | 535,398 | 7.1 |
| 14 | McDonald's Restaurants of Canada | 32,828 | 775,269 | 4.2 |
| 21 | Leon's Furniture | 25,195 | 260,538 | 9.7 |
| 25 | Canadian Tire | 24,093 | 3,013,970 | 0.8 |
| 29 | Brick Warehouse | 22,272 | N/A | N/A |
| 34 | Great Atlantic & Pacific Canada | 19,575 | 2,553,449 | 0.8 |
| 36 | F. W. Woolworth | 17,606 | 2,087,526 | 0.8 |
| 46 | Canada Safeway | 15,387 | 4,339,587 | 0.4 |
| 48 | Provigo | 15,058 | 6,711,400 | 0.2 |
| 61 | Kmart Canada | 10,738 | 1,228,144 | 0.9 |
| 63 | Royal Bank of Canada | 10,699 | 13,953,898 | 0.1 |
| 74 | Dylex | 9,117 | 1,840,391 | 0.5 |
| 81 | Woodward Stores | 8,623 | 613,349 | 1.4 |
| 89 | Multitech Warehouse Direct | 7,858 | N/A | N/A |
| 93 | Home Hardware Stores | 7,185 | N/A | N/A |
| 94 | Le Groupe Vidéotron | 6,889 | 482,109 | 1.4 |
| 96 | Canadian Imperial Bank of Commerce | 6,683 | 12,911,748 | 0.1 |

*Based on the top 100 advertisers.
†In interpreting these figures, remember that some companies have large wholesale or commercial sales.
SOURCE: Adapted from "Canada's Top Advertisers," *Marketing,* April 20, 1992, p. 20; and *The Globe and Mail: Report on Business,* July 1992.

advertising-to-sales ratios. It may be necessary to outadvertise competitors and forgo short-term profits. Growth requires investment.

Retailers should not let any method bind them. The percentage-of-sales method is quick and easy and ensures that the advertising budget is not out of proportion for the business. It may be a sound method for stable markets. But if retailers want to expand market share, they may need to use a larger percentage of sales than the industry average.

***Which Sales?***   The budget can be determined as a percentage of past sales, of estimated future sales, or as a combination of the two.

*Past Sales.* The base can be last year's sales or an average of a number of years in the immediate past. Consider, though, that changes in economic conditions can make the figure too high or too low.

*Estimated Future Sales.* The advertising budget can be calculated as a percentage of anticipated sales for next year. The most common pitfall of this method is an optimistic assumption that the business will grow. General business trends must always be kept in mind, especially if there is the chance of a slump. The directions in the industry and in the firm must be realistically assessed.

*Past Sales and Estimated Future Sales.* Future sales may be estimated conservatively based on last year's sales. A more optimistic assessment of next year's sales is to combine both last year's sales with next year's estimated sales. It is a more realistic method during periods of changing economic conditions. This method allows management to analyze trends and results thoughtfully and predict more accurately.

## Unit of Sales

In the unit-of-sales method, retailers set aside a fixed sum for each unit of product to be sold. This figure is based on their experience and trade knowledge of how much advertising it takes to sell each unit. For example, if it takes 2 cents' worth of advertising to sell a case of canned vegetables, and the object is to move 100,000 cases, management will plan to spend $2,000 on advertising. If it costs $x$ dollars to sell a refrigerator, management will need to budget 1,000 times $x$ to sell a thousand refrigerators. Managers are simply basing the budget on unit of sales rather than dollar amounts of sales.

Some people consider this just a variation of percentage of sales. The unit-of-sales method, however, does permit a closer estimate of what should be planned to spend for maximum effect. This method is based on a retailer's experience of what it takes to sell an actual unit, rather than an overall percentage of the gross sales estimate.

The unit-of-sales method is particularly useful where product availability is limited by outside factors—for example, bad weather's effect on crops. The owners estimate the number of units or cases available to them. Based on a manager's experience, they advertise only as much as it takes to sell the products. The unit-of-sales method works reasonably well with specialty goods, where demand is more stable. But it is not very useful in sporadic or irregular markets or for style merchandise.

## Objective and Task

The most difficult (and least used) method for determining an advertising budget is the **objective-and-task method.** Yet this method is the most accurate and best fulfills what all budgets should accomplish. It relates the appropriation to the marketing task to be achieved.[7] This method relates the advertising spending to the volume of expected sales. To establish a budget by the objective-and-task method, it is necessary to have a co-ordinated marketing programme. This programme should be set up with specific objectives based on a thorough survey of markets and their potential.

The percentage-of-sales or profits method first determines the amount retailers will spend, with little consideration of a goal. The task method establishes what must be done in order to meet company objectives. Only then is the cost calculated.

It is best to set specific objectives, not just "increase sales." For example, a retailer wishes to "sell 25 percent more of product X or service Y by attracting the business of teenagers." First, the manager determines which media best reaches the target market. Then the retailer estimates the cost to run the number and types of advertisements it will take to get the sales increase. This process is repeated for each objective. When these costs are totalled, the projected budget is available. As this description indicates, applying this method requires an excellent knowledge of media planning principles, often not the case among retailers. The media representatives of each medium, an advertising agency, or a media buying service may often be of assistance to a retailer.

Of course, retailers may find that they cannot afford to advertise as they would like to. It is a good idea, therefore, to rank objectives. As with the other methods, managers should be prepared to change plans to reflect reality and the resources available.

*How to Allocate the Budget*

Once the advertising budget has been determined, management must decide how to allocate the advertising dollars. A decision to use institutional (image) advertising or promotional (sales) advertising must be made. After setting aside money for the different types of advertising, retailers can allocate the promotional advertising funds. Among the most common breakdowns are (1) departmental budgets, (2) total budget, (3) calendar periods, and (4) media.

### Departmental Budgets

The most common method of allocating advertising to departments is on the basis of their sales contribution. Those departments or product categories with the largest sales volume receive the biggest share of the budget.

In a small business, or when the merchandise range is limited, the same percentage can be used throughout. Otherwise, a good rule is to use the average industry figure for each product. By breaking down the budget by departments or products, those goods that require more promotion to stimulate sales can get the required advertising dollars. The budget can be further divided into individual merchandise lines.

### Total Budget

The total budget may be the result of integrated departmental or product budgets. If the business has set an upper limit for the advertising-expense percentage, then the departmental budgets might be pared down.

In smaller businesses, the total budget may be the only one established. It, too, should be divided into merchandise classifications for distribution.

### Calendar Periods

Most executives usually plan their advertising on a monthly, or even a weekly, basis. Even a budget for a longer planning period, however, should be calculated for these shorter periods as well. This permits better control. The percentage-of-sales method is useful to determine allocations by time periods. The standard practice is to match sales with advertising dollars. If February accounts for 5 percent of sales, it might get 5 percent of the budget.

Sometimes, retailers adjust advertising allocations downward in heavier sales months in order to boost the budget of poorer periods. This is done only when a change in advertising timing could improve slow sales, as when the competition's sales trends differ markedly from those of the retailer's firm.

Monthly percentages of annual sales differ by store type and region. Also, economic conditions can affect budget plans. Other ways for allocating funds focus on the traffic-drawing power of some items or on the growth potential of key lines. Sales variations by month normally have the largest effect on advertising. Almost three fourths of the advertising budget by boating retailers, for example, is spent during March–July. In contrast, over 20 percent of the advertising budget for jewellery is spent in the month of December. Garden supplies retailers spend over 50 percent of their advertising budget during March–June. December is the largest advertising month for appliance dealers, bookstores, department stores, retail furniture dealers, hardware dealers, music stores, and shoe stores.

### Media
The amount of advertising that is placed in each advertising medium such as direct mail, newspapers, or radio should be determined by past experience, industry practice, and ideas from media specialists. Normally, retailers use the same sort of media that competitors use, because it is most likely where potential customers will look or listen.

*A Flexible Budget*

Any combination of these methods may be employed in the formation and allocation of the advertising budget. All of them — or simply one — may be needed to meet the retailer's advertising objectives. However management decides to plan the budget, it must make it *flexible,* capable of being adjusted to changes in the marketplace.

The duration of the planning and budgeting period depends upon the nature of the business. If management can use short budgeting periods, it will find that advertising can be more flexible and that it can change tactics to meet immediate trends. To ensure advertising flexibility, management should have a contingency fund to deal with specials available in local media or unexpected competitive situations.

Management should be aware of competitors' activities at all times. It should not blindly copy competitors but, instead, analyze how their actions may affect business — and be prepared to act.

*Co-Operative Advertising*

**Co-operative advertising** is a situation in which a manufacturer pays part of the retailer's advertising costs under specific conditions. Many manufacturers and wholesalers state that a significant part of the reserves they set up for co-operative advertising is not used by their retailers. It has been estimated that $600 million of the $1.5 billion in co-op funds available to Canadian retailers goes unclaimed, and the reason is that many retailers do not know about these programmes or are unsure of how they operate.[8] This is surprising. Co-operative advertising substantially lowers the cost for the retailer, since manufacturers or wholesalers pay part of the advertising cost.

For their own legal protection, and to ensure the greatest return from their investment, manufacturers set up specific requirements to be observed in co-operative advertising. The retailer should consult each vendor about the requirements that must be met to qualify. The retailer must also be aware of the procedures to follow to apply for and receive payment. Some vendors relate co-operative dollars to the amount of the retailer's business. Others figure on a percentage basis. The amount and rules for payment of co-operative dollars are at the discretion of the vendor. For more details and examples, see Retail Highlight 17–1.

Co-operative advertising as a percentage of total advertising is approximately 50 percent for department stores, shoe stores, and clothing stores, and approximately 75 percent for food stores and electrical appliance stores.[9]

## Evaluating Media Options

Each medium has its strengths and weaknesses. Retailers normally use a media mix to give them the strengths of each. Media choices include radio, newspapers, TV, magazines, direct mail, and billboards. The characteristics of each medium are

---

**Retail Highlight 17–1**

## Understanding Co-Op Advertising Programmes

When Gary Kugler decided to get more aggressive about promoting Focus Centre, his camera store in Ottawa, he increased the advertising budget by 100 percent. Through co-operative advertising, Kugler's suppliers shared the costs of his newspaper and radio ads. In return, their products got greater exposure in the local market—and everyone benefited. As his co-op relationships developed, Kugler saw his annual sales increase by 20 percent. When he added a photo-finishing centre, he marked the expansion with a two-page insert in the *Ottawa Citizen,* for which most of his 20 suppliers contributed co-op funds. The ad cost $13,000, and Kugler's share amounted to $2,000.

In many co-op programmes retailers earn co-op dollars based on a percentage of purchases made from a distributor or manufacturer—between 2 and 5 percent, although the figure can go as high as 10 percent. For example, if Kugler buys $10,000 worth of Canon cameras, his supplier will give him 5 percent of that, or $500, to be spent in advertising Canon. The supplier then pays for a portion of advertising Canon cameras (see, for example, the ad in Figure 17–2), up to the amount of co-op dollars his dealer accumulates. Most suppliers pay 50 to 75 percent of the cost for any one campaign (in some cases, they pay the full amount).

The suppliers' sales representatives are very important sources of information for these programmes. Every manufacturer has different rules, from logo size to placement of the ad in the media. They can also provide ready-made ads or help the retailer create his or her own. Local media can also help. About 68 percent of co-op dollars are spent on newspaper advertising. In order to generate more co-op business, many newspapers handle much of the co-op paperwork, such as billing agreements. Finally, co-op dollars can also be used for a wide variety of promotions—for example, direct mail or sales promotions.

Source: Jennifer Pepall, "Co-Op Advertising Builds Strength from Numbers," *Profit,* November 1990, pp. 53–54.

shown in Table 17–3. Other specialized forms of promotion not shown in the table are also available and are discussed later in the chapter.

### Finding Information on Rates and Data about the Various Media

For most media, information about rates charged to national advertisers and ad agencies, as well as various conditions offered by the media, are published monthly in *Canadian Advertising Rates & Data (CARD).*[10] However, the rates charged directly to retailers are not published in *CARD* but in an individual retail rate card that retailers obtain directly from the local medium. For example, a quick phone call to the sales office of the local newspaper will get you the retail rate card for that newspaper. To illustrate, a portion of the *Montreal Gazette* retail rate card is reproduced in Exhibit 17–1.

Some of the reasons for charging different rates are (1) the medium does not pay the 15 percent commission to advertising agencies on retail rates, since most retailers do not use an advertising agency (because of a small budget and tight

---

**TABLE 17–3    Advantages and Disadvantages of Various Advertising Media**

|  | Advantages | Disadvantages |
|---|---|---|
| Newspapers | Good flexibility<br>Timeliness<br>Good local coverage<br>Broad acceptance<br>High believability | Short life<br>Poor reproduction quality<br>Small pass-along audience |
| Magazines | Good geographic and demographic selectivity<br>Good credibility and prestige<br>High-quality reproduction<br>Long life<br>Good pass-along readership | Long production lead time<br>Some waste circulation<br>Poor position guarantee |
| Radio | Mass use audience<br>Good geographic and demographic selectivity<br>Low cost | Audio presentation only<br>Lower audience attention than TV<br>Nonstandardized rate structure<br>Fleeting exposure |
| Television | Appeals to many senses<br>Commands high attention levels<br>High reach | High absolute cost<br>High clutter<br>Fleeting exposure<br>Less audience selectivity<br>Long production lead time |
| Direct mail | Best audience selectivity<br>Good flexibility<br>No clutter<br>Good personalization | Relatively high cost<br>Sometimes poor image |
| Outdoor | Good flexibility<br>High repeat exposure<br>Low cost<br>Low competition | Poor audience selectivity<br>Limited creativity |

**Exhibit 17–1**

*Retail rate card for a newspaper*

# RETAIL RATE CARD
Effective January 1, 1992

## 1. R.O.P. VOLUME RATES (12-month contracts)

| Modular Agate Lines | Sun./Fri. | Modular Agate Lines | Sun./Fri. |
|---|---|---|---|
| Transient | 6.25$ | 50,000 | 3.53 |
| 1,000 | 4.90 | 65,000 | 3.52 |
| 2,000 | 3.97 | 75,000 | 3.45 |
| 5,000 | 3.75 | 100,000 | 3.42 |
| 7,000 | 3.71 | 200,000 | 3.40 |
| 10,000 | 3.67 | 400,000 | 3.35 |
| 15,000 | 3.62 | 500,000 | 3.32 |
| 25,000 | 3.59 | 700,000 | 3.28 |
| 35,000 | 3.58 | 1,000,000 | 3.21 |

**SATURDAY:** Add 30% to Sun./Fri. line rates.
**MULTIPLE PAGE DISCOUNTS:** Available. Separate rate card upon request.

## 2. FREQUENCY RATES

To obtain a frequency discount, the advertiser must make a commitment as to the level of frequency when placing the initial advertisement.

|  |  | Sun./Fri. |
|---|---|---|
| 2 - 6 times within | 13 weeks | $4.42 |
| 7 - 12 times within | 26 weeks | $4.10 |
| 13 - 19 times within | 26 weeks | $3.90 |
| 20 + times within | 52 weeks | $3.74 |

**Saturday:** Add 30% to Sun./Fri. modular agate line rates.

## 3. SPECIAL CLASSIFICATIONS:

■ Religious services in Metropolitan Montreal churches and synagogues, appearing on religion page
$2.35 per line
■ Fund raising activities by Metropolitan Montreal charitable organizations    Sun./Fri. $2.35 per line   Sat. + 30%
■ Community and cultural organizations that primarily serve Metropolitan Montreal    Sun./Fri. $3.30 per line   Sat. + 30%
■ Art Galleries    $3.86 per line
■ Book pages    Sat.    $3.86 per line
■ Restaurants    $3.86 per line
■ Educational institutions in Metropolitan Montreal
Sun./Fri.  $3.86 per line   Sat. + 30%

## 4. POSITION

■ No advertising on pages 1, 3 or editorial page.
■ First section guaranteed at 15% extra (no specific page).
■ Page 2: 75% extra (40 modular agate lines x 2 columns minimum, 160 modular agate lines x 4 columns maximum).
■ Pages 4 to 7 of first section: 50% extra (100 modular agate lines x 3 columns minimum).
■ All other guarantees: 30% extra.
■ Stock Table Pages:
50% extra 50 modular agate lines x 6 columns only.

## 5. COLOR ADVERTISING

| Color options | Sun./Fri. | Sat. |
|---|---|---|
| B/W + 1 color | $1,300.00 | $1,690 |
| B/W + 2 colors | $1,500.00 | $1,950 |
| B/W + 3 colors | $1,800.00 | $2,340 |

■ Under 400 modular agate lines: advertisement may not be guaranteed page exclusivity for color.
■ **Double truck:** appropriate color charge for each page used.
■ **Standby color**
B/W 1 color    Sun./Fri. $600.00    Sat. $780.00
The "standby color" rate is applicable when an advertisement is located on a page where spot color becomes available at the last moment.

## 6. BANNERS & VERTICALS

Earned rate will apply, plus the following premiums:

| 1 insertion | +75% |
|---|---|
| 6 insertions | +50% |
| 13 insertions | +45% |

## 7. BREAK PAGE BANNERS

| Section | Size | Availability |
|---|---|---|
| Business | 40 x 6 cols. | Mon. thru Sat. |
| "B" Section | 40 or 25 x 6 cols. | Mon. thru Fri. |
| Sports | 40 or 25 x 6 cols. | Mon. thru Sat. |
| Entertainment | 40 or 25 x 6 cols. | Mon. thru Fri. |

## 8. BREAK PAGE VERTICALS

One size only: 65 x 1-1/2 cols. - 97.5 lines

| Section | Availability |
|---|---|
| Living | Monday |
| Fashion (Style) | Tuesday |
| Food | Wednesday |
| Home | Thursday |
| Travel | Saturday |
| Show | Saturday |
| Living | Saturday |

## 9. ISLAND POSITION

Available Tuesday through Saturday on the Business Stock pages

| Minimum size | 100 x 2 |
|---|---|
| Maximum size | 100 x 4 |

Earned rate will apply plus the following premium:

| 1 insertion | +50% |
|---|---|
| 3 insertions | +40% |
| 6 insertions or more | +30% |

Source: Courtesy of the *Montreal Gazette*.

schedules); (2) retailers do not normally need the total audience of a medium, as their trading area is more restricted.

Most retail advertising in Canada is spent on daily newspapers, followed by radio (Table 17–4) because it effectively reaches geographic targets. Table 17–5 provides two examples of media budget allocations for a retailer.

## Media Terminology

Before discussing the various media available to a retailer, a few definitions would be useful:

- **Reach** is the number of different persons exposed at least once to a message during an ad campaign. Reach is often expressed as a percentage of the total audience.

**TABLE 17–4   Retail Advertising for Each Medium, and Share of Retail Advertising per Medium**

| Medium | Retail Expenditures (000) | Distribution (percent total retail) | Retail Share (percent total medium) |
|---|---|---|---|
| Television | $  374,917 | 13.6% | 24.4% |
| Radio | 597,399 | 21.7 | 75.9 |
| Newspapers: | | | |
|   Daily* | 1,116,892 | 40.5 | 69.4 |
|   Weekly | 621,823 | 22.6 | 90.0 |
|   Weekend supplements | 20,623 | 0.7 | 94.9 |
| Magazines | 25,270 | 0.9 | 10.0 |
|   Total retail | $2,756,924 | 100.0% | 56.3% |

*Excludes classified advertising.

SOURCE: *The Canadian Media Directors' Council Media Digest, 1992/93*, p.6.

**TABLE 17–5   Media Budget Allocations for Two Large Retailers**

| Medium | Sears Canada | | Eaton's of Canada | |
|---|---|---|---|---|
| | (in $000s) | (percent) | (in $000s) | (percent) |
| Television | $22,504 | 30.5% | $ 9,007 | 19.3% |
| Daily newspapers | 47,408 | 64.3 | 32,035 | 68.8 |
| Magazines | 3,088 | 4.2 | 5,093 | 10.9 |
| Out-of-home | 719 | 1.0 | 435 | 0.9 |
| Total | 73,719 | 100.0% | 46,570 | 100.0% |

SOURCE: "Canada's Top Advertisers," *Marketing,* April 20, 1992, p. 20.

- **Frequency** is the average number of times a person will be exposed to a message during the advertising period.
- **Cost per thousand (CPM)** is the cost of reaching 1,000 members of a desired audience with one or several ads.
- **Selectivity** is the ability of a medium to reach only specific audiences, minimizing waste (e.g., only teenagers, or men aged 24 to 45).

*Radio*

Radio follows the listener everywhere: in the home, at the beach, and on the highway. Almost every Canadian owns at least one radio. There are currently 377 AM stations and 333 FM stations in Canada.[11] Radio advertising is characterized by comparatively low rates, little or no production costs, and immediacy in scheduling. Retailers spend about 22 percent of their advertising dollars for radio (Table 17–4), and radio stations depend on retail advertisers for 76 percent of their revenues.

    Basic rates depend on the number of commercials contracted for, the time periods specified, and whether the station broadcasts on AM and/or FM frequencies.

Usually, FM broadcasting is more localized and offers wider tonal range, for technical reasons.

### Strengths of Radio

Radio allows retailers to (1) direct ads to large target audiences; (2) reach people at home, in their cars, on the beach, and almost anywhere else; (3) advertise at relatively low cost; and (4) work with short lead time.

### Disadvantages of Radio

The disadvantages of radio are (1) no pictures; (2) short messages; (3) the need to use several stations in large cities to reach a large target audience; (4) production problems, since most programming is local; and (5) large, wasted audiences for small local retailers.

Radio advertising is used to convey and reinforce distinctive images that draw shoppers to retail outlets. Such advertising typically is institutional, stressing features retailers believe customers are looking for. Humour, ad-lib dialogues, catchy music, and jingles increasingly are used to create bright images in radio advertising. Exhibit 17–2 provides some examples of radio commercials. Retailers prefer institutional advertising over price advertising because they believe that price/item advertising gets ''lost'' on air.

### Buying Radio Time

Radio advertising time is typically sold in blocks of 30- or 60-second slots, with a few stations offering 15-second slots. The 60-second slots tend to be most popular. The price of advertising time varies by time of day, size of listening audience, and length of the spots.

Radio rate schedules vary by stations, as does the system of discounts. The most expensive time is known as *drive time,* between 6 and 10 A.M. and 4 and 7 P.M. on weekdays. Advertising is very inexpensive between midnight and 5 A.M., since few people are listening to the station. Weekend rates often differ from weekly rates, depending on the composition of the audience.

Other factors affecting cost include the frequency of advertising during a given week, the number of weeks the ad is aired, and the time of year the spot is on the air. The station may select the air time or the retailer may choose a more costly fixed time slot. If the slots are part of a package, they probably consist of different time slots and frequencies for an extended period of time.

*Television*

TV has the visual impact of print and the sound impact of radio, plus colour, motion, and emotion. Canadians now spend as much time viewing TV as radio, newspapers, and magazines combined, about 25 hours per week for adults and 20 hours for children. Problems include the high cost of time and high production costs. Most people view TV at night after the stores are closed. Infrequent summer viewing is also a disadvantage, as is the increasingly fragmented audience because of cable services, either part of the basic subscription such as Vision TV or the Youth Channel, or pay-TV such as Cable News Network, The Sports Network,

**EXHIBIT 17–2**

*Radio scripts*

### WE WISH YOU A MERRY HAIRCUT

**SFX:** *(Christmas music in background)*
**TONY:** *Hi, this is Tony of Tony's Barber Shop. All the other stores here at First Canadian Place Shops, like Fairweather, Benetton and Your Jewelry, are full of shoppers looking for novel gift ideas. So, I'd just like to say, consider the gift of a haircut. 'Cause you never have to worry about a loved one getting two haircuts for Christmas...ever.*
**ANNOUNCER:** *First Canadian Place Shops at King and Bay. One hundred and sixty stores full of gift ideas.*

### WHEN DRY CLEANERS DREAM

**SFX:** *(Christmas music in background)*
**RAJ:** *Hi, this is Raj from Preeners Dry Cleaners. Other stores here at First Canadian Place Shops, like Bally Shoes, Cactus and Lipton's, are full of shoppers looking for unusual gift ideas. So, don't forget about us—Preeners Dry Cleaners—and give someone you love the gift of dry cleaning. Imagine the surprise when they open a gift and find their dry cleaning. Just imagine.*
**ANNOUNCER:** *First Canadian Place Shops at King and Bay. One hundred and sixty stores full of gift ideas.*

### COME ALL YE HEELS

**SFX:** *(Christmas music in background)*
**FRANK:** *Hi, this is Frank from Mastercraft Shoe Repair. Here at First Canadian Place Shops, other stores like Costello, Kristy Allan and Town Shoes are full of shoppers looking for unique gift ideas. So don't forget us—Mastercraft Shoe Repair. Have a heel replaced for that special someone, or if you really love somebody, consider deodorized insoles. Merry Christmas.*
**ANNOUNCER:** *First Canadian Place Shops at King and Bay. One hundred and sixty stores full of gift ideas.*

Creative Director: Terry O'Reilly

SOURCE: Courtesy of Pirate Radio.

and others. Another major problem for advertisers is the high incidence of channel switching, made so easy by remote controls, which lowers the chance of the commercial being seen.

Local TV stations carry the programmes of major networks. There are two English (CBC and CTV) and one French (Radio Canada) national commercial networks in Canada, eight regional or provincial networks, and 10 specialty networks. Canadian network programmes are viewed by about 50 percent of the TV audience (against 20 percent for the U.S. stations, 11 percent for the Canadian independents, 8 percent for the specialty channels, and 4 percent for pay-TV).[12]

The network programmes include commercials bought by national retailers such as Eaton's or Sears. The stations sell local commercial time during station breaks. Management probably should plan on using daytime, news programme times, and early evening hours before TV prime time.

### TV Ads Are Costly

The cost for a 30-second ad in prime time (8 P.M.– 11 P.M.) in a small local market such as Red Deer (Alberta) may cost between $100 and $200; in a major market such as Toronto, a similar ad may cost between $700 and $2,000.

### Cost per Viewer Is the Lowest for a National Audience

However, few retail firms other than Eaton's, The Bay, Sears, and Kmart have enough outlets to justify national TV ads. Use of local TV by large retailers is increasing, but about 14 percent of retail ad expenditures go to television. TV stations rely on local advertising for only 24 percent of their revenues (Table 17–4).

Few retailers feel that TV is the best overall medium by which to reach their audience. However, they are more prone to use television to reach a specific target audience like youth, which has been weaned on TV. Cable penetration in Canada is very high and reached 72 percent in 1992. Penetration of cable converters, to allow reception of additional stations within the basic subscription, has reached 56 percent. Pay TV, with a low penetration, does not yet have a sufficiently large audience, particularly in major markets, to attract many national advertisers.[13]

### Buying Television Time

Television time is normally sold in 15-, 30-, and 60-second time slots, with the 30-second slot being the most popular. The cost of television depends on the size of the audience, which can be described in terms of ratings and shares.

A **gross rating point (GRP)** is 1 percent of all homes with television sets in a market area. A programme with a GRP of 10 is reaching 10 percent of the television homes. In contrast, a **share** is the percentage of television sets in use that are tuned to a given programme. Thus, a programme may have a GRP of only 1, for example, at 4 A.M. on Sunday morning, but it may also have a share of 56.

*Newspapers*

About 41 percent of all retail ad dollars go to daily newspapers, and another 23 percent go to weeklies and weekend supplements (Table 17–4). Daily newspapers rely on retail advertising for about 70 percent of their revenues. The other types of newspapers depend on retail advertising for more that 90 percent of their revenues.

### Daily Newspapers

Most markets have some type of daily newspaper, and newspaper ad supplements are a popular advertising medium. **Supplements** are preprinted pages of ads that are inserted into the papers. Sunday papers are usually full of supplements, and local department stores are heavy users. There are about 109 daily newspapers in Canada with an average daily circulation of 5.3 million copies and a penetration of 60 percent of households. Almost 8 million adults read daily newspapers, spending about one hour reading them.[14]

Newspaper ad rates are quoted for short-term advertisers as weekly insertion rates, as monthly rates, and as yearly rates. Newspapers quote local retailers a retail rate that is below the general rate (charged to agencies for national advertisers).

Newspaper personnel speak in terms of modular agate lines when quoting prices. A **modular agate line (MAL)** is one (standardized) column wide and 1.8 mm deep. In addition, a **Canadian newspaper unit (CNU)** is a unit one column wide and 30 MALs deep. Newspapers have special rates for supplements, and rates for colour are higher than black-and-white rates.

The strengths of newspapers include (1) broad market coverage; (2) short lead time for ads; (3) the opportunity to advertise a large number of items together; (4) wide readership; (5) high graphic potential; and (6) assistance in ad preparation (important for a small retailer).

Newspapers have their weaknesses, too. These include (1) problems in reaching the younger market and children; (2) the chance that many readers will miss an ad; (3) accelerating ad rates; (4) limited ability to segment readers; and (5) lower suburban coverage by big-city papers.

The newspaper office can be helpful in planning the copy and layout. Many small retailers have few skills in these areas and rely on the newspaper professionals to provide the needed services.

### Community Newspapers

**Community newspapers** are published in almost every community in Canada, with the majority being published once a week. In Table 17–4, they are included in the "weeklies" category and rely almost exclusively on retail advertising. Their circulation has been increasing because their editorial coverage deals principally with local issues of interest to many readers. There are about 1,100 community newspapers in Canada, with an average weekly circulation of 12 million.[15] They tend to be well read within the community and represent an attractive audience for local retailers, and often are a very efficient buy, since there is little wasted circulation. The main drawback is the low frequency of publication.

### Shoppers

**Shoppers** go by many names, including *shopping news, pennysavers,* or *marketplace*. These papers are quite different from the traditional newspaper. They normally carry less than 25 percent editorial content. Virtually all news is syndicated feature material as opposed to local news, and shoppers are distributed free.

Shoppers offer retailers the opportunity for almost total coverage of a market area. Since they are primarily an advertising medium, the people who read them are already in a buying mood and seeking specific information. Still, the fact that the papers primarily contain advertising may cause some customers not to read them, and wasted advertising can occur.

More and more merchandisers are demanding the services of shoppers, however, since they want better market coverage. Each shopper has its own advertising rate schedule, and costs are often quite low. However, the coverage of markets in Canada is uneven, with the majority of shoppers in Ontario and a handful in Quebec, New Brunswick, Manitoba, and Saskatchewan. Suppliers in the Toronto metropolitan area provide about 6 different shoppers. Each will cover only a selected portion of the metropolitan area, such as a specific suburban community.[16]

### Special-Purpose Papers

There are newspapers for special-interest groups such as universities or community colleges (over 200), farmers (about 90 publications), and ethnic groups (about 140). General information about these media is also available in *CARD,* with retail rates from the publisher. These media are especially desirable advertising outlets for retailers who are seeking to reach highly specific audiences.

*Magazines*

As shown in Table 17–4, only 1 percent of retail ad budgets is spent on magazines. Until recently, the only retailers using magazines were national firms such as

Eaton's (10.9 percent) or Sears (4.2 percent), as illustrated in Table 17–5. However, local retailers can now place ads in regional editions of such magazines as *Reader's Digest, Maclean's,* and *Chatelaine*. There are over 540 consumer magazines in Canada, and about 30 of them offer geographic editions.

Magazine strengths include (1) carefully defined audiences, (2) good colour reproduction, (3) long ad life because they are not thrown away as quickly as newspapers, (4) low cost per thousand readers, and (5) good pass-along readership (as some magazines are read by people other than the subscribing household, such as friends and neighbours).

The primary problems are (1) high cost, (2) long closing dates (ads must be submitted several weeks before publication for monthly magazines), and (3) slower response.

### Buying Magazine Advertising Space

Advertising space is typically sold in pages or fractions of pages, such as one half or one sixth. The rates charged depend upon the circulation of the magazine, quality of the publication, and type of primary audience. Rates are higher for magazines with higher circulation. Magazines typically offer discounts for advertising depending upon the bulk and frequency of advertising. Higher prices are normally charged for special positions in the magazine and for special formats.

*Direct Promotion*    Four primary trends are responsible for the growth of **direct promotion:**

- There is an effort, because of labour shortages and high wage rates, to avoid the labour-intensive nature of in-store retailing. Direct promotions such as mail order and telemarketing (i.e., selling over the telephone) require less labour per unit of output than in-store retailing. As a result, productivity is higher than in other forms of retailing.

- The accelerating cost of land and buildings in prime locations has squeezed the profit returns on many forms of retailing. The use of direct-mail promotions allows management to avoid some of the high overhead costs associated with prime locations in major metropolitan areas.

- Shifts in the social environment explain why direct marketing is growing at two to three times the rate of in-store retailing. Most householders today are confronted with a scarcity of time. They would rather spend their limited time on leisure activities, as opposed to shopping. As a result, consumers are becoming less store loyal over time, perceive less risk in purchasing by direct marketing than in the past, and tend to be more experienced in their choices of merchandise.

- The fragmentation of markets and consumer life-styles is contributing to this rapidly growing form of promotion. Direct promotion in its various forms can allow management to carefully target mailings or to use cable TV as a way to reach narrowly defined segments of consumers. Direct promotion also allows management to expand its merchandising efforts beyond the typical trading area of a retail store and to target groups that would otherwise be difficult to reach. Technology breakthroughs, in the form of two-way cable shopping systems and developments in electronic funds transfer, are also allowing management to overcome the payment and credit problems that traditionally have plagued some forms of direct promotion.

## Direct Mail

Direct mail is the most selective form of retail advertising. But the cost per person reached is high. According to retailers, direct mail is among the top three forms of retail advertising today.

Most retailers use some form of direct mail.[17] Typical examples of catalogs are shown in Figure 17–3. The strengths include (1) the high response rate by consumers, (2) the ability to send material to a specific person, (3) not being bound by media format (it is possible to use as much space as needed to tell the story of the product and use colours or other creative effects as the budget allows), and (4) the message does not have to compete with other editorial matter.

The weakness of direct mail is its high cost compared to other media. The cost per thousand is many times higher than for other media.

There are good reasons for the popularity of direct mail. Direct mail includes bill stuffers (which are about 70 percent of direct mail), catalogs, flyers for store openings, sales letters, and everything we normally call *junk mail*. To cut costs, some retailers have resorted to hand-delivered flyers to selected targets. In addition to lower costs of printing and distribution (compared to a newspaper insert), the retailer can more effectively reach intended customers.[18]

*The Procedure for Direct Mailing.*    Mailing lists can be rented from mailing houses. The list can be selected according to consumer tastes on a variety of bases, including, for example, model of automobile, family income, tendency to buy through mail-order companies, and FSA code (forward sortation area codes are the first three digits of the postal code) or census tract. A typical mailing list will cost between $30 and $50 a thousand. An occupant list (no personalized name) of all households in a designated area may cost as little as $5 per thousand. Understandably, the more precise and well-defined the list, the higher the cost.

The frequency of mailing depends on the purpose of the campaign. However, to generate new sales leads, one consulting firm recommends one mailing every other month for continuity and long-term effectiveness, or four mailings six weeks apart for maximum short-term impact. But one annual mailing may be sufficient for a seasonal operation or for a firm that occasionally needs a limited amount of new business.[19]

## Catalogs

Many merchants now operate catalog sales departments. Sales through mail catalogs are growing. It is estimated that there are about 600 catalog firms in Canada, generating $2.2 billion in annual sales. In addition, there is very strong competition from U.S. catalog firms such as L. L. Bean and Lands' End, which generate more than $200 million in Canadian sales.[20]

**Figure 17–3**

*Direct promotion
using mail catalogs*

Source: Photo by Sandy McDougall.

Catalogs are a special form of direct-mail promotion and are often used as an advertising medium by department and specialty stores—for example, the Sears Catalog or the Regal Gifts Catalog. Most large department stores now have Christmas catalogs. Consumers like catalogs because of the convenience afforded by shopping at home, calling a toll-free number, and getting door-to-door delivery. There is even a *Catalogue of Canadian Catalogues* (Alpel Publishing). It has been estimated that about 60 percent of Canadians make a catalog or mail-order purchase during a one-year period.[21]

The following are trends in catalog marketing:

- New and better design. Recently, upscale retailers like Birks have introduced "magalogs," which are catalogs containing articles about related subjects. However, these can be very expensive to produce and distribute. In Birks' "The Spirit of Adventure," the theme of all the articles is an African safari.[22]

- Emphasis on life-style merchandising, although the term itself is defined in almost as many different ways as there are catalogs.

- A stepped-up search for cost-cutting techniques, including charging a subscription to a series of catalogs, or offering the catalog, via magazine advertising, at a charge to noncustomers.

- Growth of separate catalog operations, with full responsibility for inventory and controlling direct-mail business.

The typical department store catalog has a life of about six weeks. Two or three catalogs per year is not uncommon for some stores, and many are talking about 20 or more ''specialogs.'' For example, Sears produces about 15 catalogs per year, almost like a magazine publication. A few have over 1,000 pages, and the others 300 pages or less. The emphasis in all of the stores is on target mailing—the use of catalogs to sell separate categories of merchandise. Stores are increasingly using computers to target prime customers, instead of using blanket mailings.

*Directories*

Every retail business normally advertises in one or more directories. The most common is the Yellow Pages in the telephone directory. Directories, however, are published by various trade associations and groups, and they reach more prospective customers than virtually any other medium. Consumers have normally already made a decision to purchase before turning to a directory for help in deciding where to buy. Also, directories have a longer life than most advertising media.

Most directories are published for a minimum of 12 months, which can be a drawback. Retailers do not have the option of changing the advertisement until the appearance of a new directory. Thus, the advertisements may become obsolete quickly.

But costs are reasonable for ads such as the Yellow Pages advertising in a telephone directory. A half-column display ad can vary from $20 a month in an area with 20,000 residents to $200 a month or more in an area of 1 million.

*Out-of-Home Advertising*

Retailers are in a unique position to place advertisements near their stores, or along the roads leading to their stores. **Out-of-home advertising** may make use of a large variety of media, with the most important being transit advertising (e.g., buses) and outdoor advertising (e.g., billboards), but there are many other minor ones available at a relatively low cost (e.g., bench advertising).

**Transit Advertising**

Transit advertising includes signs placed on buses, subway cars, and commuter trains, as well as advertising placed in the terminals, platforms, and stations for such

*Painted buses make a strong statement.*

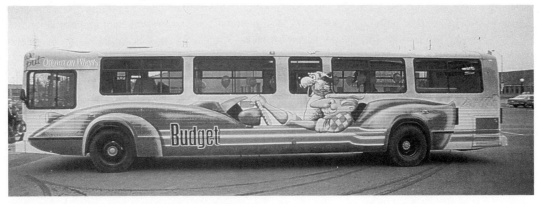

SOURCE: Courtesy of Budget Car and Truck Rentals of Ottawa.

vehicles. Painted buses, where the whole bus is painted with the message, have become popular in the last few years, although they tend to be expensive.

Transit advertising has a captive audience in the people using the vehicles. Outdoor transit advertising (on the outside of the vehicle) is especially effective for certain types of retailers. The vehicles carrying the advertising normally travel through the business area of a community and have a high level of exposure to prospective consumers.[23] Transit advertising is typically a media option only for retailers in large metropolitan areas. Small areas normally do not have public transportation.

### Outdoor Advertising Signs

Outdoor advertising signs are among the oldest forms of advertising. Outdoor signs can be found along the roads, at airports, in malls, and in the downtown areas of major cities.

Most retailers have signs outside their business even if they don't use billboards. Outdoor advertising signs have a large number of advantages, one of which is a high exposure rate. People tend to see the same outdoor billboard many times a month because they tend to follow the same traffic pattern each day. The signs are inexpensive but are heavily read by travellers and other customers seeking specific information.

The disadvantages are the relatively small amount of information that can be placed on a billboard, the large amount of display space needed, and the competition with other billboards in a community.

*Buying Outdoor Advertising.* Outdoor advertising usually is bought from companies that specialize in leasing sign space to merchants. Outdoor signs come in a variety of sizes, shapes, and locations. The typical billboard size is 3.7 metres by 7.5 metres. Outdoor advertising signs are bought in terms of a set level of GRPs. A 100 GRPs weekly in a market means that advertising space was purchased on enough posters to deliver an *exposure* level equal to 100 percent of the population in an area on the average during a week.

Nonstandard signs are normally those erected by the retailer. No standard size exists for such billboards. And the retailers arrange with each individual landowner for the space they want to lease. They have to be careful not to violate local regulations on the placement and construction of the signs, however. Billboards are becoming increasingly controversial in many communities because of concerns over quality of life and aesthetics.

### Other Out-of-Home Media

Other options for retailers include aerial advertising (e.g., balloons and skywriting), bench advertising, elevator advertising, sports advertising (e.g., in hockey arenas), taxicab and truck advertising, and theatre and videoscreen advertising. An example of the use of aerial advertising by a retailer is provided in Exhibit 17–3.

### Exhibit 17–3

#### Aerial advertising for a retailer

This balloon belongs to M.O.M. Printing, one of the largest printing firms in the Ottawa-Hull area. It cost $100,000, is 26 metres long, and sees about 100 flying days a year, depending on the weather. Rides are occasionally donated to charitable groups.

Source: "Balloons Help Printer's Message Fly," *Marketing,* June 29, 1992, p. 15.

***Video Tech***

We discussed video technology in Chapter 3 and are highlighting it again as a reminder of its growing impact on promotion plans. Video involves promoting directly to the consumer by the use of cable TV, teletext, or video discs. Technological advances in two-way interactive cable are making shop-at-home services more feasible. The primary drawback still is the high cost per purchase. Nevertheless, merchants are looking at the new technologies as ways of expanding their profit centres.

There are a number of shopping channels in Canada, either in existence or in the planning stages; these continuous cable television programmes are some of the most ambitious experiments in video shopping, and it is expected that this innovation will have a profound effect in the retailing sector.[24] In the real estate field, RE/MAX is showing 4,000 homes that are available in the Montreal market through Télémarché and the CF Cable TV. Télémarché already offers automobiles and retail sales programmes through the cable company.

Use of in-store audio and video promotion devices is one of the rapidly expanding areas of opportunity for retailers. Examples include:

- *Video screens:* These are in-store TV screens mounted at eye level that are sometimes linked together to form a video wall for presenting brief brand and price identification messages lasting for 7 to 10 seconds.
- *Audio systems:* Messages can be placed anywhere and typically are activated by motion or body heat. The devices contain a 10- to 20-second recorded selling message calling attention to a product and are typically placed within an aisle.
- *Shopping carts:* Some shopping carts today contain a video message that can be activated by the consumer.
- *In-store kiosks:* Such devices typically are placed next to a product and can operate either on constant play or be activated by a consumer who wants to see and hear a message about the product.[25]

### *Specialty Advertising*

Specialty advertising uses gift giving to customers as the advertising medium. Examples of gifts include matchbooks, fountain pens, calendars, and key chains. The gifts typically contain the name of the firm, company address, and perhaps its logo or slogan. The business endeavors to build goodwill among customers by providing useful items that will remind customers of the firm each time they use them. The specialty items chosen should match the type of merchandise sold by the firm. For example, wallpaper and paint stores often will provide a tape measure. But specialty advertising is more useful in retaining present customers than in attracting new ones.

### *Visual Merchandising*

Visual merchandising is often viewed as a form of nonmedia advertising. Visual merchandising was introduced in Chapter 12, but we want to remind you again of its critical role in communicating store image to consumers. Good displays inform the consumer about the merchandise offered and help to entertain and delight the consumer in such a way as to differentiate the outlet from competitors. As such, visual merchandising is part of a total store focus for communicating a unified image.

# Evaluating the Effectiveness of Media

Media effectiveness is usually measured in terms of (1) cost per thousand and (2) reach and frequency, in order to establish a price/value relationship between media options.

### *Cost per Thousand (CPM)*

The most common method of evaluating the cost effectiveness of several media is the cost per thousand (CPM). The CPM is measured by dividing the cost of an advertisement of given sizes (e.g., a full page) and options (e.g., four colours) by the number of households or persons reached within the target market. The general formula is:

$$CPM = \frac{Ad\ cost}{Audience\ or\ circulation\ (in\ thousands)}$$

The CPM allows comparing several different vehicles (e.g., different newspapers, magazines, or radio or TV stations) with different audiences, by standardizing the rates to the same 1,000 readers, viewers, or listeners. However, this calculation does not take into account other considerations such as quality of editorial matter or the amount of clutter (number of ads bunched together). Both of these could have an impact on ad readership.

This formula is useful only for intramedia comparisons—that is, for comparing one newspaper to another—and using the comparison for media planning purposes.[26] Intermedia comparisons of radio and a newspaper are less useful.

***Example.*** For example, a 60-second spot on radio station A provides 100,000 impressions (the audience reached by each spot in the schedule) weekly and costs $500. The same size spot on radio station B provides 200,000 impressions weekly and costs $800.

The cost per 1,000 impressions is $5 for A and $4 for B.

$$CPM\ (A) = \frac{\$500}{100} = \$5$$

$$CPM\ (B) = \frac{\$800}{200} = \$4$$

Thus, B is a better buy, in addition to providing a bigger audience.

***Reach and Frequency***

When comparing advertising programmes, it is important to select the most effective *balance* of reach and frequency. Although separate concepts, reach and frequency are closely related, and their product is the GRP (gross rating point) concept introduced earlier:

$$Reach \times Frequency = Gross\ rating\ points$$

Consider a hypothetical situation as an example. An advertiser who uses magazines for an advertising campaign has two options:

- Buy one insertion in five different magazines.
- Buy five insertions in one magazine.

Assuming that each magazine has a reach of 10, and that both options have the same cost (i.e., magazine budget), both deliver the same level of GRP (i.e., 50 GRPs—5 times 10 in both cases). However, the first option tries to reach more people by using different magazines, while the second one will reach the same people several times. The first option emphasizes reach, and the second one, frequency.

A major cause of failure in advertising programmes is insufficient frequency. It is far more effective to reduce the reach of an advertising campaign and add frequency than to reduce frequency and add reach. Unless a product or service is well known and has no competition, increasing the frequency of the advertising message will increase overall effectiveness.

# Measuring the Results of Advertising

Sales response to ads can be checked daily during the ad period. The effects of image ads are harder to measure. It is not always possible to tie a purchase to image advertising. However, the message may stay in the minds of people who have heard it. Sooner or later, it may help trigger a purchase. Research is needed to measure the success of image.

## *Tests for Immediate Response Ads*[27]

In weighing the results of the immediate response to advertisements, a number of measurements have been used in the past.

### Number of Coupons Brought In

Usually, coupons represent sales of a product. Where coupons represent requests for additional information or contact with a salesperson, management may ask if enough leads were obtained to pay for the ad. If the coupon is dated, it is possible to determine the number of returns for the first, second, and third weeks. It is possible to design a low-cost couponing experiment to determine the profitability of retailer couponing.[28]

### Number of Requests by Phone or Letter Referring to the Ad

A hidden offer can cause people to call or write. For example, included in the middle of an ad is a statement that, on request, the product or additional information will be supplied. Results should be checked over periods of one week through 6 months or 12 months because this type of ad may have a considerable carry-over effect.

### Testing Advertising Executions

Retailers can prepare two ad executions (different in some way that they would like to test) and run them during the same period. Management can identify the ads by the message or with a coded coupon so responses can be identified as to the ad or coupon that produced them. Customers can be instructed to bring in the coupon or to use a special phrase. Broadcast ads can be run at different times or on different stations on the same day with varying discount phrases. Some consumer magazines can provide a split run—that is, printing ad A in part of its press run and ad B in the rest of the run. The responses to each can then be counted.

### Sales Made of a Particular Item

If the ad is on a bargain or limited-time offer, retailers can consider that sales at the end of one week, two weeks, three weeks, and four weeks came from the ad. They may need to make a judgment as to how many sales came from in-store display and personal selling.

### Checks of Store Traffic

An important function of advertising is to build store traffic. Store traffic also results in purchases of items that are not advertised. Pilot studies show, for example, that many customers who were brought to the store by an ad for a blouse also bought a handbag. Some bought the bag in addition to the blouse, while others bought it instead of the blouse.

*Testing the Effectiveness of the Advertising Campaign*

When advertising is spread over a selling season or several seasons, part of the measurement job of campaign effectiveness is keeping records. Retailers' records of ads and sales for an extended time should be compared.

An easy way to set up a file is by marking the date of the run on tear sheets of newspaper ads (many radio stations now provide radio tear sheets, too), keeping log reports of radio and television ads, and keeping copies of direct-mail ads. The file may be broken down into monthly, quarterly, or semiannual blocks. By recording the sales of the advertised items on each ad or log, management can make comparisons.

In institutional (image-building) advertising, individual ads are building blocks of the campaign, so to speak. Together, they make up the advertising campaign over a selling season. A problem is trying to measure the effects of the ads, since they are designed to keep the name of the store before the buying public and to position the outlet in a way that harmonizes with overall marketing strategy. In contrast to institutional advertising, product advertising is designed to cover a short period of time and increase sales.

One approach to testing is making comparisons on a weekly basis. If a retailer runs an ad each week, management can compare the first week's sales with sales for the same week a year ago. At the end of the second week, managers can compare sales with those of the end of the first week, as well as year-ago figures, and so forth. Of course, the retailer should try to take into account other factors that may have influenced the sales—price reductions, advertising by competitors, or other environmental changes (e.g., a heat wave may boost the sales of fans).

# Developing the Copy

Developing an effective message is as essential as using the right media, since the message is the one that has to produce results. Good messages get noticed. In surveys of advertising awareness, many ads from retailers score very highly, among them McDonald's, Sears, Eaton's, Mr. Submarine, Canadian Tire, and Provigo. In terms of product categories, among the top 10 one finds grocery stores, drugstores, and department, furniture, and chain stores.[29]

*Creative Strategy and Execution*

Copy can be either rational or emotional. The rational approach focuses essentially on the merchandise and various facts about it. The emotional appeal addresses the psychological benefits that one can obtain by using the product. Normally, a combination of the two possibilities is very effective. For example, product benefits could be both rational (economy) and emotional (appearance). Headlines in the ad can focus on benefits, promises, or even news. Retail Highlight 17–2 describes some retail campaigns that have won awards in the past; they illustrate the role of copy in the overall advertising strategy.

The text of the advertisement can do many things, including (1) state reasons for doing something (buying the product, patronizing the store), (2) make promises or give testimonials, (3) publicize the results of performance tests, (4) tell a story, (5) report a real or imaginary dialogue, (6) solve a predicament, or (7) amuse the audience.[30]

The elements of good copy are sometimes summarized in the term *AIDCA*. This means attract *attention,* develop *interest,* arouse *desire, convince* the reader, and get *action.* For example, in the ads in Figure 17–4, humour can help attract attention and develop interest. If the need for the product is present, desire can be aroused, and the reader may be convinced to go and visit the store (i.e., action when taken).

| | |
|---|---|
| ***Major Creative Principles*** | The following are some major creative principles that can be used when developing effective print advertisements or broadcast commercials. |

- *Make each word count, and avoid unnecessary words:* Keep sentences short, use action words and terms the reader will understand, and don't use introductions—it is important to get right to the point of the message.
- *Make your ad easy to recognize:* Give the copy and layout a consistent personality and style. Avoid the cluttered look.
- *Use a simple layout:* The layout should lead the reader's eye easily through the message from the art and headline to the copy and price to the signature (i.e., name and logo of the store).
- *Use dominant illustrations:* Show the featured merchandise in dominant illustrations. Whenever possible, show the product in use.
- *Show the benefits to the reader:* Prospective customers want to know ''what's in it for me.'' But do not try to pack the ad with reasons to buy—give customers one primary reason, then back it up with one or two secondary reasons.
- *Feature the ''right'' item:* Select an item that is wanted, timely, stocked in depth, and typical of your store. Specify branded merchandise, and take advantage of advertising allowances and co-operative advertising whenever possible.
- *State a price or range of prices:* Don't be afraid to quote high prices. If the price is low, support it with statements that create belief, such as ''clearance'' or ''special purchase.''
- *Include store name and address:* Double-check every ad to make sure it contains store name, address, telephone number, and store hours.

---

**Retail Highlight 17–2**

---

# Award-Winning Retail Campaigns

Every year, organizations such as the Retail Council of Canada award retailers for their programme excellence. The campaigns of some of the past winners are as follows, and some of the winning ads are reproduced in Figure 17–4:

- *McDonald's Restaurants of Canada* won an award for a highly humorous programme promoting its low calorie/light menu. The campaign used ads in newspapers, in-store translight signs, tray liners, buttons for the staff, and crew room posters. Another award went for a campaign to introduce a line of pizzas to McDonald's menu. The campaign relied on billboards and store signs with a clever rendition of the word *pizza* with the chain's logo, a very simple message that communicates extremely well.

- *Woodward's,* Vancouver, a regional department store, produced a programme called "Look at Us Now" emphasizing

market repositioning and store renovation. It used print, television, and radio ads, a redesigned charge card and bonus programme for credit customers, a weekly consumer magazine, bulletins and a magazine for staff, and community event sponsorships.

- *The New Summerhill Hardware,* Toronto, won several awards for its newspaper ads announcing its reopening. The ads used humorous headlines such as: "What a Bunch of Knobs," and "The Only Good Bolt is a Deadbolt," and simple illustrations of the product to attract attention.

- *IKEA,* a home furnishing store, also used humour to attract attention to its ads, such as "See the Swedish Open for the 95th Time," a newspaper ad to announce the opening of their 95th store in Canada.

Source: Gail Chiasson, "Cossette Collects Golds," *Marketing,* April 27, 1992, p. 2; "The Marketing Annual Advertising Awards," *Marketing,* Section II, March 9, 1992, pp. 18–19; and Ken Riddell, "Awards for Excellence from the Retail Council of Canada," *Marketing,* October 17, 1988, p. 8.

---

### The Growing Power of Consumer Protection

The retailer must be more and more concerned with the effects of consumer protection regulations, both at the federal and provincial levels.

At the federal level, advertising is regulated by a number of agencies, including the CRTC, Health and Welfare Canada, and Consumer and Corporate Affairs. Among the regulations of the greatest importance to retailers are those concerning the use of false or misleading advertising resulting in "bait and switch" practices, forbidden by the Competition Act. There are also a number of codes, such as the Canadian Code of Advertising Standards. The media can also exercise judgment in refusing to carry an advertisement that it deems misleading, sexist, or in bad taste.

## FIGURE 17–4

*Award-winning retail advertisements*

# See The Swedish Open For The 95th Time.

| | |
|---|---|
| Älmhult, Sweden 1958 | Quebec City, Canada 1982 |
| Oslo, Norway 1963 | Uppsala, Sweden 1982 |
| Stockholm, Sweden 1965 | Duiven, Netherlands 1983 |
| Sundsvall, Sweden 1966 | Evry, France 1983 |
| Malmö, Sweden 1967 | Jeddah, Saudi Arabia 1983 |
| Tåstrup, Denmark 1969 | Löhne-Gohfeld, Germany 1983 |
| Gothenberg, Sweden 1972 | Santa Cruz, Canary Islands 1983 |
| Zürich, Switzerland 1973 | Wanchai, Hong Kong 1983 |
| Eching, Germany 1974 | Bergen, Norway 1984 |
| Dorsten, Germany 1975 | Kuwait City, Kuwait 1984 |
| Lodorf, Germany 1975 | Nossegem, Belgium 1984 |
| Sydney, Australia 1975 | Ternat, Belgium 1984 |
| Tsimshatsui, Hong Kong 1975 | Västerås, Sweden 1984 |
| Hannover, Germany 1976 | Hognoul, Belgium 1985 |
| Stuhr, Germany 1976 | Odense, Denmark 1985 |
| Vancouver, Canada 1976 | Philadelphia, USA 1985 |
| Linköping, Sweden 1977 | Vitrolles, France 1985 |
| Toronto, Canada 1977 | Wilrijk, Belgium 1985 |
| Vienna, Austria 1977 | Luzern, Switzerland 1986 |
| Wallau, Germany 1977 | Melbourne, Australia 1986 |
| Edmonton, Canada 1978 | Paris-Nord, France 1986 |
| Kamen, Germany 1978 | Perth, Australia 1986 |
| Singapore 1978 | Washington, USA 1986 |
| Stuttgart, Germany 1978 | Brisbane, Australia 1987 |
| Berlin, Germany 1979 | Manchester, England 1987 |
| Calgary, Canada 1979 | Shatin, Hong Kong 1987 |
| Kaarst, Germany 1979 | Baltimore, USA 1988 |
| Lausanne, Switzerland, 1979 | Forus, Norway 1988 |
| Ottawa, Canada 1979 | Lomme, France 1988 |
| Rotterdam, Netherlands 1979 | London, England 1988 |
| Århus, Denmark 1980 | Graz, Austria 1989 |
| Kassel, Germany 1980 | Hamburg, Germany 1989 |
| Las Palmas, Canary Islands 1980 | Melbourne, Australia 1989 |
| Freiburg, Germany 1981 | Milan, Italy 1989 |
| Gävle, Sweden 1981 | Pittsburgh, USA 1989 |
| Jönköping, Sweden 1981 | Bordeaux, France 1990 |
| Poppenreuth, Germany 1981 | Budapest, Hungary 1990 |
| Reykjavik, Iceland 1981 | Burbank, USA 1990 |
| Schwaibach-Bous, Germany 1981 | Elizabeth, USA 1990 |
| Sydney, Australia 1981 | Turin, Italy 1990 |
| Walldorf, Germany 1981 | Warsaw, Poland 1990 |
| Wels, Austria 1981 | Birmingham, England 1991 |
| Aalborg, Denmark 1982 | Dubai, United Arab Emirates 1991 |
| Amsterdam, Netherlands 1982 | Lugano, Switzerland 1991 |
| Helsingborg, Sweden 1982 | Sydney, Australia 1991 |
| Lyon, France 1982 | Long Island, USA 1991 |
| Montreal, Canada 1982 | **Burlington, Canada 1991** |
| Örebro, Sweden 1982 | |

At IKEA, opening a new store is something we've just never gotten tired of. From the very first store in Sweden, to the 95th, in Burlington.

You see we like to think that around the world, IKEA is making a difference in the way people live. Every day people everywhere see the guaranteed prices in the IKEA catalogue and realize their dreams are within reach. This year over 80 million home furnishing buyers will make their homes more colourful, comfortable and enjoyable, thanks to the wide range of affordable IKEA products.

Our goal is to create a better everyday life for the majority of people. Idealistic? Perhaps, but we've been serious about this since opening the first IKEA store in 1958. We believe that by offering well-designed, functional and low-priced home furnishings, the IKEA idea is providing a higher quality of life. And with this goal in mind, IKEA has grown from a single store in Älmhult, Sweden to 95 stores in 24 countries.

Now, we are proud to bring our unique approach to Burlington. Stop by, and see what we are doing. You could easily spend a part of the day collecting ideas in our Showroom and Marketplace. Then you can discuss those ideas over a sample of Swedish cuisine in the IKEA restaurant.

While you are browsing, your three to seven year olds can be having fun in the supervised playroom. Help yourself in the Self-Serve Warehouse, load your new furniture on your car and enjoy the evening redecorating your home. Then sit back and realize that a better everyday life is really right around the corner. And if we've said that once, we've said it 95 times.

**IKEA** **Burlington Grand Opening. July 24-27.**
INTER IKEA SYSTEMS B.V.
1065 Plains Road East, Burlington. Phone 681-IKEA. Opens Wednesday July 24.

# WHAT A BUNCH OF KNOBS.

Assorted knobs from Germany, USA and Australia.

Summerhill Hardware has reopened. And we're right inside Elte Carpets. So pull yourself in to see Canada's largest selection of decorative hardware.

## THE NEW SUMMERHILL HARDWARE

80 RONALD AVE. 1 STOPLIGHT WEST OF DUFFERIN OFF CASTLEFIELD. 785-1225.
OPEN MON TO SAT 9-6 THURS TIL 9. SUNDAYS 12-4

### February White Sale

**McChicken** 1.89
It's crispy golden on the outside, with tender and juicy chicken on the inside – topped off with lettuce, mayonnaise and served up on McDonald's own sesame seed bun.

**Filet-O-Fish** 1.49
A prime white North Atlantic fish filet made even better with process cheese and tangy tartar sauce – served up on a steamed bun!

Hurry! Sale ends February 28th.

(Store Address)

**GOOD TIME. GREAT TASTE.** **M** McDonald's

SOURCES: Courtesy of IKEA, The New Summerhill Hardware, and McDonald's.

At the provincial level, retailers must contend with bureaus of consumer affairs, Better Business Bureaus, and the Small Claims Court.

### *The Role of the Ad Agency*

The function of an agency is to plan, produce, and measure the effectiveness of advertising. Larger retailers with outlets in several communities are more likely to use an ad agency's services. An agency helps them avoid the complication of having to deal with a variety of media in each community.

Advertising agencies typically earn their incomes from commissions. As an agent for the retailer, the agency will buy space in a medium. The agency then will bill the retailer for 100 percent of the cost and pay the medium, such as a newspaper, 85 percent. The 15 percent is the normal agency commission. Agencies may also take on the accounts of small retailers on a fee basis if the normal commission of 15 percent is too small to make the project worthwhile. Also, in situations such as preparing direct-mail advertising, the agency may charge a percentage of the cost involved.

However, it is important to note that retailers are normally entitled to **retail** or *local* **rates** that are often much lower than *national* or **general rates,** provided that they are the ones purchasing the space or time from the media (no commission will be paid on retail rates). This often makes it uneconomical for a retailer to use an agency. In addition, retailers have to react very quickly to events in the marketplace, and agencies tend not to provide this service. For these reasons, retailers tend not to use an advertising agency for event advertising; when they use one, it is more likely to be for developing an image campaign.

# Sales Promotion

**Sales promotion** has been defined as "marketing activities other than personal selling, advertising, and publicity that stimulate consumer purchasing and dealer effectiveness, such as displays, sales and exhibits, and demonstrations."[31] Examples are shown in Exhibit 17–4. Perhaps the best way to introduce the varied nature of sales promotion possibilities is to highlight trends in sales promotion activities by retailers.

### *What Are the Trends in Sales Promotion?*[32]

#### Couponing

Although coupon fraud and misredemption are serious problems,[33] couponing continues to be a very popular promotion device to introduce new products, stimulate trial, and increase purchase frequency.

In 1991, 26 billion coupons were distributed, 22 billion by retailers as in-ads coupons (290 million were redeemed). This represents a huge increase since 1986, when less than 7 billion coupons were distributed, only 4 billion of which were by retailers (187 million redeemed). The redemption rate of coupons is about 4 percent for regular coupons, and .6 percent for in-ads coupons (which have short expiration dates and are only valid at one retailer). There is still a great amount of potential since, on a per capita basis, Canadian consumers received only 15 percent as many coupons as U.S. consumers, and they redeem only 25 percent as many coupons.[34]

**EXHIBIT 17–4**

*Retail sales promotion programmes*

*Gifts with purchase:* Receipt of a gift with the purchase of an item—especially popular in the promotion of cosmetics.

*Purchase with purchase:* The offer of a second item at a reduced price after a minimum purchase—plush animals have been especially popular.

*Price discount:* Short-term reduction in the price of a product, normally marked on the product.

*Coupons:* Distributed via newspapers, product packages, door to door, magazines, or direct mail, they give the consumer an opportunity to purchase an item at a reduced price based on specified terms.

*Contests:* Skill-based competitions for designated prizes.

*Sweepstakes:* Games of chance for designated prizes.

*Rebates:* Refund of a fixed amount from the purchase price.

*Premiums:* The offer of something free or at a minimal price to induce sales—free glasses with the purchase of 10 gallons of gasoline.

*Trading stamps:* Stamps issued with purchases that can be redeemed for merchandise of the consumer's choice.

*Self-liquidators:* Incentives in which consumers pay part of the cost in cash plus submit product labels as proof of purchase to obtain an item such as a T-shirt.

---

***Coupon Distribution Methods.***    The most important methods of coupon distribution are:[35]

- Free-standing newspaper inserts, usually in four colours.
- Co-operative direct mail, distributed directly to households in nonaddressed mail, according to selected postal codes.
- Selective direct mail, sent to specific customers.
- In/on pack, produced by manufacturers.
- Newspaper run-of-press, where the coupons are part of the newspaper advertisement.
- In-store coupons, distributed in store through handouts, product demonstrations, at cash registers during check-out (e.g., Catalina coupons), in special retail booklets and calendars, and on bulletin boards at the entrance (including electronic boards or kiosks).[36]
- Magazine coupons, usually in four colours, with the editorial support of the magazine, recipes, and so on.

***Trends in Couponing.***    The following trends can be identified, and one can expect more creative uses to be made in the future:

- In general, more in- and on-pack coupon usage is likely, as is continued use of retailer in-ad coupons (retailer coupons paid by manufacturers) and more combination promotions with other devices—premiums, sweepstakes, and refunds.
- Double coupons can be used to generate additional sales and combat cross-border shopping. Retailers such as A&P and Miracle Food Mart have

*More than 26 billion coupons are distributed each year in Canada.*

SOURCE: Photo by James Hertel.

successfully experimented with double coupons, doubling the face value of manufacturers' coupons for brand-name products.[37]

- An increased penetration and development of interactive electronic couponing will occur. Safeway and Kmart are experimenting with electronic kiosks. Canadian-developed technology by Qponyx International of Winnipeg allows the store to dispense coupons in 15 to 20 grocery categories, valid only the same day, at this store only. In addition, a seven-second message is played while the coupon selected by the customer is being printed. Other systems are also available in Canada.[38]

### More Sampling

Use of **sampling** is increasing, especially to new or nonusers. Quite a few services now provide selective sampling. Retailers prefer salable samples because they make a profit on them—they don't profit from free samples. Salable samples are good for manufacturers, too, because they save distribution costs.

### Fewer Cents-Off Bonus Packs

Retailers generally resist cents-off bonus packs because they necessitate additional stock-keeping units. They can also be quite costly to marketers because of the required special labelling and/or packaging. The advantages are that the benefit is passed on to the consumer, and the consumer readily sees the value in them.

### More Premiums

Some retailers are lukewarm to **premium** offers. This is especially true when they are used alone, rather than in combination with other promotion devices such as coupons. In- and on-packs, special containers, and other forms of package-related or in-store premiums are sometimes resisted because of pilferage and handling problems. Nevertheless, consumers like these types of promotions. Retailers prefer premium offers that do not require their involvement but add excitement and impact to a promotion, create consumer interest, and generate increased product movement.

The general trends are toward more expensive self-liquidators, free premiums with multiple proofs-of-purchase, and brand logo premiums that are product- or advertising-related. One example of a timely premium programme is the McDonald's/Donruss MVP Series, which offers customers four-baseball-card packs for 39 cents following the purchase of any McDonald's pizza, sandwich, or breakfast. The 33-card set from the 26 major league baseball teams, endorsed by Roberto Alamar (Toronto Blue Jays), also contains six special Blue Jays cards, a checklist card, and redemption vouchers for 1,000 Gold Series cards autographed by Alamar.[39]

### More Selective Point-of-Purchase Material

Typical **point-of-purchase materials** include end-of-aisle and other in-store merchandising and display materials. Retailers like and want p-o-p materials but generally feel that the material provided by manufacturers does not meet their needs. Retailers are highly selective in their use of p-o-p materials and prefer displays that merchandise an exciting and interesting promotion theme, support other promotion devices, adapt to storewide promotions on a chainwide and individual store basis, harmonize with the store environment, sell related products, provide a quality appearance, install easily, are permanent or semipermanent, and guarantee sales success.

Some retailers develop and produce displays in accordance with the manufacturer's budget and guidelines. Some retailers are renting floor space to manufacturers.

### More Refunds/Rebates

Refunds and rebates, similar in intent and nature, continue to grow in popularity and use. Refunds and rebates are usually handled as mail-ins with proofs of purchase. They are very effective promotion tools and will be used in more creative ways. Increasingly popular are rebates as charitable donations that show social concern, and higher price refunds for multiple products.

### Fewer Contests and More Sweepstakes[40]

Sweepstakes are generally more popular than regular contests. However, the Instant Win contests are growing in use and importance. Retailers like both sweepstakes and instant wins, especially when they bring traffic into the store to look at product packages and obtain entry blanks.

### More Mailers and Circulars

Mailers and circulars have been the biggest gainers in sales promotion over the past five years. Indeed, their share of sales promotion dollars has increased from one third to almost one half of the total dollars during this period, with the growth coming at the expense of newspapers.

### More Loyalty Programmes

A loyalty programme is one that encourages the customer to keep coming back to the store to accumulate stamps or points. An example of a loyalty programme is Zellers' Club Z. Another example for a smaller retailer is Odyssey Books and its discount stores, Empire Books. Customers earn "Empire dollars," which they can use for future purchases, and at Odyssey, they earn discount stamps on special customer cards; when the cards are complete, they can enter a monthly draw for a $25 gift certificate.[41]

*When to Use Sales Promotions?*

Table 17–6 highlights the conclusions about the effectiveness of sales promotion research based on 216 Canadian sales promotions.[42] Higher emphasis of manufacturers on the trade and the sales force would imply a different role for retailers.

---

**TABLE 17-6  Emerging Conclusions from Sales Promotion Research**

- Successful promotions depend heavily on trade support from the sales force.
- Success factors are different between consumer promotions and trade promotions.
- Promotions that are successful are more expensive to launch, but they tend to pay out more than unsuccessful ones.
- The level of incentive by itself does not relate to support from the trade—that is, a high level will not guarantee strong trade support; conversely, a low level does not always prevent strong trade support.
- For many companies, moving sales volume is more important than the profitability of the sales promotions.
- About 50 percent of sales promotions are unprofitable.
- Incentives to consumers tend to be less important to the success of a promotion than sales force support.
- More of the promotional budget should be allocated to the sales force and less to incentives to consumers.

---

SOURCE: Adapted from Kenneth G. Hardy, "Key Success Factors for Manufacturers' Sales Promotion in Package Goods," *Journal of Marketing* 50, no. 3 (July 1986), pp. 13–23.

Staple products exhibit the highest degree of price elasticity and are thus the most responsive to point-of-purchase displays. Sugar, vinegar, ketchup, coffee, and canned/powdered milk are all in the top 10 price-elastic product categories for human consumption.[43]

Suppliers often advertise directly to retailers and inform them of upcoming national campaigns so the retailer can stock sufficient merchandise to meet consumer needs and coordinate local advertising with the national advertising programme.

*Co-Operative Promotions*

Manufacturers also offer co-op funds for promotions in the same way they offer advertising co-op dollars. Suppliers often advertise directly to retailers, informing them about promotion allowances available for a product line. Suppliers then seek a commitment from the retailers for an increased volume of purchases because of the accelerated promotional programme for the product line.

# Publicity and Public Relations

**Publicity** has been defined as "any nonpersonal stimulation of demand for a product, service, or business unit by planting commercially significant news about it in a published medium or obtaining favourable presentation of it upon radio, television, or stage that is not paid for by the sponsor."[44] Publicity and public relations are known by various names. Regardless, such activities normally fit into three categories: (1) merchandising, (2) entertainment, and (3) education or community service.

*Merchandising Events*

Special events create publicity. Often, they are featured in the editorial section of a newspaper, result in an interview on a talk show, or generate other free promotion. Merchandising events require careful co-ordination between merchandising, advertising, and publicity. Such events can include fashion shows, bridal fairs, cooking demonstrations, celebrity authors, cartoon characters, sports heros, or exhibits of art, costumes, antiques, or rarities. Merchandising events may also be staged in conjunction with designers such as Alfred Sung or sports figures such as Wayne Gretzky.

For example, in 1991 (during the recession), Ogilvy, a Montreal department store, sponsored 74 special events, including book signing with authors, concerts broadcast live over CBC radio, and celebrity appearances of such U.S. supermodels as Cindy Crawford (whose appearance attracted 2,200 people in one afternoon). During a 110-day period, these special events attracted 19,000 people into the store.[45]

*Entertainment*

Retailers seek to build goodwill, store image, and name awareness through entertainment programmes. For example, several retailers participate in such events as the Quebec City Winter Carnival, the Calgary Stampede, or Canada Day festivities across the country. The results from such activities are hard to measure. Free publicity from such events can be worth hundreds of thousands of dollars.

***Education or Community Service***

Retailers sometimes sponsor education or community service activities. Such activities are provided free of charge during lunch hours. Other retailers offer fashion advice, career counselling, and even cooking courses, all on the store premises. For example, Elte Carpets of Toronto runs the "University of Fuzzy Side Up," a series of Saturday-morning courses on broadloom and rugs held at its showroom. About 20 people attend each week, learning about different kinds of carpets and how they are installed.[46]

# Chapter Highlights

- Promotion should be viewed as a sales-building investment and not simply as an element of business expense. When promotion is executed correctly, it can be an important factor in the future growth of a business.

- Promotion is communication from the retailer to the consumer in an effort to achieve a profitable sales level. Promotion includes mass media advertising, coupons, trading stamps, premium offers, point-of-purchase displays, and publicity.

- Promotion is a key element of the marketing mix. All promotion should be in harmony with pricing, product lines, and store-location decisions (place). Otherwise a poor image for the firm can result.

- Developing promotion plans begins with the goals of the firm. Retailers must decide on whom to reach, the message to get across, the number of messages to reach the audience, and the means for reaching the audience.

- After defining the goals, retailers must carefully establish their advertising budget. Typical methods include the percentage-of-sales, unit-of-sales, and objective-and-task methods. Such a budget must also be carefully allocated, and co-operative advertising programmes should be used to stretch the impact of the budget on sales.

- Numerous options exist for retail advertising, and each medium has its strengths and weaknesses, which must be studied carefully before a choice is made. Media choices include direct mail, magazines, billboards, transit ads, newspapers, radio, and television. The most commonly used media are newspapers, radio,

direct mail and distribution, and out-of-home media. Large retail chains also use television and magazines. Nonmedia advertising includes point-of-purchase displays and specialty advertising.

- Media effectiveness is normally measured in terms of cost per thousand and reach and frequency. Results tests for immediate response ads can be in terms of coupons redeemed, requests by phone or letter referring to the ad, sales made of a particular item, or an analysis of store traffic.

- Advertising copy can be either rational or emotional. The rational approach focuses on the merchandise, while an emotional appeal focuses on the psychological benefits obtained from using the product. Headlines in an ad can focus on benefits, promises, or news.

- Some retailers use an advertising agency. The function of an agency is to plan, produce, and measure the effectiveness of advertising. Agencies earn their commissions on advertisements placed for the retailers. However, retailers qualify for very advantageous retail rates (noncommissionable) if they buy directly from the media.

- Retail sales promotions include such activities as couponing, product sampling, cents-off bonus packs, premiums, point-of-purchase materials, refunds or rebates, contests and sweepstakes, and trade-in allowances.

- Publicity includes media exposure that is not paid for by the sponsor. Such activities normally fit into three categories: merchandising, entertainment, and education or community service.

# Key Terms

# Discussion Questions

1. Is it possible to increase advertising expenses as a percentage of sales while increasing the profitability of the firm?

2. Comment on the following statement: The only goal of advertising is to increase sales and profitability.

3. Discuss the following approaches to establishing an advertising budget (be sure to include in your discussion the advantages and disadvantages of each): the percentage-of-sales method; the unit-of-sales method; and the objective-and-task method.

4. What are the reasons a retailer should consider using a multimedia mix?

5. Evaluate the following media in terms of their strengths and weaknesses: outdoor, radio, television, newspapers, transit advertising, and magazines.

6. Why should a retailer consider the use of co-operative advertising funds?

7. What are the various ways by which retailers can measure advertising results?

8. The text states that the elements of good advertising copy are summarized in the term *AIDCA*. What does this statement mean?

# Application Exercises

1. Imagine you work for the promotion division of a department store and have been told that you are to prepare a campaign for a new product. Select your own new product. Plan the campaign, select the media, and prepare the message.

2. Make contacts with several dealers in a specific product line (e.g., automobiles) that has definite differences in product image, price, quality, and so on. Through interviews with the dealership managers, attempt to determine the allocation of the advertising (promotional) budget among the various media. Compare and contrast among the group. If actual dollars of promotional expenditures are not available, then utilize percentage allocations. Additionally, collect national and local ads for the same dealerships/brands and evaluate the differences and similarities noted.

3. Select several automobile dealerships that seem to project differing public images. Interview the management of each to determine its particular

image perceptions of itself and perhaps of the competition. Prepare a portfolio of ads of each dealership and also of the national ads of that same dealership's make of auto. Compare the images that

seem to be projected by the local versus the national promotions. Attempt to reach certain strategy conclusions from your investigation.

# Suggested Cases

# Endnotes

1. Ovid Riso, "Advertising Guidelines for Small Retail Firms," *Small Marketers Aid,* No. 160 (Washington, D.C.: U.S. Small Business Administration), p. 4.
2. Roger J. Calantone, David Litvack, and Charles D. Schewe, "A Canonical Analysis Approach to the Retail Segment-Media Matching Problem," *Marketing,* vol. 3, ed. Michel Laroche (Montreal: ASAC, 1982), pp. 21–30.
3. "Ad Strategy: Divide and Conquer," *Chain Store Age, General Merchandise Edition,* December 1985, p. 30.
4. Marvin J. Rothenburg, "Retail Research Strategies for the '70s," in *Combined Proceedings,* ed. Edward M. Mazze (Chicago: American Marketing Association, 1975), p. 409.
5. Riso, "Advertising Guidelines for Small Retail Firms."
6. The material on establishing and allocating the budget is based on Stewart Henderson Britt, "Plan Your Advertising Budget," *Small Marketers Aid,* No. 164 (Washington, D.C.: U.S. Small Business Administration).
7. Thomas A. Petit and Martha R. McEnally, "Putting Strategy into Promotion Mix Decisions," *Journal of Consumer Marketing* 2, no. 1 (Winter 1985), pp. 41–47.
8. Jennifer Pepall, "Co-op Advertising Builds Strength from Numbers," *Profit,* November 1990, pp. 53–54.
9. W. Haight, *Retail Advertising: Management and Techniques* (Glenview, Ill.: Scott, Foresman, 1976).
10. *Canadian Advertising Rates & Data (CARD)* is a monthly publication of Maclean Hunter. For each medium, the date for which the information was updated is indicated in the corresponding listing. For more complete information, you should request the retail rate card from the medium itself.
11. *Canadian Media Directors' Council Media Digest, 1992/93 (CMDCMD),* p. 15.
12. "Freeze Frame: A *Marketing*-Nielsen Update," *Marketing,* November 4, 1991, p. 15.
13. *CMDCMD,* pp. 7–15.
14. John Partridge, "More Canadians Are Now Reading Daily Newspapers, Survey Reveals," *Report on Business,* December 13, 1988, p. B15; see also Vernon J. Jones and Fred H. Siller, "Dimensions of Audience Exposure to the Advertising Content of a Daily Newspaper," in *Developments in Canadian Marketing,* ed. Robert D. Tamilia (ASAC, 1979), pp. 42–48.
15. *CMDCMD,* p. 20.
16. *CARD,* April 1991, pp. 59–60.
17. For further reading, see Lewis A. Spalding, "Strategies for Selling by Mail," *Stores,* September 1982, pp. 23–28.
18. Marina Strauss, "Grocers Find New Ways to Reach the Masses," *Globe and Mail,* January 14, 1992, p. B4.
19. "Advertising Small Business," *Small Business Reporter* (San Francisco: Bank of America, 1981), p. 13.
20. Gerry Blackwell, "Just What the Armchair Shopper Ordered," *Globe and Mail,* July 18, 1992, p. B22.

21. Ibid.; and Jennifer Pepall, "Selling by the Book," *Profit,* December 1990, pp. 40–41.

22. Ken Riddell, "Birks Gets into Spring with a New 'Magalog,' " *Marketing,* March 14, 1988, p. 1; Richard Siklos, " 'Magalogues' Reach Out to Upscale Consumers," *Financial Times,* December 7, 1987, p. 4; and Margaret Bream, "Hybrids on Hold," *Marketing,* February 27, 1989, p. 12.

23. Ellen Paris, "Follow the Moving Sign," *Forbes,* September 9, 1985, p. 116.

24. P. P. Yannopoulos, J. Celima, and E. Paolone, "Developing Strategies for Videotex Retailing," *Marketing,* vol. 6, ed. Jean-Charles Chebat (ASAC, 1985), pp. 351–58.

25. Ken Riddell, "Reaching Consumers In-Store," *Marketing,* July 13–20, 1992, p. 10.

26. Yvan Boivin, "Media Planning with the CPM Rule," *Marketing,* vol. 10, ed. Alain d'Astous (ASAC, 1989), pp. 39–47.

27. This material is condensed, with modifications, from Elizabeth Sorbet, "Do You Know the Results of Your Advertising?" *Management Aid,* No. 4,020 (Washington, D.C.: U.S. Small Business Administration).

28. Randall G. Chapman, "Assessing the Profitability of Retailer Couponing with a Low-Cost Field Experiment," *Journal of Retailing* 62, no. 1 (Spring 1987), pp. 19–40.

29. "Topline Results," *Marketing,* March 28, 1988, p. 16.

30. Haight, *Retail Advertising: Management and Techniques,* p. 357.

31. Committee on Definitions, *Marketing Definitions* (Chicago: American Marketing Association, 1963).

32. For further reading, see Kenneth G. Hardy, "Procedures and Problems in Evaluating Sales Promotions," *Marketing,* vol. 4, ed. James D. Forbes (ASAC, 1983), pp. 142–50; "Inside Report: Sales Promotion," *Marketing News,* June 7, 1985, p. 12; Marc Schnapp, "War Games 'In Retailing Promotions,' " *Marketing Communications,* June 1985, pp. 85–88; "Retailers Bullish on Bears," *Marketing News,* March 13, 1987, p. 18; and Corinne Berneman and

Ian Fenwick, "Using the Multinomial Logit Model to Predict the Effectiveness of In-Store Promotion," *Marketing,* vol. 10, ed. Alain d'Astous (ASAC, 1989), pp. 21–30.

33. Marina Strauss, "Fraudulent Coupon Use Costing Retailers Millions of Dollars," *Report on Business,* March 22, 1989, p. B13.

34. Ken Riddell, "Couponers Show Record Year," *Marketing,* February 10, 1992, p. 2; and Wayne Mouland, "More Exciting Times Ahead for the Consumer Promotions Industry," *Marketing,* February 20, 1989, Section CP&I, pp. 6–7.

35. René Y. Darmon and Michel Laroche, *Advertising in Canada* (Toronto: McGraw-Hill Ryerson, 1991), pp. 196–99.

36. Riddell, "Reaching Consumers In-Store."

37. Ken Riddell, "Double Coupons Perform Well for Miracle," *Marketing,* February 24, 1992, p. 7.

38. Riddell, "Reaching Consumers In-Store."

39. Ken Riddell, "McDonald's Joins the Card Craze," *Marketing,* July 13–20, 1992, p. 3.

40. Mouland, "More Exciting Times."

41. Marlene Cartash, "Catch a Falling Store," *Profit,* December 1990, p. 27.

42. Kenneth G. Hardy, "Key Success Factors for Manufacturers' Sales Promotions in Package Goods," *Journal of Marketing* 50, no. 3 (July 1986), pp. 13–23; see also Kenneth G. Hardy and Ian S. Spencer, "Managerial Problems and Research Opportunities in Sales Promotion," *Marketing,* vol. 2, ed. Robert Wyckham (ASAC, 1981), pp. 121–32.

43. "Price and Promotion Strategies for Impact at Retail," *Marketing Communications,* October 1985; see also, Corinne Berneman and Auleen Carson, "Caution: Coupo-Holics and Bargain-Hunters Ahead," *Marketing,* vol. 11, ed. John Liefeld (ASAC, 1990), pp. 46–54; "Sign of the Times: Singles' Night Shopping," *Supermarket News,* September 22, 1986, p. 1.

44. Committee on Definitions, *Marketing Definitions.*

45. Jerry Zeidenberg, "Is Upscale Dead?" *Profit,* October 1991, pp. 44–45.

46. Marlene Cartash, "Catch a Falling Store."

# 18 Developing a Customer-Focused Culture

---

## Chapter Objectives

After reading this chapter, you should be able to:

1 Understand the meaning of *customer service* versus *customer focused*.

2 Understand the strategic role of customer support services in the retailer's overall marketing plan.

3 Describe the various types of retail credit.

4 List the various types of retail credit cards.

5 Understand the laws affecting customer support services.

6 Describe customer support activities such as shopper services, educational programmes, delivery, and extended hours.

## Retailing Capsule

When asked about why they shop in the United States, many Canadians indicate that in addition to the prices, they very much like the service there. Customer service is a major problem for Canadian retailers since, according to a recent Angus Reid poll, 56 percent of Canadians said that they have not had a recent shopping experience where the customer service was excellent. Thus, Canadian retailers must learn from other successful retailers and improve their customer focus:

- A U.S. retailer that has a remarkable reputation for customer service is Nordstrom, a Seattle-based fashion specialty retailer. Nordstrom's philosophy is to offer the customer, *in the following order,* the best service, selection, quality, and value. And it is put into practice, with sales associates selected, trained, motivated, and compensated for their performance. The result is a team of outstanding individuals—friendly, knowledgeable, caring, and competent. Sales associates ask for customers' phone numbers so that they can call the customers when new merchandise, or anything else customers are looking for, comes in or is located. Sales associates walk around the store to help customers find what they want, even if it is in a different department, and even if it is located in a *competitor's store,* until the customer has found the right item! Nordstrom mythology is full of such seemingly unbelievable true stories as: a sales associate ironed a new-bought shirt so that the customer could wear it to a meeting; when a customer brought back a one-year-old pair of shoes to be repaired, he was given a new pair free; associates cheerfully gift-wrapped an item purchased from a competitor along with merchandise bought at Nordstrom.

- Although rare, such levels of service can also be found in Canada. One afternoon, a Toronto businessman bought four pairs of pants at the Mississauga store of Brettons, a Canadian-owned chain of fashion department stores. He was in a hurry since he was leaving for Japan the next morning. The pants that the businessman needed had to be shortened before the store closed, two hours from that time. He asked Patrick Kilbride, the salesman who was helping him, if it could be done. The answer was an emphatic yes. Kilbride told his customer to go home and get ready for his journey. Then Kilbride rushed to the store's alterations department, asked for the job to be done right away, and delivered the pants *personally* to the customer's home at 10:30 that night. Was this unusual behaviour for Kilbride? "No," said Kilbride, "I work at Brettons, but I work for my customers."

Sources: Ron Zemke and Dick Schaaf, *The Service Edge* (Markham, Ont.: NAL Books, 1989), pp. 352–55; and Rona Maynard, "Satisfaction Guaranteed," *Report on Business Magazine,* January 1988, pp. 58–64.

As noted in these two stories, services offer retailers the opportunity to differentiate themselves from the competition. Services are expensive, however, and many retailers do not agree on what services should be offered. Some are even reducing the number of services they offer.

Customer support services include such functions as credit, layaway, delivery, personal shopping programmes, and a variety of other activities designed to attract new customers and to strengthen relationships with existing ones. Customer support services are a primary way retailers can differentiate their outlets from those of competitors. Many retail outlets offer essentially the same merchandise at the same price with similar merchandising programmes. Services provide the opportunity to create a unique image in the minds of consumers.

Many customers now bag their own groceries, price-mark goods at warehouse outlets, serve themselves in restaurants, handle their own delivery, and pump their own gas. Shifting these functions to customers is the result of efforts by retailers to lower their costs and increase profit margins.

Retailers probably cannot eliminate all basic services if they want to stay in business. Such services include credit, repair, warranty service, and others (depending on the merchandise sold). No service should be offered, however, unless it contributes directly or indirectly to profit.

A high-fashion store such as Holt Renfrew or Fairweather that appeals to the upper-income shopper will usually offer more services than a discount store. Also, two different stores may offer wide variations in the same service. For example, a discount store may accept a bank credit card as the only means of payment other than cash, but a department store may also accept the store's credit card, a travel and entertainment card such as American Express, or offer a customer charge plan. Department stores may deliver large items such as furniture free of charge, whereas a warehouse furniture store such as Leon's may charge extra for delivery.

*Fairweather will offer a variety of services to its clientele.*

A full-service specialty outlet such as Parachute stores offers a full array of customer services, often through special promotions. In contrast, a discount outlet such as Kmart may offer identical merchandise, but without supporting services, at reduced prices. The use of services is thus part of the positioning strategy by merchants in targeting key market segments, as discussed in Chapter 6.

# Customer Service versus Customer Focused[1]

The only constant in retailing is change—in fashion, distribution channels, organization, buying patterns, customer wants and life-styles, and retail format.

Because of these constant changes, some retailers have lost sight of their primary mission—satisfying the customer. Two of the most misunderstood words today are **customer service.** Do they refer to an attitude, a function, or a result?

With increased competition, many retailers are placing greater emphasis on customer service to differentiate themselves from the competitive pack. The traditional approach to customer service, however, is not broad enough to accomplish this objective or to satisfy the needs of today's customer. To find new areas of opportunity, retailers must go beyond customer service to a **customer-focused culture.**

## *Traditional Approach*

Traditional customer service programme objectives generally fall into four categories:

1. *Integrity:* Warranties, product quality, return and exchange policies.
2. *Convenience and shopping ease:* Store layout, convenient parking, store hours, mail- and phone-order service.
3. *A pleasant shopping environment:* Valet parking services, decor and lighting, fitting-room privacy, music, credit account confidentiality.
4. *Personal shopping services:* Knowledgeable sales personnel, merchandise availability, informative product signing.

The traditional customer service approaches include a variety of organizational structures and policies aimed at making the customer happy, as illustrated in Retail Highlight 18–1.

Organizations range from a large central customer service staff, to a service/return desk at each store, to an authorized manager at each individual point-of-sale location in department and specialty stores. Return policies range from very lenient to a policy of no returns without a sales receipt to no returns at all.

### Customer Service

When the term *customer service* is used, it usually refers to cashing cheques, handling bill adjustment transactions, or managing complaints. Some stores handle complaints at the store level when they arise and provide no feedback to management on complaint types, volume, and frequency. Some companies have

---

**Retail Highlight 18–1**

# Providing Good Customer Service Pays Off

Since opening three stores in Toronto in September 1991, Talbots, a $500 million specialty retailer and cataloger of women's apparel, has been very successful and plans to open 25 additional stores in Canada. Its formula includes offering classic merchandise to professional women, at reasonable prices, and with excellent customer service. For example, Talbots offers wardrobe consulting, alterations, free gift wrapping, full refund on returned merchandise, delivery anywhere in Canada, and a highly trained sales staff. Its clubby atmosphere appeals to professional women by providing a conservative assortment of private-label merchandise, meeting their needs from head to toe: from hats, to blazers, handbags, cologne, and jewellery, to footwear.

Source: Anne Bokma, "Raking In the Dough," *The Financial Post Magazine,* January 1992, p. 34.

---

no clearly defined responsibility for pinpointing customer service, and resolve complaints slowly. Other stores have elaborate and well-defined systems for handling complaints, including procedure manuals, time standards for resolution, performance audits, and management reporting of complaints by type, store, work centre, and merchandise area. But the customer service programme is always reactive, based on some function that may not be meeting the customer's expectations.

### Customer Expectations

Retailers play a role in the development of customer expectations through advertising, store operations, and everyday marketing. When there are inconsistencies between what retailers say and do and what the customer expects, there is a problem. At best, the result is customer confusion and, at worse, the loss of a customer. The situation is further complicated by the fact that customer expectations vary, not only by type of store but also by major category of merchandise within a given store type. To make customer service proactive, retailers need to anticipate customer expectations and take action to meet or exceed them.

One simple way to identify these expectations is a customer expectation matrix by broad merchandise category. This approach identifies customer expectations of fashion, value, service, and the store facility for several types of retail store categories. It assigns a numerical value to each category as perceived by a customer. The higher the cumulative total, the higher the expectation.

By completing this format for various categories of products, one can assess how to fulfill the customers' expectations, thus reducing customer service problems.

*Roberts plans to meet and exceed customer expectations.*

SOURCE: Courtesy Roberts.

## Confusing the Customer

One of the most common ways retailers confuse the customer is by doing one thing and saying another. The following are examples of such practices:

- *Discontinuing services* such as delivery, cheque cashing, wrapping for mailing, alterations, and various repair services without offering the customer an alternative.
- Establishing *fees for support services* that are not in line with competition or that are disproportionately high for that particular service.
- Preaching customer service, but *posting restrictive negative signs* throughout the store (for example, ''No cheque cashing,'' ''Please do not

handle the merchandise,'' ''We honour only manufacturers' warranties''). These signs are most negative when posted near a ''service'' desk.

- *Aisles that are narrow or cluttered with merchandise:* No natural grouping of merchandise categories, entering and exiting traffic that collides, or high interior fixtures that restrict visibility.

- *Restrooms are difficult to find,* dirty, out of supplies, or a combination of all three.

- *Department and merchandise signing is inadequate:* Lack of up-to-date store directories, inadequate department signing, inadequate product information signing, using sales sign headers on nonsale merchandise, using a single-price sign on a fixture containing various-priced merchandise, not highlighting advertised merchandise, excessive variety of sign headers.

- *Inadequate merchandise or shelf-marking:* No price on merchandise or shelves, size information difficult to find, no standard location for merchandise tickets, merchandise tickets applied over product and size information.

- *Advertising lacks integrity:* Fictitious or overstated comparative regular prices, advertising limited-quantity merchandise without a disclaimer, unstated restrictions that apply to a special-price ad.

- Merchandise is out of stock and *the customer is not helped* by calling a different store to fill the order or providing similar merchandise at the same price (even if a markdown is involved).

One example of customer confusion occurred at Consumers Distributing. Customers wanting to buy an electric fan on a hot summer day were too often told that the product was out of stock; they also had to endure long lines, poorly worded catalogs, and a lack of merchandise displays, along with poorly trained employees who could not answer questions about the products.[2]

When measuring customer service, it is the customer's perception of a company's actions that counts, not the actions themselves.

## The Customer-Focused Culture

A customer-focused culture is one that primarily focuses on customer concerns. Some retailers with already strong reputations for customer service are reluctant to reveal their secrets of success. Other retailers may try to remedy their customer service problems by copying their competitors, erroneously believing that they then will have created a customer-focused culture.

They miss the point. A combination of many positive programmes, not a limited mix of them, produces positive results. Examples of positive programmes are:

- Knowing who the store's customers are.
- Planning an integrated approach to customer acquisition and service.

- Developing a clear statement on customer focus that is commonly shared and committed to.
- Hiring knowledgeable, consistent, motivated employees.
- Using customer information in an effective manner.
- Monitoring and measuring the results of all the combined efforts.

The two examples provided in the Retailing Capsule clearly reflect a customer-focused culture.

### Customer Definition and Knowledge

The most critical starting point is a precise definition and in-depth knowledge of the customer base. One needs to know:

- Who are they?
- What are their values and attitudes?
- What are their life-styles?
- What do they need?
- How can they be reached?
- Where do they buy?
- What do they expect?
- What are their perceptions of your customer service compared with that of the competition?

To answer these questions, a retailer must use both primary and secondary research on demographics, psychographics, media preferences, and purchasing. Primary research derives its information directly from potential customers, while secondary research derives its information from third parties. Retailers can choose from a variety of sources of research material (Chapter 10 covered these in detail). However, a retailer's own customer information base can provide useful information if it is properly coded. The closer this information can be fine-tuned to the customer base of a given store, the better the results.[3]

### A Planned Integrated Approach

A well-planned approach to customer service includes the integration of the strategies used to attract, serve, and keep customers.

Strategies to attract customers generally fall into the categories of *fashion* (newness, uniqueness, broad assortments), *value* (product/service quality, convenience, price), and *dominance* (assortment, effective presentation, strong in-stock position).

High-quality customer service strategies include:

- Qualified sales personnel in quantity.
- In-stock position.
- Integrity—doing what you say you will do.

- Consistent, timely handling of customer complaints.
- Support services, including gift wrap, delivery, repairs, credit services, child care, package checking, and consolidation.
- Clean, easy access and exit, easy traffic flow, and pleasant facilities.
- Kiosk and free-standing product information and order placement terminals.

There are many programmes that when properly timed and implemented will help to keep the customers you already have. One example is to make it easier for customers to shop and, more importantly, to purchase. Management might extend store hours (when it is legally possible); add mail- and phone-order services; develop bridal, pregnancy, and baby registry programmes; or add various financial services. All of these conveniences will make established customers happy to return to the store; they will be able to take care of many chores in the same place at the same time.

Another way to keep customers coming back is to develop programmes that build self-esteem in both customers and employees. Incentive programmes can be successful, as can programmes designed to enhance personal appearance via cosmetics. Customers will feel good when they leave the store, and employees will feel good for having satisfied the customers.

Basically, the way to retain customers is to be creative and anticipate as many of their needs as possible. Retail Highlight 18–2 indicates that a customer-focused culture can also thrive in a warehouse-type operation.

### Commitment and Communication

Underlying all of these strategies is the key factor that initiates and nurtures a customer-focused culture—a statement of customer focus that will produce the necessary drive, incentive, and awareness. Such a statement must include:

- Top-management commitment.
- Clear organizational goals.
- Specifically assigned responsibilities for each area.
- A focal point for questions and problems.
- Ongoing communication and positive examples.

Once a clear customer-focus statement has been developed containing all of these elements, all participants will have a game plan by which to achieve the goals. For example, Elte Carpets of Toronto has a clear customer focus of staff availability to answer customer questions on carpets. For that goal, it set up a 24-hour hotline service that responds to customers' questions within six hours. In addition, customers may request the salesperson's home numbers written on their receipt for future queries. Elte Carpets also set up a shop-at-home service staffed by two sales representatives who answer customer queries by phone, then take carpet-sample books (and sometimes full rugs) to the customers' homes. Customers can make a

# Big Does Not Have to Mean Poor Customer Focus

For a not-too-handy person, being in a hardware store can be an intimidating experience, especially if it is as big as two-and-one-half football fields and with over 30,000 different items. But in Aikenhead's, you have no problem. Said company president Stephen Bebis: "People have to know what to do with the things they buy." In addition, the prices are guaranteed to be the lowest: If a customer can establish that an identical item sells for less at a competitor's, Aikenhead's policy is to lower that competitor's price by 10 percent.

Among the store's 190 sales staff are licensed plumbers, electricians, carpenters, and horticulturists, all versed in Aikenhead's culture. Merely pointing customers in the right direction is discouraged. Employees are required to walk customers to various parts of the store and answer as many questions as they may have. The Aikenhead's culture encourages senior managers to wear casual clothes, and once a week they are required to visit the sales floor and mingle with customers and staff.

In addition, samples of products such as doorbells and light dimmers are installed on plywood panels to illustrate how they work. Somewhere else, a display shows, step-by-step, how to install ceramic tiles. Customers can also watch in-store project demonstrations and seminars. For the truly ambitious (or advanced), the store is equipped with computer software that can design a kitchen, a deck, or a closet organizer to fit a customer's home—then provide a perspective illustration of the completed project and a list of materials (and their prices) needed to build it.

Sources: "King Kong of Hardware," *Macleans,* April 1992, pp. 38–39; and John Heinzl, "Retailer Hammers Home Message to Suppliers," *Globe and Mail,* March 31, 1992, p. B1.

selection, ask the representatives to return with more samples, or come into the store to look at full rugs.[4]

### Customized Targeted Marketing

Another important key to developing a customer-focused culture is to effectively use marketing information. Business strategies are market driven—not product driven. Thus, one current approach toward successful marketing is to serve the needs of the customers by offering services that enhance their daily lives. The objective here is to design a shopping experience for each customer type, while offering a personal approach to the sale and handling of each individual customer. Individuality and personal preference are the hallmark of today's consumer.

The growth of "niche" catalogs and other nonstore approaches tells us that customers welcome this type of marketing. Targeted direct mail is a growing medium capitalizing on some important life-style trends. For example, one-stop shopping is becoming more and more desirable because consumers have far less leisure time, and home delivery during off hours has become an important consideration.

## Analysis for Action

There is a lot of consumer information available from both inside and outside the company. It is easier and less costly to sell to current customers than it is to attract new ones. With this in mind, there are several things that need to be accomplished in order to improve the use of customer information:

- Focusing on customer needs, not on the merchandise department's needs.
- Developing a list of merchandise classifications that customers are not buying.
- Cross-analyzing lists to use by merchandise type.
- Merging and updating internal lists with external lists.
- Determining where and how a given customer buys each product. (Department stores tend to approach all products the same way. One solution is to develop stores comprised of privately owned shops.)

## Anticipation—the Next Level

With improvements in the content and administration of customer databases, the next opportunity to develop a competitive edge in customer service is to anticipate what the customer wants. To successfully accomplish this goal, one must have a preplanned action based on information in the company's files. Here are some promotional ideas:

- If customers book vacations through the store's travel service, send them a promotional package, including information on camera and film, camcorder and videotape, photo finishing, luggage and accessories, and so on.
- When customers buy carpets, automatically send them information on carpet cleaning, drapery services, decorating services, and similar services.

Using files in this manner allows management to anticipate other related customer needs. This is where proper use of the computer can actually personalize the relationship with customers and offer additional sales opportunities.

## Organizing for the Customer

Management must have a focal point by which to gather, maintain, analyse, interpret, market, and measure the use of customer service information within the company. Functions include:

- Who buys what and where?
- Share of market surveys.
- Consumer shopping panels.
- Analysis of what current customers are buying elsewhere.
- Customer lists consolidation, development, administration, and potential communication.
- Employee feedback.
- Sales-results analyses, including test mailings and promotions.

**Summary**

Traditional customer service (as it is currently practised or not practised) in the retail industry is no longer sufficient. A broader customer-focused culture is called for today that incorporates customer life-styles and buying patterns into the strategy. The results can provide a wide range of creative, competitive opportunities. But using this information to the greatest advantage requires planning, commitment, a focal point, a merger of inside and outside information, communication, and careful measurement.

## Strategic Dimensions of Services

Given the preceding framework, services can now be analyzed on two critical dimensions—value to customers and cost. Four categories of services emerge from such an analysis, as shown in Figure 18–1: support services, disappointers, basic services, and patronage builders.[5]

### Support Services

**Support services** directly support the sale of the retailer's merchandise. They have high value to consumers but also a high cost to the retailer. Such services include home delivery, child care, gift wrapping, and personalized shopper services. Retail Highlight 18–3 provides some examples of support services.

### Disappointers

**Disappointers** include layaway and parcel pick-up. These services require high labour effort but return little value to the customer. They are candidates for elimination from the services offered by some retailers. An alternative possibility is to restructure them in such a way as to reduce their cost and increase their value to customers.

### Basic Services

Customers take some **basic services** for granted. An example is free parking. Retailers often provide such services without giving much thought to their cost, particularly if such services are a competitive necessity.

**FIGURE 18–1**

*Retail customer services profile*

SOURCE: Based on Albert D. Bates and Jamie G. Didijon, ''Special Services Can Personalize Retail Environment,'' *Marketing News,* April 12, 1985, p. 13.

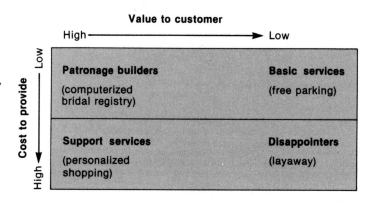

**Retail Highlight 18–3**

# Examples of Excellent Support Services

Child care and entertainment help mothers shop with their children:

- Alive and Well, a women's fashion warehouse boutique in Markham, Ontario, has a children's play area, a changing room for babies stocked with complimentary diapers, and massage chairs throughout the store for customers wanting to take a rest.
- Kiddlywinks, a children's clothing and toy store in Orangeville, Ontario, offers a children's play area, a weekly story-reading hour, and face painting for preschoolers.

Conveniences that make shopping easier:

- Alive and Well has 25 change rooms, each with four hooks, a shelf, and a mirror, and there is no limit on the number of items the customer can bring into the room.

Personalized services:

- Harry Rosen's 24 stores across Canada are all linked by computer, with a database of customers that allows salespeople to know what a particular customer has bought in the past, and to assist him in selecting the proper sizes, fit, and items (to avoid duplications). This data is also used to improve the merchandise mix, so that the right items are always in stock.
- Korry's Clothiers to Gentlemen offers potential clients a free one-hour wardrobe analysis, and this information will be stored and used whenever the client has a need.

Sources: Stephen Forbes, "This Retailer Is Alive and Well," *Marketing,* October 15, 1990, pp. 15–17; Angela Bianchi, "Retailers Are Cashing In by Catering to Kids," *Marketing,* October 15, 1990, p. 20; Leslie C. Smith, "Dressing Up Customer Service," *Globe and Mail,* June 11, 1992.

*Patronage Builders*

**Patronage builders** are the services that receive the most strategic attention from retailers. They include such services as birthday reminders and gift certificates. The services have high consumer value and can be provided at nominal cost. As such, they provide the opportunity to increase the store's customer base, especially if competitors are unable to provide comparable services at the same price. Computers have allowed retailers to shift some services from the high-value/high-cost category to one of high consumer value but low cost. Computerized bridal registries, for example, can be accessed from multiple store locations, and purchases can be entered on virtually a real-time basis.

Management may want to charge for support services, eliminate disappointers, and use patronage builders as a way to expand the customer base. Regardless, management needs to periodically re-evaluate services and make sure that patronage builders do not drift into the support services category.

# A Services Audit

A services audit can help management evaluate the firm's services offering relative to competition and on the basis of value to customers, as discussed above. The end result will likely be a more customer-driven services programme. Identifying what services consumers really value is no simple task, partly because consumers may have difficulty articulating their preferences. Additionally, customers often form opinions about the quality and quantity of services by using competitors as a reference point.[6]

Customer services cannot be an afterthought. A quality services programme can help to differentiate the firm from competition, generate new sales leads, discourage consumers from switching to alternative retail outlets that may offer the same merchandise, and reinforce customer loyalty. Asking questions such as the following helps management integrate services as a strategic element of its customer support plan:

1. What are the company's customer service objectives on each service offered—to make a profit, break even or, in order to remain competitive, to sustain the loss?
2. What services does the company provide (customer education, financing arrangements, predelivery preparation, complaints handling, repair service, etc.)?
3. How does the company compare with the competition on the customer services provided?
4. What services do customers want?
5. What are the customer service demand patterns?
6. What trade-offs in terms of cost versus service are customers prepared to make?
7. What level of service do customers want and at what price? For example, is an 800 telephone number adequate, or is selling in person necessary?[7]

Effective implementation of the services programme is critical after the completion of the audit. Services response systems should be standardized whenever possible, and a pricing policy should be established in those situations where management decides to charge for various services.

The value of a services audit can be seen in Table 18–1. The information in the table is based on interviews with more than 1,000 female shoppers in five major metropolitan areas to determine the types of services that most influence their decision on where to shop. As shown, money-back satisfaction was ranked more important than any other factor. Convenience factors such as available parking close to the store, quick check-out service, and restrooms were the other services that would sway 50 percent of the women to change their shopping habits. It may come as a surprise that merchants could enhance their total service package simply by making sure such mundane things as restrooms meet customer expectations.[8]

Today's shopper is busy, so it should also come as no surprise that 45 percent would shop a certain store if they were notified in advance of sales and other events.

---

**TABLE 18–1    Would It Influence Your Decision Where to Shop if You Were Confident of . . . ?**

| | Percent Saying It Would |
|---|---|
| Money-back satisfaction | 77.9% |
| Convenient parking | 61.0 |
| Quick check-out service | 52.8 |
| Women's restroom | 50.7 |
| Advance notice of sales/events | 45.9 |
| Private fitting rooms | 43.8 |
| Sales assistance | 43.3 |
| Store charge card | 37.0 |
| Phone orders | 24.6 |
| Low-cost home delivery | 21.1 |
| Gift wrapping | 19.7 |
| Someone in the store who knows you by name | 19.5 |
| Background music | 8.5 |

SOURCE: "Service: Retail's No. 1 Problem," *Chain Store Age, General Merchandise Trends,* January 1987, p. 19.

Also important to over 40 percent of the women were private fitting rooms and quality sales assistance.

Let's now look at the range of services offered by many retailers to see how they fit into a customer-focused culture.

# Retail Credit

Understandably, credit in one form or another is one of the most basic customer support services many retailers can offer. *Consumer credit* can be defined as sums that are borrowed, or financial obligations incurred, for a relatively short period of time. Historically, retailers have used a number of forms of retail credit to encourage patronage and purchases in their premises. The advantages and disadvantages of the various types of retail credit systems are shown in Table 18–2.

## In-House Credit

Credit is expensive, and write-offs are very costly, as illustrated in Table 18–3. However, well-managed, large-scale credit operations can be very profitable. One estimate is that 40 percent of the operating profit for Sears and The Bay comes from their credit card operations.[9]

Most retailers believe that granting credit is necessary. Consumers apparently feel the same way since they often shop only in stores where credit cards are honoured.

### What Types of Store Credit Should Be Offered?

Management has five choices in offering store credit, as shown in Figure 18–2: (1) instalment payments, (2) open-charge credit, (3) revolving credit, (4) deferred billing payment, and (5) layaway.

**TABLE 18–2    Advantages and Disadvantages of Retail Credit Systems**

| Option | Advantages | Disadvantages |
|---|---|---|
| Maintaining in-house credit | Builds strong identification with customer<br>Retains customer loyalty<br>Facilitates customer purchase decision<br>When outside agency purchases credit contract, bad debt risk is transferred<br>Special consumers may be targeted with credit plan | Bad debt may be incurred<br>Must staff and equip credit department<br>Clerical work involved with transaction<br>When credit contract is sold to outside agency, retail firm loses a percentage of credit contract |
| Accepting bank cards | Attracts more diverse clientele<br>Outside agency may accept responsibility for collection of bad debts<br>Reduces pressure on sales personnel to grant credit<br>Loss due to bad debts accepted by outside agency<br>Credit offered to customers who otherwise would not qualify<br>Steady cash flow can be maintained<br>Broadens customer base<br>Supplements firm's credit options | Fees paid to third party<br>Clerical work involved with transaction<br>With large purchases, liability for nonpayment may rest with retail outlet if proper authorization and/or signature is not obtained<br>Depersonalizes relationship between firm and customer |
| Accepting travel and entertainment cards | Attracts more diverse clientele<br>Card holders are usually more responsible, affluent customers<br>Broadens customer base<br>Supplements existing credit options<br>Responsibility for processing applications, credit authorization, and collection rests with outside agency | Fee charged to firm for using card<br>Clerical work involved with transaction<br>Proper authorization and/or signatures must be secured from cardholder (firm may be liable for debt if not)<br>Depersonalizes customer/firm relationship<br>Types of purchases may be restricted |
| Buying a private-label credit system | Bank handles details of processing, promotion of plan, credit authorization, and collection<br>Identity of third party is hidden since name of a retail firm is on card<br>Customer loyalty is retained<br>Strong identity with retail firm is built<br>No fee assessed firm outside of cost for programme | Up-front fee assessed firm by sponsoring bank |
| Payment by cheque or cash | Discounts may be given for cash-only purchases<br>Salesperson/customer relationship enhanced since paperwork held to minimum | Depending on type of firm, cash-only basis may restrict growth<br>Bad debt may be incurred with cheques<br>Greater chance of employee fraud<br>Identification requirements for cheque writers may diminish firm/customer relationship |

**TABLE 18–3    Every Dollar Written Off Requires a Fortune in New Business to Break Even**

| Your Profit Percent | Write-Offs of | | | | | | | |
|---|---|---|---|---|---|---|---|---|
| | *$250* | *$500* | *$1,000* | *$2,000* | *$3,000* | *$5,000* | *$7,500* | *$10,000* |
| | **Equivalent to Sales of** | | | | | | | |
| 2% | $12,500 | $25,000 | $50,000 | $100,000 | $150,000 | $250,000 | $375,000 | $500,000 |
| 3 | 8,333 | 16,667 | 33,333 | 66,667 | 100,000 | 166,667 | 249,975 | 333,333 |
| 4 | 6,250 | 12,500 | 25,000 | 50,000 | 75,000 | 125,000 | 187,500 | 250,000 |
| 5 | 5,000 | 10,000 | 20,000 | 40,000 | 60,000 | 100,000 | 150,000 | 200,000 |
| 6 | 4,165 | 8,333 | 16,667 | 33,333 | 50,000 | 83,333 | 124,950 | 166,667 |
| 7 | 3,572 | 7,143 | 14,286 | 28,571 | 42,857 | 71,429 | 107,145 | 142,857 |
| 8 | 3,125 | 6,250 | 12,500 | 25,000 | 37,500 | 62,500 | 93,750 | 125,000 |
| 9 | 2,778 | 5,556 | 11,111 | 22,222 | 33,333 | 55,556 | 83,340 | 111,111 |
| 10 | 2,500 | 5,000 | 10,000 | 20,000 | 30,000 | 50,000 | 75,000 | 100,000 |

Example: If you decide to write off $2,000 in bad debts and are averaging 6 percent profit, you must sell an additional $33,333 to recover that $2,000.

SOURCE: I.C. System, Inc. (St. Paul, Minn.).

**FIGURE 18–2**

*Types of in-house credit*

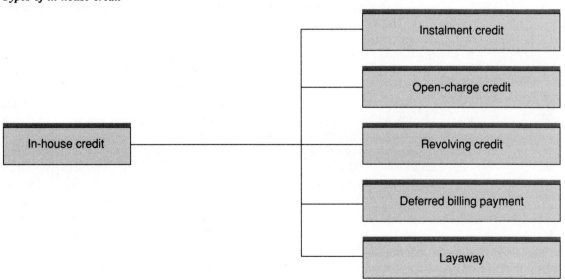

**Instalment credit** (a monthly payment account) means that a customer pays for a product in equal monthly instalments, including interest. Automobiles and major appliances are often paid for in this way.

**Open charge credit** means that the customer must pay the bill in full when it is due, usually in 30 days. Credit limits are set that the customer cannot exceed; also, part payments on the account are not allowed.

**Revolving credit** means that a customer charges items during a month and is billed at the end of that month on the basis of the outstanding balance. Such a plan allows the customer to purchase several items without having a separate contract for each purchase.

A business can also offer **deferred billing credit.** Deferred billing occurs when a retailer allows customers to buy goods and defer payment for an extended time with no interest charge. During the Christmas season, many stores advertise "No down payment, and first payment not due for 90 days."

A **layaway plan** is another type of credit. This plan allows a customer to make a small deposit, perhaps two or three dollars, to hold an item. The retailer retains possession of the item until the customer completes paying for it. The advantage to customers is not having to worry about whether the item will be in stock when they need it. And retailers do not have to worry about collection problems.

### The Credit Card Phenomenon in Retailing

A *credit card* is basically a convenient way for customers to obtain credit without having to go through the approval process. It is, in fact, a modern form of revolving credit.

Credit cards were first introduced in 1968 by the Royal Bank. Its card was called the Chargex card (which became Visa). In 1991, it was estimated that 46 million credit cards were in circulation in Canada (i.e., 2.3 for each adult), and that credit card balances exceeded $11 billion.[10] Of these, 24 million were bank cards (Visa and MasterCard), 14 million were retail store cards, and 3 million were gasoline retailers. Visa and MasterCard were used for more than 617 million transactions and accounted for $40 billion in sales. In addition, in 1991, there were 857,000 merchant accounts in Canada.[11] The most popular cards in Canada are shown in Table 18–4.

Most retailers today honour some type of credit card. A retailer has two basic choices with credit cards: It can (1) provide its own card or (2) participate in a third-party programme.

**Third-party credit** can consist of (1) a *bank card* such as Visa or MasterCard, (2) a **private-label credit card** for the store that is issued by a third party such as a bank, and (3) *travel and entertainment cards* such as American Express or Diner's Club.

Today, independent department stores and petroleum companies are practically the only stores that have internal credit operations (and even those are declining). These stores believe they get a strong marketing advantage from in-house credit. Many have added bank credit card plans to their programmes, primarily to take advantage of out-of-town business. Others such as Woodward's have sold their

---

### TABLE 18-4   Credit Cards in Canada

**Financial Institutions**
Visa (at least nine institutions)
MasterCard (at least seven institutions)

**Retail Stores**
Canadian Tire
Eaton's
Home Hardware
The Bay
Sears
Simpsons'
Woodward's
Zellers

**Gasoline Retailers**
Esso*
Husky Oil*
Irving Oil*
Petro Canada
Shell (now a MasterCard with Royal Trust)
Sunoco*
Ultramar

**Travel and Entertainment Cards**
American Express*
Carte Blanche
Diner's Club
en Route

---

*For these cards, full payment of the balance is required each month.
SOURCE: "Credit Card Interest Charges," *Information,* April 1992, Minister of Supply and Services Canada, pp. 2–4.

credit card business to financial institutions.[12] Thus, in-house credit probably is on its way out for many merchants.

***Third-Party Credit***

Bank credit cards such as Visa, or travel and entertainment cards such as Diner's Club, are not controlled by the merchant. Rather, the bank or the entertainment company receives applications and issues cards and is responsible for customer billing and collection. The firms then bill the merchants accepting the card at a flat percentage of all credit sales.[13]

In a third-party programme, banks handle (1) credit applications, credit processing, and authorization; (2) customer inquiries; (3) promotion; and (4) issuing each customer a card with the name of the participating store on it. Recently, Visa has gone this route and will place a store name on the face of its card. The advantage is that the retailer gets more loyal customers plus the wide acceptability of Visa.

In summary, more and more retailers are dropping in-house credit as a service. Many are (1) going to a private-label, third-party system, (2) honouring bank cards such as Visa, (3) honouring travel and entertainment cards, or (4) structuring a programme to encourage the use of cheques and cash. Some retailers—for example, Canadian Tire—give rebates of 3 to 5 percent in the form of store money on cash purchases. This discount is the equivalent of what merchants pay the banks for the right to allow customers to make purchases with a bank credit card such as Visa.

***Managing Internal Credit***

Most firms issuing credit use an application form. The application requests information that allows the firm to decide whether the person should be granted credit. The forms may ask for such information as the size of savings and chequing account balances, extent of debts, and various other personal information. Often information on the credit worthiness of the applicant is obtained from a credit bureau.[14]

*Credit Scoring*

Many firms use **credit scoring** in screening credit applicants. This method assigns points to various types of personal information concerning the applicant. The points are determined through a study of information obtained from other good and bad accounts. Depending on the number of points received, a person may be given a credit limit or may be rejected. Experience can help decide on the minimum number of points necessary to approve an application.

Scoring gives the retailer the following advantages: (1) better control over credit, (2) ease in training new personnel, (3) lower cost of processing loan application, and (4) a more legally defensible way of granting or denying credit.

On this last point, retailers must comply with the antidiscrimination sections of the Canadian Human Rights Act and some provincial Human Rights Codes, some provisions of the Bank Act and the Interest Act, as well as the appropriate provincial Consumer Protection Act and Cost of Credit Disclosure Act. To a lesser extent, the Competition Act (section 49) and the Small Loan Act may apply to credit.

The retailer also needs to decide how credit will be verified when a credit purchase is made. Some firms still have *manual credit verification*, where a clerk calls the credit department when a sale is made and asks for approval. Today most credit authorization is done electronically. The clerk enters the account number and the amount of the sale at the cash register. The system then automatically checks the accounts receivable information stored in the computer and indicates whether a credit charge should be approved.

The stand-alone credit authorization terminal is rapidly becoming a thing of the past. Instead, high-credit-volume retailers are integrating credit authorization into POS terminals. Currently, only 19 percent of mass merchants and 50 percent of apparel retailers, including department stores, use stand-alone credit authorization terminals.[15]

*Promoting Credit*

In spite of the possible losses from a credit operation, many retailers aggressively promote their credit plans because they can result in increased merchandise sales. College students are often a special target. They are perceived as upwardly mobile, soon-to-be young professionals, with high income potential. As well, the population turnover in a community can easily equal 15 percent per year, and an ongoing programme of credit promotion is necessary to maintain a strong customer base for a retail outlet.

# Handling Cheques

Historically, a customer with a chequebook at the head of a check-out line was sure to bring moans and grumblings from customers waiting in line. The process of paying by cheque can easily take 5 to 10 minutes and create great customer frustration. Stores have turned to on-line cheque acceptance services that make payment by cheque as simple as using a credit card and just as quick.

Many retail customers still prefer to pay by either cash or cheque. Making it easy for them to pay by cheque generates customer goodwill and a substantial amount of ''plus'' business. Some supermarkets such as Provigo offer cheque-cashing privileges to their customers with the store card. A customer can not only pay for groceries with a cheque (no hassle for approval) but also write a larger amount to obtain cash in return.

# Shopping Services

Retailers are always trying to make it possible for customers to buy goods without having to spend an extended time in the store. Shopping services thus are being experimented on by large food retailers like Provigo. The most common shopper services are (1) telephone shopping, (2) in-home shopping, and (3) personal shopping.

*Telephone Shopping*

*Telephone shopping* is pushed by retailers because many people have less time for shopping. Often, the store will issue a catalog to the consumer. After looking at the catalog, the customer calls the store, orders the merchandise, and charges the goods to an account or credit card. The goods are then delivered to the shopper's home.

Some retail outlets also offer toll-free 800 service as a way of increasing sales. Harrod's Department Store, in London, England, was the first store in Europe to join AT&T's international 800 service. Shoppers were able to order goods during th⌐ store's post-Christmas sale by dialing direct—even before the store opened for business to Londoners.[16]

*In-Home Shopping*

In-home demonstrations remain popular for such services as home decoration. Employees bring samples of draperies, carpeting, and wallpaper to a customer's home and the customer can then see how the materials look under home lighting conditions. One such example is Elte Carpets, discussed earlier in this chapter.[17]

*Personal Shopping Services*

**Personal shopping services** are one of the fastest-growing customer services. The customer goes to the store and provides a list of needed measurements, style, colour preferences, and life-style information. After that, the person can call the store and indicate the types of items wanted. Store personnel can then assemble several choices and have them ready at the customer's convenience.[18]

# Other Customer Support Services

Additional customer support services are (1) warranties, (2) delivery, (3) extended shopping hours, (4) automatic bill payment, (5) helping customers with special needs, and (6) registries.

*Warranties*

Most services are designed to help sell merchandise and are offered at no extra cost. But retailers can offer some additional services for which customers may gladly pay. An example is an *extended warranty* or a service contract.[19] The store agrees to extend a manufacturer's warranty for a period of time, commonly a year or so. The customer does not have to pay a repair bill during the agreed period of time regardless of how much the repair service may cost. Extended warranties are common on major household appliances and television sets.

Retailers should be aware of warranty legislation, however, when offering extended warranties, in particular the Competition Act and the appropriate provincial Consumer Protection Act. "Satisfaction Guaranteed" is a phrase often heard, but today such a statement may be interpreted as a contract, not just a courtesy. Some laws also determine where and how warranty information must be displayed. Many retail catalogs inform consumers that they can obtain warranty information by mail before purchasing from the store.

## Delivery

Delivery can be a large expense for big ticket items such as furniture and household appliances. Stores are often pressured not to charge extra for delivery. Retailers can help their image as full-service retailers by having their own trucks for delivery. The delivery schedule can then be more flexible, but the cost of delivery trucks is high.

Another method of delivery is to use parcel post and service express. Retailers may want to use these services in addition to independent delivery services. Parcel post is a good way to deliver small packages to customers who may live a long distance from the store. Mail-order retailers often arrange delivery in this way.

## Extended Shopping Hours

Where it is legal, more and more retailers are offering consumers longer shopping hours, either late night or 24-hour shopping. Utility charges are about the same, since store equipment runs most of the time anyway. Additional sales generated by longer hours can help spread the fixed costs over a larger sales base.

*Customer support services are an important part of Sears strategy.*

SOURCE: Copyright Sears Canada Inc., 1988.

Merchants may do very well with such a service, since in many communities only a few stores are open 24 hours a day. But it is important to study such a move carefully before making a decision. Retailers will have to pay overtime to employees or add part-time workers. The chance of being robbed is greater, and energy bills will go up somewhat.

Retailers should also remember that **blue laws** (laws against opening on Sunday) are enforced in some areas. Enforcement is spotty, but a retailer can be fined if a pressure group pushes the police to enforce the law. Blue laws are likely to be a thing of the past in the next few years since most consumers seem to want Sunday shopping.

*Automatic Bill Payment*

Retailers are increasingly offering bill-payment programmes that allow bills to be paid by telephone, preauthorization, or electronic terminals as an alternative to paying by cheque.

One such system is the **debit card,** introduced in Canada in 1986 by several banks such as the National Bank, the Toronto-Dominion Bank, and the Canadian Imperial Bank of Commerce. At the retail level, the transaction is as follows:

1. The client presents the debit card to the cashier.
2. The cashier hands the client a keyboard that is attached to the cash register.
3. The client inserts the card into the terminal.
4. The client verifies the amount of purchase indicated, chooses the bank account from which the withdrawal should take place, and then authorizes the transaction by keying in a personal identification number (PIN).
5. The money is transferred electronically from the client's to the retailer's bank account.
6. The client receives a statement of the full transaction.

The whole operation lasts only a few minutes. With the current system, the debit card works only within the network of merchants signed on by the issuing bank. As an increasing number of banks and merchants adopt this type of service, the whole automatic debit system is expected to be integrated with the Interac banking system, allowing customers to use their cards almost anywhere.[20]

The advantages of such systems include (1) the elimination of bad cheques, (2) lower labour costs to the retailer, (3) lower cheque processing fees because of a smaller cheque volume, and (4) reduced postage.

The disadvantages include (1) the loss of direct contact with the consumer, (2) the loss of the opportunity to send stuffers with monthly statements, (3) misunderstandings with consumers over the timing of the payments, which can lead to loss of goodwill, and (4) the loss of an audit trail that would help in catching dishonesty and fraud. Automated bill paying is likely to increase in popularity in the future because consumers react positively to saving time by this means of payment.

**Customers with Special Needs**

Opportunities exist to meet the needs of special consumers, including those who don't speak English—or French in Quebec—the aged, and the infirm (including people who are deaf, blind, or confined to wheelchairs). More than 3 million people have physical or sensory disabilities.

The federal government mandated the push toward barrier-free environments in education, employment, and nonemployment situations. Now, many provinces also have legislation requiring architectural compliance regarding barrier-free environments. Some progressive stores offer programmes to assist and inform handicapped and aged shoppers.

Large retailers in such metropolitan markets as Toronto, Vancouver, and Montreal, or in places popular with tourists such as Banff, Niagara Falls, or Charlottetown, offer multilingual signing to attract and serve foreign tourists. They also maintain lists of employees with foreign language ability. In addition, store directories and information pamphlets are sometimes printed in foreign languages.

**Registries**

Computerization is giving department stores a convenience and flexibility in their registry systems that were previously unavailable. The benefits these retailers have seen in a computerized bridal registry are broadbased. The most obvious advantage is in access and updating capabilities. Because a complete registry can be printed from the computer within a matter of minutes, stores on the system can provide customers with an instant shopping list for a betrothed couple—a list they can carry with them from department to department as they make their selections.

But perhaps of most interest to store executives is the merchandising aspect, providing buyers and merchandise managers with complete, up-to-the-minute sales information, right down to details on vendor, patterns, size, or colour of each gift purchased.

# Handling Complaints and Returns

Retailers need a policy for dealing with customer complaints and merchandise returns. Customers are allowed to return items in most stores, and some retailers feel the customer should be satisfied at any price. Almost all retailers, while not guaranteeing satisfaction, do try to be fair to the customer. There may be many problems in addition to returns, including complaints about products, poor installation, problems with delivery, damaged goods, errors in billing, and so forth.

Complaints and returns can be handled on either a centralized or decentralized basis. Stores with a *centralized policy* handle all issues at a central level in the store; in this way, they can be sure that a standardized policy is followed for all departments. In a *decentralized approach,* problems are handled on the sales floor by the person who sold the item, and the customer gets greater personal attention.

Stores normally prefer not to give a cash refund when handling a complaint or return. Most retailers try to get the customer exchanging an item to accept a slip (or *due-bill*) that allows them to purchase an item at the same price in the future. This policy is designed to keep the customer coming back to the store. Some retailers may feel, however, that the consumer should be given a refund. They believe this better satisfies customers and builds better customer relations.

Stores also have to decide whether to put the emphasis on the customer or the store when handling complaints and returned merchandise. Again, a cost-benefit analysis is required. Providing an elaborate system for handling complaints and returns is costly, especially when the consumer wants money instead of merchandise upon returning an item. Still, stores may be better off viewing returns primarily from the viewpoint of the consumer and generating goodwill by going out of their way to have a liberal returned-goods policy, as illustrated in Retail Highlight 18–4.

## Evaluating the Cost-Effectiveness of Services

All services offered cost the firm money. Employees may need to be added to offer certain services. The cost must be balanced against anticipated revenues, or the loss of goodwill if the services are not offered.

It is not possible to precisely determine the revenue-generating effects of each service. Also, if certain services are offered by the competition, the firm may have to offer them to remain competitive.

Many factors must be considered in deciding to offer or discontinue a service. The same is true when the retailer is deciding whether to charge for a service such as accepting merchandise returned through no fault of the retailer. Consider the

---

**Retail Highlight 18–4**

## Proper Handling of Customer Complaints and Returns Requires a Conversion

The following story illustrates a customer-focused perspective on complaints and returns. Tom Sieciechowicz pondered service long and hard after he and his wife Anna opened their first Odyssey Books store in Kanata, Ontario, 11 years ago. After deciding that he was doing most things wrong by using his own preferences, he concluded that his store would have to capture loyal book buyers first and adjust inventory to suit their tastes. He then began a policy of exchanging any book a reader found to be unsatisfactory—for whatever reason. But *carrying out* the policy required a conversion of faith. He recalls a pitched battle with a customer over a refund. In mid-argument, he suddenly realized that he had to stand behind his policy and

give the refund. The experience changed his thinking: "What is service? It's what the customer thinks is service. The customer wanted to be able to return books without questions being asked. Whether he even bought it at a different store, he wanted to have a fair trade, to feel that everything was guaranteed. That was logical from the customer's point of view, so it became logical from mine."

Another telling example is the story of the sales associate at a Nordstrom Department Store who gave a customer his money back for a set of tires for which he was claiming a refund, even though Nordstrom does not sell tires!

Sources: Marlene Cartash, "Catch a Falling Store," *Profit,* December 1990, pp. 26–27; and Ron Zemke and Dick Schaaf, *The Service Edge* (Markham, Ont.: Penguin Books, 1989), p. 353.

issue of credit: Management must balance the additional revenue from additional customer sales against the cost of offering credit. For example, the funds that are used for the credit programme are not available to be invested, so interest is lost. Also, management cannot use the funds for other purposes.

Other costs of credit include the discounting of receivables—for example, when a financial institution buys the credit accounts from a retailer at a discount. The advantage to the retailer is that the cash is immediately available and no risks of collection are assumed. Still, the discount paid to get quick access to the funds can result in lower net profit. Outside costs also include the time salesclerks spend in charging a sale to a bank credit card or a travel and entertainment card.

## Chapter Highlights

- Many features of a store affect how customers view it and whether they will continue to shop at the outlet. The kind and quality of services are key factors.

- Traditional customer service in the retail industry is no longer sufficient. A broader customer-focused culture is called for today that incorporates customer life-styles and buying patterns into the strategy. The results can provide a wide range of creative, competitive opportunities. But using this information to the greatest advantage requires planning, commitment, a focal point, a merger of inside and outside information, communication, and careful measurement.

- There are four categories of services that retailers must evaluate carefully (through a service audit): support services, disappointers, basics, and patronage builders.

- Retailers face a variety of decisions in deciding whether to offer credit. They can offer in-store credit or have credit handled by an outside agency such as a bank by honouring bank credit cards. They may also issue a store credit card of their own, or have a card with their name on it but have the bank handle the administrative details. Consumer pressure in favour of bank credit cards is increasing, and most stores now honour them.

- Most types of credit are offered by the retailer at a loss. However, credit normally is a necessary customer service.

- Retailers can offer a variety of other services as part of the customer support mix. These include extended hours and Sunday openings, delivery, services such as baby sitting, interior-design counselling, nonstore shopping opportunities, appliance installation, and an almost endless variety of other services. However, it is important to try to balance likely revenue against the cost of the services.

- Retailers should closely monitor the legal issues relating to many of the services they offer.

## Key Terms

Basic services     499
Blue laws     509
Credit scoring     506
Customer-focused culture     490
Customer service     490
Debit card     509
Deferred billing credit     504
Disappointers     499
Instalment credit     504

Layaway plan     504
Open charge credit     504
Patronage builders     499
Personal shopping service     507
Private-label credit card     504
Revolving credit     504
Support services     498
Third-party credit     504

# Discussion Questions

1. What might be the major reasons for a retailer to offer selected services? Why are many retailers cutting down on the number of services they offer?

2. Why should a retailer offer a store's own card for credit? What problems or disadvantages exist when a store has its own card?

3. What are some retailers doing to encourage customers to pay cash for purchases?

4. What are some of the methods retailers use to determine to which applicants credit should be extended?

5. What are the advantages and disadvantages of offering customers liberal merchandise return privileges?

6. Explain the concept of a debit card. Describe its advantages and disadvantages for both the customer and the retailer.

7. What are some of the things retailers are doing to be more responsive to customers who have special needs?

8. What are the advantages and disadvantages of a centralized versus a decentralized procedure for handling consumer complaints?

# Application Exercises

1. Talk to the credit manager at two local department stores in your community and to the loan officer at two banks to determine how they evaluate customer applications for credit. Try to get a copy of the forms they use, if possible. Find out if they use credit scoring. If not, what do they do in order to be objective in their evaluations? Find out if they are reasonably current on the regulations granting credit to women.

2. Select a department store, supermarket, discount store (e.g., Kmart), and national chain like Sears. Develop a list of services that the stores might offer

(from the text listing). Then interview a group of students at random. Have each student check the services he or she perceives are offered by each type of store chosen. Write a report on the findings and suggest what they mean to you in terms of the material included in the chapter.

3. Discuss with several friends complaints that they may have had against a store or stores. Describe how each was handled by (1) the customer and (2) the store. Evaluate the process of complaint handling.

# Suggested Cases

# Endnotes

1. This section on customer service versus customer focus is reproduced with permission from Roy Burns, "Customer Service vs. Customer-Focused," *Retail Control,* March 1989. Copyright © National Retail Merchants Association. All rights reserved.

2. Michael Salter, "Sorry, We're Out of It," *Report on Business Magazine,* September 1987, pp. 66–70.

3. Leslie C. Smith, "Dressing Up Customer Service," *Globe and Mail,* June 11, 1992, p. D1.

4. Marlene Cartash, "Catch a Falling Store," *Profit,* December 1990, p. 29.

5. Albert D. Bates and Jamie G. Didion, "Special Services Can Personalize Retail Environment," *Marketing News,* April 12, 1985, p. 13.

6. Gordon McDougall and Terry Levesque, "The Measurement of Service Quality: Some Methodological Issues," in *Marketing, Operations and Human Resources Insight into Services,* ed. Pierre Eiglier and Eric Langeard (Aix, France: I.A.E., 1992), pp. 411–31; J. Joseph Cronin, Jr., and Steven A. Taylor, "Measuring Service Quality: A Reexamination and Extension," *Journal of Marketing* 56 (July 1992), pp. 55–68; and Gaston LeBlanc, "The Determinants of Service Quality in Travel Agencies," in *Marketing,* vol. 11, ed. John Liefeld (ASAC, 1990), pp. 188–96.

7. Hirotaka Takeuchi and John A. Quelch, "Quality Is More than Making a Good Product," *Harvard Business Review,* July–August 1983, pp. 139–45.

8. Larry Forester, "Service Ain't What It Use to Be," *Chain Store Age, General Merchandise Trends,* January 1987, p. 5; and "Pul-eeze! Will Somebody Help Me?" *Time,* February 2, 1987, pp. 48–57.

9. Karen Howlett, "Woodward's Strikes Deal to Sell Credit Card Business," *Globe and Mail: Report on Business,* November 2, 1988, p. B8.

10. "Credit Card Interest Charges," *Information,* April 1992, Minister of Supply and Services Canada, pp. 2–4.

11. Murray Campbell, "The Credit Card Comes of Age," *Globe and Mail,* March 25, 1989, p. D5.

12. Howlett, "Woodward's Strikes Deal."

13. See David P. Schulz, "Plastic Practices," *Stores,* October 1986, pp. 34–39.

14. For further reading, see "Coping with Growing Personal Bankruptcies," *Stores,* April 1986, p. 47.

15. "Credit Authorization Stand-Alones Decrease," *Chain Store Age Executive,* January 1989, pp. 100–104.

16. "London's Harrod's Department Store," *Sales and Marketing Management,* January 13, 1986, p. 83.

17. Cartash, "Catch a Falling Store," p. 29.

18. Smith, "Dressing Up Customer Service"; and "Career Dressing," *Stores,* January 1987, pp. 51–56.

19. C. A. Kelly, J. S. Conant, and J. J. Brown, "Extended Warranties: Retail Management and Public Policy Implications," in *Proceedings of the American Marketing Association,* eds. Gary Frazier et al. (Chicago: American Marketing Association, 1988), pp. 261–66.

20. Nancy Durnford, "Loss of Interest One Pitfall of Automatic Debit Service," *Montreal Gazette,* March 4, 1989, p. K-2.

# IV EVALUATING THE RETAIL STRATEGY

In Part IV, the tools used to determine how well the retail strategy is doing are explained. Internal evaluation is critical to the retail manager, including the elements involved in developing control systems (Chapter 19), and evaluation of performance through an accounting system (Chapter 20).

# 19   EVALUATION AND CONTROL OF MERCHANDISE AND EXPENSE PLANNING

## Chapter Objectives

After reading this chapter, you should be able to:

1 Explain the relationship between planning and control.

2 Illustrate how to establish a dollar control and open-to-buy system to control dollar merchandise investment.

3 Explain unit control of inventory investment.

4 Understand expense control.

**Retailing Capsule**

The task of merchandise planning in a supermarket—a store that typically carries between 8,000 and 12,000 items—is easier today than a few years ago, thanks to computer systems. Loblaws is among the 1,100 supermarket outlets in Canada that have computerized check-out price scanners and in-store computers. Loblaws stocks more than 1,000 new national-brand products each year, but it also drops an equal number. Computer systems allow Loblaws to identify both high- and low-volume items and make adjustments to shelf allocation—the low-volume items may be dropped and the high-growth products get more space. As well, computer systems can track inventories and allow the retailer to adjust quickly to changes in consumers' buying patterns.

Sears Canada has approximately 1,600 catalog stores across Canada to handle the sales generated through its catalogs. The company has continued to fine-tune its catalog systems, including the installation of a fully integrated, on-line, inventory control system. This allows Sears to closely monitor inventory levels, ensure prompt delivery of goods to customers, and provide up-to-date information about merchandise availability.*

New computer systems are being developed that will allow customers to select merchandise, insert a tag attached to the merchandise along with a credit card into a scanner, and validate the purchase. The scanner deactivates the tags, and the customer puts the merchandise in a bag and leaves the store. With these systems, the retailer can use the information to improve inventory control and product selection and make better use of existing floor or shelf space.†

*Sears Canada, Annual Report, 1991.

†Susan Gitlins, "Computers 'Check Out' for Groceries," *The Financial Post,* November 14, 1988, p. S5; and Andrew Lamb, "Want to Shop until Your Computer Drops?" *Globe and Mail,* March 13, 1989, p. C1.

These examples illustrate the importance retailers place on merchandise management in the competitive struggle in today's marketplace. A good merchandise planning and control system allows the retailer to monitor what's going on so that better decisions can be made to attain a productive investment in inventory (i.e., not too much, not too little). This chapter emphasizes the basics of the control of merchandise and expense management. Of primary interest is the evaluation of planning activities through control. Planning, discussed in detail in Chapter 13, was presented as an effort to obtain a competitive advantage in the marketplace. The merchandise and expense budgets were noted as key plans utilized by management to reach specific objectives.

This chapter is a companion to the Chapter 13 material since it approaches the evaluation of these plans to achieve certain objectives. Planning is useless unless retailers monitor operating results to determine whether goals are being met. If plans are not being followed, corrective action must be taken to improve the situation. The monitoring process is the *control* aspect of retail management. Without control, planning is a wasted effort.

# The Relationship between Planning and Control

The relationship between planning and control is essential, direct, and two-way. As shown in Figure 19–1, control records are needed to develop plans. And once a plan is developed, control records are needed to determine how well the retailer is doing.

In Chapter 13, the merchandise plan was discussed in terms of developing the following aspects of stock balance: (1) dollars, (2) width, and (3) depth. A merchandise budget in dollars and a model stock were developed for planning the width and depth factors. In this chapter, attention is given to the systems used to control these aspects of the merchandise plan. Figure 19–2 illustrates the relationship between the merchandise planning and control systems.

Note from Figure 19–2 that two systems are used for controlling the merchandise plan: **Dollar control** is the way of controlling dollar investment in inventory; **unit control** is used to control the width and depth aspects of stock balance. Figure 19–3 shows how these two types of control— dollar and unit—work together.

## *Dollar Merchandise Inventory Control*

Dollar control is important to retail management as a way of controlling dollar investment in inventory. To control dollar inventory investments, the retailer must know the following:

1. The beginning dollar inventory.
2. What has been added to stock.
3. How much inventory has moved out of stock.
4. How much inventory is now on hand.

To determine the value of inventory at the end of the period, the retailer may (1) take a *physical inventory* (actually count all of the inventory on hand) or (2) set up a book inventory or *perpetual inventory system*. A **book inventory** is the

**FIGURE 19–1**

*The planning and control process*

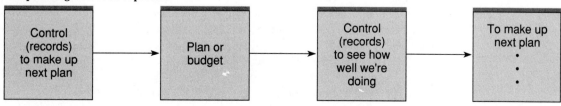

**FIGURE 19–2**

*From planning to control*

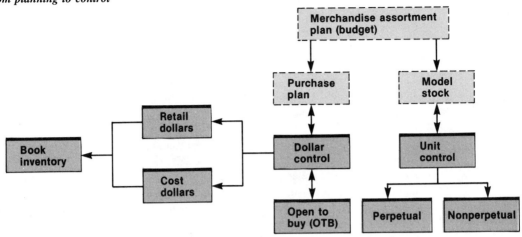

**FIGURE 19–3**

*Diagram of merchandise planning and control*

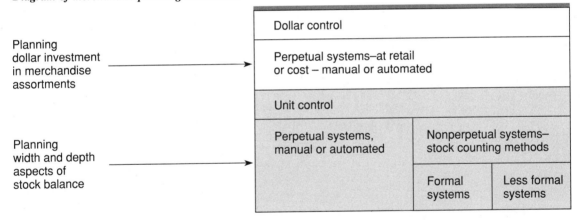

continual recording of all additions to and deductions from a beginning stock figure so that the ending inventory figure is always current. It is impractical to take a physical inventory every time the manager wants to know how much inventory is on hand. Thus, retailers set up a book inventory system. This enables them to know the dollar value of inventory on hand without having to take a physical inventory.

To have efficient and effective dollar control, a book inventory system is needed. Information must be collected and recorded continually. The information can be recorded in retail dollars or in cost dollars, manually or by computer.

## Retail Dollar Control

Figure 19–4 includes the typical items in a retail dollar control system. The system is a perpetual one and provides answers to the following questions:

- *What dollar inventory did the retailer start with?* The BOM (beginning of month) inventory dated 3/1 gives the answer to this question. This March

**FIGURE 19–4**

*Retail dollar book (perpetual) inventory—sweat suits*
March

| Items Affecting Dollar Value of Inventory during Month | | | | Necessary Explanations of Certain Items | Where to Get Information |
|---|---|---|---|---|---|
| BOM inventory, 3/1 | | | $10,000 | | EOM February inventory |
| Additions to stock: | | | | | |
| Purchases | $2,000 | | | | Purchase records or invoices |
| Less: Vendor returns | (100) | | | Goods go back to source | Vendor return records |
| Net purchases | | $1,900 | | | |
| Transfers in | $ 200 | | | In multistore firm, goods transfer from one store to another | Interstore transfer forms in multistore firm |
| Less: Transfers out | (100) | | | | |
| Net transfers in | | 100 | | | |
| Additional markups | | 300 | | Price increase after goods in stock | Price change forms |
| Total additions | | | 2,300 | | |
| Total available for sale | | | $12,300 | | |
| Deductions from stock: | | | | | |
| Gross sales | $2,500 | | | | Daily sales report |
| Less: Customer returns | (100) | | | | Return forms |
| Net sales | | $2,400 | | | |
| Gross markdowns | $ 500 | | | Reduction from original price | Price change forms at start of a sale |
| Less: Markdown cancellations | (100) | | | | Price change cancellation at end of sale to bring prices back to regular |
| Net markdowns | | 400 | | | |
| Employee discounts | | 200 | | Employee pays less than merchandise price | Form completed at sale |
| Total deductions from stock | | | $ 3,000 | | |
| EOM inventory, 3/31 (including shortages) | | | $ 9,300 | A book inventory figure so actual amount is somewhat different (physical inventory necessary for actual) | Derived figure from additions and deductions from BOM inventory |

BOM inventory figure is the EOM (end of month) February figure, or $10,000.

- *What has been added to stock?* The additions to stock are purchases, transfers, and additional markups that add dollars to the beginning inventory. Total additions are $2,300. The total available for sale is $12,300.

- *How much inventory has moved out of stock?* The deductions from stock are sales, markdowns, and employee discounts, which reduce the total dollars of inventory available for sale. Total deductions are $3,000.

- *How much inventory is on hand now?* The EOM inventory, dated 3/31, is the difference between what was available and what moved out of stock. This is the book inventory figure, $9,300.

The explanations in Figure 19–4 should be studied carefully since it is important to fully understand the items that affect retail book inventory. This information, however, should not be confused with an accounting statement discussed in the next chapter: Accounting statement information comes from accounting data, but it is for control purposes only.

Note at the bottom of Figure 19–4 the notation "including shortages" for EOM inventory. Since these are "book" figures, a chance for error exists. The only way to determine the accuracy of the book figure is by taking a physical inventory.

The retail book figures indicate the value of on-hand inventory to be $9,300. Assume that when a physical inventory is taken, the retail value of on-hand stock is $9,000. This situation represents a shortage of $300. A **shortage** occurs when the physical inventory is smaller than the book inventory. Shoplifting, internal theft, short shipments from vendors, breakage, and clerical errors are common causes of shortages. If, on the other hand, the physical inventory had indicated the value of stock on hand to be $10,000, then the retail classification has incurred an overage of $700. An **overage** occurs when the physical inventory is larger than the book inventory. In retailing, an overage situation is usually caused by clerical errors or miscounts.

### Open-to-Buy

One of the most valuable outputs of a retail dollar control system is **open-to-buy (OTB)** (see Figure 19–2). OTB exists to control the merchant's utilization of the planned purchase figure (see Chapter 13, Planned Purchases section). Dollar control provides the essential information to set up an OTB system. These essentials are the BOM and EOM inventories.

As illustrated in Figure 19–5, OTB is determined by deducting from planned purchases commitments that have been made. The two commitments are (1) merchandise on order that has not been delivered and (2) merchandise that has been delivered. Remember, planned purchases relate to one particular month (in the case above, to February). So, OTB relates to only one month. If, for example, merchandise was ordered in January to be delivered in March, that amount would not be a February commitment and would not affect OTB for February.

**FIGURE 19–5**

*Open-to-buy illustration*

| | | |
|---|---|---|
| Planned purchases = | $25,000 | (EOM February or BOM March at retail) |
| + | 2,500 | (Planned sales—February) |
| + | 600 | (Planned reductions—February) |
| = | $28,100 | (Dollars needed) |
| − | 24,000 | (BOM February at retail/EOM January) |
| = | $ 4,100 | (Planned purchases) |

Commitments against
 planned purchases
 during the month of
 February:

On order to be delivered
 in February:    $1,000

Merchandise received
 as of February 15:    $1,500 − $ 2,500    (Commitments against planned purchases)

OTB as of February 15    = $ 1,600    (Note: The $1,600 figure is in retail dollars and must be converted to cost to use as a buying guide in the market.)

*Controlling inventory is critical to retail success.*

From the illustration, one can see that as of February 15, the buyer has $1,600 (in retail dollars) to spend for merchandise to be delivered in February. At the beginning of any month with no commitments, planned purchases and OTB are equal. Assume, however, that by February 20 all of the OTB has been used up and that, in fact, the buyer has overcommitted by $100. This situation is called *overbought* and is not a good position to be in.

This leads to another point that must be made about OTB: OTB must be used only as a guide and must not be allowed to actually dictate decisions to the merchant. A merchant, however, always wants to have OTB to take advantage of unique market situations. The system must also allow for budget adjustments. If the buyer needs more OTB for certain purposes, management approval must be obtained. This can be done by (1) convincing management of the importance of a contemplated purchase and obtaining a budget increase for planned sales; (2) increasing planned reductions or taking more markdowns than have been budgeted; or (3) increasing the planned EOM inventory in anticipation of an upswing in the market.

Each of these is a legitimate merchandising option and indicates that the OTB control system is flexible, as any budget control system must be.

Figure 19–6 presents a sample open-to-buy report form. Of course, this form would vary by company based on what the retailer feels is needed for decision making. By using this form, OTB could be derived by: Line 11 + Line 7 + Line 14 − Line 5 = Planned purchases − Line 17 = OTB (Line 18). (Numbers from Figure 19–5.)

### Cost Dollar Control

Retail dollar control is used more often than cost dollar control. The major problem in using cost versus retail control is *costing* each sale. Costing means converting retail dollars to cost dollars after a sale has been made.

Because of this costing problem, a cost dollar control system is used only when (1) merchandise is of an unusually high unit value and (2) there are relatively few transactions. With merchandise such as furniture or automobiles, cost dollar control is practical. However, for merchandise classifications such as the sweat suit illustration in Figure 19–4, retail dollar control is used. Figure 19–7 shows the kind of information needed for a perpetual cost control system. When using a cost dollar control system, it is not possible to record additional markups and reductions such as markdowns and employee discounts because all of the figures are in cost dollars.

### Unit Merchandise Inventory Control

Unit control is the system used to control the width and depth aspects of stock balance (see Figures 19–2 and 19–3). Unit control is simpler than dollar control since fewer factors affect units than affect dollars invested. The difference is that the price changes do not affect units carried. As Figures 19–2 and 19–3 indicate, the two types of unit control are perpetual and nonperpetual (or stock-counting) systems.

**FIGURE 19–6**

*Open-to-buy report*

Department _____ Classification _____ Date prepared February 15

**Last Month (January)**

| Line | | | $ |
|---|---|---|---|
| 1 | **Sales** | Actual last year | |
| 2 | | Adjusted plan this year | |
| 3 | **Stock** | Actual this year | |
| 4 | | Adjusted plan EOM this year | |
| 5 | | Actual EOM this year | 24,000 |
| 6 | | Actual last year | |
| 7 | **Sales** | Adjusted plan this year | 2,500 |
| 8 | | Month to date this year | |

**This Month (February)**

| 9 | **Stock** | Balance of month this year | |
|---|---|---|---|
| 10 | | Actual EOM last year | |
| 11 | | Adjusted plan EOM this year | 25,000 |
| 12 | | Actual as of this report | |
| 13 | **Markdowns** | Actual last year | |
| 14 | | Adjusted plan this year | 600 |
| 15 | | Actual as of this report | |
| 16 | | Balance of month this year | |
| 17 | **On order** to be received and received to date | | 2,500 |
| 18 | **Open-to-buy** | | 1,600 |

**FIGURE 19–7**

*Perpetual cost dollar control*

| Date | BOM Inventory | Cost of Items Received | Cost of Items Sold | Net Change |
|---|---|---|---|---|
| March 1 | $15,000 | $1,500 | $1,000 | +$  500 (1,500 − 1,000) |
| March 2 | 15,500 | — | 2,000 | − 2,000 |
| March 3 | 13,500 | 400 | 1,200 | −  800 (+ 400 − 1,200) |
| March 4 | 12,700 | | | |

## Perpetual Unit Control

Perpetual unit control, like perpetual dollar control, is a book inventory. Figure 19–8 provides an illustration of perpetual unit control.

Note in Figure 19–8 the notation "including shortages," which appears at the end of the illustration. As with dollar control, this is a book figure—thus, there is a chance for error. Again, the only way to determine the accuracy of the book figure is to take a physical inventory. The concepts of shortages and overages apply here

FIGURE 19–8

*Perpetual unit control—sweat suits March*

| | | | |
|---|---:|---:|---:|
| BOM inventory, 3/1 | | | 1,000 |
| Additions to stock: | | | |
|   Purchases | 250 | | |
|   Less: Vendor returns | (40) | | |
|   Net purchases | | 210 | |
|   Transfers in | 41 | | |
|   Less: Transfers out | (20) | | |
|   Net transfers in | | 21 | |
|     Total additions | | | 231 |
|     Total available for sale | | | 1,231 |
| Deductions from stock: | | | |
|   Gross sales | 225 | | |
|   Less: Customer returns | (8) | | |
|   Net sales | | 217 | |
|     Total deductions from stock | | | (217) |
| EOM inventory, 3/31 (including shortages) | | | 1,014 |

just as they do in dollar control. The only difference is that shortages and overages are expressed in terms of number of units rather than in dollars.

A perpetual book inventory for unit control is the most sophisticated of the unit systems. Since perpetual book systems require continuous recording of additions and deductions from stock, they are expensive to operate and involve a great deal of paperwork. The technology of point-of-sale systems offers great potential. It costs less and saves time in collecting the information needed for a perpetual unit control system.

### Nonperpetual Unit Control

**Nonperpetual unit control** systems are also called *stock-counting methods*. These include *formal* and *less formal* systems.

Stock-counting systems are *not* book inventory methods. Thus, the retailer will not be able to determine shortages or overages since there is no book inventory against which to compare a physical inventory.

*Formal Systems.*     The requirements of *formal, nonperpetual systems* are:

1. A planned model stock.
2. A periodic counting schedule.
3. Definite, assigned responsibility for counting.

The tie classification is an example. Every tie in stock might be counted once a month. The retailer might select the first Tuesday of each month for the count schedule. Based on the stock on hand, the stock on order, and the stock sold, the buyer will place a reorder as the information is reviewed each count period.

A nonperpetual system for unit control is actually a compromise. Perpetual control is better and the retailer gets more and better information. But sometimes the benefits simply do not justify the cost. Under certain conditions, however, the formal system that is nonperpetual can work quite successfully. The rate of sale of the items being controlled must be predictable. For example, the retailer can predict quite well the sales behaviour of a seasonal item such as beach towels. The formal system *does* account for items on order (which the less formal system does not). The items controlled by this system should not be of such a fast-moving, fashionable nature that the retailer needs to know the status of stock more often than the periodic count schedule will permit. Of course, the alert merchant will spot-check between count dates to catch any out-of-stocks that occur.

*Less Formal Systems.*   Some kinds of merchandise can be controlled with a less formal system. If immediate delivery of goods is possible, there is no need to account for merchandise on order. However, the retailer still must have a planned model stock and a specific time for visually inspecting the stock.

Under this less formal system, there will be a minimum stock level (e.g., shelf level or number of cases in the stockroom) below which the stock must not go. When the stock reaches that level, a reorder is placed. In the canned goods department in a supermarket, this system might be used quite effectively.

# Expense Control

The final objective of this chapter is to introduce expense control. In Chapter 13, we discussed the development of the expense plan (budget). As with the merchandise plan, retailers must control the expense plan. They must look at expenses on a routine basis to see how actual expense commitment compares with planned expenses. If differences are found, action can be taken.

An expense report is similar to an open-to-buy report in merchandising. The expense report, however, is referred to as an **open-to-spend report.** Figure 19–9 shows how a budget form for operating expenses might be set up for both planning and control.

**FIGURE 19–9**

*Open-to-spend report based on expense budget—sweat suit classification\**
*Fall season*

| Expenses[†] | January | February | ... | Total |
|---|---|---|---|---|
| Plan | $1,000 | | | |
| Committed | 400 | | | |
| Open-to-spend | 600 | | | |
| Actual at end of month | ‡ | | | |

\*As of January 15.

[†]Other expenses handled similarly.

‡Actual put in at end of month.

# Chapter Highlights

- Planning is useless unless retailers monitor operating results to determine whether goals are being met. If plans are not being followed, corrective action must be taken to improve the situation. The monitoring process is the control aspect of merchandise and expense management.

- The relationship between planning and control is essential, direct, and two-way. Control records are needed to develop plans, and plans are evaluated by these control data.

- Two systems are used for controlling the merchandise plan: *Dollar control* for controlling dollar investment and *unit control* for controlling the width and depth aspects of stock balance.

- To control dollar inventory investment, the retailer must know: (1) the beginning dollar inventory, (2) what has been added to stock, (3) how much inventory has moved out of stock, and (4) how much inventory is now on hand.

- One of the most valuable outputs of a retail dollar control system is open-to-buy (OTB), which exists to control the retailer's utilization of the planned purchase figure.

- Retail dollar control is used more often than cost dollar control because of the problems of costing each sale for the latter system.

- Unit control is the system used to control the width and depth aspects of assortments and is simpler than dollar control since fewer factors affect units than affect dollars invested. For example, price changes do not affect units.

- The two types of unit control are perpetual and nonperpetual (or stock-counting systems); the latter can be formal or less formal.

- The expense budget demands control just as does investment in merchandise. The open-to-spend report is of valuable assistance in this management task.

# Key Terms

# Discussion Questions

1. Explain the relationship between *planning* and *control*.

2. What is dollar control? What is its value to retail management?

3. What is the relationship between dollar control and book inventory?

4. Distinguish between *shortages* and *overages*. How are they determined?

5. Explain open-to-buy. How can a buyer who is overbought make adjustments to get more open-to-buy? Why should a retailer always attempt to have open-to-buy available?

6. What is the major problem faced in cost dollar control (versus retail)? When is a retailer likely to use cost dollar control?

7. Compare the mechanics of maintaining a dollar versus a unit control system.

8. Compare the formal and less formal systems of nonperpetual unit control systems. Can a retailer determine shortages in a nonperpetual unit control system? Explain your answer.

# Problems

1. Given the following data for a certain department as of June 10, calculate *(a)* planned purchases and *(b)* open-to-buy:

| | |
|---|---|
| Planned sales for the month | $47,000 |
| Planned reductions for the month | 1,500 |
| Planned EOM inventory | 52,550 |
| Planned BOM inventory | 47,800 |
| Merchandise received to date for June | 14,980 |
| Merchandise on order, June delivery | 6,850 |

2. The following data are for a certain department as of January 20. Calculate *(a)* planned purchases and *(b)* open-to-buy:

| | |
|---|---|
| Planned sales for the month | $142,000 |
| Planned BOM inventory | 177,000 |
| Planned reductions for the month | 4,200 |
| Planned EOM inventory | 165,000 |
| Merchandise received to date for January | 130,000 |
| Merchandise on order, January delivery | 4,200 |
| Merchandise on order, February delivery | 2,200 |

3. Given the following data for a certain department as of September 20, calculate *(a)* planned purchases and *(b)* open-to-buy:

| | |
|---|---|
| Planned sales for the month | $ 9,200 |
| Planned reductions for the month | 100 |
| Planned BOM inventory | 14,600 |
| Planned EOM inventory | 15,500 |
| Merchandise received to date for September | 9,800 |
| Merchandise on order, September delivery | 500 |

4. Given the following information for the month of July, calculate *(a)* planned purchases and *(b)* open-to-buy:

| | |
|---|---|
| Planned sales for the month | $27,000 |
| Planned reductions for the month | 650 |
| Planned EOM inventory | 36,000 |
| Stock-to-sales ratio for July | 1.5 |
| Merchandise received to date for July | 13,800 |
| Merchandise on order, July delivery | 5,250 |

5. Find open-to-buy for March given the following figures:

| | |
|---|---|
| Stock on hand, March 1 | $72,500 |
| Planned stock on hand, April 1 | 80,000 |
| Merchandise on order for March delivery | 49,875 |
| Planned sales for March | 63,500 |

6. Given the following information for November, calculate open-to-buy *(a)* at retail and *(b)* at cost:

| | |
|---|---|
| Planned sales for the month | $24,600 |
| Planned reductions for the month | 300 |
| Planned EOM retail stock | 32,300 |
| Planned BOM retail stock | 30,800 |
| Merchandise received for the month of November | 16,300 |
| Merchandise on order, November delivery | 4,000 |
| Merchandise on order, December delivery | 2,575 |
| Planned initial markup at retail | 35% |

7. Given the following information for August, calculate open-to-buy *(a)* at retail and *(b)* at cost:

| | |
|---|---|
| Planned sales for the month | $57,000 |
| Planned reductions for the month | 1,200 |
| Planned EOM retail stock | 72,000 |
| Stock-to-sales ratio for the month of August | 1.2 |
| Planned initial markup at retail | 42% |
| Merchandise received for the month of August | 35,000 |
| Merchandise on order, August delivery | 16,400 |

# Application Exercises

1. If you have a friend who is a retailer, make an appointment with that person and ask to see *(a)* the types of controls that are used in the store and *(b)* what they are used for. Report your findings to the class.

2. Visit a local grocery store. See if the store has scanning equipment at the check-out counter. If it does, ask to see the manager and tell that person you are a student and want to ask a few questions. Design your questions so you can find out if information received from the new equipment is being used for control. If not, what is it being used for?

3. If you can, find a person who sells to retailers. Ask that person what he or she knows about retailers' open-to-buy. Report your findings to your class.

# 20   PERFORMANCE EVALUATION

## Chapter Objectives

After reading this chapter, you should be able to:

1 Review the key financial statements.

2 Utilize the strategic profit model (SPM) as a framework for monitoring performance results.

3 Explain how inventory turnover affects profitability (performance) by utilizing the concept of gross margin return on inventory investment.

4 Examine the problems that management faces in determining the cost and value of merchandise inventory.

## Retailing Capsule

In the recession of 1991–92, Mark's Work Wearhouse, the Canadian retail chain, had a difficult time and did not meet its financial objectives of (1) earning a 20 percent return on shareholders' equity and (2) earning a 20 percent contribution margin by region. In fact, Mark's Work Wearhouse suffered a loss of $6.4 million from operations in fiscal 1991 and a further loss of $4.8 million in fiscal 1992. The retailer has a plan to return to profitability based, in part, on an extensive performance review and a revision of its retail strategy. In fact, the loss of $4.8 million from operations in fiscal 1992 reflected some positive signs for the future. Consider the following comparisons between 1991 and 1992 based on the company's performance review:

- *Total chain sales:* Declined by 23 percent (from $172 million to $133 million) due, in part, to the recession.
- *Contribution margin:* Increased by 14 percent (from 11.5 to 15.9 percent) due to an improvement in initial markup, reduced markdowns, and reduced shrinkage.
- *Sales per square metre:* Declined by 18 percent (from $3185 to $2615), which was less than the overall sales decline due to the closing of some unprofitable stores.
- *Fixed expense per square metre:* Was reduced by 12 percent (from $517 to $452), reflecting the effort that went into reducing controllable expenses, including personnel, advertising, and other variable expenses.
- *Inventory turnover:* Was virtually unchanged (from 2.5 to 2.4) in spite of the sales decline reflecting an improved inventory control system.

The new target for Mark's Work Wearhouse is to achieve an annual after-tax profit on sales of 4 percent by fiscal 1995. With improved economic times, continual monitoring of performance, and the appropriate strategy, the target is attainable.

Source: Mark's Work Wearhouse, Annual Report, 1992.

Clearly, the future strategy and success of Mark's Work Wearhouse depends, in part, on the results of the performance review. This is a critical component of retailing and provides the basis for improving the financial results of the firm. The information for this performance review is generated by the accounting system.

In Chapter 19, we addressed the control information necessary to take proper action relative to merchandise and expenses. This tracking data comes from the accounting function of the organization. Here, the focus is entirely on that accounting function as it relates to actions taken not for control purposes but for appraisal of the firm's profitability. As well, the importance and contents of an accounting system for retailers is discussed. A good accounting system can solve problems of cash flow, assist in taking timely discounts on merchandise, and signal problems within the firm before they become difficult to handle. We begin by looking at the key financial statements.

# Key Financial Statements

The balance sheet, the income statement, and the various ratios derived from them give management the information needed to evaluate the effectiveness of strategy in financial terms.

## *The Balance Sheet*

Exhibit 20–1 lists the components of the **balance sheet—assets** (**current** and **fixed**), liabilities, and net worth. The simplest expression of the balance sheet equation is:

$$\text{Assets} = \text{Liabilities} + \text{Net worth}$$

Net worth (also referred to as *shareholders' equity*) is the owners' claim on the assets of the business—that is, the owners' investment or equity. Figure 20–1 (on p. 535) is an example of a balance sheet.

## *The Income Statement*

While the balance sheet is a snapshot of a business's financial health on a specific date, the **income statement** is more like a moving picture of the firm's financial performance over time. The income statement shows whether investments in assets and the implementation of strategy were successful during a particular time period (see Figure 20–2 on p. 537).

Analysis of this statement shows (1) how much gross margin was made ($85,645), (2) how much was spent on total expenses ($70,655), and (3) how much profit (after taxes) has been made ($10,040). *Gross margin* is the difference between net sales and cost of goods sold. Cost of goods sold is computed as follows:

|   |   |
|---|---|
|   | Beginning inventory |
| + | Purchases |
| = | Goods available for sale |
| − | Ending inventory |
| = | Cost of goods sold |

Notice that the key elements of the income statement are also stated in percentages. For example, the gross margin percentage is calculated by dividing gross margin dollars by net sales dollars (or $85,645 divided by $192,300 = 44.54 percent). Percentages help the manager compare present performance with performances (1) in prior periods or (2) of similar stores.

Information from the income statement assists the manager in making any adjustments deemed necessary. For example, if expenses are higher than in the past and higher than in similar stores, the manager may decide that corrective action is needed. In general, the income statement is a valuable tool for measuring the results of operations.

**Exhibit 20–1**

*Balance sheet*
How the Business Looks on a Specific Date

| *Assets* | *Liabilities and Shareholders' Equity* |
| --- | --- |
| What the business owns | This side of the balance sheet shows the claims on the assets by both the creditors and the owners of the business. The claims of creditors are debts of the business—the *liabilities.* The owners' claim is their investment in the business—the *shareholders' equity* (or net worth). |
| *Current assets:* Expected to be turned into cash within the next year.<br>Cash: Money on hand or in the bank.<br>Accounts receivable: What customers owe the business for merchandise or services purchased.<br>Inventory: Merchandise on hand. | *Current liabilities:* Debts owned by the business that are expected to be paid within one year.<br>Notes payable: to banks or trade creditors.<br>Accounts payable: to trade and suppliers.<br>Income taxes: taxes payable to governments. |
| *Fixed assets:* Used in the operation of the business—not intended for resale.<br>Real estate: Land and buildings used by the business—valued at original cost.<br>Leasehold improvements: Permanent installations—remodelling or refurbishing of the premises.<br>Machinery, equipment, vehicles—used by the business, valued at original cost.<br>Less accumulated depreciation: These assets (except land) lose value through usage and age. The business claims this loss of value as an expense of doing business. The running total of this expense is the accumulated depreciation.<br>Net fixed assets: Cost of fixed assets − Depreciation = Current value. | *Long-term liabilities:* Debts owed by the business to be paid beyond the next year.<br>Mortgage: On property.<br>Shareholders' equity (or net worth): Owners' (or shareholders') assets of the business; owners' investment; owners' equity in the business.<br><br>*For sole proprietorship or partnership:*<br>Owner, capital: Owners' original investment plus any profit reinvested in the business.<br><br>*For corporation:*<br>Capital stock: Value assigned to the original issue of stock by the directors of the corporation. If the stock sold for more than the assigned value, the excess will show as:<br>Surplus, paid-in: The difference between the assigned value and the selling price of the original issue of stock. (The subsequent selling price of the stock does not change the assigned value.)<br>Retained earnings: Profits revealed by the firm after paying dividends. |

Balance sheet equation: Assets = Liabilities + Net worth

## The Strategic Profit Model

An important purpose of this section is to utilize the **strategic profit model (SPM)** as a framework for monitoring performance results. The SPM is derived from information obtained in the balance sheet and the income statement. The SPM provides the essential ratios for performance evaluation needed here, as illustrated in Figure 20–3 on p. 537.

The object of all retailing is to make a profit; but exactly what does ''making a profit'' mean? Perhaps the most common way to describe profit is net profit after taxes—the bottom line of the income statement. Profit performance is often

## FIGURE 20–1

*Balance sheet*
December 31, 19—

*Assets*
Current assets:

| | | |
|---|---|---|
| Cash | $15,000 | |
| Accounts receivable | 24,000 | |
| Merchandise inventory | 84,000 | |
| Prepaid expenses | 10,000 | |
| Total current assets | | $133,000 |

Fixed assets:

| | | |
|---|---|---|
| Building | $85,000 | |
| Furniture and fixtures | 23,000 | |
| Total fixed assets | | 108,000 |
| Total assets | | $241,000 |

*Liabilities and Shareholders' Equity*
Current liabilities:

| | | |
|---|---|---|
| Accounts payable | $20,000 | |
| Wages payable | 18,000 | |
| Notes payable | 32,000 | |
| Taxes payable | 5,000 | |
| Interest payable | 3,000 | |
| Total current liabilities | | $ 78,000 |

Fixed liabilities:

| | | |
|---|---|---|
| Mortgage payable | $75,000 | |
| Total fixed liabilities | | 75,000 |
| *Total liabilities* | | $153,000 |

Shareholders' equity:

| | | |
|---|---|---|
| Capital surplus | $80,000 | |
| Retained earnings | 8,000 | |
| Total shareholder's equity | | 88,000 |
| Total liabilities and shareholders' equity | | $241,000 |

evaluated in terms of sales volume—that is, profit as a percentage of sales. For strategic purposes, the most valuable way to view profit, however, is in terms of a return on investment (ROI).

The two ways of looking at ROI from a strategic point of view are (1) return on assets (ROA) and (2) return on net worth (RONW). ROA reflects all funds invested in a business, whether they come from owners or creditors. RONW is a measure of profitability for those who have provided the net worth funds—that is, the owners.

*Purposes of the SPM*

Figure 20–4 on p. 538 diagrams the SPM. Boxes 1 through 5 provide the basic ratios (derived from the key financial statements) that comprise the model. A simple algebraic representation of the model would look like this:

*Inventory is a current asset for the retailer.*

SOURCE: Courtesy BiWay.

$$\underset{(1)}{\frac{\text{Net profit}}{\text{Net sales}}} \times \underset{(2)}{\frac{\text{Net sales}}{\text{Total assets}}} = \underset{(3)}{\frac{\text{Net profit}}{\text{Total assets}}} \times \underset{(4)}{\frac{\text{Total assets}}{\text{Net worth}}} = \underset{(5)}{\frac{\text{Net profit}}{\text{Net worth}}}$$

Figure 20–4 also indicates the various paths to profitability and what each component of the model measures. Specifically, the SPM:

1. Emphasizes that a firm's principal financial objective is to earn an adequate or target rate of return on net worth (RONW).
2. Provides an excellent management tool for evaluating performance against the target RONW and high-performance trade leaders.
3. Dramatizes the principal areas of decision making—*margin management, asset management,* and *leverage management.* A firm can improve its rate of RONW by (1) increasing its profit margin, (2) raising its rate of asset turnover, or (3) leveraging its operations more highly. **Leveraging** occurs when assets worth more than the amount of capital invested by the owners are acquired.

**FIGURE 20–2**

*Income statement*
Year Ending December 31, 19—

| | | | |
|---|---|---|---|
| Gross sales | | $208,600 | |
| Less: Returns and allowances | | 16,300 | |
| Net sales | | $192,300 | 100.00% |
| Cost of goods sold: | | | |
|    Opening inventory | $ 21,650 | | |
|    Net purchases | 113,500 | | |
|    Goods available for sale | | $135,150 | |
|    Less: Closing inventory | | 28,495 | |
|    Cost of goods sold | | 106,655 | 55.46 |
|    Gross margin | | $ 85,645 | 44.54 |
| Expenses: | | | |
|    Rent | $ 19,400 | | |
|    Payroll | 32,950 | | |
|    Advertising | 8,825 | | |
|    Insurance | 1,475 | | |
|    Travel | 2,160 | | |
|    Utilities | 5,265 | | |
|    Miscellaneous | 580 | | |
|     Total expenses | | 70,655 | 36.74 |
| Profit before taxes | | $ 14,990 | 7.80 |
| Income tax | | 4,950 | 2.57 |
| Net profit after taxes | | $ 10,040 | 5.22% |

**FIGURE 20–3**

*Role of the strategic profit model*

**The Impact of Turnover on Profitability**

The concept of turnover (either stock or merchandise) was discussed in Chapter 13 in some detail. The SPM shows that a basic path to profitability is asset management. In this discussion, we focus on how inventory turnover affects profitability. *Managing turnover* helps management achieve the return on investment targeted. Through accounting systems, management is able to *monitor turnover* as an evaluation tool for performance. If the performance is less than planned, then corrective action can be taken. (We are not addressing margin or leverage management here. The attention is on asset management.)

**FIGURE 20–4**

*Strategic profit model*

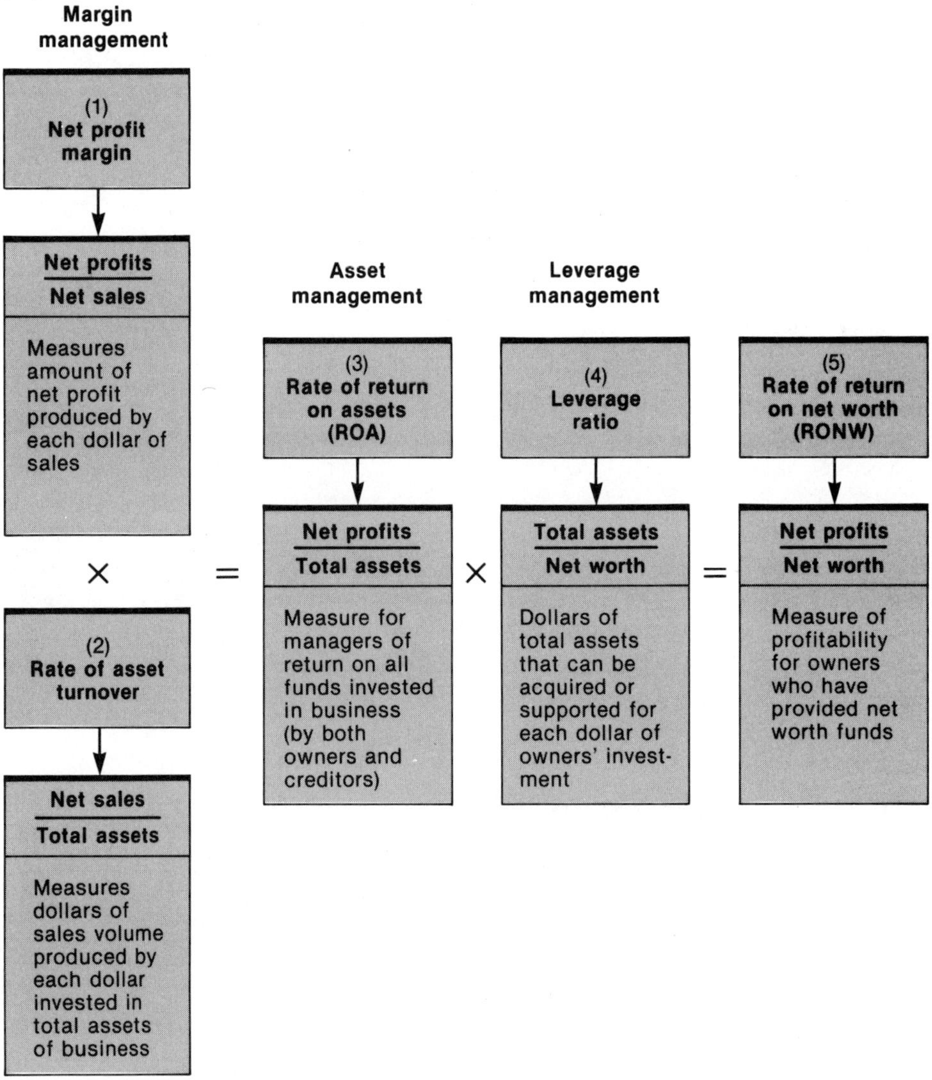

**Margin management**

| (1) Net profit margin |
|---|
| **Net profits** / **Net sales** |
| Measures amount of net profit produced by each dollar of sales |

×

| (2) Rate of asset turnover |
|---|
| **Net sales** / **Total assets** |
| Measures dollars of sales volume produced by each dollar invested in total assets of business |

=

**Asset management**

| (3) Rate of return on assets (ROA) |
|---|
| **Net profits** / **Total assets** |
| Measure for managers of return on all funds invested in business (by both owners and creditors) |

×

**Leverage management**

| (4) Leverage ratio |
|---|
| **Total assets** / **Net worth** |
| Dollars of total assets that can be acquired or supported for each dollar of owners' investment |

=

| (5) Rate of return on net worth (RONW) |
|---|
| **Net profits** / **Net worth** |
| Measure of profitability for owners who have provided net worth funds |

To be meaningful, turnover goals must be planned for similar merchandise groupings. Planning for large, diverse categories is unsound. Today's computer technology allows classification planning and thus better turnover information for managing that asset.

No one can say whether a particular turnover figure is good or bad or whether a particular ratio is efficient. Turnover goals must be related to a particular operation, and a raw turnover figure is virtually meaningless. Comparisons within and among the various kinds of businesses illustrate the range of performance results.

*Gross Margin Return on Inventory Investment (GMROI)*

**Gross margin return on inventory investment (GMROI)** can be stated as follows:

$$\text{GMROI} = \frac{\text{Gross margin dollars}}{\text{Average inventory investment}}$$

This single ratio does not indicate clearly the focus we want to emphasize—the important relationship between profit return (margin) and sales-to-retail stock (which is inventory turnover). Consequently, it is more useful to express GMROI as follows:

$$\text{GMROI} = \frac{\text{Gross margin dollars}}{\text{Total sales}} \times \frac{\text{Total sales}}{\text{Average inventory investment}}$$
$$\text{(expressed in retail dollars)}$$

We must emphasize that gross margin return on *retail* inventory investment is *not* a real measure of return on investment because investment is in *cost* dollars. But many retail managers with a planning focus maintain retail book inventory figures. Thus, *retail* value GMROI can be calculated more frequently using the more common and more easily obtainable turnover component. Sales-to-cost inventory ratios are more accurately ROI ratios. In this particular discussion, however, the value of utilizing retail GMROI outweighs the somewhat different terminology. Our intent is to focus on the impact of turnover on profitability—thus, retail value is important.

The value of the turnover and margin components of the GMROI concept can be seen in Figure 20–5. Three hypothetical retail classifications each produce the same GMROI, although they have differing gross margin percentages and turnover components. This indicates the impact that turnover and margin management has on the return on each dollar invested in inventory. For illustration, let us keep the gross margins constant at 40.0 percent and change only the turnover ratios, as in Figure 20–6. This illustration dramatically indicates how turnover can affect profitability and stresses the importance of turnover goals.

**FIGURE 20–5**

*Differing retail operations, margins, and turnovers resulting in identical GMROI*

| Type of Store | Gross Margin (percent) | × | Turnover Ratio | = | GMROI (percent retail) |
|---|---|---|---|---|---|
| Discount store sport shirt classification | 25.0 | | 4.0 | | 100.0 |
| Specialty store sport shirt classification | 40.0 | | 2.5 | | 100.0 |
| Department store sport shirt classification | 33.3 | | 3.0 | | 100.0 |

FIGURE 20–6

*Impacts on classifications of constant gross margins and varying turnover rates*

| Type of Classification | Gross Margin (percent) | × | Turnover Ratio | = | GMROI (percent) |
|---|---|---|---|---|---|
| A | 40.0 | | 4.0 | | 160.0 |
| B | 40.0 | | 2.5 | | 100.0 |
| C | 40.0 | | 3.0 | | 120.0 |

## Determining Cost and Value of Inventory

The focus of this section is on the importance of merchandise inventory in performance evaluation and the problems that arise in determining its cost and value. The importance of merchandise inventory is reflected in several ways. As previously noted, merchandise inventory is typically the largest current asset on the balance sheet. The cost of merchandise sold, reported on the income statement, is critical in determining gross profit. Thus, an error in determining the inventory figure will cause an equal misstatement of gross profit and net income in the income statement. Errors of this nature, due to faulty information and a bad accounting system, can lead to disaster, as was the case in the bankruptcy of Bargain Harold's (Retail Highlight 20–1). The amount of assets noted on the balance sheet will also be incorrect by the same amount. The effects of understatements and overstatements of inventory at the end of a period are demonstrated in Figure 20–7 on p. 542, which includes abbreviated income statements and balance sheets.

### Determining Inventory Cost

A major problem in determining inventory cost arises when identical units of a product are acquired over a period of time at various unit cost prices. Consider the purchase of sport shirts during the spring season. With the sample shown in Figure 20–8, the average cost per unit has increased by over 28 percent in just three months.

In some departments and/or classifications, it may be possible to identify units with specific expenditures. This can occur when assortments and varieties of merchandise carried and the sales volume and transactions are relatively small. More often, however, as in the sport shirt classification, specific identification procedures are too complex to justify their use.

Consequently, one of two costing methods may be adopted to simplify the problem of inventory costing.

### FIFO

The assumption of the **first-in, first-out (FIFO)** method of costing inventory is that costs should be charged against revenue in the order in which they were incurred—that is, the first shirts purchased are the first ones sold. Thus, the inventory remaining at the end of an accounting period is assumed to be of the most recent purchases, as calculated in Figure 20–9 on p. 543.

---

**Retail Highlight 20–1**

# Bargain Harold's: Faulty Performance Evaluation Leads to Bankruptcy

In early 1992, Bargain Harold's, a 160-store discount chain, went bankrupt, throwing over 4,000 people out of work and leaving suppliers with over $52 million in unpaid bills. While a number of factors led to its demise, including poor management and a recession, a central cause of the failure was a faulty performance evaluation system.

In 1990, a group of investors led by Dean Muncaster purchased Bargain Harold's from Kmart in a highly leveraged financial arrangement. Among the many changes introduced at Bargain Harold's by the new management team was a computerized information system that was installed in just 21 of the 160 stores. Management decisions were based on the information from this system. As it turned out, information coming into the head office from the other stores was often inaccurate, inflating margins. Stores using the old system could, for example, charge $3.79 for a box of detergent, while the head office was assuming that the price was $3.99. Miscalculations were made on everything from inventory to profits. The results were excess inventory, inadequate analysis of financial data, and unreliable profit projections. In a year-end audit at the end of 1991, management discovered the errors, but by then it was too late. The weight of decisions based on a faulty information system wrecked a company. As one retail expert noted: "It's a textbook case of a company that had a great concept and just blew it."

Sources: John Heinzl, "Good Strategy Gone Awry, Top Retailer's Tale of Woe," *Globe and Mail*, March 7, 1992, pp. B1, B4; Harvey Enchin, "Bargain Harold's in Receivership," *Globe and Mail*, February 29, 1992, p. B5; and Dunnery Best, "The Man behind Bargain Harold's Mess," *Financial Times*, April 13, 1992, pp. 1, 4.

---

Let's assume that the physical inventory at the end of the fiscal year (January 31) is 130 shirts. Based on the assumption that the inventory is composed of the most recent purchases, the cost of the 130 shirts is as calculated in Figure 20–10.

If we deduct the end-of-period inventory of $2,020 from the $2,990 available for sale during the period, we get $970 as the cost of merchandise sold. FIFO is generally in harmony with the actual physical movement of goods in a retail firm. Thus, FIFO best represents the results that are directly tied to merchandise costs.

### LIFO

The costing method known as **last-in, first-out (LIFO)** assumes that the most recent cost of merchandise should be charged against revenue. Thus, the ending inventory under LIFO is assumed to be made up of the earliest costs. Using the same example, Figure 20–11 shows the ending inventory value under LIFO.

If we deduct the inventory of $1,550 from the $2,990 of merchandise available for sale during the accounting period, we get $1,440 as the cost of merchandise sold.

**FIGURE 20–7**

*Effects of correct statement, understatement, and overstatement of ending inventory on net profits*

| *Income Statement—19___* | | | *Balance Sheet—19___* | |
|---|---|---|---|---|
| Net sales | | $200,000 | Merchandise inventory | $ 20,000* |
| Beginning inventory | $ 30,000 | | Other assets | 80,000 |
| + Purchases | 110,000 | | Total | $100,000 |
| = Available for sale | 140,000 | | Liabilities | 30,000 |
| − Ending inventory | 20,000* | | Net worth | 70,000 |
| = Cost of goods sold | | 120,000 | Total | $100,000 |
| Gross profit | | 80,000 | | |
| − Expenses | | 55,000 | | |
| = Net profit | | $ 25,000 | | |
| Net sales | | $200,000 | Merchandise inventory | $ 12,000† |
| Beginning inventory | $ 30,000 | | Other assets | 80,000 |
| + Purchases | 110,000 | | Total | 92,000 |
| = Available for sale | 140,000 | | Liabilities | 30,000 |
| − Ending inventory | 12,000† | | Net worth | 62,000 |
| = Cost of goods sold | | 128,000 | Total | $ 92,000 |
| Gross profit | | 72,000 | | |
| − Expenses | | 55,000 | | |
| = Net profit | | $ 17,000 | | |
| Net sales | | $200,000 | Merchandise inventory | $ 27,000‡ |
| Beginning inventory | $ 30,000 | | Other assets | 80,000 |
| + Purchases | 110,000 | | Total | $107,000 |
| = Available for sale | 140,000 | | Liabilities | 30,000 |
| − Ending inventory | 27,000‡ | | Net worth | 77,000 |
| = Cost of goods sold | | 113,000 | Total | $107,000 |
| Gross profit | | 87,000 | | |
| − Expenses | | 55,000 | | |
| = Net profit | | $ 32,000 | | |

*Ending inventory correctly stated.
†Ending inventory understated $8,000 (thus income, assets, capital also).
‡Ending inventory overstated $7,000 (thus income, assets, capital also).

**FIGURE 20–8**

*The effect of increasing unit costs*

| | Sport Shirts | Units | Unit Cost | Total Cost |
|---|---|---|---|---|
| February 1 | Inventory | 50 | $ 9 | $ 450 |
| April 15 | Purchases | 40 | 13 | 520 |
| May 1 | Purchases | 30 | 14 | 420 |
| Total | | 120 | | $1,390 |
| Average cost per unit | | | | $11.58 |

**FIGURE 20–9**

*Shirts available for sale*

| | | | | | | | |
|---|---|---|---|---|---|---|---|
| February 1 | Inventory: | 50 | shirts @ | $ 9 | = | $ 450 |
| April 15 | Purchases: | 40 | shirts @ | 13 | = | 520 |
| May 1 | Purchases: | 30 | shirts @ | 14 | = | 420 |
| October 1 | Purchases: | 100 | shirts @ | 16 | = | 1,600 |
| Available for sale during year | | | | | | $2,990 |

**FIGURE 20–10**

*End-of-period inventory of shirts under FIFO*

| | | | | | |
|---|---|---|---|---|---|
| Most recent purchases (October 1) | 100 shirts | @ | $16 | = | $1,600 |
| Next most recent (May 1) | 30 shirts | @ | 14 | = | 420 |
| Inventory, January 31 | 130 shirts | | | = | $2,020 |

**FIGURE 20–11**

*Ending inventory under LIFO*

| | | | | | |
|---|---|---|---|---|---|
| February 1 | 50 shirts | @ | $ 9 | = | $ 450 |
| April 15 | 40 shirts | @ | 13 | = | 520 |
| May 1 | 30 shirts | @ | 14 | = | 420 |
| October 1 | 10 shirts | @ | 16 | = | 160 |
| Inventory, January 31 | 130 shirts | | | | $1,550 |

**FIGURE 20–12**

*Comparison of FIFO and LIFO*

| | FIFO | LIFO |
|---|---|---|
| Merchandise available for sale | $2,990 | $2,990 |
| Inventory, January 31 | 2,020 | 1,550 |
| Cost of merchandise sold | $ 970 | $1,440 |

As seen in Figure 20–12, FIFO yields the lower cost of merchandise sold and thus yields higher gross profit and higher inventory figures on the balance sheet. On the other hand, LIFO yields a higher figure for cost of goods sold and lower figures for gross profit, net income, and inventory. For income determination purposes, Revenue Canada accepts LIFO, but FIFO is not accepted.

*Conservative Valuation of Inventory*

***Cost or Market, Whichever Is Lower.***     Another problem in determining the cost of merchandise inventory is placing a conservative value on the inventory—that is, at cost or market, whichever is lower. This approach is an alternative to valuing inventory at cost. With either course, it is first necessary to determine the cost of inventory. *Market* means the cost required to replace the merchandise at the time of the inventory, whereas *cost* refers to the actual price of merchandise at the time of its purchase.

Figure 20–13 demonstrates the impact on profits of valuing the ending inventory at (1) actual cost, (2) depreciated value, and (3) appreciated value. In addition, it provides a rationale for the acceptance of the conservative practice of valuation—at cost or market, whichever is lower. At any given time, some merchandise in stock may not be valued at the amount originally paid for it. The merchandise may have declined in value because of obsolescence, deterioration, or decreases in wholesale market prices. It may have increased in value because of inflation, scarcity of materials, and the like. The first column in Figure 20–13 indicates that the profit is $5,000 after the valuation of inventory at its actual cost (determined by one of the methods discussed earlier). The second column indicates that, if the retailer were to replace the same inventory at the time of valuation, it would be depreciated to $4,000 (a $6,000 decline in value from the actual cost); instead of a $5,000 profit, a $1,000 loss would be incurred. The information in the third column reflects a $12,000 valuation of the ending inventory resulting in a $7,000 profit, rather than a $5,000 profit based on actual cost.

The depreciated ending inventory value relative to the actual cost results in an increased cost of goods sold and thus reduces gross profit. The appreciated ending inventory relative to the actual costs results in a decreased cost of goods sold, an increased gross profit, and, with the same expense amount, an increased net profit. Comparing each method with the actual cost, the conservative rule would dictate that the inventory value should be taken at the depreciated value—column (2)—and at actual cost—column (1)—when compared with market increase. Let's investigate the logic of such a practice.

**FIGURE 20–13**

*The impact on profits of valuation of ending inventory at actual cost, or depreciated or appreciated market value*

|  | (1) Actual Cost | | (2) Depreciated | | (3) Appreciated | |
|---|---|---|---|---|---|---|
| Net sales |  | $100,000 |  | $100,000 |  | $100,000 |
| Merchandise available for sale | $70,000 |  | $70,000 |  | $70,000 |  |
| Ending inventory | 10,000 |  | 4,000 |  | 12,000 |  |
| Cost of goods sold |  | 60,000 |  | 66,000 |  | 58,000 |
| Gross profit |  | $ 40,000 |  | $ 34,000 |  | $ 42,000 |
| Expenses |  | 35,000 |  | 35,000 |  | 35,000 |
| Net profit |  | $ 5,000 |  | $ (1,000) |  | $ 7,000 |

### Rationale for the Conservative Rule

If management values the ending inventory at $4,000 rather than the cost of $10,000, the loss resulting will be taken in the period in which it occurs. This is logical, because the ending inventory of one period becomes the beginning inventory of the next. Thus, by placing a realistic depreciated market value on ending inventory, the lowered figure, which will be the next beginning inventory value, will give the merchant the opportunity to reflect a proper beginning inventory cost in the next period. This lets the merchant show realistic, and perhaps profitable, performance in the next period. This ending inventory figure also becomes an asset item on the balance sheet.

A realistic valuation reflecting declining value is wise because otherwise the assets of the firm, and consequently its net worth, will be overstated. Finally, if the market value were declining and the inventory were taken in at cost, the firm would show a profit, as illustrated in Figure 20–13. Income taxes would be paid on "paper profits."

To emphasize the concept of paper profits, consider what the results would be if the inventory were valued at an appreciated value—column (3)—of $12,000, rather than a cost of $10,000. The $7,000 profit, rather than the $5,000, represents anticipated profits on merchandise that has not been sold and thus should not be reported.

In summary, retail inventories should be valued at cost or market, whichever is lower. As with the method chosen for the determination of inventory cost (LIFO or FIFO), the method elected for inventory valuation (cost, or lower of cost or market) must be consistent from year to year.

# Methods of Valuation of Inventory

The final objective of this chapter is to introduce the accounting practices that assist management in valuation decisions. Retailers invest large sums of money in merchandise and must know at all times the value of this inventory investment. The information is needed for tax reasons, to compute gross margins as measures of performance, and to make day-to-day decisions. How *is* a value placed on inventory in retailing? Basically, the two ways are (1) *the cost method* and (2) *the retail method*.

## *The Cost Method*

The cost method provides a book valuation of inventory, and the system uses only cost figures. All inventory records are maintained at cost. When a physical inventory is taken, all items are recorded at actual cost including freight. The cost of sales and cost of markdowns (depreciation) are deducted from the total merchandise available to provide the book inventory at the lower of cost or market value, which can be checked by means of a physical inventory. The limitations of the cost method are difficulty in determining depreciation; difficulty for large retailers with many classifications and price lines; daily inventory is impractical; and costing out each sale, allocating transportation charges to the cost of the sales, and reducing markdowns to cost are extremely difficult. The cost method is appropriate in operations with big-ticket items, where there are few lines and few price changes, where the rate of sales is rapid, and/or where management has very sophisticated computer expertise.

Because of the limitations with the cost method, the retail method of inventory was created early in this century.

*The Retail Method*

### Advantages of the Retail Method

The retail method of inventory is a logical extension of a retail book (perpetual) inventory utilized for dollar control. The following list gives advantages of the retail method. Items 1–3 are advantages that exist because the retail method is a perpetual, book inventory method. Items 4 and 5 are advantages that are uniquely related to the system of the retail method of inventory.

1. Accounting statements can be drawn up at any time, especially with the new technology. Income statements and balance sheets are normally available once a month.

2. Shortages can be determined. The retail method is a book inventory, and this figure can be compared to the physical inventory. Only with a book inventory can shortages (or overages) be determined.

3. The retail method, through its book inventory, serves as an excellent basis for insurance claims. In case of loss, the book inventory is good evidence of what *should* have been in stock. Records should be kept in a safe, fireproof vault or cabinet.

4. The physical taking of inventory is easier with the retail method. The items are recorded on the inventory sheets at *only* their selling prices, instead of their cost and retail prices.

5. The retail method gives an automatic, conservative valuation of ending inventory because of the way the system is programmed. This means that the retail method gives a valuation of ending inventory at cost or market, whichever is lower.

The retail method is in actuality an income statement that follows certain programmed steps in the final determination of net profits. These steps are illustrated in Figure 20–14. The methodology provides a format for computing net profit. The steps are described next.

### Steps of the Retail Method

***Step 1: Determine the Total Dollars of Merchandise Handled at Cost and Retail.***
As indicated in Figure 20–14, we start with a beginning inventory that we assume is an actual, physical inventory from the end of the previous period. To this figure we add purchases (minus vendor returns and/or allowances), any interstore or departmental transfers, and transportation charges (at cost only). The price change, which is a part of Step 1, is additional markups. Suppose the retailer has a group of sport shirts in stock that were received recently. They are carried in stock at $14.95.

**Figure 20–14**

*Statement of retail method of inventory*

| Calculations | Step | Items | Cost | Retail | Cost | Retail | Percent |
|---|---|---|---|---|---|---|---|
| | 1 | Beginning inventory | | | $ 60,000 | $105,000 | |
| | | Gross purchases | $216,000 | $345,000 | | | |
| | | Less: Returns to vendor | (9,000) | (14,100) | 207,000 | 330,900 | |
| | | Transfers in | 3,000 | 4,800 | | | |
| | | Less: Transfers out | (4,500) | (7,200) | (1,500) | (2,400) | |
| | | Transportation charges | | | 4,500 | | |
| | | Additional markups | | 2,100 | | | |
| | | Less: Cancellations | | (600) | | 1,500 | |
| | | Total merchandise handled | | | 270,000 | 435,000 | |
| ($270,000 ÷ $435,000) | 2 | Cost multiplier/cumulative markup | | | | | 62.069/37.931 |
| | 3 | Sales, gross | 309,000 | | | | |
| | | Less: Customer returns | (9,000) | | | 300,000 | |
| | | Gross markdowns | 12,000 | | | | |
| | | Less: Cancellations | (1,500) | | | 10,500 | |
| | | Employee discounts | | | | 1,500 | |
| | | Total retail deductions | | | | 312,000 | |
| ($435,000 − $312,000) | 4 | Closing book inventory @ retail | | | | 123,000 | |
| | | Closing physical inventory @ retail | | | | 120,750 | |
| ($123,000 − $120,750) | | Shortages | | | | 2,250 | 0.75 |
| ($120,750 × 0.62069) | | Closing physical inventory @ cost | | | 74,949 | | |
| ($270,000 − $74,949) | 5 | Gross cost of goods sold | | | 195,051 | | |
| ($300,000 − $195,051) | 6 | Maintained markup | | | 104,949 | | 35.0 |
| | | Less: Alteration costs | | | (3,000) | | |
| | | Plus: Cash discounts | | | 6,000 | | |
| ($104,949 + $3,000) | | Gross margin | | | 107,949 | | 36.0 |
| | | Less: Operating expenses | | | 75,000 | | 25.0 |
| | | Net profit | | | 32,949 | | 11.0 |
| | 5 | Gross cost of goods sold | | | 195,051 | | |
| | | Less: Cash discounts | | | (6,000) | | |
| | | Net cost of goods sold | | | 189,051 | | |
| | | Plus: Alteration costs | | | 3,000 | | |
| | | Total cost of goods sold | | | 192,051 | | |
| ($300,000 − $192,051) | 6 | Gross margin | | | 107,949 | | 36.0 |
| | | Less: Operating expenses | | | 75,000 | | |
| | | Net profit | | | 32,949 | | 11.0 |

Wholesale costs have increased since the delivery, and the wholesaler suggests that we take an additional markup of $3.00 per unit, bringing the retail price to $17.95. We take a physical count and find we have 700 shirts in stock; thus, we take an additional markup of $2,100 to accommodate the price increase. Immediately after processing the price change, we find that the count was incorrect, or the amount of the additional markup was too high due to a misunderstanding. At any rate, the retailer wants to cancel $600 of the additional markup so that the mistake can be corrected. (See step 1 in Figure 20–14 for the handling of this situation.) Cancellation of an additional markup is *not* a markdown, which reflects market depreciation. Cancellation is rather a procedure for adjusting an actual error in the original additional markup. Summing all the items that increase the dollar investment provides the total merchandise handled at cost and retail ($270,000 and $435,000, respectively).

***Step 2: Calculate the Cost Multiplier and the Cumulative Markup.***    As indicated in Figure 20–14, the computation of the cost multiplier (sometimes called the *cost percentage* or the *cost complement*) is derived by dividing the total dollars handled at cost by the total at retail (that is, $270,000 ÷ $435,000 = 62 percent). This is a key figure in the retail method and in fact involves the major assumption of the system. This cost multiplier says that for every retail dollar in inventory, 62 percent, or 62 cents, is in terms of cost. The assumption of the retail method is that if cost and retail have this relationship in goods handled during a period, then that same relationship exists for all the merchandise remaining in stock (i.e., the ending inventory at retail).

The *cumulative markup* is the complement of the cost multiplier (i.e., 100.00 − 62.07 = 37.93) and is the control figure to compare against the planned initial markup. (See Chapter 15, where this planned figure is discussed.) For example, let's assume that the planned initial markup is 37 percent. If our interim statement shows, as ours does, that our cumulative markup is 37.9 percent, then management will consider that operations are effective, at least as they relate to the planned markup percentage. The initial markup is planned so as to cover reductions (markdowns, employee discounts, and shortages) and provide a maintained markup (or gross profit or margin) at a level sufficient to cover operating expenses and to ensure a target rate of profit return.

***Step 3: Compute the Retail Deductions from Stock.***    Step 3 includes all the retail deductions from the total retail merchandise dollars handled during the period. Sales are recorded and adjusted by customer returns to determine net sales. Markdowns are recorded as they are taken.

As an example, let's assume that during this period, a group of 1,200 sport shirts retailing for $25.95 are put out for a special sale at $15.95. We would thus take a markdown of $12,000 before the sale. After the sale, we want to bring the merchandise back to the regular price; an additional markup is not appropriate since we are merely cancelling an original markdown. Consequently, we put a markdown cancellation through the system for the remaining number of shirts—in this case, 150 that were not sold, making a cancellation of $1,500, which will reestablish the original retail price of $25.95. Employee discounts are included as deductions because employees receive, for example, a 20 percent discount on items purchased for personal use. If a shirt retails for $19.95, the employee would pay $15.96. If the discount were not entered as a separate item in the system, the difference between the retail price and the employee's price would cause a shortage. Recording employee discounts as a separate item also gives management a good picture of employee business obtained and affords a measure of control over use of the discount.

### Step 4: Calculate the Closing Book (and/or Physical) Inventory at Cost and Retail.

The statement thus far has given us a figure for the dollars at retail that we had available for sale ($435,000) and what we have deducted from that amount ($312,000). Thus, we are now able to compute what we have left ($435,000 − $312,000), or the ending book inventory at retail—$123,000. We are assuming, in this particular illustration, that this is a year-end statement and that we have an audited, physical inventory of $120,750. Consequently, we can now determine our shortages by deducting the amount of the physical inventory from the book inventory ($123,000 − $120,750 = $2,250) or 0.75 percent of sales.

Let's assume that we were working with an interim statement rather than a fiscal year statement. If this were the case, we would include in our retail deductions from stock (step 3) an *estimated* shortage figure, which would give us as accurate a figure as possible for total deductions, and thus a figure for closing book inventory at retail. If we have an interim statement, then the cost multiplier is applied to the book inventory at retail to determine the cost value: If there is a physical retail inventory figure, as in Figure 20–14, then we use that figure for cost conversion, since the physical inventory figure is accurate.

The key to the retail method, as noted, is the reduction of the retail inventory to cost by multiplying the retail value by the cost multiplier ($120,750 × 0.6207). In our illustration, we get a value of $74,949.

### Step 5: Determination of Gross Cost of Goods Sold.

Since we know the amount of the merchandise handled at cost ($270,000), and know what we have *left* at cost ($75,949), we can determine the cost dollars that have moved out of stock ($195,051).

### Step 6: Determination of Maintained Markup, Gross Margin, and Net Profit.

Two procedures may be followed at this step. (We prefer the first method because of the emphasis given to the concept of maintained markup in Chapter 15.) The gross margin and net profit figures in either case are identical—slightly different accounting philosophies are the determining factor. The justification of either method is neither appropriate nor valuable here; we simply show the two ways to let you see the differences between them. Gross cost of goods sold is deducted from net sales to determine maintained markup ($300,000 − $195,051). Alteration costs (or workroom expenses) are traditionally considered in retailing as merchandising, nonoperating expenses and in this first method are offset by cash discounts earned (nonoperating income). The net difference between the two is added or subtracted from the maintained markup to derive the gross margin ($104,949 − $3,000 + $6,000 = $107,949), from which operating expenses are deducted to calculate net profit before taxes ($107,949 − $75,000 = $32,949). The various percentages appearing on the statement are all based on net sales (with the exception of the cost multiplier and the cumulative markup).

The second process for determining gross margin and net profit differs in that cash discounts earned are deducted from gross cost of goods sold ($195,051 − $6,000) to derive *net* cost of goods sold ($189,051). Alteration costs are added to that figure to obtain *total* cost of goods sold ($189,051 + $3,000 = $192,051). Total cost of goods sold is deducted from net sales ($300,000 − $192,051) to obtain the gross margin figure of $107,949.

### Evaluation of the Retail Method

Determination of profits using the retail method of inventory is not a new system, and over the years it has been criticized. A major complaint is that it is a method of averages. This refers to the determination of the cost multiplier as the average relationship between all the merchandise handled at cost and retail, and the application of this average percentage to the closing inventory at retail to determine the cost figure. Such a disadvantage, more real in the past than today, can be largely overcome by classification merchandising or dissection accounting—that is, breaking down departments into small subgroups with similar margins and turnover. The new technology in point-of-sale systems affords unlimited classifications and thus allows the similarity necessary for implementation of the retail method, giving management a good measure of the actual effectiveness of operations.

The retail method of inventory is not applicable to all departments within a store. For example, unless the purchases can be "retailed" at the time of receipt of the goods, the system will not work. The drapery workroom could not be on the retail method. Consequently, there are certain cost departments within many establishments. Such a condition does not lessen the value of the system where it is appropriate.

Finally, the retail method is easily programmed for computer systems and has proved most effective for management decisions. All accounting entries into the system can be automated, and the management reports that can use such data are virtually limitless.

# Chapter Highlights

- Accounting systems are essential in monitoring the performance of a retail firm.
- The strategic profit model (SPM) dramatizes the principal areas of decision making—margin, asset, and leverage management—and is the framework for profitable retail management.

- Inventory turnover has a direct impact on profitability. The gross margin return on inventory investment (GMROI) concept effectively illustrates this impact.
- Inventories should be valued at the lower of cost or market. The retail method of inventory valuation provides this information.

# Key Terms

Assets, current    533
Assets, fixed    533
Balance sheet    533
FIFO (first-in, first-out)    540
GMROI (gross margin return on inventory investment)    539

Income statement    533
Leveraging    536
LIFO (last-in, first-out)    541
Strategic profit model (SPM)    534

# Discussion Questions

1. Distinguish between the balance sheet and the income statement. Illustrate a format for each.
2. Explain the problems related to defining the terms *profit* and *investment*.
3. What are the significant purposes of the strategic profit model (SPM)?
4. Discuss the practical value of the strategic profit model.
5. Discuss your reaction to the following statement made by the manager of a large, full-line department store: "I am very pleased that my store had a 3.6 turnover rate for 1992."

6. Discuss the impact that turnover and margin planning have on the return of each dollar invested in inventory using a GMROI format.
7. Why is it difficult to determine cost of ending inventories? How do (a) FIFO and (b) LIFO relate to this problem? Explain the assumptions of and contrast the two methods.
8. Describe the cost method of inventory valuation. What are the limitations of the cost method? Under what conditions would this method be more appropriately used?

# Problems

Use the retail method of accounting. Prepare a well-organized statement and determine for each of the three problems the following sets of figures:

a. Cumulative markup percentage.
b. Ending inventory at retail.
c. Ending inventory at cost.
d. Maintained markup in dollars and percent.
e. Gross margin of profit in dollars and percent.
f. Net profit in dollars and percent.

1.

| Item | Cost | Retail |
|---|---|---|
| Beginning inventory | $20,000 | $ 35,000 |
| Gross purchases | 72,000 | 115,000 |
| Purchase returns and allowances | 3,000 | 4,700 |
| Transfers in | 1,000 | 1,600 |
| Transfers out | 200 | 400 |
| Transportation charges | 1,216 | |
| Additional markups | | 700 |
| Additional markup cancellations | | 400 |
| Gross sales | | 111,000 |
| Customer returns and allowances | | 11,000 |
| Gross markdowns | | 4,500 |
| Markdown cancellations | | 1,000 |
| Employee discounts | | 500 |
| Estimated shortages, .4 percent of net sales | | |
| Cash discounts on purchases | 1,600 | |
| Workroom costs | 800 | |
| Operating expenses | 16,000 | |

2.

| Item | Cost | Retail |
|---|---|---|
| Additional markup cancellations | | $    620 |
| Estimated shortages, .05 percent of net sales | | |
| Gross markdowns | | 8,000 |
| Workroom costs | $    500 | |
| Sales returns and allowances | | 12,000 |
| Transportation charges | 2,094 | |
| Beginning inventory | 44,000 | 64,000 |
| Purchase returns and allowances | 2,200 | 5,200 |
| Markdown cancellations | | 1,200 |
| Gross purchases | 65,600 | 105,240 |
| Gross additional markups | | 2,480 |
| Gross sales | | 102,000 |
| Employee discounts | | 1,400 |
| Cash discounts on purchases | 1,500 | |
| Operating expenses | 11,000 | |

3.

| Item | Cost | Retail |
|---|---|---|
| Gross sales | | $27,200 |
| Beginning inventory | $14,300 | 20,100 |
| Sales returns and allowances | | 200 |
| Gross markdowns | | 2,200 |
| Gross additional markups | | 650 |
| Transportation charges | 418 | |
| Purchase returns and allowances | 830 | 1,720 |
| Employee discounts | | 500 |
| Gross purchases | 17,200 | 27,520 |
| Markdown cancellations | | 300 |
| Operating expenses | 3,800 | |
| Cash discounts on purchases | 200 | |
| Additional markups cancelled | | 150 |
| Alteration and workroom costs | 300 | |
| Ending physical inventory | | 16,500 |

# Application Exercises

1. Interview at least three types of retailers, such as managers of department stores or catalog showrooms. Discuss the issue of LIFO versus FIFO methods of inventory valuation. See if the retailers understand the advantages and disadvantages of each. Summarize their perceptions and degree of sophistication. Try to draw some conclusions from this exercise.

2. Interview several small retailers and perhaps a large one (e.g., several dress shops, men's stores, and a

department store). Ask if you could speak with the person in charge of the accounting records. Find out if any of the retailers are using the retail method of accounting. If not, find out how they operate the cost method. How do they determine shortages? Try to strike up a conversation that covers the subject of this chapter. Report back your findings.

3. Secure an annual report of a retail firm and construct (to the best of your ability) an SPM for that organization.

## Suggested Cases

# CAREERS IN RETAILING

Retailing has been, and will continue to be, an important sector in the Canadian economic scene. Retailing offers many career opportunities for those interested in a dynamic, ever-changing field. As well, there are opportunities available for retail entrepreneurs. Budding entrepreneurs should consider the field of retailing as a likely, long-term choice for one's own business. However, we hasten to caution all students against going into retailing as entrepreneurs immediately following an educational experience. We are strong believers in "making mistakes for someone else" before investing one's own capital in any business, especially retailing.

This appendix addresses the concerns of the average student who will probably go into the job market to seek a job with someone else. Consequently, the purposes of this appendix are to:

1. Focus your attention on career orientation.
2. Describe the characteristics of retailing careers.
3. Review the job skills needed to succeed in retailing.
4. Provide some tangible tips on:
    *a.* The value of internships/experience.
    *b.* Preparing a game plan for job finding.
    *c.* Interviewing dos and don'ts.
    *d.* Reviewing questions you can ask in an interview.
    *e.* Getting together an up-to-date résumé.
    *f.* Common mistakes job hunters make.
5. Illustrate typical training programmes and career paths that exist in retail organizations.
6. Offer suggestions for career progress and success.

Students considering the possibility of retailing as a career probably have a particular type of retailing in mind because of personal knowledge. However, they may not realize where the jobs really are. Department stores, for example, although highly visible, are just one source of entry-level opportunities. Retailing, of course, takes place in many kinds of operations—specialty stores (Runner's World), off-price stores (BiWay), and discount firms (Nabours); the national chains (Sears and Eaton's); national, regional, and local food organizations (Safeway, Loblaws, and Sobeys); the specialty chains (Toys Я Us); and many other types of firms. Students interested in retailing careers may also consider direct sellers (Mary Kay and Tupperware); shopping centre developers and managers (Cambridge); mail-order firms (Eddie Bauer); and services retailing (Century 21 and Air Canada). This is quite a list, though still incomplete, to add to The Bay and Zellers.

Students must recognize that retailing is not without disadvantages. Retailing suffers from some image problems. For example, young people expecting to get ahead in retailing will probably be required to work long hours at the beginning of their careers, particularly during evenings and weekends. Retailing trainees can also expect to do some menial tasks as part of the learning process.

Still, the skills gained in retailing are transferable to other fields. Retailing can be a good experience for anyone who enjoys buying and selling. If you are excited about ''making your day''—seeing how well you did compared to the same day in the previous year—retailing can be a challenge.

Not everyone who studies retail management wants a career in the field. For those of you who are curious about retailing opportunities, however, this appendix can help you discover what to expect after graduation.

# Career Development

Students are at various stages of career development. The continuum shown below suggests the degrees of career development or orientation that you may be experiencing. You probably have friends who are at each phase. Students who are career ''disoriented'' may not have given any thought to the future. As time passes, however, they usually think of possible careers they may enjoy (initial orientation) and then, with more experience, decide on a specific career (definitive orientation).

```
x ──────────────── x ──────────────── x
Disoriented        Initial orientation    Definitive orientation
```

We encourage you to seek career counselling at all phases of your career development, especially when a concern about careers surfaces. Also, don't confuse ''getting a job'' with career development. We suspect that a great deal of early attrition in first jobs results from both a desire to get a job simply to earn money and uncertainty about a career. A job without career direction is likely to prove unsuccessful in the long run.

The following sections offer information on careers in retailing and on careers in general to assist you in finding the right direction for your career.

# Characteristics of Retailing Careers

Employment in retailing exceeds 1.6 million persons in Canada. The diversity of opportunities is staggering and can fulfill almost every kind of ability, ambition, and desire. Retail establishments are located in the smallest rural village and the most sophisticated metropolitan area.

### Security

Security in a job is important to many people. Retailing offers a good degree of job security. Even during periods of economic stagnation, retailing usually suffers fewer employment declines than manufacturing or wholesaling. The reason is that consumers must continue to buy merchandise regardless of the state of the economy.

### Decentralized Job Opportunities

No matter where they live, people must purchase merchandise on a regular basis to maintain their standards of living. This means you can have a successful career in retailing even if you do not want to move far from home. On the other hand, people who want to move frequently can find the opportunity for employment in retailing wherever they go.

### Opportunities for Advancement

Many executive positions exist because of the large number of retail establishments in Canada. Retailing is continuing to expand, and positions in management are being created on a basis proportionate to this expansion.

### Reward for Performance and Entrepreneurship

Retailing offers a daily performance measure because sales and profits can be read and evaluated daily. For high performers, such tangible measures are a delight; for the nonperformers, each day is painful. Obviously, not everyone is right for retailing (and the same can be said for all career options). A graduate who performs well may become a buyer for a high-dollar-volume department in a large department store organization within two or three years. As a buyer responsible for producing a profit in the department, such an achiever will really be acting as an entrepreneur in the security of an established firm.

### Women in Retailing

A recent survey found that the retail industry offers women good opportunities for advancement. Women have moved into all middle-management positions and beyond. In the 1990s, women hold top management positions—president, general merchandise manager, and divisional merchandise manager—and in numbers revealing that rather dramatic changes are taking place. Women were locked into advertising, publicity, fashion coordinating, or personnel training 15 or 20 years ago. "Though women in retailing haven't yet made it to the top in equal numbers as men, by the end of the decade we expect they will earn genuine parity with their male counterparts."[1]

### Salaries in Retailing

Starting salaries for graduates entering retail training programmes vary widely— from $17,000 to $30,000 annually. The contrast in starting salaries reflects the variation in training programmes, location, cost of living, and the competitive market for trainees.

### Nonmonetary Rewards

A person's ability and effort—or the absence of these qualities—are quickly recognized in retailing. The position of store manager appeals to persons with the ability to organize and direct the activities of others. As store manager, you set your own sales and profit goals as well as control expenses, compensate employees, and perform other vital management functions. In effect, you have the opportunity to manage your own business with someone else's money. A management career in retailing also offers the opportunity to work with ideas. Managers create ways of increasing sales and profit through imaginative use of the retailing mix.

# Job Skills Needed in Retailing

Cashiers and salesclerks are the positions many people imagine when retailing is mentioned. These jobs are only two of the many available. A substantial number of "behind the scenes" jobs exist in all retail settings.

The different types of job opportunities in retailing can be grouped into five employment categories that are common to most retail firms.

*Merchandising.* Merchandising is buying and selling goods. Merchandising is one of the most important areas of employment. Trainees often start out in this area, because it is the heart of the store. Buyers work with suppliers in acquiring goods for the outlet. They also help coordinate advertising and display, and may travel worldwide to acquire the latest fashions. An ambitious and successful buyer may become a merchandise manager, which means overseeing several buyers.

*Operations.* Operations means sales support. The jobs include store management, warehousing, receiving, delivery, security, and customer service.

*Sales Promotion.* Sales promotion is closely related to merchandising. Sales promotion involves advertising, display, publicity, and other sales promotion activities. Creativity and originality are needed for these jobs; for example, writing and artwork skills are important in advertising. Jobs include copywriter, decorator, and art director.

*Control.* Persons working in the control area manage the company's assets. Knowledge of statistics, accounting, or data processing are needed for these jobs. Credit, accounts payable and receivable, auditing, and data processing are some of the jobs found in this area.

*Personnel.* Jobs in personnel involve recruiting, selecting, and training employees. People in this area also work with employee compensation and other benefits, and they handle union problems.

# Tangible Career Tips

For this discussion to be meaningful, we must assume that you have moved along the career orientation continuum to at least the initial orientation phase. We also want to note here that this section is generic: We think the tips herein are valuable even if retailing is not your career objective.

### Job-Finding Game Plan

We urge you to develop a job-finding game plan with which you can live. Exhibit A-1 includes four proven strategies you will find very helpful.

### Questions to Ask in an Interview[2]

"If you really want the job, you ask probing, intelligent questions." The following 10 questions are suggested:

1. How would you describe a typical day on the job?
2. When was my predecessor promoted?
3. What kind of training can I expect in the first three months?
4. What specific skills or experience would help someone do well in this job?
5. Do most managers have advanced degrees? If so, which ones?
6. When will the first job performance evaluation take place?
7. To whom would I report?
8. Will I have a chance to meet people who would be my co-workers?
9. Would I be assigned to a specific department or rotate throughout the organization?
10. Does the company anticipate changing the current structure soon?

### EXHIBIT A-1
*Job-finding game plan*

Here are four proven strategies that will help you in your job quest.

1. Develop a game plan. Think about the kind of job you want. Where do you want to work? How do you plan to approach the job search? What information do you need? Where can you get it? Who are the resource people who can help you?

2. Organize your job search. Work as hard at getting a job as you would on the job. Plan job search activities on a daily basis. Set goals. Keep detailed records. Maintain deadlines.

3. Utilize all available resources. Go to the placement centre, employment agencies, and community organizations. See what services they offer. Learn what their strengths and weaknesses are. Respond to want ads, and use personal and direct contacts. Go to lectures, workshops, and seminars. Attend professional meetings and conferences. The more resources you utilize, the better your chances are for success.

4. Continually evaluate your game plan. If your strategy isn't working, look realistically at what you're doing. Get help if you need it. Remember that the job search is a process, not an outcome. Nothing is irreversible. Résumés can be rewritten, interviewing techniques can be improved. What is most important is that you try to remain flexible at all times.

SOURCE: *Business Week's Guide to Careers,* Spring–Summer 1984, p. 65.

## Have a Good, Up-to-Date Résumé

Check with the placement office for ideas, but above all, make sure that the résumé is neat, has no spelling errors, and points out your skills and work-related background. Focus on the jobs you have held and on your skills, talents, and interests. Exhibit A–2 shows you the organization of a typical résumé for a person in college seeking retailing employment. Exhibit A–3 is a checklist for résumé preparation. Other useful tips are found in Exhibit A–4: interview dos and don'ts presented along with typical interview questions to contemplate in your initial career search activities and the job-interviewing process.

EXHIBIT A–2

*A résumé*

---

Julie K. Ashman
Post Office Box 123
Main City
Province Code
(111) 222-3333

### Objective

Retail management—Aiming for employment with a retail firm where a strong sense of responsibility, strong technical skills, and a willingness to learn and grow are valued characteristics.

### Retail Experience

September 1993 (present)—Part-time salesperson, home furnishings department, Jackson's Department Store, Prairie City

Summer 1993—Intern to Mr. S. C. Jackson, Owner/Manager of Jackson's Department Store, Prairie City

Summer 1992—Worked in the receiving and marking department at Saska Discount Stores, Anycity

Summer 1991—Cashier at Saska Discount Stores, Anycity

### Education

B.A., The University of the Prairies (1993)

Major: Marketing with a concentration in Retail Management
Grade Point Average: B overall and in major

### Activities/Honours

College: Retailing Association (president and treasurer); The Marketing Club (membership chair); Student Government Association (senator); Member of the Student Executive Council of the College of Commerce and Business Administration; Retailing Achievement Award, Dean's List (3 years)

High School: Valedictorian; Student Council Vice-President

### References

To be supplied on request

---

## Exhibit A–3

### *Résumé (or data sheet) checklist*

1. Give your résumé an informative heading worded for the appropriate degree of selling.
   a. Identify your name, type of work desired, and (preferably) the company to which addressed.
   b. Be sure you apply for work, not a job title.
2. For appropriate emphasis, ease of reading, and space saving:
   a. Balance the material across the page in tabular form.
   b. Use different type and placement for emphasis and to show awareness of organization principles.
   c. Use centred heads that carry emphasis and help balance the page.
   d. Capitalize the main words in centred heads and underline the heads unless in solid caps.
   e. If you have to carry over an item, indent the second line.
   f. Remember to identify and number pages after the first.
3. Lead with whatever best prepares you for the particular job, but account for the chronology of your life since high school. (Gaps of more than three months may arouse suspicion.) When older and extensively experienced, such complete coverage is less necessary.
4. Education details should point out specific preparation.
   a. Show the status of your education early: degree, field, school, and date.
   b. Highlight courses that distinctively qualify you for the job. Listing everything takes away emphasis from the significant and suggests an inability to discriminate.
   c. In listing courses, give title or descriptions that show their real content, or briefly give specific details of what you did.
   d. Give grade averages in an understandable form (letters, quartiles, or percentages).
   e. Avoid belittling expressions like ''theoretical education.''
5. Experience—for jobs listed:
   a. Give job title, duties, firm or organization name, full address, specific dates, *responsibilities,* and immediate superior's name.
   b. If experience is part time, identify it as such.
   c. Consider reverse chronology or other arrangement to emphasize the most relevant and important.
   d. Use noun phrases and employ action verbs that imply *responsibility.*
6. If you include a personal details section, it should present a clear, true picture. (Though law prevents employers from asking about race, religion, age, health, and marital status, no law prohibits you from volunteering such information.)
   a. Tabulate, but try combining ideas to save words:

   | | |
   |---|---|
   | Born in Medicine Hat, | Married, no children |
   |   Alberta, 1973 | Member of (list appropriate organizations) |
   | 1.80 metres, 85 kg. | Like fishing and reading |
   | Good health, glasses for close work | |

   b. Give your address(es)—and phone(s) if likely to be used—in minimum space where easily found but not emphasized.
7. List or offer to supply references. When you list references (to conclude your résumé or supply later on request):
   a. Give the names, titles, full addresses, and telephone numbers of references for all important jobs and fields of study listed.
   b. Unless obvious, make clear why each reference is listed.
8. Remember these points about style:
   a. A résumé is ordinarily a tabulation; avoid paragraphs and complete sentences.
   b. Noun phrases are the best choice of grammatical pattern.
   c. Items in any list should be in parallel form.
   d. Keep opinions out of résumés; just give facts. Use impersonal presentation, avoiding first- and second-person pronouns.

SOURCE: Adapted from C. W. Wilkinson, Peter B. Clarke, and Dorothy C. M. Wilkinson, *Communicating through Letters and Reports* (Homewood, Ill.: Richard D. Irwin, 1980), p. 343.

## Exhibit A–4

### *Interview dos and don'ts*

Ninety-nine out of 100 bright-as-a-penny candidates who are wearing their best dressed-for-success outfits and have all the credentials necessary to impress St. Peter at the gates of heaven won't make the effort necessary to answer the following typical inverview questions:

- How did you happen to select X as a career choice?
- What are the qualities necessary for success in X?
- What do you consider your chief strengths in this profession?
- What are some of the weaknesses that might hinder your success?
- Why should we hire you rather than one of your equally competent classmates?
- What are your long-term career objectives at this point?
- Why do you think you would like to work for our company?

There is no way you can answer these questions without also revealing whether or not you have done your homework about yourself, your career decisions, and the company.

**Do:**

- Anticipate probing questions about any obviously difficult career episode on your résumé, such as a job briefly held, or a summer job that did not result in a permanent offer.
- Control your desire to run the interview. Instead, concentrate on adopting a pleasant and cordial tone throughout.
- Be succinct.

**Don't:**

- Oversell and make promises you will live to regret once you are actually on the job.
- Project a self-centred perspective, such as "What's in this for me?" Don't be negative about any employer or company. Don't blame others in the course of explaining situations.

Allan Sarn, an executive search consultant who sees the mistakes that experienced candidates make while interviewing for executive jobs, emphasizes that candidates must know the following about the company before an interview:

- The dollar volume of the company's annual business.
- The number of employees who work for the company.
- The products manufactured or services provided by the company.
- The names of the top executives in the company.
- The scope of the business—whether domestic or international.
- The general content of the company's most recent annual report as well as information contained in major articles written about it.

### Common Job-Hunting Mistakes[3]

''You'll find a job faster and more easily—and even enjoy the quest—if you steer clear of these frequently made errors.''

- Not knowing what you want to do.
- Not taking the initiative.
- Going to too few prospects.
- Not viewing employment from the employer's perspective.
- Asking too directly for a job.
- Not targeting the people with whom you would be working.
- Approaching prospects in an impersonal way.
- Having an unfocused résumé.
- Overlooking selling points.
- Not following through.

# Job Training and Career Paths

Thus far, this appendix has focused on career orientation, the characteristics of retailing careers, the job skills needed to succeed in retailing, and some generic, tangible career tips. This concluding section is concerned with job training programmes and career paths.

### Training Programmes

Training programmes often involve rotation among the various departments/ functions within a firm until the trainee is familiar with the operations. Programmes vary in detail and reflect the philosophy of the particular retail organization.

### Career Paths

A career path can be thought of as the route taken within a particular company. The progression through a retailing organization depends at least in part on the organizational structure. For example, in a highly centralized structure, more executive-level opportunities exist in the corporate or division headquarters. In a more decentralized operation, where most of the necessary functions are at the local level, additional opportunities may exist in the individual stores.

A career path can also be viewed as a life-time pattern of advancement. This longer time frame will undoubtedly involve multiple organizations; different industries; and apparent total changes in direction.

### Conclusions

We do not believe it is our role to sell you on a retailing career. We have presented information for you to think about. Retailing career paths are rather definite and understandable, and can result in high-level performance for the right person. Retailing offers many excellent training programmes. You must evaluate them in terms of your own career aspirations. We do encourage you to consider retailing as a career possibility—we ask no more.

# Appendix Highlights

- Retailing offers many diverse opportunities but suffers from an image problem as far as a career is concerned.
- Students are at various stages of career development or orientation—from disoriented, through initial orientation, to definitive orientation. Students are encouraged to become oriented as soon as possible.
- Characteristics of retailing careers are a good degree of job security; decentralized job opportunities; opportunities for advancement; daily performance measures with tangible rewards;

good opportunities for women; and salaries that, although varying, are basically competitive at the entry level.

- The different types of job opportunities can be grouped into the following areas of employment: merchandising, operations, sales promotion, control, and personnel.
- The following career tips are useful: get a head-start through some kind of experiential learning activity; create a job-finding game plan; prepare carefully for interviews; have a good, up-to-date résumé; and avoid the 10 common job-finding mistakes.

# Discussion Questions

1. What are the major advantages and disadvantages of a career in retailing?
2. What are the main qualities that a person should have to succeed in retailing?
3. What are the employment possibilities for women in retailing? What are the reasons women should consider a career in retailing? Are the reasons different for men? Explain your answer.
4. What are the major types of jobs in retailing?
5. If you are planning to own your own retail business in the future, what types of experience should you first have?
6. What recommendations would you give other students to help them prepare for a job interview?

# Application Exercises

1. Write to several retail organizations and ask for any career information they have. Then make up a summary chart contrasting and comparing the various career components a potential trainee in retailing would want to evaluate. Try to get information on beginning salaries, promotional paths, career options, and so on.
2. Assume you have been out of school for several years. You have been in a nonretailing position (assume anything you desire) and want to change career patterns. You look at retailing as a career possibility. Outline the steps you might go through to assist you in your decision. Assume you decide on retailing as a career. What sources are available in your job search? Do an inventory of steps you

will take and information you can develop. Then do a marketing job on yourself and prepare to offer your services to the firm you believe offers a good future.

3. Many companies do not recruit college or university graduates in the student placement office, if one exists. Thus, in your local community, find out the different choices that exist in the retail field for university and college graduates. Find out the entry level for grads; kind and length of training programme, if one exists; steps up the management ladder; and, if possible, beginning salaries and chances for promotion in each firm. Prepare a career chart for the city as a result of your findings.

# Endnotes

1. Janice Harayda, "Internships: Getting a Head Start," *Business Week's Careers,* September 1986, pp. 21–23.

2. Marilyn Moats Kennedy, "Questions You Can Ask the Interviewer," *Business Week's Careers,* September 1986, pp. 26–30.

3. Robert B. Nelson, "10 Common Mistakes Job Hunters Make," *Business Week's Careers,* November 1986, pp. 91–93.

# CASES

---

## 1.
## VIDEOFILE

Ms. Alice Chaffe, the owner of Videofile, an independent video rental store located in a neighbourhood shopping plaza, was deeply concerned. She had just received a call from Murray Blain, the owner of another neighbourhood video store about 3 kilometres away. Mr. Blain told her he was closing his store. "I can't make a go of it," he told Ms. Chaffe. "My customers are all going to the superstores like Jumbo and Major. I'm renting less than 20 movies a day." He finished the conversation by wishing her luck. "I'll need it," Alice thought to herself. "I'm doing better than Murray, but not by much." Alice had opened the store in early 1985 to cash in on the rapidly growing video rental market. However, in the past year or two, the market had changed significantly and competition had increased. Sales at Videofile had been declining and Alice wondered if there was still room in this dynamic market for a neighbourhood video store.

### Video Industry in Canada

The market for video rentals has developed as an offshoot of the videocassette recorder (VCR) market. Since 1980, the number of households owning VCRs—and, so, in a position to rent videos—has escalated from approximately 45,000 in 1980 to about 7.1 million in 1992. This represents about 70 percent of all the households in Canada. Until recently, growth in video rentals had paralleled VCR sales. Typically, nearly 60 percent of a VCR's user-time was spent playing rented videos. Surveys had indicated that VCR households rented an average of about two videos per week. However, in the past two years, total revenues from video rentals had actually declined in North America, due in part to the increase in the pay per view market offered by cable companies.

### The Video Business

Ms. Chaffe reflected on the changes that had occurred in the business since she began operations in 1985. The most common type of video store at that time was like

This case was prepared by Arlene Bennett and Gordon McDougall, Wilfrid Laurier University.

hers—neighbourhood video stores that were located in strip malls. Her store was located in such a mall, which included a supermarket, hairdresser, bank, pizza take-out, convenience store, and laundromat. Her customer base was the immediate neighbourhood. Typically, people would rent a movie on their way home from work and return it the following day.

While many competitors entered the market—including major department stores like Eaton's and, on the other extreme, gas stations—her major competition was the convenience store in the mall that introduced video rentals in 1986 and other neighbourhood stores (the closest being her competitor who had just closed).

However, in 1987, the market changed significantly. The first superstore in the area, Major Video, opened eight blocks away. Major Video was one of the first operations to begin franchising on a regional—then a national—basis. Major carried a wide range of titles and benefited from economies of scale (mass media advertising, quantity discounts on movie purchases), expertise in store/strategy development, and convenience to customers (drop off of videos at any location). Efficiencies were also gained through computerized inventory systems.

If that wasn't enough, in early 1988, Jumbo Video, another developing national chain, opened a store just six blocks from her location in another strip mall. Now she faced two video superstores, both in close proximity to her store.

Both Major Video and Jumbo Video were large (approximately 740 square metres) and stocked over 5,000 titles. Jumbo was open 24 hours a day.

These superstores used membership cards (usually free) to keep track of customers and their rentals. They also used economies of scale and efficiency through computerization to keep their costs down.

A further threat was the video vending machine (VVM). These machines are accessed with a major credit card or a store-issued card; some machines require cash payment, others automatically charge the purchaser's account. The machines only hold from 100 to 500 movies. The VVM can be accessed 24 hours a day, but are subject to vandalism when placed at remote (and convenient) locations. They can also be located in 24-hour convenience stores or in controlled-access areas of other stores—to control vandalism, to make optimum use of limited store space, to reduce lineups, and for 24-hour access. Some machines are equipped to handle reservations of videos, at an additional charge. VVMs allow independents to expand geographically with relatively low capital expenditures.

## Recent Trends

When Alice returned home that night, she mentioned the closing of Mr. Blain's store to her husband Jack, a plant manager for a metal fabrication factory. Jack had encouraged her to go into the business and had a continuing interest in the progress of the store. He responded, "Maybe you should think about the future of the store. Last weekend I made some notes on the articles I found on the video business. Let me read some of them." With that, Jack began reading his notes, which included the following comments about the video industry.

- The neighbourhood stores are being squeezed on the one hand by the big chains and on the other hand by automated videocassette dispensing machines in grocery and convenience stores, subway stations, apartment buildings, and other high-traffic locations.

- The video rental industry is not unlike the corner grocery store before Mac's Milk and the hamburger business before McDonald's. It's dominated by unsophisticated operators. Over the next few years, there will be a consolidation of the market. This appears to be happening in that many convenience stores no longer stock movies, more video chains are appearing (although Bandito Video went bankrupt in 1991), and the largest chains are now advertising.

- Another major change that is occurring is the increase in sales of videos as opposed to rentals. Estimated at $200 million, or 15 percent of the total Canadian video market, video sales were made primarily by the large video chains in Canada.

- The latest trend in video retailing—which may deal the knockout blow to the small operators—is video superstores (like Jumbo) that stock thousands of titles. The industry is changing to larger stores, larger selections, and more convenient hours.

- Video store rentals have declined (and may continue to) due to the increase in pay per view films being offered by cable companies and because the price of buying the popular videocassettes (e.g., the "blockbuster" movies) has dropped sharply, from a regular price of $89.95 only two years ago to less than $20.00 today. The majority of movies were priced at around $30.

- The strategies of the large chains are changing to reflect the new environment. For example, Jumbo Video is devoting less space to rentals and more space to video sales and other "entertainment" products, including audio books, film merchandise, relaxation tapes, and computer software. Other chains are rearranging their space to make their stores more entertaining.

Jack paused for a moment, then said, "That's the bad news. But some people see some hope for the independent." With that, he read the following notes.

- Some customers who have switched from the neighbourhood to the superstores are returning and willing to pay higher prices for better service. These customers are overwhelmed by the size of the superstores and they can't find anything. As well, they may be willing to drive four or five miles to get a video, but they are not keen about returning them. Also, the superstores may advertise a large selection, but most of their titles are "B movies" and customers quickly become disappointed.

- The key for the independent operator to keep a strong customer base is a knowledgeable sales staff and personalized service—service with a smile.

Alice reflected on the comments and then responded, "I'm going to take a close look at what I offer versus Jumbo and Major. Let's talk about this again tomorrow night."

## The Current Situation

The next day, Alice prepared a sheet listing the major characteristics of Videofile, Jumbo, and Major (Exhibit 1). She then did some rough calculations on her costs and revenues.

Videofile had 1,800 members, although many were inactive—they had not rented a movie in the past six months. Videofile was open 75 hours a week, and Alice worked 40 of those hours and had part-time help whom she paid $8 an hour to cover the remaining hours. While the cost per movie varied, she calculated she bought three new movies a week at an average price of $25. Occasionally, a discount of 15 percent was offered if a video store purchased six copies of a new movie. Alice had never purchased more than two copies of any movie. She estimated that total monthly fixed costs including rent, insurance, and so on were $500.

**Exhibit 1**

*Profile on Videofile, Jumbo Video, and Major Video*

|  | *Videofile* | *Jumbo Video* | *Major Video* |
|---|---|---|---|
| *Hours* | Mon.–Sat., 10:00 A.M.– 9:00 P.M. Sunday, noon–9:00 P.M. | Open 24 hours | Daily, 10:00 A.M.– 10:00 P.M. |
| *Rental Rates* | $2.99/day Classics $1.49/day Children's $1.99/day | $2.99/day Children's and "specials" $.99/day $3.99 for three-day rental | New arrivals $3.33/day Regular $2.99/day Lunchtime (12–1 P.M.), $2.00/day Happy hour (8–9 P.M.), two for $2.00/day |
| *VCR Rentals* | $4.99/day | $4.99/day | $4.99/day |
| *Laser Disc Rental Rates* |  | $2.99/day | $2.99/day |
| *Laser Disc Player Rentals* |  | $4.99/day | $4.99/day |
| *Membership* | Free | Free | Free |
| *Number of Movies Available* | 2,000 | Thousands | Thousands |
| *Physical Size* | 5.5 m × 9.1 m | 21.3 m × 21.3 m | 21.3 m × 27.4 m |
| *Other Features/ Services* | Reservations Nintendo video games and cartridges for rent Small selection of snack foods | Free popcorn Nintendo video games and cartridges for rent Camcorders for rent ($19.99/day) Snack foods for sale Movies for sale Blank tapes, posters for sale | Nintendo video games and cartridges for rent Camcorders for rent Small selection of snack foods |

Alice then looked at her sales for the last two months. She found that she had rented an average of 40 movies a day at $2.50. As well, the rental of VCRs (she had six in stock) added another $500 a month to her revenues. "If I pay myself $8 an hour, this store is barely breaking even," she thought.

## The Future

That night, she showed Jack her analysis. "Maybe I should get out before things get worse," she said. "Before you do that," said Jack, "let's look at all the options, then decide." With that, they did some brainstorming and listed a number of ideas that included the following:

- Video rental stores compete on the basis of convenience, service, selection, and price. Convenience includes store hours, location, parking, and store layout. Service includes the attitude of the staff, their knowledge of the movies (and customers), a reservation policy, and when movies are returned. Selection includes the number and quality of titles and the availability of a movie on a particular night. Pricing includes the price of the movie on a weekday or weekend and whether it is a new release, older movie, or a children's movie.

- With price, a number of further options exist, including selling coupons for movies, a monthly price that would allow a customer 30 movies for the month, and reduced prices for older movies.
- With promotion, options include mailings to customers, signs within the store, neighbourhood pamphlets, and temporary signs.
- With product, options include selling the older movies at reduced prices, considering new product lines (compact discs, VCRs, other accessories, snacks, and selling new movies).

After they generated the list, Alice and Jack agreed to think about it for a day and make the decision the next night. As Alice turned out the lights, she thought, "I really want to make a go of this, but I'm not sure. There must be something I can do to turn this around and make it a viable operation."

## Questions

1. What further changes, if any, will take place in the video rental market?
2. Recommend a strategy for Ms. Chaffe, assuming she plans to stay in the business?
3. Should Ms. Chaffe stay in the business?

---

## 2.
## RETAILING NEWSWATCH

Choose an article from a business magazine that addresses a topic/event/issue of importance to retail management. The topics can be wide-ranging but must be related in some way to the *practice* of retail management.

The article must have been published over the last two years. Likely sources for the articles include the following:

| | |
|---|---|
| *Business Week* | *Globe and Mail* |
| *Business Quarterly* | *Harvard Business Review* |
| *Canadian Business* | *Marketing* |
| *The Financial Post* | *Marketing and Media Decisions* |
| *Financial Times* | *Marketing News* |
| *Forbes* | *Report on Business Magazine* |
| *Fortune* | |

This case was prepared by Rosemary Polegato, Saint Francis Xavier University.

There are many possibilities for topics: Sunday shopping, cross-border shopping, auxiliary services, profiles of retailing entrepreneurs, shopping malls, warehouse retailers, Canadian retailers in the United States, U.S. retailers in Canada, strategic and operational analysis of a retailing operation (e.g., Wal-Mart, Canadian Tire, or McDonald's), universal product code, display/merchandising techniques (e.g., planograms), home shopping, shrinkage, and so on. You may also know of some issues in finance, accounting, industrial relations, or MIS that have a bearing on retail management. The more wide-ranging the topics, the greater the contribution to the class!

### Your Task

1. Sign up for a presentation date.
2. Choose one article, as described above.
3. Prepare a 10-minute presentation on the content of the article and on the implications for retail management.
4. *Five days before your presentation,* please deliver to the instructor a legible copy of the article.
5. Have fun choosing your topic and figuring out what it's all about!

---

## 3.
## THE SINGLES' LIFE-STYLES MARKET

A major department store chain is taking a fresh look at a potential target market—singles—and is asking some important questions about their life-styles and habits.

The retailer, through its consumer feedback programme, conducted a study of singles—the never-married, the widowed, and the divorced—who number over 23 percent of all Canadian households. More specifically, the goals of this study were to increase understanding of the life-styles of singles 25–39, whose incomes ranged from $17,500 to $50,000 for women, and from $25,000 to $50,000 for men.

As well, the project attempted to understand the values that underlie these life-styles; to identify the changing needs and expectations of singles at home, at work, and in the marketplace; and to suggest some of the implications resulting from the project.

What emerged were three issues for marketers to consider. First, being single is an acceptable life-style choice. Second, there are three basic types of singles' life-styles—changing, focused, and settled—and a person will move from one to another as circumstances and attitudes change. Third, independence is a common value throughout all singles' life-styles.

For each of the three singles life-styles groups, there was an emphasis on self, relationships, and career. Among the topics these groups addressed were their personal, career, and consumer choices.

Source: *Stores* Magazine, National Retail Merchants Assoc., 1986.

Some of the characteristics of the three basic life-style groups as consumers were illustrated by their attitudes on eight issues.

The *changing* singles "buy to satisfy short-term needs; buy anywhere; and are concerned with fashion and price." Their approach to shopping is "sometimes impulsive, but willing to shop for the best price." This group reported "ads, signing, and friends were influences on buying behaviour." They are the least brand oriented, most sales oriented, and least service oriented, although "return policy is important."

The *focused* singles (focused on self or career—those focused on children/relationships did not fit clearly in these categories) will generally "buy what they want, and shop primarily in specialty stores and better department stores." Their emphasis is on "fashion and quality," and they are described as "time pressured."

Some of the things that influence the buying behaviour of the focused singles are "convenient location, appropriate selection, personal service, and knowledgeable salespeople." This group has a "strong interest in designer/national brands, which provide desired styling and quality, are least sale oriented, and are most service oriented."

The *settled* singles, the survey indicated, buy "according to priorities in an overall plan, and select stores for products and reputation." Quality and value are important to this segment. They are described as "planned shoppers." Sale ads for desired merchandise and comparative price shopping are characteristic of their buying influences. They have "strong interest in national brands and private labels with proven quality and value, but wait for a sale in planned purchases. Postpurchase service and return policy are important."

Some general features of the life-style types identified through the study are:

In terms of him- or herself, the changing single is building self-confidence; seeking life direction; adapting to single status; finding a new environment. The focused single is concentrating on personal interests, avoiding commitments, and working for the money. The settled single has come to terms with being single and pursues interests for personal satisfaction.

Each of the groups is also distinguished by the types of relationships characteristic of it. Changing singles are considering marriage, contemplating parenthood, looking for relationships. The focused group is committed to a relationship with an adult or child and tries to balance relationships with self and career. The settled group has its social network in place and has resolved family relationships.

Where career is concerned, changing singles are seeking more—more challenge, more dollars, more satisfaction. Some are exploring a second career or considering their own businesses. The focused singles are committed to career—for advancement, money, or recognition. Settled singles are secure in their jobs, have adequate income, feel satisfied with their careers, and want to grow where they are.

## Questions

1. Compare and contrast the life-styles of the three types of singles identified: changing, focused, and settled.
2. How do the shopping behaviours of the three groups mentioned differ?
3. What types of retailing strategies are likely to be the most successful in attracting these three groups of shoppers?

## 4.

## CANADIAN LIFE-STYLES

Compusearch, a Canadian market research firm, has evaluated over 200 different demographic and socioeconomic variables and, by clustering neighbourhoods, has isolated 10 major urban groups and three major rural groups. The percentage of Canadian households by province in each of these life-styles and the life-style definitions are contained in Tables 1 and 2.

### Questions

Provide examples, by analyzing the data, as to how this life-style information can be useful for retailers in the following situations:

1. A regional chain of clothing stores that carries mid-range prices wishes to go national.
2. A successful sporting goods store in Toronto that targets upper income households wants to expand to another province.

**TABLE 1   Canadian Life-Styles**

| | Percentage of Households, by Province | | | | | | | | | | |
|---|---|---|---|---|---|---|---|---|---|---|---|
| | Canada | Nfld. | P.E.I. | N.S. | N.B. | Que. | Ont. | Man. | Sask. | Alta. | B.C. |
| Affluent | 1.99 | .22 | .12 | .65 | .31 | 1.33 | 2.88 | 1.24 | .76 | 3.67 | 1.22 |
| Upscale | 7.92 | 4.32 | 4.17 | 4.16 | 1.94 | 4.93 | 11.50 | 6.65 | 4.57 | 9.53 | 7.10 |
| Middle class | 17.12 | 10.75 | 6.62 | 9.54 | 12.67 | 17.31 | 19.39 | 13.53 | 10.74 | 18.18 | 17.10 |
| Working class | 14.79 | 16.95 | 17.94 | 24.08 | 18.59 | 20.89 | 11.32 | 8.06 | 7.78 | 13.74 | 13.92 |
| Lower income | 6.41 | 1.91 | 4.29 | 3.64 | 4.50 | 8.68 | 6.76 | 7.00 | 4.32 | 4.18 | 4.64 |
| Older and retired | 4.58 | 1.27 | 4.09 | 1.79 | 1.67 | 4.11 | 5.31 | 5.05 | 2.79 | 1.89 | 7.91 |
| Empty nesters | 10.13 | 5.69 | 7.97 | 8.61 | 7.13 | 6.31 | 12.22 | 14.91 | 9.38 | 8.72 | 13.89 |
| Young singles | 4.91 | .18 | .77 | 2.84 | 1.42 | 4.52 | 3.76 | 5.14 | 5.84 | 8.41 | 8.33 |
| Young couples | 4.56 | .77 | .00 | 2.39 | .88 | 7.35 | 4.09 | 3.97 | 1.34 | 3.79 | 3.90 |
| Ethnics | 2.50 | .00 | .00 | .15 | .00 | 1.21 | 5.05 | .78 | .40 | .49 | 2.18 |
| Rural upscale and middle class | 10.31 | 6.75 | 11.42 | 11.86 | 9.39 | 5.75 | 10.42 | 10.70 | 15.91 | 16.09 | 12.37 |
| Rural working class | 12.51 | 50.61 | 38.72 | 29.83 | 41.26 | 16.87 | 5.96 | 14.85 | 20.06 | 5.58 | 7.16 |
| Farming | 2.27 | .61 | 3.88 | .47 | .24 | .74 | 1.33 | 8.11 | 16.12 | 5.73 | .29 |
| Total | 100.00 | 100.00 | 100.00 | 100.00 | 100.00 | 100.00 | 100.00 | 100.00 | 100.00 | 100.00 | 100.00 |
| Total number of households (000) | 9,735 | 169 | 44 | 315 | 246 | 2,563 | 3,516 | 399 | 365 | 888 | 1,205 |

SOURCE: Canadian Markets 1992, *The Financial Post,* 1992.

## TABLE 2   Definitions of Canadian Life-Styles

**Affluent:** Extremely wealthy, highly educated households living in exclusive neighbourhoods, parents mostly over 35 years of age with teenaged children. Average household income, $122,935.

**Upscale:** Wealthy, well-educated, middle-aged families with school-aged children living in expensive, single detached houses. Average household income, $77,300.

**Middle (and upper-middle) class:** Families with children living in suburban, single detached houses, moderate education level. Average household income, $56,750.

**Working class:** Families with children often living in rented multiple dwellings with below average education level. Average household income, $41,511.

**Lower income:** Low education level, young households with blue-collar or low-level white-collar positions in rental units. Average household income, $30,701.

**Older and retired:** Older couples and widow(er)s living in high-rise apartments, low education levels. A wide range of incomes averaging $32,003.

**Empty nesters:** Husband and wife families over 55 years of age where their children have left home; wide range of incomes and types of dwellings. Average household income $50,582.

**Young singles:** Highly mobile, young one- or two-person households in rented dwellings, highly educated, many working women. A wide range of incomes averaging $33,411.

**Young couples:** Young, one- or two-person households in rental high-rise accommodations, slightly above average education. Average household income, $35,709.

**Ethnics:** Large ethnic families whose primary language is neither English nor French, low education, many blue-collar workers. A wide range of incomes averaging $47,061.

**Rural upscale and middle class:** Large families with young children, above average incomes for small urban and rural areas, primarily white-collar positions. Equivalent of Affluent, Upscale, and Middle class living in a more rural setting. Average household income, $47,212.

**Rural working class:** Large households with children, below average incomes, living in older, inexpensive, single detached houses. Low mobility households with much below average education levels, blue-collar employment with low female participation rate in labour force, often older individuals. Average household income, $34,085.

**Farming:** Households whose primary source of income is agriculture. Large families with children, middle-aged and older parents, living in older, single detached farmhouses. Farmers with a wide range of household incomes averaging $40,319.

SOURCE: Canadian Markets 1992, *The Financial Post,* 1992.

3. A franchise concept that plans to market lower-priced home furnishings wants to rank the provinces in terms of attractiveness.

4. A Nova Scotia home improvement centre that targets households with incomes under $30,000 wants to expand into other provinces.

## 5.

## CANADIAN POPULATION, HOUSEHOLD, AND RETAIL SALES TRENDS

An important aspect of retailing is determining the future implications of population and household trends. Tables 1, 2, 3, and 4 provide past and future data on the Canadian population by age group, geographic area, and household and retail sales by region.

### Questions

1. Analyze the tables and prepare a discussion on the retailing implications for the decade from 1991 to 2001. Contrast these changes with those that occurred in the decade from 1981 to 1991.

2. Between now and 2001, what retail sectors should experience the greatest growth? The least growth? Why?

### TABLE 1   Population, Actual and Projected, by Age Group
1951–2006 (in thousands)

| Year | Population | Under 9 | 10–19 | 20–34 | 35–49 | 50–64 | 65 and Over |
|------|-----------|---------|-------|-------|-------|-------|-------------|
| **Actual** | | | | | | | |
| 1951 | 14,010 | 3,120 | 2,190 | 3,260 | 2,610 | 1,740 | 1,090 |
| 1956 | 16,080 | 3,790 | 2,600 | 3,540 | 3,020 | 1,890 | 1,240 |
| 1961 | 18,240 | 4,340 | 3,290 | 3,670 | 3,400 | 2,150 | 1,390 |
| 1966 | 20,020 | 4,500 | 3,930 | 3,950 | 3,630 | 2,470 | 1,540 |
| 1971 | 21,570 | 4,070 | 4,420 | 4,790 | 3,760 | 2,780 | 1,750 |
| 1976 | 22,990 | 3,620 | 4,620 | 5,760 | 3,850 | 3,140 | 2,000 |
| 1981 | 24,340 | 3,560 | 4,240 | 6,560 | 4,220 | 3,400 | 2,360 |
| 1986 | 25,600 | 3,630 | 3,730 | 6,940 | 4,980 | 3,590 | 2,730 |
| 1991 | 26,610 | 3,570 | 3,610 | 6,750 | 5,820 | 3,690 | 3,170 |
| **Projections** | | | | | | | |
| 1996 | 27,810 | 3,550 | 3,710 | 6,280 | 6,630 | 4,060 | 3,580 |
| 2001 | 28,280 | 3,140 | 3,650 | 5,850 | 6,980 | 4,800 | 3,860 |
| 2006 | 29,050 | 2,810 | 3,610 | 5,890 | 6,800 | 5,680 | 4,280 |

SOURCE: *Marketing Research Handbook,* Statistics Canada, Catalogue 63-224, various years. Projections based on moderate fertility rates, average net international migration, and a migration flow within Canada that partially reflects the late 1960s pattern. Reproduced with the permission of the Minister of Supply and Services Canada, 1992.

TABLE 2  **Population, Actual and Projected, by Geographic Area**
1951–2006 (in thousands)

| Year | Total Population | Maritime Provinces | Quebec | Ontario | Prairie Provinces | B.C. and Yukon/NWT |
|------|------|------|------|------|------|------|
| **Actual** | | | | | | |
| 1951 | 14,010 | 1,620 | 4,050 | 4,600 | 2,550 | 1,190 |
| 1956 | 16,080 | 1,760 | 4,630 | 5,410 | 2,850 | 1,430 |
| 1961 | 18,240 | 1,900 | 5,260 | 6,230 | 3,180 | 1,670 |
| 1966 | 20,020 | 1,980 | 5,780 | 6,960 | 3,380 | 1,920 |
| 1971 | 21,570 | 2,060 | 6,030 | 7,700 | 3,540 | 2,240 |
| 1976 | 22,990 | 2,180 | 6,240 | 8,260 | 3,780 | 2,530 |
| 1981 | 24,340 | 2,230 | 6,400 | 8,630 | 4,230 | 2,810 |
| 1986 | 25,600 | 2,320 | 6,630 | 9,110 | 4,510 | 3,030 |
| 1991 | 26,610 | 2,360 | 6,750 | 9,410 | 4,800 | 3,290 |
| **Projections** | | | | | | |
| 1996 | 27,810 | 2,350 | 6,920 | 10,280 | 4,800 | 3,460 |
| 2001 | 28,280 | 2,330 | 6,920 | 10,530 | 4,930 | 3,570 |
| 2006 | 29,050 | 2,330 | 7,010 | 10,890 | 5,100 | 3,720 |

SOURCE: *Marketing Research Handbook,* Statistics Canada, Catalogue 63-224, various years. Projections based on moderate fertility rates, average net international migration, and a migration flow within Canada that partially reflects the late 1960s pattern. Reproduced with the permission of the Minister of Supply and Services Canada, 1992.

TABLE 3  **Households, Actual and Projected, by Geographic Area**
1951–2006 (in thousands)

| Year | Total Households | Maritime Provinces | Quebec | Ontario | Prairie Provinces | B.C. and Yukon/NWT |
|------|------|------|------|------|------|------|
| **Actual** | | | | | | |
| 1966 | 5,180 | 450 | 1,390 | 1,880 | 910 | 550 |
| 1971 | 6,030 | 500 | 1,600 | 2,230 | 1,020 | 680 |
| 1976 | 7,170 | 600 | 1,900 | 2,640 | 1,190 | 840 |
| 1981 | 8,280 | 670 | 2,170 | 2,970 | 1,450 | 1,020 |
| 1986 | 9,220 | 750 | 2,340 | 3,430 | 1,590 | 1,110 |
| 1991 | 10,110 | 820 | 2,510 | 3,780 | 1,760 | 1,240 |
| **Projections** | | | | | | |
| 1996 | 11,010 | 870 | 2,870 | 3,960 | 1,890 | 1,420 |
| 2001 | 11,970 | 910 | 3,120 | 4,290 | 2,080 | 1,570 |
| 2006 | 12,810 | 960 | 3,330 | 4,590 | 2,240 | 1,690 |

NOTE: Households include single-detached, single-attached, apartments and flats, and mobile homes.
SOURCE: *Marketing Research Handbook,* Statistics Canada, Catalogue 63-224, various years. Projections based on moderate fertility rates, average net international migration, and a migration flow within Canada that partially reflects the late 1960s pattern. Reproduced with the permission of the Minister of Supply and Services Canada, 1992.

TABLE 4    **Retail Sales, by Geographic Area**
1951–1997 (in $ millions)

| Year | Total Retail Sales | Maritime Provinces | Quebec | Ontario | Prairie Provinces | B.C. and Yukon/NWT |
|------|-----|-----|-----|-----|-----|-----|
| **Actual** | | | | | | |
| 1951 | 10,693 | 898 | 2,443 | 4,130 | 2,122 | 1,100 |
| 1956 | 14,774 | 1,209 | 3,463 | 5,734 | 2,728 | 1,640 |
| 1961 | 16,073 | 1,380 | 4,108 | 6,207 | 2,774 | 1,604 |
| 1966 | 22,678 | 1,861 | 5,881 | 8,621 | 3,810 | 2,505 |
| 1971 | 30,660 | 2,533 | 7,682 | 11,883 | 4,929 | 3,633 |
| 1976 | 58,468 | 4,795 | 14,529 | 21,629 | 10,522 | 6,993 |
| 1981 | 92,821 | 8,098 | 22,578 | 32,428 | 18,248 | 12,469 |
| 1986 | 138,131 | 8,803 | 34,246 | 53,054 | 23,967 | 15,780 |
| 1991 | 213,975 | 16,324 | 53,971 | 83,110 | 34,101 | 26,469 |
| 1992E | 233,298 | 17,615 | 58,717 | 91,385 | 36,793 | 28,788 |
| **Projections** | | | | | | |
| 1994 | 256,459 | 18,849 | 63,582 | 101,984 | 40,013 | 32,031 |
| 1997 | 334,611 | 23,796 | 81,639 | 134,631 | 52,018 | 42,577 |

NOTE: Data for the years 1951 and 1956 are not strictly comparable with data for later years. Data for 1992 are estimated.

SOURCE: Canadian Statistical Review, Catalogue 11-003, various years, and *The Financial Post,* Survey of Markets, various years.

# 6.
# THE CANADIAN MARKETPLACE: PROSPECTS FOR RETAILERS

The dramatic changes that are occurring in the Canadian marketplace create threats and opportunities for virtually all retailers seeking to grow and remain profitable. The key to success is to fully understand the impact these changes will have on a particular retail business, and to take the appropriate steps to benefit from them. Consider the following trends:

1. By the beginning of the next decade, Canada will be in a steady state of population growth.
2. Household size has been declining for many years, from 4 persons per household in 1951 to 2.7 persons per household in 1992. About 23 percent of Canadian households consist of a single adult. About 14 percent of families have one parent at home (82 percent of them female), and 34 percent of families consist of childless couples.
3. The baby-boom generation (those born between 1946 and 1966) are in 1993 between 27 and 47 years of age. There are about 9 million baby boomers, and their influence will always be felt as they move through the various stages of life.

4. A number of new affluent segments are of interest to retailers:
   a. Skoties (spoiled kids of the eighties): With smaller families, many children have lots of money and the time and freedom to spend it. According to one survey, the average 10-year-old has $11 per week to spend.
   b. Yuppies (young urban professionals): This is a subgroup of the baby-boom generation, living in urban areas, with professional white-collar jobs and earning more than $50,000 yearly. They number about 2 million.
   c. Dinks (dual income, no kids): These tend to be families with working spouses who have decided not to have children, and family income exceeding $50,000 yearly.
   d. Muppies (middle-aged urban professionals): Similar to the yuppies but older, they number about 300,000. This segment will become bigger as the baby boomers reach the 50–64 age bracket.
   e. Woopies (well-off old people): These are Canadians over 65 and with incomes over $50,000. They have little debt (only 8 per cent of Canadians over 65 are still paying a mortgage), and a lot of leisure time.
   f. The Countdown Generation: These are the 12 percent of Canadians who expect to retire in the next few years; they control about half of the personal wealth in Canada.

5. Many changes are occurring within the family, which will affect the way retailers relate to their customers:
   a. Teenagers (more than 2.5 million in Canada) have very different attitudes and behaviours when compared to the adult population. They tend to have a sizable income (according to one study, the average teenager has $38 per week to spend), which is usually spent buying clothing, personal care products, and tapes and compact discs. Also, a very large percentage of teenagers cook, and half do a lot of shopping, as well as influence the family's brand choice for many supermarket items.
   b. The increased participation of women in the work force puts these two-income families into a higher income and social-class category, with the corresponding changes in consumption behaviour. Also, working wives use their time differently from wives who don't work outside the home.
   c. The changing role of women is forcing some changes among men, with an increasing percentage of men cooking and doing the main food shopping.

## Questions

1. Considering the above trends, what are the major threats and opportunities facing Canadian retailers in the next few years?
2. What are the implications of these trends for retailers in terms of:
   a. Clientele mix.
   b. Training retail employees.
   c. Merchandise decision.
   d. Brand and store loyalty.
   e. Store design, layout, and merchandise presentation.
   f. Pricing.
   g. Retail advertising.
   h. Customer support functions—for example, opening hours.
   i. Retail research.

## 7.

## BUYING AN ORIENTAL RUG

Janet Gordon was admiring her three new rugs and feeling a little bit guilty at spending so much money. Trying to understand these mixed emotions and her own behaviour, she looked back at the events of the past few weeks.

Janet, a recent university graduate, is employed as a computer programmer in Calgary. Soon after she started working, she married John Gordon, a young production supervisor. They bought a small older house in a well-maintained neighbourhood about 2 kilometres from the city centre. Shortly after moving in, they felt the need to do some decorating. They bought some traditional-style furniture, but Janet thought the rooms felt empty without rugs. She remembered that her parents had wall-to-wall solid colour carpets, and how she came to dislike them. Janet also remembered the neighbours' house, and how the furniture was enhanced by the use of patterned rugs. Looking for ideas in home magazines, she kept noticing the use of patterned rugs in the decorating ideas presented in the articles and advertisements.

During her lunch hour, she visited the rug department in a leading department store. She was quickly overwhelmed by the quantity and variety of rugs displayed on the floor. She had some trouble lifting them up to examine them, and no salesperson was available to offer assistance. Confused about what to do, she left the department store. On her way back to the office, she passed by Ali Baba, a small store specializing in patterned rugs. A sign on the window advertising "One-third Off" attracted her attention. She decided to take a look inside and was met by the store owner, who asked what she was looking for. In the ensuing discussion, she learned that there were a variety of rugs of different quality and price. Some were machine made and tended to be cheaper, while others were hand made in various countries such as Iran (Persian rugs), Pakistan, India, Turkey, China, or Morocco. Some were made of pure wool, others (more expensive) of silk, and others were blends. As the time was passing quickly and the owner kept pressuring her to buy, Janet said that she needed to talk to her husband, and went back to the office.

In the afternoon, she had trouble remembering and trying to sort out all the information the store owner had provided. That evening, she related her experiences to her husband. They agreed that a patterned rug would be nice in the dining and living rooms, but that they had to be careful about their finances since they were carrying a large mortgage and still paying for the furniture. They also found it difficult to decide on a particular design. They decided to postpone the decision.

Janet realized that she was talking more and more to her friends and colleagues about decorating with rugs and noticing ads about them in the newspaper and magazines. The following Saturday, she and her husband were invited to dinner at the home of John's boss. As they arrived, they immediately noticed that all the rugs in the house were beautiful Bokharas. They found out later that the rugs were from Pakistan. The following week, Janet talked to two friends who seemed knowledgeable about decorating, read articles in magazines about oriental rugs, and compared prices in newspaper ads. She noticed that the department store she had previously visited was having a one-third-off sale beginning the following Saturday. Janet and John decided to see what was on sale.

This case was prepared by Anne H. Laroche.

On Saturday morning, they went to the store and noticed that the rug department was very busy. This time, a young clerk offered some help and was able to answer most of their questions. Both he and John were able to lift the rugs, so that all of a rug could be seen for its effect. At one point, the clerk left for a minute and came back with the department manager, Mr. Barton. The manager was much more at ease discussing the advantages and prices of different types of rugs. After asking a few questions about their furnishings and decor, Mr. Barton asked them where they lived and realized that they were neighbours. He suggested that the simplest thing would be for him to bring a few rugs over to their house so that they could see what style and size of rug would do best.

On the following Monday evening, Mr. Barton arrived at their house with several rugs. Both Janet and John were impressed with Mr. Barton's advice on decorating. After trying out these rugs in different rooms, they found three rugs that they liked very much, two Bokharas and one Kirman. Mr. Barton suggested that they keep them for a few days to see how they liked "living" with them. He emphasized that they were under no obligation to buy any rug from him. If they decided not to buy any, they had only to call the store and a delivery truck would pick them up. He also indicated that they could pay in four instalments without interest.

After having the three rugs on the living-room and dining-room floors for two days, they decided that they liked them all and called Mr. Barton to announce that they were keeping all three. Looking at each other, they seemed surprised by their decision. They were also pleased that they had bought three rugs for the price of two.

## Questions

1. What needs were Janet and John attempting to satisfy in purchasing the rugs?
2. What and who influenced Janet and John in purchasing the rugs?
3. What were the major events that occurred in the buying process?
4. Evaluate the actions of the salespeople in the two retail stores. What were the advantages and disadvantages of their actions?

---

## 8.
## A Buying Experience

"I really enjoyed that last movie," Doug said to his wife Jean. Doug Bell and his family had just finished watching four movies on a weekend in mid-January, something they had done once a month or so for the past five years. Typically, they rented a VCR and 4 or 5 movies from Steve's TV, a local store, and had a "weekend binge" where the four family members (Doug, Jean, and the two children, Kathy, age 15, and Jason, age 11) each picked out a movie and spent much of the weekend watching the shows.

As they were returning the VCR and movies to Steve's TV, Doug mentioned to Jean that over the course of a year they probably did this eight or nine times, at a cost of $30 to $40.

© David Gillen and Gordon McDougall, School of Business and Economics, Wilfrid Laurier University, 1992.

He thought that maybe they should buy a VCR instead of renting one. "We'd probably pay for it in a couple of years. I've been watching the prices on VCRs in the paper and they've come down a lot in the past two years but the prices don't seem to be getting lower." Jean agreed and after returning home they mentioned the idea of buying a VCR to the children and both Kathy and Jason thought it was a great idea.

The Bells owned a colour TV set and had the basic cable service which provided 10 channels. They had not purchased any of the seven pay TV channels available, nor did they have the converter system which added eight more channels to the basic service. They had never discussed purchasing these extra services.

Doug, an associate professor in the Economics Department at the University of Waterloo, knew very little about VCRs. Many of his friends had VCRs and he knew they had paid as much as $900 for them two years earlier. Often when he was reading the daily newspaper he looked at ads for VCRs and observed that the prices had come down to around $500 for a basic unit but had not declined further. He thought that VCR prices probably wouldn't go much lower and, in fact, had noticed that new model VCRs had more features such as stereo. He felt that prices might start going up a bit because of these features.

Doug wanted to get some information on VCRs and the type of machine he'd probably buy before he visited any stores. On January 20th, Doug went to the university library and spent about an hour looking up all the articles he could find on VCRs. He photocopied two he thought were useful, went back to his office, and spent about an hour reading them. He noted the wide range of options available and the strengths and weaknesses of the various types of machines.

The next day Doug picked up a recent copy of *Consumer Reports* that had an extensive article on VCRs and listed the characteristics and strengths and weaknesses of over 40 machines. While reading the article Doug was amazed at the number of features available in VCRs. He also noted that the article emphasized that an important factor to consider in buying a VCR was that the instructions and programming were easy to follow and do. It struck Doug that as more features were added—the bells and whistles—it became increasing complex to use the recording features. He knew that he wanted to use a VCR for recording and he didn't want to get a machine where he'd have to spend hours learning how to programme it.

After reading the article, Doug felt comfortable with what he had learned. The article had pointed out the key questions a buyer should ask himself, explained the technical jargon, and described the features to get for a good basic VCR, including on-screen programming and one-touch recording. Doug examined the extensive list of models received and decided that Magnavox and Panasonic looked like good brands. These two brands were rated highly for both the high-priced, full-feature models and the low-priced basic units. As well, both brands had excellent repair records. Doug thought he'd like to buy a VCR that had multiple channels, more than two tracks to increase the clarity, and easy programming. He did not want any other features such as "stop action" because he wasn't going to be taping sports like football where that feature might be useful.

In early February, Doug felt he was ready to buy a VCR and one night he told his family what he had learned. They talked about what they'd use the VCR for and Doug suggested the kinds of features he thought were important, what was available, and what they shouldn't get. He pointed out that it would be nice to get stereo but it was difficult to get stereo on a VCR without having all the bells and whistles. Since stereo was a new feature, it was also the most expensive and they probably wouldn't get their money out of it. The family finally concluded that what they really needed was a VCR that was capable of getting multiple channels, provided clarity, was easy to record, and had a good repair record.

At work the next day, Doug was talking with one of his students who knew a lot about stereos and VCRs. Doug mentioned what he was looking for and asked him where he could pick up a good quality VCR with those features. The student said that he often dealt with Natural Sound and it was a good store. On his way home from work Doug went into Natural Sound, where he found only a few VCRs on display. He talked to the owner of the store who said that Natural Sound was getting out of the VCR business: "We can't compete with places like Steve's TV and Krazy Kelly." Doug decided that if Natural Sound wasn't going to service it, he wasn't going to buy it there and he left.

Doug had planned to go to Steve's TV but it was getting late and he went home for dinner. At dinner he mentioned he was going over to Steve's TV to buy the VCR and the family decided they'd all go. They drove over to Steve's TV and went to the aisle where the VCRs were located. The newer stereo VCRs were set up on the right side of the aisle and the basic VCRs were on the left side of the aisle. The movie *Back to the Future* was playing on the top-of-the-line stereo VCR. The four stereo models on display were all made by Panasonic and ranged in price from $750 to $1,100. Doug and his family were immediately attracted to the movie, which had a very catchy soundtrack, and stood watching it.

A salesman approached and asked if he could help them. Doug told him they were interested in buying a VCR. The salesman then went to the lowest priced stereo VCR ($750) and asked if they were familiar with all the features. Doug replied that he had talked to a number of people who had owned VCRs and had read a lot about them in *Consumer Reports*. Jean said that she knew very little. Doug said; "I'm interested in three features; easy programming, multiple channels, and a good repair record." The salesman replied: "This low price VCR has linear stereo and is not true hi-fidelity. Do you know the difference?" "No," replied Doug and Jean. "With linear stereo you can record and play back in stereo but the sound range is narrower than the true hi-fi." The salesman then moved to the next model, priced at $850. "This model has on-screen programming, an MTS decoder, and four heads for better picture clarity. It has on-screen programming which makes it easy to programme." He then moved to the next model which was priced at $1,000. "Now, this model has true hi-fi." Doug interjected that they were not interested because it was too much money. They then moved back to the two lower priced stereo models. The salesman compared the two models and explained that the higher priced one had a number of features which made it very compatible with the new stereo television sets that were coming onto the market. Jean said, "We don't watch much TV and we probably won't buy a stereo TV." Doug and Jean then said they did like some of the features on this mid-range model priced at $850.

At that point, Jean and the children began talking and thought that the difference between a basic $500 VCR and an $850 stereo VCR was probably going to be worth it because of the added features they would get in addition to stereo. Jean said, "You know, we're renovating the basement and we plan to move two stereo speakers down there and attach them to the television. Once we get the stereo speakers hooked up it wouldn't cost much more to get the stereo VCR."

Doug was a little unhappy with this turn of events. He had planned to spend $500. He didn't watch much television and felt that $850 was more than they should spend. He thought to himself that if they watched a lot of television and rented movies every week, then he might feel differently. Maybe, he thought, with a stereo unit we'll use it more. Doug then asked the salesman: "How easy is it to get these VCRs repaired?" The salesman replied, "We can do all the repairs here in the store."

After some discussion the Panasonic model they chose was the "one-up" from the lowest priced stereo VCR. They were impressed with the stereo sound and agreed it had the features they wanted. Doug then gave the salesman a credit card. The total price, including tax, came to $909. The salesman brought out a boxed VCR, Doug put it in the trunk, and five minutes later the VCR was home and downstairs. Doug and his son began to hook it up. They set up the VCR and immediately discovered that in order to hook up the stereo speakers you needed an amplifier. Unfortunately, their amplifier was located upstairs. This was something that Doug was not aware of and they stopped setting up the VCR. Doug decided to think about it a little bit more and find out what it cost to buy an amplifier. The whole family went to bed that night somewhat disappointed.

At work the next day he spent an hour phoning several stores asking about prices of amplifiers and found out he would have to spend at least $100 to $150 to get even a used amplifier. He then decided buying the stereo VCR was a mistake. He was going to go home and take the VCR back and get what he wanted to get in the first place, which was a basic VCR.

He went home and packed up the VCR, making sure he had all the materials in the box and that it was packed properly and protected. He took it upstairs and was about to leave when Jean and the children came up and asked him what he was doing. He told them that he felt they had made the wrong decision. "We're spending way too much money, we don't really need this, it's got too many features, and the whole cost is adding up much too quickly." They agreed and Doug said, "I'm going to take it back and get the VCR we went to buy in the first place."

On the way over to Steve's TV, Doug was a little hesitant. He had unpacked everything and wondered if he'd have any problems returning it. He was upset with himself in that he hadn't known how these stereo systems worked. "I should have known that," he thought.

He took the VCR into Steve's TV and found the salesman from whom he'd purchased it. The salesman asked what the problem was, Doug explained what had happened, and the salesman immediately said, "No, we don't have a policy about taking these machines back." Doug's heart sank at that point because he didn't want to end up spending another $150 for an amplifier. The salesman brought out the manager. Doug explained his problem to him and he immediately tried to sell him an amplifier. Doug knew at this point that he was not going to have his mind changed—he wanted to return the VCR.

The sales manager told Doug he was making the wrong decision and that Doug was getting a lot of new features and extra technology in this VCR. He pointed out that if he wanted to upgrade the system in a couple of years, the additional cost would be much higher than what Doug would pay now. Doug told him his family didn't watch that much television and didn't rent movies that often. Doug also said he didn't want all of this extra technology because he felt the cost was simply too high. "What I want is a basic VCR. I'm more than happy to purchase it here and I'm sorry to have caused this kind of problem." The manager said: "Fine, that's what we will do." The salesman took Doug over to the basic VCR models. There was a large selection of brands and models available. Doug remembered the reason why he had agreed to buy the stereo Panasonic was that Panasonic was rated very well in *Consumer Reports*. He knew Panasonic was a good name and said that he was interested in the Panasonic basic VCR. The salesman showed him two different Panasonic models, and Doug took the lower priced one without any bells and whistles on it but with the features he wanted, including easy programming.

Doug gave the salesman his credit card, the purchase was wrung through, and Doug got a credit receipt for $350, the difference between his original purchase ($909) and the basic VCR ($559). Doug felt good because now he was getting the product he wanted in the first place. He was also pleased with the way in which the store had handled the matter. He didn't feel that there had been any upmanship on his part. He was going home with what he wanted but it had simply taken him a long time to get there. On the way home, Doug thought the salesman had been very kind. After the transaction had been completed he had given Doug two free VCR movie tickets. When he got home, Doug and his son immediately took the VCR downstairs and hooked it up. Jean and Kathy decided that it would be nice to have popcorn and watch their first movie on the new VCR. They took one of the tickets, went over to Steve's TV, got a movie, brought it home, and had a very enjoyable night. They commented on the terrific sound, how easy it was to programme and how much they enjoyed it.

About a month later Doug and Jean were talking about the VCR. Doug said: "I'm happy with it. The best thing is, we can rent movies when we want—and we're not paying for the VCR." Jean replied: "I agree, but I wonder how we would feel if we had the first VCR we bought?" Doug laughed and said: "That's a good question—I'm glad I don't have to think about that."

## Questions

1. What needs was Doug attempting to satisfy in purchasing a VCR?
2. Evaluate the salesperson's performance at Steve's TV.
3. Evaluate the sales manager's performance at Steve's TV.
4. What implications does Doug and his family's behaviour have for retailers of VCRs?

---

# 9.
# York Furniture Company

Mrs. Carol King has been operating the York Furniture Company for 10 years and has slowly built sales to $900,000 a year. Her store is located in the downtown shopping area of a city with a population of 150,000. It is basically a factory town, and she has deliberately selected blue-collar workers as her target market. She carries some higher-priced furniture lines but places great emphasis on budget combinations and easy credit terms.

Mrs. King is concerned because she feels the store may have reached the limit of sales growth—sales have not been increasing during the last two years. Her newspaper advertising seems to attract her target customers, but many of these people come in, look around, and then leave. Some of them come back, but most do not. She feels her product selections are very suitable for her target market, and she is concerned that her salespeople do not close more sales with potential customers. She has discussed this matter several times with her salespeople. They say they feel they ought to treat all customers alike—the way they personally want to be treated. They feel their role is just to answer questions when asked—not to make suggestions or help customers arrive at their selections. They feel this would be too much of a "hard sell."

This case was prepared by E. Jerome McCarthy, Michigan State University.

Mrs. King argues that this behaviour is interpreted as indifference by the customers who are attracted to the store by her advertising. She feels that customers must be treated on an individual basis—and that some customers need more encouragement and suggestions than others. Moreover, she feels that some customers would actually appreciate more help and suggestions than the salespeople themselves might. To support her views, she showed her salespeople the data from a study about furniture store customers (Tables 1 and 2). She tried to explain to them about the differences in demographic groups and pointed out that her store was definitely trying to aim at specific groups. She argued that they (the salespeople) should cater to the needs and attitudes of their customers—and think less about how they would like to be treated themselves. Further, she suggested that she may have to consider changing the sales compensation plan if they don't ''do a better job.'' Now they are paid a salary of $13,000 to $20,000 per year (depending on years of service) plus a 1 percent commission on sales.

## TABLE 1

| In Shopping for Furniture I Found (Find) That | Demographic Groups | | | | Marital Status | |
| | Group A | Group B | Group C | Group D | Newlyweds | Married 3–10 years |
| --- | --- | --- | --- | --- | --- | --- |
| I looked at furniture in many stores before I made a purchase | 78% | 57% | 52% | 50% | 66% | 71% |
| I went (am going) to only one store and bought (buy) what I found (find) there | 2 | 9 | 10 | 11 | 9 | 12 |
| To make my purchase I went (am going) back to one of the stores I shopped in previously | 48 | 45 | 39 | 34 | 51 | 49 |
| I looked (am looking) at furniture in no more than three stores and made (will make) my purchase in one of these | 20 | 25 | 24 | 45 | 37 | 30 |
| No answer | 10 | 18 | 27 | 27 | 6 | 4 |

## TABLE 2  The Sample Design

*Demographic Status*

**Upper Class—Group A (13% of Sample)**
Managers, proprietors, or executives of large businesses. Professionals, including doctors, lawyers, engineers, college professors and school administrators, and research personnel. Sales personnel, including managers, executives, and upper-income salespeople above level of clerks.
Family income over $50,000.

------

**TABLE 2** *Continued*

------

*Demographic Status*

------

**Middle Class—Group B (37% of Sample)**
White-collar workers, including clerical, secretarial, sales clerks, bookkeepers, etc. Also includes
  school teachers, social workers, semiprofessionals, proprietors or managers of small businesses,
  industrial foremen, and other supervisory personnel.
Family income between $25,000 and $50,000.

  **Lower Middle Class—Group C (36% of Sample)**
Skilled workers and semiskilled technicians, along with custodians, elevator operators, telephone
  linemen, factory operatives, construction workers, and some domestic and personal service
  employees.
Family income between $15,000 and $40,000.
No one in this group had above a high school education.

**Lower Class—Group D (14% of Sample)**
Nonskilled employees and day labourers. Also includes some factory operatives, domestic and
  servicepeople.
Family income under $18,000.
None had completed high school; some had only a grade school education.

------

## Questions

1. What recommendations would you make to Mrs. King?
2. Justify your recommendations.

------

## 10.
## THE PERFECT PACE

Early in March 1987, Patricia Cameron, 25, sat at her parents' kitchen table reviewing the
hectic schedule of the previous two months and began to map out what likely would be an
even busier schedule for the two months ahead. At the start of the year, she had returned to
her hometown, Antigonish (pronounced Auntie-gun-ish), Nova Scotia, to open a fitness club
for women. Since her return, Patricia had created a name for the club; found a suitable
location; contacted several equipment suppliers, local contractors, and office furnishings
dealers to obtain estimates or quotations; studied the Antigonish market; met with insurance
agents, media reps, bankers, and government officials; and had tentatively lined up two
experienced instructors. In the weeks ahead, Ms. Cameron knew that she would have to
supervise and finalize all of these arrangements as well as develop in some detail a tentative
programme of activities for members, price and sell memberships, and effectively promote
the opening. The target date for the opening of the club was May 1.

This case was prepared by Ian Spencer and Shauna White, Saint Francis Xavier University.

Ms. Cameron had chosen Antigonish not only because it was her hometown but also because Antigonish had no fitness club to serve the needs of women. From her experience as the assistant manager of a fitness club in Truro, Nova Scotia, and having taught fitness and aerobics classes at the Halifax YWCA and Mount Saint Vincent University during the previous four years, she believed that The Perfect Pace could achieve a membership base of 400 by the end of the first year. As she sat at the table, Ms. Cameron realized that the long-standing dream of owning her own business soon would come true. She was excited, enthusiastic, and determined to succeed.

## The Fitness Craze

In the mid 1970s, Participaction generated widespread awareness of a massive Canadian fitness problem. The average 60-year-old Swede, Participaction had discovered, was fitter than the average 30-year-old Canadian. Widespread awareness soon led to widespread guilt that, in turn, led to widespread action. In the early to mid-1980s, hundreds of thousands of Canadians made a commitment to better physical health. Some did it on their own and some through company or recreation department–sponsored programmes. Others did it through television (The 20 Minute Workout) or books (Jane Fonda's or Christine Brinkley's plans) or joined private fitness centres.

By 1986, all Canadian cities and most larger Canadian towns had one or more fitness centres that offered members workout gymnasiums, exercise mats and equipment, weight equipment for body building and muscle toning programmes, a variety of fitness and aerobics classes, fitness assessments, diet planning, saunas, showers, and locker facilities. Some centres even had squash and racquetball courts, colour and beauty consultations, tanning beds, and child-minding services.

## The Antigonish Market

Although the population of the Town of Antigonish was only 5,290, the Antigonish trading area contained an estimated 35,000 people. Most families from Antigonish County (population 18,775) and Guysborough County (population 12,720) shopped in the Town of Antigonish with some regularity. As well, a minority of families from Richmond, Victoria, and Inverness Counties to the east and Pictou County to the west shopped in Antigonish. Antigonish County occupies the northeast corner of mainland Nova Scotia and is about 250 kilometres west of Sydney and 250 kilometres northeast of Halifax. Antigonish Town is the home of Saint Francis Xavier University, which generates an annual influx of 2,300 students each September to April. The Antigonish Town Office had provided Ms. Cameron with age, gender, and labour force profiles for Antigonish County (Exhibit 1).

Ms. Cameron had not conducted any formal marketing research but, from informally listening to her peers and some of her mother's friends, she sensed a strong interest in the idea of a women's fitness club. Patricia felt that they were tired of doing nothing, that many had been bored for too long, and that her club would be an ideal outlet for them.

As a further indication of interest, Ms. Cameron discovered that Linda Steeghs, one of the two qualified instructors she had approached about working for her, had offered fitness classes for women with great success during 1984 and 1985 through a franchise called Dance Fit. Linda had been unable to continue these classes after 1985 because the large and very inexpensive space that she had rented became unavailable when the building was sold and later torn down.

## Exhibit 1

*Population and labour force statistics for Antigonish County*

| Age Group | Male | Female | Total |
|-----------|------|--------|-------|
| 0–14      | 2,615 | 2,465 | 5,080 |
| 15–24     | 1,725 | 1,705 | 3,430 |
| 25–34     | 1,375 | 1,405 | 2,780 |
| 35–44     | 1,255 | 1,240 | 2,495 |
| 45–64     | 1,385 | 1,450 | 2,835 |
| 65+       | 920   | 1,220 | 2,140 |
| Total     | 9,275 | 9,485 | 18,760 |
| **Labour Force** | | | |
| Population 15+     | 6,610 | 6,940 | 13,550 |
| Labour force       | 4,810 | 3,545 | 8,355 |
| Participation rate | 73%   | 51%   | 62% |
| Employed           | 4,145 | 2,935 | 7,080 |

SOURCE: Statistics Canada, 1986 Census. Reproduced with the permission of the Minister of Supply and Services Canada, 1992.

Ms. Cameron also discovered that the university posed limited competition on two fronts. First, some physical education students had offered aerobics classes for a nominal fee to their fellow students. Second, the university offered public memberships in a Fitness and Recreation Association. Ms. Cameron was not too concerned about this competition. The aerobics classes were taught by students just trying their hand at it, not by qualified personnel. The Fitness and Recreation Association offered no fitness classes and tended to be a do-it-yourself facility. Its main attraction for families was access to the only indoor swimming pool in the area. It also offered a weight room, squash, racquetball, handball, and tennis courts, and access to the university gymnasium. The only overlapping activities with The Perfect Pace Ms. Cameron could see were the weight room, the sauna, and showers. A family membership in the Association cost $195 and a single adult membership, $160. To Ms. Cameron's knowledge, there were no other fitness organizations in Antigonish, but the ever-present risk that someone else might be planning to start one heightened the urgency to get The Perfect Pace open as soon as possible.

## The Hectic January and February Pace

Ms. Cameron's first two actions in January were to see the family's bank manager and to decide on a name. The bank manager indicated that with favourable revenue and profit projections he could probably lend her up to 100 percent of the value of her equipment, repayable over five years, if the equipment were pledged as security. She would have to raise the balance of the initial investment privately but believed that with favourable projections, this would be possible.

The club needed an appropriate name—one that was somewhat feminine, connoted fitness, and suggested a club without also suggesting exclusiveness or snobbishness. After much deliberation and some consultation with family members, she chose the name The Perfect Pace.

A few days later, Ms. Cameron heard about some space available above a dry cleaning business just off Main Street at the east end of town. Substantial renovations and improvements would be required, and available parking on the short side street would not always be easy for members to find. However, the room was large enough, had windows on three sides, a fairly high ceiling, a solid floor, and a rent of only $650 per month plus utilities. Near the end of January, Ms. Cameron signed a one-year lease with an option to renew for two years at a rent to be determined. Her sketch for utilizing the space is reproduced in Exhibit 2.

Ms. Cameron solicited cost estimates from several equipment suppliers, two general contractors, several tradesmen, and two office furnishings dealers. By early March, the file folder of estimates was both thick and virtually complete. It appeared that renovations and improvements—all wiring, plumbing, heating, insulation, carpentry, tiling, drywalling, and painting—would cost about $16,000. The fitness equipment, including mats, bikes, benches, rowing machines, a central weight machine, a quality tape deck, and assorted hoops and balls, would come to about $15,000. The office furniture and furnishings, including carpeting, chairs, a table, a stool, locker room benches, a reception counter, planters, and pictures, would come to $6,000.

With a little assistance from a friend, Ms. Cameron estimated that monthly operating expenses, aside from rent and interest on the loan, would be about $3,500. This figure included salaries and benefits, utilities, telephone, office supplies, maintenance supplies, instructional supplies, insurance, property taxes, and advertising. In developing the expense estimates, she had assumed that The Perfect Pace would be open approximately 70 hours each week from Monday to Saturday. As the membership wished or needed, this assumption could change. The instructors would be paid on an hourly basis at a higher rate for teaching

**EXHIBIT 2**

*Sketch of the layout*

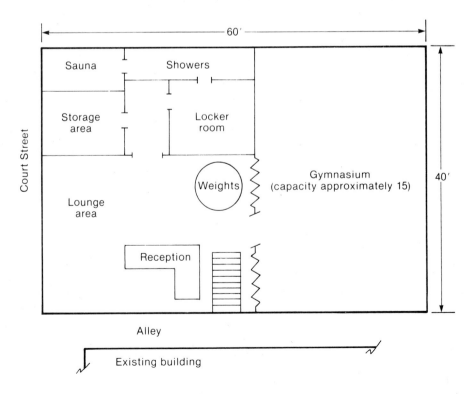

a class and at a lower one for working at the reception desk. Ms. Cameron planned to act as both manager and instructor and expected to work 60–70 hours per week for the first year, if necessary.

Ms. Cameron also had a file folder on the programme of activities to be offered, which contained a summary of the Truro club's facilities and services and some of her own programming notions. The Truro club (her former employer) charged a membership fee of $325 per year. The membership bought unlimited access to all facilities and classes. The facilities available to members were a series of exercise machines, called the Nautilus System, on which an individual programme of body building and muscle toning could be developed, six stationary bikes, free weights, a sauna, two tanning beds, showers, a change area with hair dryers, and a lounge area with a television and a videocassette recorder. The two classes offered were introductory and advanced aerobics. Each class, including change, warm-up, cool-down, and class time, ran about an hour. Some days, there were only a few classes, while other days, the exercise gym was booked solid. Ms. Cameron recalled that the average was about five classes per day. The Truro fitness club was open Monday to Thursday from 7 A.M. to 10 P.M., Friday from 7 A.M. to 9 P.M., Saturday from 9 A.M. to 5 P.M., and Sunday from 11 A.M. to 6 P.M.

Ms. Cameron planned to offer aerobics classes at the beginner, intermediate, and advanced levels, weight toning and body-building programmes, and fitness assessments. In time, if demand seemed to warrant it, The Perfect Pace would add a child-minding service for mothers. She wanted The Perfect Pace to be known for quality instruction and service. Each member would be assured careful attention and guidance as she advanced in the programme. She also wanted to ensure that members who were inexperienced did not injure themselves, become discouraged, or lose interest. She was highly committed to the proper education of every member.

## The Hectic Pace Ahead

Ms. Cameron believed that 90 percent of the members of The Perfect Pace would be women from Antigonish County, including some of the students at the university. She felt that few women from the adjacent counties would travel the 50 to 100 kilometres to take advantage of her fitness classes and facilities. Hence, to create awareness and sign up members, she planned initially to focus on the town, the county within about 30 kilometres of town, and the university campus.

The price of a Perfect Pace membership would be a critical decision. Ms. Cameron felt that the Truro club's fee might be a little too high, while the university Fitness and Recreation Association's fee might be a little too low. She had thought about offering introductory memberships for three or six months in addition to the regular full-year memberships, but she was unsure whether they would lead to a larger membership base. She had also thought about a user pay plan whereby someone could pay by the hour or by the activity, but she wondered what the regular members might think of sharing the facility with casual users. Finally, she believed that she should offer an eight-month student membership but had not determined what this might be.

Decisions on advertising and promotion also would be critical to the success of The Perfect Pace. From her discussions with the media reps, Ms. Cameron had learned that the local newspaper had a weekly circulation of 8,500, with most copies sold in Antigonish County. A very small ad one-column wide and 1-inch high would cost $4, a one-eighth-page ad would cost $60, and a one-quarter-page ad, $120. The local radio station had a total six-county reach of over 70,000 different people each week. On average, the number of listeners during a quarter-hour time period between 6 A.M. and midnight was about 8,000.

The radio station would charge $15 for each 30-second commercial. Advertising in the campus newspaper would cost about half as much as the local newspaper, while advertising on the campus radio station would cost about a quarter as much as the local radio station. Flyers could be printed and distributed for as little as $.10 each for a one-colour, one-side-only, 8½ × 11-inch page. Larger, four-colour flyers printed on both sides could cost as much as $2 to $3 or more. To date, Ms. Cameron had not done any detailed planning for advertising, special promotions, or publicity. In the operating expense budget, she had tentatively estimated advertising at $1,000 for the first year.

As she began to mull over issues such as pricing memberships and advertising for the opening, Ms. Cameron became a bit concerned. She certainly had not lost her enthusiasm nor her determination to succeed. However, the importance of these factors in motivating women to join The Perfect Pace, coupled with the uncertainty of making the right decisions, really made her wish she had someone else she could turn to for help.

### Questions

1. What are the uncertainties facing Ms. Cameron as she considers opening her fitness salon? Does she have any information that will help her address the uncertainties? What additional information might be helpful?

2. What is the concept of The Perfect Pace? What competitive reaction might occur after its opening?

3. What are the possible marketing strategies for The Perfect Pace? Design a marketing mix for the opening of The Perfect Pace in terms of the prices, facilities, classes to offer, hours of operation, and promotion.

4. How likely is Ms. Cameron to reach her goal of 400 members by the end of the first year of operation?

---

## 11.
## DIEGO'S

Dr. Albert Collins, a Montreal physician, faced a difficult decision as to whether or not to invest in a new fast food franchise concept specializing in Mexican food. Dr. Collins had made several good business investments and while he thought this was a great opportunity, he recognized that there was a chance it wouldn't succeed. He decided to discuss the concept with his friend Jack Timlin, a marketing consultant, who had advised him on a number of earlier ventures. Dr. Collins arranged a meeting and presented the following information to Mr. Timlin.

### The Concept

About six months ago, Dr. Collins had read an article in a major U.S. magazine about a relatively new but already successful fast food franchisor based in Phoenix, Arizona. In operation for less than 5 years, this franchisor had opened in 55 locations (some franchised, some corporately owned) in Arizona and several other southwestern states and had sold (to one firm) the franchise rights for 80 locations in Florida and had sold many other, soon to be built, franchises in the midwestern states.

Although Mexican food is very popular in the southern United States, this firm in all of its advertising and store signs always uses the phrase ''We serve marinated charbroiled chicken and Mexican food'' to indicate that it offers a choice of items so that people who don't like Mexican food can also patronize the chain.

On the door of each location is a sticker stating that this restaurant is approved by the American Heart Association as a healthy place to eat away from home. Dr. Collins believed that this endorsement was obtained because of the manner in which the chicken is prepared. First it is marinated in a secret recipe of natural fruit juices and herbs and then it is charbroiled so that the fat drips out of the meat. Chicken prepared this way is lower in cholesterol than fried chicken and is juicier than barbecued (B.B.Q.) chicken. To further enhance its healthy image the chain does not serve french fries but does offer baked potatoes and an assortment of salads.

A quote from the article provided a very strong endorsement from at least one customer: ''I do not have a great deal of experience in eating Mexican food, but the dishes were different than what I expected. The chicken was tender and juicy and had a subtle flavour—for my taste it was better than B.B.Q. chicken. The other dishes were very tasty and definitely not spicy. If this is what Mexican food is like, I am a convert.''

Dr. Collins investigated further and found out that the recipes could not be protected by patent or copyright. In fact, he learned that the Arizona chain found out how a California chain of chicken restaurants marinated their chicken and then they used the recipe themselves. Dr. Collins then purchased some of the American marinated chicken, had it analyzed by a laboratory, and then had a food technologist develop and test the formula and the correct procedures to cook the chicken.

He gathered a group of investors (primarily friends and acquaintances) who liked the concept and were willing to put up most of the money required to open up one or two locations to show that the concept would be successful in Canada. The plan was to sell franchises across the country.

For each location, franchisees would be charged an initial fee plus an ongoing 5 percent royalty on the gross sales of the franchises. In return for these fees the franchisee would have the right to use the trade name, which the investors decided would be Diego's. The franchisee's staff would be trained to prepare the food as per set procedures and the franchisee would purchase the chicken marinade from the franchisor. The franchisee would be assisted in site selection, construction of the restaurant, and the purchasing of the required equipment and would receive ongoing managerial assistance. In addition, the franchisee would benefit from a co-op advertising programme to be funded by a charge of 4 percent of gross sales levied on each location—franchised or corporately owned.

## Preliminary Research

Dr. Collins met with the investment group several times and although nothing was formalized, a considerable amount of preliminary research had been conducted. A location was found for the first Diego's restaurant in a relatively new suburban residential area where most of the homes have been built in the last 10 years. New homes were still being built in the area and there was enough vacant land to more than double the population of the area. Most of the homes sold for $150,000 to $225,000 (compared to the current Montreal average price of $89,500 per home). Census data suggested that the typical home owner in this area was raising a young family and had a managerial job or was a professional with a practice that had not yet developed fully.

Studies have shown that most people will travel about 2.5 to 3.5 km (5 minutes) to go to a fast food restaurant. Since Diego's would be very distinctive, the first few locations probably would draw customers from a slightly larger trading area. Information was obtained from recent census data for the census tracts that would likely constitute the trading area (Table 1).

## Investor Group Meeting

After the information was collected, the investors held a meeting where a lively debate took place about the proposed image of Diego's, the target markets, and other matters.

The investment group couldn't agree what image Diego's should have and what types of customers they should concentrate on satisfying. Some of the members wanted to concentrate the efforts on attracting and satisfying families with young children (e.g., offering free magic shows on selected evenings and on weekends, offering children free balloons, and perhaps offering a special children's menu of items that would appeal to children).

One member argued that this market segment appeared to be important. A recent newspaper article reported the results of an American study that, in 85 percent of the cases when parents go out to eat with their young children, the children make the final decision on which restaurant the family will go to.

Some of the group argued that children are known as very finicky eaters and maybe they wouldn't like Diego's food. They suggested that Diego's should go after the teenage market or possibly Diego's should concentrate on the adult fast food market.

One member of the investment group had conducted an analysis of the competition in the trading area (Table 2). He noted that at least two competitors in the trading area, McDonald's and Chi Chi's, had special strategies for attracting children. Another group member provided some data prepared by Statistics Canada that dealt with food purchased from restaurants (Table 3).

## TABLE 1    Trading Area Demographic Data

| | |
|---|---|
| Total population | 114,858 |
| Private households | 38,500 |
| Total families: | 31,535 |
|   With 1 child at home | 6,355 |
|   With 2 children at home | 8,980 |
|   With 3 children at home | 3,950 |
|   No children at home | 12,250 |
| Ages of children: | |
|   0 to 4 years | 8,860 |
|   5 to 9 years | 9,035 |
|   10 to 14 years | 8,425 |
|   15 to 19 years | 8,975 |

SOURCE: Statistics Canada, 1992. Reproduced with the permission of the Minister of Supply and Services Canada, 1992.

## TABLE 2    The Competition

The competition is located in the Dollard/Pointe Claire area (Montreal suburbs located about 30 minutes by car from downtown Montreal).

On the 2 km stretch of St. John's Road North from the TransCanada Highway to the proposed location of Diego's, there are 10 restaurants, including:

| | |
|---|---|
| McDonald's | It is estimated that an average McDonald's has sales of between $2 million and $2.5 million per year. McDonald's places special emphasis on children and some locations have playgrounds. |
| Chenoy's | A deli which has been at this location for at least 15 years. |
| Chi Chi's | A restaurant which features Americanized Mexican food. Runs special promotions to attract children, e.g., Shirley Temples (a nonalcoholic cocktail) and a special children's menu. It is estimated that Chi Chi's total sales volume is good but it is thought that more than 50 percent of its revenue comes from its bar. |
| Le Vieux Duluth | A Greek restaurant featuring popular priced meals in the $8 to $12 range. Most Saturday evenings there is a line-up to get into this restaurant. |
| Nan Wah Restaurant | Located in the small shopping centre across the street from the proposed Diego's location. It has been there for several years. Monday to Friday they offer a nice lunch buffet for $4.95 plus tax. While eating there a few times, we observed the lunch trade arrive just after 12:00 noon and a second small group arrive just after 1:00 P.M. On the days that we were there, it appeared that their lunch volume was between 30 and 50 patrons per day. (Many businesses located on the TransCanada Highway are outside the 5 minute trading area.) |

Along the 2 km stretch further north from the proposed Diego's location to the end of St. John's Road, there are 6 additional restaurants including a St. Hubert B.B.Q. St Hubert's offers sit down at the table service and take out. A quarter chicken (dark meat), french fries, sauce and bun costs $5.95 plus tax and tip. It is estimated that an average St. Hubert B.B.Q. has sales in the $1 million per year range.

Sources Boulevard, about 1.5 km away from St. John's, is the next major artery that runs parallel to St. John's. On Sources there are many other restaurants including a Swiss Chalet B.B.Q., which has been at its location for at least 20 years and is considered to be a very successful operation. This restaurant is part of a chain that frequently uses coupons to offer very good value meals—e.g., 1/4 chicken (dark meat), french fries, a bun, sauce and a soft drink for $3.75 plus tax and tip. Swiss Chalet features sit down at the table service and take out.

Next to the Swiss Chalet on Sources Blvd. is one of the few Wendy's locations in Quebec that is currently profitable.

NOTE: Please remember that all this information is based on general discussions with various people and extrapolations of available facts. There is no assurance that any of the estimated sales figures are accurate.

One of the members of the investor group was a practising accountant. He estimated that if the average bill at a restaurant was $3.75 (excluding tax) and the actual cost of the food and the packaging was 30 percent of the selling price, the restaurant would need to serve 225,000 meals a year to break even.

Information on traffic flows was also collected. One Thursday, Dr. Collins went to the proposed site and between 12:00 noon and 1:00 P.M. counted 2,000 cars moving in the four directions at the intersection. Between 5:00 P.M. and 6:30 P.M. the street heading north in front

---

### Table 3    Weekly Food Purchases from Restaurants per Family

Canada, 1990

|              | Food Purchases | Income before Taxes |
| ------------ | -------------- | ------------------- |
| Average      | $27.28         | $45,708             |
| 1st quintile | 12.63          | 11,808              |
| 2nd quintile | 22.39          | 25,333              |
| 3rd quintile | 32.11          | 39,453              |
| 4th quintile | 45.39          | 55,813              |
| 5th quintile | 63.51          | 96,133              |

NOTE: The average weekly food purchases from restaurants in the Montreal Metropolitan Area were $33.83.

SOURCE: *Family Food Expenditures in Canada—17 Metropolitan Areas,* Statistics Canada, 1992, Catalog 62-554. Reproduced with the permission of the Minister of Supply and Services Canada, 1992.

of the site became a "parking lot" as people headed home. He felt that this was a positive sign in that people could stop on the same side of the street as they were already travelling (and not have to cut across traffic), pick up food for supper, and then continue home.

Related to the decision as to which target market(s) to appeal to, some members wondered if people would be confused if the restaurant was simultaneously promoted as a chicken restaurant and as a Mexican food restaurant. That is, would potential customers perceive the chicken as a Mexican dish or would they consider the chicken to be a suitable alternative to B.B.Q. chicken or fried chicken?

Various members then raised the following questions and issues:

- Will consumers recognize the fact that Diego's is really two different restaurants in one and even if a person does not like Mexican food (or is afraid to try it) he or she can order a very tasty chicken or will some stay away because they view Diego's as a Mexican restaurant? Perhaps Diego's is too strong a Mexican name for what we would like to achieve?

- Both images should be positive. Diego's proposed first location is not far from Chi Chi's which exposed the consumer to and expanded the market for Mexican food. According to comparisons made by some of the group members, our Mexican dishes taste better and will cost less than the same items at Chi Chi's.

- On the other hand, for many years chicken has been more popular in Quebec than in other parts of the country. It may be due to cultural differences or may be the result of the success of the St. Hubert B.B.Q. chain which started in Quebec (Table 4).

- In addition, over the last three or four years the consumption of chicken across Canada has increased significantly as people switched away from red meats which are higher in cholesterol than chicken. This ties in very nicely with the emphasis that the American chain firmly places on the health aspect of its chicken meals.

Some members debated whether legally they could use an approach similar to the one Americans use and were not convinced that the "healthy" image will be a unique selling proposition that will cause people to pick our restaurant over the competition. They argued

---

## TABLE 4   Per Capita Regional Differences in Food Consumption

National average = 100 percent

|                    | *Chicken* | *Italian* | *Chinese* | *Greek* |
|--------------------|-----------|-----------|-----------|---------|
| National           | 100%      | 100%      | 100%      | 100%    |
| Quebec             | 125       | 120       | 145       | 130     |
| Ontario            | 90        | 75        | 85        | 80      |
| Prairies           | 90        | 165       | 35        | 25      |
| B.C.               | 90        | 120       | 100       | 85      |
| Atlantic provinces | 175       | 80        | 55        | 45      |

---

that the Canadian laws concerning food advertising were different and more restrictive than the U.S. laws. In Canada the advertising of the cholesterol content of food (with the exception of vegetable oils such as Mazola) is prohibited. In addition, it appears that, even if it wanted to, the Canadian Heart Association would be unable, given the present legal environment, to endorse the restaurant. As well, they argued that many Quebecers are not especially health conscious when it comes to food.

One member had obtained a copy of a research study conducted in Montreal about bakery products. This study concluded that French speaking respondents were less concerned with food additives than the English speaking segment of the population. It was also found that older people were less concerned with this issue than the younger generation. Quebecers consumed large amounts of especially greasy french fries and poutine (french fries, sauce, and melted cheese). In other parts of Canada the preference was for crispier, less oily french fries.

Some research conducted in the Montreal area by one of the members indicated that more than half of the respondents want french fries with their B.B.Q. chicken. Consumers like and expect the combination and that is what the chicken restaurants offer with their meals.

In spite of this information other members would like to follow the lead of the American firm and not serve french fries but instead offer a choice of baked potatoes or Mexican rice.

One member pointed out that Quebecers love fine food and are receptive to ethnic foods. However, for some reason Mexican food has not caught on in Quebec. Taco Bell, a large U.S. Mexican fast food chain which has opened in Ontario does not, at this time, have any Quebec locations. In Montreal proper, several small Mexican restaurants have opened. None of them appears to be especially successful.

In addition, one member visited about a dozen supermarkets (some in the area of the proposed location, others in various parts of Montreal and other suburbs). Each store has a small section of packaged Mexican foods. The managers of these stores described the sales of Mexican foods as "slow but steady."

Because there was a lot of money at stake, the investors paid for some basic research. They conducted focus groups in a restaurant setting similar to what was being considered and the respondents had the chance to taste the food. (Table 5 provides a summary of the comments.) The results of the research were interesting in that in two cases the findings went against what the investors thought the consumer might want or accept.

First, it was planned to prepare the food out in the front of the restaurant where it could be seen by people inside and outside. This was intended to show that Diego's had nothing to hide and that the food was prepared under hygienic conditions. In addition, it was hoped that seeing the golden brown chicken on the grill and the aroma of cooking chicken would

## TABLE 5    Focus Groups Comments

**Positive Comments**

The food is delicious.

Great food.

I never tasted Mexican food before, it is really good and not at all spicy.

I am happy that you don't serve french fries. My seven-year old son just ate nutritious food, not the junk food that he prefers.

I enjoyed the food. The chicken was moist but not greasy.

I liked it. I would come back again.

I hope it opens soon. I am bored and fed up with the traditional fast foods.

**Negative comments**

The chicken looks yellow. What's wrong with it? Is it cheaper quality chicken?

I don't think French Canadians are ready to eat B.B.Q. chicken on paper plates using plastic cutlery.

I don't want to see the chicken being cooked. I don't want to know that it was once a living thing.

The chickens were brought to the grill in a pail. Do they use the same pail to wash the floors?

For me B.B.Q. chicken and french fries go together. Something is missing and the meal is not enjoyable without french fries.

encourage people to order. According to the focus groups some people viewed this as a strong negative.

Secondly, while travelling through New England, Dr. Collins came across a very successful chain of seafood restaurants which, in order to keep prices low, serves on paper plates and provides plastic cutlery. This makes sense because Harvey's and other fast food chains also use disposables. Again, based on the results of the focus groups, there seems to be resistance in Montreal to eating chicken in this way.

Another research finding was of special interest and required more study. When respondents were offered a choice between traditional B.B.Q. sauce and salsa, a Mexican sauce, the vast majority opted for the B.B.Q. sauce. Was it because it was something unknown? Was it the fear of something spicy? Or, perhaps it was just a habit.

## The Decision

Dr. Collins concluded the presentation to Mr. Timlin with the following comments: "As you can see there is a lot of information to consider. In fact, I am confused as to what I should do. I know that the concept is successful in Arizona but I have also obtained a great deal of information, some of which is not positive, about duplicating this concept in Canada and particularly in Quebec.

"I don't know if I should invest in this project or not. If it succeeds, it will be the chance of a lifetime to make a lot of money. Should I go into it, or not? What, if anything, can be done to improve the concept so that the risk of failure will be reduced?"

## Questions

1. What would you recommend that Dr. Collins do?

2. Justify your recommendation.

## 12.

## THE UNDERCOVER AGENCY

In July of 1989, Bill Jones and Ruth McDonald had one of their many meetings to discuss a business venture. Over the past two years, Bill and Ruth had identified, studied, and finally rejected a variety of potential enterprises. At last they believed they had come across an idea that would be successful: a woman's intimate apparel store.

"Listen Bill, we have conducted the market research and calculated the financial analysis. I believe this idea is sound and will make money. After all, your financial projections show we will meet our objective of showing a profit by the second year. I say we should go for it."

But Bill raised several objections. "I realize the financial projections and industry analysis do look good. But what if this trend toward intimate apparel is just a fad? Also, the rent for the store location is very high. Perhaps it would be better to find a different location. I think we should review our analysis and see if it is really as good an opportunity as we think."

Ruth agreed to further review the information; however, she reminded Bill that this was Friday night and that a decision would have to be made by Monday since the mall manager would not hold the lease option open any longer than that.

### Background

Bill and Ruth felt that together they formed a good business partnership, since they both held business degrees and their areas of interest complemented each other. For the past five years, Bill had been employed as a chartered accountant with a firm in St. Catharines, Ontario. He was able to contribute a strong financial background to the partnership. Ruth had a good knowledge of the retailing industry. After rapid advancement over the last five years, she had recently been promoted to assistant buyer with a major department store chain.

Because of their business knowledge, both partners had actively participated in conducting the feasibility study for the lingerie store. Each was also willing to contribute $25,000 to the venture. Any further financing requirements would have to be met by borrowing from a bank. Neither Bill nor Ruth had actually owned or operated a business. However, given the nature of the product and Ruth's merchandising experience, both partners felt she would be able to manage the store, and that Bill would provide part-time assistance, primarily on the accounting side of the venture.

### The Idea

Bill and Ruth first became interested in opening an intimate apparel specialty store they would call The Undercover Agency after Ruth read an article in *Marketing* about *Linrich,* a new fashion magazine catering specifically to women's intimate apparel. The article stressed that consumer interest in intimate apparel was growing in Canada. They began to formalize plans for The Undercover Agency after conducting some initial investigations, as well as seriously discussing the proposal.

The product assortment they were considering would consist of bras, panties, camisoles, teddies, slips, nightwear, and matching sets. These items would be highly fashionable and would be offered in a variety of colours and sizes. Bill was uncertain whether he wanted the

This case was prepared by Scott Edgett, McMaster University, with the assistance of Louise Gauthier.

store to carry basic products, which included mainly packaged bras; however, Ruth felt these items were a necessity. Suppliers would be mainly Canadian: Canadelle (Wonderbra), Warner's and Vogue for intimate apparel products, as well as Kayser, Papillon Blanc, and French Maid nightwear. These suppliers offered high-quality, high-fashion products, ranging in price from medium to high. Bill estimated these prices would allow for gross margins in the range of 30 to 50 percent.

An ideal location for the store had become available in the Pen Centre, a regional shopping mall located in St. Catharines, Ontario. At the time Bill and Ruth were considering their business venture, the Pen Centre was the only large shopping centre in Ontario's Niagara region. The traffic flow through the mall averaged 129,000 people per week; however, this figure was expected to increase after completion of a major addition to the mall.

The potential store location measured 100 square metres. Bill and Ruth estimated that 15 square metres would be sufficient for the storage room, as most of the products would be displayed on the sales floor. Ruth had designed a layout to provide maximum exposure to the fashion items located at the front of the store, while maintaining some visibility to the basic products at the rear of the store. The fashion items at the front of the store obstructed the sight line to the rear. This would enable browsers to feel more comfortable while shopping. Ruth had suggested that the store be richly decorated in warm pastel colours, with wood-coloured trim. The fixtures, racks, and change rooms would be custom made of wood and brass, and the lighting would be very soft. The store would be perfumed with mild fragrances, and relaxing music would be played.

Ruth felt a promotional plan would be needed to develop a strong position in the market as well as to gain a competitive edge. One idea she had been toying with was to start a registry system, which would include a customer's personal preferences, previous purchases, as well as her home address to enable the store to mail announcements of new product arrivals and upcoming sales. The customer would also be invited to disclose information regarding her husband/boyfriend, to facilitate the mailing of reminder notices to them for events such as birthdays and anniversaries. Gift wrapping and delivery services would also be provided for male customers. Bill had suggested a grand opening be held to create a high level of initial awareness among consumers.

## The Industry

The lingerie market in Canada was estimated to be worth more than $2 billion in 1987, with the intimate apparel segment estimated at $570 million in retail sales. This segment of the industry is currently at the maturity stage of its life cycle and experiencing limited growth. However, the specialty store segment of this industry is experiencing a growth in retail sales due to the increasing interest among women in stylish lingerie.

As Bill and Ruth collected information from discussions with various manufacturers and retailers, they were able to put together a profile of the intimate apparel market. Department stores accounted for about 30 percent of the market, discount stores another 15 percent, specialty stores 50 percent, and other types of outlets the remaining 5 percent. By combining St. Catharines/Niagara region population figures with the area's combined retail sales, Bill had determined that the total intimate apparel sales for the area were approximately $7 million. Although pantyhose accounted for another $300 million in industry sales, Bill and Ruth decided after a lengthy debate not to carry the product due to the diverse range of the line and the display space this type of product would require. With her experience and knowledge as a buyer, Ruth was able to provide a breakdown of industry sales by product line (Exhibit 1).

## EXHIBIT 1

### *Total women's intimate apparel market*

| Product | Percent of Market |
|---|---|
| Bras | 37% |
| Panties | 18 |
| Camisoles | 5 |
| Teddies | 1 |
| Full slips | 4 |
| Half slips | 4 |
| Hostess gowns, loungewear | 2 |
| Negligees | 2 |
| Nightshirts | 4 |
| Nightgowns | 17 |
| Pyjamas | 6 |
| Total | 100% |

## The Competition

Recognizing that competition would be strong in a mature industry, the partners conducted a competitive analysis for the local trading area. After surveying local stores, Ruth categorized the competitors as direct and indirect competition. Direct competitors included all intimate apparel specialty stores, whereas indirect competitors consisted of a local department store called The Right House, as well as all stores selling apparel in the Pen Centre. These were comprised mostly of department stores and discounters (Exhibits 2 and 3).

## The St. Catharines Market

St. Catharines is located in southern Ontario and is the main shopping area for the Niagara region. This region accounts for 1.42 percent of all retail expenditures in Canada. The Pen Centre is no more than a 30-minute drive for Niagara region residents. Population and income information from the 1986 Canadian Census is provided in Exhibits 4 and 5.

Ruth felt that further segmentation could be conducted but was unsure about how to do this. She wondered how important ages of potential consumers would be. Although males purchase gifts for their wives/girlfriends, she was also unsure of the extent to which males should be considered potential customers.

## Financial Analysis

Bill had estimated that the approximate start-up costs and operating expenses would be as follows:

| | |
|---|---|
| Insurance | $ 1,000 |
| Fixtures | 60,000 |
| Computer system | 8,000 |
| Office supplies | 500 |
| Professional fees | 1,000 |

**EXHIBIT 2**

*Direct competition*
Table of Attributes

| Scale: | 4 = Excellent selection | 3 = Good selection |
|--------|------------------------|-------------------|
|        | 2 = Fair selection     | 1 = Poor selection |

| Product | Annabelles | Charlotte's | Intimate Memories | Phoebes |
|---------|-----------|-------------|-------------------|---------|
| Bras | 2 | 2 | 3 | 4 |
| Panties | 1 | 1 | 3 | 4 |
| Camisoles | 1 | 1 | 2 | — |
| Teddies | 1 | 1 | 3 | 1 |
| Full slips | 1 | 2 | 2 | — |
| Half slips | 2 | 3 | 1 | — |
| Negligees | 1 | 1 | 1 | — |
| Nightshirts | 1 | 1 | 4 | 2 |
| Nightgowns | — | 2 | 1 | 2 |
| Pyjamas | — | 2 | — | — |
| Hostess/loungewear | — | 1 | 2 | — |
| Pantyhose | 1 | 1 | — | — |
| Service | Good offered assistance | Good offered assistance | Good offered assistance | Good offered assistance |
| Location | Downtown | Lakeshore Plaza | Ridley Square | Downtown |
| Visibility | High | Low | Moderate | Low |
| Accessibility | Restricted | Good | Good | Restricted |
| Parking | Restricted Pay | Ample — | Ample — | Restricted Pay |
| Square metres | 90 | 70 | 120 | 30 |
| Hours | Mon.–Fri., 9:30–9:00 Saturday, 9:30–5:30 | Mon.–Fri., 9:30–9:00 Saturday, 9:30–6:00 | Mon.–Fri., 10:00–9:00 Saturday, 10:00–6:00 | Mon.–Wed., 10:00–5:30 Thur.–Fri., Sat. 10:00–5:00 |
| Price | Medium | Medium | Medium | High |
| Target | 25–44 yrs. | 35–45 yrs. | 25–45 yrs. | 30–45 yrs. |

| Rent | $ 3,500/month plus .5% of gross sales |
|------|---------------------------------------|
| Salaries per year | 26,000 |
| Advertising: Opening | 1,000 |
| During year | 4,500 |
| Freight and shipping | 1,400 |
| Utilities | 1,800 |
| Interest (on loan principal) | 11,500 |

Bill estimated that sales for the first year would be $240,000, and for the second year they would be $280,000. The cost of goods sold was calculated to average 58 percent of sales. It is an industry custom by manufacturers to allow 60-day terms for opening inventory requirements.

**EXHIBIT 3**

*Indirect competition*
Table of Attributes

| | | | | |
|---|---|---|---|---|
| Scale: | 4 = Excellent selection | 3 = Good selection | | |
| | 2 = Fair selection | 1 = Poor selection | | |

| Product | Right House | Eaton's | Robinson | Sears |
|---|---|---|---|---|
| Bras | 4 | 4 | 4 | 3 |
| Panties | 4 | 4 | 3 | 4 |
| Camisoles | 1 | 1 | 1 | 1 |
| Teddies | 1 | — | 1 | — |
| Full slips | 4 | 3 | 2 | 3 |
| Half slips | 4 | 3 | 2 | 3 |
| Negligees | 2 | 1 | 1 | — |
| Nightshirts | 3 | 2 | 2 | 2 |
| Nightgowns | 3 | 3 | 2 | 3 |
| Pyjamas | 2 | 2 | 2 | — |
| Hostess/loungewear | 1 | 1 | 3 | 2 |
| Pantyhose | 4 | 3 | 3 | 2 |
| Service | Moderate assistance available | Moderate, only one salesperson for dept. | Moderate assistance offered | Poor, no salesperson available |
| Location | Fairview Mall | Pen Centre Plaza | Pen Centre Square | Pen Centre |
| Visibility | Moderate | High | High | High |
| Accessibility | Good | Excellent | Excellent | Excellent |
| Parking | Ample | Ample | Ample | Restricted |
| Square metres | 210 | 270 | 280 | 270 |
| Hours | Mon.–Fri., 9:30–9:00 Saturday, 9:30–6:00 | Mon.–Fri., 9:30–9:00 Saturday, 9:30–5:30 | Mon.–Fri., 9:30–9:00 Saturday, 9:30–5:30 | Mon.–Wed., 9:30–9:00 Saturday, 9:30–5:30 |
| Price | Medium to low | Medium to low | Medium to low | Medium to low |
| Target | 18–45 yrs. | 13 and over | 13 and over | 13 and over |

## Summary

Bill and Ruth settled in for a long night. By Monday morning, a decision would have to be reached on whether or not to go ahead with the venture. If a "go" decision were to be made, the partnership would need a more tailored target market and a marketing plan before presenting a proposal to a bank for financing consideration.

## Questions

1. Conduct a situational analysis for The Undercover Agency business venture.
2. Conduct a segmentation analysis of the market. Who should the target market be?
3. Would you recommend a "go" or a "no go" decision for this business venture?

**Exhibit 4**

*St. Catharines/Niagara population*

| Age Groups | Male | Female |
|---|---|---|
| 15–19 years | 14,020 | 13,350 |
| 20–24 years | 14,505 | 14,260 |
| 25–34 years | 25,830 | 26,770 |
| 35–44 years | 22,885 | 23,530 |
| 45–54 years | 17,790 | 18,635 |
| 55–64 years | 18,700 | 20,490 |
| 65–74 years | 12,770 | 15,355 |
| 75 years and over | 6,470 | 11,115 |
| Total | 132,970 | 143,505 |

**Exhibit 5**

*Income levels by gender*

| Income Levels | Males, 15+ | Females, 15+ |
|---|---|---|
| Population with income | 124,420 | 115,455 |
| Under $9,999 | 32,055 | 68,475 |
| $10,000–$19,999 | 25,670 | 29,825 |
| $20,000–$29,999 | 25,030 | 10,885 |
| $30,000 and over | 41,665 | 6,270 |
| Average income | $23,809 | $10,975 |
| Median income | $21,799 | $ 8,486 |

4. If the recommendation is "go," develop a marketing strategy; if "no go," write a report that will show the partners why the idea is not viable.

# 13.

# Donna Holtom

## Introduction

"Hello, Santé Restaurant." Donna Holtom, owner and manager, flipped open the reservation book. "Can I make a reservation for 4 at 7:30 tonight?" This used to be a simple question. But after three and a half years in business, Donna found herself planning and replanning the reservation book before replying, "I could serve you at 8:30." It was Friday night, and once again she was losing potential revenues, even after setting four extra tables in the gym.

Santé is part of a group of businesses Donna operates at the corner of Sussex and Rideau Streets, in the heart of downtown Ottawa. The major business components are:

- The Sussex Club, a women's club centred around a fitness program but also offering its members access to a wide range of personal services (the spa, hair salon and "dining-room").
- Santé Restaurant, a fine dining facility offering an eclectic blend of Caribbean, Californian and East Asian dishes.
- Holtz Health & Beauty Centre, a health spa offering aesthetic services (facials, manicures, pedicures, electronic muscle toning, etc.), massage and hair styling.

## Background

After three years managing a womens' credit union, and a dozen before that working as Executive Assistant to Alderman and later Mayor Marion Dewar, Donna's first step in establishing her own business had been a big one, starting the three businesses together, from scratch. She had expected the three businesses to develop a synergistic relationship—and they had.

The Sussex Club had developed a strong reputation as Ottawa's premier womens' facility because it could offer its members a quality dining facility and a wide range of personal services that the membership of a private club just could not support. At the same time, the club members provided a solid core of regular clientele for the restaurant and spa, reducing their marketing requirements.

Santé had also been very successful in establishing a reputation, based on its innovative cuisine, fine service and central location. Donna takes full advantage by promoting the spa and club facilities to restaurant diners. Her most effective technique is the "fishbowl." Diners have the opportunity to win a complimentary massage (or some similar service) by dropping a business card into the bowl. Even the "losers" are called with the offer of a discount on the service being promoted at the moment.

Each of these entities attracts differing, but overlapping clienteles. The Sussex Club services predominantly professional and business women 30 to 60 years old. The restaurant attracts diners of both sexes, but offers "fine dining" and an elegant decor attractive to the upper third in income terms. Ninety-five percent of spa clients are women (a few men utilize the massage services), but they cover a wider age and income range than Club members.

What Donna hadn't counted on was that the three businesses would be so diverse in their management and operating requirements. When the hired managers proved to be unsuccessful, she found herself learning three new business areas "on the job."

The start-up period was difficult, and the nature and range of services offered have gradually been refined with experience, adding some elements, and deleting others. Overall the group is now profitable (see Table 1), and the challenge is how to continue growing and avoid turning business away.

## The Facility

The businesses are located in a small eight-story office building at a major intersection, two blocks from the Parliament Buildings, with the By-Ward Market restaurant district a block behind, and a major downtown shopping centre across the street. The two best known downtown hotels (the Chateau Laurier and the Westin) and the convention centre are all

## TABLE 1  Operating Income

### SANTÉ RESTAURANT

| | Period Ending | |
| --- | --- | --- |
| | *May 1988* | *May 1989* |
| Revenue: | | |
| Food | $484,200 | $615,651 |
| Liquor | 143,114 | 201,976 |
| Other | (8,523) | (10,827) |
| Total revenue | $618,791 | $806,800 |
| Cost of sales | | |
| Cost of food | $177,835 | $257,012 |
| Cost of liquor | 69,654 | 91,476 |
| Credit card discounts | 8,867 | 13,716 |
| Miscellaneous | 3,138 | 1,656 |
| Total cost of sales | $259,494 | $363,860 |
| Contribution margin | $359,297 | $442,940 |
| Expenses | | |
| Salary waiting | $ 75,397 | $109,896 |
| Salary kitchen | 95,607 | 101,944 |
| Other labour costs | 3,486 | 3,885 |
| Total wage and salary | $174,490 | $215,725 |
| Rent and occupancy | $ 79,011 | $ 81,784 |
| General administration | 24,008 | 23,060 |
| Advertising | 27,197 | 14,617 |
| Printing | 0 | 8,736 |
| Laundry | 4,246 | 5,937 |
| Equipment/smalls | 8,822 | 33,132 |
| Other | 3,970 | 11,410 |
| Total other expenses | $147,254 | $178,676 |
| Total expenses | $321,744 | $394,401 |
| Operating profit (loss) | $ 37,553 | $ 48,539 |

within a block. As a result, there is considerable pedestrian, vehicle and bus traffic at the corner and in the immediate area. Most downtown employment, however, is across the Canal, several blocks away.

There is no parking associated with the building, and although there is considerable parking in the immediate area, most of it is in parking structures and virtually no free parking is available.

The first floor of the building is occupied by a major bank branch. The businesses occupy all of the second floor, and part of the third. Customer access is by a stairwell and elevators common to the office floors further up.

The layout of the second floor is shown in Figure 1. There are two entrances to the complex, one for the restaurant, and one for the spa, hair salon and fitness facility. This allows the restaurant to establish a somewhat separate identity, a useful approach, particularly in attracting male diners to a complex that is otherwise primarily "female."

**TABLE 1**  *(concluded)*

**HOLTZ HEALTH & BEAUTY (including the Sussex Club)**

| | Period Ending | |
|---|---|---|
| | *May 1988* | *May 1989* |
| **Health Spa** | | |
| Revenue | | |
| Retail sales | $ 82,058 | $ 237,850 |
| Aesthetic services | 147,700 | 243,047 |
| Massage services | 54,802 | 91,939 |
| Hair services | 50,113 | 41,828 |
| Prepaid items | 91,342 | 245,285 |
| Less: Certificates used | (62,118) | (129,321) |
| Total revenue | $363,897 | $ 730,628 |
| Cost of sales | | |
| Cost of products sold/used | 54,362 | 140,188 |
| Payroll aesthetics | 61,532 | 120,292 |
| Payroll massage | 24,601 | 44,625 |
| Hair commissions | 29,687 | 21,826 |
| Advertising | 1,455 | 19,421 |
| Supplies and expenses | 11,605 | 9,812 |
| Total cost of sales | $183,242 | $ 356,164 |
| Gross profit | $180,655 | $ 374,464 |
| **Fitness Programme** | | |
| Revenue | | |
| Membership sales | $110,563 | $ 123,968 |
| Other sales | 19,103 | 10,553 |
| Total revenue | $129,666 | $ 134,521 |
| Cost of sales | | |
| Payroll | 65,937 | 66,035 |
| Advertising | 2,955 | 9,117 |
| Services purchased from spa | 7,835 | 12,012 |
| Expenses | 6,619 | 7,539 |
| Total cost of sales | $ 83,346 | $ 94,703 |
| Gross profit | $ 46,320 | $ 39,818 |
| Other/unallocated | $ (350) | $ (11,104) |
| Total gross profit | $226,625 | $ 403,178 |
| Corporate expenses: | | |
| Salaries and benefits | $ 42,996 | $ 69,126 |
| Rent | 116,475 | 118,605 |
| Administrative | 39,114 | 55,505 |
| Advertising | 14,798 | 14,238 |
| Maintenance/cleaning | 3,810 | 3,937 |
| Credit card discounts | 6,714 | 14,306 |
| Bank charges | 4,277 | 3,278 |
| Other | 15,463 | 3,429 |
| Total corporate expenses | $243,647 | $ 282,424 |
| Operating profit (loss) | $ (17,023) | $ 120,754 |

NOTE: The data has been disguised.

**FIGURE 1**

*Facility layout, main floor*

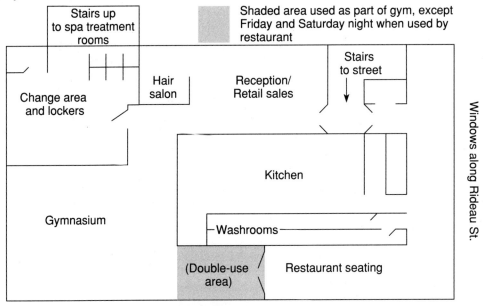

Windows along Sussex Dr.

The restaurant offers a very pleasant, relatively formal atmosphere. There are very few "poor tables," with most of the seating along the floor-to-ceiling windows along both Sussex and Rideau, offering interesting views of some fine older buildings and the activity along the street below. There are 62 seats at 22 tables, and another six tables with 20 seats are set up in part of the gym most Friday and Saturday evenings (on long weekends, and in January and February they generally aren't required).

This extra seating has helped deal with the rising demand in the evenings, but they can't be used when the gym programme is running, and they could be filled most Friday lunches, and an average of 10 extra seats would be useful for Thursday lunches. It takes two waiters an hour and a half to "convert" the gym space to restaurant seating so it is not a useful response to an unexpected group of "walk-in" patrons. There are five evenings a month (on average) when the 20 seats could be used for walk-ins or large parties that cannot be accommodated now. In fact there are probably an equal number of Friday or Saturday evenings when another 20 seats could be useful.

The nicely decorated gym facility is relatively small, accommodating aerobic classes of 10 to 15 persons, and a small selection of Nautilus and Lifecycle equipment.

The spa originally had six treatment rooms and a small lounge area on the third floor. This space can be reached by a private stairway from the change area, which is used by aesthetic clients. As a result of the increasing demand for services, however, the spa recently took over some vacant space across the public hallway from the third floor treatment rooms, adding four treatment areas. However, the need to cross the public hallway to reach this area is a distinct disadvantage for clients dressed in housecoats between treatments. The space allocation for the three businesses is provided in Table 2.

---

TABLE 2    **Space Allocation (in square metres)**

|                | Sussex Club | Santé Restaurant | Holtz Health & Beauty Spa | Rent/$m^2$ [*] |
|----------------|-------------|------------------|---------------------------|----------------|
| Second floor   | 163         | 279              | 70                        | $207.21        |
| Third floor    |             |                  | 186                       | $182.99        |

*Quoted as "net, net." Landlord charge an additional $86.11/sq. metre for taxes, maintenance, etc. Lease has three years to run, and a five year option to renew, subject to arbitration on rent level.

## The Spa

Holtz Health & Beauty is the largest aesthetic salon in Ottawa, and is unique in the regional focus of its market. Aesthetic salons are generally based on a clientele that works or lives in the area of the business, and uses it out of convenience. They tend to be small operations, usually an aesthetician/manager and two or three staff with gross revenues in the $80 to $120,000 range. Although there were two other large salons with a more substantial staff and clientele, the central location of Holtz, the wide range of services it provides, and the promotional approaches it pioneered give it a different focus.

One third of Holtz's revenues come from the sale of "gift certificates" and "prepaid" items, and about half of those sales come in the pre-Christmas period. If the revenues from repeat visits by clients introduced by gift certificates and the retail products purchased by those clients were included, the significance of this marketing approach would be even more obvious.

The gift certificates are specially promoted for Christmas, Valentine's Day, and Mother's Day, but are also advertised throughout the year as "A Perfect Gift for the Woman Who Deserves Everything" for birthdays, graduations, weddings, corporate recognition, etc. Most of these sales are for the "Supreme Day of Beauty," a $165 package. The gift certificate sales are promoted through radio and newspaper advertising (the results from the newspaper are obvious, those from radio are not), by donations as door prizes for community events and through flyers and direct mail campaigns and at the annual "Bridal Fair."

Effective promotion is part of the programme's success, but so is Holtz's reputation as the "best and biggest" salon in the city, with the widest range of services. Donna plans to maintain this reputation by continuing to improve the facilities and expand the range of services offered. Holtz is still weak in the area of water treatments, for example, and a whirlpool used for treatments should generate at least two clients a day for a $35 treatment. The cost of a treatment is $6.

Although not all gift certificates are in fact redeemed for services, the success of the gift certificate programme is having a dramatic impact on the level of activity in the spa. Holtz was the first salon to introduce this concept in Ottawa, and in the three years they have offered it, sales have increased dramatically. Although the facilities have been expanded once, they still cannot keep up with the demand, and the location of the manicure area (where clients tend to be fairly chatty) adjacent to the massage rooms (where clients tend to be fairly drowsy) is less than ideal.

## The Sussex Club

The situation with the gym facility is quite different. Fitness facilities in the region fall into two categories:

- Volume oriented, high pressure sales, well advertised "meet markets," focused on weights and aerobic programmes.
- Higher priced, generally suburban sports clubs that offer a wide range of facilities for racquet sports, swimming, running, weights, etc.

The Sussex Club is a very small facility, relative to the others, and has a totally female clientele that tends to be older, less fit, and higher income. It serves business and professional women who pay a little more to receive more individual attention, and to have their bodies shielded from the masses, at least until they are improved a little. But this part of the business has never been very profitable and after paying its share of the rent has never broken even. It certainly raises the question that perhaps this space could be used more profitably. On the other hand, Donna feels that with a more aggressive and effective sales effort, membership could be increased. The average price of a Sussex Club annual membership is $495. In the past, membership sales appeared to be related to the level of skills and motivation of the sales staff. Both newspaper advertising and door to door distribution of flyers had been used and did show some effect. The club also offers incentives to members to bring referrals (three extra months of your membership, etc.).

## Santé Restaurant

The restaurant requires an entirely different promotional approach. The best promotions have been the least "in control"—nothing did more for business than a restaurant review in the daily newspaper. Another period of increased sales could clearly be related to the major exhibition that ran following the opening of the nearby National Gallery. A good week always results from a major production at the neighbouring National Arts Centre. Conversely, the newspaper advertising that works well for the other businesses produced no measurable results for the restaurant.

But one promotional activity has worked well. The "Entertainment Card" was introduced to Ottawa just as the restaurant opened. A coupon booklet put out across North America featured a section in which restaurants could offer a free entrée with any dinner for two. Santé was featured in the first booklet and each annual edition subsequently. It had also placed the same offer in a widely distributed coupon booklet put out for "Wheelchair Sports."

The results are very noticeable. Particularly in the periods shortly after the books come out, and shortly before they expire, as many as half the tables in the restaurant any given night could be using a coupon as partial payment for their meals. This results in a higher cost of sales and lower profit margin than some restaurants show, and brings the average dinner bill down from $28/seat "sold" to $25/seat actually collected. For a while this resulted in poor service as overstretched waiters and kitchen staff tried to push tables through. More recently, it was resulting in reservations refused and walk-ins turned away. The coupons are less noticeable at lunch, and receipts are only marginally below the $12/head "sold" at menu prices.

## Alternative Directions

"I think we are ready to expand," Donna said, "but I am not sure which direction we should take.

"Sometimes it seems we should eliminate the Sussex Club. The fitness programme is not a big revenue generator, in fact if you take into account the rent on the space it occupies, it loses money."

Figure 2 shows one option for the re-allocation of this space. It would add 40 seats (including the 20 already used some evenings) and a corresponding expansion to the kitchen (56 square metres) to the restaurant.

The remaining 107 square metres would be allocated to the spa, relocating the hair salon and manicure areas to take advantage of the windows along Sussex Drive, and allowing the development of water treatment rooms and an expansion of the massage facilities. Donna estimates the hair salon revenues would double with the improved environment, while the water treatment facility should average \$35/treatment, with two to three treatments per day.

This sounded like an excellent idea until the cost of making these changes was estimated as follows:

| | | |
|---|---|---:|
| A) | Converting gym space to restaurant seating | \$20,000 |
| B) | Extending kitchen | 15,000 |
| C) | New hair salon/manicure area | 15,000 |
| D) | New water treatment area | 10,000 |
| E) | Changes to change area | 10,000 |
| F) | New massage treatment rooms | 8,000 |
| | Total cost | \$78,000 |

At current rates, a bank loan to finance these changes would cost 15 percent per annum. It would be nice to know the expenditure was worthwhile before taking on that kind of commitment. Since the lease has three years to run and a five year option to renew, these improvements will be amortized over an eight year period.

**FIGURE 2**

*Optional facility layout, main floor*

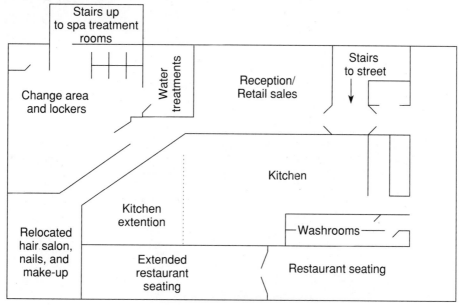

Windows along Sussex Dr.

Although she feels that the above mentioned estimates are realistic, she also wants to determine the effect that the proposed changes will have on profits under a more pessimistic scenario. She wonders what would happen if: hair salon revenues would increase by only 50 percent and if 25 percent of the members of the Sussex Club would not return to take advantage of the spa and restaurant. Sussex Club members, on average, have been spending $200 per year at the spa and the same amount at the restaurant.

Donna is also considering an alternative strategy, one that would involve increasing promotion to get new members for the Sussex Club while leaving all other conditions unchanged. She would spend $25,000 for another salesperson and an additional $10,000 for newspaper advertising. The variable costs for each member are $80 per year and the average price for an annual membership is $495. Each new member can be expected to spend $200 per year at the spa and the same amount at the restaurant.

Before making any decision, Donna wants to know the effect of each of the scenarios on the operations' total profits.

### Questions

1. How will the proposed changes affect profitability *(a)* under the current scenario, and *(b)* under the most pessimistic scenario?
2. How many new members would be needed to cover the cost of the proposed promotional campaign?
3. What recommendation will you offer Donna?

## 14.
## WOODWARD'S DEPARTMENT STORES: HOLIDAY TRAVEL

During the summer of 1987, executives of Woodward's, a multiunit western Canadian department store chain with headquarters in Vancouver, had to decide about their involvement in the travel agency business. The decision boiled down to a choice between accepting an offer from Maple Leaf Travel, Ltd., to operate agencies within Woodward Stores as a licensee or developing agencies owned and operated by the department store.

Holiday Carousels, Ltd., which had operated travel agencies in eight Woodward Stores, went out of business in early summer of 1987. The Holiday Carousels organization had created a unique physical unit to house its agencies. Called carousels, they were semicircular in design, attractively decorated, and occupied about 28 square metres of floor space.

The management of Woodward's considered the sales growth of Holiday Carousels promising, with average sales of approximately $700,000 to $800,000 per unit per month in the spring of 1987. Each unit employed the equivalent of four full-time agents. (Industry rules of thumb suggest that an experienced agent should sell about $300,000 of travel per month.)

The executives decided to continue to offer travel agency service to their customers for the following reasons:

This case was prepared by Dr. Robert G. Wyckham, Simon Fraser University.

1. The results of the Holiday Carousel experience were promising.

2. Increasing disposable incomes, smaller families, and larger numbers of senior citizens suggested a growing travel market.

3. Travel was seen as a natural complement to a full-line department store image and to the existing level of customer traffic.

4. That level of customer traffic, plus customer confidence and loyalty to Woodward's, provided an excellent opportunity for travel sales.

5. There was a high potential profit per square metre of space occupied.

6. A travel agency service was necessary in order to remain competitive with other department store chains that were in the travel business.

After receiving proposals from a number of travel agencies, Woodward's management decided to compare the Maple Leaf offer with the alternative of setting up its own travel agencies.

Maple Leaf Travel, Ltd., was a Vancouver-based travel agency with all national and international accreditations. It was owned, in part, by the credit unions of the province, which had more than 600,000 members. Total revenue of the travel agency in 1986 exceeded $4 million, the bulk of which was developed by direct mail to credit union members.

The Maple Leaf proposal was based on the immediate reopening of the Park Royal, West Vancouver, travel office. Other offices would be opened when, by mutual agreement, a sufficiently smooth operating system had been achieved. Additional openings would occur first on the lower mainland of British Columbia and later Alberta.

Maple Leaf required about 28 square metres of space for an initial staff of two. Hours would be 9:30 A.M. to 5:30 P.M., Monday to Friday. Experiments with evening and Saturday openings would also be carried out. Location of the travel office within each store was to be based on a trade-off between the need for traffic flow and visibility, the consumers' need for privacy, and the travel agents' need for relative quiet.

The lease agreement requested by Maple Leaf was as follows:

1. Five years with a five-year renewal clause.

2. Twenty-eight square metres of space initially; option to increase to 56 square metres as business warrants.

3. Rent formula:
   1.0 percent of net sales of less than $250,000.
   1.5 percent of net sales of $250,000 to $499,999.
   2.0 percent of net sales of $500,000 to $999,999.
   1.5 percent of net sales of $1 million to $1.5 million.
   1.0 percent of net sales of more than $1.5 million.

Assuming an average commission rate of 9 percent, Maple Leaf Travel estimated a break-even point of sales of $411,000 in the first year. Pro forma contribution for the first year was estimated conservatively at $4,000 and optimistically at $16,000.

Three markets were identified for potential development: credit union members in the Woodward's trading areas, current Woodward's customers, and the general public. Co-operative direct-mail and newspaper advertising were suggested as the most productive forms of promotion.

In analyzing the alternative possibility, the creation of wholly owned and operated units, Woodward's executives outlined some financial and other advantages:

1. The contribution to overhead and profit of travel outlets owned by Woodward's was estimated to be 2.6 percent on annual sales of $1 million compared to 1.625 percent from Maple Leaf Travel.

2. Because of the fixed nature of many expenses, it was thought that the contribution rate from owned agencies would increase as sales grew.

3. Advantageous advertising rates and in-house advertising expertise could be extended to a travel business operated directly by Woodward's.

4. Having control over an important service to Woodward's customers was felt to be an advantage. Ownership was also seen as leading to greater flexibility in promotion, rate of growth, and operating characteristics.

5. Through various merchandising and promotions activities, Woodward's already was generating customer traffic; owned travel agencies would result in greater benefits to Woodward's from this traffic.

6. Woodward's had a "built-in" market, the corporate travel of executives, and direct access to a large number of employees.

7. Individual experts in the travel business were available, and accounting services with travel agency experience could be retained.

A number of disadvantages of ownership were pointed out. In any new business, the first weeks and months are difficult. A large amount of executive time would likely have to be allocated to the travel business, a business in which Woodward's executives had no prior experience. Fairly substantial losses would probably occur in the initial period before accreditations were received and the business was built up.

A number of advantages would also be forgone if the Maple Leaf proposal was not accepted. The major potential loss was the opportunity to have more direct exposure to hundreds of thousands of credit union members. Also, Woodward's rather than Maple Leaf Travel would have to absorb any losses incurred in the start-up period. Any lease arrangements with Maple Leaf, in contrast, would be based on that firm's sales. There would, therefore, always be a positive contribution to Woodward's even if the travel agencies did not make a profit. Finally, Maple Leaf had marketing and operating systems already in place. Hence, the amount of time Woodward's executives would have to apply to the travel business would be greatly reduced.

## Questions

1. Which of these two alternatives should Woodward's select?
2. How would you support the recommendation?

## 15.
## WEST COAST FURNITURE

West Coast Furniture is a high-line furniture dealer active in the Vancouver area. The company specializes in expensive luxury furnishings that are purchased by upper-middle- to high-income consumers who want fine craftmanship and quality—and who are prepared to pay for it. West Coast deals in products such as oak burl inlaid coffee tables ($4,000), dining-room suites ($10,000–$15,000), bedroom suites ($6,000–$10,000), sofas and couches ($6,000), and executive desks ($8,000).

A slowdown in total company sales began in the mid-1980s. With the onset of the 1990 recession, sales started to deteriorate seriously. This trend became apparent to the owners, Stan and Susie, when they reviewed the historical sales of their two main market segments (see Exhibit 1). West Coast had originally relied on its wholesaling operation to other retail furniture dealers, but the company also sold direct to consumers through its own discount retail showroom.

Aside from the difficulties related to declining sales, West Coast was also under pressure from its retail dealers to stop selling direct to consumers. Retail dealers argued that West Coast was supposed to act as their wholesaler, and that operating a discount retail showroom made it a direct competitor.

A review of West Coast's performance was definitely in order, so the owners, together with a consultant, examined the firm's two market segments. Their marketing mix analysis included the following insights.

### EXHIBIT 1

*West Coast Furniture sales ($000)*

|  | 1984 | 1985 | 1986 | 1987 | 1988 | 1989 | 1990 |
|---|---|---|---|---|---|---|---|
| Wholesale | $1,351 | $1,329 | $1,304 | $1,271 | $1,216 | $1,137 | $1,002 |
| Direct retail | 821 | 831 | 843 | 867 | 905 | 983 | 951 |
| Total company sales | $2,172 | $2,160 | $2,147 | $2,138 | $1,121 | $2,120 | $1,953 |

### Wholesale Distribution to Retail Dealers

***Product.*** West Coast's retail distributors concentrated on the low- and mid-range product lines in terms of quality and brand image. Retailers used a very limited selection of West Coast's luxury name-brand product lines to provide an option to those consumers who found the quality and craftmanship of their regular product lines to be unacceptable. While the retailers carried a good selection of the low- and mid-range product lines in their showrooms (and in immediately available inventory), the brand names distributed by West Coast were available only through catalog ordering. Retailers followed this policy to minimize their inventory carrying costs for the expensive West Coast product lines.

This case was written by Dr. Lindsay Meredith, Simon Fraser University.

*Price.*     The retailers' price structures were heavily concentrated in the low and medium ranges. For comparative purposes, a consumer could expect to pay approximately 40 percent more for the cheapest product lines distributed by West Coast than for the most expensive mid-priced products offered by the retailers. This price spread reflected the manufacturing costs and quality of materials used in the furniture. Low- and medium-priced furniture, for example, is made of a thin layer of oak veneer glued to particle board. The brands distributed by West Coast are made from solid oak.

*Place.*     All of the retail dealers were located in the suburban areas of Greater Vancouver. The retailers preferred mall locations in regions where low- to medium-priced townhouses and medium-priced single detached housing starts were increasing most rapidly. The general consensus in the industry was that these areas of new family formation represented the largest demand for potential furniture sales. Three of West Coast's retailers had declared bankruptcy in 1990, which left Stan and Susie with $18,000 in bad debts.

*Promotion.*     The retailers supplied by West Coast had over recent years begun to rely heavily on advertising their price competitiveness as a means of attracting the young marrieds who comprised the family formation groups. Retail dealers rarely advertised the expensive furniture lines supplied by West Coast because they didn't wish to scare off potential customers who wanted to avoid high-priced home furnishings.

### Direct Discount Retail Sales to Consumers

*Product.*     West Coast's product lines were very high quality with a good assortment of name-brand furnishings. Depth of the company's product mix was substantial. Approximately 12 percent of inventory in dining-room suites averaged one to two turns per year. The total 1990 inventory in dining-room suites was approximately $300,000.

*Price.*     West Coast's retail discounting strategy gave customers an approximate 20 percent price advantage over its four major luxury furniture competitors. Prices weren't actually shown on the majority of stock on the showroom floor because Stan and Susie wanted the customers personally to approach the sales staff for help. The sales representatives could then provide price data as well as information about West Coast's fine product quality and competitive value.

*Place.*     West Coast was strategically located in close proximity to three major upscale suburbs in the Greater Vancouver area. Other high-income areas in Vancouver were closer to competitors' locations, but Stan and Susie believed that people who were prepared to spend an average of $8,000 on a home furnishing item were also inclined to spend more search time looking for high quality at good prices.

West Coast's 2,500-square-metre showroom floor was a bit large, but necessary to carry its substantial product mix.

*Promotion.*     West Coast relied solely on word of mouth for its advertising. The sales force was, by necessity, made up of Stan and Susie plus one receptionist/clerk because low cash flows coupled with poor retail sales didn't justify any more help.

The segmental analysis raised a number of questions and concerns regarding West Coast's total operations:

1. While the wholesale operation of the company still accounted for over slightly half of its revenues, what was causing the decrease in West Coast's sales to its retail dealers since 1985? (See Exhibit 1.)

2. Should the company get out of direct selling to consumers since a number of West Coast's retailers didn't like it acting as a competitor? If West Coast chose to remain a wholesaler as well as selling direct to consumers, what could it do about the negative reaction of those retailers who feared direct competition from West Coast?

3. Direct consumer retail sales (see Exhibit 1) indicated a moderate but consistent level of growth over the 1984 to 1989 period. But 1990 sales gave cause for concern. Stan and Susie couldn't understand why they weren't getting a better response from upper-income consumers of luxury home furnishings. After all, the other luxury furniture stores in Vancouver certainly appeared to be getting business. The owners wondered if all of the elements in their market mix were operating effectively.

4. Finally, Stan and Susie wondered if they should try advertising, but this involved answering a number of questions: What media should they use: direct mail, newspapers, radio, TV, or magazines? Even if they chose some of these media, where in the newspaper should they advertise, for example? What radio station should they use? If all of the magazines were similar, should they look for the cheapest one? Where would they get the money to pay for the advertising since poor sales meant that their cash flow was limited?

### Questions

1. Would you recommend that West Coast drop its own direct sales programme?
2. If not, what changes would you make in that programme?
3. What about advertising?

---

## 16.
## EATON CENTRE (EDMONTON)

In June 1990, Sandy McNair faced an extremely difficult task—to rejuvenate a dying mall in Edmonton, the mall capital of Canada. He had no retail experience—his background was in sales and marketing for a software company. Then, in 1990, he joined Confed Realty Services, which owned 11 shopping malls, including Edmonton's Eaton Centre. He was hired to build Confed's property portfolio, but as troubles increased at the Eaton Centre, he was asked to find a way to turn around the mall.

The situation he faced was grim. During the 1980s, shopping centre developers built hundreds of malls in Canada, and retail chains opened thousands of stores in those malls. In 1980, Edmonton had five main malls; by 1990, that had grown to 12, one of which was the

Source: Based on information contained in John Southerst, "The Reinvention of Retail," *Canadian Business*, August 1992, pp. 26–31.

Eaton Centre, built in the downtown core in 1987. In 1989, Eaton Centre sales totalled $2,270 per square metre; the typical break-even point for retailers was about $2,700. The Eaton Centre competed with the Edmonton Centre mall, directly across the street, for an ever-declining share of the downtown shopping dollar. The Eaton Centre was losing the battle, and in late 1989, of the Eaton Centre's 49,000 square metres of rental space, vacancies stood at 4,650 square metres and were growing.

Morale among the managers and staff of stores in the mall was low. As the country went into a recession in 1990, sales and profits for the stores in the mall continued to decline. Mall management did little to arrest the decline. The problem was further complicated by the fact that half the mall belonged to Triple Five Corporation, the owner of the giant West Edmonton Mall and also the Westmount Mall, another Edmonton shopping centre. The Ghermegian brothers, owners of Triple Five Corporation, were not prepared to spend money on the Eaton Centre as its flagship in West Edmonton was experiencing trouble. When Sandy McNair was given the assignment, the first thing he did was to buy the Triple Fives 50 percent interest. He paid $1, an indication of how the Ghermegians felt about the Eaton Centre.

As of June 1990, when he took over full control of the Eaton Centre, Sandy McNair faced the following situation:

- Of the 120 stores in the mall, 20 shops were vacant and most of the remaining 100 retailers were demanding rent rollbacks.
- Many of the store managers had little experience or formal training in retailing. This was due in part to the rapid expansion of malls and stores during the 1980s, when clerks rose quickly to become store managers.
- Few chain store executives could spend time on the problems of one store. With the recession, these executives were busy trying to hold the entire chain together.
- The recession, coupled with the introduction of the Goods and Services Tax in January 1991, had created a dramatic decline in retail sales across Canada.

His objective was to turn the mall's fortunes around. He knew that the typical response in these desperate times was to provide rent concessions to tenants in the hope that they wouldn't leave the mall. He decided on another tack—take the money that would normally be lost to rent concessions and put it into a programme to rejuvenate mall retailers. He took the plan, which included a massive $7.9 million renovation budget, to senior executives at Confed. Recognizing it was a gamble, the executives approved the plan. While Sandy McNair was pleased, he realized that this was just the start of a long-term strategy to return the mall to profitability. The real task lay ahead.

## Questions

1. What options could Mr. McNair consider?
2. Prepare a strategy for the Eaton Centre for the next two years.

## 17.
## THE MAACO FRANCHISE

Martin Klyne sat back and reflected on the analysis he had just completed. Now he had to make the decision—whether or not to obtain a Maaco auto-painting and body work franchise. He was impressed with the franchise and his first-year financial projections for the Regina market looked great. However, he thought, I'll just review everything again before I decide.

### The Idea

Mr. Klyne became interested in obtaining a Maaco franchise while working with the Canadian Imperial Bank of Commerce during a co-operative work semester. He was a finance major in the bachelor of administration programme at the University of Regina. During his work semester, he had been involved in approving loans, some of which were for individuals purchasing various franchises. In his spare time, he studied the franchise field and identified Maaco as an up-and-coming franchise in Canada. He expressed his interest to a friend, Dale Schick, an experienced auto-body repairman. Dale had 13 years' experience in all phases of the business, from wreck dismantler, auto-body man, painter, and estimator, to shop supervisor. Together, they agreed to investigate obtaining a Maaco franchise. Martin had a small inheritance and Dale had some money set aside, and they determined that each partner could invest $40,000 in the business.

The potential partners then gathered some information on the Maaco franchise concept, the Regina market, the competition, and the investment required for the franchise.

### The Maaco Franchise Concept

The typical Maaco Centre focused on quality, with job specialization and a production-line approach enhancing the centre's performance. In addition to auto painting, a shop handled auto-body repairs, from minor fender bender to the most extensive collision repairs.

The highest profit resulted from completing as many total paint jobs as possible, with only minor or cosmetic body repairs. Retail paint jobs were the most lucrative, but to ensure the shop operated at full capacity year-round, Maaco also sought trade or wholesale paint jobs (marginally less profitable). Collision repair, also profitable, kept the shop busy during the winter months. The high efficiency of the shop was complemented by aggressive advertising and promotion, quality service, reasonable prices, and particularly effective ways of closing sales.

*Franchisor Support.*    The first Maaco franchise opened in 1972, and by 1987, there were more than 450 centres, including 30 in Canada. Based on accumulated knowledge and experience, Maaco had developed a uniform system for the financing, location, construction, and operation of its centres. The relationship between Maaco and the franchisee was thoroughly laid out in a 14-page franchise agreement. Maaco provided the following support:

This case was prepared by Jim Mason, University of Regina.

1. Finance: Maaco assisted with obtaining and negotiating financing.
2. Site selection: Maaco assisted in locating and negotiating the lease for an existing location or a build-to-suit facility.
3. Education: Every new owner/manager attended a five-week training programme. There, the owner/manager learned painting and auto-repair techniques, as well as how to make service estimates, close sales, evaluate technical performance, supervise personnel, and manage a shop environment. Maaco covered the training, travel, and lodging expenses as part of the franchise agreement.
4. Advertising: Maaco created and coordinated placement of all advertising for television, radio, local newspapers, and the Yellow Pages. Franchisees contributed $400 per week to the advertising fund in the United States. Because Maaco advertising was in its infancy in Canada, Canadian franchisees co-ordinated their own advertising and promotions using American materials. With more Maaco centres, franchisees would be expected to pay $400 per week to a Canadian advertising pool.
5. Equipment: A Maaco service technician organized and supervised the installation of all equipment and utilities inside the centre. The franchise package covered this service along with equipment and installation costs.
6. Signs: Maaco furnished both freestanding and affixed outdoor signs. The package included the signs and all freight charges. The owner/operator paid for the pole, mounting attachments, electrical hookup, and installation.
7. Operations: Maaco furnished full operating support for a centre's first three weeks. Thereafter, their operations person constantly monitored the centre's operation and management. Within 20 days of month end, franchisees submitted monthly profit-and-loss statements. Maaco had an automated accounting system capable of complex statistical analysis.

Maaco's professional staff provided guidance, training, and field and telephone supervision, and help was readily available from other centres. Maaco held regular operations meetings where franchisees exchanged ideas, resolved problems, and received additional training. Further, a weekly newsletter listed the performance of all shops and highlighted new ideas.

Business for a Maaco franchise came from three areas: the retail market (people repainting their cars), the trade and wholesale market (used car dealers, auto rental, etc., who wanted cars repaired or painted), and the collision repair market (cars that were in an accident and usually covered by insurance).

## The Regina Market

*Retail Market.* Martin and Dale contacted another Maaco franchisee, in operation for eight years, who advised them that a Regina Maaco Centre should easily secure a retail market (no collision/claims repair) of $150,000 per year. The average retail complete job was $550 ($350 for paint plus $200 in cosmetic body work). Therefore, securing a market of $150,000 would mean painting 273 retail cars.

Martin did some quick calculation on the retail market. The population of Regina was 175,000, and the number of households was 58,695. Assuming that 90 percent of the households had cars and that 25 percent of these households had two cars, the total number of cars in Regina was 66,030.

How many of these cars would require completes? Perhaps 1 in 10, or 6,603. How many of these car owners could afford to or would care to paint these cars? How many could be enticed if the price was reasonable and the end product was a quality finish? Perhaps one in four, or 1,650 (2.5 percent of the total car population). How many of these 1,650 could be enticed by Maaco's aggressive advertising and marketing to inquire further? Maybe one in four, or 412. Maaco's retention rate—that is, how many inquiries they closed on—was 50 percent. In summation, then, Maaco Regina should attain 206 cars (0.31 percent of the total car population) at $550 each, for a total retail of $113,300.

This did not take into account cars repaired under an insurance claim. A good majority of these car owners would have their entire car painted while it was in for collision repair, if the price was right. As the car was already being handled for body work, paint preparation, and painting, Maaco could afford to reduce its rates.

Could a Maaco Centre handle 206 cars? The season for retail completes was April to August inclusive—22 weeks. This added up to 110 working days, of which perhaps 5 were statutory holidays, leaving 105 days available. This meant approximately two cars per day on average—well within a Maaco Centre's capacity.

***Trade and Wholesale Market.***   Numerous trade sources (used car dealers, auto brokers, fleet and lease disposal specialists, and auto rental centres) were contacted by telephone to determine the amount of trade business available. This market excluded collision/claim repairs. Fleet owners (i.e., City of Regina, SaskTel, Genstar, federal and provincial supply and services, etc.) were not contacted. It was judged that they purchased new vehicles (paint finish, factory ordered) and would, therefore, fall into the collision/claim repair market. The resale (and refurbishing) of these fleets would be included in collision/repair business.

Individuals contacted were briefed on the concept: quality work, reasonable prices, and relatively quick turnaround time. Of those who responded favourably, only one (Regina Mazda Sales) would be reluctant to provide 100 percent of their available work. They considered it important to spread this around among those shops that purchase Mazda parts. Based on their survey, Martin and Dale estimated that the following work was available:

| | | |
|---:|---|---:|
| 473 | completes @ $380 | $179,740 |
| 64 | completes @ $425 | 27,200 |
| 325 | touch-ups/half cars @ $175 | 56,875 |
| 862 | | $263,815 |

For those customers who would provide more than 25 complete paint jobs per annum, a discount was included. Average trade complete job was $425, which the 10 percent discount lowered to $380.

To be realistic, Martin reduced the total by 40 percent to approximately $150,000 per year. Thus, the forecast for trade work was 517 cars handled in one year over 249 working days. On average, the centre would have to handle approximately two cars per day. Again, well within the capacity of a Maaco Centre.

***Collision Market.***   Regina's total collision market was $25 million. They estimated a Maaco franchise should get 1 to 2 percent of that market with an aggressive advertising and promotion budget. This would mean revenues of $250,000 to $500,000 from collision repairs. They felt they should be able to get at least $405,000 from this market. A typical Maaco Centre easily had the capacity for $675,000 of business in collision repair alone.

## Competition

Leading competition in the auto-body industry were A & B, Arcola, Queen City, Regina, and Western. In the best sense of the Maaco concept, competition was very limited. Maaco would ultimately be the industry leader. Most shops were averse to complete paint jobs versus collision repair due to perceived lower margins. Maaco's efficient operations welcomed both paint and collision markets. With an aggressive advertising budget and quality service at a reasonable price, Maaco would become a key player in short order.

## The Investment

The summary of investment in Exhibit 1 was based on a Maaco "Analysis of Investment" and discussions with the franchisor's representatives, other Maaco franchisees, and local body shop owners and suppliers.

The total investment was $180,000—$80,000 cash investment and $100,000 in seven-year term debt that could be arranged under the Small Business Loans Act. This investment secured a turnkey operation.

With respect to the advertising, Maaco collected an initial $2,500 for classified advertising in the *Leader Post* to hire a start-up crew, and for preopening and grand opening retail advertising. With the support of the regional operations representative, Martin planned to ask Maaco to return the $2,500. He would then coordinate his own preopening and grand opening advertising.

With a budget of $6,800 he judged that he would be able to undertake the following:

- An educational brochure circulated to *Leader Post* subscribers in selected areas. The brochure would outline who and where they were, and what services they provided.
- An on-location radio setup for the grand opening.
- A full-page ad in the *Leader Post* (grand opening) in conjunction with their suppliers and contractors.

## Exhibit 1

### *Summary of investment*

| Description | Investment |
| --- | --- |
| License and service fee | $ 15,000 |
| Initial advertising | 6,800 |
| Working capital fee | 6,000 |
| Equipment—including installation, freight, rigging, and provincial sales taxes and custom duties where applicable | 106,890 |
| Inventory—paint, supplies, and stationery | 11,550 |
| Sign package—not including installation | 5,760 |
| Total franchise package | $152,000 |
| First month's rent and security deposit (estimated) | 8,000 |
| Miscellaneous start-up costs (estimated) | 20,000 |
| Total investment | $180,000 |

Martin then worked out a couple of scenarios for the business. A "most likely" scenario projected gross sales at $665,000, resulting in a 60 percent return on the cash investment (Exhibit 2). Sales at $575,000 ("pessimistic" scenario—15 percent reduction, very conservative) resulted in a net loss of $2,405. However, this was after meeting all loan payments, having no accounts payable, and setting aside a $17,800 cash balance to start the second year of operations. Break-even revenue was approximately $584,000.

In these scenarios, Martin felt that expenses were projected very realistically and were overstated in some areas. The second year under both scenarios improved substantially, since one-time start-up expenses were not incurred. Under the "most likely" scenario, the returns were 15 percent and 33 percent; under the worst, the returns were 4 percent and 9 percent.

## The Decision

Martin knew that people brought their cars to an auto-body shop for many reasons:

- To provide normal maintenance, like tune-ups, brakes, and tires.
- To spruce up the family's second car.
- To refurbish their present car until they decide on a new model.
- To protect and restore the original beauty of a special car.
- To repair damage from an accident.

They would bring their car specifically to Maaco because it offered:

- Quality paint services for every budget.
- Written warranties honoured at more than 400 locations.
- State-of-the-art paint finishes.
- Timely service.
- Expert body repairs.
- Full collision repair services, from the minor fender bender to the most extensive collision repairs.
- Extensive experience from servicing more than 3 million customers.

The needs of the Regina market had never before been met economically. Auto dealers, body shops, and "cheap paint" shops had attempted to satisfy the market with various

**EXHIBIT 2**

*Financial projections (first year)*

| | |
|---|---|
| Total sales | $665,000 |
| Cost of sales | 364,234 |
| Gross profit | 300,766 |
| Operating expenses: | 238,913 |
| Net income before tax | 61,852 |
| Tax | 15,463 |
| Net income | 46,389 |
| Add: Depreciation | 10,400 |
| Less: Principal | 16,000 |
| Cash flow | $ 40,789 |

alternatives—limited colour selection, air-dry coating (an inferior process), spot or partial painting, and the high-priced paint job.

Martin was convinced of the merits of the Maaco franchise but wondered if his analysis was sound. Did he and Dale have the administrative and managerial skills and technical expertise to successfully operate the franchise? Should he obtain the franchise?

### Questions

1. Should the partners conduct any further analysis before making the decision?
2. What are the advantages and disadvantages of the Maaco franchise?
3. Should the partners invest in the franchise?

---

## 18.
## WHO'S THE BEST CANDIDATE?

Howard Goldman, the president of David and Charles, a department store in Halifax, Nova Scotia, had a buying vacancy in his misses coat department, and three candidates to choose from to fill it.

The misses coat department was not in good shape. The previous buyer, who had just been let go, had left a lot of distress stock behind, following a season in which sales had dropped nearly 8 percent. Mr. Goldman recognized that the department needed new blood, which was why he was eager to make the best possible choice.

### Paul Coward

The first candidate was the current assistant in the department, Paul Coward. Coward was 28 years old, and had come to the store directly from school five years earlier. He had joined the training group, served as a branch manager, and worked in various coat departments since then. He was familiar with the coat market and the department's vendors, and, of course, knew all store people and systems thoroughly. He had consistently received excellent reviews, but had lost a chance to become misses dress buyer to a candidate with comparable qualifications six months earlier. He had a pleasant personality and was well liked throughout the store.

### Marie Whipple

The second choice was Marie Whipple. Two years younger than Coward, she had been with the store three years, all of which had been in the children's area. Currently, she was associate buyer of children's wear, with full responsibility for buying girls' coats. She had bought these coats for one full season, and her figures showed a respectable 20 percent growth. She had only completed two years of college (as opposed to Coward's four), but was

This case was prepared by David Ehrlich, Marymount University.

known as a hard-driving, no-nonsense kind of buyer. The children's executives thought extremely well of her and recommended her strongly to Mr. Goldman.

### Frank Coyle

Finally, Goldman had received a résumé of an older candidate, Frank Coyle, from an employment agency. Coyle had just been released by one of the Simpson's stores, which had recently undergone a belt-tightening. He had an impressive résumé—20 years of buying coats, and his sales figures and gross margin had always been superior, even in years when the coat business had been difficult. He knew everyone in the coat manufacturing business and had many friends and supporters there. Goldman wondered, though, whether he might not favour too many of his old friends as he came to a new store. Coyle would also cost the store more to hire. His salary would be at least $10,000 higher than what Goldman would pay the other two, and there would be relocation and agency expenses.

### Questions

1. As Howard Goldman, which candidate would you pick?
2. Justify your recommendation.

---

## 19.
## DIAMOND CLOTHIERS

Ruth Diamond, president of Diamond Clothiers, was concerned that sales in her store appeared to have flattened out, and was considering establishing a different method of compensating her salespeople.

Diamond was located in an affluent suburb of Toronto, Ontario. Ruth's father had founded the company 40 years earlier, and she had grown up working in the business. After his retirement in 1980, she moved the store into an upscale shopping mall not far from its previous location, and sales had boomed almost immediately, rising to just over $1 million in five years. However, once it had reached that level, sales volume remained there for the next three years, making Ruth wonder whether her salespeople had sufficient incentive to sell more aggressively.

Diamond's staff was all women, ranging in age from 27 to 58. There were four full-timers and four part-timers (20 hours a week), all of whom had at least three years of experience in the store. All of them were paid at the same hourly rate, which was $10; there was also a liberal health benefit plan. Employee morale was excellent, and the entire staff displayed strong personal loyalty to Mrs. Diamond.

The store was open 78 hours a week, which meant that there was nearly always a minimum staff of three on the floor, rising to six at peak periods. Diamond's merchandise

This case was prepared by David Ehrlich, Marymount University.

consisted exclusively of designer coats and jackets, ranging in price from $750 to more than $5,000 each. The average unit sale was about $2,000. Full-timers' annual sales averaged about $160,000, and the part-timers' were a little over half of that.

Mrs. Diamond's concern about sales transcended her appreciation for her people's loyalty. She had asked them, for example, to maintain customer files and call their customers when new styles came in. While some of them had been more diligent about this than others, none of them appeared to want to be especially aggressive about promoting sales.

So she began to investigate commission systems, and discussed them with some of her contacts in the trade. All suggested lowering the salespeople's base pay and installing either a fixed or a variable commission rate system.

One idea was to lower the base hourly rate from $10 to $7 and let them make up the difference through a 4 percent commission on all sales, to be paid monthly. Such an arrangement would allow them to earn the same as they currently did.

However, she realized that such a system would provide no incentive to sell the higher-priced coats, which she recognized might be a way to improve overall sales. So she considered offering to pay 3 percent on items priced below $2,000 and 5 percent on all those above.

Either of these systems would require considerable bookkeeping. Returns would have to be deducted from commissions, and she was also concerned that disputes might arise among her people from time to time over who had actually made the sale. So she conceived a third alternative, which was to leave the hourly rates the same, but to pay a flat bonus of 4 percent of all sales over $1 million, and divide it among the people on the basis of the proportion of hours each had actually worked. This "commission" would be paid annually, in the form of a Christmas bonus.

## Questions

1. What is your opinion about the various alternatives Mrs. Diamond is considering?
2. Do you have any other suggestions for improving the store's sales?

---

## 20.
## THE GOURMET PALACE

Beverly Long had just finished reviewing with her daughter Alison the results of a survey that she had conducted the previous week. She kept shaking her head, not really understanding the situation. She had thought all along that research would give her the answers she was looking for, but now she wasn't sure.

Mrs. Long is the owner of the Gourmet Palace, a food store specializing in gourmet foods and exotic items from around the world. It is located in an upscale shopping mall situated in the downtown area of an east coast city with a total population of 103,000. The store was opened a year ago, and business has been very uneven and rather disappointing, with large variations during the week and during the year. She confided her problems to a friend, and he suggested that she needed to do some customer research. Her friend worked for a company that often purchased marketing research. He did not have any expertise himself, but he strongly encouraged Mrs. Long to conduct a study of her customers. He added that it shouldn't be too hard for Beverly to design, distribute, and analyze a simple questionnaire on why people shop at her store.

After thinking about this idea for a few days, she sat down and developed the questionnaire shown in Exhibit 1, which seemed to deal with the questions that were bothering her. She had the questionnaires copied by the print shop located in the mall. The following Saturday, she put up a sign inside the store indicating that, in exchange for filling the questionnaire, she would give the customer a free can of tuna. She collected 50 questionnaires that way, which she spent Sunday tabulating.

The results were very disappointing. Many questions were left unanswered, such as addresses, age, and income. In the questions about the store, respondents wrote down one or two words, often quite general and not very useful. About half the respondents shop there once a week, and the other half occasionally. In the second question, several answered milk, bread, and cheeses. In the third question, most said quality and freshness. What they liked least were the high prices. They found out about the store by walking through the mall. For question 7, very few provided a suggestion. Among those who did, some said sushi, caviar, and quails. Most said yes to question 8, and question 9 was not answered by anyone.

Beverly then showed the questionnaire and the results to her daughter Alison who was visiting her from Fredericton. Alison had recently graduated from the University of New Brunswick with a Bachelor of Commerce. Alison immediately reacted with confidence and pride. She said to her mother that she would develop a set of hypotheses, a new questionnaire, a sampling plan, and a plan for analysis before she returned to Fredericton.

## Questions

1. Evaluate the research design and the questionnaire prepared by Mrs. Long.

2. Take the role of Alison and complete the assignment.

**EXHIBIT 1**

*Questionnaire used
by Beverly*

### The Gourmet Palace

Hi! I am conducting a survey today in order to find out your impressions about the Gourmet Palace, and how I can better serve you. Upon completing this questionnaire, you will receive a free can of tuna.

**Information about you:** Please indicate below

Your address  _____

Your age  _____     Your sex  _____

Your occupation  _____

Your approximate family income  _____

Size of your family  _____

**Information about the Gourmet Palace**

1. How often do you shop here?  _____

2. What kinds of food items are you looking for?  _____
   _____

3. What do you like best about the Gourmet Palace?  _____
   _____

4. What do you like least about the Gourmet Palace?  _____
   _____

5. How did you find out about the Gourmet Palace?  _____
   _____

6. How do you find the prices at the Gourmet Palace?  _____
   _____

7. Are there other food products you would like to buy at the Gourmet Palace?  _____
   _____

8. Have you recommended the Gourmet Palace to your friends?  _____
   _____

9. Any other comments?  _____
   _____

*Thank you very much.*

## 21.
# F. B. Smith/McKay Florists Ltd.

In April 1990, Marie Robbins, owner of F. B. Smith/McKay Florists Ltd. of Hamilton, Ontario, was considering whether or not to relocate one of her retail stores. The lease was up for renewal at the end of August. Marie believed that any decision she made would have a profound impact on the future of that store, in particular, and her business, in general.

## Company Background

In 1990, Smith/McKay Florists consisted of three separate outlets. Marie, a native of Hamilton, purchased F. B. Smith Florists in 1980 and McKay Florists in 1983. These two established florists were among the oldest flower stores in Hamilton, having been opened in 1919 and 1907, respectively. Marie blended the two business names in 1985 before establishing a third outlet in 1988.

Prior to 1980, Marie had been a Family Studies teacher for grades 8 to 12 in the public school system. Although she had little experience in the florist business, Marie valued her independence and saw the store as an outlet for her entrepreneurial spirit and creative energies. Lacking both floral design and business experience, Marie worked over the summer of 1980 with the former owners before launching out on her own.

The location in question was the original site of F. B. Smith Florists. Located between the Pioneer Restaurant and the Canadian Imperial Bank of Commerce, the building was on the south side of King Street West, between James and MacNab Streets. Her other two locations were 238 James Street North (the original site of McKay Florists) and 1685 Main Street West. All three locations had a reputation for quality, service, and rapid delivery.

In 1990, Marie had 12 employees at the King Street store who served customers and arranged flowers. The centre of her operations was the James Street store where she combined a retail outlet with storage, office space, and a floral design production facility. Daily flower deliveries were handled by a local delivery service. Smith/McKay Florists belonged to the FTD (Florist Transworld Delivery), the AFS (American Florist Service), and the Teleflora networks. Phone-in sales accounted for 75 percent of the King Street store's current business.

The average customer spent $22 at Marie's stores—$28 at a holiday time. On average, Marie did $300 to $500 per day in business at the King Street store. Her product mix was relatively simple: cut flowers, silk flowers, potted plants, and arrangements. She had found that items priced under $5 tended to be purchased as impulse goods on a cash and carry basis. The King Street store was open from 8:00 A.M. to 5:30 P.M. daily and closed early at 4:00 P.M. on Saturday.

## The Florist Business in Hamilton

Between 1985 and 1990, the florist business in Hamilton flourished. Approximately 33 shops were opened, bringing the total number to 95 stores. According to Marie, the rapid expansion of the market created a "neighbourhood phenomenon." Almost every neighbourhood in the city had at least one florist.

This case was prepared by Marvin Ryder, McMaster University.

The flower business was seasonal by nature. The sales peaks were Valentine's Day, Easter, Mother's Day, and Christmas. The worst months for flower sales were June, July, August, October, November, January, February (except for February 14), and March. On the other hand, December flower sales accounted for 25 percent of her yearly revenue. For the remainder of the year, anniversary, funeral, wedding, birthday, and hospital arrangements accounted for the majority of the sales volume.

Smith/McKay Florists faced competition on three fronts. First, it competed directly for the phone-in business with any florist shops listed in the Yellow Pages. Second, it competed for walk-in traffic with other nearby florist shops. Third, there was competition from the grocery stores, which carried both plants and cut flowers. Because of their buying power, they could offer flowers at a cheaper price. They did not offer arrangements or delivery. All the florist shops in Hamilton purchased their flowers from the same suppliers.

In some ways, Marie believed the grocery store sales might actually be beneficial. "Grocery stores may help encourage people to purchase flowers. Getting them into the habit of buying flowers will help my business. Further, when they visit my store, they should be able to see the extra quality that I offer."

In addition to the Yellow Pages, Marie participated in many promotional activities. She placed a bimonthly ad in the classified section of *The Hamilton Spectator* between the birth and death notices. She also used a limited amount of radio ads. She advertised during the "Garden Doctor" radio show on a local station for a couple of weeks prior to a special holiday. She also had occasion cards printed (with her company name and address) for customer use.

## The Location Decision

Since Marie first bought the store, Smith/McKay Florists had been renewing its lease on an annual basis. The monthly rental, $800, had been unchanged since 1984. That figure included one third of the property taxes on the store (the landlord paid the rest) and did not include heat ($2,500 per year) or hydro ($225 per month). However, as of August 1990, the monthly rent would increase 50 percent. In addition to the proposed rent hike, Marie was concerned about persistent rumours that the block in which the store was located would be torn down to make way for a large office building. She knew that the Canadian Imperial Bank of Commerce had been buying up the properties around the store for the last few years and had expressed an interest in this property, too. Marie was anxious, therefore, to explore alternative locations for her shop.

## Alternatives

Although in theory Smith/McKay Florists could relocate anywhere in the city, Marie had a preference for the downtown Hamilton area, where her target market—the upscale suburban consumer—lived and worked. She felt that she must stay downtown, so any potential location should be within four to five blocks of her current location. If she were too remote, loyal customers might not be able to find her. The alternative locations, therefore, were selected with this criterion in mind.

*Park Place.*    Park Place, a recently opened shopping/office complex, was located on the northwest corner of King and Hughson Streets. The building had been home to a furniture store for nearly 75 years until it closed in 1987. Sand blasted and completely renovated inside, the mall was targeted to the luxury consumer. Only a few stores and businesses had moved into the building so far. The complex managers had a prime 46-square-metre location that they felt was proper for a flower store. The King Street store had over 186 square metres of space.

The rent at Park Place was $359 per square metre per year, and heating was included. Management indicated that there would be no trouble negotiating a five-year lease. Marie estimated hydro costs to be $70 per month. No parking was available at the mall, but there were two large municipal lots within three blocks of the building. As the only florist in this mall, Smith/McKay would get all the florist business. Yet business would have to improve to cover her increased costs.

Starting with the concrete floors and unfinished walls, and given the mall's luxury image, Marie estimated that her renovation costs would be about $40,000. As well, there would be a delay in the completion date of any renovations, as the management was waiting for a special carpeting that all stores were supposed to use. This location was three blocks east of her current store, and she estimated that moving costs would be about $3,000. All the one-way streets in the downtown core added to the total time a move would take.

Marie was uncertain about this location for two reasons. First, the mall was new. There was little traffic through the mall, as there were very few stores. As far as business traffic was concerned, so few companies had taken office space that she was unable to predict any level of walk-in sales. She also questioned her ability to maintain a high profile in the larger Hamilton community. She felt that the downtown core was expanding to the west and a move to the east could really isolate her business.

*Jackson Square.*    Jackson Square, a major development, first opened in 1972, and two expansions to the mall were completed in 1977 and 1989. The mall was situated opposite her current King Street location. The mall complex included the recently-opened Sheraton Hotel and Victor K. Copps Coliseum. The development was bounded by King, James, York, and Bay Streets. The density of housing was high with many apartments and condominiums nearby. Four office towers had been incorporated into the complex. As well, three underground parking lots were available for up to 1,000 cars.

The trading area for the mall was defined to be the downtown business community and apartment dwellers. Few people from outside the city or from the Hamilton Mountain area shopped at the mall on a regular basis. Over the past few years, many suburban malls had opened (Eastgate Mall and Centre Mall in the east end and Lime Ridge Mall on the mountain), yet few customers had been lured away. There already was one florist, Brandi's House of Flowers, in Jackson Square, which had just opened for business. Given the large number of shoppers who frequented the mall, Smith/McKay Florists, as the only other florist, would benefit substantially.

The length of the lease was negotiable, but Marie felt that five years would be the maximum that she could obtain. In spite of the obvious advantages offered by a dynamic mall, Marie was concerned about the monthly rent. Mall managers were asking $452 per square metre per year rent, which included heating and air conditioning. She estimated that her hydro costs would be $75 per month. Marie wondered whether the potential increase in walk-in business would offset the increase in rent.

Mall management were offering her a 39-square-metre space, which was about one-fifth the size of her current location. Even with that small size, she estimated that renovations to the location would cost $35,000 and could take up to two months to complete. Moving and purchases of new furnishings could cost another $1,500. Marie also wondered what impact extended mall hours (Monday, Tuesday, Wednesday, and Saturday—9:30 A.M. to 5:30 P.M.; Thursday and Friday—9:30 A.M. to 9:00 P.M.) would have on her staffing. She had found it difficult in the past to find and train good staff.

***King Street.***     The King Street location was the bottom half of a car rental agency, situated at the very busy intersection of Caroline and King Streets, two blocks from the exclusive Hess Village shopping area of Hamilton. Marie would purchase the building for between $125,000 and $140,000 rather than lease. The top floor could be used for office and storage space and, perhaps, a one-bedroom apartment could be created and rented out. Marie estimated total renovation costs to be about $75,000. Other pertinent costs included a large illuminated sign ($1,500), property taxes ($7,750 per year), heating and hydro (same as current location). Total usable floor space amounted to 149 square metres.

Marie believed that the volume of drive-by traffic would increase the store's visibility. King Street was one of the city's main traffic arteries. The traffic flow, at the end of the day when people might want to take flowers home to a loved one, was going the "correct" way. Ten parking spaces were available on the property, and four major bus routes had stops nearby.

Although Marie felt that aesthetically the location had great potential, she had reservations. Though the property was zoned for commercial business, Marie felt that she would have to spend $4,000 in legal fees to purchase the building. As well, in light of her success downtown, Marie was concerned that the location was too isolated from other retail outlets and the office building workers that she relied upon for her business. A used car lot, a maternity clothing store, and a print shop occupied the other three corners of the intersection—residential housing, some of it newly renovated, apartments, and some small shops made up the rest of the immediate area.

Marie's friends and business associates urged her not to move away from the downtown core where Smith/McKay Florists was an established member of the retail community.

If she decided to move, Marie knew she would have to promote to tell people where the store was going. With the alternatives in mind, Marie wondered what she should do.

## Questions

1. What location would you recommend?
2. Justify your recommendation.

22.

# Housewares Unlimited

Paul Crowne had a decision to make—which one of five possible locations to select within the Conestoga Mall for his new housewares store. After working for eight years as a buyer for Sears, Paul had returned to his hometown of Waterloo to open his own store.

With the experience gained at Sears, Paul had been able to identify many suppliers in both North America and Europe who manufactured top-quality housewares at very competitive prices. In many cases, these manufacturers were not well-known and, as a result, sold primarily on the basis of price, as opposed to brand name. Paul was convinced that a store that offered a wide and shallow range of housewares would succeed. His plan was to offer the best value product in each area with very limited choice. For example, he would offer only one line of coffee-makers—from a Swedish manufacturer—that were quality products at competitive prices. His total merchandise line would consist of all the items necessary in the preparation and serving of food (excluding major appliances). The line would include pots, pans, mixing bowls, utensils, kettles, small appliances, baskets, cannisters, place mats, napkins, table cloths, and other items in the houseware line.

Paul had grown up and gone to college in Waterloo, Ontario. During his years with Sears he had worked in Toronto and Montreal but always had the desire to return to Waterloo. While working, he had saved sufficient funds to open his store, which he planned to call Housewares Unlimited, and in the summer of 1989, he resigned from Sears and returned to Waterloo.

Paul spent the next two months contacting the suppliers and establishing his merchandise line. As well, he looked for a site for his new store. Waterloo is one of the two twin cities (Kitchener being the other) located 100 kilometres west of Toronto. The population of Waterloo is 70,000 and of Kitchener is 130,000. Both cities are part of a census metropolitan area (CMA) that has a population exceeding 322,000. Both personal incomes and retail sales in the CMA are above the Canadian average.

After examining a number of possible sites, Paul decided that a shopping mall would be a desirable location because of the traffic volume generated by the mall. After studying each of the malls in the area, he decided that the Conestoga Mall, located in North Waterloo, would be ideal. Many new housing developments were springing up in the area, and the majority of stores in the mall stocked medium-priced merchandise, which would be consistent with Paul's plan to sell quality items at competitive prices.

The Conestoga Mall was a regional enclosed mall that had 80 stores and parking for 1,868 cars. The primary market (within 5 kilometres of the mall) included 89,000 people and 44,000 households. The secondary market (within 7 kilometres of the mall) included 97,500 people and 22,000 households. The average household income in the prime market was $46,100 per year. The anchor tenants in the mall were Robinson's, a department store chain, Kmart, another department store chain, and Zehrs, a supermarket chain owned by Loblaws. Exhibit 1 provides a layout of the mall.

Paul's major competitor in the mall would be Robinson's, which offered medium-priced houseware goods. Although Robinson's would be a strong competitor, Paul felt that his merchandise line offered a unique alternative to customers. Kmart was another competitor, but the houseware items offered were lower priced and of lower quality. Paul felt he was targeting a different group of customers from Kmart's. The only other competitor was Pot

**EXHIBIT 1**

*The Conestoga Mall*

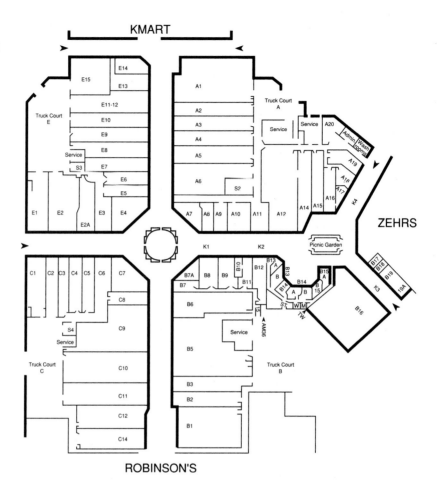

Pourri, which offered specialty houseware items at medium prices. However, Pot Pourri focused mainly on kitchen items, whereas Paul would offer a far wider range.

Much to Paul's delight, upon inquiring about spaces for lease in Conestoga Mall, he discovered that due to a recent remodelling of the mall, five locations would be available for lease. The locations that would be available were A3, B7A, C4, B2, and A16. The corresponding sizes and costs per square metre are given in Exhibit 2.

Rents are based, among other things, on the traffic flow in various parts of the mall. The shops in the centre square paid the highest rent per square metre as most people passed through the centre square at least once while in the mall. The largest parking lot is located outside sections E and C, and therefore stores along that strip had the highest traffic flow. This is followed by the strips leading to Kmart and Robinson's. The traffic flow was considered to be equal along these two strips, and there were parking lots of equal size outside both Kmart and Robinson's. The strip between section A and B was the least travelled section. People going to Zehrs generally parked in the lot outside Zehrs, did their shopping, and left.

## EXHIBIT 1 *(concluded)*

**Ladies'**

| | |
|---|---|
| A9 | Cotton Ginny |
| B5 | Fairweather |
| E8 | Irene Hill |
| B1 | Northern Reflections |
| C12 | Pennington's |
| C10 | Reitmans |
| E6 | Smart Set |
| B6 | Suzy Shier |
| C9 | The Loft |
| B3 | Town & Country |
| C11 | Venus Lingerie |
| B2 | Zacks |
| B7A | N·K·D |
| E4 | Tan Jay |
| E11/12 | D'Allaird's |

**Men's**

| | |
|---|---|
| B5 | Big Steel |
| C9 | Jack Fraser |
| A6 | Tip Top |

**Unisex**

| | |
|---|---|
| C4 | Athlete's World |
| C5 | Bootlegger |
| C6 | Class Reunion |
| B12 | Joggers |
| E9 | Thrifty's |

**Children's**

| | |
|---|---|
| E10 | Young Canada |
| B1 | UB Anywear |
| A8 | Dr. Denton |

**Junior Department Stores**

| | |
|---|---|
| A1 | BiWay |
| A12 | Marks & Spencer |

**Shoes**

| | |
|---|---|
| E13 | Agnew |
| E5 | Belinda & Brother |
| B7 | Dolan |
| A5 | Kinney's |
| E7 | Maher |
| E15 | Shoeworld |
| A10 | Julia |

**Jewellery and Gifts**

| | |
|---|---|
| C7 | Mappins |
| A7 | Peoples |
| B11 | Young's |

**Drugs, Stationery, Books, and Records**

| | |
|---|---|
| C2 | A & A Records |
| A14 | Coles Books |
| C14 | Carlton Cards |
| E14 | Direct Film |
| A11 | Hallmark |
| B18 | Japan Camera |
| B16 | Shoppers Drug Mart |
| A18 | Smokers Den |
| A2 | W.H. Smith |

**Sporting Goods, Hobbies and Toys**

| | |
|---|---|
| A17 | Leisure World |
| E2A | Dufferin Games Room |

**Specialty Shops**

| | |
|---|---|
| C8 | Baronessa |
| B9 | Flowers N' Fancies |
| K2 | Faces |
| A4 | Kitchener Textiles |
| A15 | Radio Shack |
| E12 | Singer |

**Home Furnishings**

| | |
|---|---|
| E3 | Pot Pourri |
| A3 | St. Clair Paint & Paper |
| C3 | Atlantique Sound & Video |

**Specialty Food**

| | |
|---|---|
| A19 | General Nutrition Centre |
| B8 | Laura Secord |
| E2 | Timothy's Coffees |

**Restaurants**

| | |
|---|---|
| E2 | Tiffany Restaurant |

**Fast Food**

| | |
|---|---|
| B13 | Treats |
| B13A | Grandma Lee's |
| B13B | Arthur Treachers Fish & Chips |
| B14 | Mrs. Vanelli's |
| B14A | Sizzling Wok |
| B14B | Sailor's Steamer Hot Dogs |
| B15 | A&W |
| B15A | Spatz Frozen Yogourt Emporium |

**Services**

| | |
|---|---|
| K3 | Battery 1 Stop |
| K4 | Express |
| K1 | Infoplace |
| B17 | Meissner Travel |
| B10 | Things Engraved |
| A20 | Trillium Dental |
| B19/19A | Total Image |

**Financial**

| | |
|---|---|
| C1 | Canada Trust |
| E1 | Canadian Imperial Bank of Commerce |

**Major Tenants**

Kmart
Robinson's
Zehrs
Leamon Auto Service

| | |
|---|---|
| **82** | **Stores and Services** |

Exhibit 2

**Information on store sites**

| Store | Physical Size | Total Square Metres | Rent per Square Metre per Year |
|-------|---------------|---------------------|-------------------------------|
| A16 | 7.3 × 15.8 m | 116 | $215.00 |
| A3 | 7.3 × 20.4 m | 149 | 237.00 |
| B7A | 7.9 × 5.8 m | 46 | 269.00 |
| C4 | 7.9 × 16.8 m | 133 | 247.00 |
| B2 | 7.3 × 18.9 m | 138 | 237.00 |

Paul was somewhat concerned about the rental cost, as his cash flow would be tight in the first few months of operation. However, he also felt that he needed a location with a reasonable amount of traffic flow to ensure people became aware that his store existed. Paul estimated that the ideal size for a store to hold his merchandise line would be around 120 square metres, but he also knew that a slightly smaller store would be more economical.

## Questions

1. What store site would you recommend?
2. Justify your recommendation.

---

## 23.
## THE BEST DISPLAY?

A major department store, one of the three oldest in Canada, recognized that the first-floor selling fixtures in its main branch had become outmoded and had set aside funds to renovate. The main floor had not been changed appreciably since the store was built in the 1920s. There were a number of handsome mahogany-panelled counter islands, which had always given the store an aura of tasteful elegance.

Jim Lewis, director of store fixturing, was debating the merits of several possible display systems. The selling departments that would be affected by the renovation were cosmetics; fine and costume jewellery; women's handbags, scarves, and belts; men's shirts, ties, and furnishings; women's sweaters; and gifts.

As Lewis saw it, the two major issues surrounding his decision were incompatible. On the one hand, the store wanted to make merchandise as accessible to customers as possible; on the other hand, experience had indicated that open-selling fixtures inevitably led to more shoplifting. As an experiment, the store had tried substituting self-service fixtures in its upstairs men's sweater department a year earlier. Sales jumped 30 percent, but inventory shrinkage in the department had gone from 2 to almost 5 percent.

A further consideration was that the size and quality of the staff on the selling floor had

This case was prepared by David Ehrlich, Marymount University.

declined dramatically. In 1929, there were always two salespeople behind every counter, and customers could count on never having to wait for service. However, selling costs had since escalated, and the store's staff was less than half what it had been then. Furthermore, the store had instituted modern point-of-sale cash registers that enabled every salesperson to ring up a sale from any department in the store at any register. Most of the clerks were paid minimum wage and were only working there until something better turned up. Although some were able to provide useful selling information to the public, most could do little more than ring up sales.

The kind of open-selling fixtures Lewis was considering were contemporary and very attractive. They allowed the customer to pick up, unfold, or unpackage merchandise, try it on if appropriate, and then return it to the fixture. Such fixtures would unquestionably lead to more sales, especially since the customer could merely look for any salesperson or perhaps go to a central cashier to pay. However, it was equally unquestionable that such easy access to merchandise, especially to small goods, would encourage shoplifting and increase the need for ongoing stock-keeping.

Another disadvantage to the new type of fixturing was that in addition to being contemporary, it was somewhat trendy, which would lead to the need to replace it in a few years, thereby adding to capital costs.

An alternative system would be to retain the old counter islands, or a portion of them, but to put more goods on the countertops to encourage a measure of self-service. The disadvantage here, of course, would be the blocking of sight lines. Salespeople could not see customers, customers could not see salespeople, and the store security personnel could not see either. There would also need to be more policing by the store's display and merchandising staff to be sure the countertops looked inviting at all times. Manufacturers often contribute countertop displays to stores as part of the merchandise buying, and many of them might not be in harmony with the store's overall appearance.

Lewis recognized that he would have to make some compromises. Every affected department has its own peculiarities, and his job was to minimize those differences, rather than allow them to get out of hand. Some merchandise, such as fine jewellery, would obviously have to remain behind glass, but other departments would probably do much better by opening up their stocks to the public.

## Questions

1. What display system would you recommend? Why?
2. Would you make the same recommendation for each of the affected departments? Why or why not?

## 24.
## NOBLE FOODSTUFFS

James Noble was puzzled by the design layout he had just received for his new supermarket (Exhibit 1). He was very uncomfortable with it, but could not quite say why, and if it needed to be changed, he did not know what should be done.

   James Noble is a young entrepreneur. He graduated two years ago from the University of Calgary with a Bachelor of Commerce. He immediately started working for a supermarket chain in Penticton, British Columbia. However, he soon realized that he did not like working for a large corporation, and that he really wanted to be his own boss. With a bank loan, and money lent to him by his father, he had rented a corner location in a newly built shopping mall in a mixed working–middle class neighbourhood of Calgary. The mall had rented all 18 stores. Noble Foodstuffs was the only supermarket in the mall. There were also a small department store and several small boutiques. The mall had a 100-car parking lot.

**EXHIBIT 1**   *Proposed layout for Noble Foodstuffs*

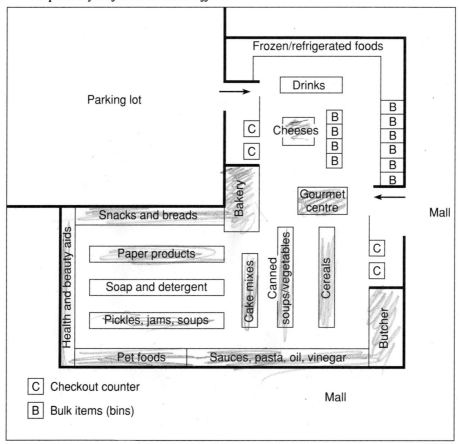

James Noble decided to use a store design consultant to help in planning the layout for the new store. He had asked his designer to take into account a number of current trends that he found in various newspaper and magazine articles:

- The trend toward more bulk items, and items that are not damaging to the environment.
- The trend toward gourmet items, as well as freshly baked breads, muffins, and pastries.
- The trend toward fresh fish, seafood, and specialty cuts of meat.
- The trend toward adding nonfood items in supermarkets.

The designer had just brought a first draft of her work, and James Noble needed to approve the layout before work could start. He was bothered by a number of decisions the designer had made, including the location of check-out counters, the placement and size of the different departments, and the flow of traffic in the store. He also had to decide on the interior design of the store—that is, what kind of atmosphere and image did he want to create inside his supermarket?

## Questions

1. Evaluate the design proposed by the consultant.
2. What changes, if any, would you recommend? Why?

## 25.
## JIM'S SPORTING GOODS

Jim's Sporting Goods, a large store, offers a complete range of sporting goods and accessories to both beginners and experts. The store consists of 16 departments (labelled A to P), each carrying a sports line (e.g., hockey, baseball) or types of clothing (e.g., beach wear, hiking). Recently, an issue arose concerning space allocations for two departments.

The two adjacent departments have space, sales, and sales per square metre as follows:

|         | Square Metres | Annual Sales | Sales per Square Metre |
|---------|---------------|--------------|------------------------|
| Dept. A | 84            | $ 63,000     | $750                   |
| Dept. B | 93            | 50,000       | 538                    |
|         | 177           | $113,000     | $638                   |

Department A is in urgent need of 19 square metres of additional space to provide adequate display and storage space for a line that is enjoying an upward trend in popularity. There is considerable evidence that a good deal of potential business is being lost because of

This case was prepared by Aldo J. Cimpello, Algonquin College of Applied Arts and Technology.

the inadequate space. The manager is convinced that he can generate $750 a square metre from the additional space requested.

   The only practical way to do this is to take away 19 square metres from Department B, where space does not seem to have been used to best advantage and where volume is barely holding its own. Better layout planning should increase the average sales per square metre in B to $592. But dollar sales, nevertheless, will be reduced considerably in B, to which the manager of that department objects.

## Questions

1. If management decides to make the proposed change, how much may total sales of the two departments combined be increased?
2. What will be the increase in sales per square metre for the total area?

---

## 26.
## BETTY'S FASHIONS

Anne Lemont, the buyer for Betty's Fashions, was preparing the merchandising plan for the store for the spring season (February–July). Betty's Fashions is a women's fashion accessory store located in Charlottetown, Prince Edward Island. As a first step, Anne filled in the previous year's sales, stock, markdowns, and purchases as well as this year's targets (initial markup, gross margin, etc.) on the six-month merchandising plan (Exhibit 1). She then reviewed the information she had, which included:

- The planned sales increase for the forthcoming season was 20 percent.
- The planned markdown rate was 15 percent.
- Last year, Betty's Fashions underwent a major renovation and expansion that was completed on May 1st. This resulted in a 30 percent sales increase for that month, and an average 25 percent sales increase for the balance of the season.
- A new shopping centre located approximately 3 kilometres from the store is presently under construction and is scheduled to open on April 1st. Betty, the store owner, has estimated that it may attract up to 10 percent of the store's customers.
- Betty feels very strongly that for the type of merchandise the store offers (fashion accessories—jewellery, handbags, scarves, hats, etc.), the major seasonal clearance should be held back until July—rather than June, as it was done last year.
- Anne noted that she had just confirmed with one of the store's major suppliers that Betty's Fashions would be given an exclusive promotion of 50 percent off on a wide assortment of fashion jewellery for the month of March. Anne had bought $30,000 at retail for this promotion.
- A two-week strike at a major local plant last year in February resulted in a 5 percent decrease in sales for this period.

   With this information in mind, Anne began preparing the merchandising plan.

This case was prepared by B. Chevallier, Sheridan College of Applied Arts and Technology.

**Exhibit 1**

*Merchandising plan form*

| | | Betty's Fashions | |
|---|---|---|---|
| | | Plan *(this year)* | Actual *(last year)* |
| **Six-Month Merchandising Plan** | Initial markup (%) | 48.0 | 47.5 |
| | Gross margin (%) | 42.0 | 41.7 |
| | Cash discount (% cost purchase) | 7.9 | 7.8 |
| | Season stock turnover (rate) | 3.0 | 2.8 |
| | Shortage reserve (%) | 1.6 | 1.7 |
| | Advertising expense (%) | 3.5 | 3.0 |
| | Selling salaries (%) | 8.4 | 8.6 |

| *Spring 199—* | | *Feb.* | *Mar.* | *Apr.* | *May* | *June* | *July* | *Season Total* |
|---|---|---|---|---|---|---|---|---|
| **Sales** | Last year | 105 | 140 | 160 | 225 | 175 | 155 | 960 |
| | Plan | | | | | | | |
| | Percent of increase | | | | | | | |
| | Revised | | | | | | | |
| | Actual | | | | | | | |
| **Retail Stock (BOM)** | Last year | 330 | 360 | 360 | 410 | 340 | 290 | 320 |
| | Plan | | | | | | | |
| | Revised | | | | | | | |
| | Actual | | | | | | | |
| **Markdowns** | Last year | 20 | 24 | 28 | 20 | 25 | 20 | 137 |
| | Plan (dollars) | | | | | | | |
| | Plan (percent) | | | | | | | |
| | Revised | | | | | | | |
| | Actual | | | | | | | |
| **Retail Purchases** | Last year | 155 | 164 | 238 | 175 | 150 | 205 | 1087 |
| | Plan | | | | | | | |
| | Revised | | | | | | | |
| | Actual | | | | | | | |

Note: All figures in thousands of dollars.

## Questions

1. Prepare the merchandise plan for the next six months.
2. Provide a rationale for each month's planned sales increase or decrease.

---

## 27.
## ROGER'S DEPARTMENT STORE

A new general merchandise manager was recently appointed at Roger's large urban department store. He arrived with a reputation as an aggressive merchant, a believer in low inventories and high turnover and in taking advantage of unusual buying opportunities whenever possible.

His credo was, "If we could fill our stores with new merchandise *every single day,* we would be the smartest buyers in the country. I want us to run *lean and mean.* I want us to be bringing in fresh goods every day. And I want everything we buy to be bought at the best possible prices."

The store had tended to be quite lax under the previous management, allowing inventories to pile up early in the season, and leaving little open-to-buy available to make advantageous late-season market breaks.

At his first meeting with his buyers, he issued the following instructions: "Please come back to me with a plan that will improve sales by at least 10 percent, and will reflect a stockturn of at least 3.25 times next fall season."

The handbag buyer took out her last year's sales figures and tried to put together a plan that she could achieve and that would also meet her new boss's guidelines.

Last year's results in sales dollars were as follows (in thousands):

| Month | Beginning Inventory | Purchases | Sales | Ending Inventory |
|-------|---------------------|-----------|-------|------------------|
| August | 225 | 135 | 60 | 300 |
| September | 300 | 75 | 100 | 275 |
| October | 275 | 95 | 70 | 300 |
| November | 300 | 165 | 90 | 375 |
| December | 375 | 25 | 200 | 200 |
| January | 200 | 20 | 60 | 160 |
| Total | | 515 | 580 | 262 (average) |

Last year's stockturn, she calculated, was only 2.21 times, and she had to agree that she had been careless. However, she was concerned that she would only be able to meet the new guidelines if she were allowed several ads.

This case was prepared by David Ehrlich, Marymount University.

## Questions

1. As the buyer, work out a plan that will produce sales of $650,000 and that will meet the merchandise manager's goal of 3.25 turns.

2. After doing this, you feel the requirements are too tough without a lot of advertising. Work out an advertising programme that you think will help you achieve the 10 percent sales increase. Be specific about what kinds of merchandise you will want to advertise and when.

---

## 28.
## THE LYON'S DEN

The Lyon's Den had been a winner ever since Jane and Jim Lyon opened their gift shop in an old renovated home in Victoria, British Columbia, and moved in over it. The business was started in 1950. Over the years, it had become *the* place for gifts and, eventually, decorating services in a city of some 260,000. Their apartment was a showcase for the many lines of fine silver, china, crystal, and decorator furniture items that were carried in the shop.

Over the years, their lines expanded. To the traditional gift lines they added cosmetics and linens. Nothing in the shop was carried anywhere else in the trade area, and their lines were unique in that they were all Canadian made. Jane and Jim felt that exclusivity was a major advantage for The Lyon's Den.

Several years ago, Jane, who does the bulk of the buying (Jim is the decorator and takes care of the books), felt that she had secured a market exclusive for the area. She was able to acquire the finest and most prestigious lines of stainless Hensen. The name was not known in the market, but the quality was unsurpassed. Jane knew that, given an exclusive, she could develop a demand for the line that would make her a leading outlet for the merchandise. She had done this before; she knew good products and was a retailer with foresight—an entrepreneur who liked a challenge. The salesperson, whom she met at a regional trade show, assured her of market protection, and thus she set out to launch the new line.

She ran ads and invited special customers to attend a reception to meet the manufacturer. The market had probably never had such a dramatic introduction and perhaps never would again. After a year and a half, the line was one of the most profitable in the shop. Brides were convinced that, without Hensen from The Lyon's Den, marriage was out of the question. Jane had done what she set out to do—create a market demand for the line and bring in new customers because of it.

Just this morning, Jane got a phone call from the Toronto office of Hensen's. The national sales manager was on the phone with some distressing news for The Lyon's Den. Lucille's Table Top, a new market entrant carrying medium- to high-priced table accessories, had just been into the Toronto showroom and had bought the Hensen line. The sales manager felt that since Lucille's was in a shopping centre in Victoria some distance from The Lyon's Den, the competition would be negligible. In addition, the sales manager said that company policy was actually not to give exclusives in a market. The salesperson who originally opened the Lyon's account had not been aware of the policy.

## Questions

1. What options are available to Jane?
2. What are the advantages and disadvantages to a supplier of granting a retailer the exclusive right to sell a line of merchandise?

---

## 29.
## Ashley's

Sally Jones, sweater buyer for Ashley's, a 10-unit department store, was making her plans for a forthcoming buying trip to the Far East. Ashley's, an upper-crust store, had made its first direct buying venture to Hong Kong last year and had been quite successful, with several knitwear purchases totalling some $1 million at retail. It was anxious to expand its direct importing.

For this trip, Ashley's intended to examine the advisability of transferring its entire shetland sweater business to this market, and Sally had been asked to evaluate the desirability of substituting Hong Kong shetlands for a domestic programme that had been successful for the last five years.

Last fall's shetland sales were approximately 6,000 units (500 dozen), and the store hoped to increase sales to 7,200 pieces this year. The price was $32 each, and nearly all units were sold without a markdown.

Banner, Ashley's source last year, is a large domestic sweater producer, operating in an old Montreal mill. It buys its yarn abroad and turns out its production on somewhat antiquated machinery. It is known for an unusual colour sense and reliability for on-time delivery and ability to fill in sizes and colours on a one-week basis. Last fall, Ashley had placed two orders for 2,400 units each on July 25 and September 25, as well as weekly fill-ins. This year's wholesale price had already been announced: $15.75 less 8 percent.

In a price list received from Yu Pei Mee, a Hong Kong supplier, Sally noticed shetland sweaters that appeared of a quality comparable to Banner's being offered at $7.60 net. The colour range was just as broad as Banner's.

Making the Hong Kong buy would require accepting a single shipment of all 7,200 sweaters in July, and also, the store would have to tie its money up in a letter of credit from February until July.

Further investigation disclosed that Canadian customs duty on wool sweaters was 25 percent of the cost, and that air freight and other expenses associated with buying abroad would come to about $10,000.

Sally's final consideration was that shetland sweaters just might fall out of fashion favour next fall, causing huge markdowns, although she doubted that.

Her choice, therefore, was between the higher markup afforded by the Hong Kong sweaters, and the reliable service provided by the domestic supplier.

This case was prepared by Professor David Ehrlich, Marymount University.

## Questions

1. Figure the difference in gross margin between buying domestically and abroad, assuming all units are sold at full price.

2. As Sally, would you recommend buying (1) in Hong Kong, (2) domestically, or (3) some kind of third option?

---

## 30.
## COURTNEY'S

For the last two years, Courtney's, an upscale gift store, has carried a sweet-smelling potpourri in a plastic bag with an attractive ribbon at Christmastime. The mixture is heavily scented with cloves and gives a pleasant holiday aroma to any room, including the store at holiday time.

Two years ago, the mixture cost $4.50 a bag, and Courtney's, the only store in town that carried it, sold 300 pieces for $9.50. Courtney's supply ran out 10 days before Christmas, and it was too late to get any more.

Last year, the manufacturer raised the price to $5.00, and Courtney's raised its retail to $9.95. Even though the markup was lower than the previous year, the store owner, Linda Courtney, felt there was "magic" in the $10 price. As before, the store experienced a complete sellout, this time five days before Christmas. Sales this year were 600 units.

This year, the wholesale price has gone up to $5.50, and store personnel are trying to determine the correct retail price. Linda's feeling is once again to hold the price at $10 ($9.95), but the buyer, Jason Blue, disagrees:

"It's my job to push for the highest possible markup wherever I can. This item is a sure seller, as we're still the only store around with it, and we had some unsatisfied demand last year. I think we should market it at $12.50, which will improve the markup to 56 percent. Staying at $10 will penalize us unnecessarily, especially considering the markup would be even lower than last year. Even if we run into price resistance, we'll only have to sell 480 to maintain the same dollar volume."

Linda responded: "This scent is part of our store's ambience. It acts as a draw to get people into the store, and its pleasant smell keeps them in a free-spending state of mind. I think we should keep the price at $9.95, despite the poorer markup. And if we can sell many more at this price, we'll realize the same dollar gross margin as last year. I think we should buy 1,000. Furthermore, if people see us raising the price of a familiar item by 25 percent, they might wonder whether our other prices are fair."

## Questions

1. What price should Courtney's charge?
2. What do you think sales would be at each price level?
3. Which price would result in the most profits?

This case was prepared by Professor David Ehrlich, Marymount University.

4. What other factors should Courtney's consider?

5. How many units would you order?

---

## 31.
## CLASSY FORMAL WEAR

Stephen Hecht, grandson of Marcus Hecht, the founder of Classy Formal Wear, and now executive vice president and chief operating officer of the company, was considering how his new line of tuxedos, made in Korea and carrying the Yves Saint Laurent label, should be priced. It was June 1987. A large quantity of new, black, pure wool tuxedos would be arriving in early 1988 at a cost that would permit a retail price well below any comparable tuxedo in the market. However, a low price might have an unfavourable impact on the firm's marketing image among its most important customers. Stephen Hecht was pondering both the tactical and strategic consequences of alternative prices, in preparation for choosing a price for the new line.

### History and Growth

Marcus Hecht had founded the firm in 1919. It was one of the first formal wear rental stores in Canada. At the time, formal wear—tuxedos, full-dress black tailcoat outfits, and morning suits—was worn almost exclusively by well-to-do men. They wore formal attire to such events as weddings, balls, concerts, and school graduations. Hecht felt that the appeal of this type of dress could be broadened if quality formal garments were made available at prices that the growing middle class could afford. Hence, he founded Classy as a formal wear rental company. By renting tuxedos, tailcoats, and morning suits at a fraction of their retail selling prices, Hecht believed that he could attract substantial numbers of new customers who would otherwise not dress in formal wear.

From a one-store operation located near Montreal's downtown core, he gradually expanded the business so that by the late 1940s there were five stores in the city as well as one in Ottawa. By the 1950s, his sons had assumed management positions in the company and stores were opened in Toronto and Hamilton. During the 1960s, Marcus Hecht handed the presidency of the company over to his eldest son Jack, and he continued Classy's expansion with the successful opening of stores in Vancouver and Quebec City.

Parallel to the growth in formal wear rentals experienced in the six cities where Classy now had stores, the company began to offer formal wear for sale on a limited basis. A narrow range of shirts was made available, and tuxedos were offered for sale on a made-to-order basis with an average delivery time of six weeks.

### The Market and Competition

By the 1970s, retail and wholesale sales still accounted for only about 5 percent of total company volume. These sales were basically regarded as an add-on, as opposed to a

This case was prepared by V. H. Kirpalani and Harold J. Simpkins, Concordia University.

mainstream contribution to corporate revenues from rentals. Toward the latter part of this decade, two new trends began to make their presence strongly felt.

The first trend was a levelling off in the number of weddings taking place. This is mainly because the baby-boom generation born in the late 1940s and early 1950s had by now moved through the early marriage age. Close to 80 percent of formal wear rentals were for weddings, and the stabilization in the number of weddings was not encouraging. The other 20 percent of the market was split about evenly between school graduations and other formal occasions. The second trend was increased competition. In each of the Montreal, Vancouver, and Hamilton markets, Classy had two major competitors, while in Toronto there were four.

In 1978, Jack Hecht passed away and left no heirs. His brother Joseph became Classy's president, and the trends in the marketplace concerned him as well as his son Stephen, who had been appointed executive vice president and chief operating officer in the early 1980s. A recent MBA graduate from the University of Western Ontario, Stephen brought a pronounced marketing emphasis to Classy's way of doing business. His research and analysis of the formal wear market showed that the levelling off in the number of weddings was being more than offset by an increasing number of weddings "going formal." In other words, although there was no growth in weddings actually taking place, there were more formal weddings. However, he could not be sure how long this phenomenon would continue.

## Classy's Strategy

Stephen decided to establish two fundamental marketing objectives for Classy. The first was to significantly increase the company's share of the formal wear rental market across the country. The second was to substantially increase the level of Classy's retail and wholesale sales.

One of the key strategic tools the company used to help it achieve these objectives was the location and design of Classy stores. First, the company opened stores in new cities— Edmonton, Calgary, Winnipeg, and Kitchener. Also, it developed firm plans to open in other major centres. Second, Classy opened additional stores in Vancouver, Toronto, Ottawa, and Montreal. Third, all the new stores were located in prime retail areas, either in downtown cores or in major regional shopping malls. Finally, all of the company's stores, including the older ones, were fitted with retail merchandising fixtures such as suit racks, shirt display units, and point-of-purchase shelving for formal wear accessories.

Another key strategic action Classy deployed was to increase the availability and inventory levels of its retail merchandise. All stores now carried and displayed a basic line of tuxedos priced from $399 to $599, formal shirts from $39 to $49, and bow tie and cummerbund accessory sets priced from $37. By comparison, very few of Classy's competitors carried any retail stock whatsoever, although they all offered used as well as custom-ordered tuxedos for sale.

By late 1987, Classy had 38 retail stores and over 1,000 wholesale agents across Canada and was by far the dominant formal wear company in the country. Retail sales now accounted for about 10 percent of company revenues. But, in Stephen Hecht's assessment, Classy had barely scratched the surface of the potential retail sales market. Moreover, he felt the company was now well positioned to dramatically increase its sales revenues.

## Planning Its Sales Revenues

It was with this in mind that Stephen Hecht developed an aggressive plan to make Classy the leading Canadian formal wear retailer. In early 1987, he visited a number of manufacturers of men's suits in Korea. During his three-week stay in that country, he discovered that the quality of suits being produced there was equal to and, in many cases, better than those being made in Canada. He also determined that any of the major Korean manufacturers could make quality tuxedos at about 60 percent of the cost of Classy's Canadian suppliers. The same cost structure proved to be the case with the Korean shirt manufacturers. Toward the end of his trip, Stephen Hecht gave an order for 2,000 black pure wool tuxedos to one of the suit manufacturers for delivery in early 1988. He also placed a substantial order for formal shirts.

On his return to Canada, he actively pursued and secured the exclusive license for the Yves Saint Laurent name and pattern. As a result of this, all of the tuxedos he had ordered from Korea would carry the Yves Saint Laurent label, and Classy would be the only formal wear specialist in Canada permitted to sell Yves Saint Laurent tuxedos.

The total landed cost to Classy for these Korean-produced Yves Saint Laurent tuxedos came to $137.50, including licensing fees. To begin the process of developing a pricing strategy for the new tuxedos, Stephen Hecht called a meeting of his three key executives on June 26, 1987. It was a Friday afternoon, so there was less likelihood of interruptions.

## Marketing Decision Time

Attending the meeting were Stephen Hecht and Classy's vice presidents of finance, operations, and marketing. Stephen opened the meeting by reviewing the highlights of the plan he had put together. He stated that the company's goal should be to sell 2,000 tuxedos during 1988. He then asked the group for suggestions regarding a retail selling price for the tuxedos.

The vice president of finance remarked that this purchase of tuxedos by Classy was the largest investment in retail stock that the company had ever made. He went on to say that the company's overall objectives would be best served by recouping this investment as quickly as possible, so that funds for expansion would not be tied up for any appreciable amount of time.

The vice president of operations expressed his agreement with this point of view but was quick to add that in the company's 68-year history, it had never sold more than 500 tuxedos in any one year.

The vice president of marketing added that while the quality and designer name associated with the new tuxedos were inherently attractive, there were three key factors to consider when pricing them. First, consumer research in the United States indicated that the typical tuxedo purchaser was over 35 years of age and was most likely to go to a menswear or department store, rather than to a formal wear store, for his purchase. Second, most of Classy's current customers were under 35 years of age. Third, within the past two years, there had been strong competition in the retailing of tuxedos. According to the vice president of marketing, competition could be categorized as in Table 1.

Finally, he pointed out that Classy is not perceived as a formal wear retailer by the 35 and over age group, and that in establishing a retail selling price, the average rental price of $85 should be kept in mind. The vice president of operations reminded the group that the $85 rental price included a shirt, bow tie, and cummerbund or vest, as well as cuff links and shirt studs, and that this should be kept in mind as well.

The next issue that came up at the meeting was the market size. How many men are there who are considering a tuxedo purchase? Should the retail price be set at a low enough level to attract those men who have not as yet considered buying a tuxedo, or should it be set to appeal mainly to those who are already thinking about buying one? Given the company's

---

**TABLE 1**

| Type of Store | Type of Tuxedos Offered | Designer Labels | Retail Prices |
|---|---|---|---|
| Better menswear stores | Very high quality 100% wool Italian, German, and American imports | Giorgio Armani Mario Valentino Gianni Versace Hugo Boss Polo by Ralph Lauren | $749–$1500 |
| Better department stores | High quality 100% wool Italian and British imports and Canadian garments | Mani by Giorgio Armani Emmanuel Ungaro Hardy Aimies | $499–$749 |
| Regular menswear stores | Good quality polyester/wool blends from Korea and Canada | Private label | $295–$349 |
| Classy formal wear stores | Good quality polyester/wool blends from Korea and Canada | Private label | $399–$599 |
| Discount menswear stores and boutiques | Adequate quality polyester/wool blends from Korea and Eastern Europe | Private label | $179–$229 |

---

objective of turning over the 2,000 tuxedos now on order in one year, it was agreed to set a price that would be attractive to both groups.

At this point, the vice president of operations suggested a $299 retail selling price. The vice president of marketing supported this suggestion since it seemed to offer broad appeal to potential consumers and, from an advertising standpoint, could create strong impact. The vice president of finance remarked that the 54 percent markup reflected by this price was slightly above the markup level now being generated by Classy's other retail items. Therefore, he also supported the $299 price.

As the meeting began to wind down, Stephen Hecht said that the $299 price was deserving of consideration. But he was going to take a few days to think about it before making a firm recommendation to Joseph Hecht, Classy's president. In Stephen's mind, there were a number of questions that remained to be answered. First and foremost was his concern that Classy might be missing a major short-term profit opportunity by not pricing the tuxedos higher, say at $349 or $379 or $399. Given the high-quality pure wool fabrication of the garments, he felt that the market might be willing to pay up to $100 more. Second, if the tuxedos were to be sold to Classy's wholesale agents, the price to them would have to be approximately $150. This would generate a negligible margin to Classy. Although the company could possibly push the majority of sales through its own stores, doing this at a $299 price would effectively close off any wholesale sales opportunity. Also, he was concerned about supply lines. If tuxedos sold out very quickly, Classy would be caught in an out-of-stock situation. The lead time for delivery from Korea was six months. The last thing Stephen Hecht wanted was to have to turn away customers because there were no $299 Yves

Saint Laurent tuxedos left for sale. On the other hand, he did not want the company to be holding large quantities of unsold stock at the end of the year.

Finally, Stephen Hecht realized that the price would have strategic implications for the kinds of customers that Classy might appeal to, and the image that Classy might create relative to the competition. But he was less sure of the best marketing strategy for Classy to pursue, and how alternative prices might help or hinder the chosen strategy.

### Questions

1. What factors should be evaluated in this pricing decision?
2. What marketing strategy and price would you recommend? Why?

---

## 32.

## DUNCAN DEPARTMENT STORE

Donald Claxton, the confectionary buyer for the Duncan Department Store, was concerned. He had purchased $35,000 (at retail) of candy for the Easter selling season. The initial markup was 30 percent, or $10,500. Here it was the Saturday morning following Good Friday and he was holding $16,000 worth of inventory he would have to sell in one day or "give it away" after Easter. Mr. Claxton quickly reviewed the events leading up to this situation. The purchase of $35,000 was an increase of $20,000 from the previous Easter season. He based this increase on two factors:

1. Last year, he ran out of stock on the Thursday before Easter by 12 noon, thereby losing two full selling days.

   Store hours:    Thursday    9:00 A.M. to 9:00 P.M.
                           Friday        Closed (Good Friday)
                           Saturday    9:00 A.M. to 6:00 P.M.

2. He recognized that the Thursday and Saturday before Easter represent approximately 65 percent of his total Easter candy sales.

The sales plan and actual results to date were:

| | Plan | Actual |
|---|---|---|
| Weeks prior to Easter week | $ 4,500 | $4,400 |
| Monday | 2,000 | 1,800 |
| Tuesday | 2,500 | 2,600 |
| Wednesday | 4,000 | 3,900 |
| Thursday | 10,000 | 6,300 |
| Friday | — | — |
| Saturday | 12,000 | |

This case was prepared by Aldo J. Cimpello, Algonquin College of Applied Arts and Technology.

Thursday at closing he pondered the actual sales to date in comparison to his plan. Saturday morning, on his way to work, he was still troubled by the amount of inventory remaining. He knew that after the store closed on Saturday, the remaining candy would be sold at 50 percent off the retail price during the following week.

## Questions

1. What options are available to Mr. Claxton?
2. What would you do in this situation?

---

## 33.
# How Good Are Tire Warranties?

Jim Reed was really upset about the poor customer service and the inconsistent warranties from the Dunlop Tire Company and was wondering if there was anything that could be done.

It all started when Jim Reed, a professor at the University of Ottawa, was returning from a sabbatical at San Diego State University. Jim and his wife Joan had taken her V.W. Jetta to San Diego, instead of Jim's Volvo, because the Jetta was still under warranty. The return trip, some 5,600 kilometres, was not a comfortable drive. The Jetta did not seem to be able to take the heavy load that was packed in the car, and Jim was convinced that the shocks would need to be replaced.

They arrived home in early June, and three days later Jim took the Jetta into Desjardins Inc., in Hull, to get it serviced. They changed the oil, the oil filter, and added a litre of transmission fluid. The shocks were fine, but the manager claimed that the car needed four new tires. This bothered Jim since the tires had only 42,000 kilometres on them. He figured that he might have ruined them by overloading the car on the trip from California, or perhaps the manager was being overly cautious and saw a chance to make a large sale, especially during the recession when business was down. In any case, since he was planning to return to San Diego next January, Jim felt that he could replace them at a lower price and not have to pay the exorbitant 15.56 percent combined GST (goods and services tax) and PST (provincial sales tax). In the meantime, neither Jim nor Joan would do much driving in the Jetta.

At the end of July, their daughter Julie and son-in-law David found a job in Washington, D.C., and asked to borrow the Jetta to carry their possessions to their new home. While driving to Washington, one of the tires exploded, and they replaced it. They were told that the other three tires were not very good.

When they returned with the car on August 12, Jim took it to Desjardins and bought three tires that would be compatible with the new tire. The invoice shows that three P185/60HR14 Dunlop D89 ETE tires were purchased at \$84.92 each, and the total invoice, including taxes, was for \$294.40. The odometer reading was 45,516 km. The same day, upon the advice of the technician at Desjardins, the car was given a four wheel alignment, which with two small parts costs \$83.27.

© 1991, Faculty of Administration, University of Ottawa. This case was written by Professor David Litvack.

On December 11, Jim drove the Jetta to Swedish Garage to get it serviced. After 6,000 km, it was time to have the oil changed. On the way there, Jim felt a shimmy in the steering and he asked the mechanic to check it. He balanced the tires but the shimmy was still there. He looked at the tires and discovered that two of them were defective. The odometre reading was 48,640, or 3,124 km of driving on the tires.

After he left Swedish, Jim drove directly to Desjardins where the defects were confirmed. Two new tires were ordered and an appointment was made for the following Tuesday to have them installed. That day, Jim arrived at 3 P.M., and within a half hour the car was ready to go. He was surprised to hear that he would have to pay for partial use of the defective tires. Since the tires had a 96,000 km warranty, Jim figured that he would owe Desjardins about $6. He became very upset when the cashier presented him with a bill for $44.50. He went to see the manager, who told him that he was being charged according to the policy of the Dunlop Tire Company, and that if he did not like it, he could replace the new tires with the old ones.

Jim argued that he was being treated unfairly, and that the policy did not make sense. He insisted that the manager get someone from Dunlop on the phone. The man at the other end of the line, who claimed to be in public relations at Dunlop, defended the policy, adding that he had been in the tire business for 38 years. After more discussions, he offered to cut the price in half, stating that he still did not agree with Jim that the policy was unfair. Since there seemed to be little choice, Jim decided to accept his offer, but deep inside, he was still angry.

When he got off the phone, two customers who had overheard the conversation approached him and told him that he was absolutely right. André Lefort, a service agent at Desjardins, joined the discussion and expressed some sympathy at Jim's predicament.

Feeling a little bit better, Jim returned home and put the invoices and receipts into his "car file." In flipping through the file, he discovered an invoice dated from early June (shortly after they returned from San Diego) for four new tires for his Volvo which had been sitting idle since the previous January. The invoice read: four 185/70R14 Dunlop Elite 4S BW at $85 each plus tax. Along with the tires came a warranty which states:

> **UP TO 50% WORN/NO CHARGE:** If during the first five thirty-seconds of an inch (5/32") of tread wear, the tire becomes unserviceable for a condition covered by this warranty, it will be replaced by a comparable new Dunlop tire. No charge will be made for mounting, balancing or taxes.

At this point, Jim was extremely angry but he did not know what to do next.

## Questions

1. Analyze the buying decision process of Jim Reed, using three decision cycles.
2. What lessons can a retailer learn from these events?
3. What other retailing concepts are illustrated in this case?

## 34.
## AN ADVERTISING PLAN

A major department store in the Toronto area is planning a major sale of rugs in its suburban Brampton warehouse over the three-day Labour Day weekend (Saturday through Monday). Nearly $2 million worth of rugs will be on sale, assembled both from the company's inventory and from various market purchases. The average sale price of each rug is approximately $300, and the company hopes to realize at least $900,000 in sales during the three days.

This is the first time the store has sold rugs from its warehouse, but previous experience with coats and furniture has been successful. Two factors in particular were common to the previous events:

1. The first day's sales are 50 percent of the total; the second day's, 35 percent, and the last day's, 15 percent.
2. One of every two customers who come makes a purchase.

It is known further that large numbers of people always flock to such sales, some from as far away as 50 miles. They come from all economic levels, but are all confirmed bargain hunters.

You are the assistant to the general merchandise manager, and he has asked you to plan the advertising campaign for this event. You have the following information at your disposal:

1. A full-page ad in the *Toronto Star* costs $10,000, a half-page ad is $6,000, and a quarter page is $3,500. Furthermore, in order to get the maximum value from a newspaper campaign, it is company policy to always run two ads (not necessarily the same size) for such events.
2. Using the local Brampton paper, which is printed weekly and distributed free to some 15,000 households, costs $700 for a full page and $400 for a half page.
3. In order to get adequate television coverage, at least three channels must be used, with a minimum of eight 30-second spots on each channel at $500 per spot, spread over three or more days. The cost of producing a television spot is $3,000.
4. The store has contracts with three radio stations: one that appeals to a broad general audience aged 25–34; one that is popular with the 18–25 group; and a classical music station with a small but wealthy audience. The minimum costs for a saturation radio campaign (including production) on the three stations are $8,000, $5,000, and $3,000, respectively.
5. To produce and mail a full-colour flyer to the store's 80,000 charge customers costs $10,000. When the company used such a mailing piece, its experience was that about 3 percent would respond.

This case was prepared by Professor David Ehrlich, Marymount University.

## Questions

Knowing that the company wants a mixed-media advertising campaign to support this event, prepare an advertising plan for the general merchandise manager that costs no more than $40,000.

1. Work out the daily scheduling of all advertising.
2. Work out the dollars to be devoted to each medium.
3. Justify your plan.

---

## 35.
## THE M&G ADVERTISING AGENCY

Sandra Malik has just been given a new assignment: to prepare and deliver a report to her vice president within a week on the various aspects of retail advertising.

Sandra is the account executive for the newly created account on retail operations within the M&G advertising agency. The agency has recently decided to expand its customer base into the retail field, and the assignment was given to Sandra. Her mandate was to develop a complete understanding of retail advertising, and to use this knowledge to develop new clients.

Sandra has been with the M&G agency for two years. She joined the firm after doing an internship during her Bachelor of Business Administration studies. Toward the end of the internship, one of the vice presidents came to appreciate her marketing savvy and her ability to work hard and produce effective results. After she obtained her degree, she was hired by the agency as a junior account executive, and assigned small accounts, none in the retail field.

Sandra realized that retail advertising is very different from product advertising. Although products and services are sold by retailers, the main objective of a particular retailer is to make sure that product or service is bought at his or her store. In order to succeed, a retailer begins by carefully defining the target market, and learning as much as possible about these customers. Then, the retailer must know the role and goals of advertising within the overall mix decisions. There are a variety of goals that a retailer may want to pursue, including:

- Define or improve the image of the store, or some specific aspects of it.
- Obtain customer acceptance for a particular merchandise line or group of lines.
- Attract new customers to improve store traffic.
- Create store loyalty.
- Increase frequency of patronage by existing customers.
- Promote special events.
- Announce sales and clearances in order to smooth out sales during the year, increase inventory turnover, and liquidate old inventory.

Sandra also realized that retailers use different kinds of media, partly because of smaller budgets, and partly because of their target audiences. Most print retail advertising can be found in daily newspapers and weekend supplements, community newspapers and shoppers, local magazines, out-of-home media (billboards, mall, transit), direct mail, catalogs, and directories. Retailers also use radio, and a few use television. However, due to the time constraint, it was agreed that for this initial assignment, she will devote her report to the print media only.

Sandra can see how she can structure her report as well as her oral presentation. However, she needs some examples to illustrate the various advertising goals that a retailer may have, and it would be more effective to have examples of good and bad retail advertisements. As she will be asked to justify her evaluation of each one, she must carefully examine each one of them in terms of intended target, goal, creative approach, and effect. Now she is starting to work on her report.

### Questions

1. Assume the role of Sandra Malik and provide examples of good and bad retail print advertisements.
2. Include your justification along the lines indicated in the case.

---

## 36.
## SHOE KINGDOM

Sam McGuire was meeting this morning with Joan LeBlanc, the account executive of the small advertising agency that he hired to develop an advertising campaign for Shoe Kingdom. Both were relatively new to the game of advertising. Sam had just been hired as marketing manager, and Joan's agency had recently been established by a former vice president at McKim, Vancouver. Both parties were hoping to benefit from this relationship.

Shoe Kingdom was a national chain of 105 stores situated in the 28 major metropolitan areas of Canada. It was founded in 1972 to provide good-quality shoes at reasonable prices for every member of the family. It was a successful formula, and in 1992, the chain had total revenues of $30 million. In the past two years, sales had increased marginally, a reflection of the difficult economic times in Canada. However, during the same period, a number of retail shoe chains had declared bankruptcy.

The retail chain had never advertised on a national basis, leaving it to the discretion of store managers to advertise special sales or events. However, when Sam took over as marketing manager, he realized that the chain did not have a very clear and consistent image across Canada. Also, individual store advertisements projected different images, contributing to the lack of a strong identity. In the excitement of developing the business, no one had even thought of developing a slogan that would capture the chain's strategy. At this time, he approached Joan's agency for some help in developing a national advertising campaign for Shoe Kingdom. Sam had known the owner of the new agency for many years, since McKim had handled the advertising business for National Foods, where he had previously worked as a market analyst.

As Sam explained to Joan, his objective was to create a strong image for Shoe Kingdom, which in turn would generate consistent store traffic over the year and make the cash register ring more often. Another objective was to attract some of the price-conscious consumers who were cross-border shopping in the United States.

Although the initial strategy had been successful, sales were uneven across the country and during the year (see Exhibit 1). Also, the initial target market (i.e., every member of the family) did not fully materialize; most of the sales were for children's and younger women's shoes (see Exhibit 2).

What Sam wanted was a strong slogan that would project a positive image of Shoe Kingdom. He had made up one slogan: "Shoes Fit for a King, at Prices His Servants Would Like." The messages should reflect a number of attributes such as:

- Comfort with quality.
- Leadership and authority.
- Fashionable yet practical shoes.
- Reasonable prices and good values.
- One-stop shopping for the whole family.
- Very attentive, superior service.

In the past, store managers had mainly used newspaper advertisements, and some had distributed fliers, all announcing a special sale—for example, "Back to School Sale." However, Sam felt there was some merit in using radio, television, billboards, mall posters, or even magazines. Exhibit 3 provides some rate benchmarks for a preliminary budget exercise. Of course, Joan would have access to more accurate information by looking at the last issue of *Canadian Advertising Rates & Data*. Sam figured that he could get final approval for a total budget of $300,000, with 15 percent of it devoted to preparing the ads, and the rest to media expenditures.

The meeting was coming to an end. Joan had agreed to come back in two weeks and present Sam with a preliminary advertising plan, complete with a slogan, some sample advertisements and/or commercials, and a rough media plan.

## Exhibit 1

### Sales distribution by province and month

| Province | Population | Sales | Number of Stores | Month | Sales |
|----------|-----------|-------|------------------|-------|-------|
| Newfoundland | 2.1% | 3.0% | 1 | January | 2% |
| P.E.I. | 0.5 | 0.0 | 0 | February | 4 |
| Nova Scotia | 3.3 | 3.6 | 2 | March | 5 |
| New Brunswick | 2.8 | 3.1 | 2 | April | 4 |
| Quebec | 25.8 | 29.1 | 36 | May | 10 |
| Ontario | 36.0 | 38.1 | 44 | June | 8 |
| Manitoba | 4.2 | 4.0 | 4 | July | 2 |
| Saskatchewan | 4.0 | 3.5 | 4 | August | 10 |
| Alberta | 9.3 | 8.1 | 5 | September | 19 |
| British Columbia | 11.4 | 7.5 | 7 | October | 15 |
| Yukon | 0.1 | 0.0 | 0 | November | 11 |
| N.W.T. | 0.2 | 0.0 | 0 | December | 10 |
| Total Canada | 100.0 | 100.0 | 105 | | 100 |

**Exhibit 2**

*Distribution of sales by demographic group*

| Group | Age | Population | Sales |
|-------|-----|------------|-------|
| Women | 13–19 | 4.7% | 15% |
|       | 20–34 | 12.5 | 10 |
|       | 35–54 | 13.5 | 8 |
|       | 55+ | 11.2 | 7 |
| Children | 0–6 | 9.8 | 22 |
|          | 7–12 | 8.4 | 27 |
| Men | 13+ | 40.0 | 11 |
| Total | All | 100.0 | 100 |

**Exhibit 3**

*National costs guidelines*

| | |
|---|---|
| Television | $700 per GRP (30-second commercial) |
| Radio | $400 per GRP (60-second commercial) |
| Newspaper | $ 80 per modular agate line, black & white |
| Magazine | $20,000 per page, 4 colours (6 major magazines) |
| Outdoor/transit | $200 per GRP |

NOTE: A GRP represents 1 percent of the corresponding population that is reached by the medium (e.g., with TV sets, radio sets, with access to outdoor/transit). A modular agate line (MAL) is a newspaper space 1.8 mm deep by one standard column. A full page is 1,800 MALs for a broadsheet and 900 MALs for a tabloid. For fractional sizes, use the proportional rule. For more details, consult the appropriate sections in Chapter 17. For actual rates for vehicles, consult the latest *CARD* catalog and discount them by 30 percent, or ask each vehicle for its retail rate card.

## Questions

1. Prepare a preliminary advertising campaign for Shoe Kingdom.
2. Be prepared to justify your recommendations.

## 37.
## ANNE'S BOUTIQUE

Anne Lyton, a fashion designer for a large women's clothing manufacturer, had always had a desire to own and operate her own retail business. Her goal was accomplished when she purchased a small retail business that specialized in women's fashion clothing. She renamed

**TABLE 1**

| Ratio | Anne's Boutique | Industry Average |
|---|---|---|
| Net profit margin | 4.8% | 10.2% |
| Rate of asset turnover | 1.7× | 1.5× |
| Rate of return on assets | 8.2% | 15.3% |
| Leverage ratio | 4.0% | 2.8% |
| RONW | 32.6% | 35.1% |

the store, calling it Anne's Boutique, introduced a number of new fashion lines, and changed the interior of the store.

Anne's strengths were in design and product selection—she did not feel comfortable with the ''numbers'' side of the operation. At the end of the first full year of running her business, she hired an accountant to prepare a balance sheet and operating statement. When the accountant submitted the information, he also provided her with a table consisting of a number of ratios (Table 1). Anne looked at the table and wondered what it meant.

## Questions

1. Interpret the data in the table. What are the strengths and weaknesses of Anne's Boutique?
2. What areas need particular attention?

**Above the competition pricing**　A pricing strategy in which retailers set prices above the level of competitors.

**Action close**　A sales-closing technique where the salesperson takes a positive step toward clinching the order, such as immediate delivery.

**Adaptive behaviour**　A theory about retail institution change based on the premise that institutions evolve when environmental conditions are favourable.

**Advisory boards**　A cross section of community citizens appointed by a retailer to offer advice and counsel to management on a variety of issues.

**Anchor tenants**　The major tenants in a shopping centre that serve as the primary consumer-attracting force.

**Arbitration**　The settlement of a dispute by a person or persons chosen to hear both sides of a dispute and come to a decision.

**Area-development franchise**　An individual purchases an extensive territory and then opens a large number of franchises within the territory.

**Area sampling**　A method of selecting respondents in a survey, where first the trading area is defined on a map; next, some blocs are randomly selected (for example, census tracts or enumeration areas); third, some streets are randomly selected; and finally, houses or apartments are either systematically or randomly selected.

**Assets, current**　Primarily cash, accounts receivable, and inventory. They are in varying states of being converted into cash within the next 12-month period.

**Assets, fixed**　Used in the operation of the business; they are not intended to be resold. They include real estate, leasehold improvements, machinery, equipment, and vehicles.

**Assortment**　The number of different choices available within a particular merchandise line.

**Assumptive close**　A sales-closing technique that asks a question about preferred colours, method of payment, or type of delivery that can help the salesperson to quickly determine whether a customer is ready to make a purchase.

**At the market pricing**　A pricing strategy in which retailers set prices at the level of competitors.

**Autonomous decision**　A decision within the family that is made over time independently by the husband and the wife.

**Backward integration**　A development that occurs when a retailer or wholesaler performs some manufacturing functions.

**Balanced tenancy**　An arrangement whereby the types of stores in a planned shopping centre are chosen to meet all of the consumers' shopping needs in that trading area.

**Balance sheet**　The financial statement that expresses the equation: Assets = Liabilities + Net worth. (Net worth is the owners' equity or claim to the assets of the business.)

**Basic services**   Services that customers expect to have available at all retail outlets. An example is free parking.

**Basic stock method**   The amount and assortment of merchandise sufficient to accommodate normal sales levels.

**Below the competition pricing**   A pricing strategy in which retailers set prices below the level of competitors.

**Benefits**   Holidays and paid vacations, insurance, health care, pensions, social insurance, disability payments, and various other forms of support for employees.

**Benefit summary**   A transition to the close technique, where the salesperson summarizes the product benefits, to demonstrate that the product is the right one for the customer.

**Blind check**   A checking method in which the checker lists the items and quantities received without the invoice in hand and then compares the list to the invoice.

**Blue laws**   Provincial laws that prohibit retailers from opening on Sundays.

**Book inventory**   Continually recording all additions to and deductions from a beginning stock figure so that the ending inventory figure is always current. (Also called perpetual inventory.) The book inventory must be compared to the actual physical inventory to determine shortages or overages.

**Boutique layout**   Merchandise classifications are grouped so that each classification has its own ''shop'' within the store.

**Breadth (or width)**   The number of different merchandise lines carried.

**Business format franchising**   An ongoing relationship between a franchisor and a franchisee that includes not only the product, service, and trademark, but the entire business format.

**Canadian Advertising Rates & Data (CARD)**   A monthly publication providing updated general rates and other information for most media in Canada.

**Canadian Human Rights Commission**   An agency of the federal government with the responsibility to eliminate discrimination on the basis of race, national or ethnic origin, sex, colour, age, religion, or other variables in job hiring, retention, and promotion.

**Canadian Newspaper Unit (CNU)**   A unit of measure of newspaper space that is one standardized column wide and 30 MALs deep.

**Cash datings**   Payment terms that call for immediate payment for merchandise. Cash datings include COD (cash on delivery) and CWO (cash with order). Cash datings do not involve cash discounts.

**Cash discount**   A premium granted by the supplier for cash payment prior to the time the entire bill must be paid.

**Census tract**   A permanent small census area established in large urban communities of 50,000 or more population; the population of a census tract must be between 2,500 and 8,000 people.

**Central business district**   The area of the central city that is characterized by high land values, a high concentration of retail and service businesses, and high traffic flow.

**Central buying**   A method of buying in which the authority and responsibility for merchandise selection and purchase are vested in the headquarters office rather than in the individual store units that comprise the chain.

**Chain**   A retail organization consisting of two or more centrally owned units that handle similar lines of merchandise.

**Channel of distribution**   System through which products, commodities, or services are marketed.

**Checking**   A phase of the physical handling process that involves matching the store buyer's purchase order with the supplier's invoice (bill), opening the packages, removing the items, sorting them, and comparing the quality and quantity of the shipment with what was ordered.

**Classification dominance**   Displaying and arranging merchandise in such a way that psychologically the consumer is convinced the firm has a larger assortment of merchandise in the category than competitors.

**Cognitive dissonance**   A feeling whereby consumers, when making a major purchase, are afraid that they may have spent their money foolishly.

**Committee buying**   A form of central buying where more than one person shares the buying responsibility.

**Community newspapers**   Local newspapers that are usually published once a week.

**Community shopping centre**   A shopping centre in which the leading tenant is a variety store or junior department store. The typical leasable space is 15,000 square metres, and the typical site area is 40,000 square metres. The minimum trade population is 40,000 to 150,000.

**Compensation**   The amount of salary and fringe benefits to be paid for a particular job.

**Consignment** A situation in which suppliers guarantee the sale of items and will take merchandise back if it does not sell.

**Consumer co-operative** A type of retail store owned by consumers and operated by a hired manager.

**Consumer-dominated information sources** Information sources over which the retailer has no influence. Examples include friends, relatives, acquaintances, and others.

**Consumerism** An organized expression of consumer dissatisfaction with selected business practices.

**Consumer rebates** A situation in which a manufacturer pays the consumer a sum of money in the form of a price reduction when a purchase is made.

**Convenience goods** Frequently purchased items for which consumers do not engage in comparison shopping before making a purchase decision.

**Convenience sample** A nonprobability sample in which researchers simply talk to the most readily available individuals.

**Co-operative advertising** Promotional programmes in which wholesalers or manufacturers pay a portion of the retailer's advertising cost under specified conditions.

**Co-ownership and comanagement franchises** Franchise arrangements in which a franchisor has an ownership interest in the operation.

**Corporate culture** The values of greatest importance to the organization.

**Corporate systems competition** A type of competition that occurs when a single management ownership links resources, manufacturing capability, and distribution networks.

**Corporation** A group of people who obtain a charter that grants them collectively the rights, privileges, liabilities, and legal powers of an individual, separate and apart from the individuals making up the group. The corporation can sell, buy, and inherit property. The corporation owns assets and is liable for the debts it contracts.

**Cost per thousand (CPM)** A measure of the relative cost of advertising that is determined by the number of households or persons reached.

**Coupon** A sales promotion technique consisting of a certificate offering a given price reduction for a given item or service.

**Creative selling** A type of higher-level selling in which the salesperson needs complete information about product lines, product uses, and the technical features of products.

**Credit scoring** A method used by retailers to screen credit applicants based on various types of personal information about the applicant.

**Cross-border shopping** A form of outshopping, where Canadians travel to the United States to make purchases on a regular basis.

**Culture** A set of values, attitudes, traditions, symbols, and characteristic behaviour shared by all members of a recognized group.

**Customer-focused culture** An integrated approach to dealing with customers that incorporates customer lifestyles and buying patterns into the overall strategy of the retail firm.

**Customer service** Additional services provided to customers such as cashing cheques or managing complaints.

**Debit card** A bank-issued card that, with the help of special terminals attached to the cash register, allows a customer to pay for purchases by an electronic transfer of funds from the client's to the retailer's bank account.

**Deferred billing credit** A payment plan in which a retailer allows customers to buy goods and to defer payment for an extended period of time with no interest charge.

**Demand merchandise** Merchandise purchased as a result of a customer coming into the store to buy that particular item.

**Departmentalization** An organizational principle that determines how jobs are grouped.

**Depth** The number of items carried in a single merchandise line.

**Dialectic process** A theory of change in retail institutional structure based on the premise that retailers mutually adapt in the face of competition from "opposites." When challenged by a competitor with a differential advantage, an established institution will adopt strategies and tactics in the direction of that advantage, thereby negating some of the innovator's attraction.

**Direct check** A checking method whereby the shipment is checked against the vendor's invoice.

**Direct close** A sales-closing technique where the salesperson takes the position that the customer is ready to buy.

**Direct promotion** A form of promotion of the store and its merchandise directly to customers through the use of direct mail or catalogs (printed or electronic).

**Disappointers** Services offered by a retailer that have a high labour content and return little value to the consumer.

**Distributor allowances** Discounts and/or extended payment terms to retailers designed to encourage them to purchase additional merchandise from a wholesaler or manufacturer.

**Distributorships** Franchise systems whereby franchises maintain warehouse stocks to supply other franchises. The distributor takes title to the goods and provides services to other customers.

**Dollar control** A system for controlling the dollar investment in inventory. To work, the system must record the beginning dollar inventory, what has been added to stock, how much inventory has moved out of stock, and how much inventory is now on hand. Involves perpetually recording additions and deductions at retail or cost.

**EcoLogo** A seal of approval by the Federal Minister of the Environment given to products that do not damage the environment.

**Employee compensation** Wages or salary, commissions, incentives, overtime, and benefits.

**Enumeration area** A small federal electoral area of about 100 to 200 households, the smallest geographic unit for which census data are available.

**Event campaign** An advertising campaign to promote a very specific sale, during a specific period (e.g., after-Christmas sale).

**Exclusive dealing** A situation in which a supplier prohibits a retailer from selling the product of a competitor.

**Experimental design** A type of research design that allows management to make inferences about cause-and-effect relationships in variables of interest.

**Exploratory research** A research process characterized by flexibility in design and the absence of a formal research structure.

**External data** Previously published data gathered by other groups or organizations and made available to the firm.

**External environment** The political, technological, economic, and social forces that affect the organization.

**External factors** In a situation analysis, variables over which store management has no control.

**Factory outlet centre** Shopping areas occupied by manufacturers selling directly to the public.

**Family life cycle** The various stages individuals go through as they get married, have children, and so on until retirement.

**Feature-benefit relationship** Understanding the reasons why customers buy, relating products to those reasons, and describing the products or services to the customers.

**Field work** The steps involved in actually collecting information from respondents in a survey.

**FIFO (first-in, first-out)** An inventory costing method that assumes that costs should be charged against revenue in the order in which they were incurred; in other words, the first items purchased are the first ones sold. The method is generally in harmony with actual movement of goods.

**Financial risk** The monetary loss from a wrong decision.

**Fixed-payment lease** A rental agreement in which rent is based on a fixed payment per month.

**Flex-time** A system by which workers arrive to work on a variable schedule.

**Focus group** A type of exploratory research, where a group of 8 to 12 suppliers, customers, or noncustomers gather around a table to talk informally about an issue with the assistance of a trained interviewer.

**Forward integration** A situation in which a manufacturer establishes its own wholesale and retail networks.

**Franchise contract** A legal document that enables an independent businessperson to use a franchisor's operating methods, financing systems, trademarks, and products in return for the payment of a fee.

**Franchisee** An individual who pays a fee for the right to use a franchisor's product, service, or way of doing business.

**Franchisee association** A situation in which individual franchisees join an organization to represent the individual owners in dealing with a franchisor.

**Franchisor** An organization that has developed a unique product, service, or way of doing business and allows another firm to use the product, service, or business concept in return for payment of a fee.

**Free-flow layout** Merchandise and fixtures are grouped into patterns that allow an unstructured flow of customer traffic.

**Free Trade Agreement (FTA)** An agreement whereby, on January 1, 1989, Canada and the United States started a 10-year process of lowering tariff barriers and liberalizing trade practices.

**Frequency** The average number of times a person will be exposed to a message during an advertising period.

**Future datings** A type of dating other than cash dating; includes DOI (date of invoice), ROG (receipt of goods), EOM (end of month), and extra datings.

**General rate** The advertising rate charged to agencies for national advertising.

**General salary increases** Increases granted to employees to maintain real earnings as required by economic factors and in order to keep pay competitive.

**Generics** Unbranded merchandise offerings carrying only the designation of the product type on the package.

**GMROI (gross margin return on inventory investment)** Expression of the relationship between margin and sales-to-retail stock (turnover), stated to effectively indicate the impact on profitability as:

$$\frac{\$ \text{ GM}}{\$ \text{ Sales}} \times \frac{\$ \text{ Sales}}{\$ \text{ Average inventory investment}}$$

**Gravity models** Methods for trading area analysis that are based on population size and driving time or distance as the key variables in the models.

**Green marketing** Marketing products that do not harm the environment.

**Grid layout** Merchandise is displayed in straight, parallel lines, with secondary aisles at right angles to these.

**Gross rating point** One percent of all homes with television sets in a market area (and generalized to other media).

**Group buying** The joint purchasing of goods by a number of noncompeting, nonaligned stores.

**High involvement** Consumer's shopping characterized by a high level of search in an effort to obtain information about products or stores.

**Husband-dominant decision** A decision within the family that is made most of the time by the husband.

**Image** The way consumers feel about a store or merchandise.

**Impulse merchandise** Merchandise bought on the basis of unplanned, spur-of-the-moment decisions.

**Income statement** Operating results of a period indicating if investments in assets and strategy have been successful and if a profit has resulted.

**Initial markup** The difference between the cost of merchandise and the original retail price.

**Instalment credit** A payment plan in which a customer pays for a product in equal monthly instalments, including interest.

**Institutional advertising** An advertising campaign to communicate the total character or image of the store; no merchandise or prices are featured.

**Institutional reliance** A belief that members of society should turn to government for solutions to their problems.

**Intangibility** The characteristic of a service that indicates that a service cannot be seen, touched, smelled, or handled.

**Internal data** Data that helps management systematically determine what's going on in the firm.

**Internal environment** Forces within the organization that affect the activities of the firm.

**Internal factors** In a situation analysis, variables that are largely under the control of store management.

**Intertype competition** Competition between different types of retail outlets selling the same merchandise.

**Intratype competition** Competition among retailers of the same type.

**Job analysis** A method for obtaining important facts about a job.

**Job classification** Comparing jobs with the aid of a scale that evaluates job complexity and the length of time the respective responsibility and qualifications are utilized during an average workday.

**Job description** The part of a job analysis that describes the content and responsibilities of a job and how the job ties in with other jobs in the firm.

**Job evaluation** A method of ranking jobs to aid in determining proper compensation.

**Job ranking** Ranking jobs on the basis of how valuable they are to the organization and the complexity of the job.

**Job sharing** A situation whereby two workers voluntarily hold joint responsibility for what was formerly one position.

**Job specification** The part of a job analysis that describes the personal qualifications required of an employee to do a job.

**Labelling violation** A situation encountered by consumers where some important information—for example, fibre content —is missing from the product label.

**Layaway plan** A situation in which a customer can make a small deposit that ensures that the retailer will hold the item until the customer is able to pay for it.

**Lead time** The length of time between order placement and receipt of goods.

**Leased departments** Departments of a retail business that are operated and managed by an outside person or organization rather than by the store of which they are a physical part.

**Leveraging** When assets worth more than the amount of capital invested by the owners are acquired. Leveraging is the ratio of total assets to net worth. The higher the ratio, the higher the amount of borrowed funds in the business.

**Licensing** A tool of marketing in which the licenser or owner of a ''property'' (the concept to be marketed) joins with a licensee (the manufacturer of the licensed product) and attempts to sell to retail buyers.

**Life cycle** The stages through which retail institutions evolve, including innovation, growth, maturity, and decline or stagnation.

**Life-style cluster** Urban shopping areas that cater to a specific life-style with a combination of food stalls, specialty shops, and restaurants.

**Life-styles** How consumers spend their time, what interests them, and how they view themselves; consumers' patterns of living as reflected in the way merchandise is purchased and used.

**Life-style segmentation** Dividing consumers into homogeneous groups based on similar activities, interests, and opinions.

**LIFO (last-in, first-out)** An inventory costing method that assumes that the most recent cost of merchandise should be charged against revenue. LIFO yields a higher figure for cost of goods sold than FIFO and thus lower figures for gross profit, net income, and inventory. LIFO is popular during inflationary periods.

**Likert scale** A type of scale that allows respondents to express their level of agreement or disagreement with a statement.

**Loss-leader pricing** A situation in which merchandise is sold with less than the normal markup or margin in an effort to increase store traffic.

**Low involvement** Consumer's shopping characterized by a very low/no effort to compare products or stores; the product that will satisfy the consumer's needs will be purchased at the most convenient outlet.

**Maintained markup** The difference between invoice cost and sales retail.

**Management by objectives** Goals established with salespersons that give direction to their efforts and permit them to evaluate their progress.

**Management information system** The structure of people, equipment, and procedures necessary to gather, analyze, and distribute information needed by management.

**Manufacturer's brand** A brand, often referred to as a national brand, owned by a manufacturer who may sell to anyone who wants to buy the brand.

**Margin** The percentage markup at which inventory is sold.

**Markdown** A reduction in the original selling price of an item.

**Market development** A strategy option that focuses either on attracting new market segments or completely changing the customer base.

**Marketer-dominated information sources** Sources of information under the control of the retailer. Examples are advertising, personal selling, displays, sales promotion, and publicity.

**Marketing** The process by which individuals and groups obtain what they need and want through creating and exchanging products and value with others.

**Market penetration** A strategy option whereby retailers seek a differential advantage over competition by a strong market presence that borders on saturation.

**Market positioning** Developing a unique position in a market segment relative to other retailers by the use of merchandise, price, hours of operation, services offered, and a clear understanding of consumer demographics.

**Market saturation** A situation that occurs when such a large number of stores are located in a market that low sales per square metre, compared to the industry average, are the result.

**Market segments**   The grouping of consumers based on homogeneous responses to merchandise offerings.

**Marking**   A phase of the physical handling process that involves putting information on the goods or on merchandise containers to assist customers and to aid the store in the control functions.

**Master franchise**   An individual buys the right to an extensive geographic area and sells the rights within the territory to individual franchisees.

**Merchandise approach**   A retail sales approach that begins with a statement about the merchandise.

**Merchandise budget**   A plan of how much to buy in dollars per month by classification based on profitability goals.

**Merchandise distribution**   An aspect of merchandise management in multiunit organizations related to getting merchandise from consolidation points/distribution centres to the individual stores.

**Merchandise information systems**   Computer-based systems that provide retail managers with better and faster information on their merchandising activities. The product of a merchandise information system is a series of computerized reports that can give almost instant answers to queries.

**Merchandise line**   A group of products that are closely related because they are intended for the same end use, are used together, or are sold to the same customer group.

**Merchandise management**   The management of the product component of the marketing mix.

**Merchandise planning**   Includes all the activities needed to plan a balance between inventories and sales.

**Merchandising**   Having the right merchandise, at the right price, at the right place, at the right time, and in the right quantities.

**Merit increases**   Pay increases granted to recognize superior performance and contributions.

**Message**   The development of an idea in transmittable form.

**Micromarketing**   Marketing to smaller and smaller market segments, in order to focus on very specific needs.

**Mission statement**   A statement that describes what a firm plans to accomplish in the market in which it will compete for customers it wants to serve.

**Mobile franchise**   Business is done from a mobile vehicle.

**Model stock plan**   A fashion merchandiser's best judgment about what demand will be at specific times of the year.

**Modular Agate Line (MAL)**   A unit of measure of newspaper space that is one standardized column wide and 1.8 mm deep.

**Motivation**   Getting people to do what is best for the organization.

**Multiattribute model**   A model that explains how attitudes toward stores are formed based on a number of attributes, their stated importances, and beliefs by consumers.

**National brands**   The brands of a manufacturer such as Procter & Gamble that are sold through a wide variety of retail outlets.

**Neighbourhood shopping centre**   A shopping centre in which the leading tenant is a supermarket or drugstore. The typical leasable space is 5,000 square metres and the typical site is 20,000 square metres. The minimum trade population is 7,500 to 40,000.

**Neutral sources of information**   Sources of information such as government rating agencies and state and local consumer affairs agencies that consumers perceive as trustworthy.

**Nonperpetual unit control**   (Also called stock-counting methods). This is *not* a book-inventory method. A nonperpetual unit system requires the retailer to have a planned model stock, a periodic counting schedule, and definite, assigned responsibility for counting. The beginning and ending inventories are counted and the differences are the sales (and shortages).

**Nonstore retailing**   The sale of merchandise other than through retail stores. Examples include mail order, telephone shopping, door to door (direct selling), and vending machines.

**Nonstore shopping**   The purchase of merchandise by use of catalogs, telephone, or ways other than physically entering an outlet.

**Nutritional labelling**   Information provided on the label that helps people with allergies or on some form of diet or who are interested in knowing what they're eating.

**Objective-and-task method**   A method of setting the advertising budget that relates the dollar appropriation to the advertising goals to be achieved.

**Objectives**   Statements of results to be achieved.

**Observation**   A type of primary data collection where the behaviour of customers or competitors is monitored and analyzed.

**Off-price retailers**   Outlets offering well-known brands of merchandise at substantial discounts compared to conventional stores handling the same products.

**Open charge account**   A charge account in which the customer must pay the bill in full when it is due, usually in 30 days.

**Open code dating**   Information provided so that the consumer can tell the date after which a product should not be used.

**Open-ended close**   A sales-closing technique where the salesperson asks open-ended questions that imply readiness to buy.

**Open-ended question**   A type of question where the respondents are simply asked to give their opinions without a formal response structure.

**Open-to-buy (OTB)**   A control system devised to control the retailer's utilization of the planned purchase figure. Dollar control provides the essential component of the system. OTB records the commitments made against the planned purchases amount.

**Open-to-spend report**   A report recording commitments against planned expenses for a period.

**Operational evolution**   Changing competitive strategy over time by focusing on a new target market and developing a business concept different from the existing one.

**Opinion leader**   A person whose product-specific competence is recognized by others.

**Order ceiling**   A level of stock sufficient to maintain a minimum order point level of stock sufficient to cover sales between ordering intervals.

**Order interval**   The amount of time between merchandise orders.

**Order point**   The level of stock below which merchandise is automatically reordered.

**Original retail price**   The first price at which an item is offered for sale.

**Out-of-home advertising**   All the advertising media that are physically outside the home, such as outdoor, transit, aerial, bench, taxicab, and so on.

**Outshopping**   Travelling out of one's local area to make purchases.

**Overage**   The physical inventory (either in dollars or units) is larger than the book inventory.

**Panel**   A selected group of customers or suppliers who are asked to keep a record of their purchases over time or give their opinions about merchandising issues.

**Partnership**   A voluntary association of two or more persons to operate a retail outlet for profit as co-owners. The rights, responsibilities, and duties of the partners are stated in the articles of partnership.

**Patronage builders**   A classification of services that provides high customer value and can be provided by the retailer at nominal cost. An example is a computerized bridal registry.

**People care programmes**   Programmes by some retailers to give employees paid time off to deal with personal matters such as taking a driving test, applying for a mortgage, or doing volunteer work in the community.

**Percent deviation method**   An inventory method where the actual stock on hand during any month varies from average planned monthly stock by only half of the month's variation from average estimated monthly sales.

**Performance risk**   The chance that merchandise purchased may not work properly.

**Perishability**   The characteristic that a service is lost forever if not consumed within a specific period.

**Personal shopping service**   A situation in which a retailer will assemble wardrobes for men and women at their request and have the items ready for inspection when the customer comes to the store.

**Physical handling**   Activities involved in receiving, checking, and marking merchandise.

**Physical risk**   The likelihood that a purchase decision will be injurious to one's health or will cause physical injury.

**Planned shopping centre**   A shopping centre developed with balanced tenancy, parking, and architecture.

**Point-of-purchase material**   A sales promotion technique that includes end-of-aisle and other in-store merchandising and display material.

**Point-of-sale (POS)**   A point-of-sale terminal that records a variety of information at the time a transaction occurs.

**Positioning**   The design and implementation of a retail mix to create an image of the retailer in the customer's mind relative to its competitors.

**Power strip centre**   An oversized strip centre typically anchored by destination-oriented retailers or superstores (e.g., Toys Я Us).

**Predatory pricing**   Setting prices to deliberately drive competition out of business.

**Premiums**   A sales promotion technique that offers something free or at a minimal price to induce sales.

**Preretailing**   The practice of determining merchandise selling prices and writing these prices on the store's copy of the purchase order at the time it is written.

**Price discrimination**   Varying the prices charged to different retailers for identical merchandise without an economic justification for doing so.

**Price elasticity**   The ratio of the percentage change in the quantity demanded to the percentage change in price.

**Price lining**   Featuring products at a limited number of prices that reflect varying levels of merchandise quality. Price lining may occur either in the context of rigid price points or price zones.

**Price points**   Offering merchandise at a small number of different prices. For example, a merchant might price all ''good'' suits at $175, all ''better'' suits at $225, and ''best'' suits at $350.

**Price zones**   Pricing strategy in which a merchant establishes a range of prices for merchandise of different quality. For example, prices for ''good'' suits might be between $175 and $200, while prices for ''better'' suits might be between $225 and $275.

**Primary data**   Needed information that is unavailable either internally or externally to the firm and that must be collected especially for the purpose at hand.

**Primary trading area**   The area around the store that includes the majority of the store's customers who live within a certain range of the store.

**Private brands**   Brands of merchandise that retailers develop and promote under their own label.

**Private corporation**   A corporation owned by a few people. Persons outside the corporation cannot buy the stock on the open market.

**Private label credit card**   A credit card that is imprinted with the name of the issuing retail outlet but for which the administrative details of the credit transaction are handled by a third party such as a bank.

**Probability sample**   A sample in which each unit has a known chance of selection.

**Product**   A tangible object, service, or idea.

**Product and trade-name franchising**   An independent sales relationship exists between a supplier and a dealer, but the dealer acquires some of the identity of the supplier. Primary examples are automotive and truck dealers, gasoline service stations, and soft drink bottlers.

**Product benefit**   A customer's basic buying motive that is fulfilled by a product feature.

**Productivity improvement**   A strategy that focuses on improved earnings through cost reductions, increased turnover through an improved merchandise mix, and increased prices and margins.

**Promotion**   Any form of paid communication from the retailer to the consumer.

**Promotional allowance**   A discount from list price given by suppliers to retailers to compensate them for money spent on promoting particular items.

**Promotional increases**   Salary increases given to employees assigned a different job and a higher pay level.

**Promotion plan**   A written document detailing the complete promotional programme, including communication goals, targets, budgets, media, and messages.

**Prospecting**   The first step in the selling process; involves identifying and qualifying possible customers.

**Psychographics**   Ways of defining and measuring the life-styles of consumers.

**Psychological risk**   The probability that the merchandise purchased or the store shopped will be compatible with the consumer's self-image.

**Public corporation**   A corporation in which the stock of a firm can be purchased on the open market.

**Publicity**   Any nonpersonal stimulation of demand for a product, service, or business unit by planting commercially significant news about it in a published medium or obtaining a favourable presentation about it on radio, television, or in other ways that are not paid for by the sponsor.

**Quality violation**   A situation encountered by consumers whereby the quality of a product is found to be lower than claimed by the retailer or the manufacturer.

**Quantity discount**   A reduction in unit cost based on the size of an order.

**Quantity violation**   A situation encountered by consumers whereby the quantity of a product was significantly less than claimed by the retailer or the manufacturer.

**Questionnaire**   A sequence of questions that elicit from respondents the information that needs to be collected to meet the objectives of the survey.

**Random sample**   A sample in which each unit has a known and equal chance of selection.

**Reach**   The number of persons exposed at least once to a message during an ad campaign.

**Receiving**   A phase of the physical handling process that involves taking possession of the goods and then moving them to the next phase of the process.

**Reduce, reuse, and recycle logo**   A triangular logo with three arrows that indicate that a product or package can be recycled or reused, or that the amount of packaging has been reduced.

**Reference group**   Any group for which the consumer is a ''psychological'' participant, one with which he or she will identify and accept its norms or judgment.

**Regional centre**   A shopping centre in which the leading tenants are one or more full-line department stores. The typical leasable space is 40,000 square metres, and the typical site is 120,000 square metres. The minimum trade population is 150,000 or more.

**Regional dominance**   A location strategy whereby a retailer decides to compete within one geographic region—for example, the Maritimes.

**Resale price maintenance**   A situation in which manufacturers set minimum prices at which their products must be sold.

**Retail accordion**   A theory about institutional change based on the premise that retail institutions evolve from broad-based outlets with wide assortments to specialized narrow lines, then return to the wide-assortment pattern.

**Retail decision support system**   The structure of people, equipment, and procedures to gather, analyze, and distribute the data that management needs for decision making.

**Retailing**   Consists of all activities involved in the sale of goods and services to the ultimate consumer.

**Retailing mix**   Those variables—product, price, presentation, promotion, personal selling, and customer services—that can be used as part of a positioning strategy for competing in chosen markets.

**Retail rate**   Rate given by the media to retailers, which is considerably lower than for a national advertiser or an ad agency.

**Retail saturation**   The extent to which a trading area is filled with competing stores.

**Retail the invoice**   The practice of determining merchandise selling prices and writing these prices on the copy of the invoice in the receiving room.

**Revolving credit**   A customer is billed at the end of a month on the basis of an outstanding credit balance.

**Role playing**   A sales training situation in which one person plays the part of the customer, while another person plays the part of the salesperson.

**Routine selling**   A type of selling that involves the sale of nontechnical items.

**Safety stock**   The level of stock sufficient to maintain adequate inventory for accommodating unexpected variations in demand and variations in supplier delivery schedules.

**Sales promotion**   Marketing activities other than direct selling, advertising, and publicity that stimulate consumer purchasing. Examples include displays, sales, exhibits, and demonstrations.

**Sales retail price**   The final selling price, or the amount the customer pays for the merchandise.

**Sample**   A selected group of respondents in a survey.

**Sampling**   A sales promotion technique where the product is provided free or at nominal cost for trial.

**Seasonal discount**   A special discount given to retailers who place orders for seasonal merchandise in advance of the normal buying period.

**Seasonal merchandise**   Merchandise in demand only at certain times of the year.

**Secondary data**   Secondary data is existing data that has been previously collected for other purposes.

**Secondary market expansion**   Development of retail outlets in communities with under 50,000 population.

**Secondary trading area**   The area around the store, beyond the primary trading area, which includes the majority of the store's customers who live within a certain range of the store (the rest is called the fringe trading area).

**Seek agreement**   A transition to the close technique where salespersons try to get customers to agree with them on a number of points, leading to making the order.

**Selectivity**   The ability of a medium to reach only specific audiences, minimizing waste (e.g., only teenagers, or men aged 24 to 45).

**Semantic differential scale** A type of scale that allows respondents to select the point representing the direction and intensity of their feelings between two bipolar words.

**Service approach** A weak approach in personal selling in which salespersons simply ask if they can be of assistance to a potential customer.

**Service franchises** Franchises in which franchisors license persons to dispense a service under a trade name.

**Share** The percentage of television sets in use that are tuned to a given programme.

**Shoppers** Newspapers that carry primarily advertising and very little news; they are distributed free to the homes of consumers.

**Shopping goods** Merchandise for which consumers will make comparisons between various brands in a product class before making a purchase.

**Shortage** The physical inventory (either in dollars or units) is smaller than the book inventory.

**Single-line store** A retail outlet specializing in the sale of one product line of merchandise such as family shoes.

**Single-price policy** All merchandise in a store is sold at the same price.

**Situation analysis** An assessment of internal strengths and weaknesses and external threats and opportunities.

**Social classes** Divisions of society that are relatively homogeneous and permanent, and in which individuals or families share the same values, life-styles, interests, and types of behaviour.

**Social risk** The likelihood that the merchandise or store will not meet with peer approval.

**Sole proprietorship** A situation where the retail outlet is owned and operated by one person who has title to the assets and who is subject to the claim of all creditors.

**Solo location** A location with no other retail stores nearby.

**Source** The originator of the promotion message.

**Source marking** The practice of the vendor rather than the retailer marking the goods.

**Span of control** A principle of organization that addresses the question of how many persons should report to a supervisor.

**Specialization** A principle of organization stating that the content of individual jobs should be narrowly defined.

**Specialized functional area** Self-defining urban shopping areas such as entertainment districts, medical districts, or high-fashion districts.

**Specialty goods** Products that consumers know they want and for which they are willing to make a special effort to acquire.

**Specialty store** An outlet specializing in the sale of one item in a product line. An example is a store specializing in athletic shoes.

**Staple merchandise** Items of merchandise generally in demand year-round, with little change in model or style.

**Stock-keeping unit (SKU)** One (or more) unit of a distinctive item.

**Stock-to-sales ratios** Used in planning monthly stocks in relation to expected sales for the month.

**Store design** Refers to the style or atmosphere of a store that helps project an image to the market.

**Store layout** Planning of the internal arrangement of selling and sales-supporting departments, and deciding on the amount of space for each department.

**Store planning** Includes exterior and interior building design, the allocation of space to departments, and the arrangement and location of departments within the store.

**Strategic planning** Defining the overall mission/purpose of the company, deciding on objectives that management wants to achieve, and developing a plan to achieve those objectives.

**Strategic profit model (SPM)** A model from the basic ROI model that focuses on the firm's primary profit paths—margin, assets, and leverage.

**Structure (retail institution)** The arrangement of parts, elements, or constituents considered as a whole rather than a single part.

**Suggestion selling** Using a customer's original purchase decision as a basis for developing suggestions about related or additional items in which the customer might be interested.

**Supermarket retailing** A type of retailing characterized by self-service and self-selection, large-scale but low-cost physical facilities, strong price emphasis, simplification and centralization of customer services, and a wide variety and broad assortment of merchandise.

**Supplements** Preprinted pages of ads that are inserted into newspapers.

**Support services** Services offered by a retailer that directly support the sale of the retailer's merchandise. Examples include home delivery or gift wrapping.

**Survey research** Collection of data on the opinions or perceptions of persons in a market segment by the use of a structured questionnaire.

**Syncratic decision**    A decision within the family that is made jointly by both spouses.

**Syndicated services**    Services offered by firms that specialize in collecting and selling information to clients.

**Systematic sampling**    A type of probability sample in which researchers choose a random beginning and then choose every *n*th number thereafter.

**Target markets**    The markets that management decides to serve.

**Tenure increases**    Pay increases given to employees for time worked with the company.

**Test market**    A selected testing area that allows the retailer to help decide on whether to make changes in the merchandise mix, decor, store layout, or similar variables.

**Third-party arbitration**    A process by which two parties agree to have an impartial third party or panel resolve a difficulty with a final and binding decision.

**Third-party credit**    A situation in which a customer uses a card such as Visa or MasterCard to charge merchandise purchased at a retail outlet.

**Time loss risk**    The likelihood that the consumer will not be able to get merchandise adjusted, replaced, or repaired without loss of time and effort.

**Trade discount**    A reduction off the seller's list price that is granted to a retailer who performs functions normally the responsibility of the vendor.

**Trading area**    The area from which a store primarily attracts its customers.

**Traffic count**    A method used to determine the character and volume of traffic (both vehicular and pedestrian) passing a particular site.

**Transaction processing**    A situation in which employees serve as check-out clerks or cashiers and do little selling.

**Trial close**    A transition to the close technique where a question is asked to determine the customer's readiness to buy.

**Turnover**    The number of times the average inventory is sold, usually in annual terms.

**Unit control**    System used to control the width and support aspects of stock balance. The system records (perpetual) beginning inventory and all additions and deductions to stock to obtain the ending inventory. (See *Nonperpetual unit control* for the other system in use.)

**Unit pricing**    A situation in which price is stated in such terms as price per kilogram or litre.

**Unity of command**    A principle of organization that states that no person should be under the direct control of more than one supervisor in performing job tasks.

**Universal product code (UPC)**    A standardized form of product marking for electronic reading of price and other information that is used for food and health products and beauty aids.

**Universal transverse mercator (UTM)**    A system that provides the coordinates of every location in Canada.

**Universal vendor marking (UVM)**    A standard vendor-created identification system for marking merchandise items at the vendor level.

**Urban arterial development**    Shopping areas usually found in an older part of the city.

**Urgency close**    A sales-closing technique where the salesperson advises the prospect of some compelling reason for ordering immediately.

**Variable-payment lease**    A situation in which the retailer makes a guaranteed monthly rental payment to the landlord in addition to a specified percentage of sales.

**Variety**    The width of a store's selection of merchandise.

**Vertical merchandising**    A form of displaying merchandise vertically instead of horizontally to increase space productivity.

**Wand**    An electronic device that can be passed over items for reading machine-coded information.

**Weeks' supply method**    Used in planning weekly stocks in relation to the desired turnover.

**Wheel of retailing**    A theory about institutional structure change based on the premise that institutional innovations in retailing penetrate the system on the basis of price appeal and gradually trade up over time in terms of store standing, quality, store services, and prices.

**Width**    (See Breadth.)

**Wife-dominant decision**    A decision within the family that is made most of the time by the wife.

**Work sharing**    A situation that occurs during economic recessions where employees are required to cut back on their work hours rather than face layoffs and are paid accordingly.

question 20> answer is A

calculations in m/c

Chapters 11 + 12

20 m/c
20 T/F